KITCHEN PRINCESS

OMNIBUS

1

Natsumi Ando

Story by Miyuki Kobayashi

Translated by Satsuki Yamashita

Adapted by Nunzio DeFilippis and Christina Weir

Lettered by North Market Street Graphics

Kitchen Princess Omnibus volume 1 is a work of fiction. Names, characters, places, and incidents are the products of the author's imagination or are used fictitiously. Any resemblance to actual events, locales, or persons, living or dead, is entirely coincidental.

A Kodansha Comics Trade Paperback Original.

Published in the United States by Kodansha Comics, an imprint of Kodansha USA Publishing, LLC, New York.

Publication rights for this English edition arranged through Kodansha Ltd., Tokyo.

First published in Japan in 2005 by Kodansha Ltd., Tokyo, as *Kitchen no Ohime-sama* volumes 1 and 2.

ISBN 978-1-935429-44-9

Printed in the United States of America.

www.kodanshacomics.com

9 8 7 6 5 4

Translator: Satsuki Yamashita
Adaptor: Nunzio DeFilippis and Christina Weir
Lettering: North Market Street Graphics

Contents

Honorifics Explained

Throughout the Kodansha Comics books, you will find Japanese honorifics left intact in the translations. For those not familiar with how the Japanese use honorifics and, more important, how they differ from American honorifics, we present this brief overview.

Politeness has always been a critical facet of Japanese culture. Ever since the feudal era, when Japan was a highly stratified society, use of honorifics—which can be defined as polite speech that indicates relationship or status—has played an essential role in the Japanese language. When addressing someone in Japanese, an honorific usually takes the form of a suffix attached to one's name (example: "Asuna-san"), as a title at the end of one's name, or in place of the name itself (example: "Negi-sensei," or simply "Sensei!").

Honorifics can be expressions of respect or endearment. In the context of manga and anime, honorifics give insight into the nature of the relationship between characters. Many translations into English leave out these important honorifics and therefore distort the "feel" of the original Japanese. Because Japanese honorifics contain nuances that English honorifics lack, it is our policy at Kodansha Comics not to translate them. Here, instead, is a guide to some of the honorifics you may encounter in Kodansha Comics.

-san: This is the most common honorific and is equivalent to Mr., Miss, Ms., or Mrs. It is the all-purpose honorific and can be used in any situation where politeness is required.

-sama: This is one level higher than "-san." It is used to confer great respect.

-dono: This comes from the word "tono," which means "lord." It is an even higher level than "-sama" and confers utmost respect.

-kun: This suffix is used at the end of boys' names to express familiarity or endearment. It is also sometimes used by men among friends, or when addressing someone younger or of a lower station.

-chan: This is used to express endearment, mostly toward girls. It is also used for little boys, pets, and even among lovers. It gives a sense of childish cuteness.

Bozu: This is an informal way to refer to a boy, similar to the English terms "kid" and "squirt."

Sempai/
Senpai: This title suggests that the addressee is one's senior in a group or organization. It is most often used in a school setting, where underclassmen refer to their upperclassmen as "sempai." It can also be used in the workplace, such as when a newer employee addresses an employee who has seniority in the company.

Kohai: This is the opposite of "sempai" and is used toward underclassmen in school or newcomers in the workplace. It connotes that the addressee is of a lower station.

Sensei: Literally meaning "one who has come before," this title is used for teachers, doctors, or masters of any profession or art.

[blank]: This is usually forgotten in these lists, but perhaps the most sig- nificant difference between Japanese and English. The lack of hon-orific means that the speaker has permission to address the person in a very intimate way. Usually, only family, spouses, or very close friends have this kind of permission. Known as yobisute, it can be gratifying when someone who has earned the intimacy starts to call one by one's name without an honorific. But when that intimacy hasn't been earned, it can also be very insulting.

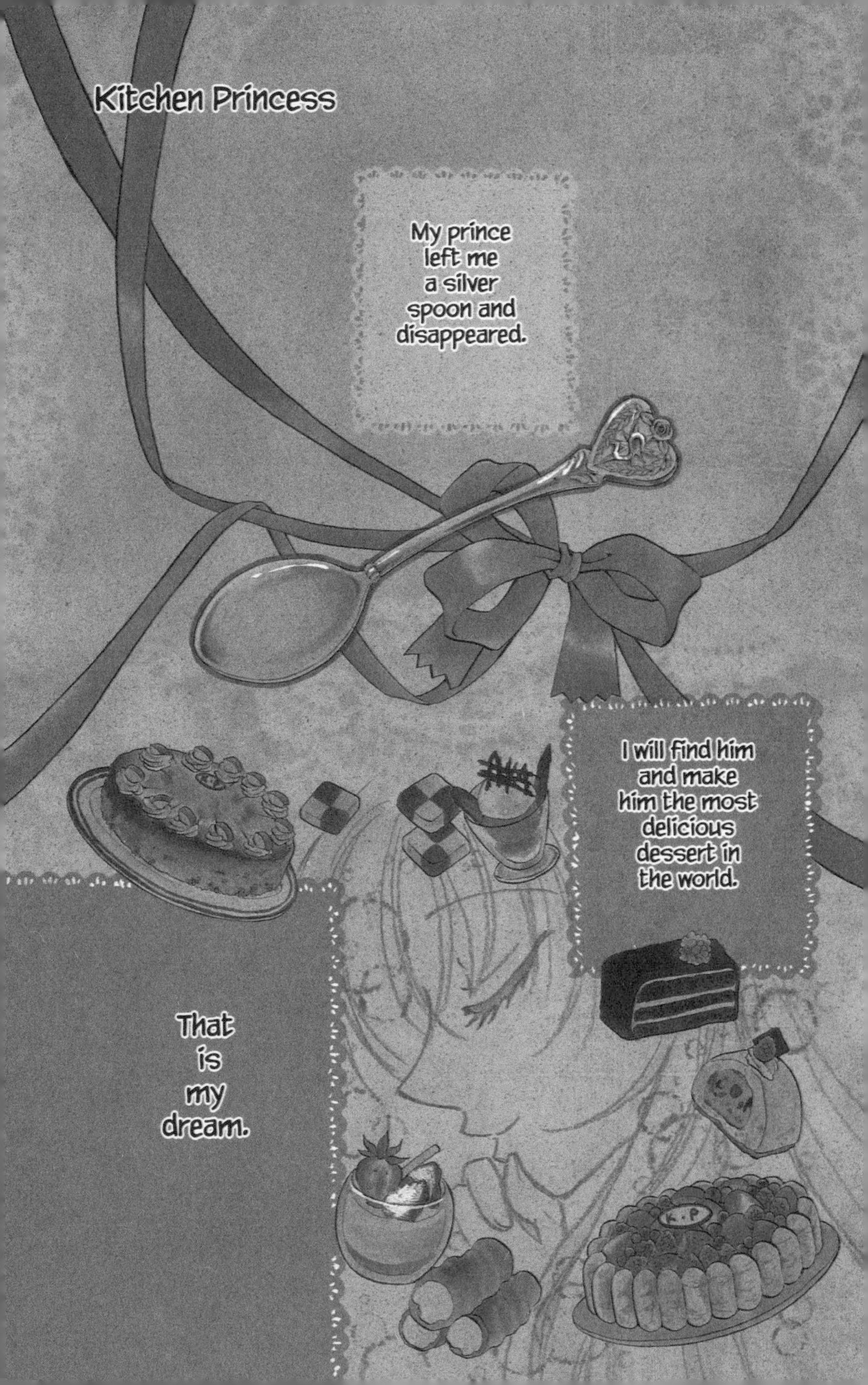
Kitchen Princess
My prince left me a silver spoon and disappeared.
I will find him and make him the most delicious dessert in the world.
That is my dream.
K.P

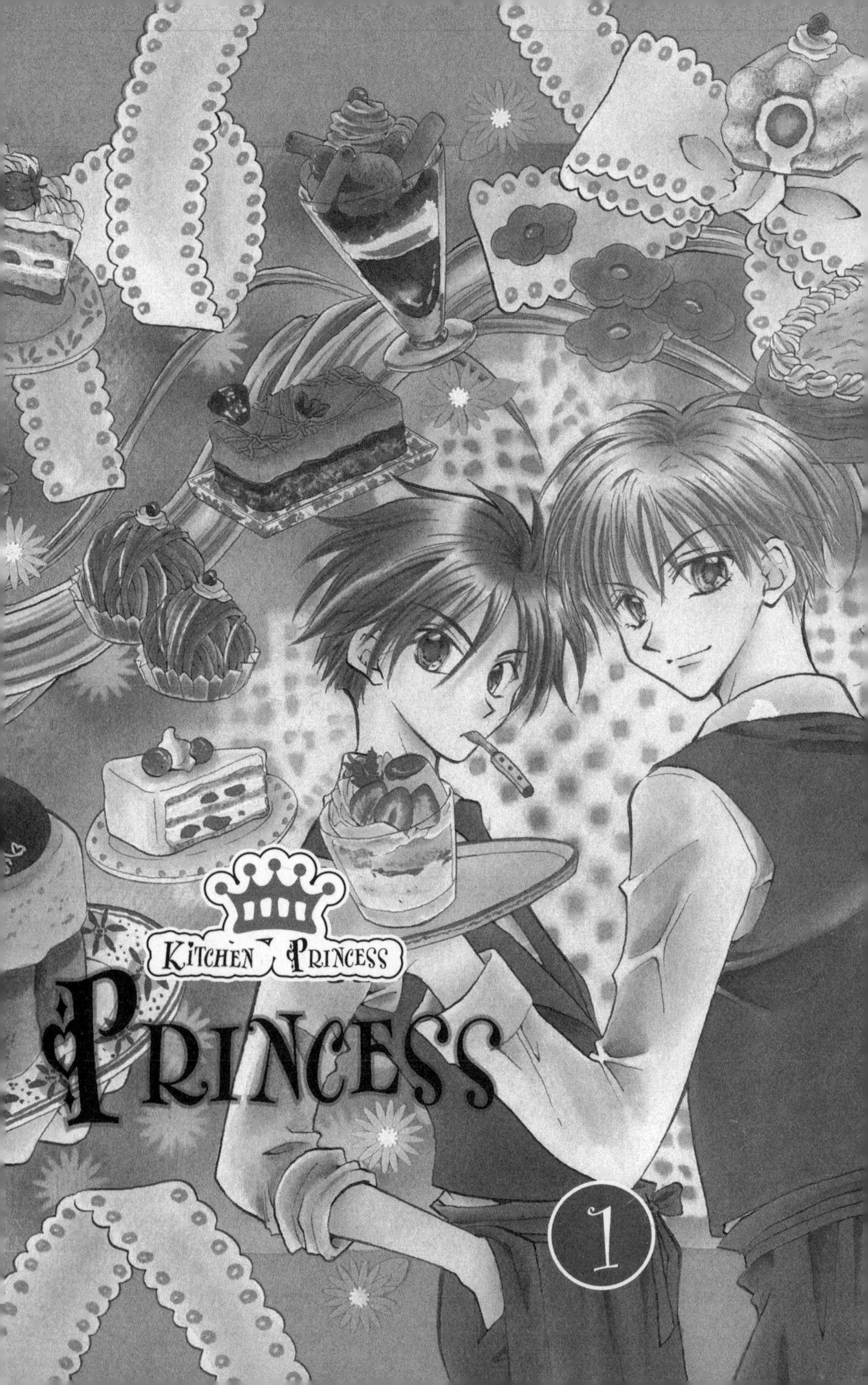

KITCHEN PRINCESS
PRINCESS
1

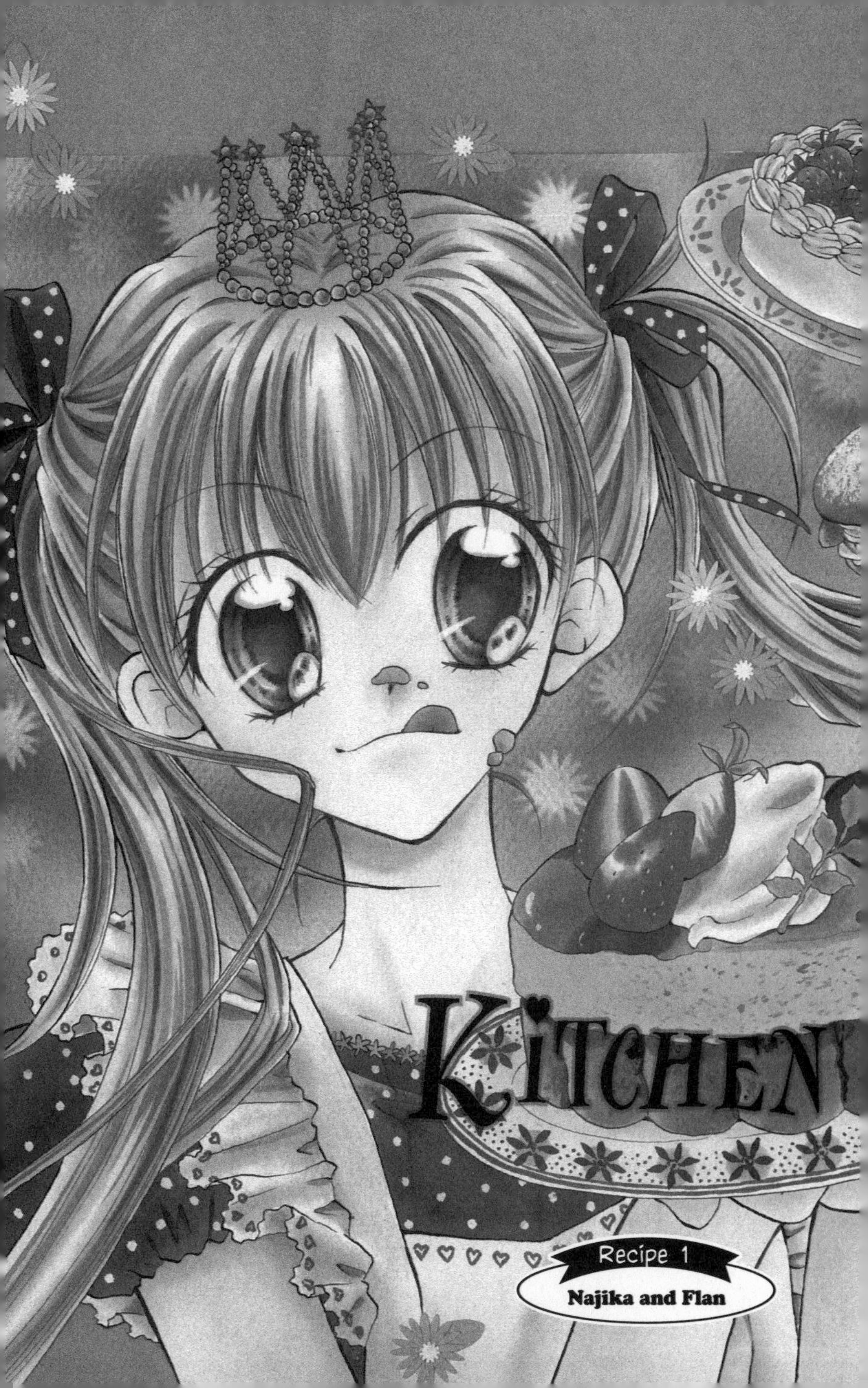
KITCHEN
Recipe 1
Najika and Flan

Kitchen Princess

Table of Contents

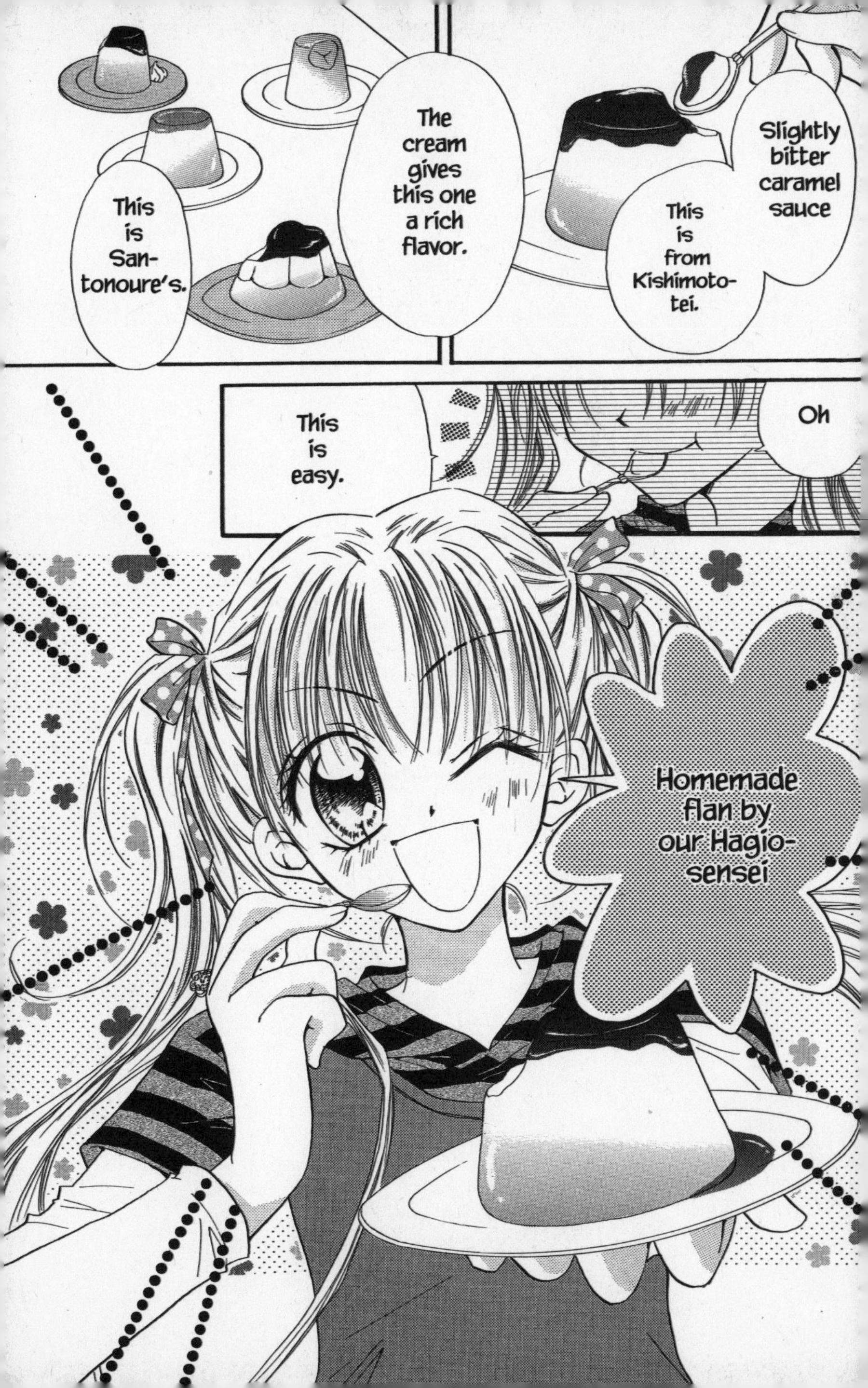
Slightly bitter caramel sauce
This is from Kishimoto-tei.
The cream gives this one a rich flavor.
This is San-tonoure's.
Oh
This is easy.
Homemade flan by our Hagio-sensei

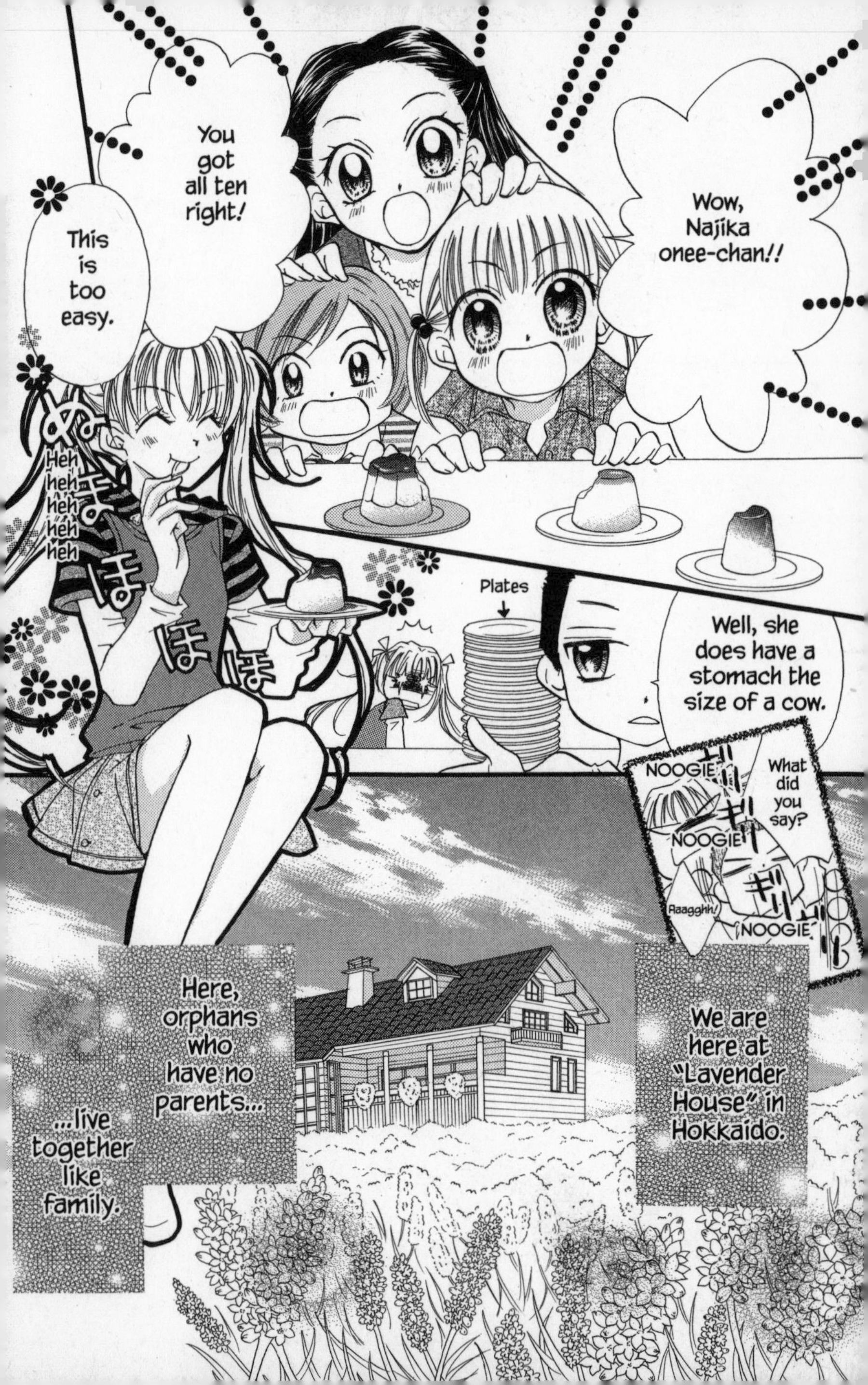
Wow, Najika onee-chan!!
You got all ten right!
This is too easy.
Heh heh heh heh heh
Plates
Well, she does have a stomach the size of a cow.
What did you say?
NOOGIE
NOOGIE
NOOGIE
Raaagghh!
We are here at "Lavender House" in Hokkaido.
Here, orphans who have no parents...
...live together like family.

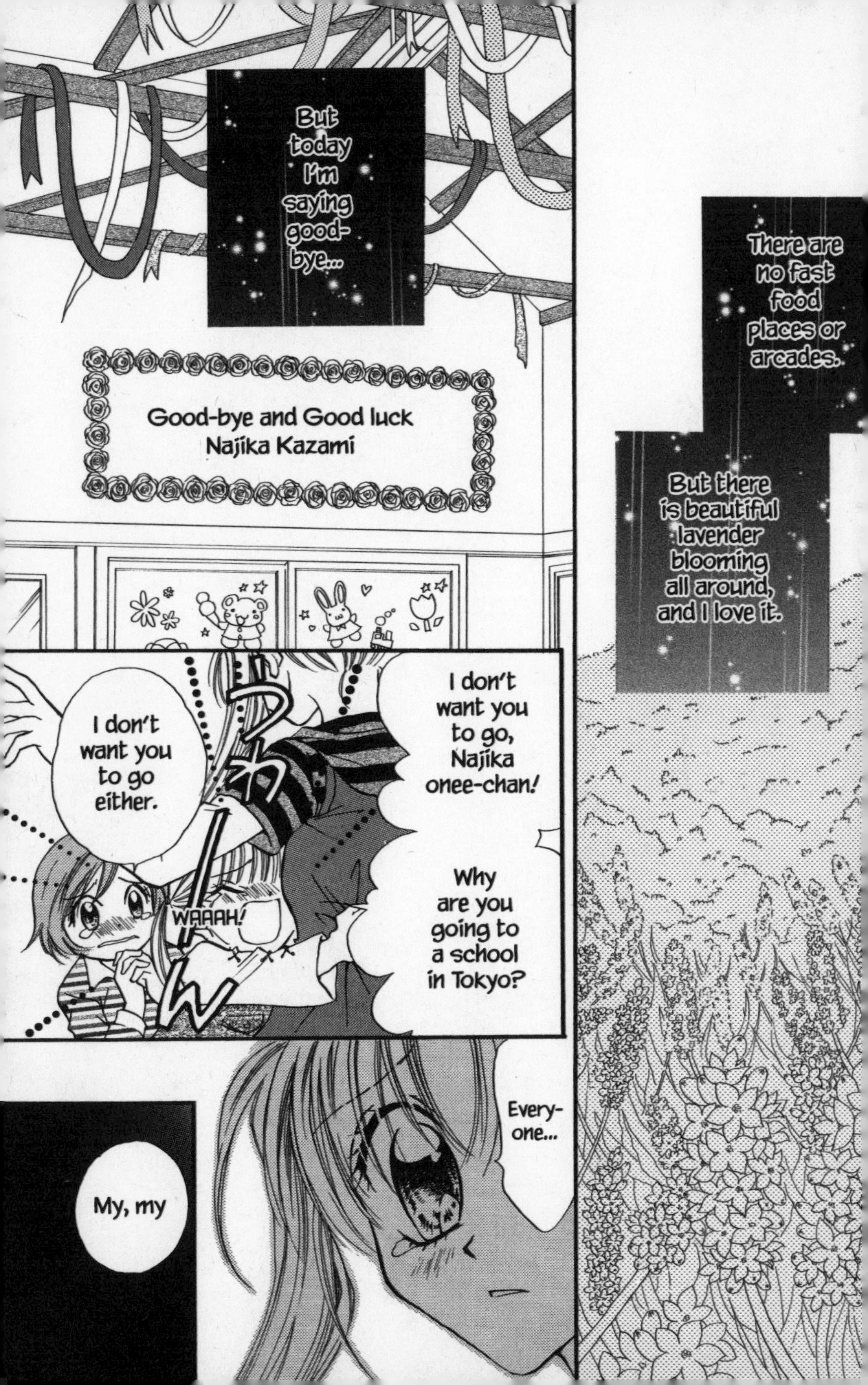
There are no fast food places or arcades.
But there is beautiful lavender blooming all around, and I love it.
But today I'm saying good-bye...
Good-bye and Good luck Najika Kazami
I don't want you to go, Najika onee-chan!
Why are you going to a school in Tokyo?
WAAAH!
I don't want you to go either.
Every-one...
My, my

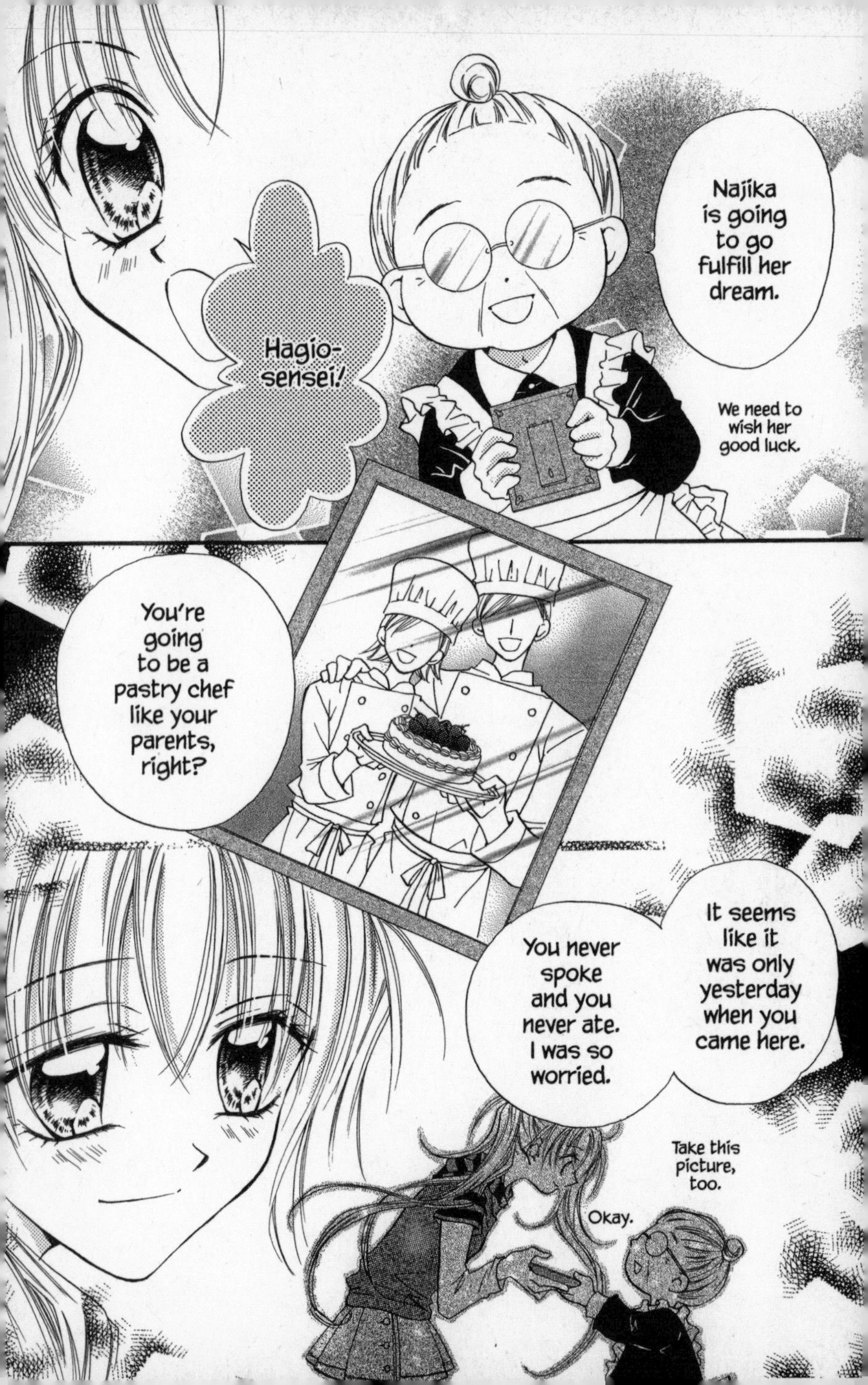

Najika is going to go fulfill her dream.
We need to wish her good luck.
Hagio-sensei!
You're going to be a pastry chef like your parents, right?
It seems like it was only yesterday when you came here.
You never spoke and you never ate. I was so worried.
Take this picture, too.
Okay.

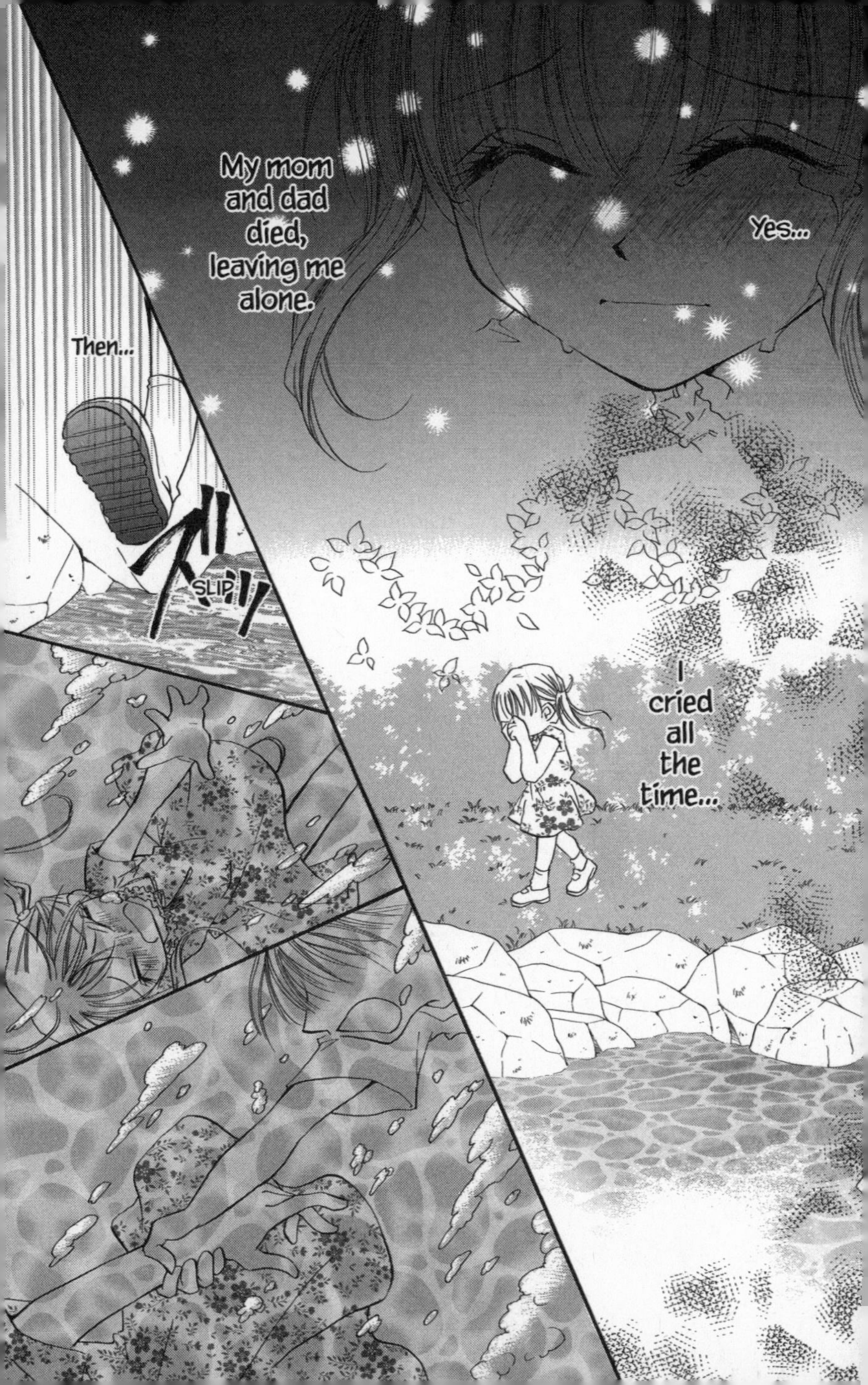
Yes...
My mom and dad died, leaving me alone.
I cried all the time...
Then...
SLIP

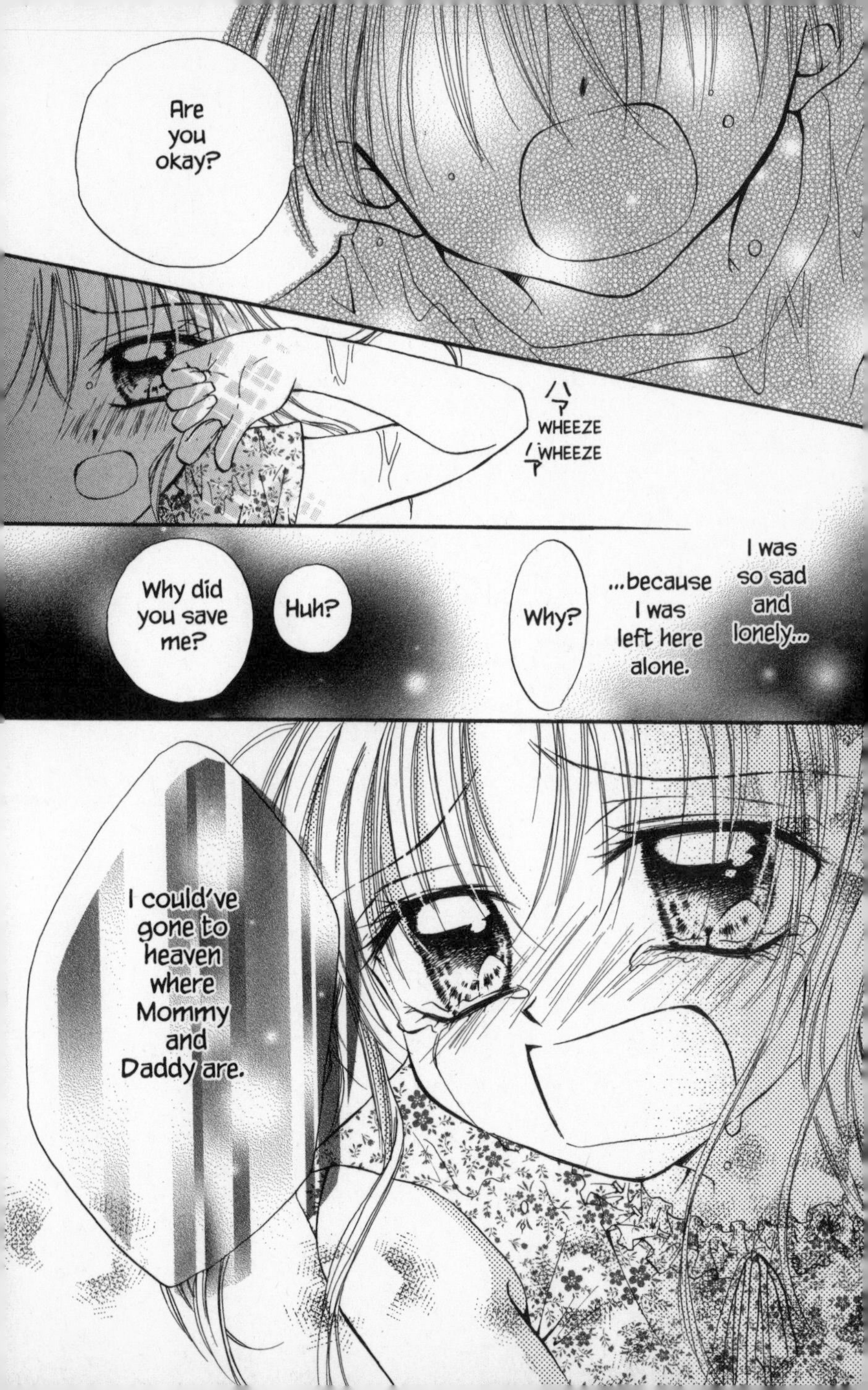
Are you okay?
ハァ WHEEZE
ハァ WHEEZE
I was so sad and lonely...
...because I was left here alone.
Why?
Huh?
Why did you save me?
I could've gone to heaven where Mommy and Daddy are.

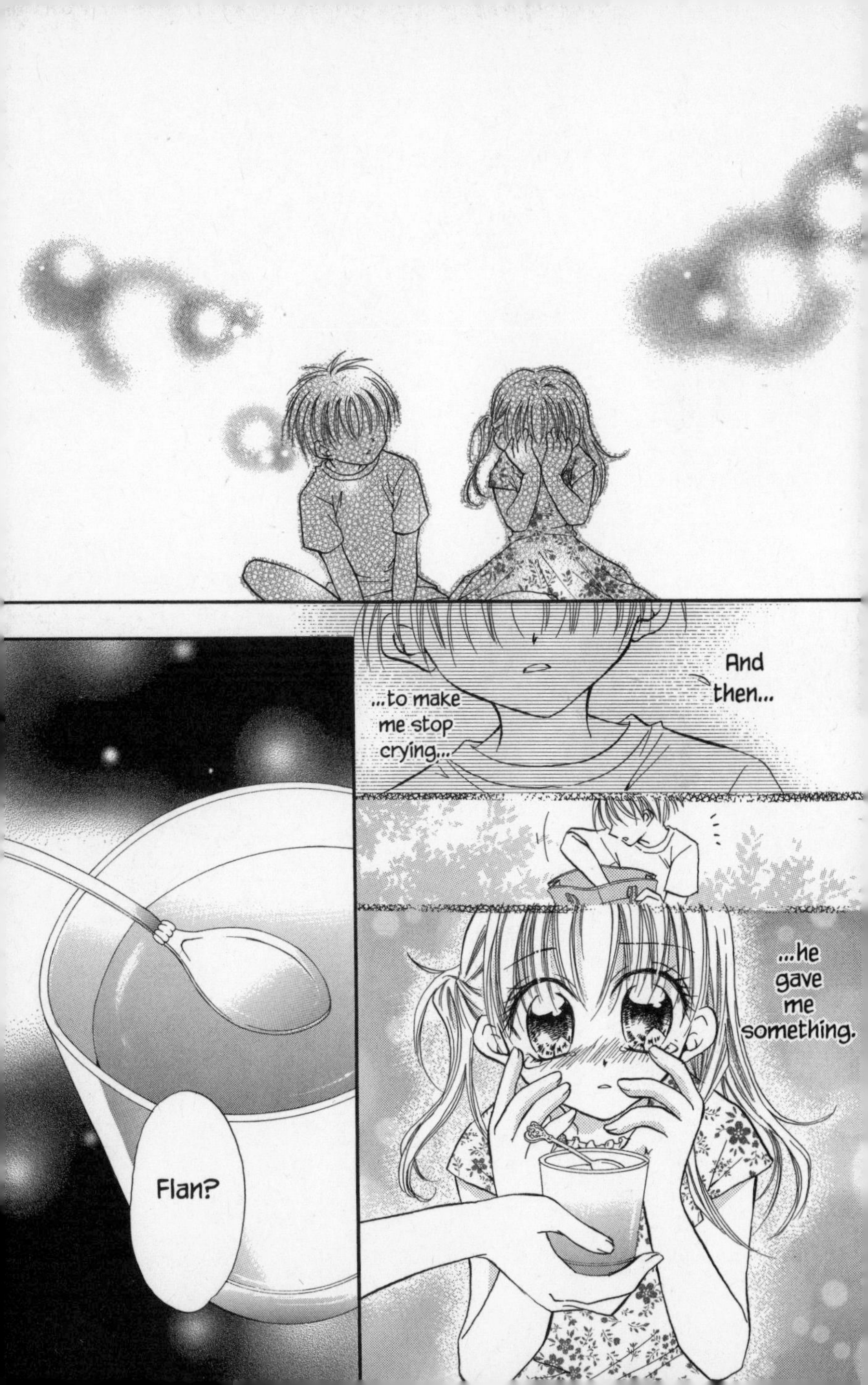
And then...
...to make me stop crying...
...he gave me something.
Flan?

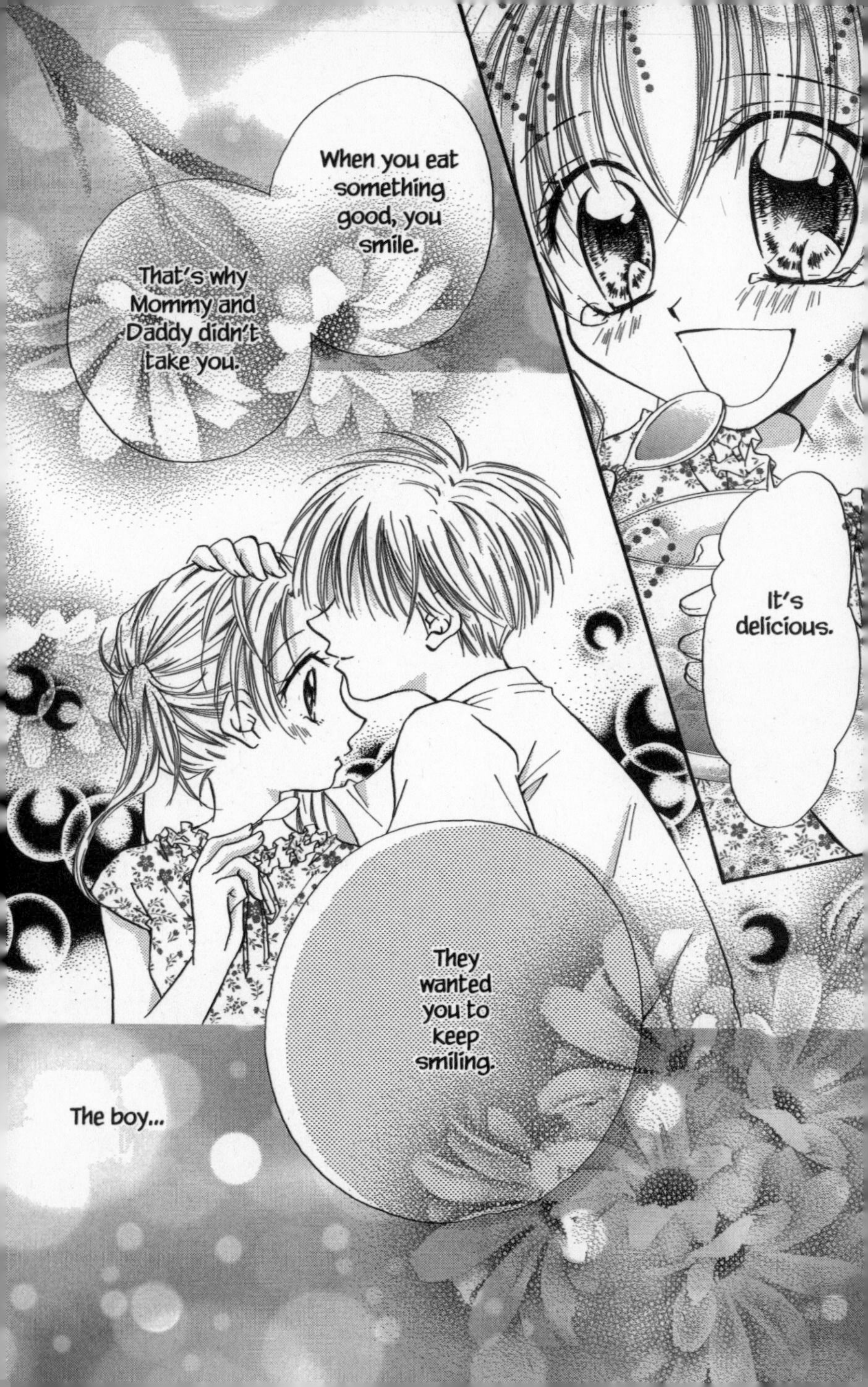
It's delicious.
When you eat something good, you smile.
That's why Mommy and Daddy didn't take you.
They wanted you to keep smiling.
The boy...

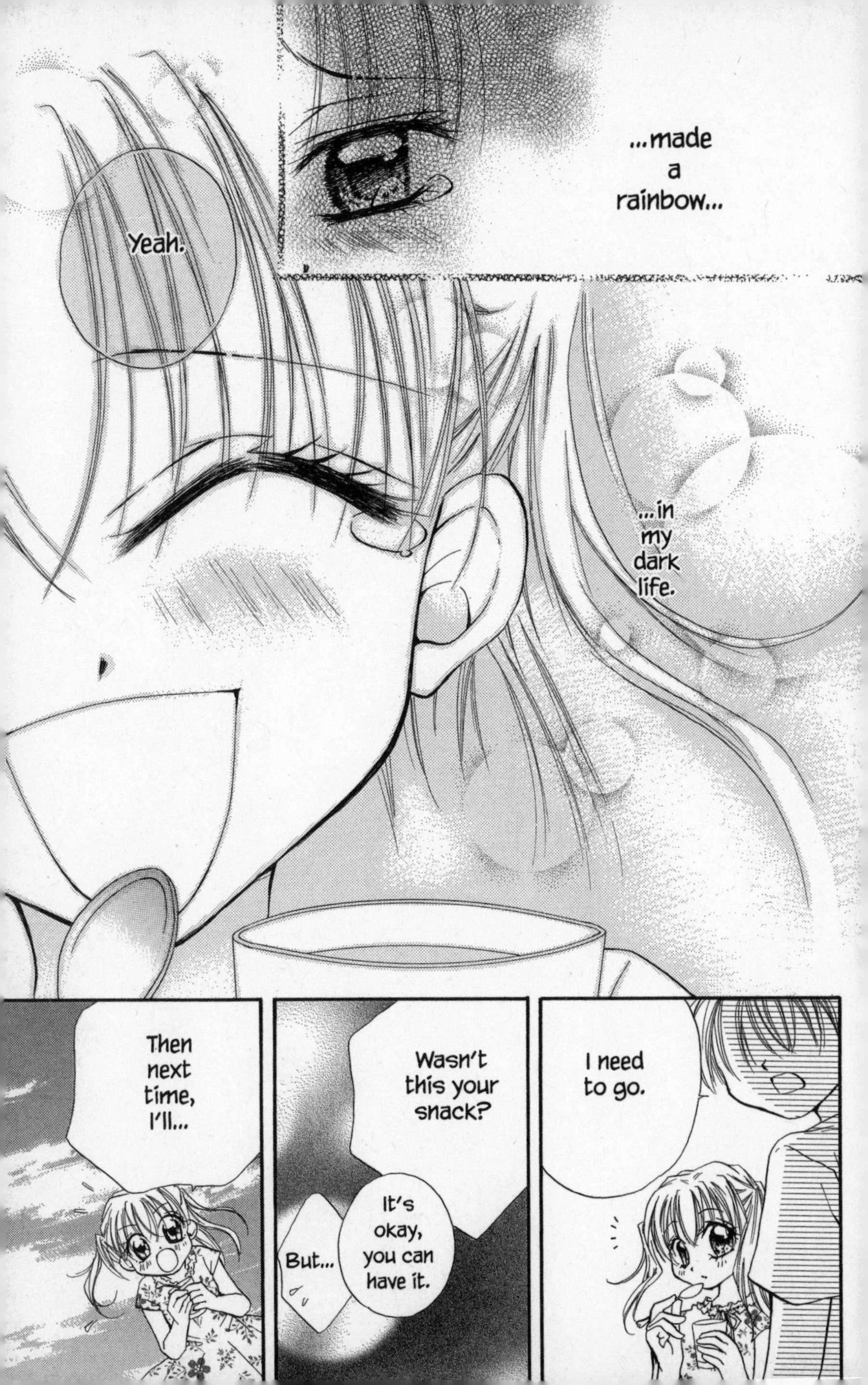
...made a rainbow...
...in my dark life.
Yeah.
I need to go.
Wasn't this your snack?
It's okay, you can have it.
But...
Then next time, I'll...

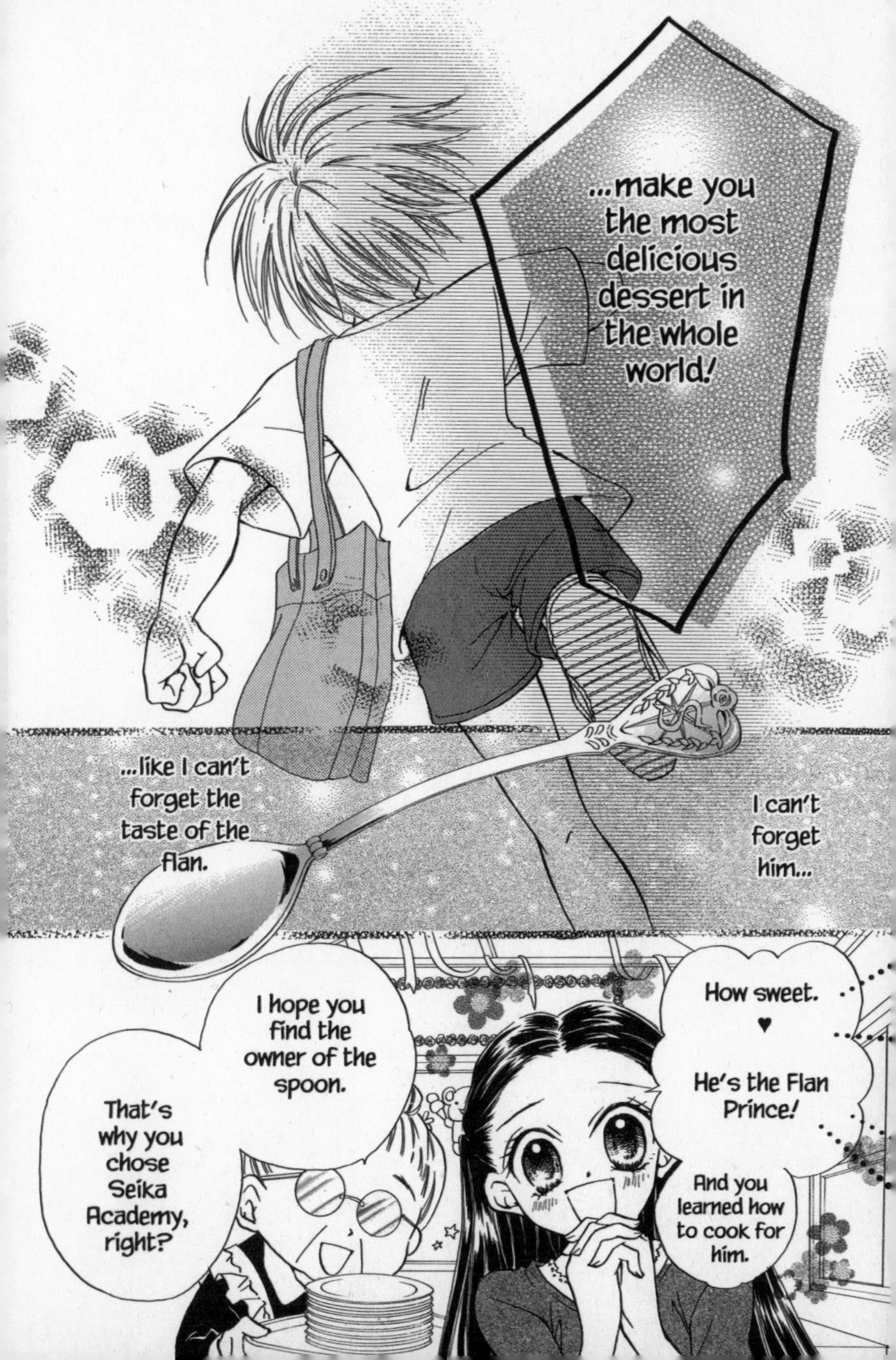
...make you the most delicious dessert in the whole world!
I can't forget him...
...like I can't forget the taste of the flan.
How sweet. ♥
He's the Flan Prince!
I hope you find the owner of the spoon.
And you learned how to cook for him.
That's why you chose Seika Academy, right?

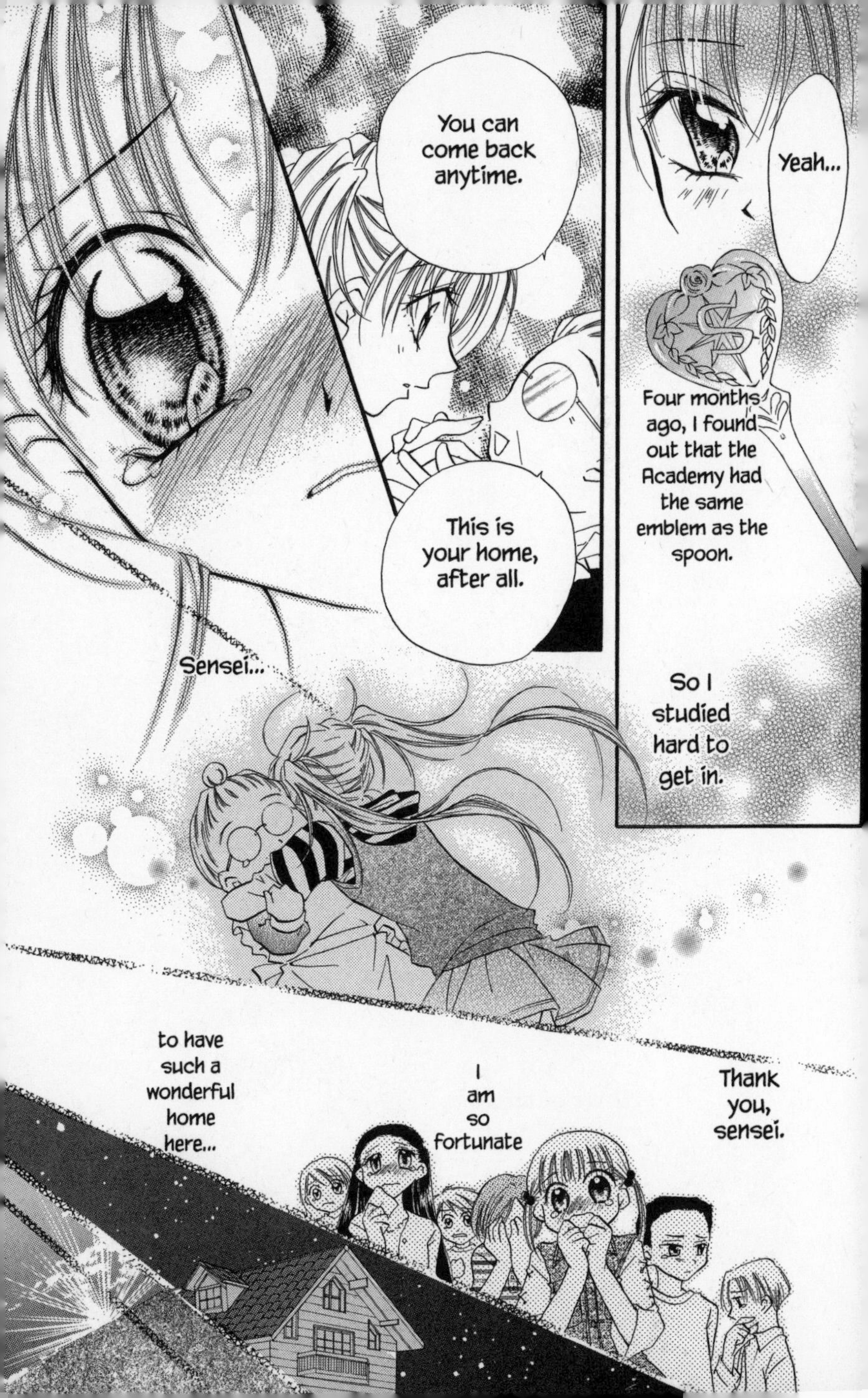
Yeah...
Four months ago, I found out that the Academy had the same emblem as the spoon.
So I studied hard to get in.
You can come back anytime.
This is your home, after all.
Sensei...
Thank you, sensei.
I am so fortunate
to have such a wonderful home here...

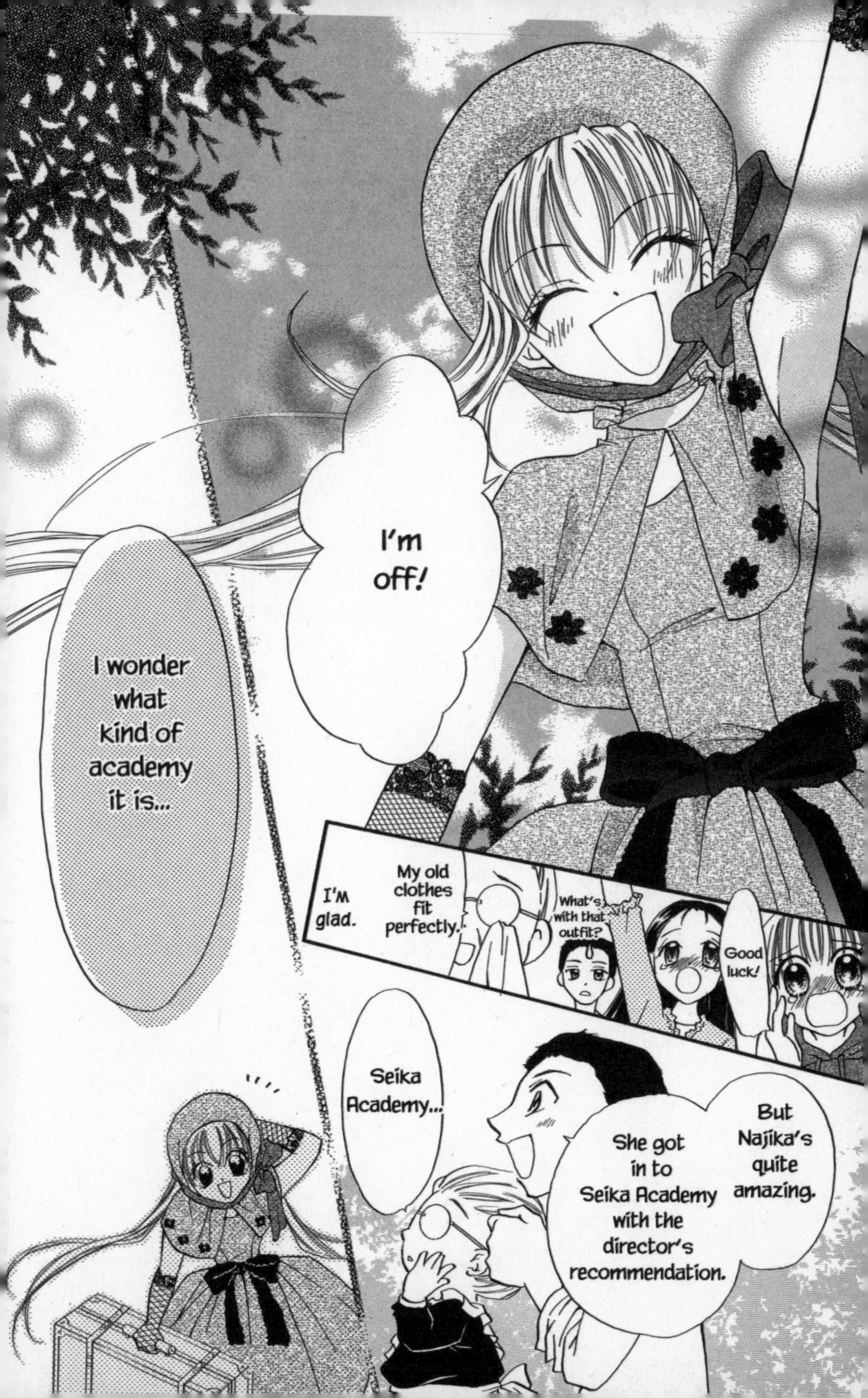
I'm off!
I wonder what kind of academy it is...
Good luck!
What's with that outfit?
My old clothes fit perfectly.
I'm glad.
But Najika's quite amazing.
She got in to Seika Academy with the director's recommendation.
Seika Academy...

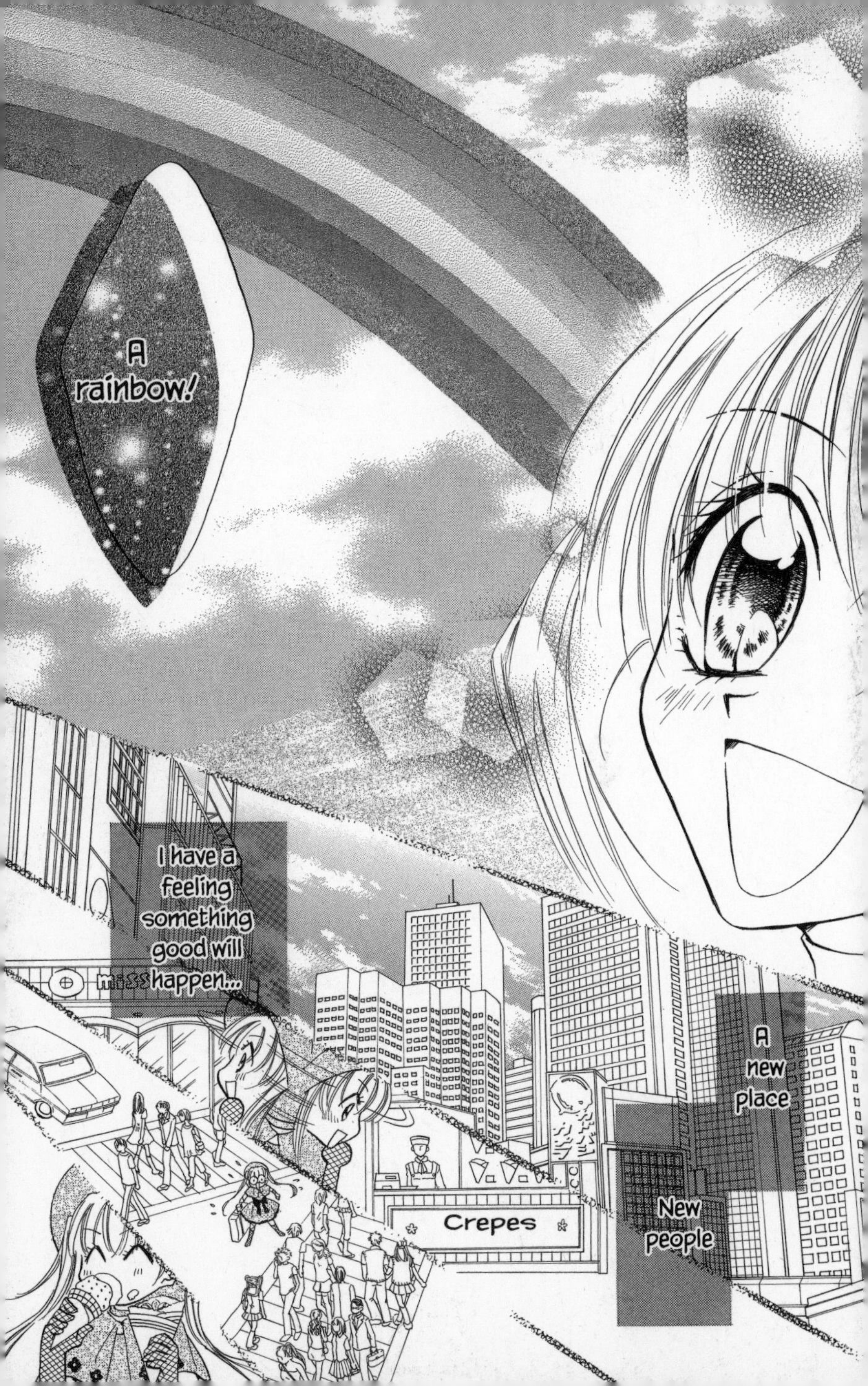
A rainbow!
A new place
New people
I have a feeling something good will happen...
Crepes

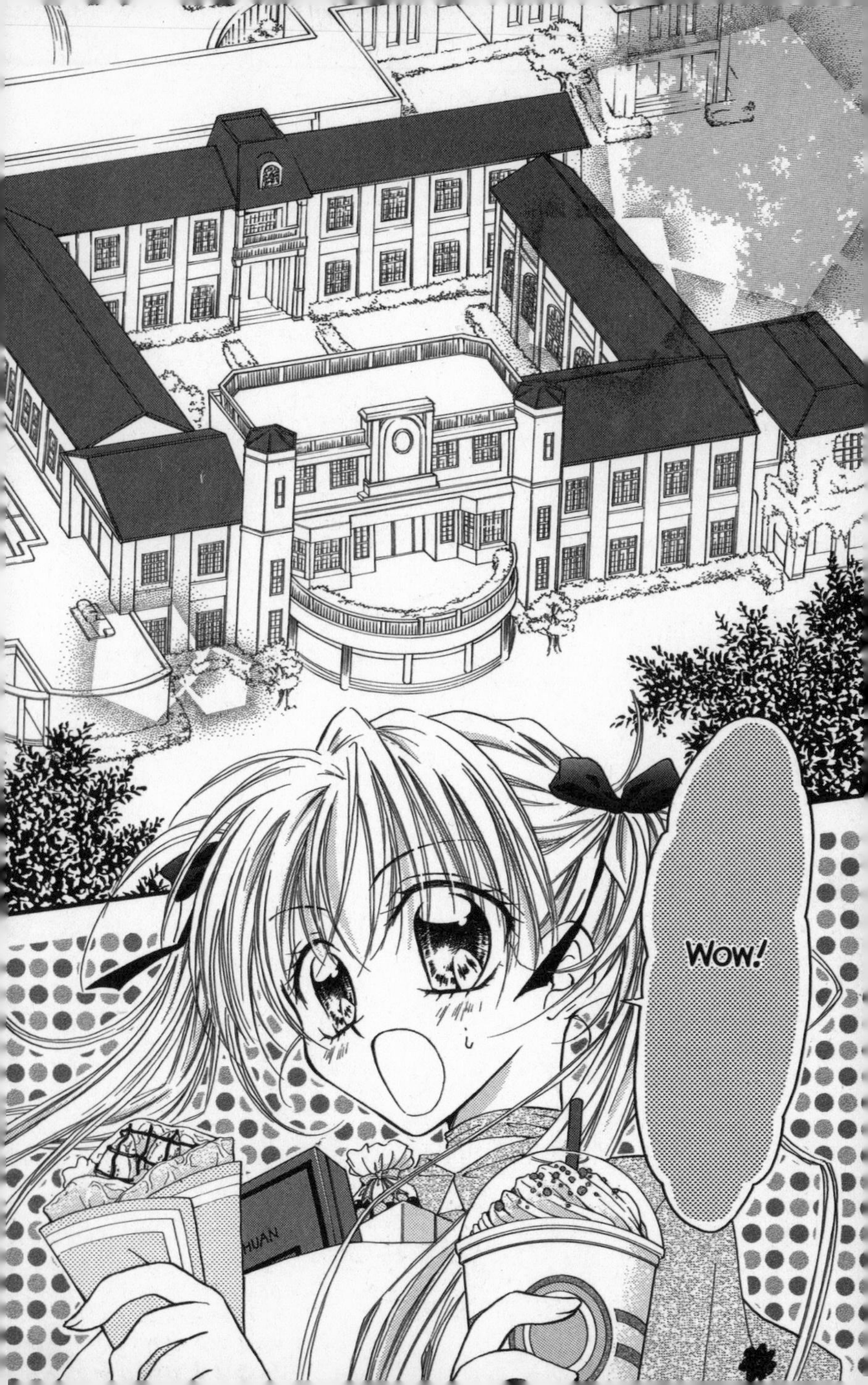
WOW!
HUAN

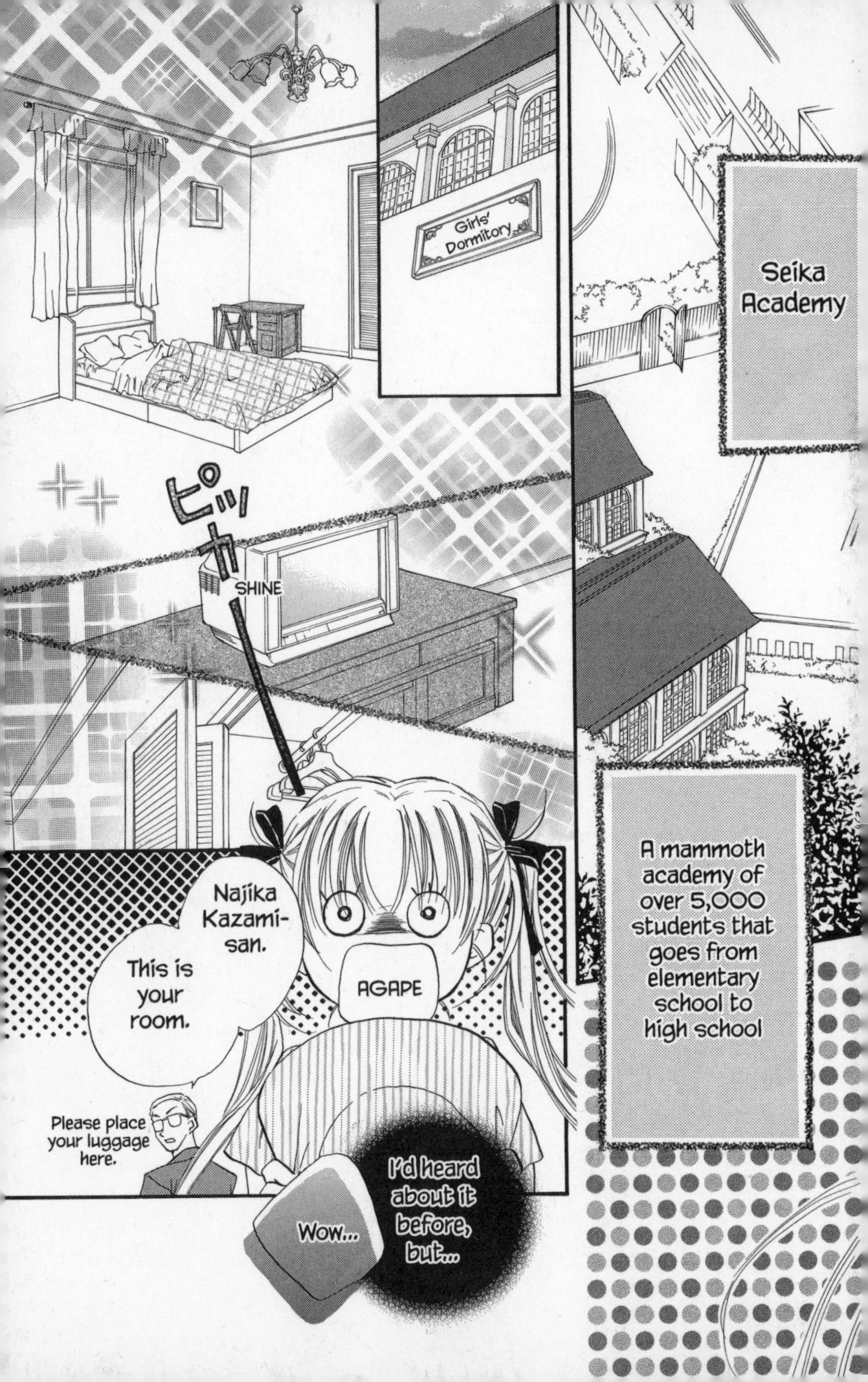
Seika Academy
A mammoth academy of over 5,000 students that goes from elementary school to high school
Girls' Dormitory
ピカッ
SHINE
AGAPE
Najika Kazami-san.
This is your room.
Please place your luggage here.
I'd heard about it before, but...
Wow...

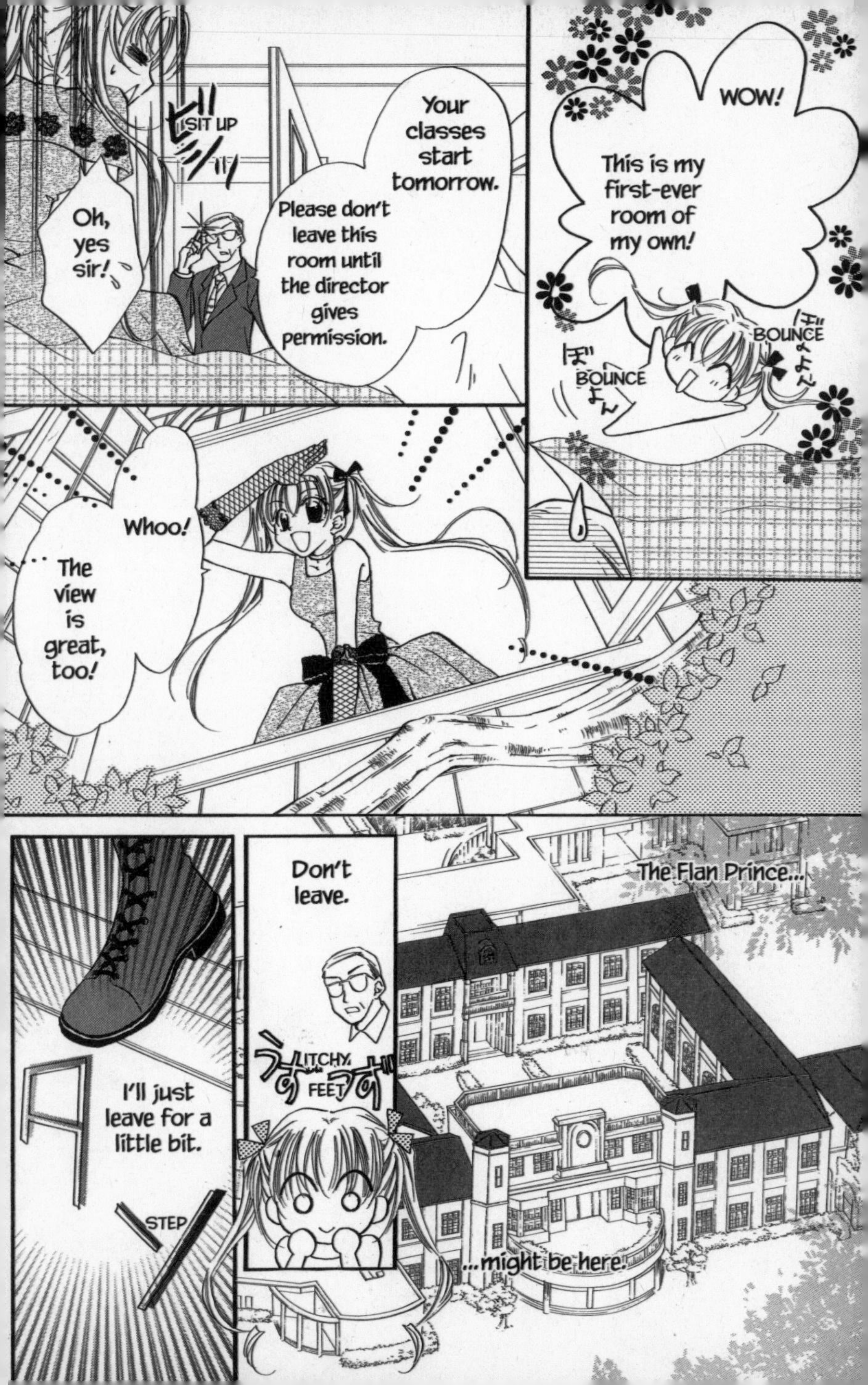
WOW!
This is my first-ever room of my own!
BOUNCE
BOUNCE
Your classes start tomorrow.
Please don't leave this room until the director gives permission.
SIT UP
Oh, yes sir!
Whoo!
The view is great, too!
The Flan Prince...
...might be here.
Don't leave.
ITCHY, FEET
I'll just leave for a little bit.
STEP

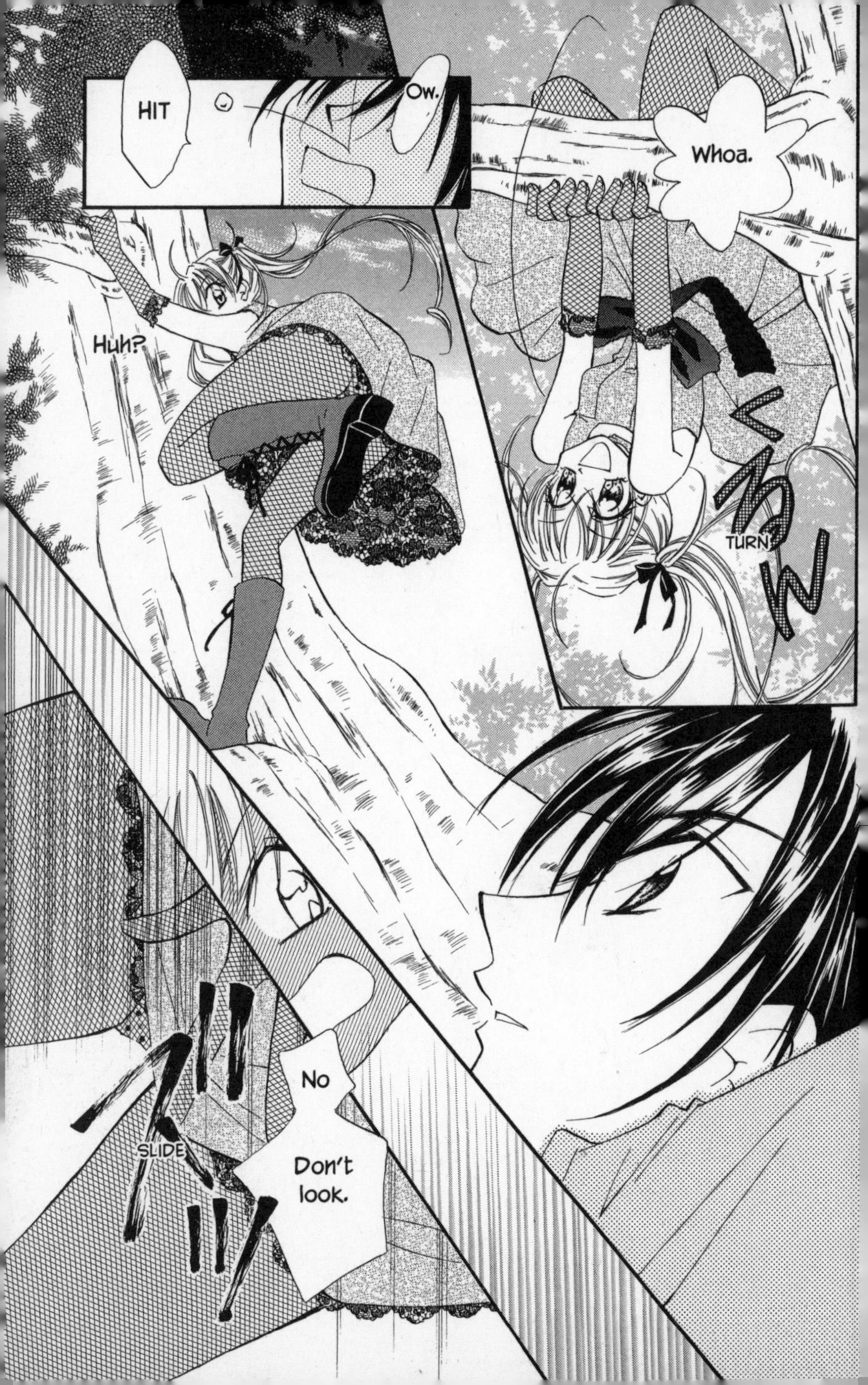
Whoa.
TURN
Ow.
HIT
Huh?
No
Don't look.
SLIDE

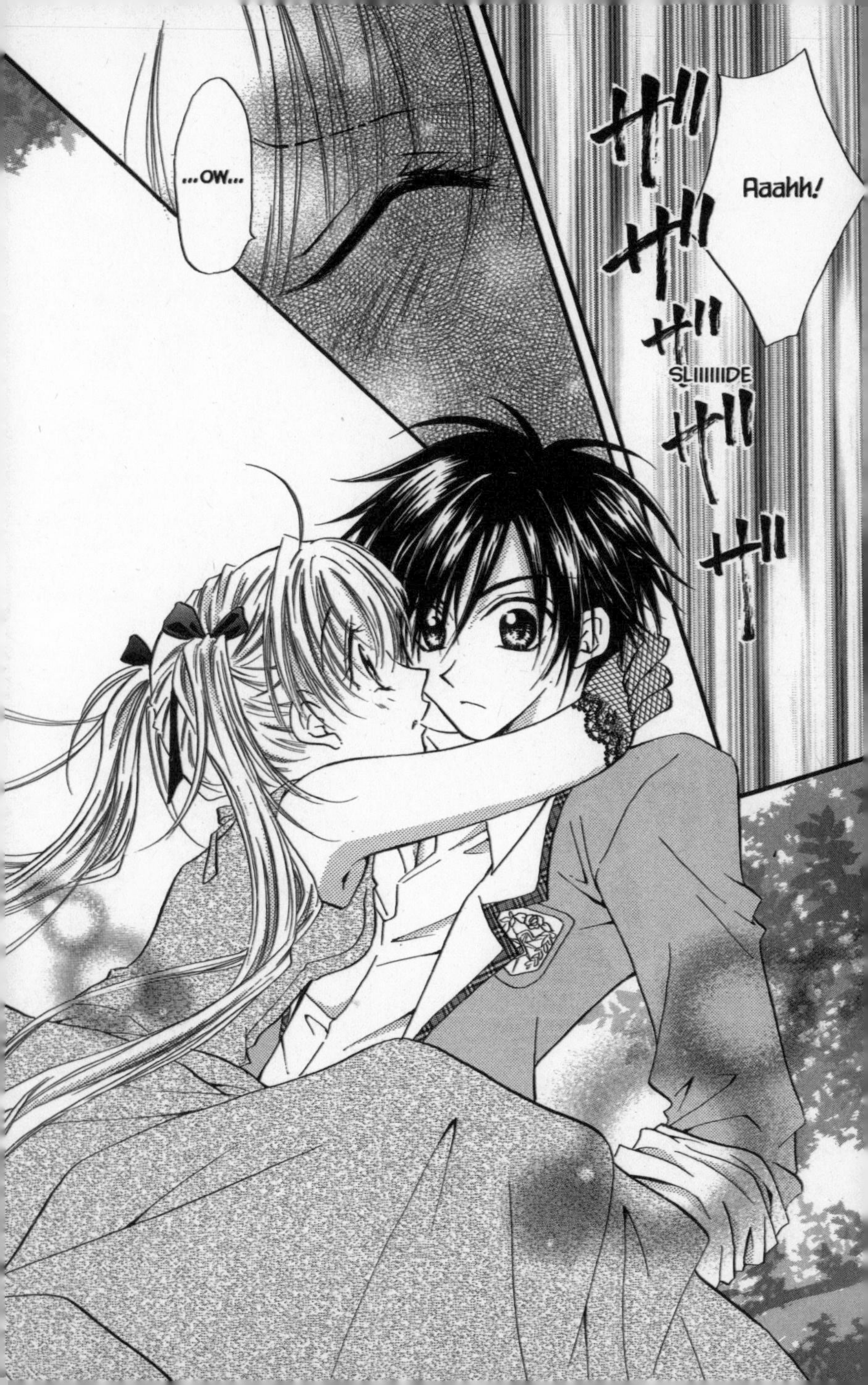
Aaahh!
SLIIIIIIDE
...OW...

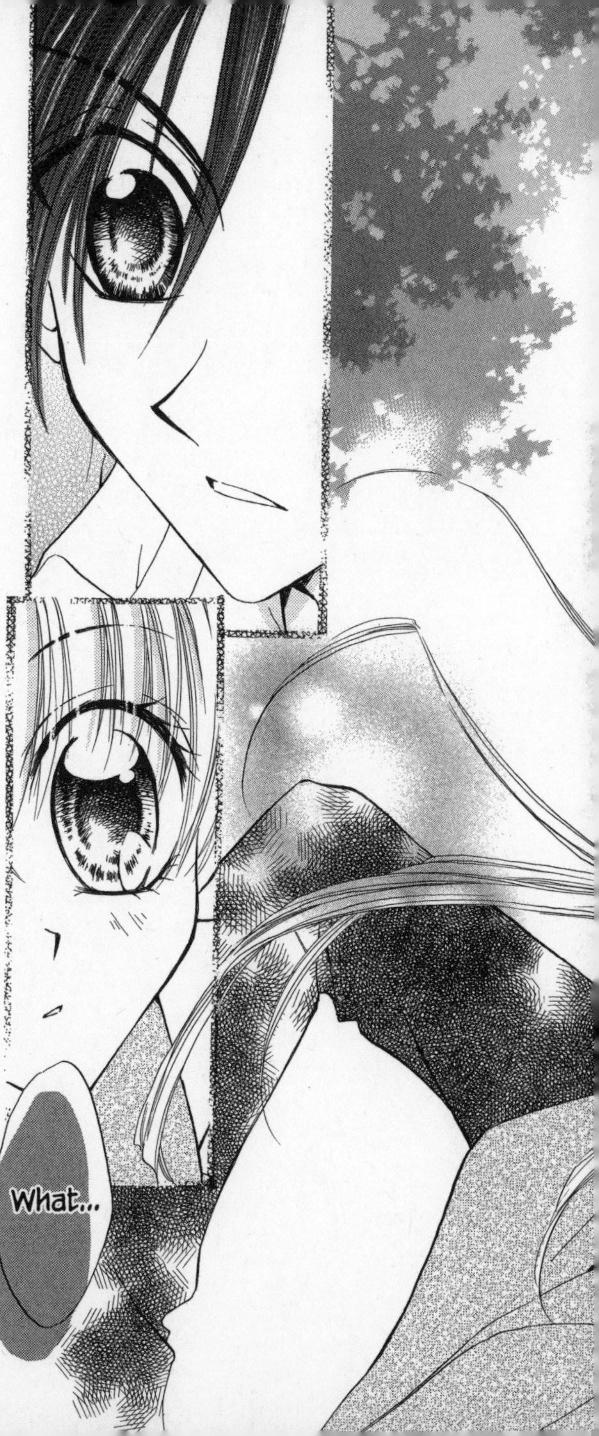
What...

Hello

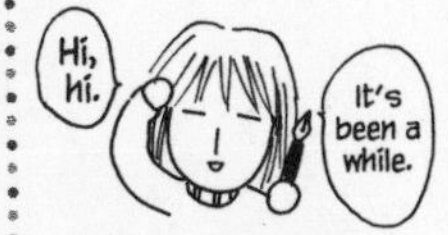
Hi, hi.
It's been a while.

This is Ando. I've been sleeping at night and waking up in the morning, and living like a normal human being.
Now, "Kitchen Princess" was something I wanted to do. I always wanted to do something related to cooking.
I am trying my best to show the deliciousness of the food, so please wish me luck!!
I was dieting until this series started, but I felt that I should be eating delicious food if I'm drawing it, so now I'm eating a lot.♪
But I lost 7 kg so maybe my diet was a success...
I didn't like the fact that I couldn't eat any carbs...that was a killer.

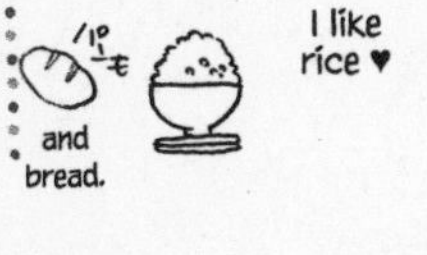
I like rice ♥
and bread.

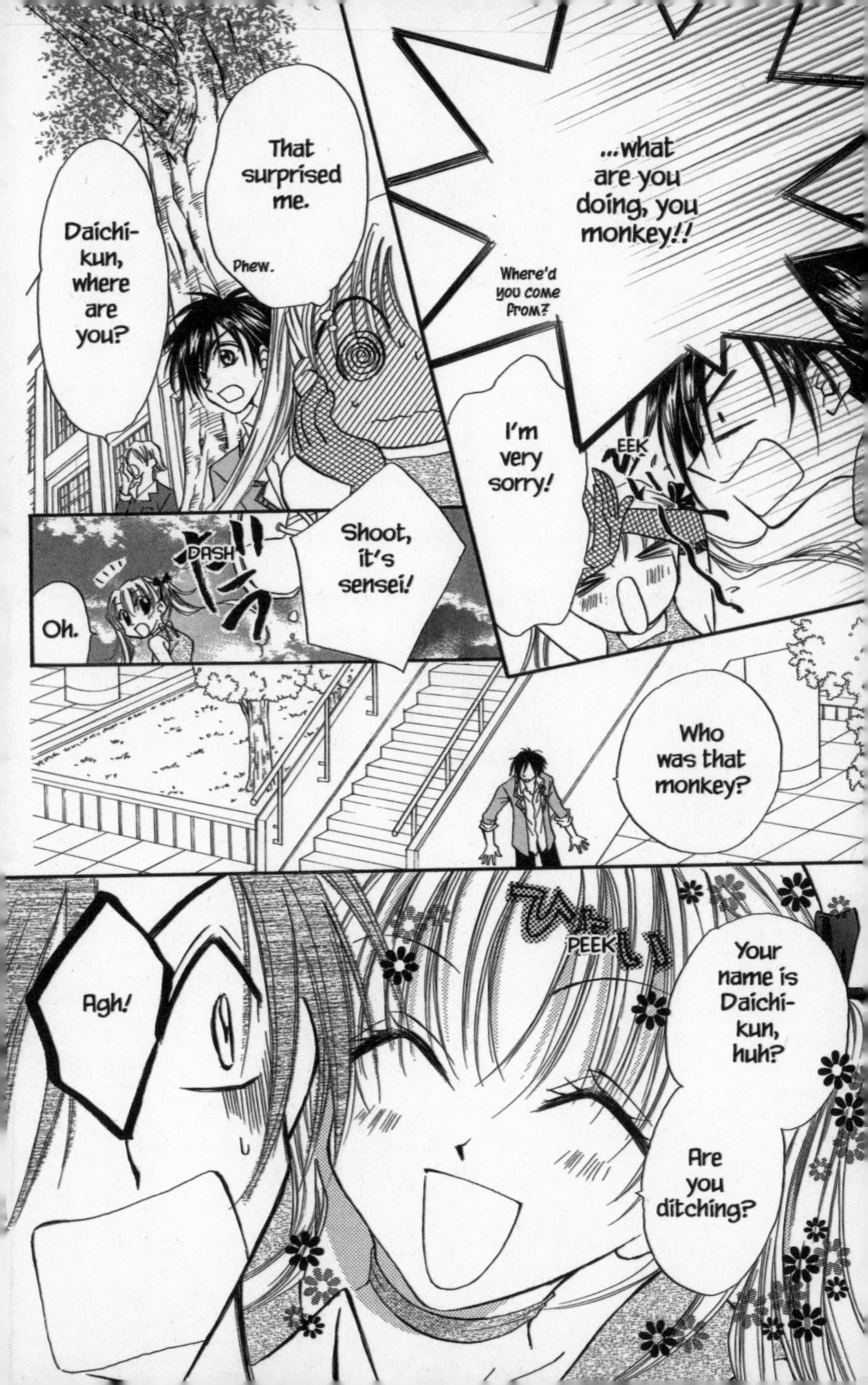
...what are you doing, you monkey!!
Where'd you come from?
EEK
I'm very sorry!
That surprised me.
Phew.
Daichi-kun, where are you?
Shoot, it's sensei!
DASH
Oh.
Who was that monkey?
PEEK
Your name is Daichi-kun, huh?
Are you ditching?
Agh!

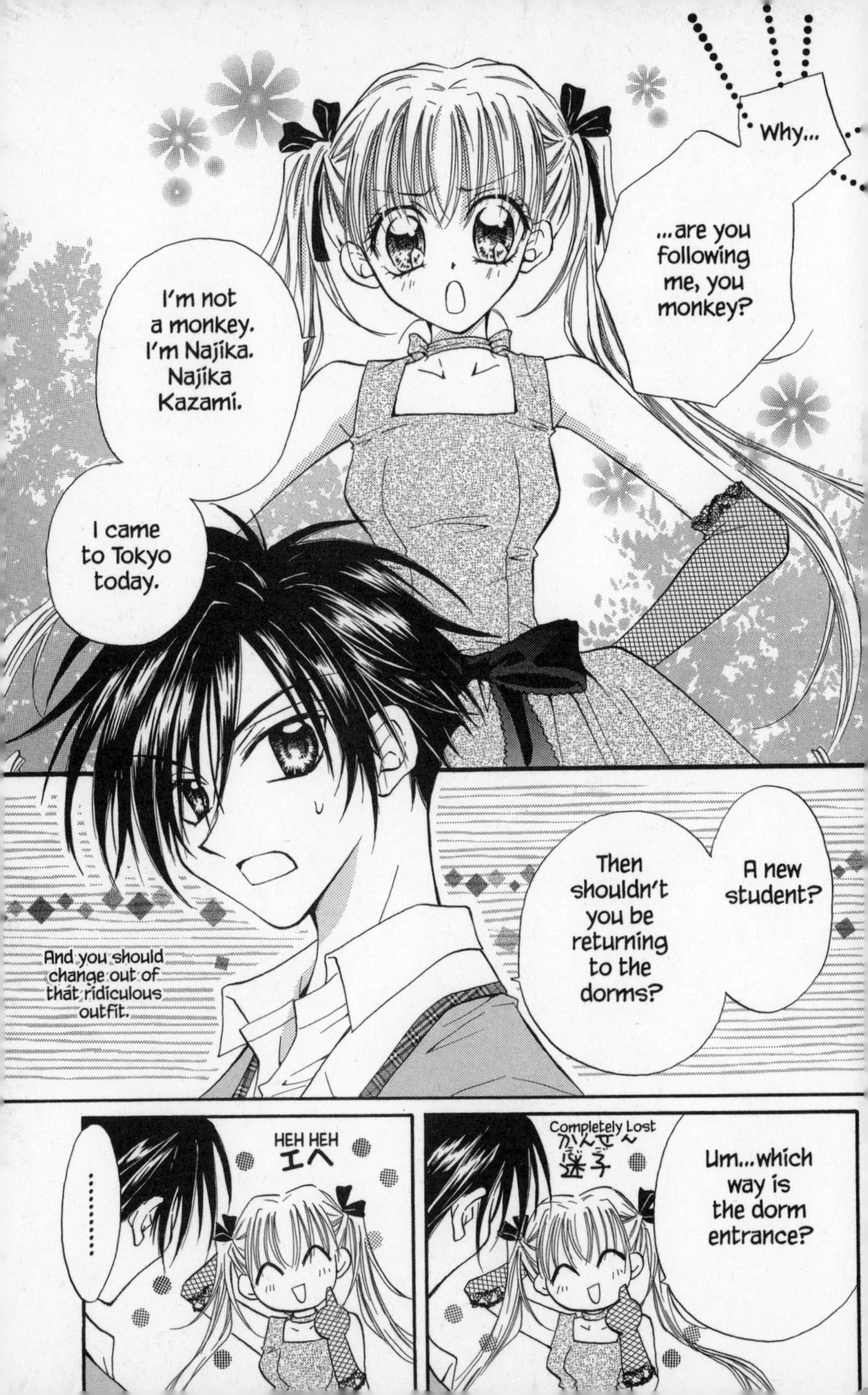
Why...
...are you following me, you monkey?
I'm not a monkey. I'm Najika. Najika Kazami.
I came to Tokyo today.
A new student?
Then shouldn't you be returning to the dorms?
And you should change out of that ridiculous outfit.
Completely Lost
かんぜん迷子
Um...which way is the dorm entrance?
HEH HEH
エヘ
......

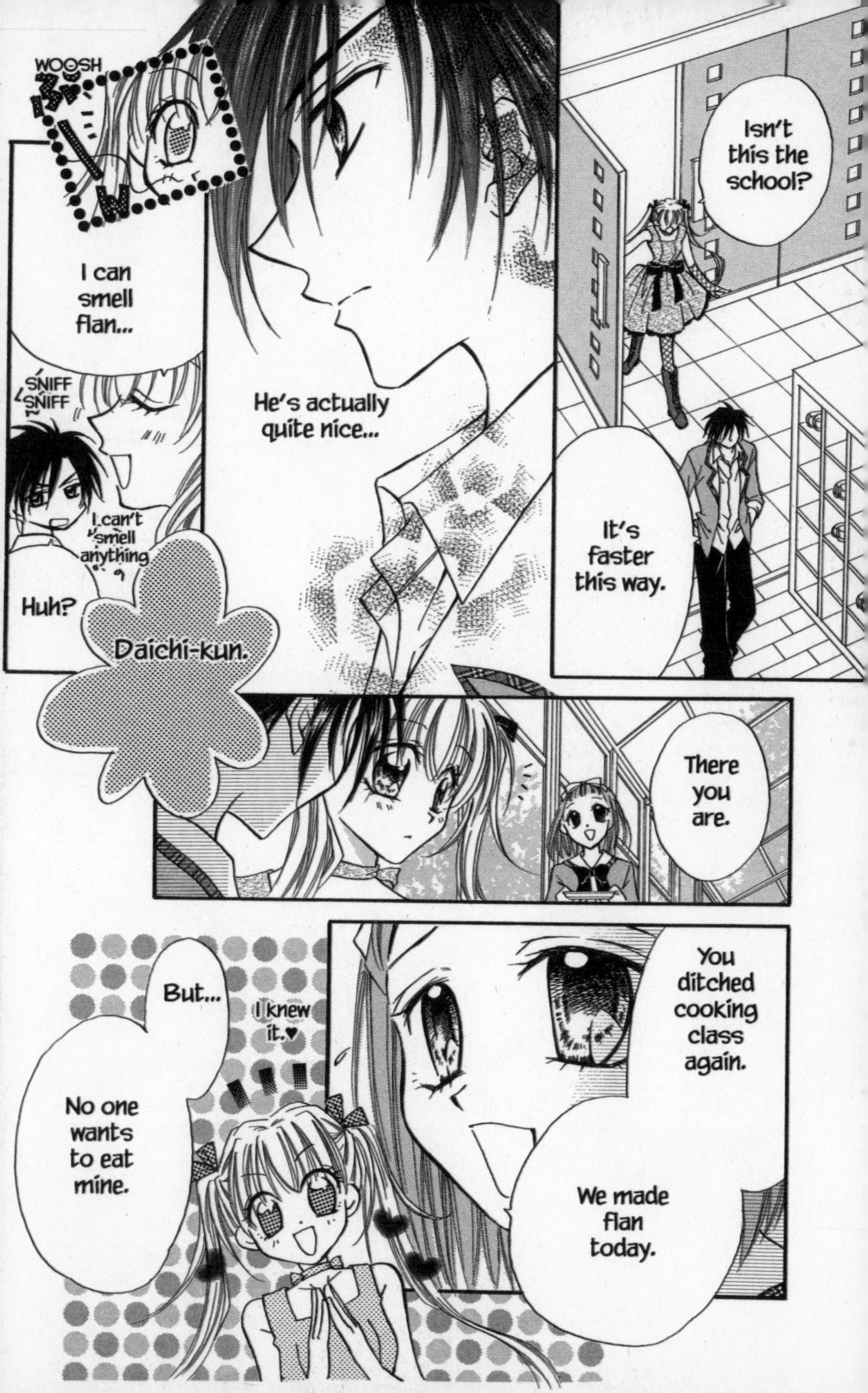
Isn't this the school?
It's faster this way.
He's actually quite nice...
WOOSH
I can smell flan...
SNIFF SNIFF
I can't smell anything
Huh?
Daichi-kun.
There you are.
You ditched cooking class again.
We made flan today.
But...
I knew it.♥
No one wants to eat mine.

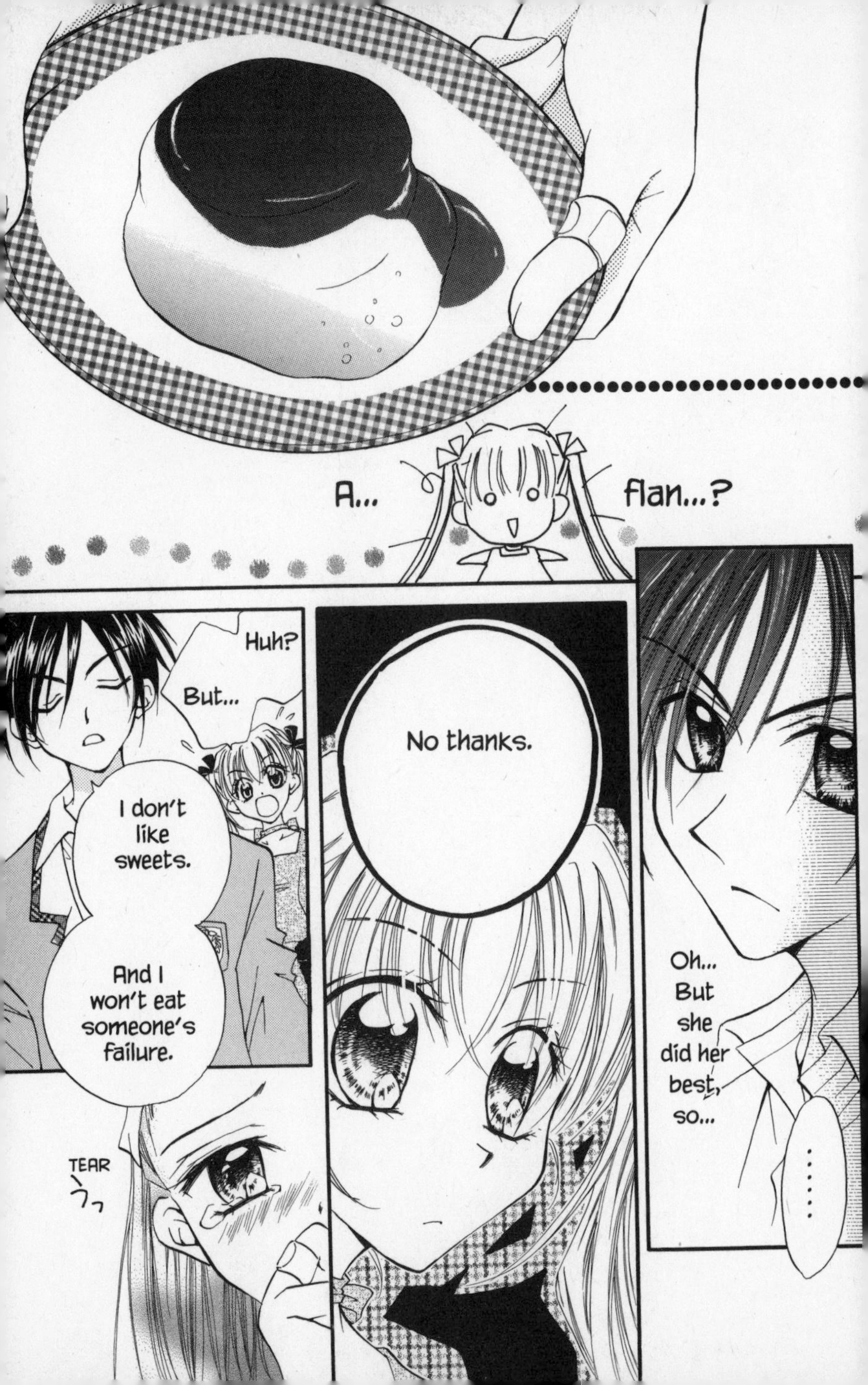
A... flan...?
Oh... But she did her best, so...
......
No thanks.
Huh?
But...
I don't like sweets.
And I won't eat someone's failure.
TEAR

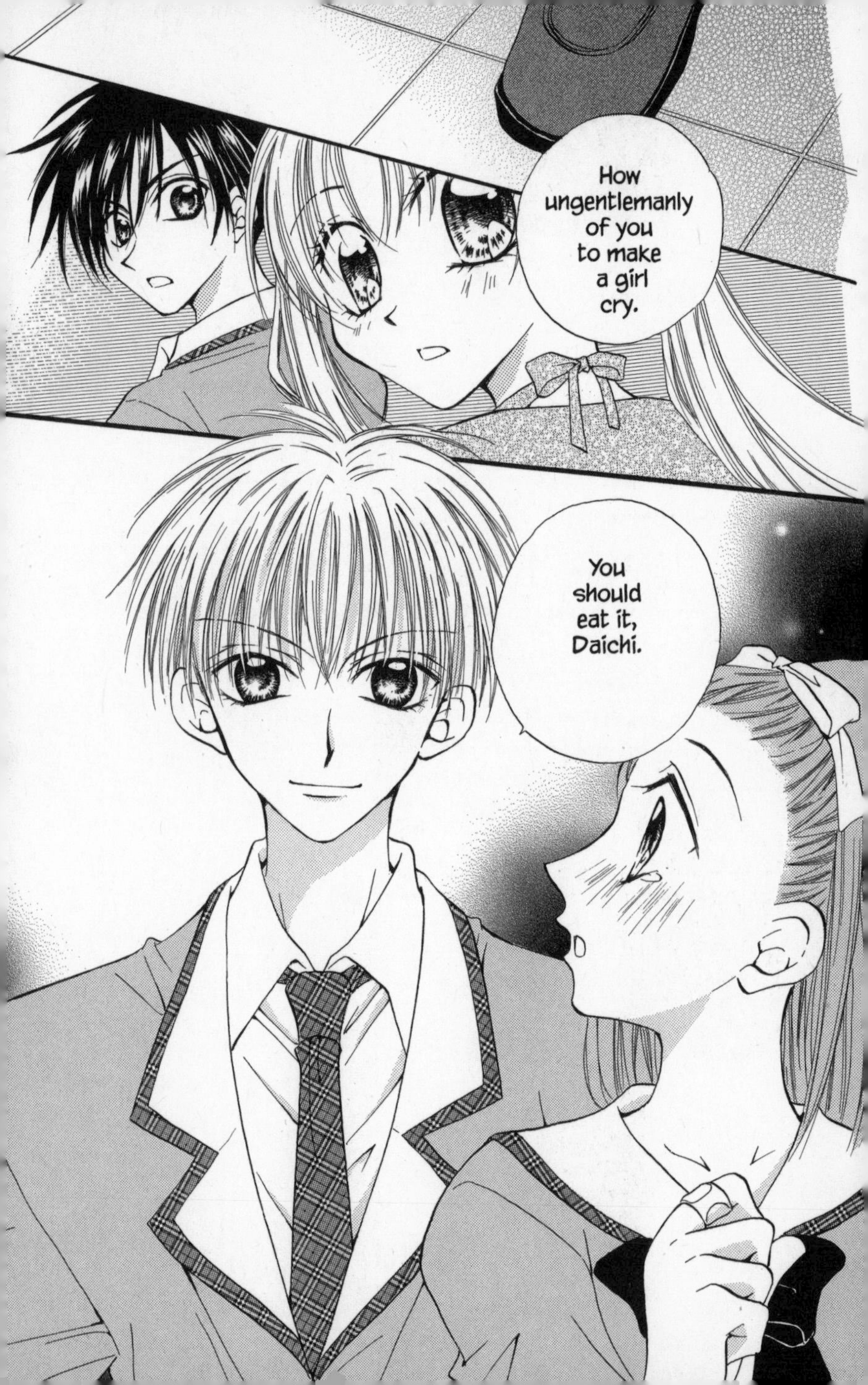
How ungentlemanly of you to make a girl cry.
You should eat it, Daichi.

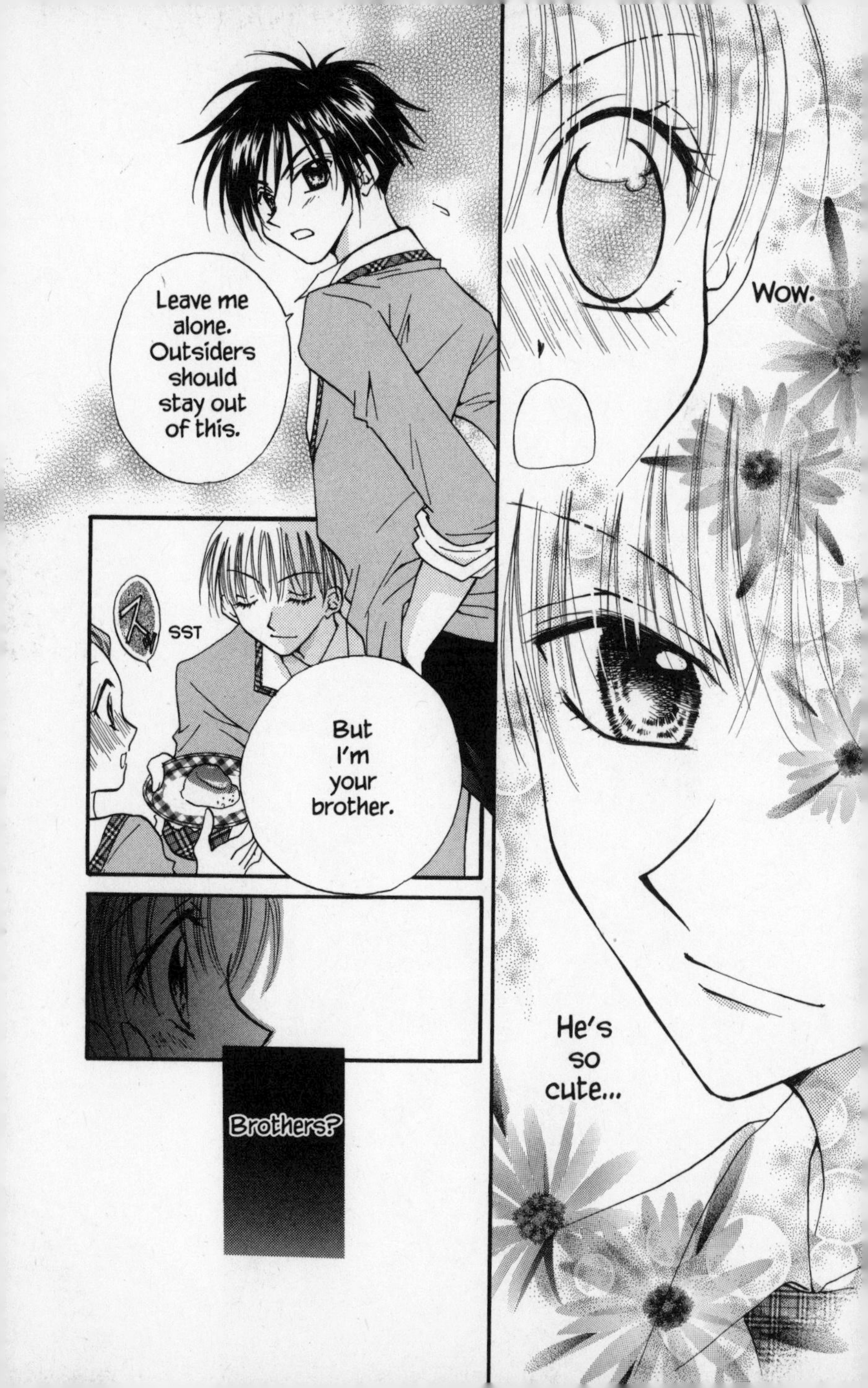
Wow.
He's so cute...
Leave me alone. Outsiders should stay out of this.
SST
But I'm your brother.
Brothers?

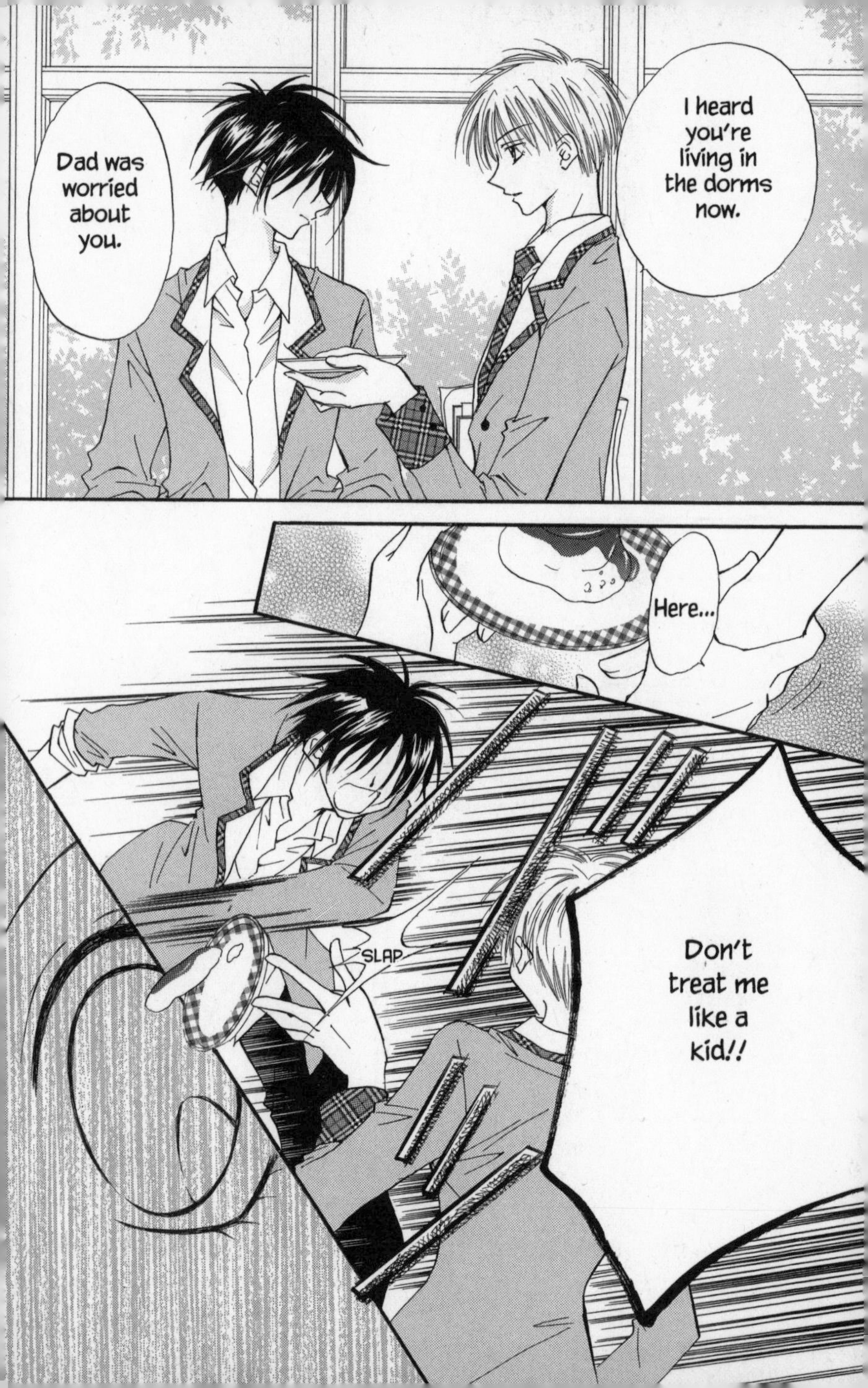

I heard you're living in the dorms now.
Dad was worried about you.
Here...
Don't treat me like a kid!!
SLAP

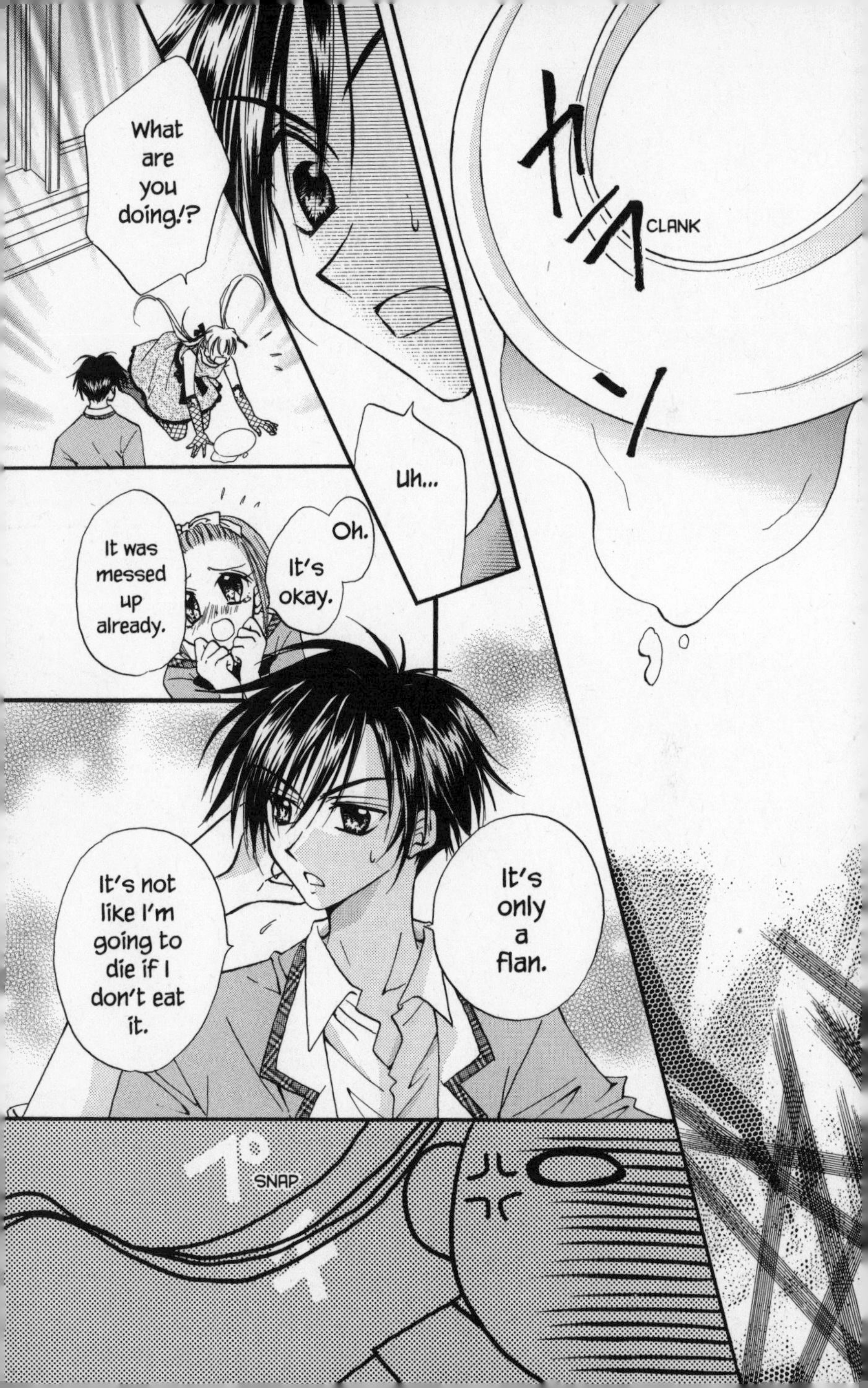
CLANK
What are you doing!?
Uh...
Oh. It's okay.
It was messed up already.
It's only a flan.
It's not like I'm going to die if I don't eat it.
SNAP

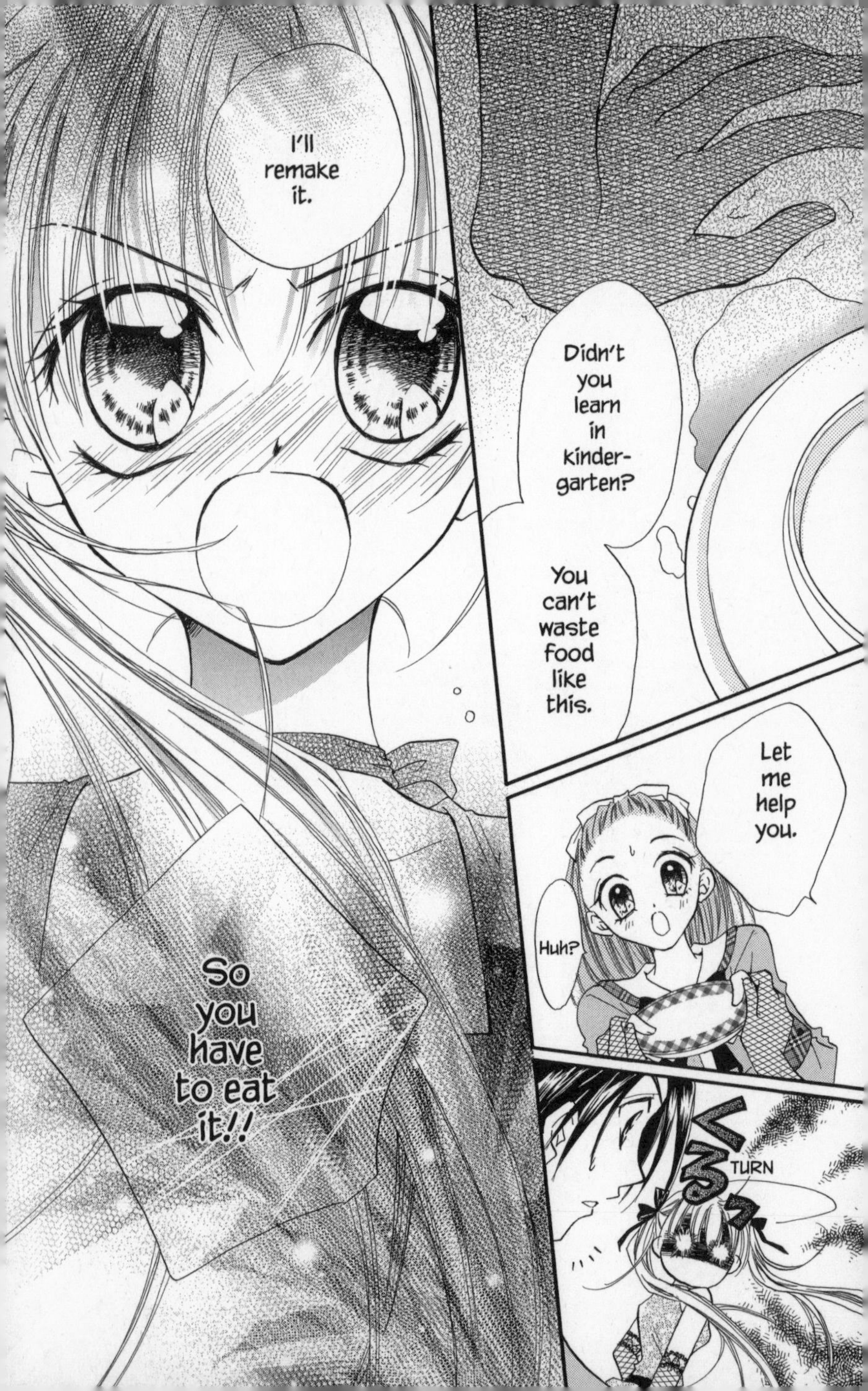
Didn't you learn in kinder-garten?
You can't waste food like this.
Let me help you.
Huh?
TURN
I'll remake it.
So you have to eat it!!

Food

Since I'm doing a manga on food, I'll try to talk about my likes and dislikes. Not that anyone cares. ♪

- **Green Tea**

  I choose this flavor for everything—drinks, ice cream, cake, flan, you name it! I love it!! When a friend told me that I could make pancakes using the rice cooker, I made them green tea-flavored. ♪

- **Hacchou Miso**

  Since I'm from Nagoya, I love this taste. It's so sweet! I usually don't like pork cutlets, but if they're topped with hacchou miso, they become my favorite food. ♥

  For miso soup, I prefer red miso, too.

- **Seasoning**

  I usually don't use seasoning other than miso. I don't pour soy sauce on my fish, and I don't dip tempura in the tempura sauce.

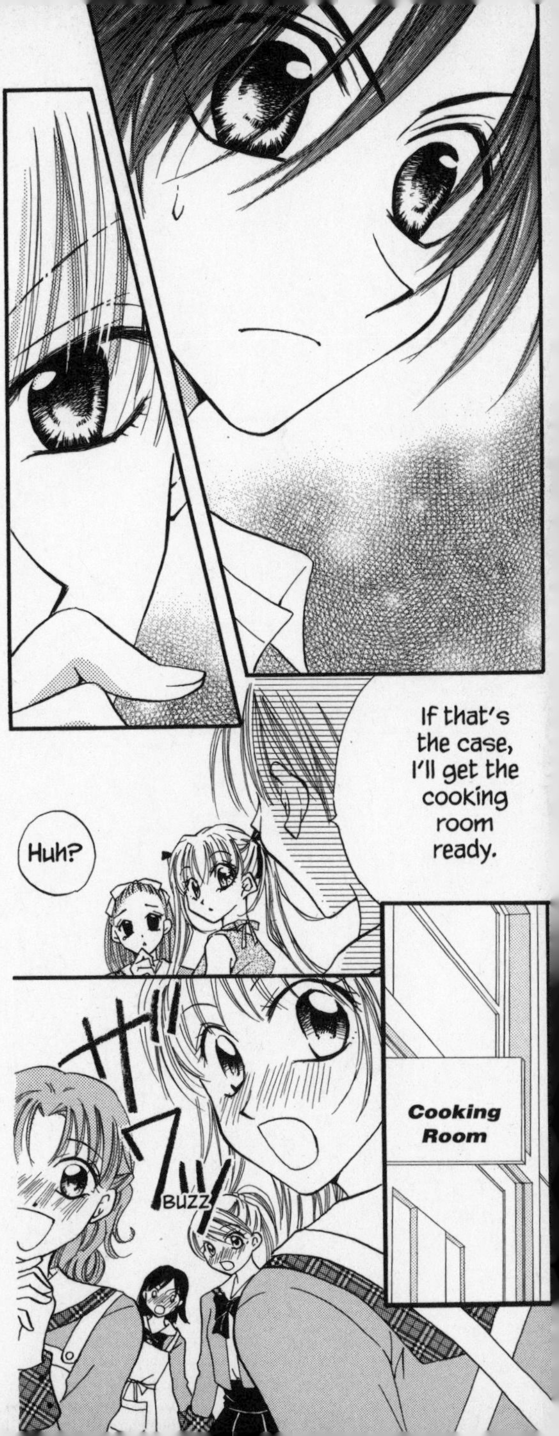
If that's the case, I'll get the cooking room ready.
Huh?
Cooking Room
BUZZ

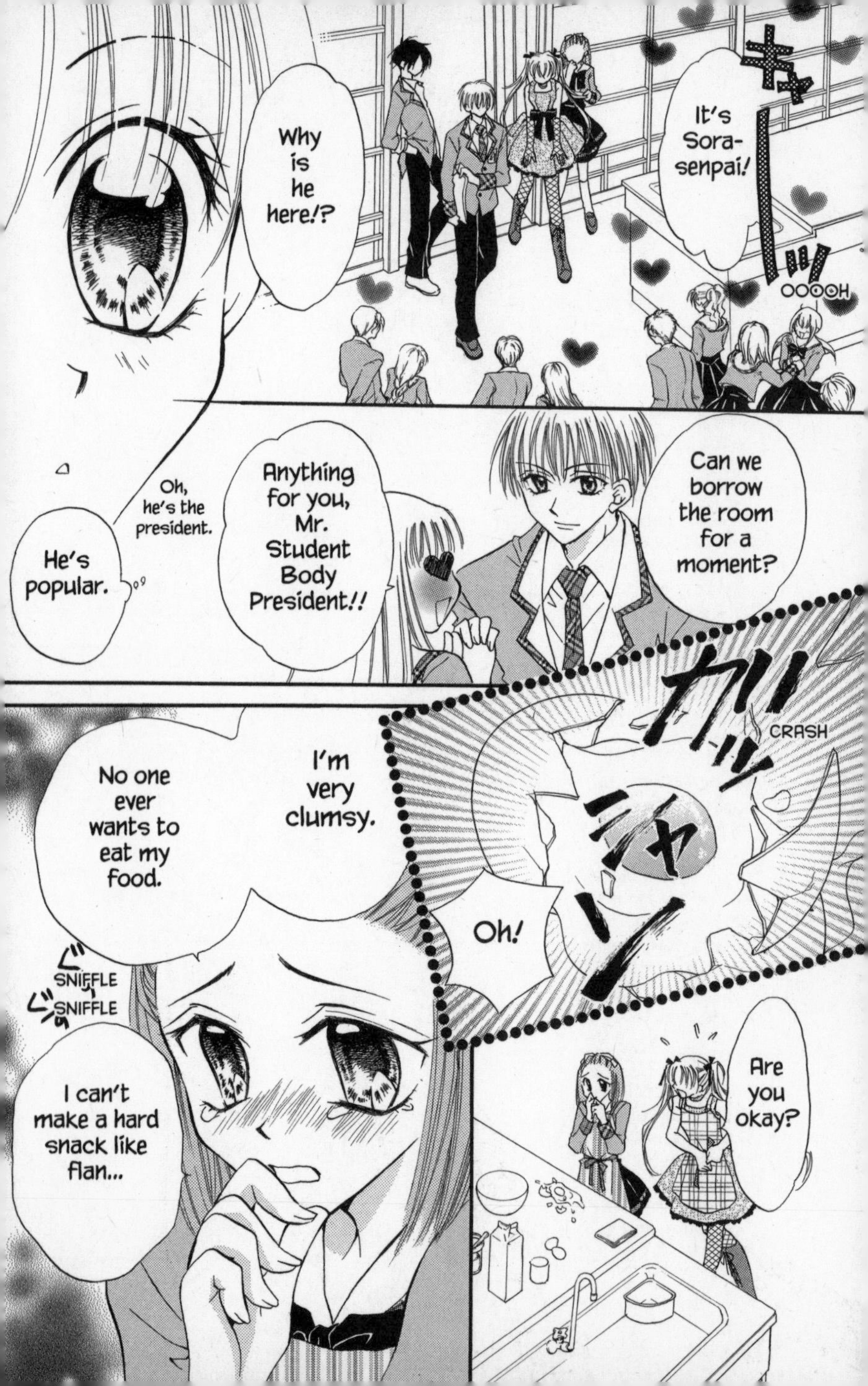
It's Sora-senpai!
キャー!!
OOOOH
Why is he here!?
Can we borrow the room for a moment?
Anything for you, Mr. Student Body President!!
Oh, he's the president.
He's popular.
ガッシャーン
CRASH
Oh!
Are you okay?
I'm very clumsy.
No one ever wants to eat my food.
SNIFFLE
SNIFFLE
I can't make a hard snack like flan...

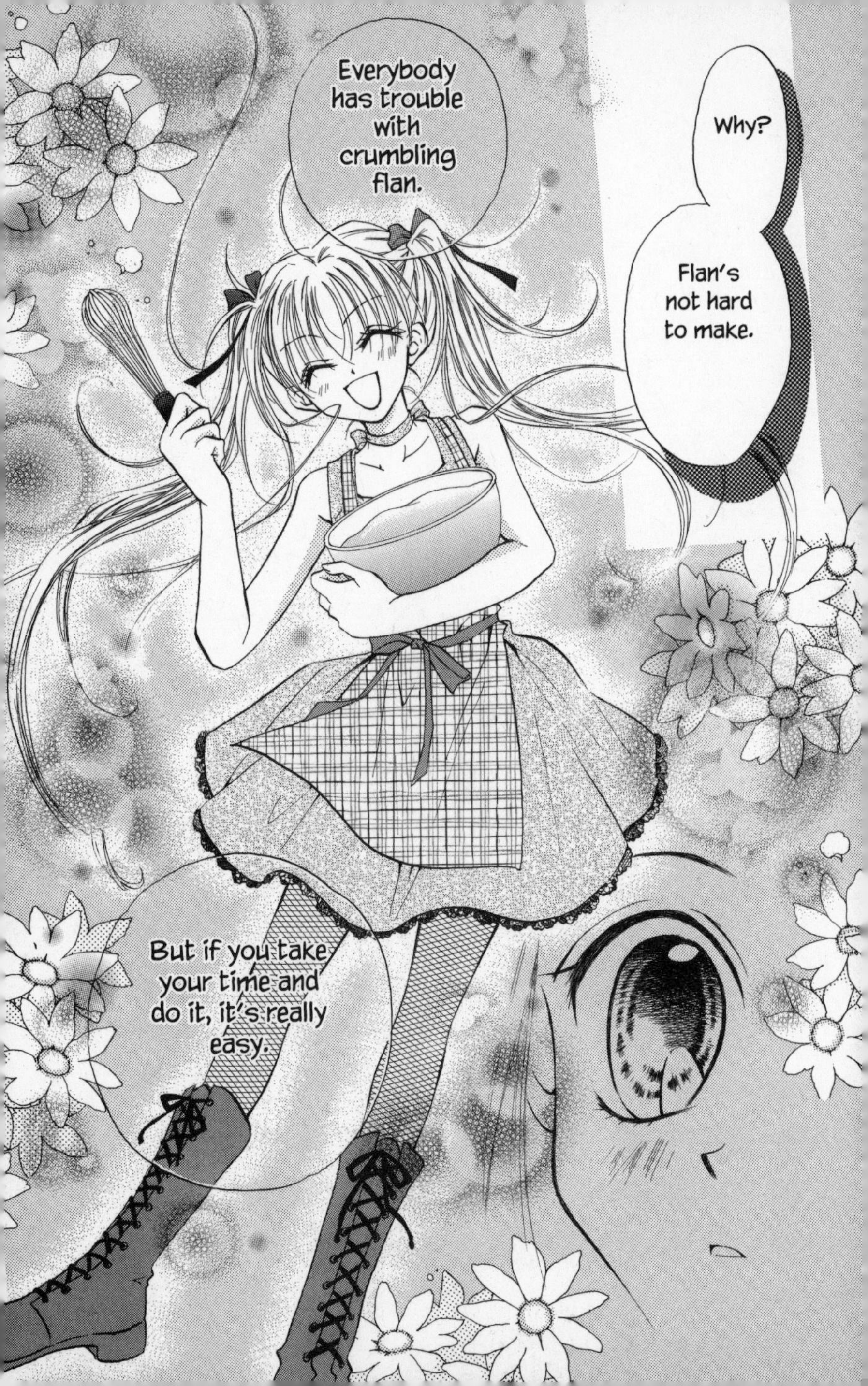
Why?
Flan's not hard to make.
Everybody has trouble with crumbling flan.
But if you take your time and do it, it's really easy.

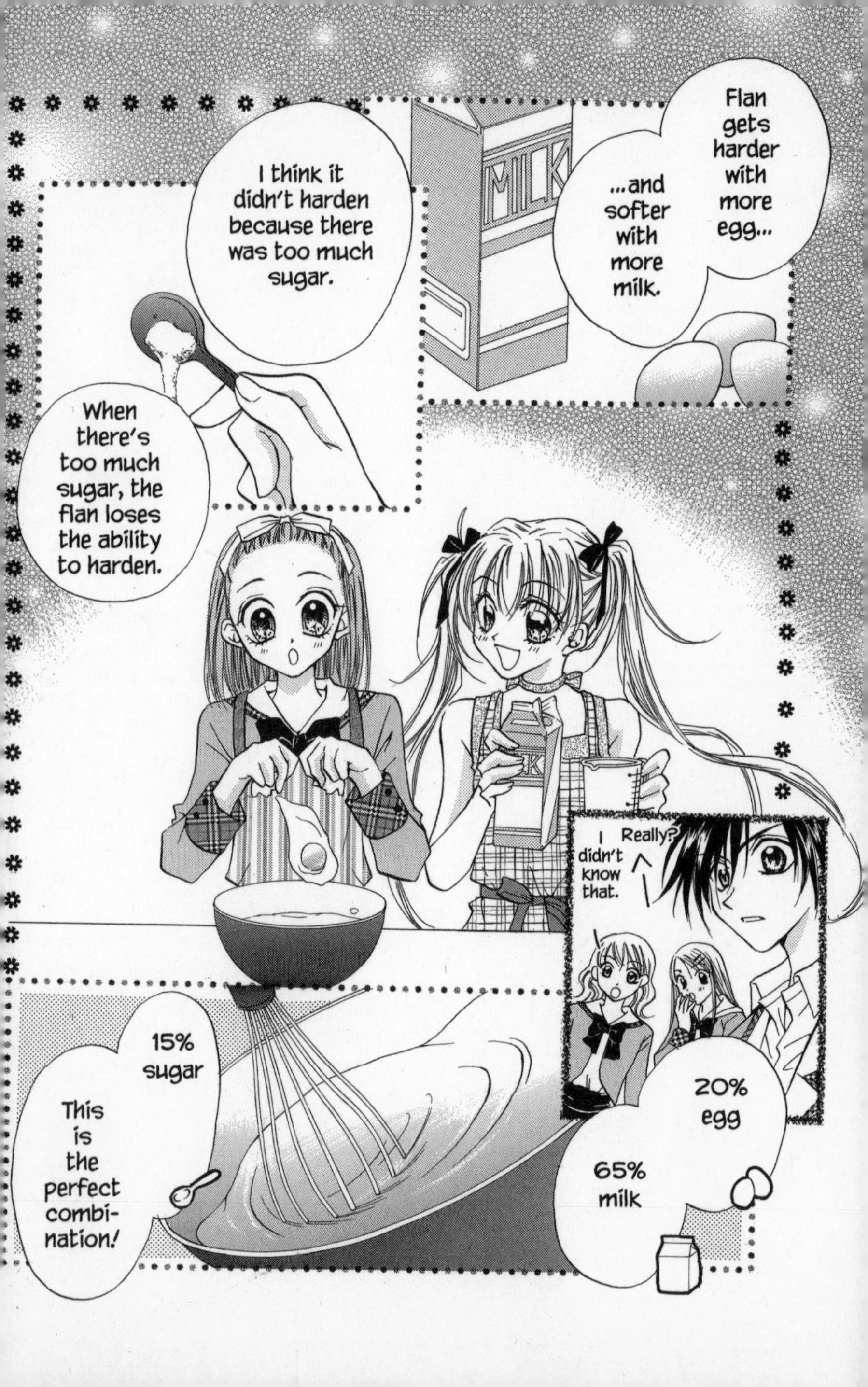
Flan gets harder with more egg...
...and softer with more milk.
I think it didn't harden because there was too much sugar.
When there's too much sugar, the flan loses the ability to harden.
Really?
I didn't know that.
20% egg
65% milk
15% sugar
This is the perfect combination!

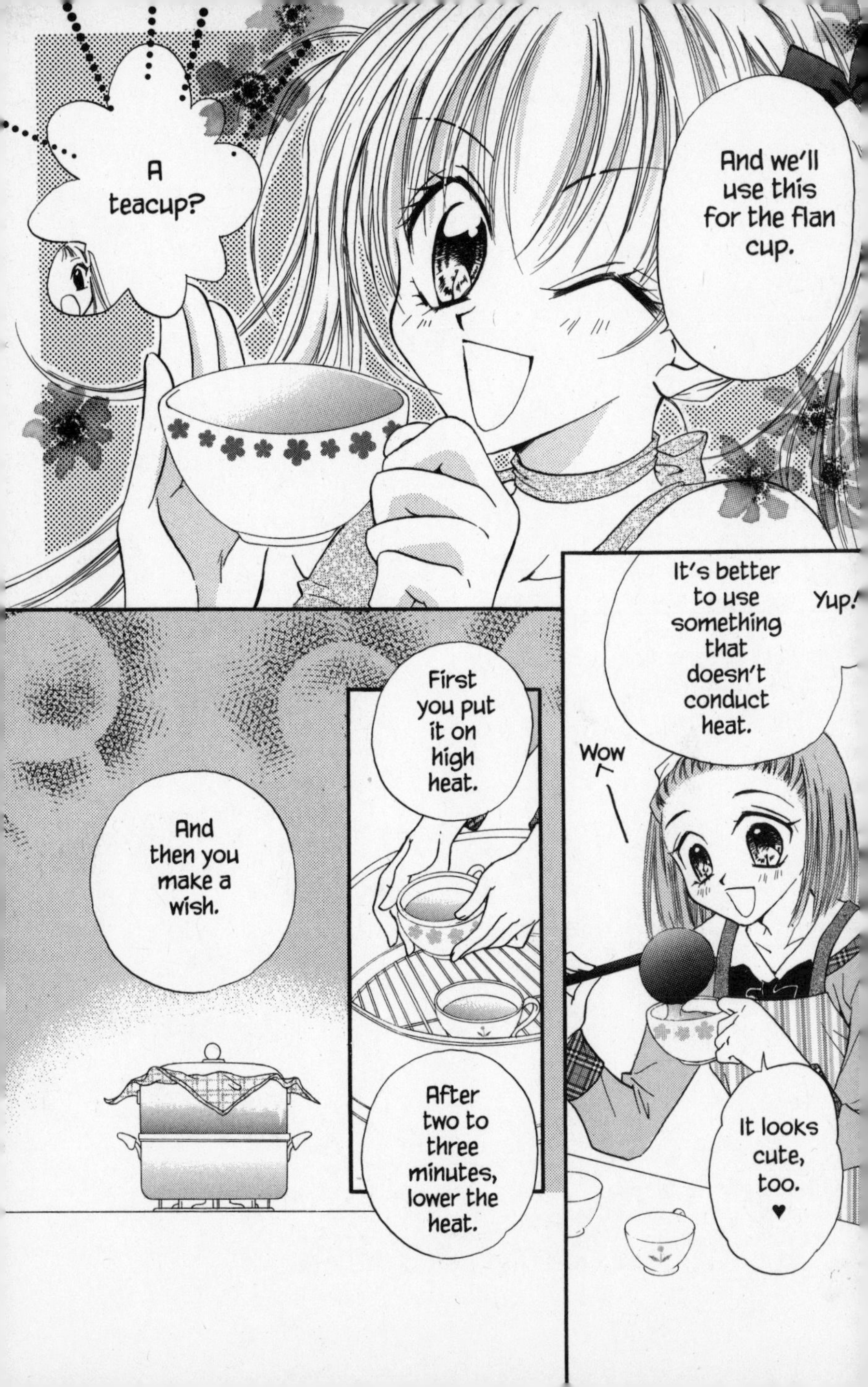
And we'll use this for the flan cup.
A teacup?
It's better to use something that doesn't conduct heat.
Yup!
Wow
It looks cute, too. ♥
First you put it on high heat.
After two to three minutes, lower the heat.
And then you make a wish.

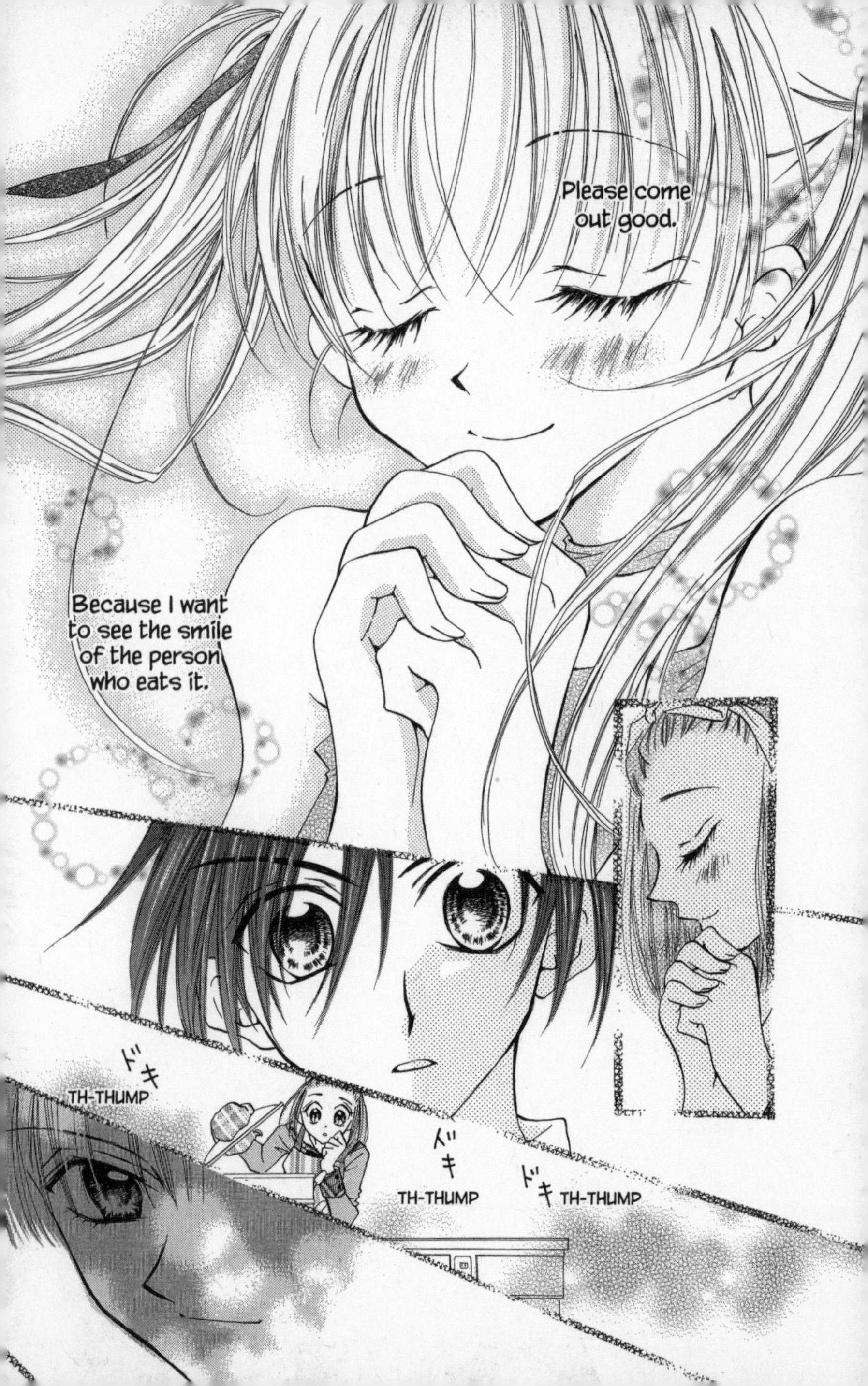
Please come out good.
Because I want to see the smile of the person who eats it.
ドキ
TH-THUMP
ドキ
TH-THUMP
ドキ
TH-THUMP

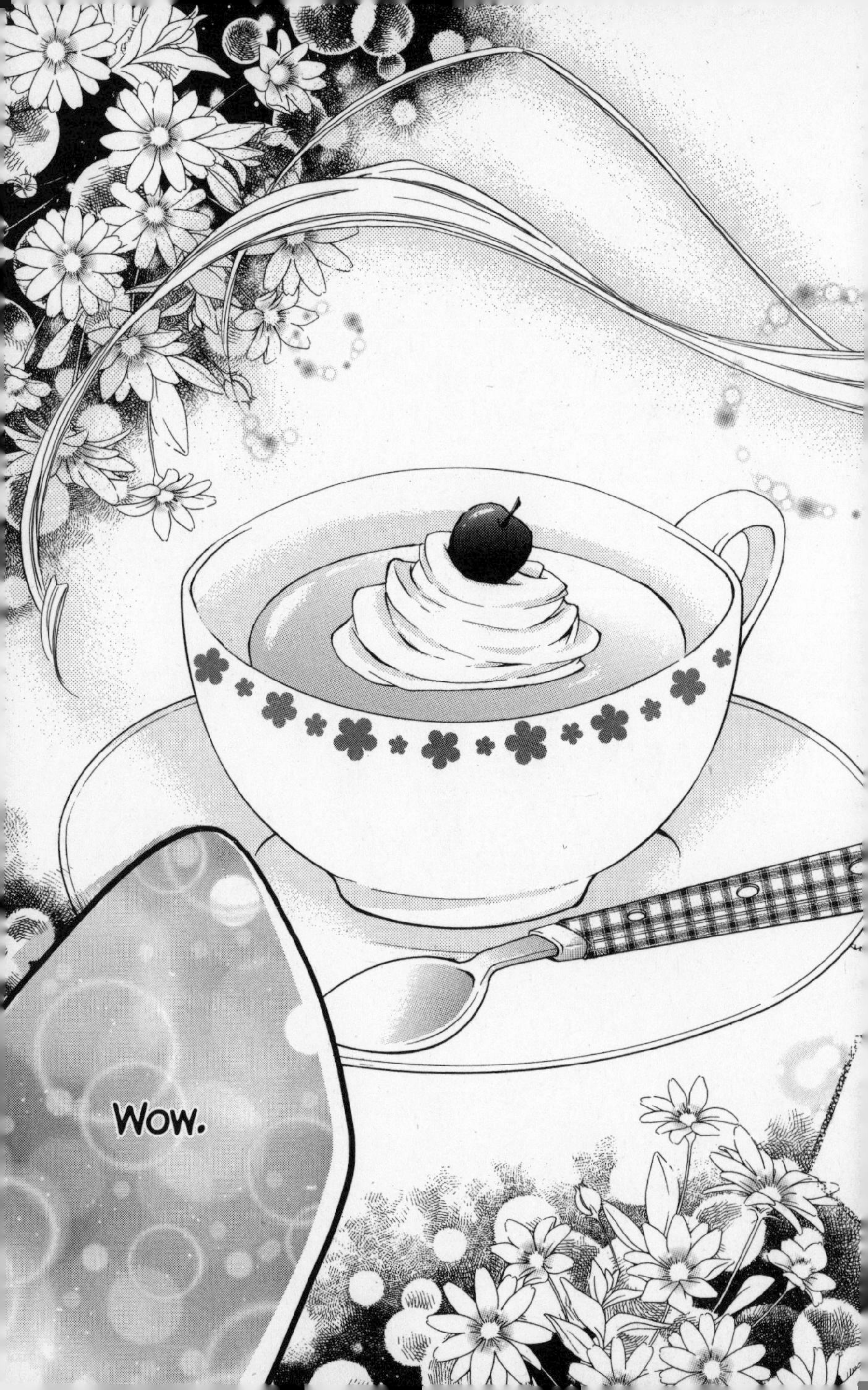
Wow.

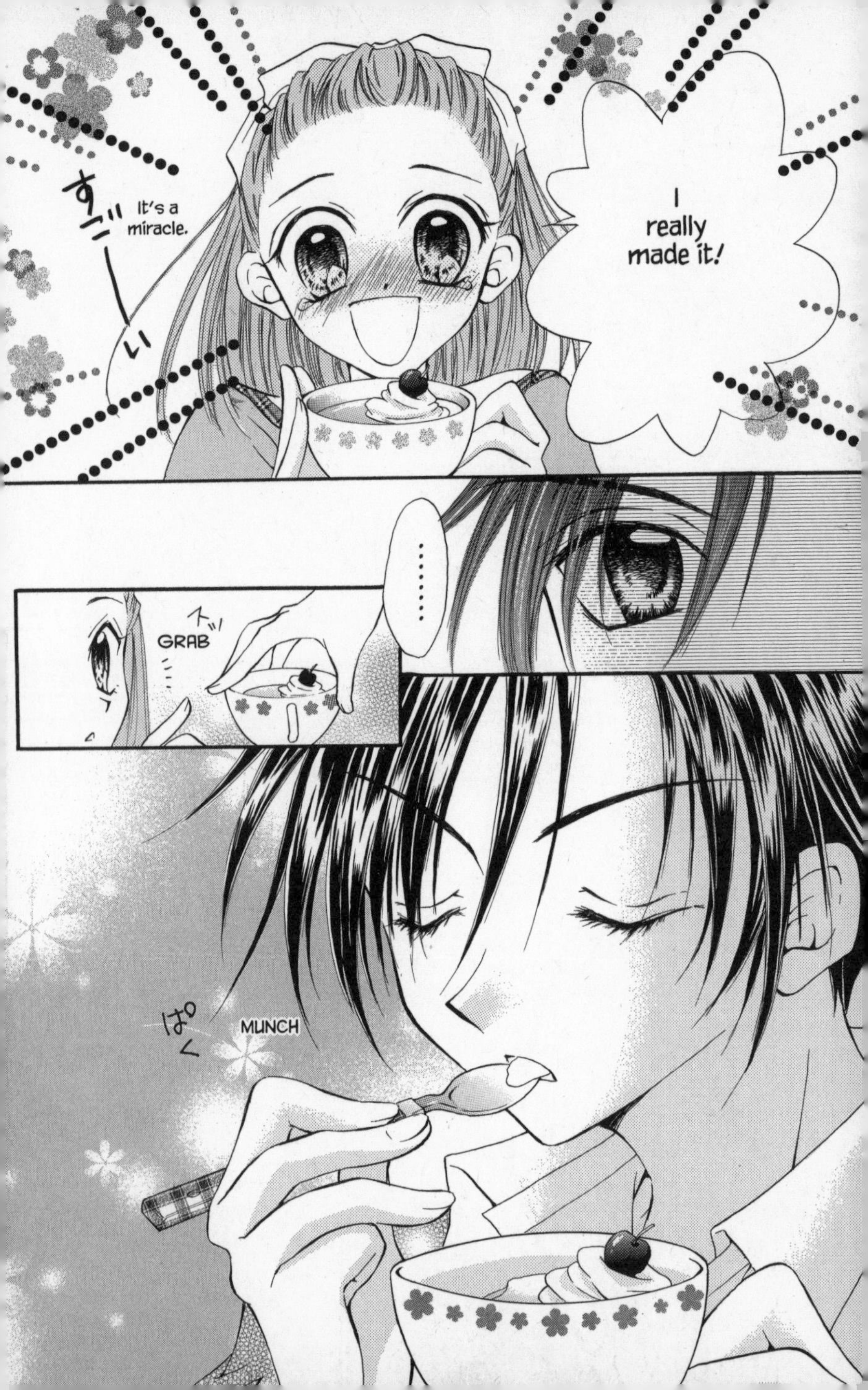
I really made it!
すごーい
It's a miracle.
......
ズッ
GRAB
ぱく
MUNCH

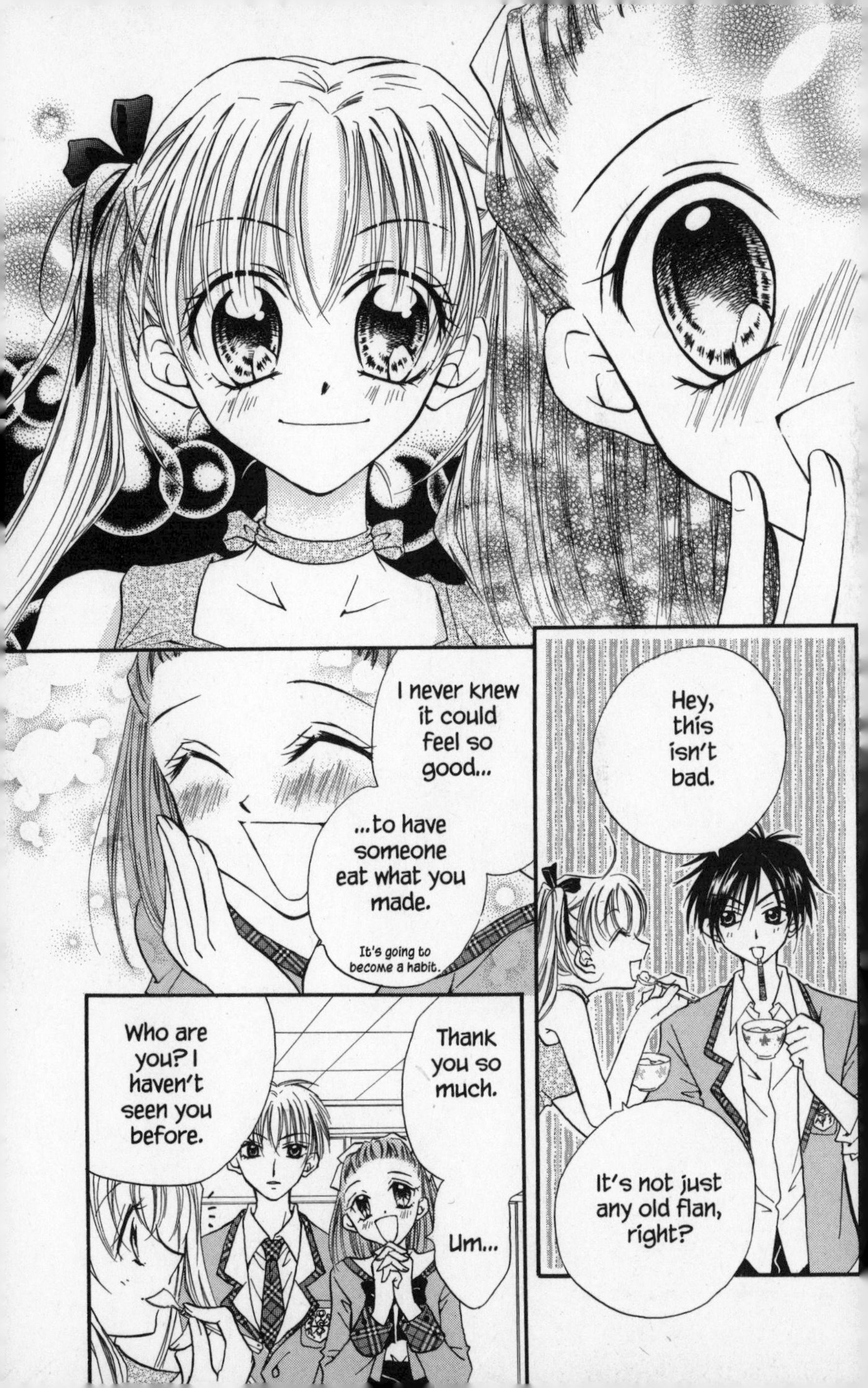
Hey, this isn't bad.
It's not just any old flan, right?
I never knew it could feel so good...
...to have someone eat what you made.
It's going to become a habit.
Thank you so much.
Um...
Who are you? I haven't seen you before.

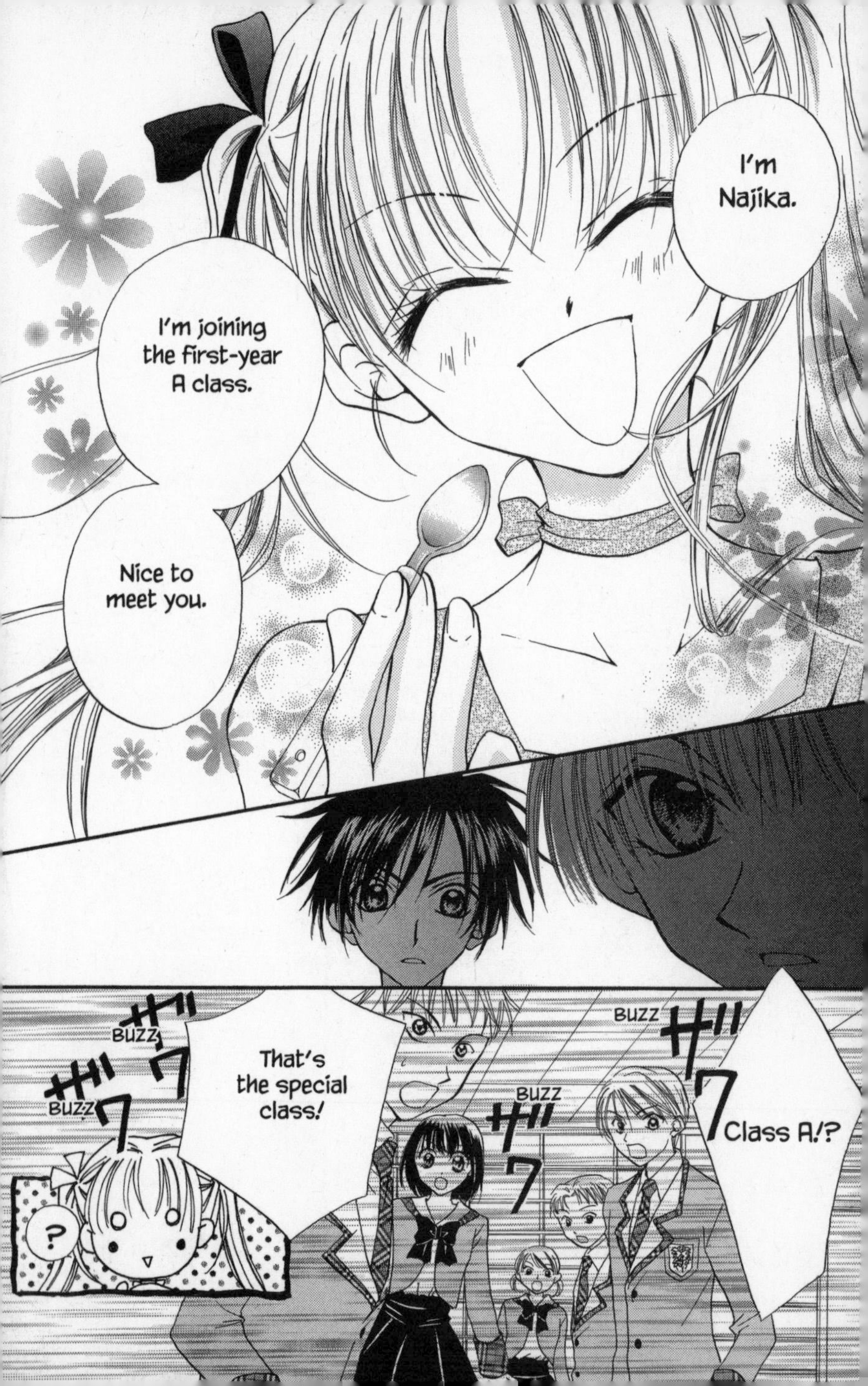
I'm Najika.
I'm joining the first-year A class.
Nice to meet you.
BUZZ
ザワ
Class A!?
BUZZ
ザワ
That's the special class!
BUZZ
ザワ
BUZZ
ザワ
?

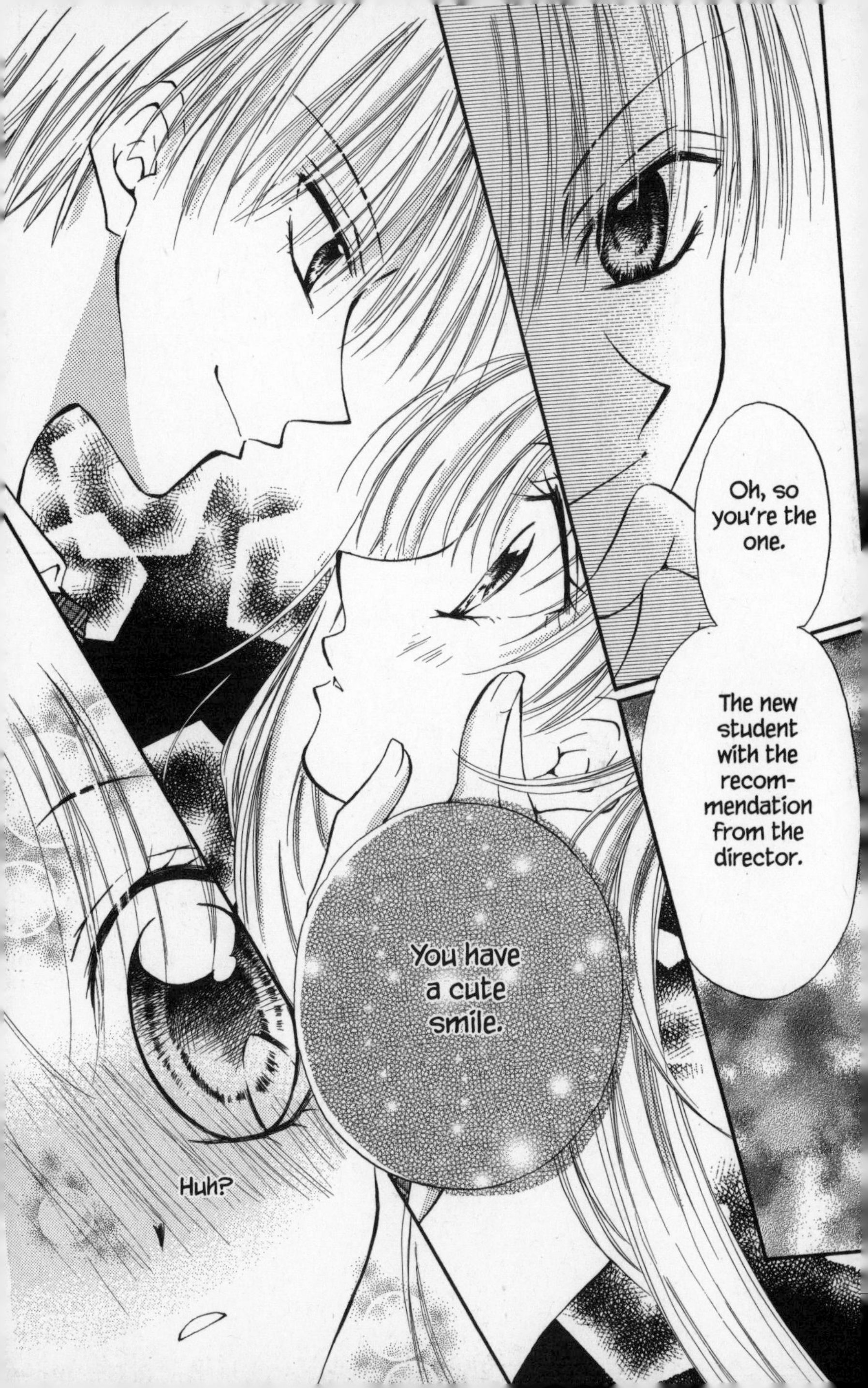
Oh, so you're the one.
The new student with the recom-mendation from the director.
You have a cute smile.
Huh?

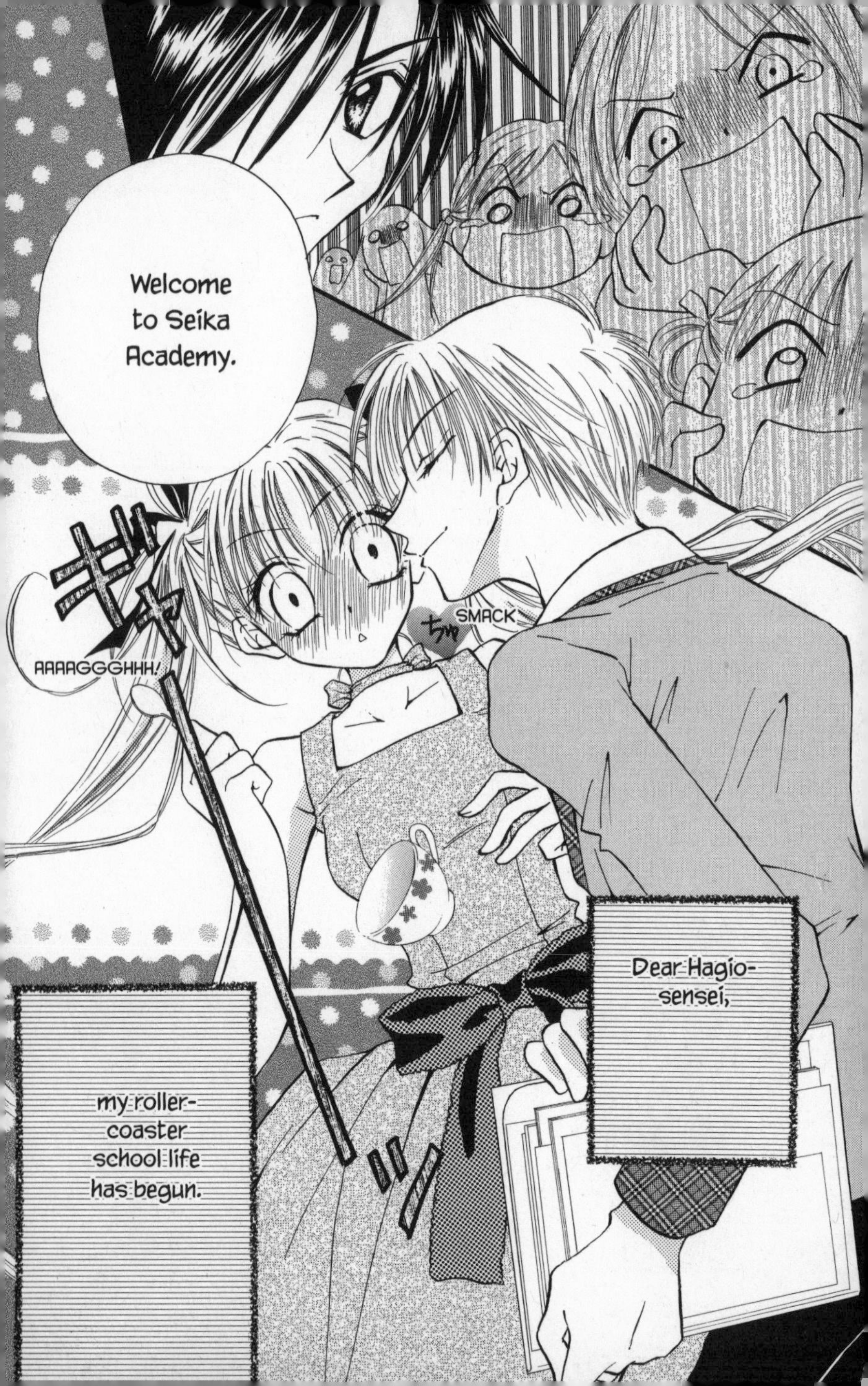
Welcome to Seika Academy.
Dear Hagio-sensei,
SMACK
AAAAGGGHHH!
my roller-coaster school life has begun.

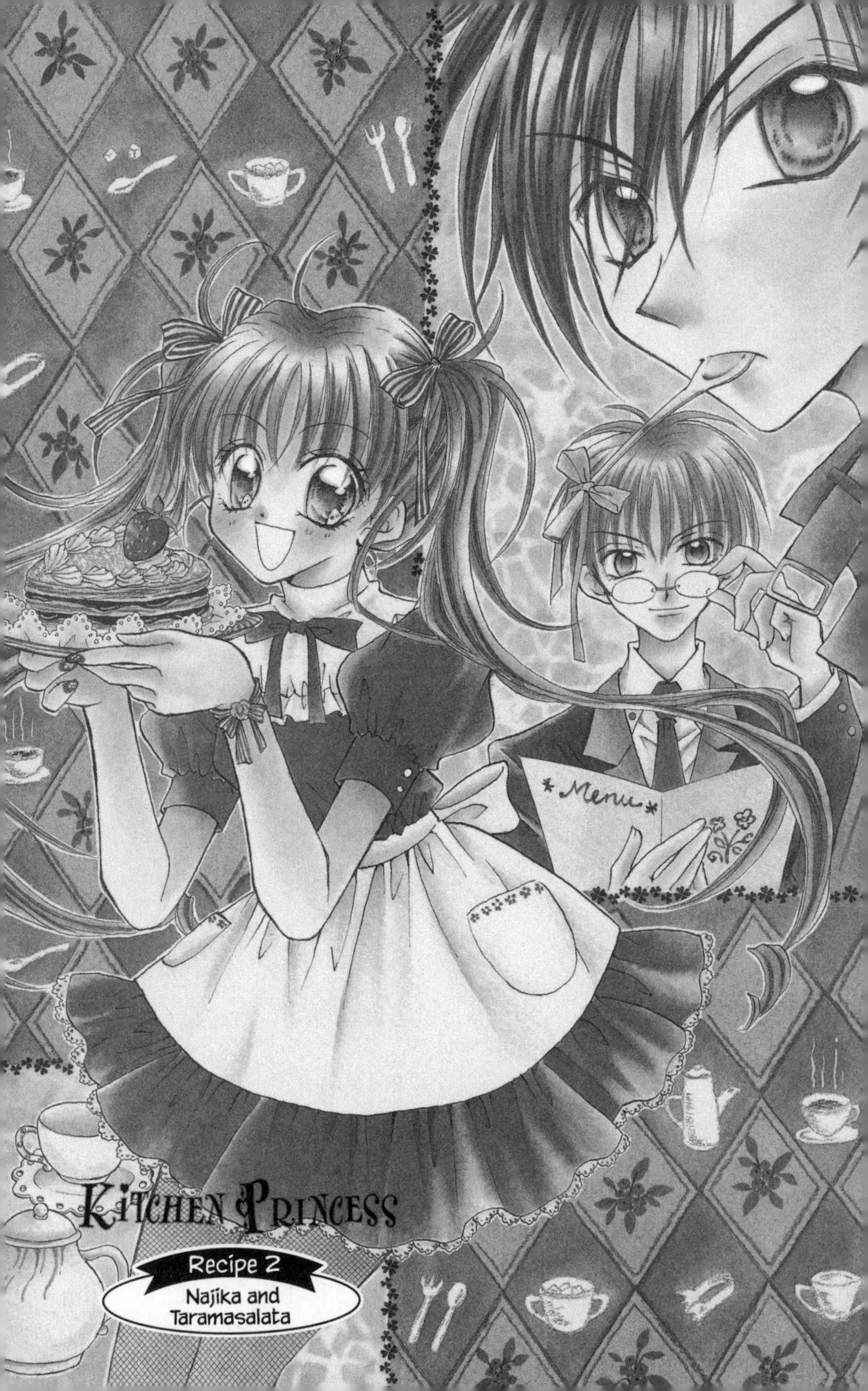

Menu
Kitchen Princess
Recipe 2
Najika and Taramasalata

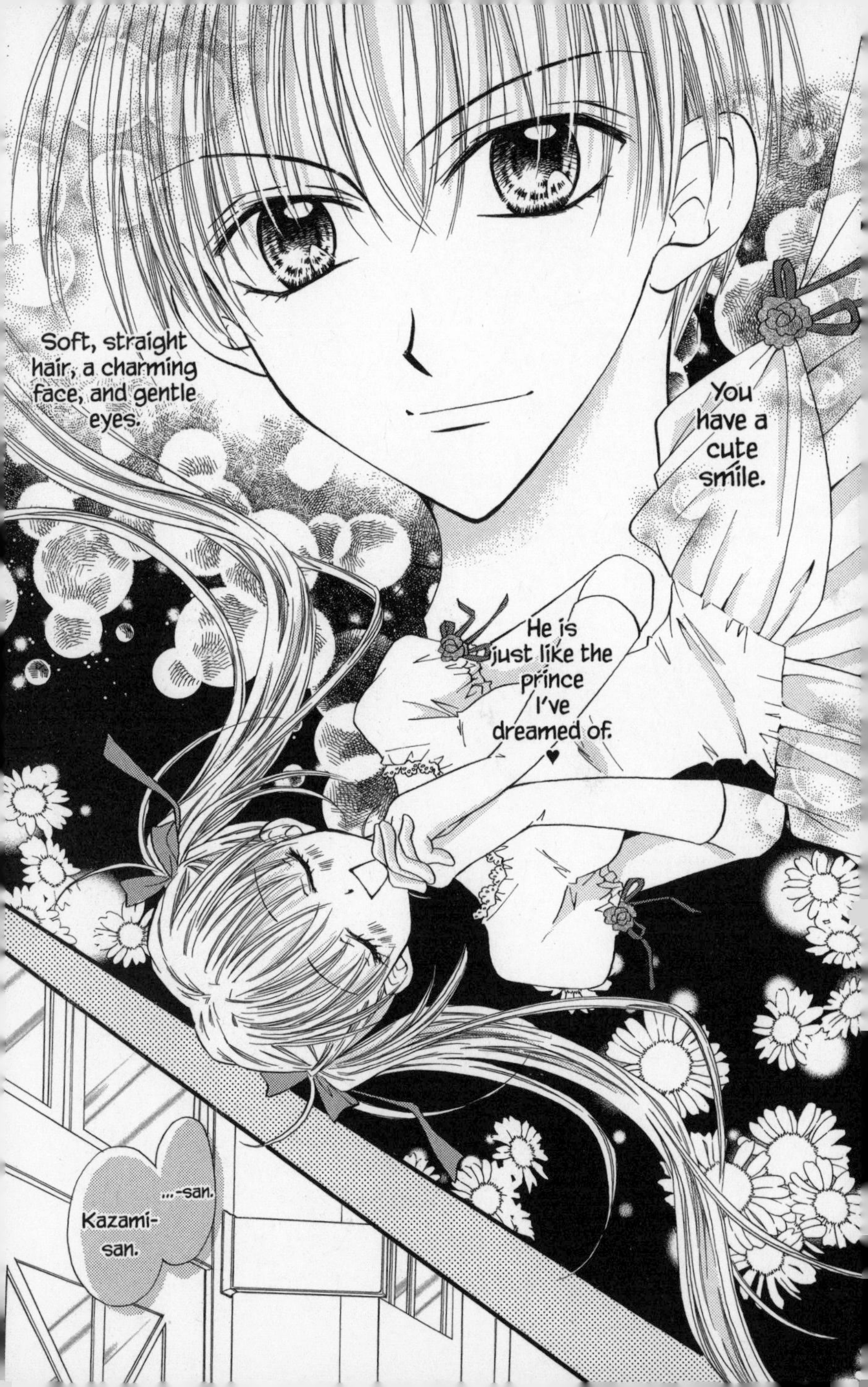
You have a cute smile.
Soft, straight hair, a charming face, and gentle eyes.
He is just like the prince I've dreamed of. ♥
...-san.
Kazami-san.

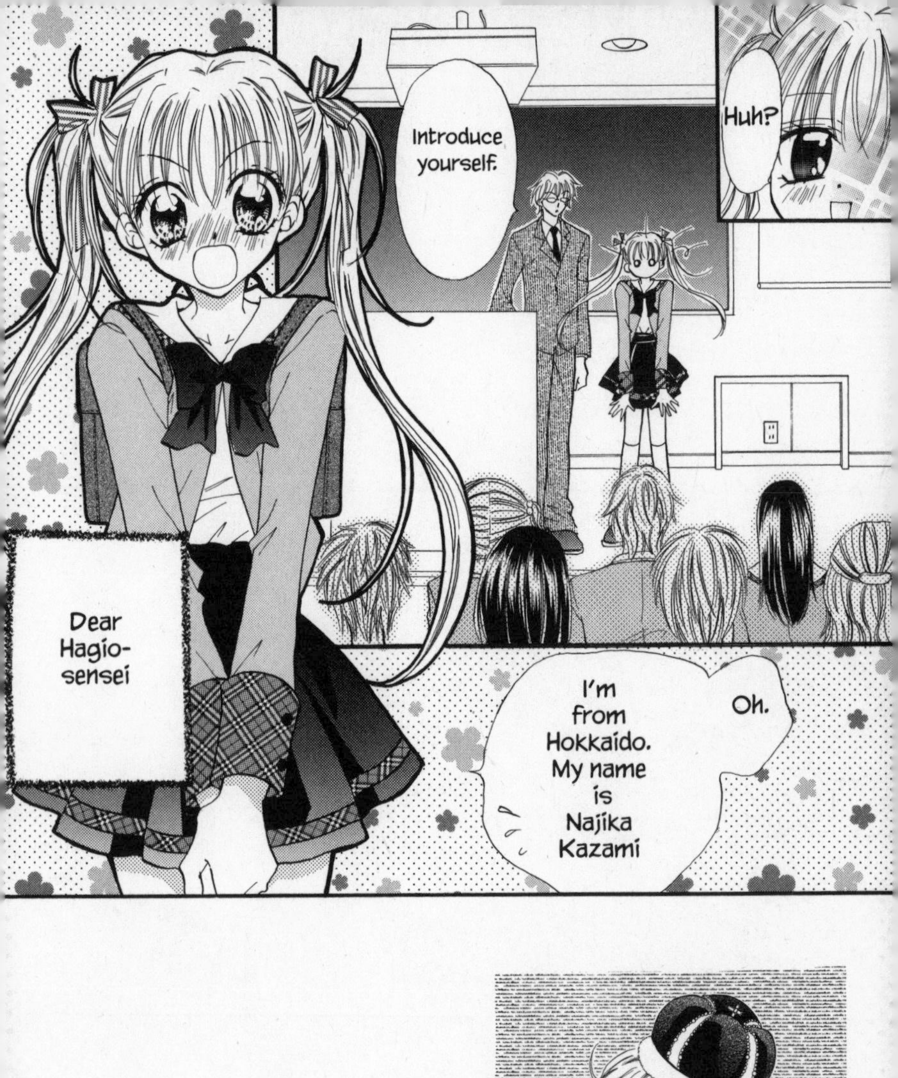
Huh?
Introduce yourself.
Oh.
I'm from Hokkaido. My name is Najika Kazami
Dear Hagio-sensei

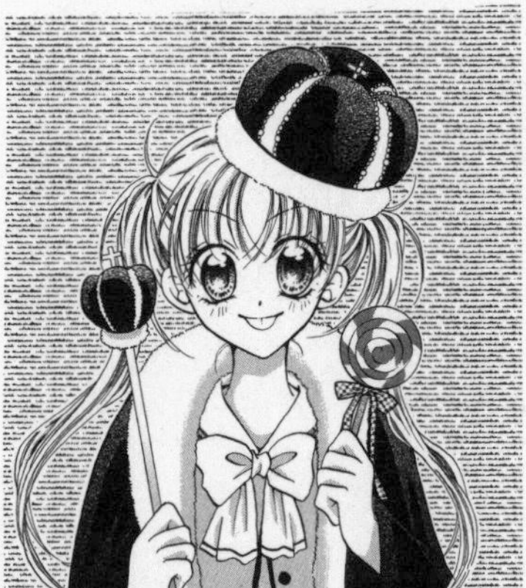

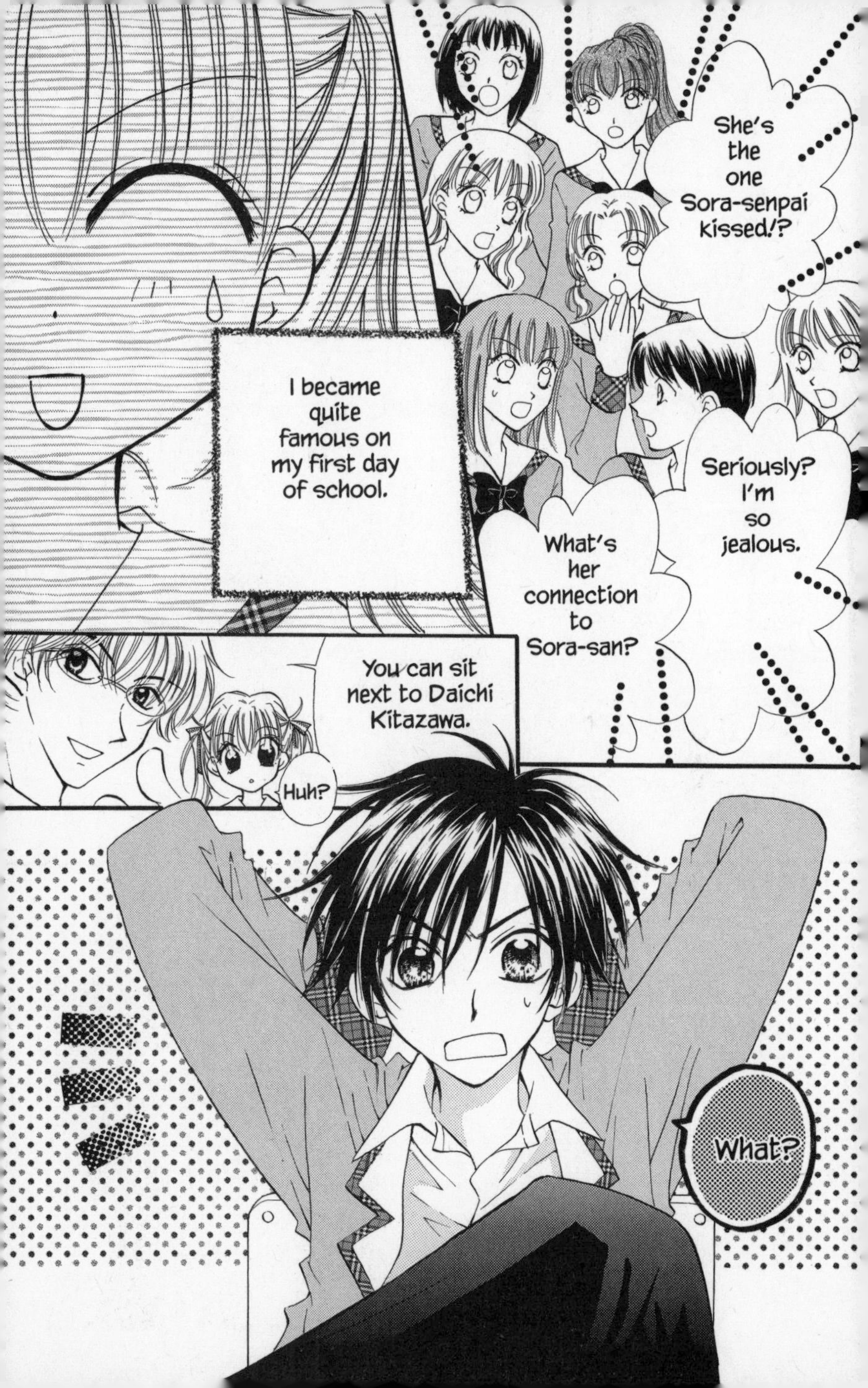
She's the one Sora-senpai kissed!?
Seriously? I'm so jealous.
What's her connection to Sora-san?
I became quite famous on my first day of school.
You can sit next to Daichi Kitazawa.
Huh?
What?

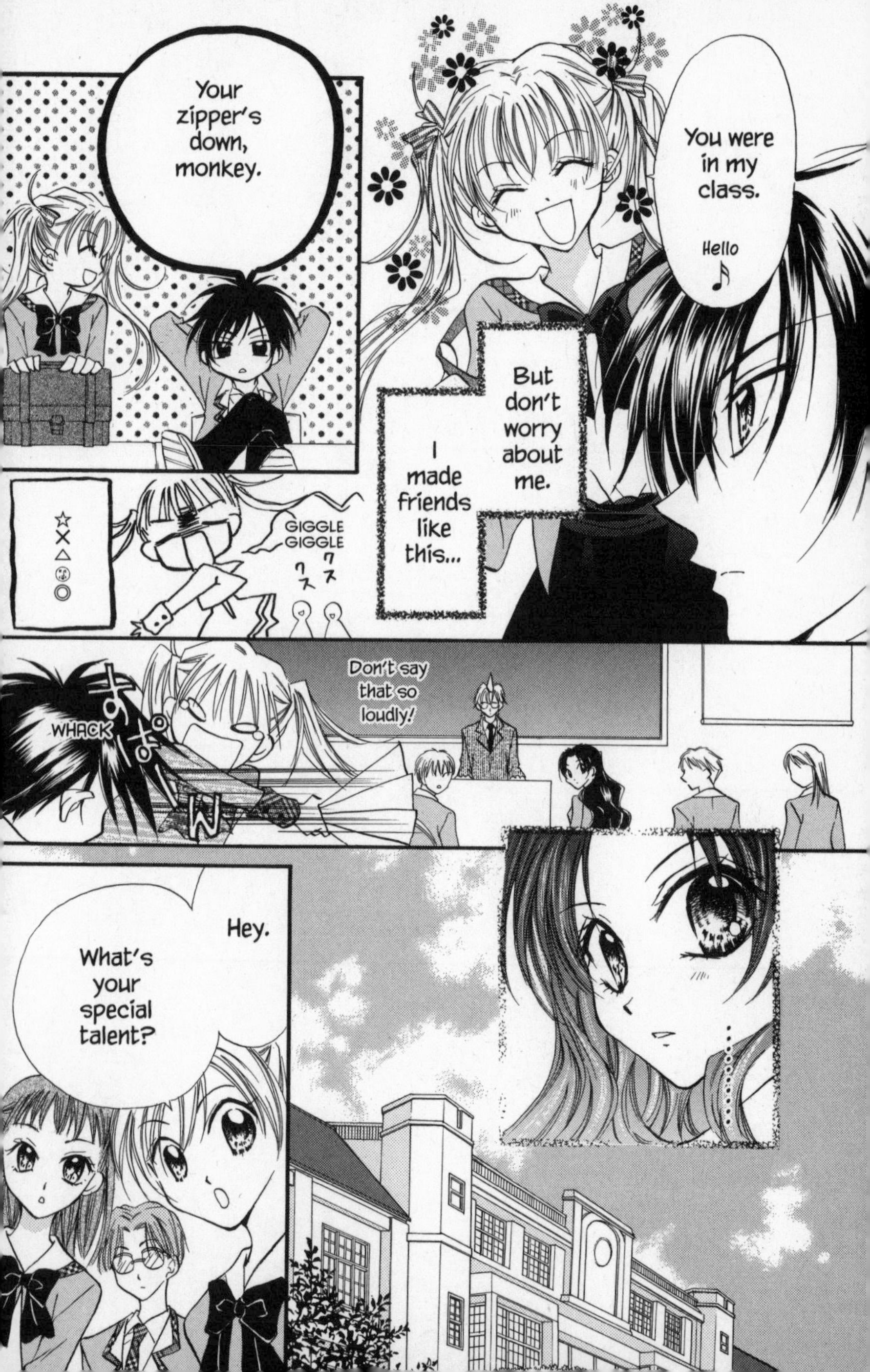
You were in my class.
Hello ♪
But don't worry about me.
I made friends like this...
Your zipper's down, monkey.
☆ × △ ◎
GIGGLE GIGGLE
クス クス
Don't say that so loudly!
WHACK
Hey.
What's your special talent?

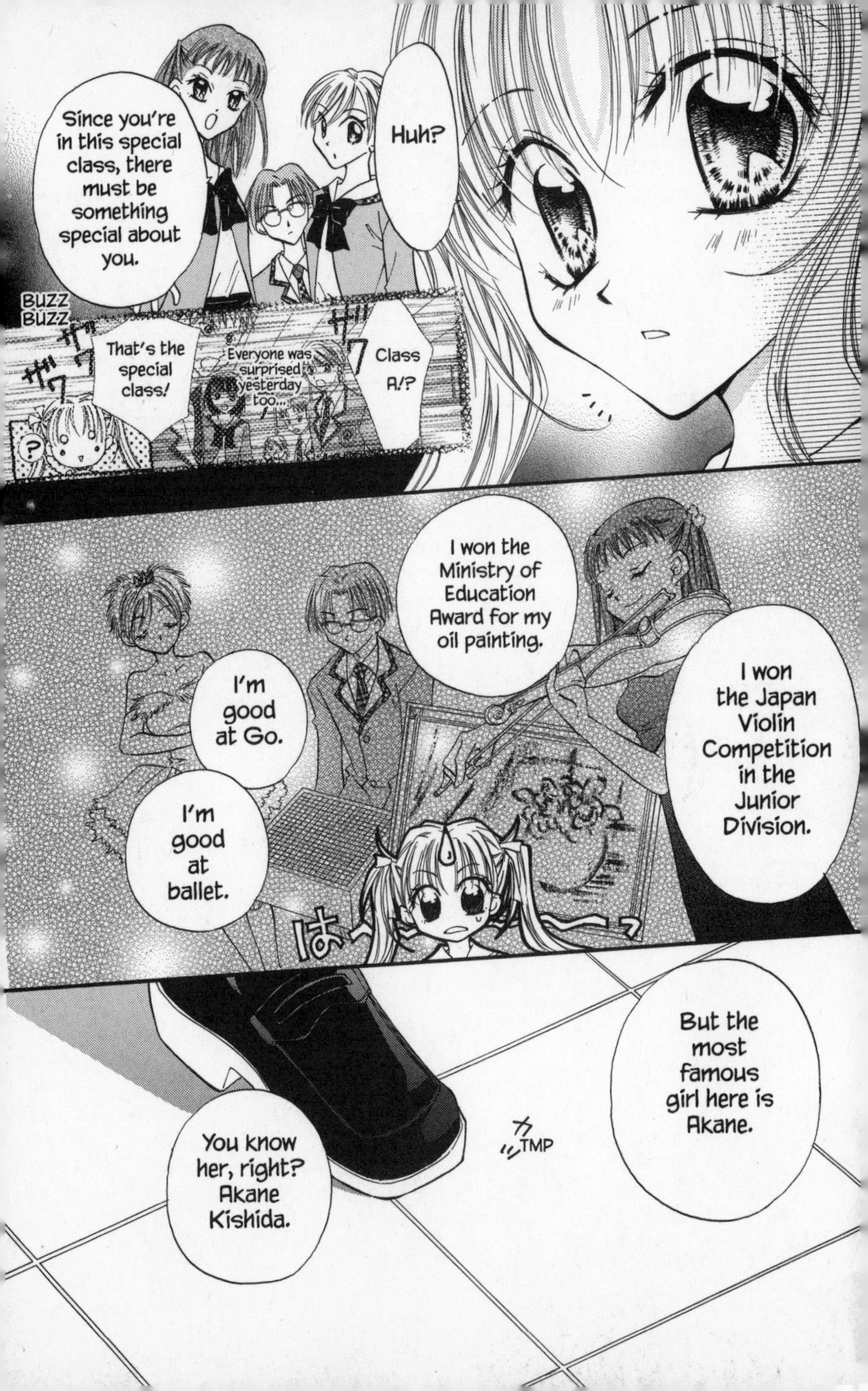
Since you're in this special class, there must be something special about you.
Huh?
Class A!?
Everyone was surprised yesterday too...
That's the special class!
BUZZ BUZZ
I won the Japan Violin Competition in the Junior Division.
I won the Ministry of Education Award for my oil painting.
I'm good at Go.
I'm good at ballet.
But the most famous girl here is Akane.
TMP
You know her, right? Akane Kishida.

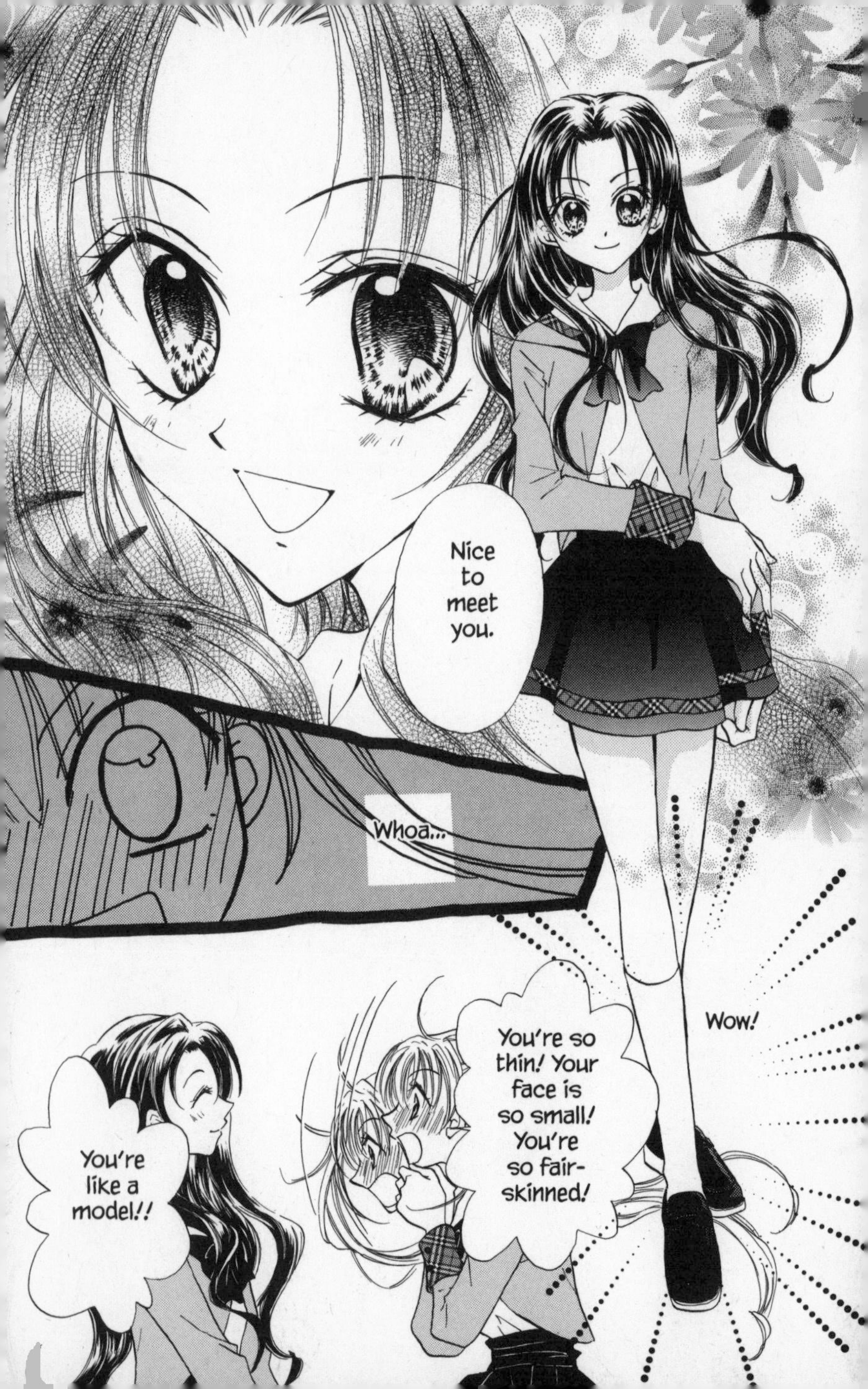
Nice to meet you.
Whoa...
Wow!
You're so thin! Your face is so small! You're so fair-skinned!
You're like a model!!

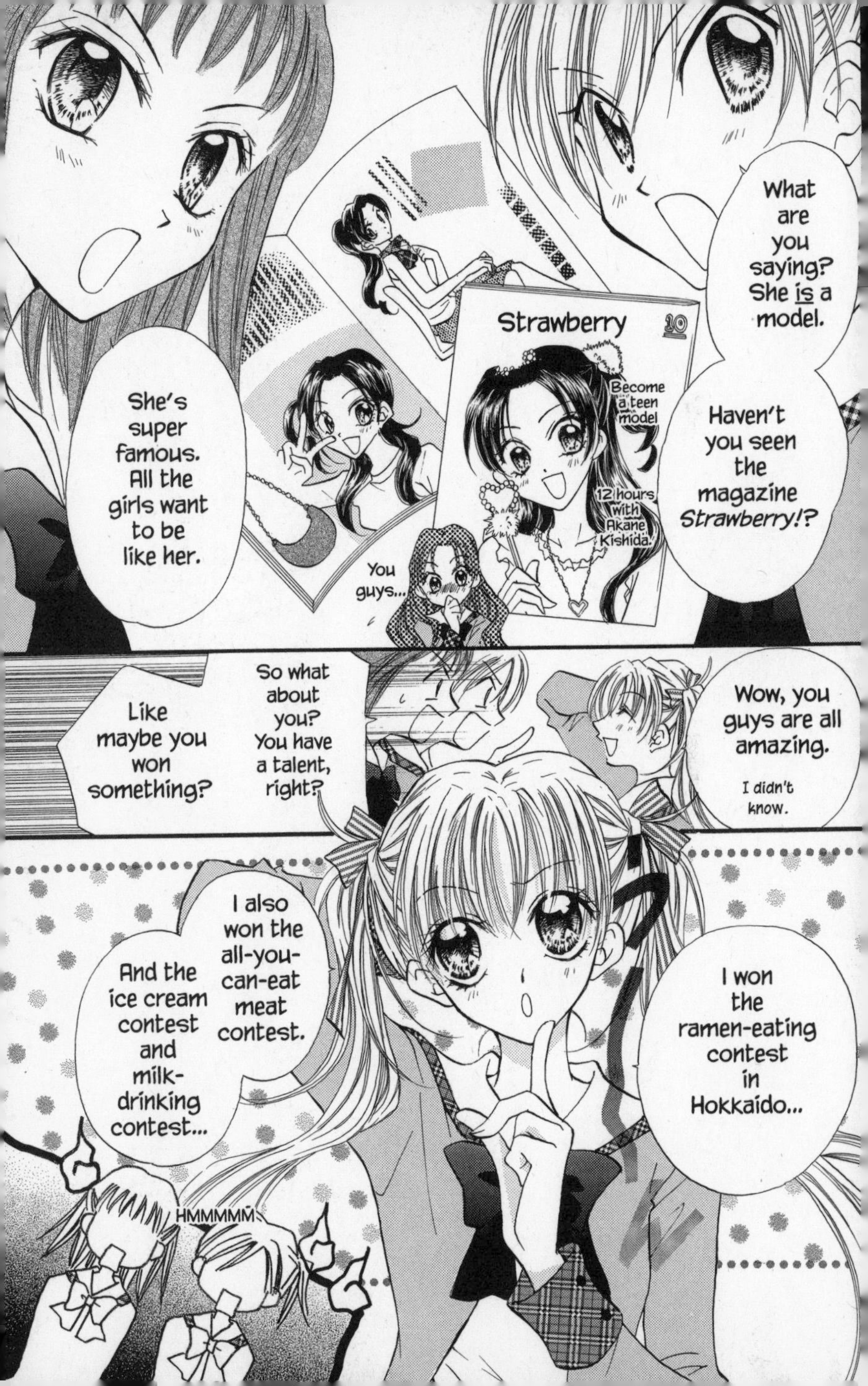
What are you saying? She is a model.
Haven't you seen the magazine Strawberry!?
Strawberry
10
Become a teen model
12 hours with Akane Kishida.
You guys...
She's super famous. All the girls want to be like her.
Wow, you guys are all amazing.
I didn't know.
So what about you? You have a talent, right?
Like maybe you won something?
I won the ramen-eating contest in Hokkaido...
I also won the all-you-can-eat meat contest.
And the ice cream contest and milk-drinking contest...
HMMMMM

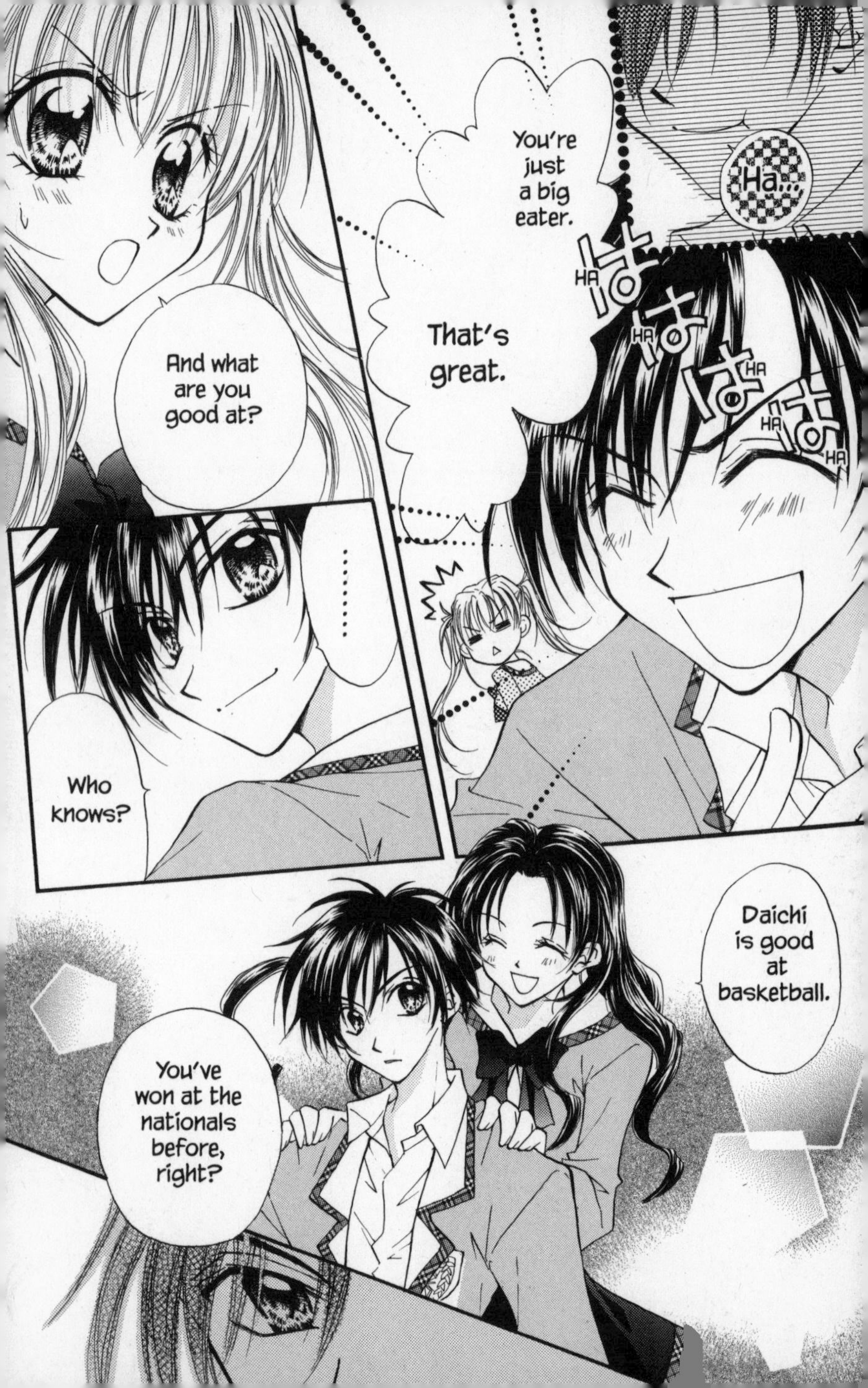
Ha...
You're just a big eater.
That's great.
HA HA HA HA HA
And what are you good at?
Who knows?
Daichi is good at basketball.
You've won at the nationals before, right?

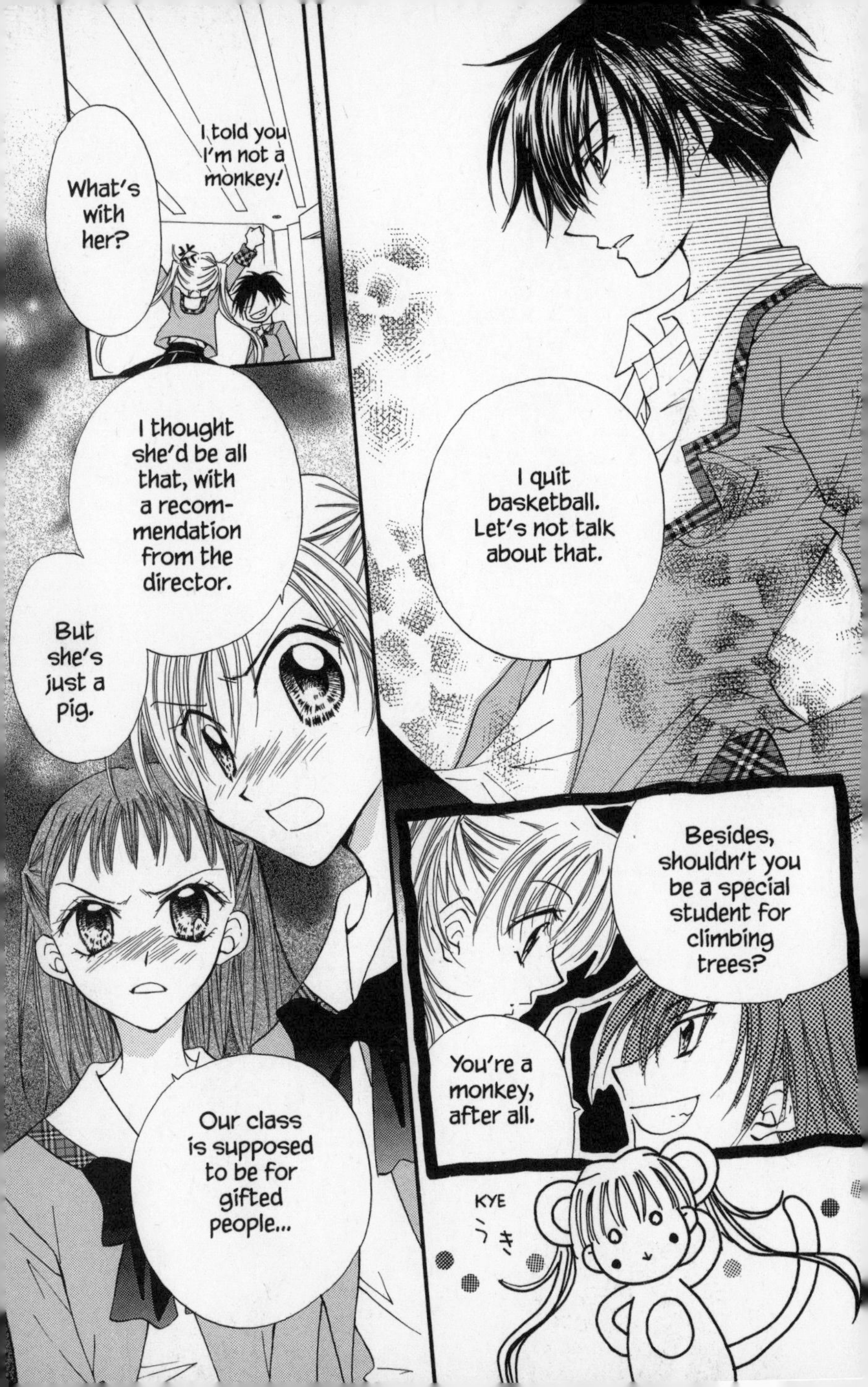
I quit basketball. Let's not talk about that.
Besides, shouldn't you be a special student for climbing trees?
You're a monkey, after all.
KYE
うき
I told you I'm not a monkey!
What's with her?
I thought she'd be all that, with a recommendation from the director.
But she's just a pig.
Our class is supposed to be for gifted people...

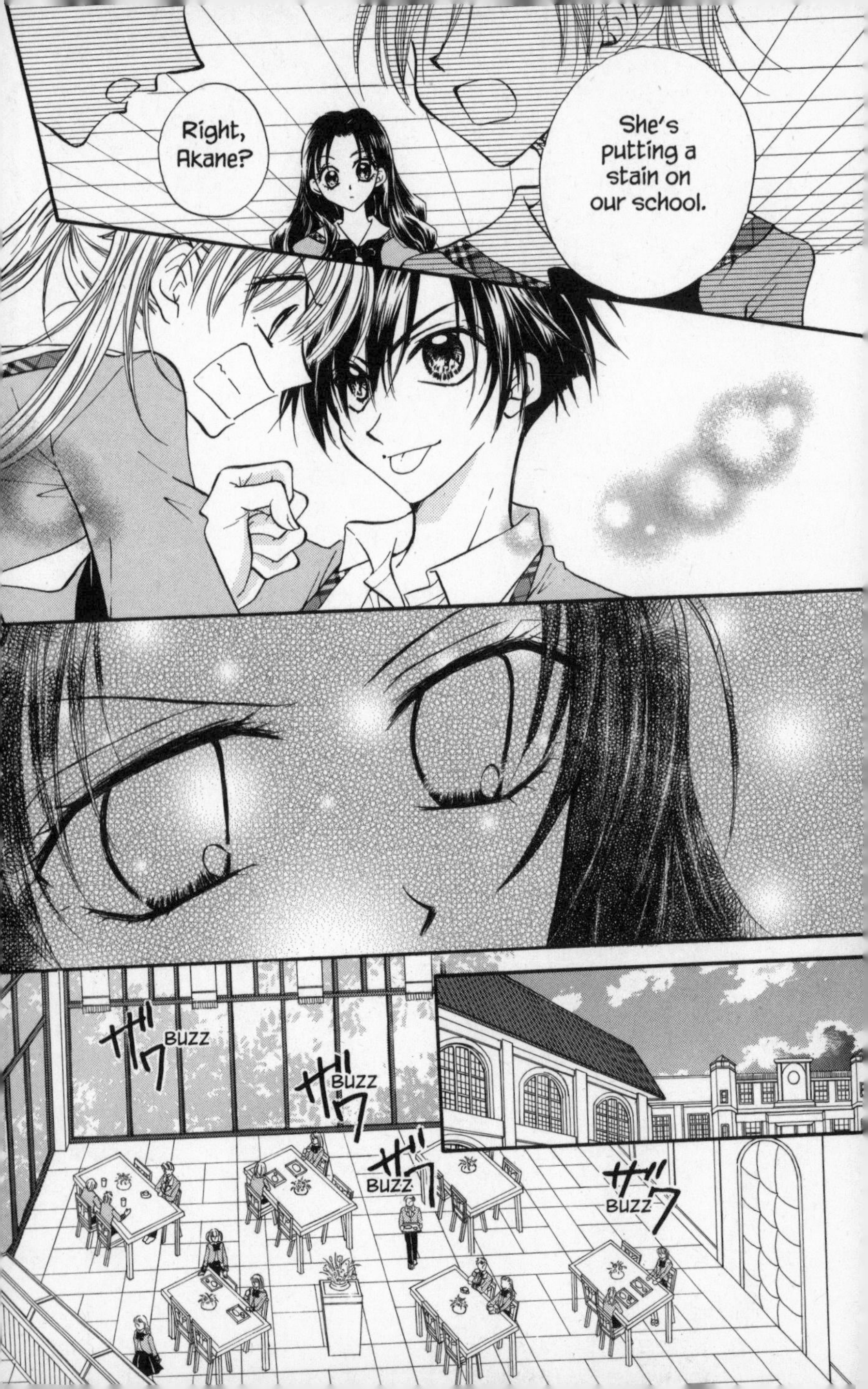
She's putting a stain on our school.
Right, Akane?
ザワ BUZZ
ザワ BUZZ
ザワ BUZZ
ザワ BUZZ

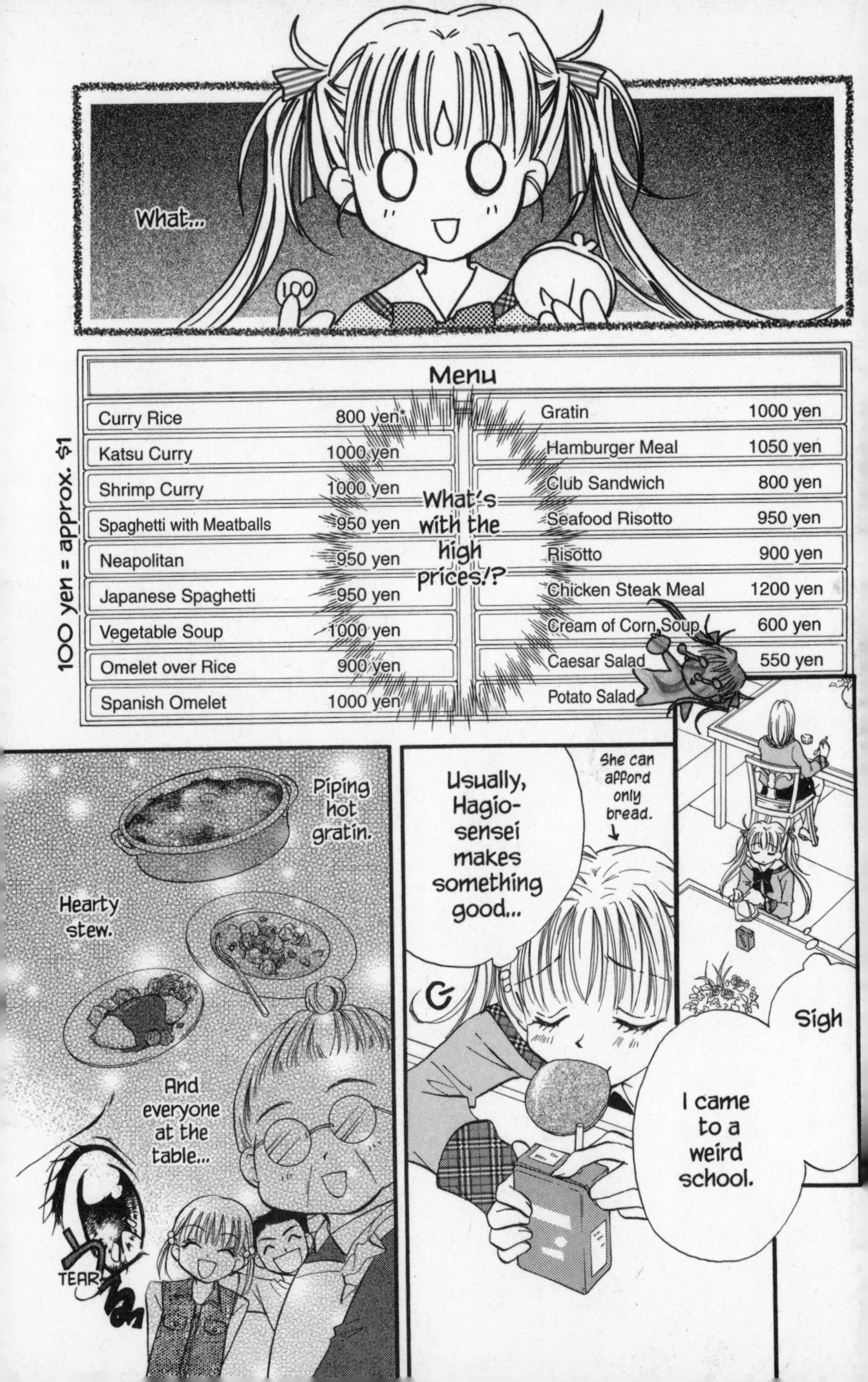
What...
Menu
Curry Rice 800 yen*
Katsu Curry 1000 yen
Shrimp Curry 1000 yen
Spaghetti with Meatballs 950 yen
Neapolitan 950 yen
Japanese Spaghetti 950 yen
Vegetable Soup 1000 yen
Omelet over Rice 900 yen
Spanish Omelet 1000 yen
Gratin 1000 yen
Hamburger Meal 1050 yen
Club Sandwich 800 yen
Seafood Risotto 950 yen
Risotto 900 yen
Chicken Steak Meal 1200 yen
Cream of Corn Soup 600 yen
Caesar Salad 550 yen
Potato Salad
What's with the high prices!?
*100 yen = approx. $1
Sigh
Usually, Hagio-sensei makes something good...
She can afford only bread.
I came to a weird school.
Piping hot gratin.
Hearty stew.
And everyone at the table...
TEAR

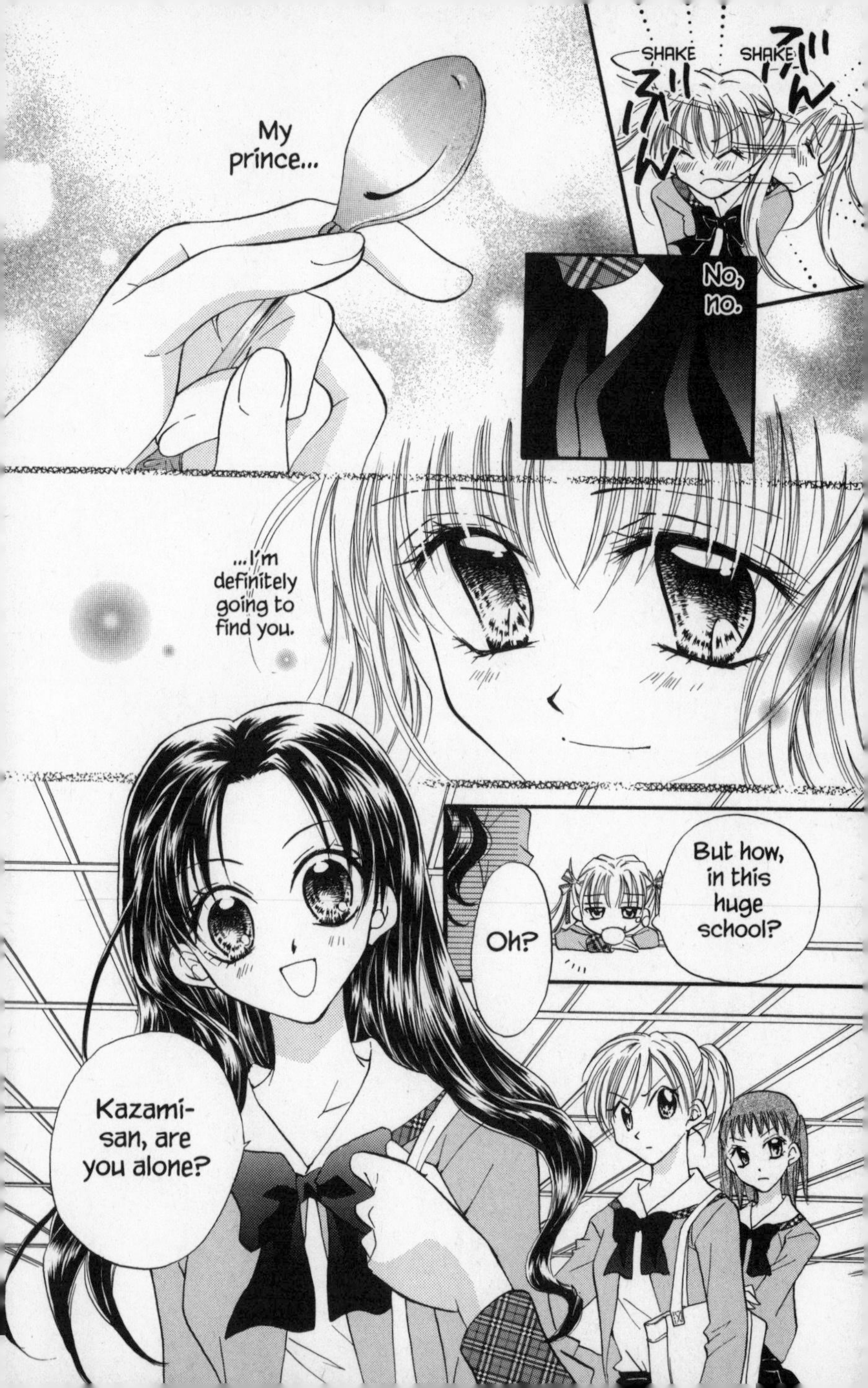
SHAKE SHAKE
No, no.
My prince...
...I'm definitely going to find you.
But how, in this huge school?
Oh?
Kazami-san, are you alone?

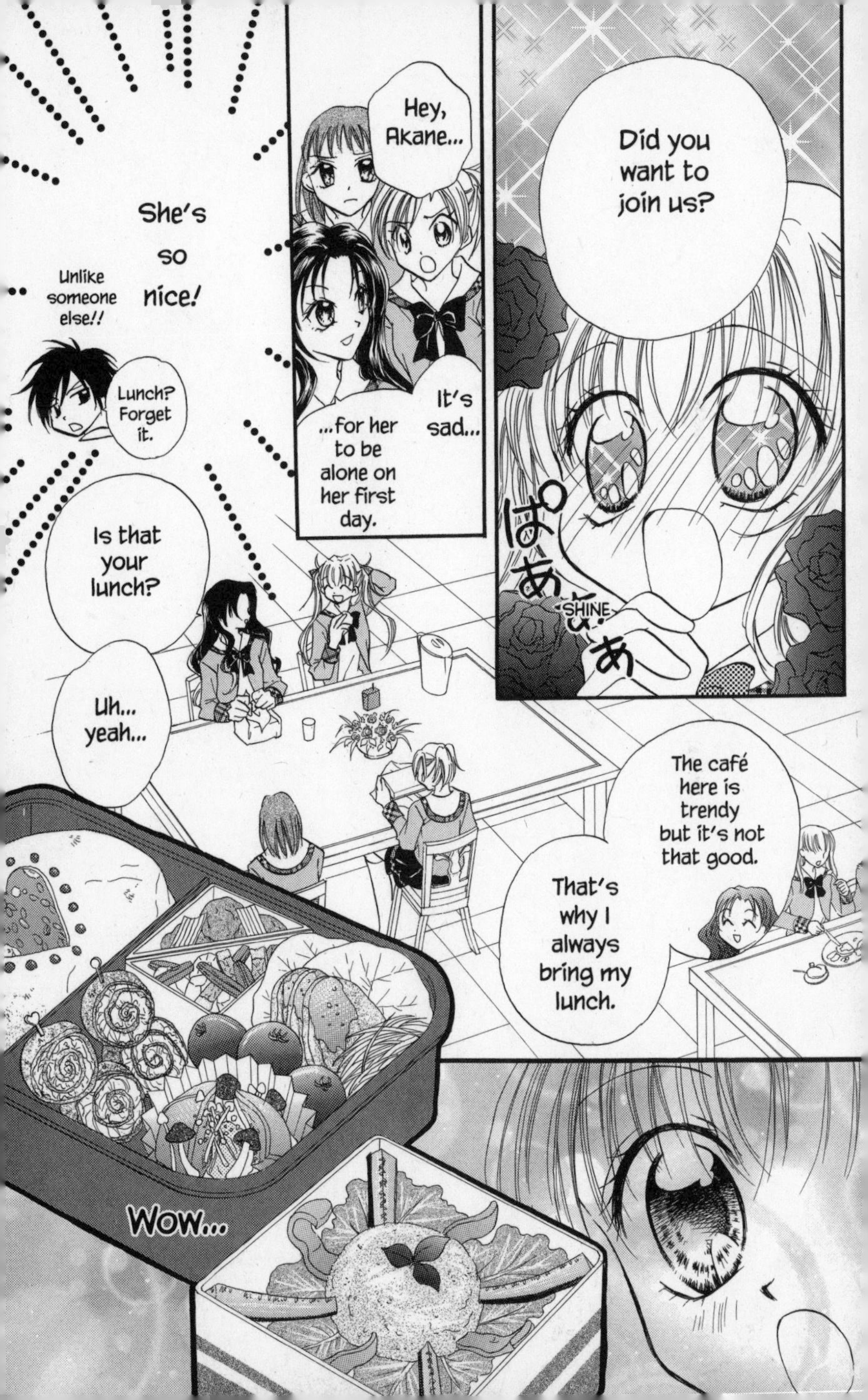
Did you want to join us?
ぱあ
SHINE
ぱあ
Hey, Akane...
It's sad...
...for her to be alone on her first day.
She's so nice!
Unlike someone else!!
Lunch? Forget it.
Is that your lunch?
Uh... yeah...
The café here is trendy but it's not that good.
That's why I always bring my lunch.
Wow...

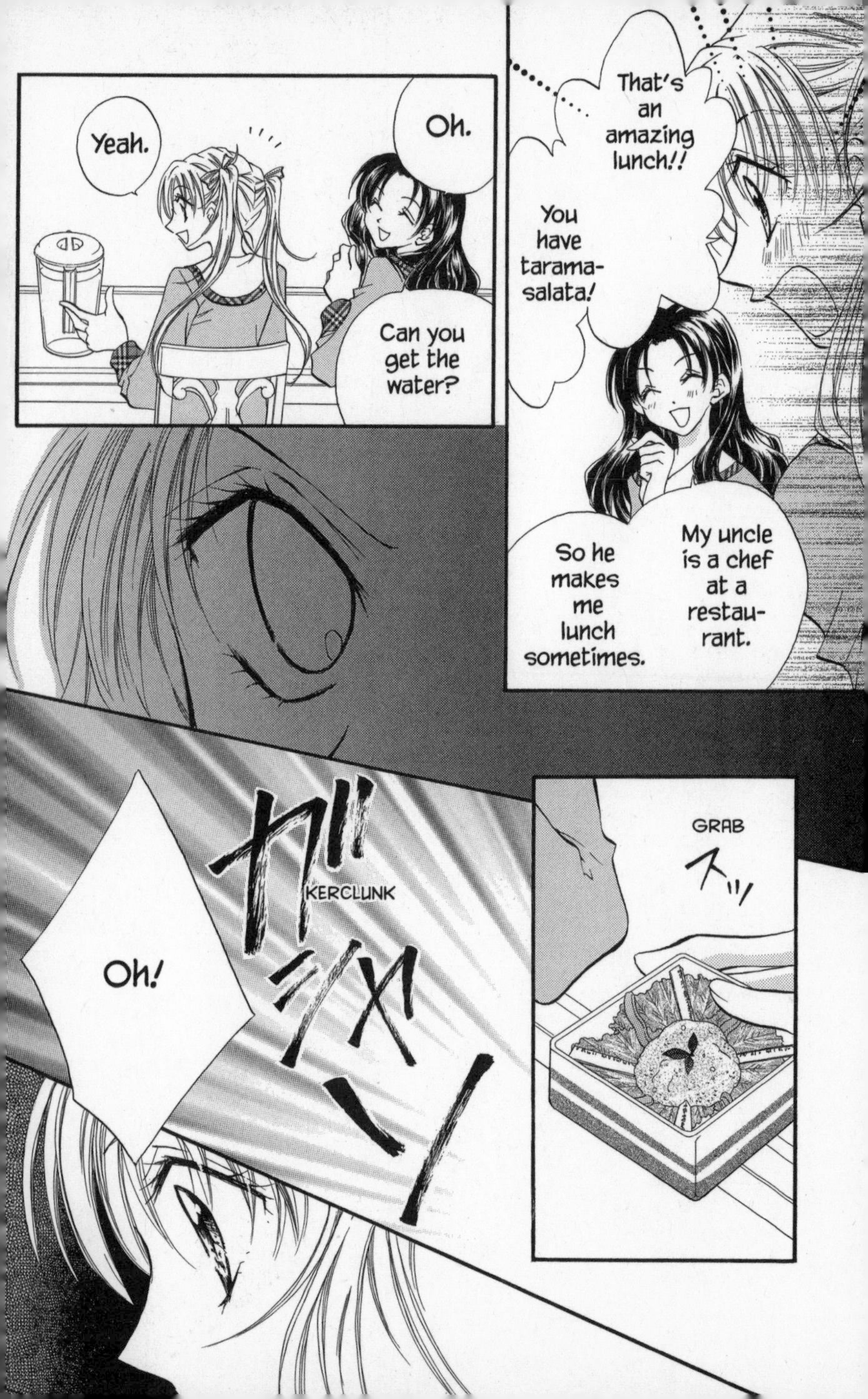
That's an amazing lunch!!
You have tarama-salata!
My uncle is a chef at a restau-rant.
So he makes me lunch sometimes.
Oh.
Can you get the water?
Yeah.
GRAB
KERCLUNK
Oh!

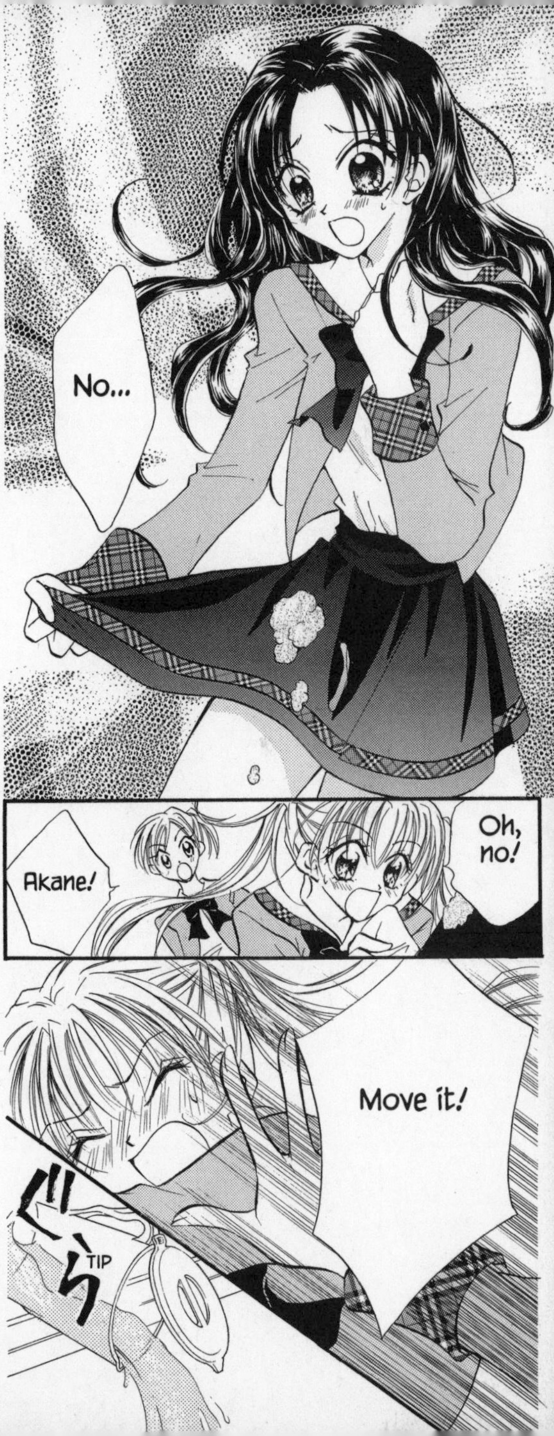
No...
Oh, no!
Akane!
Move it!
TIP

● Crab

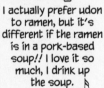

...I can't eat it. I hear it was one of my favorite foods when I was younger, but I guess I had a bad one once (I don't remember) and ever since, I can't eat it... I hear it's so good. Dang it!!

● Vinegar

I can't eat it... So I can't eat any vinegar-based salad, or any Chinese food with gravy over it (sweet and sour pork, shrimp chili sauce). But vinegar is good for your body! I hope I find a way to be able to eat vinegar...

● Ramen

I actually prefer udon to ramen, but it's different if the ramen is in a pork-based soup!! I love it so much, I drink up the soup. ♪

● Snacks

I love little candies. I can eat them all day if there's enough.

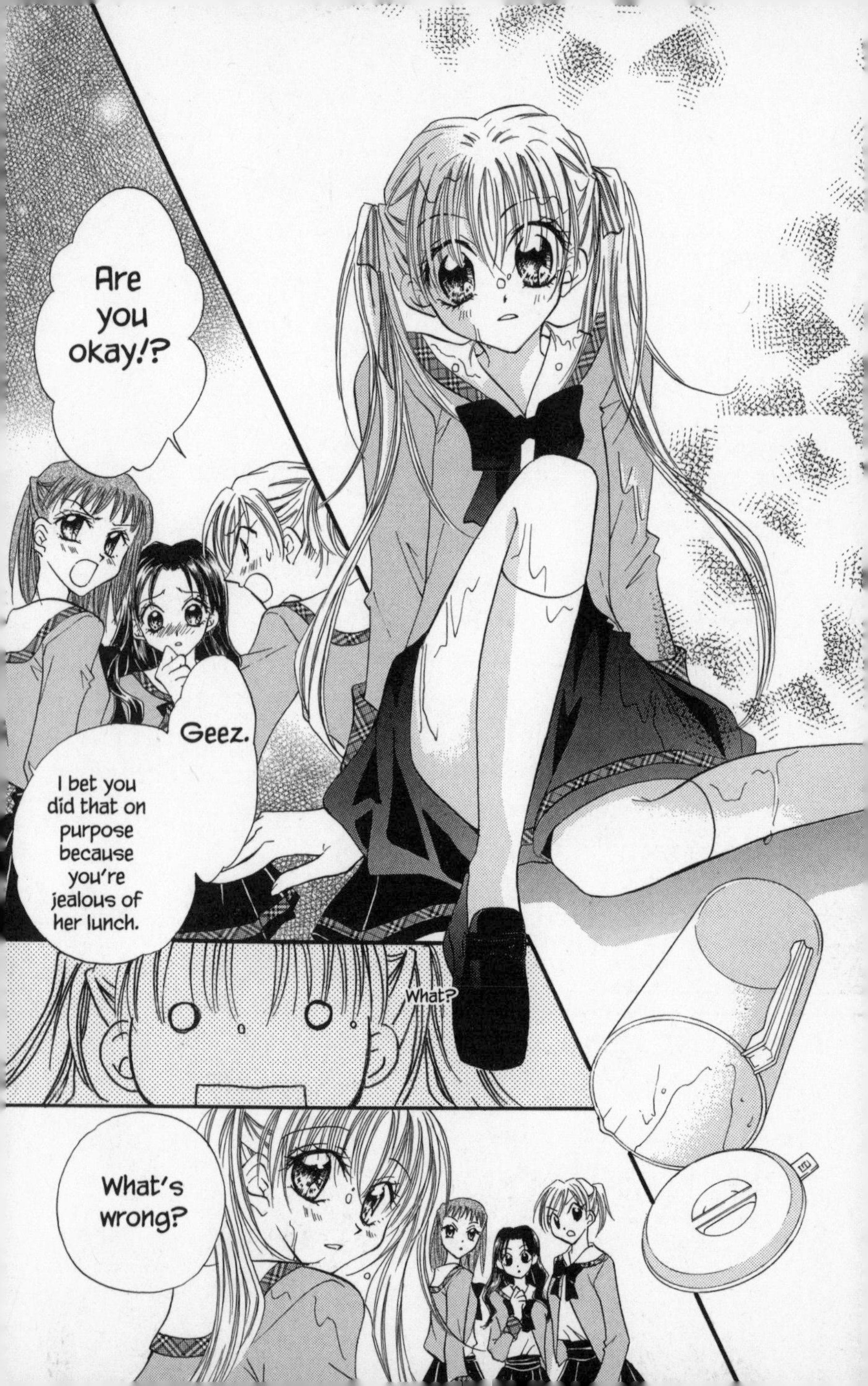
Are you okay!?
Geez.
I bet you did that on purpose because you're jealous of her lunch.
What?
What's wrong?

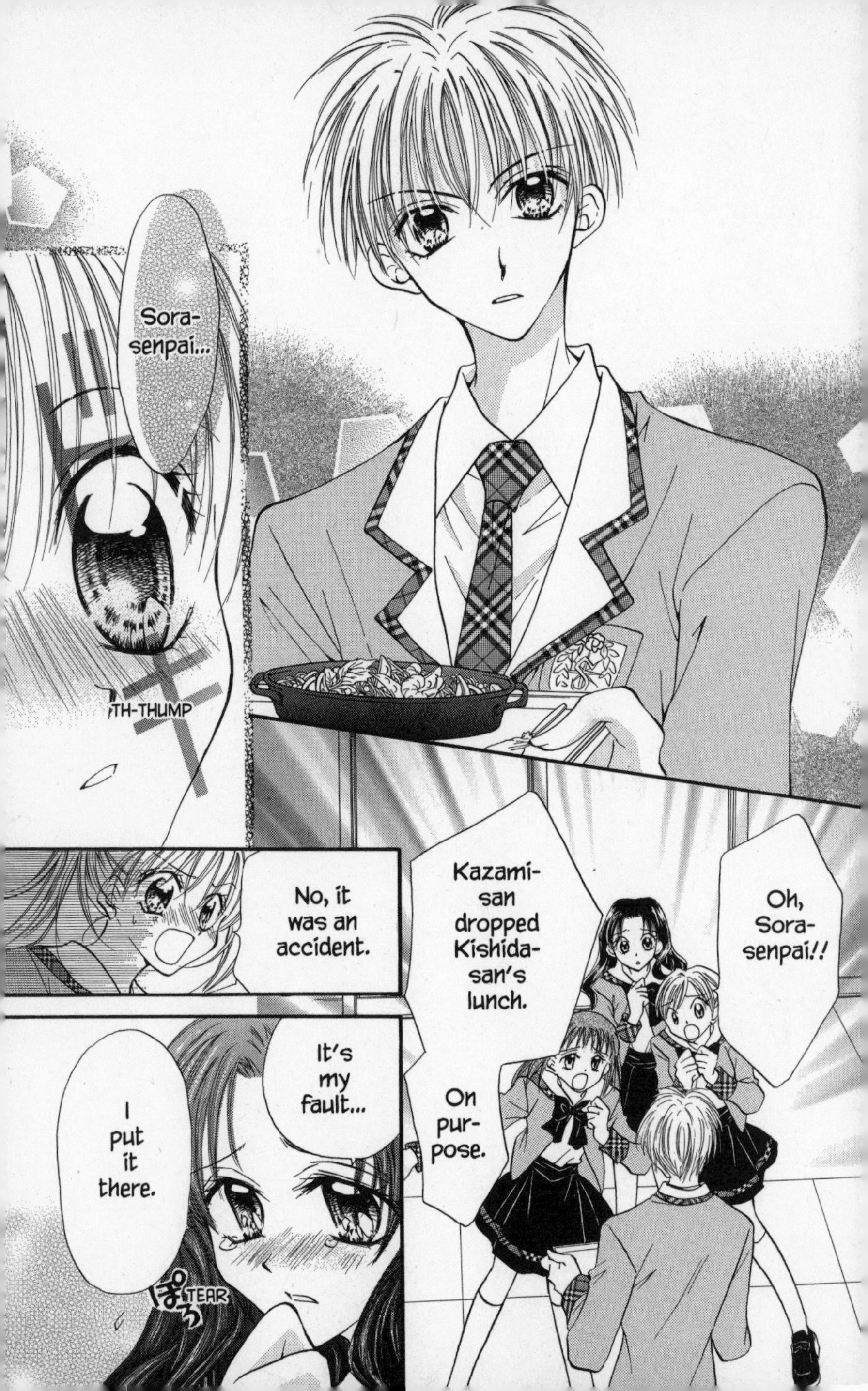
Sora-senpai...
TH-THUMP
Oh, Sora-senpai!!
Kazami-san dropped Kishida-san's lunch.
On pur-pose.
No, it was an accident.
It's my fault...
I put it there.
ぽろ TEAR

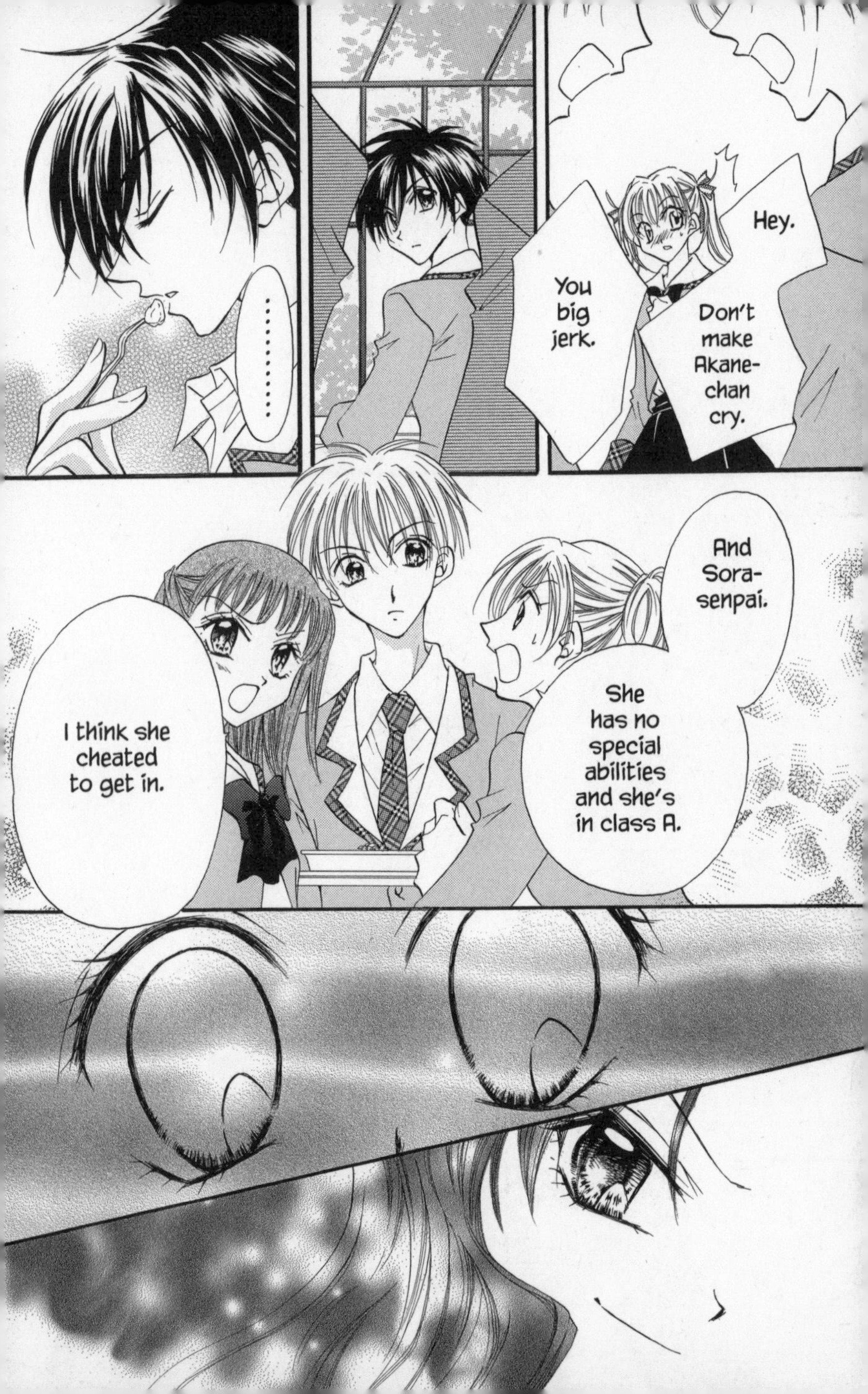
Hey.
Don't make Akane-chan cry.
You big jerk.
......
And Sora-senpai.
She has no special abilities and she's in class A.
I think she cheated to get in.

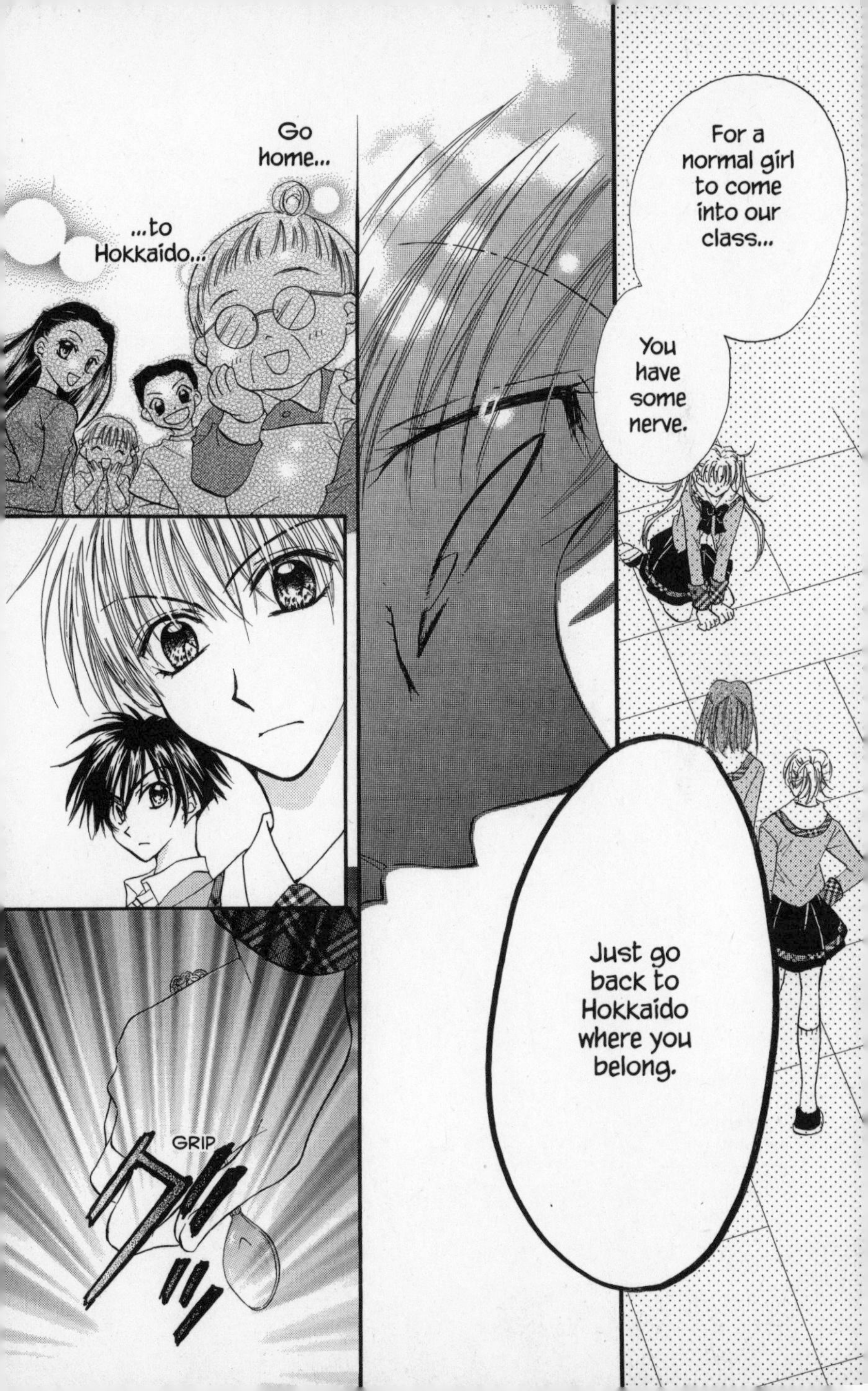
For a normal girl to come into our class...
You have some nerve.
Just go back to Hokkaido where you belong.
Go home...
...to Hokkaido...
GRIP

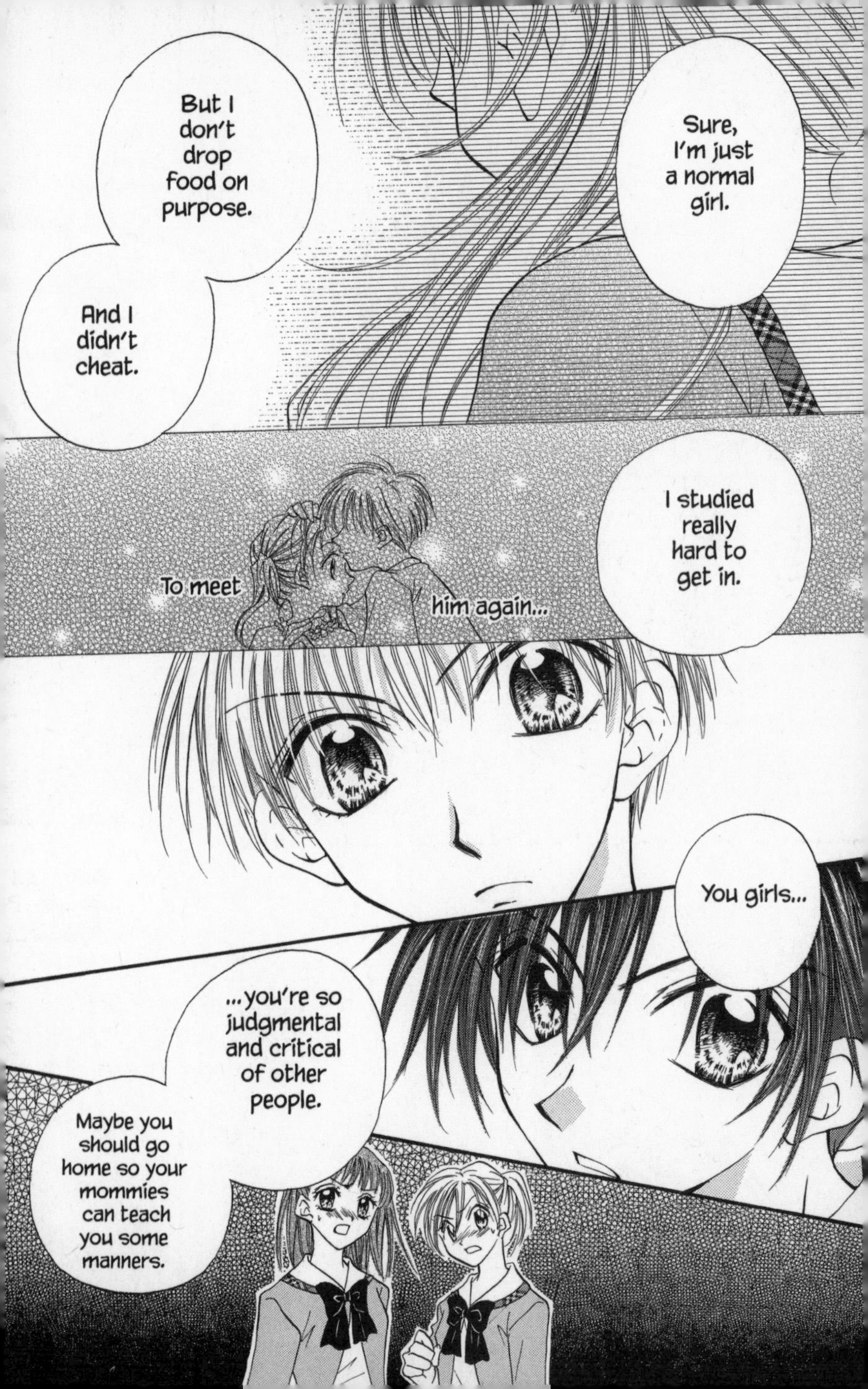
Sure, I'm just a normal girl.
But I don't drop food on purpose.
And I didn't cheat.
I studied really hard to get in.
To meet
him again...
You girls...
...you're so judgmental and critical of other people.
Maybe you should go home so your mommies can teach you some manners.

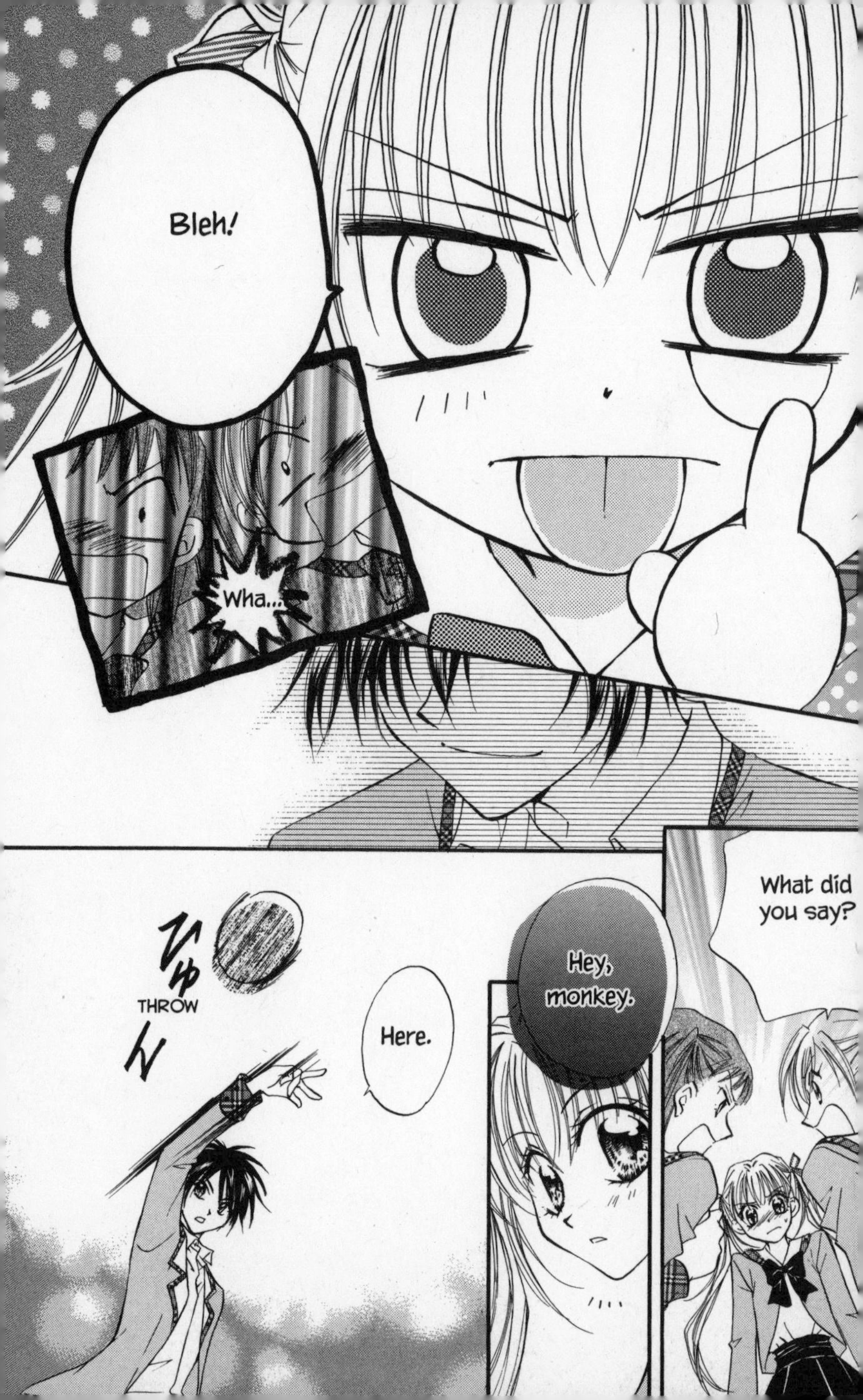
Bleh!
Wha...
What did you say?
Hey, monkey.
Here.
ひゅん
THROW

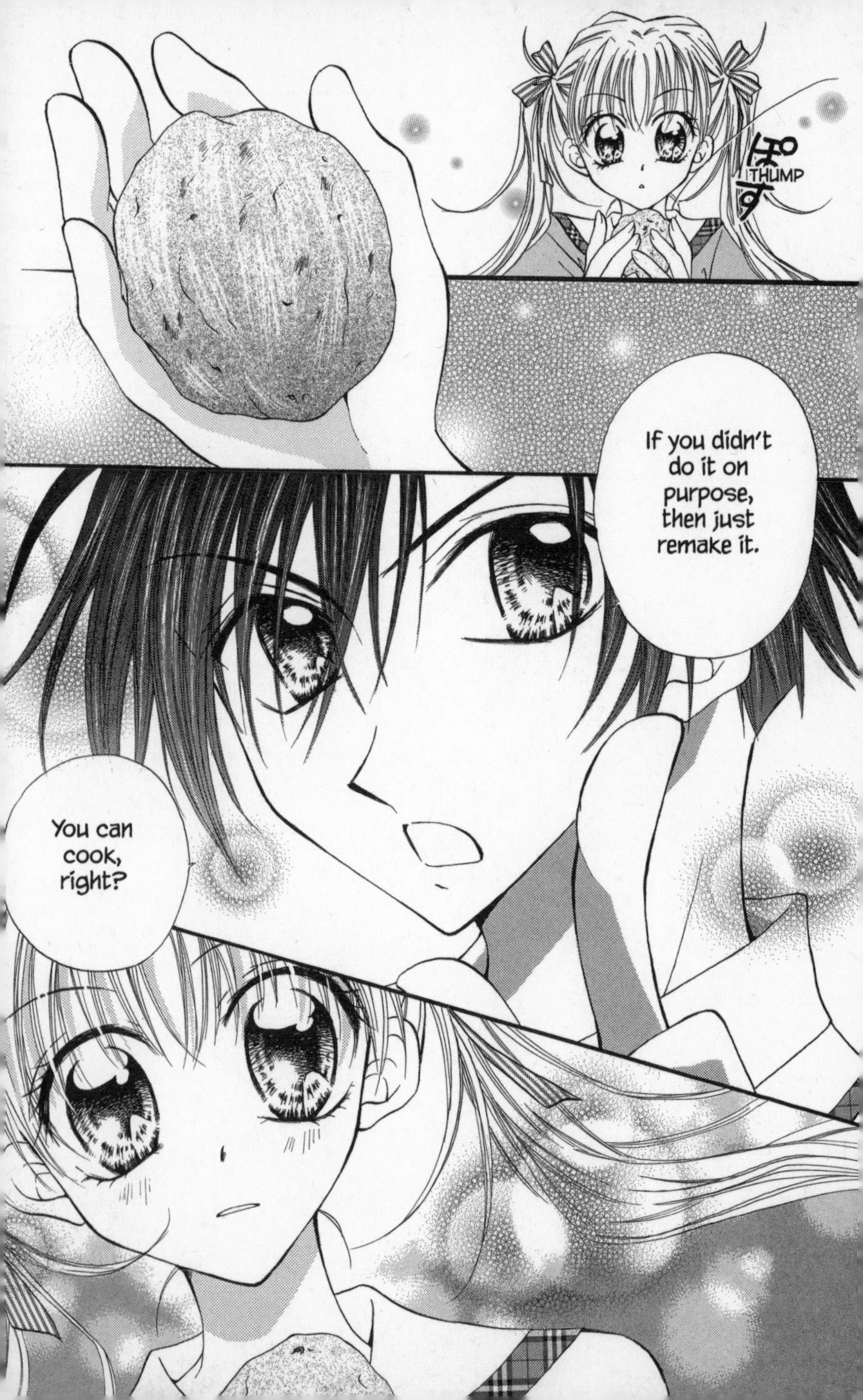
ぽす
THUMP
If you didn't do it on purpose, then just remake it.
You can cook, right?

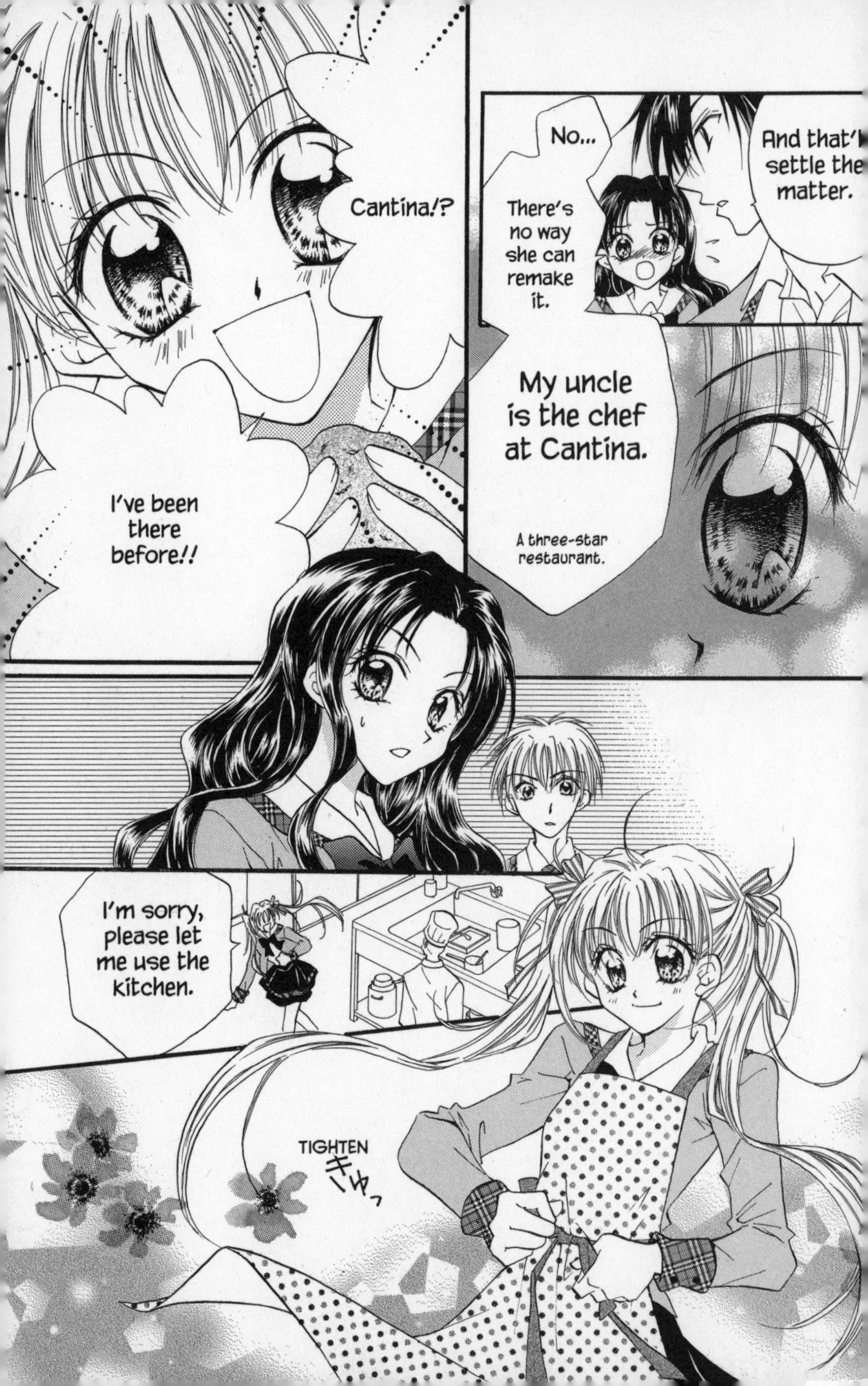
And that'l settle the matter.
No...
There's no way she can remake it.
My uncle is the chef at Cantina.
A three-star restaurant.
Cantina!?
I've been there before!!
I'm sorry, please let me use the kitchen.
TIGHTEN
きゅっ

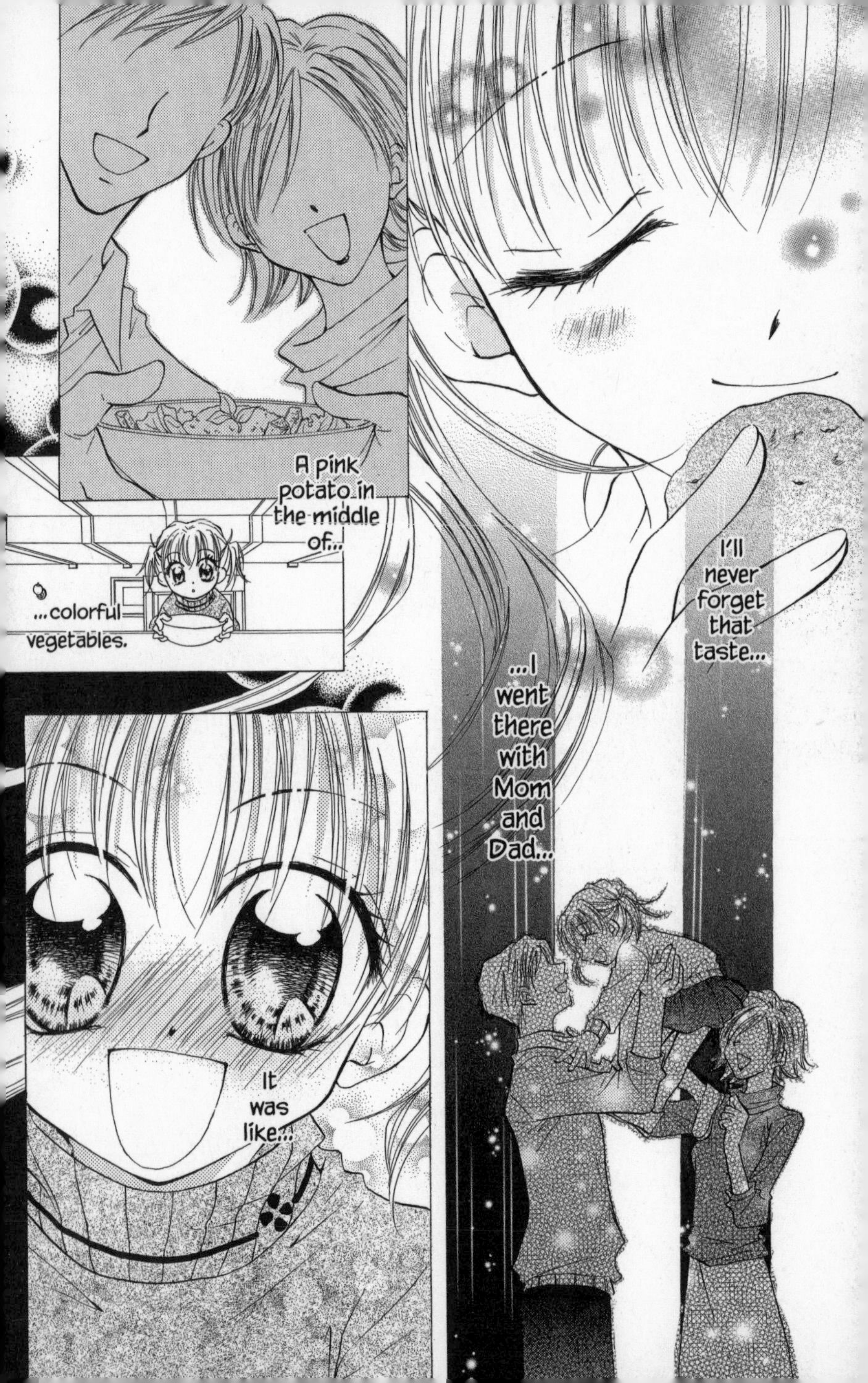
I'll never forget that taste...
...I went there with Mom and Dad...
A pink potato in the middle of...
...colorful vegetables.
It was like...

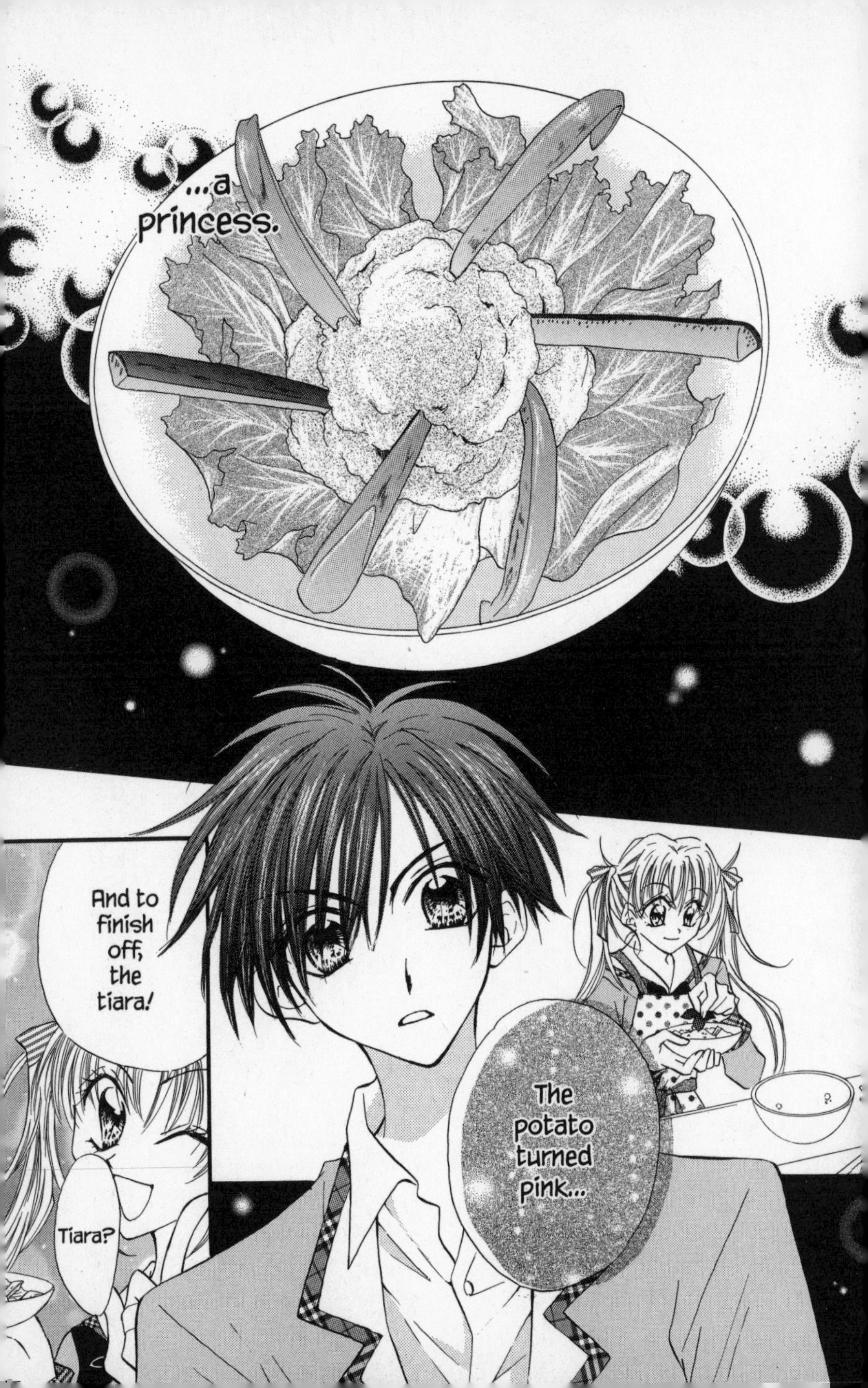
...a princess.
The potato turned pink...
And to finish off, the tiara!
Tiara?

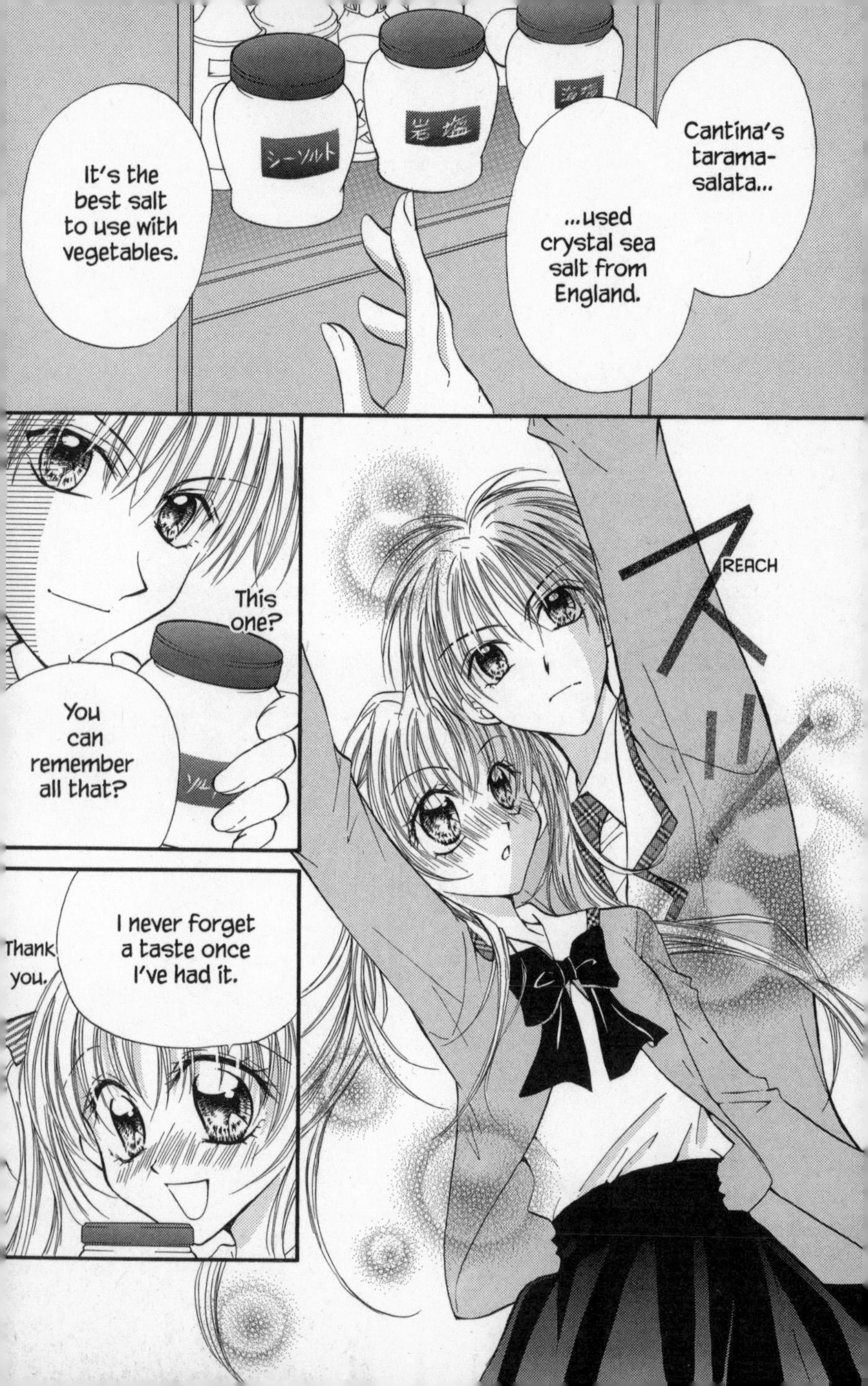

Cantina's tarama-salata...
...used crystal sea salt from England.
岩塩
シーソルト
It's the best salt to use with vegetables.
REACH
This one?
You can remember all that?
I never forget a taste once I've had it.
Thank you.

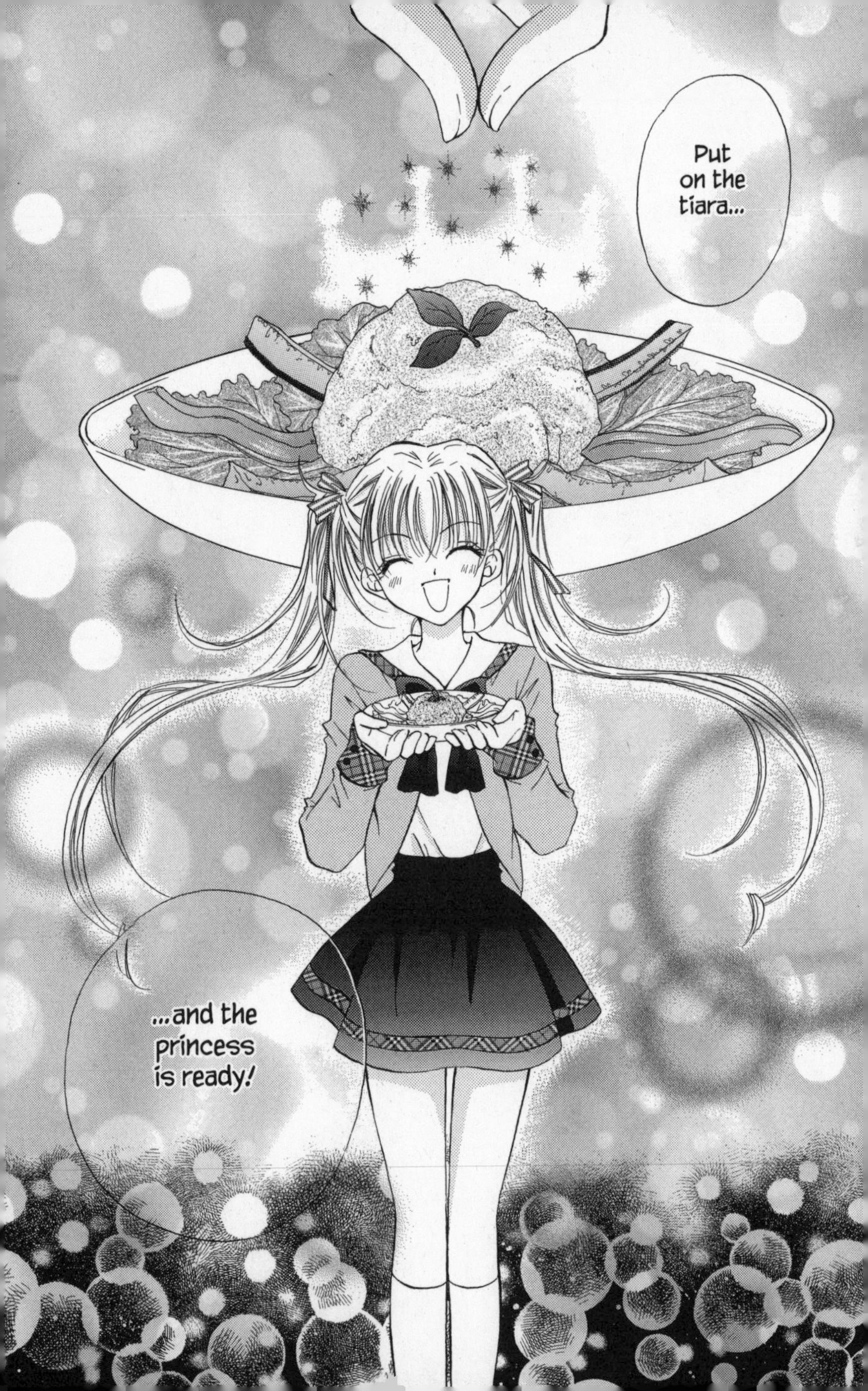
Put on the tiara...
...and the princess is ready!

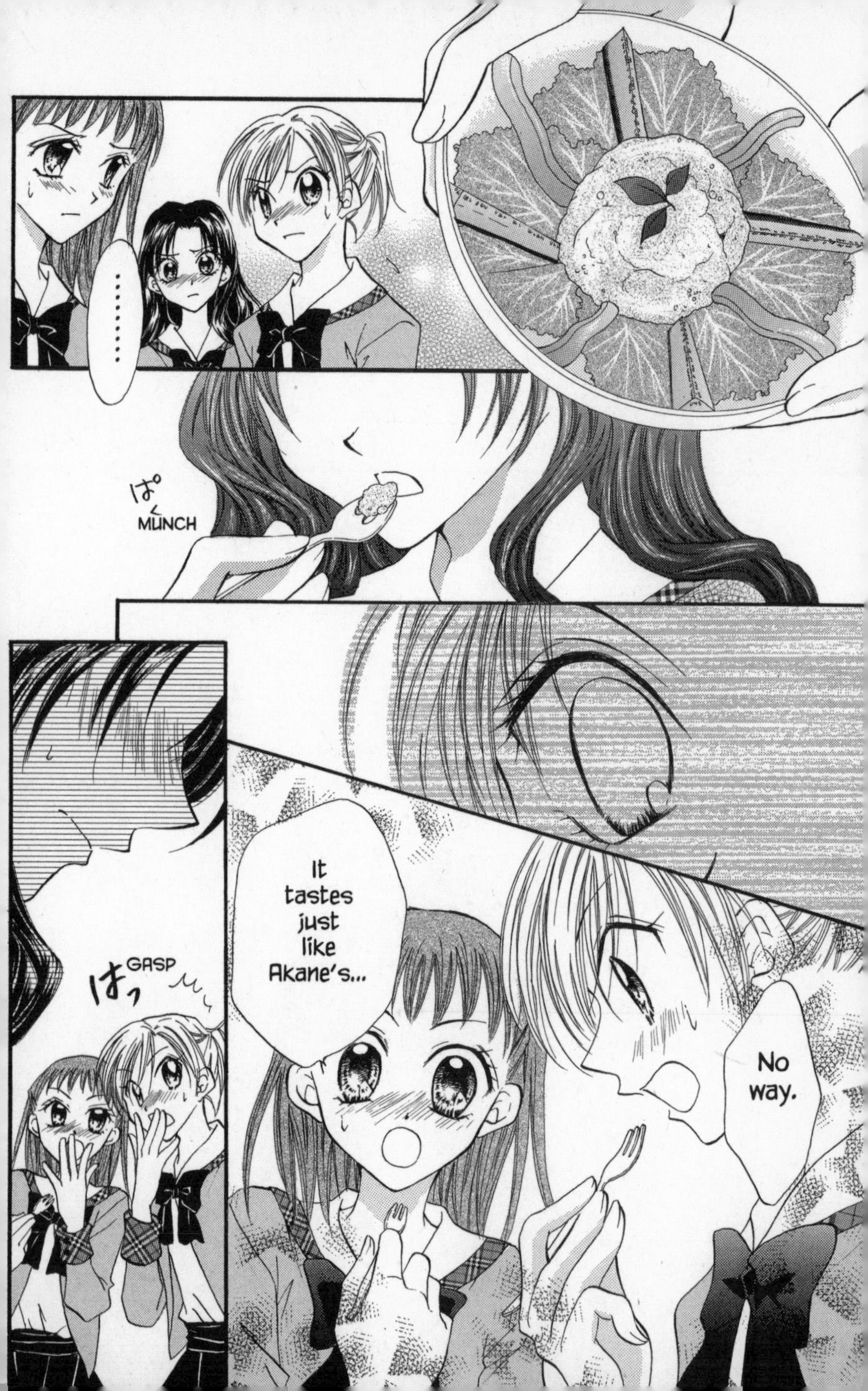
......
ぱく
MUNCH
No way.
It tastes just like Akane's...
はっ
GASP

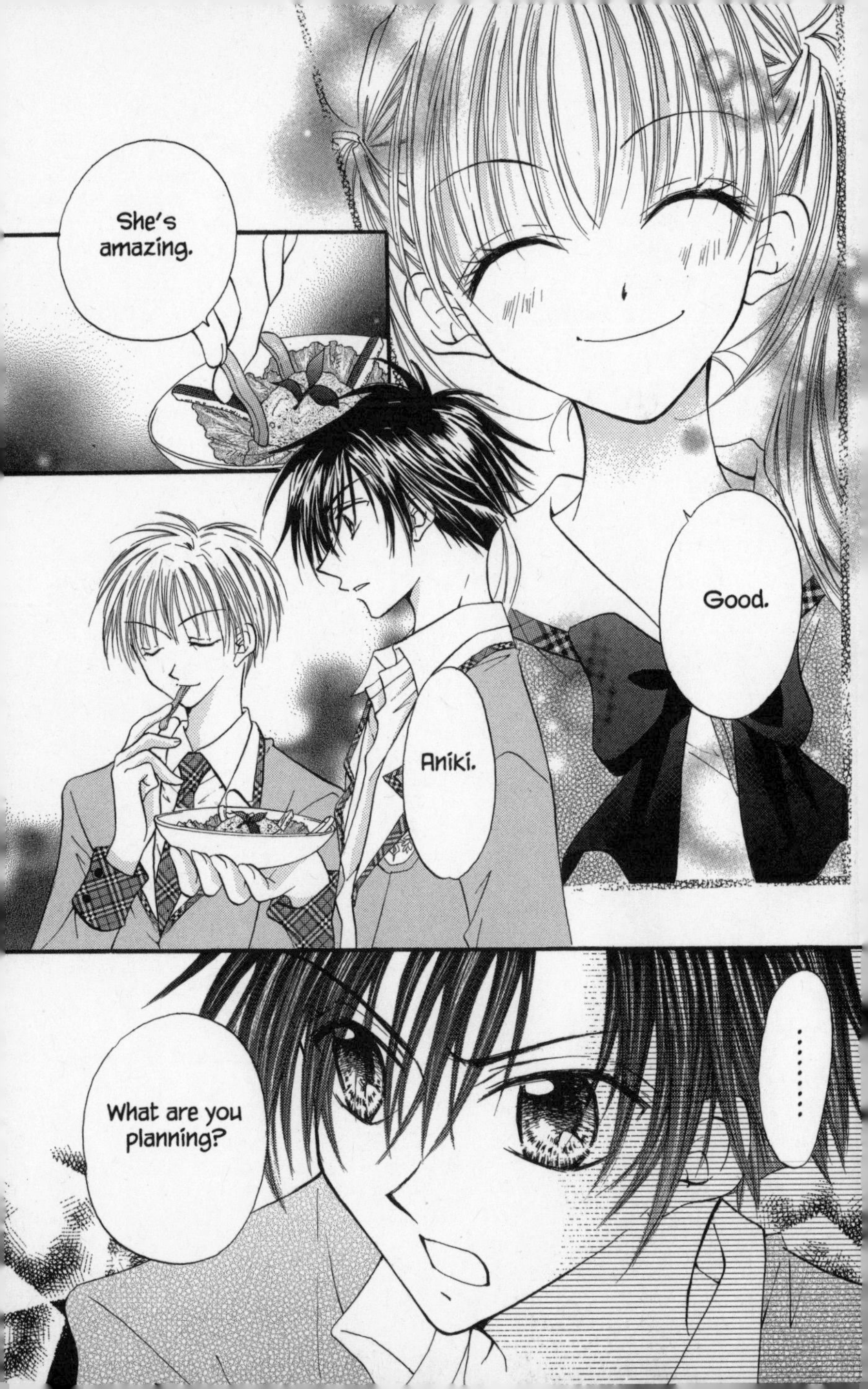
She's amazing.
Good.
Aniki.
......
What are you planning?

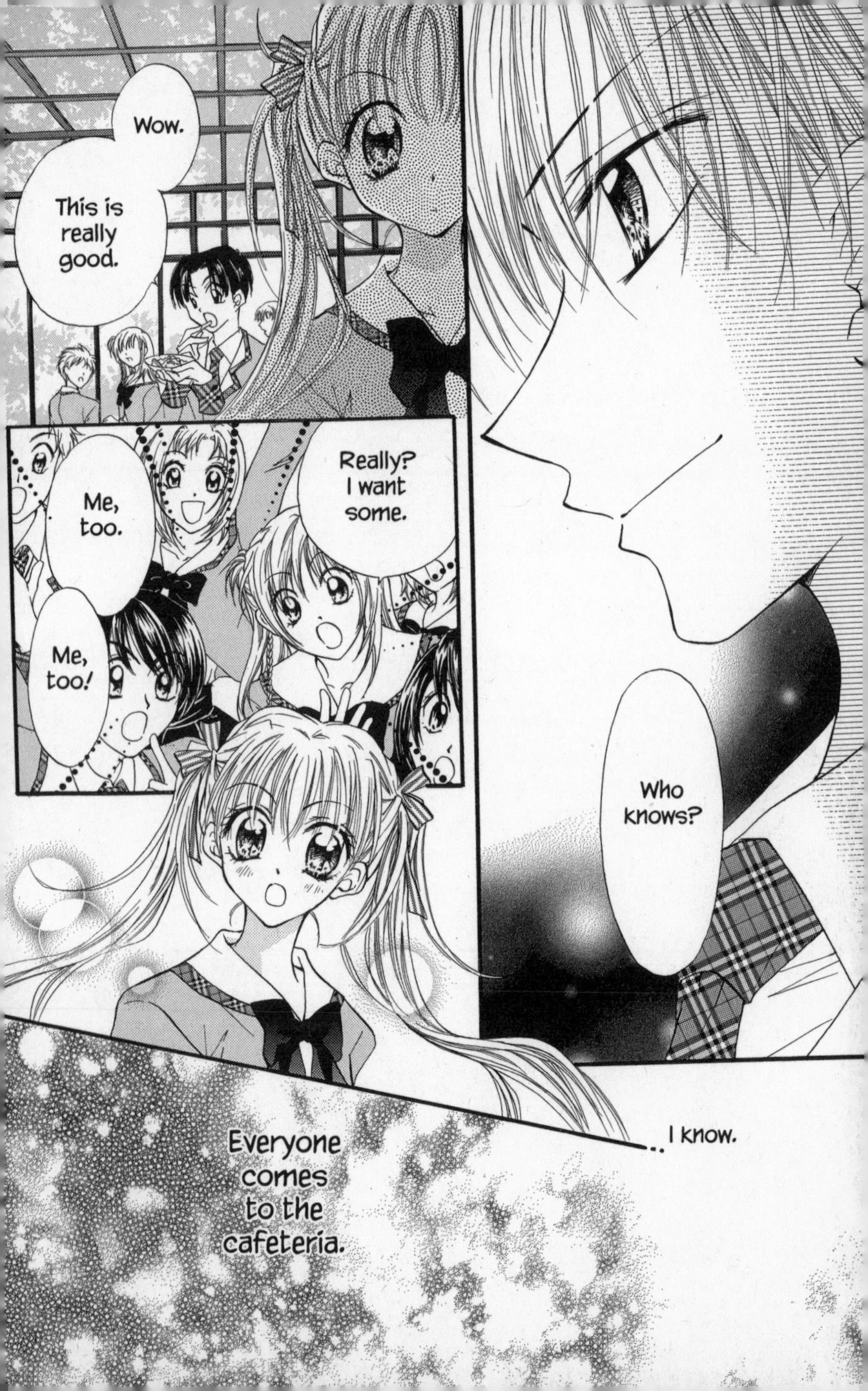
Who knows?
Wow.
This is really good.
Really? I want some.
Me, too.
Me, too!
...I know.
Everyone comes to the cafeteria.

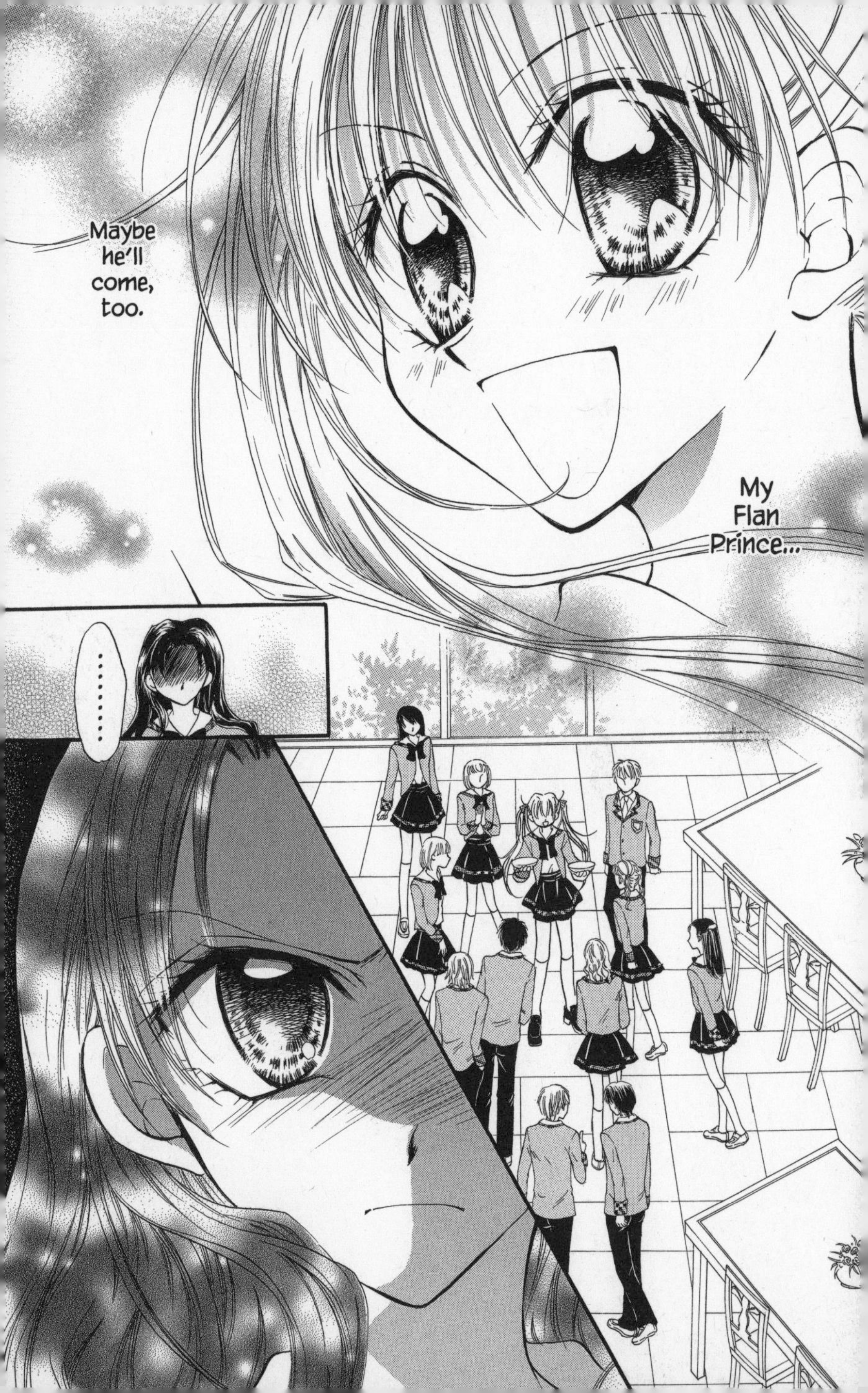
My Flan Prince...
Maybe he'll come, too.
......

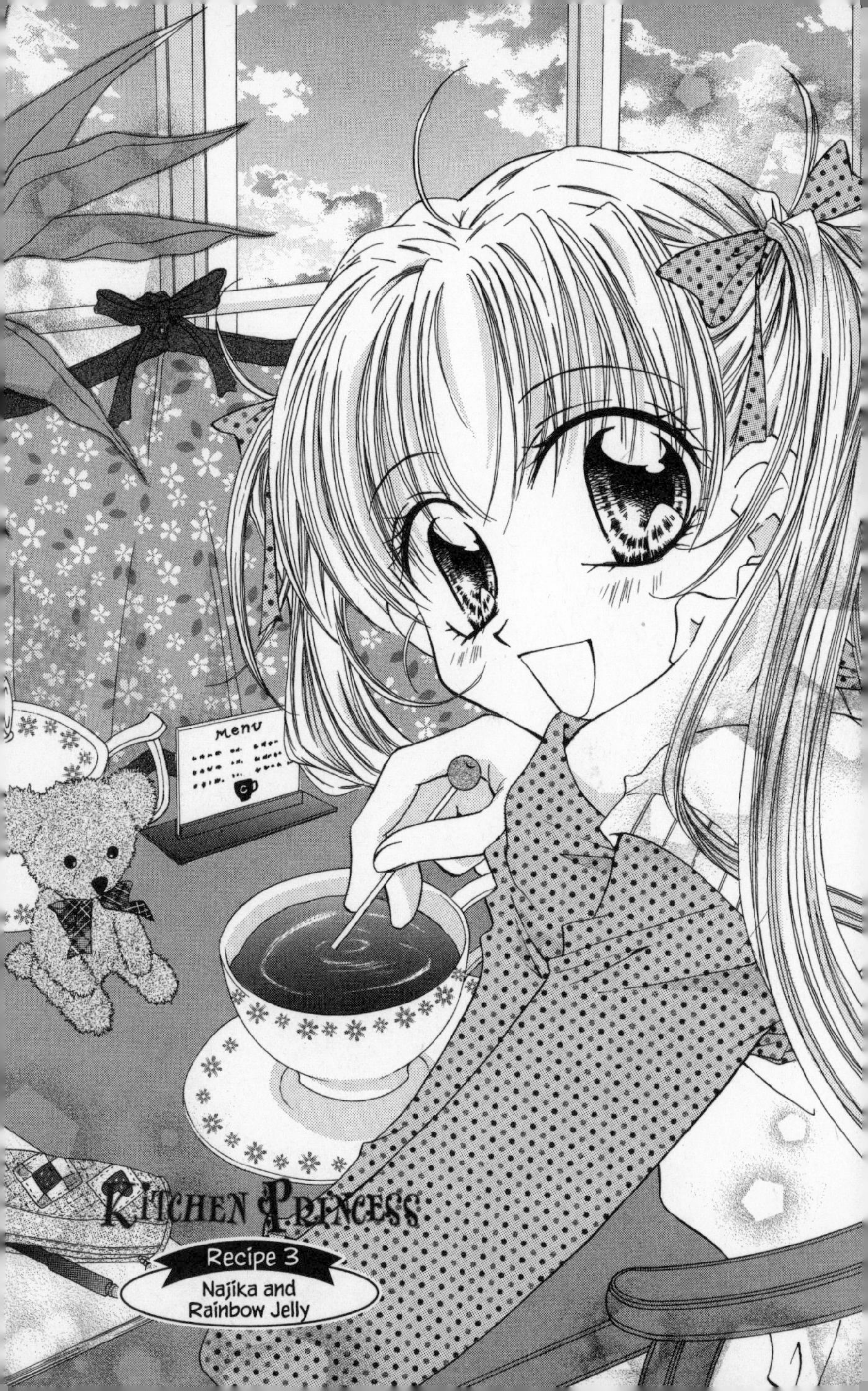
Menu
Kitchen Princess
Recipe 3
Najika and Rainbow Jelly

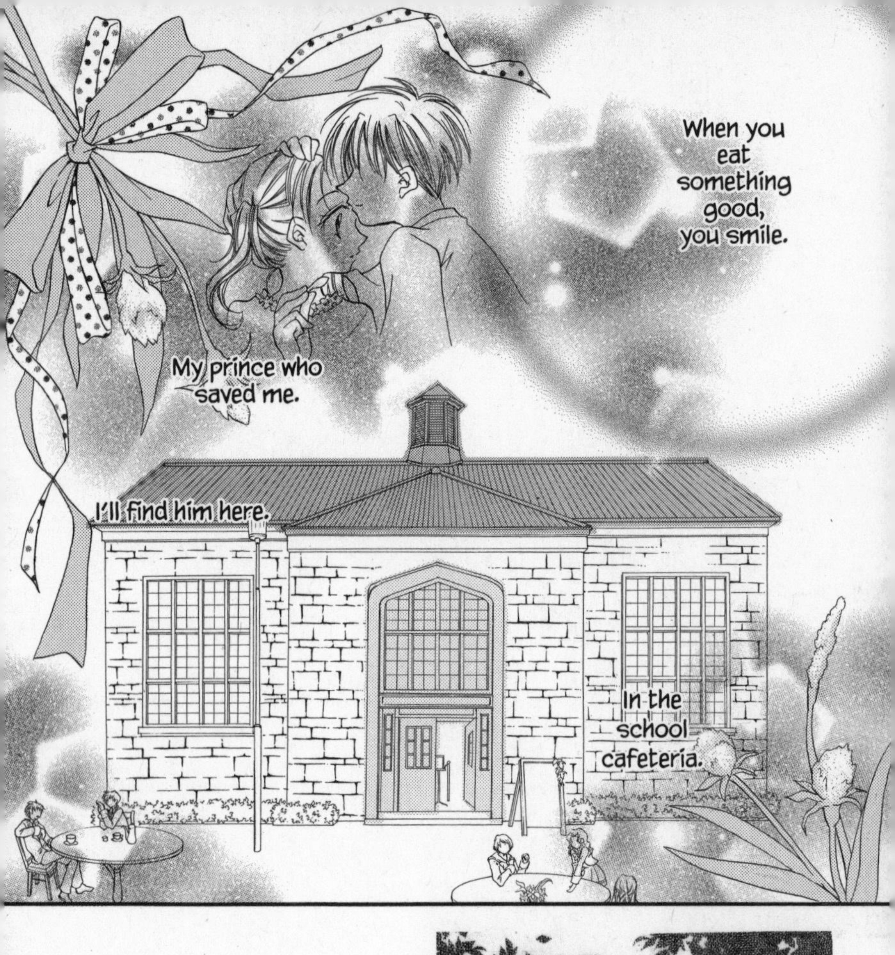
When you eat something good, you smile.
My prince who saved me.
I'll find him here.
In the school cafeteria.
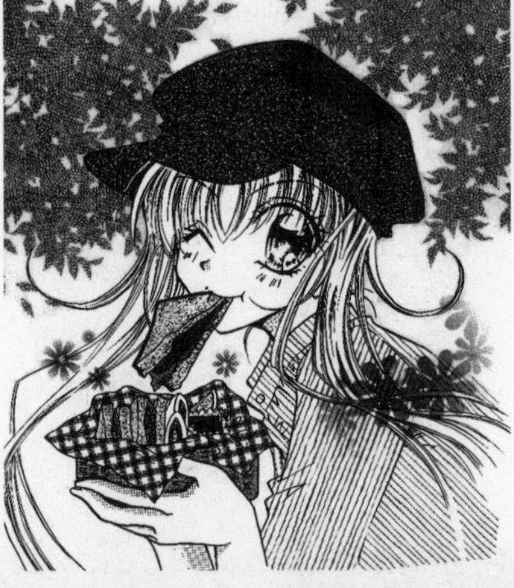

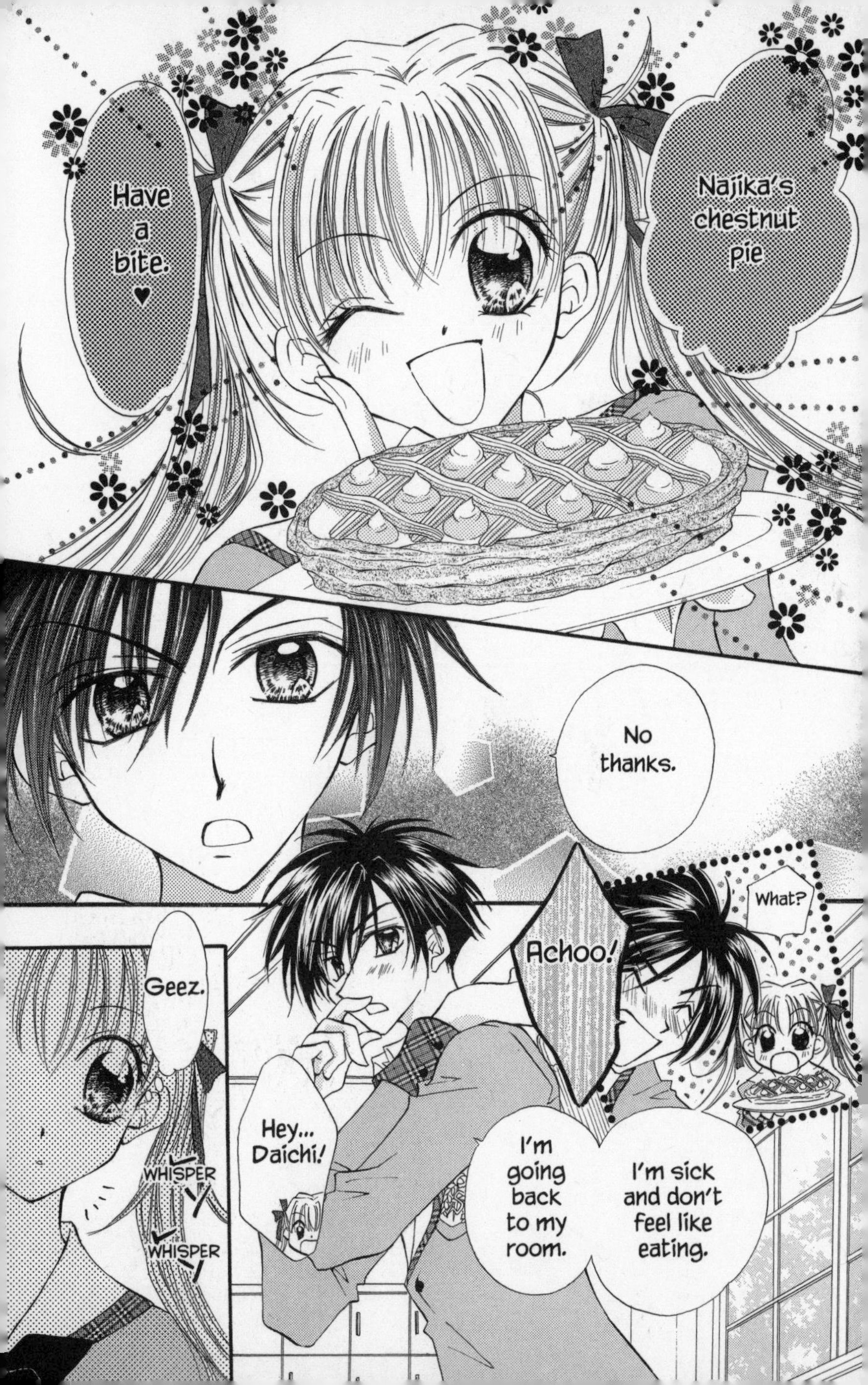
Najika's chestnut pie
Have a bite. ♥
No thanks.
What?
Achoo!
I'm sick and don't feel like eating.
I'm going back to my room.
Hey... Daichi!
Geez.
WHISPER
WHISPER

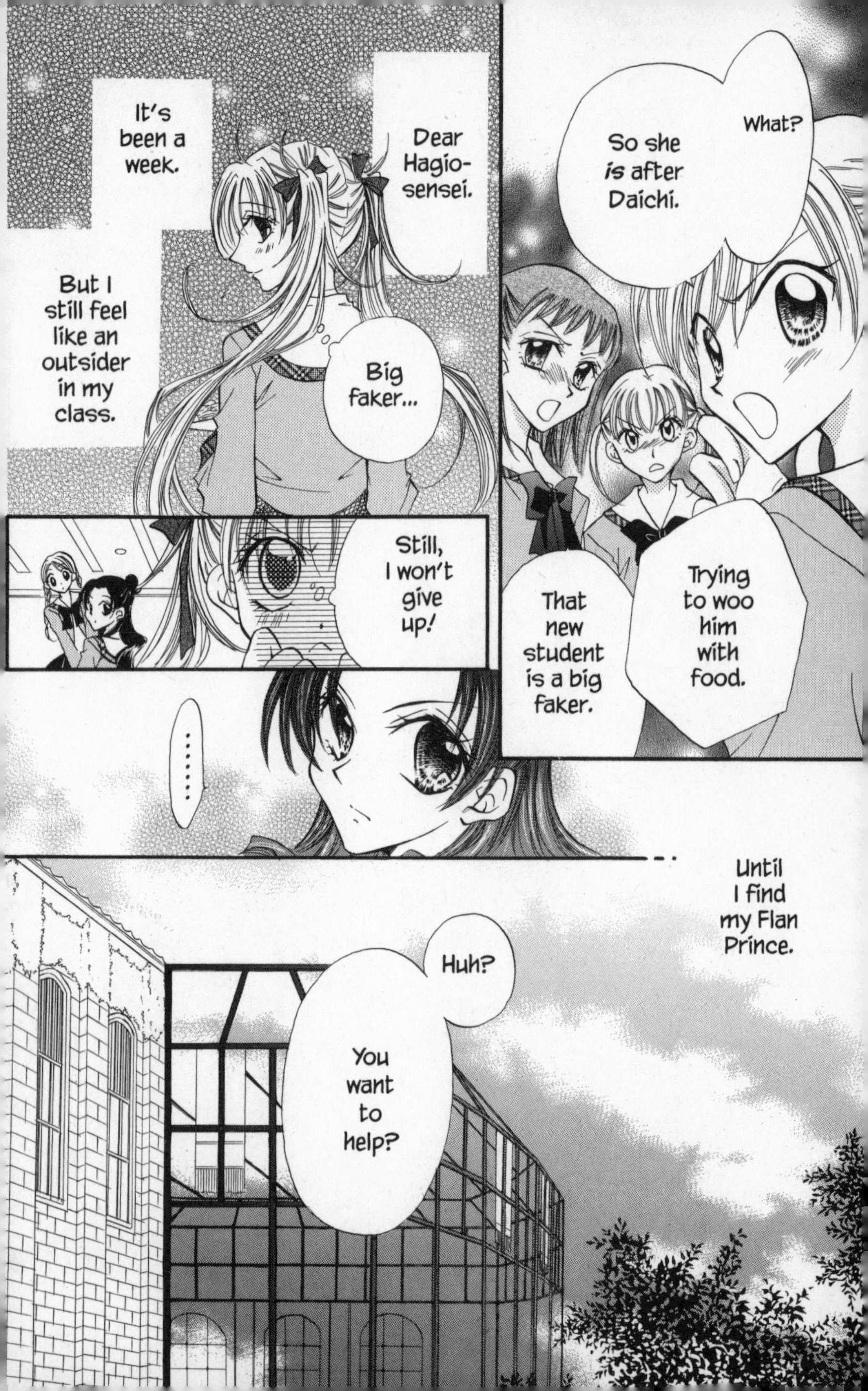
What?
So she *is* after Daichi.
Trying to woo him with food.
That new student is a big faker.
Dear Hagio-sensei.
It's been a week.
But I still feel like an outsider in my class.
Big faker...
Still, I won't give up!
......
Until I find my Flan Prince.
Huh?
You want to help?

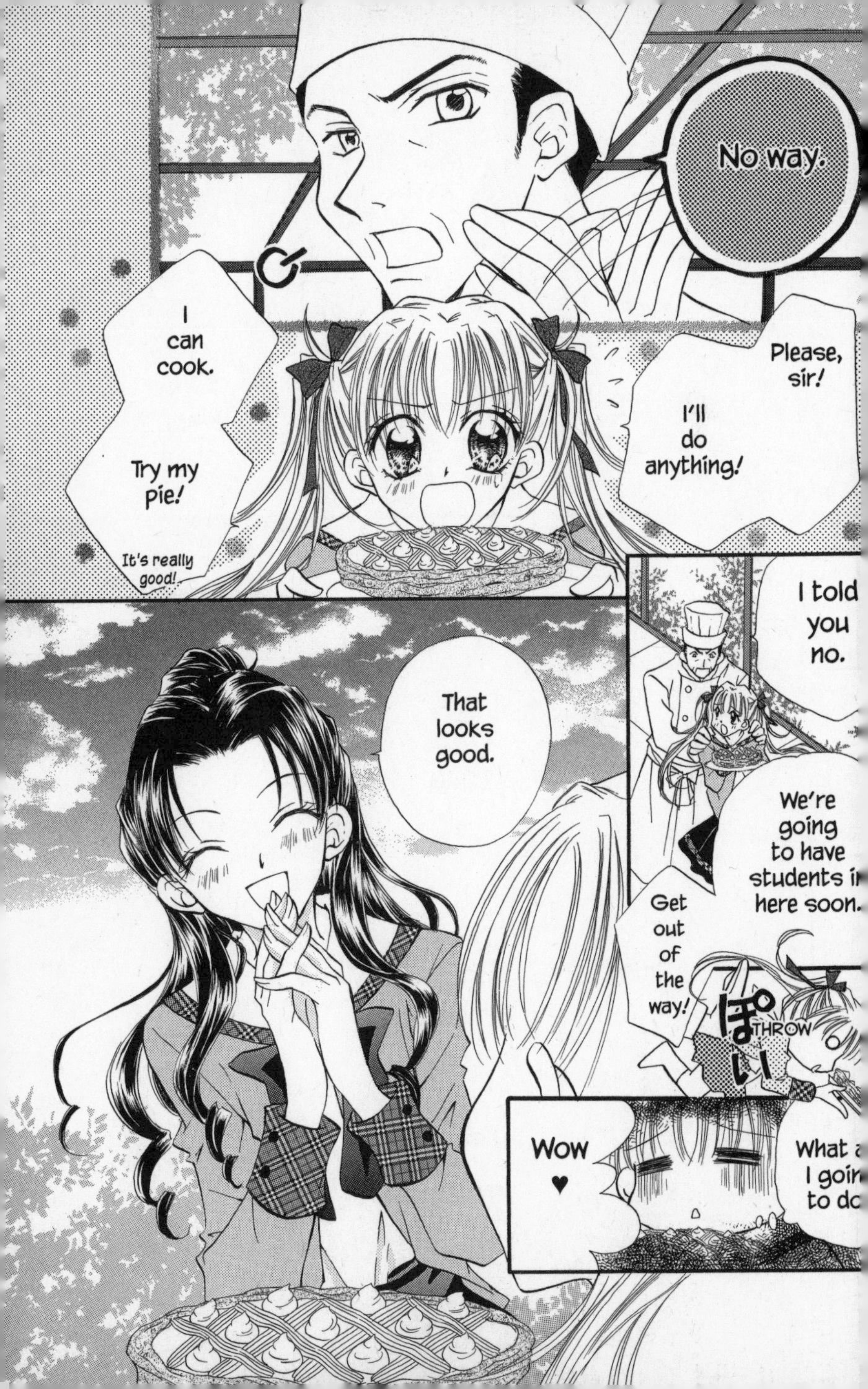
No way.
Please, sir!
I'll do anything!
I can cook.
Try my pie!
It's really good!
I told you no.
We're going to have students i
here soon.
Get out of the way!
THROW
ぽい
What a
I goin
to do
Wow ♥
That looks good.

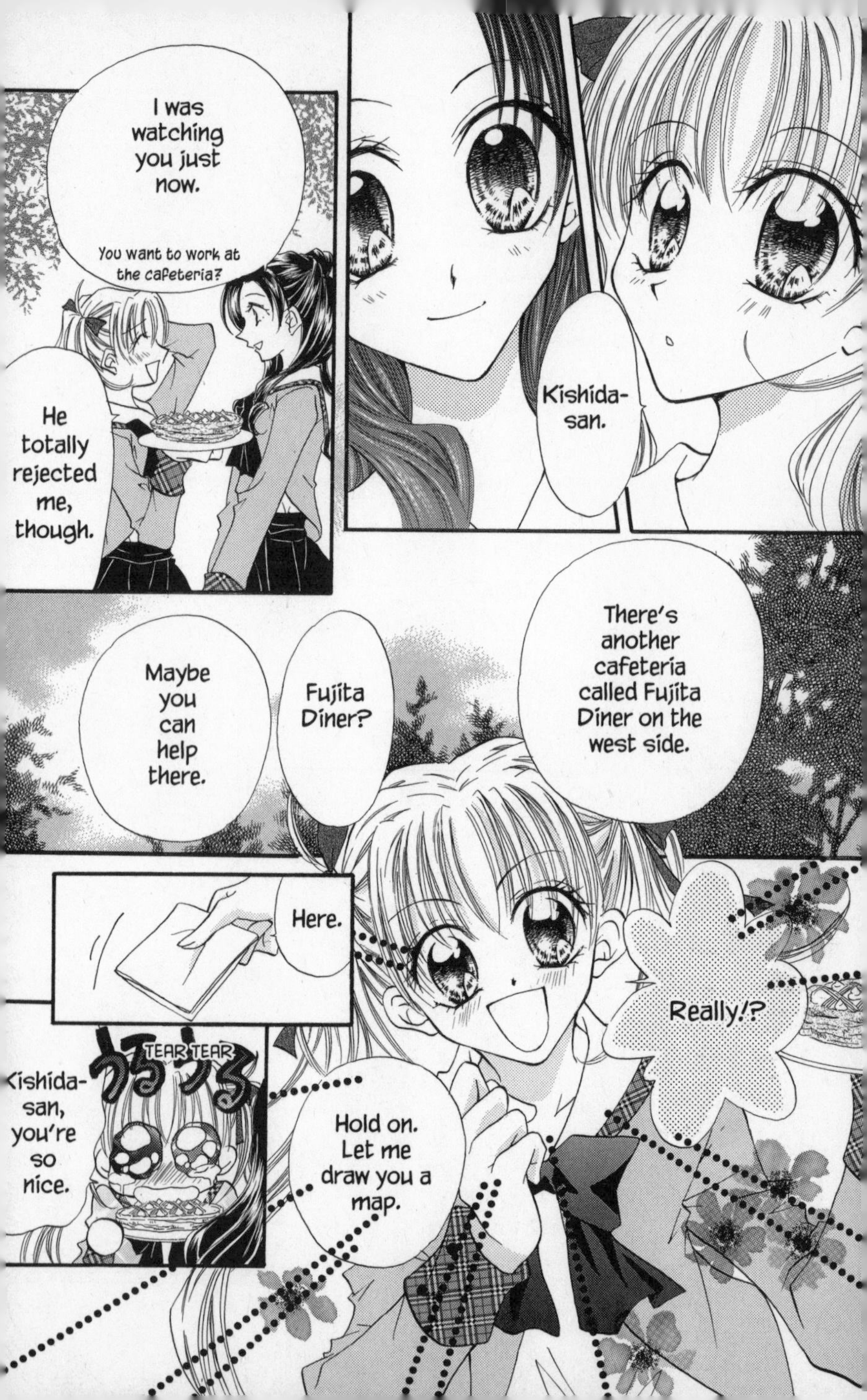
Kishida-san.
I was watching you just now.
You want to work at the cafeteria?
He totally rejected me, though.
There's another cafeteria called Fujita Diner on the west side.
Fujita Diner?
Maybe you can help there.
Really!?
Hold on. Let me draw you a map.
Here.
うるうる
TEAR TEAR
Kishida-san, you're so nice.

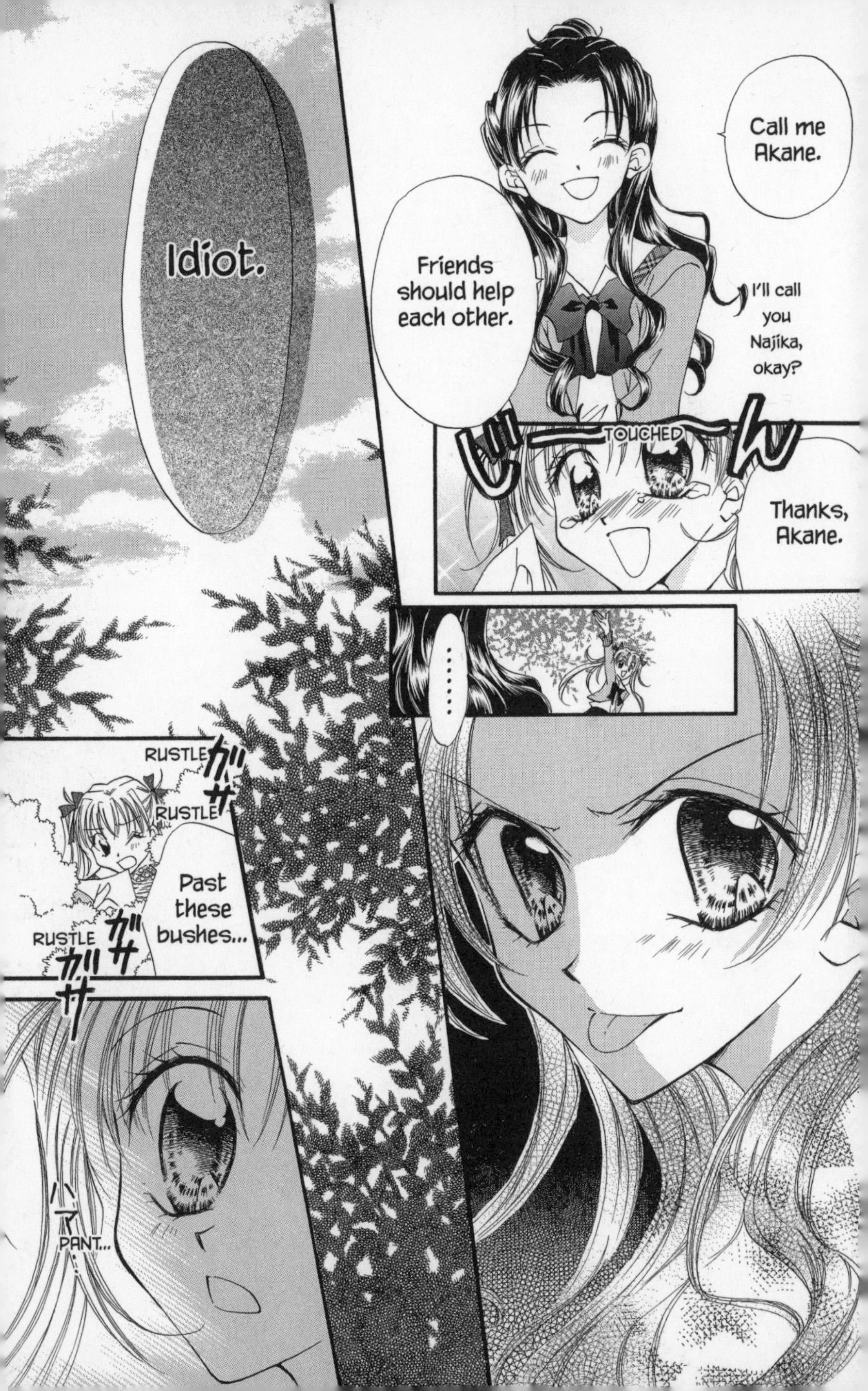
Call me Akane.
Friends should help each other.
I'll call you Najika, okay?
TOUCHED
Thanks, Akane.
Idiot.
......
RUSTLE
RUSTLE
Past these bushes...
RUSTLE
PANT...

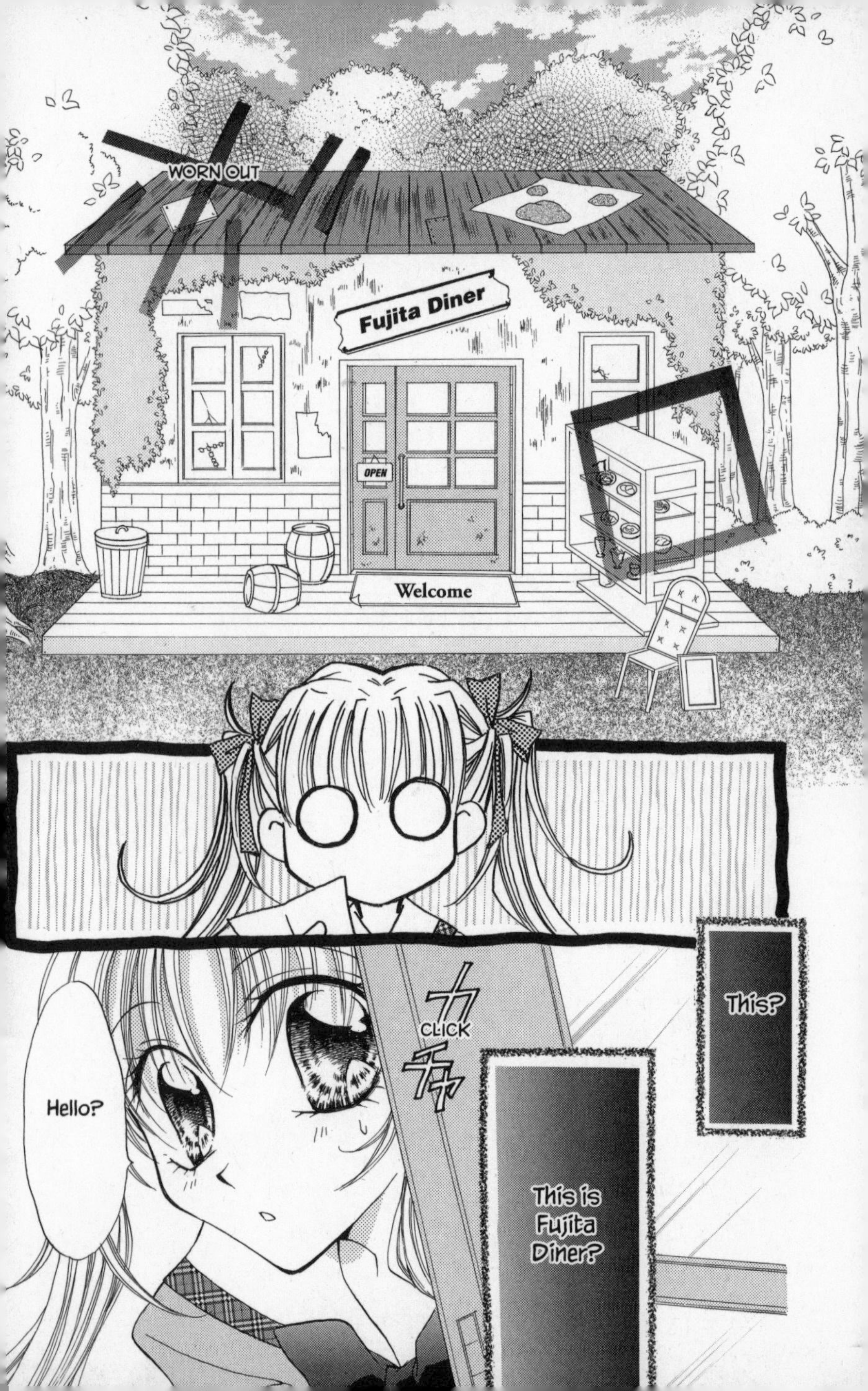
WORN OUT
Fujita Diner
OPEN
Welcome
This?
This is Fujita Diner?
カチャ
CLICK
Hello?

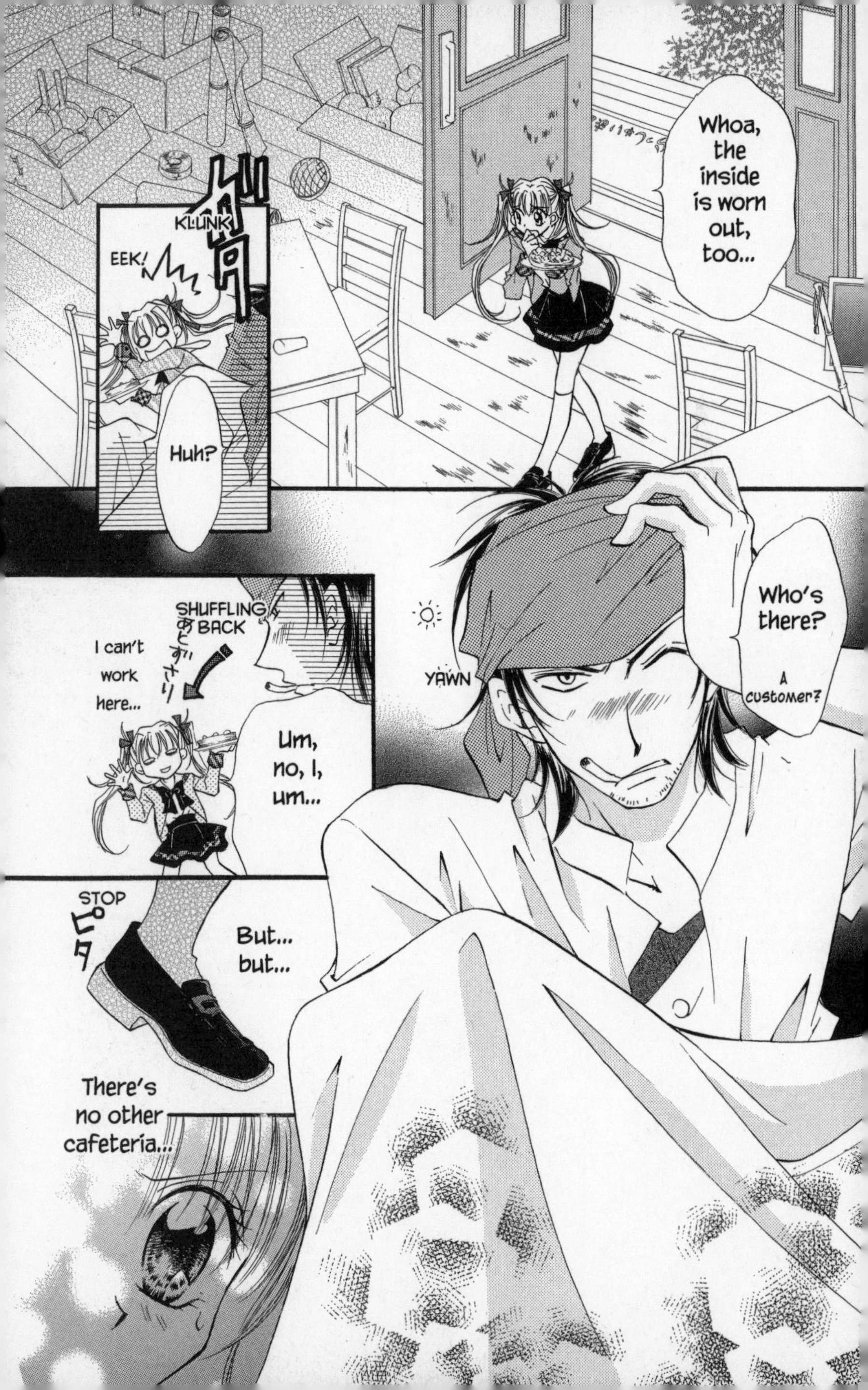
Whoa, the inside is worn out, too...
KLUNK
EEK!
Huh?
Who's there?
A customer?
YAWN
SHUFFLING BACK
Um, no, I, um...
I can't work here...
STOP
But... but...
There's no other cafeteria...

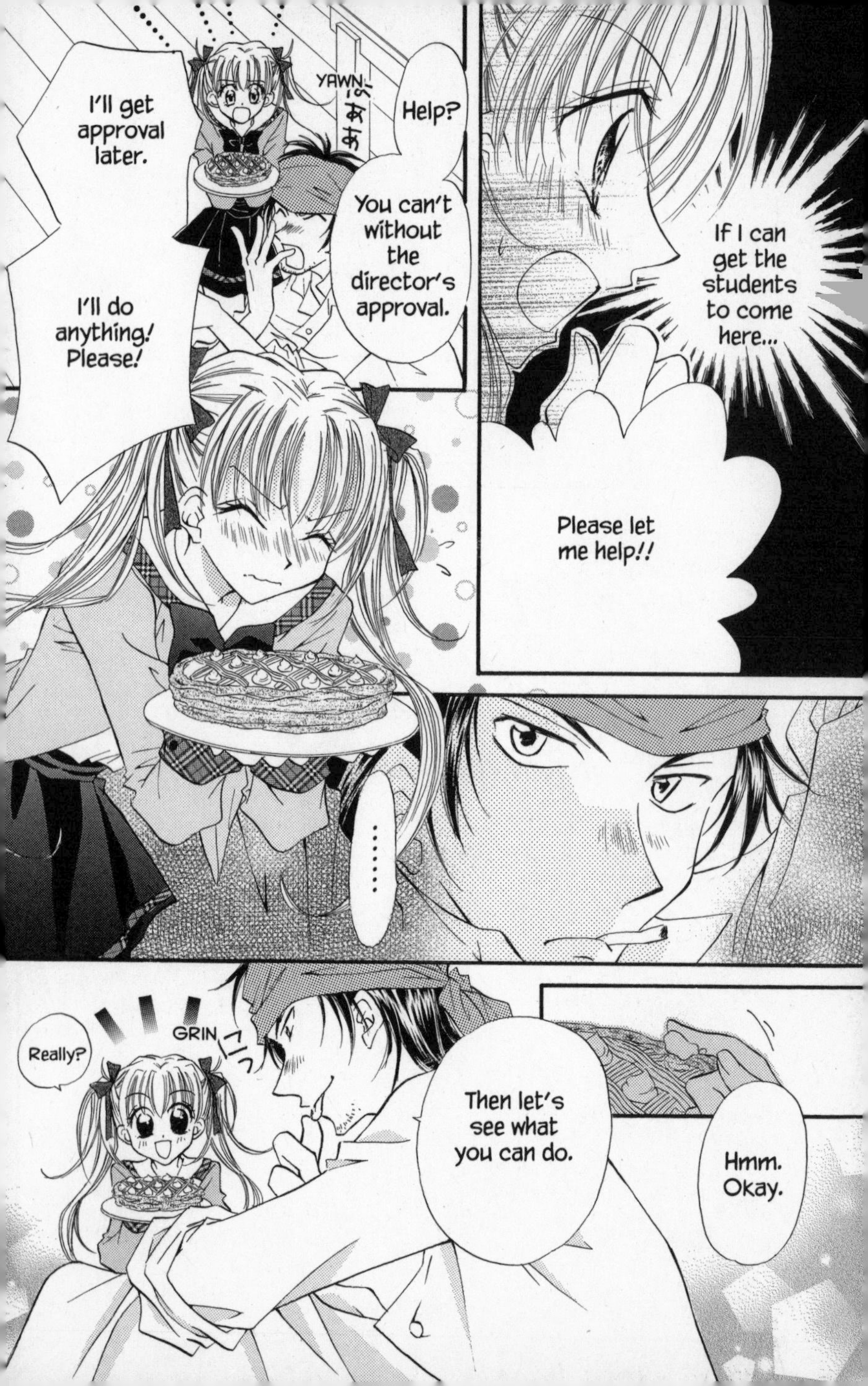

If I can get the students to come here...
Please let me help!!
Help?
YAWN
You can't without the director's approval.
I'll get approval later.
I'll do anything! Please!
......
Hmm. Okay.
Then let's see what you can do.
GRIN
Really?

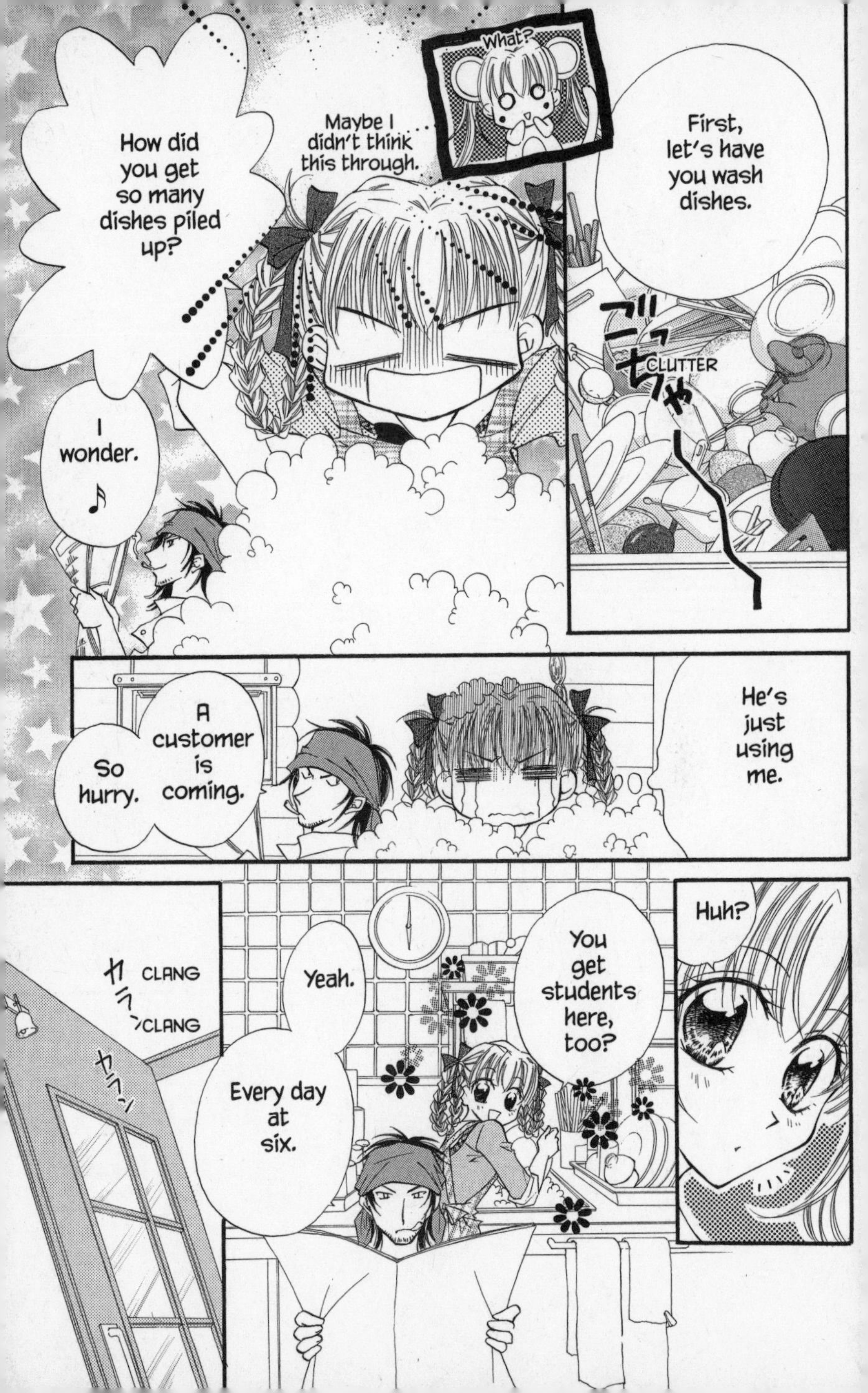
First, let's have you wash dishes.
CLUTTER
What?
Maybe I didn't think this through.
How did you get so many dishes piled up?
I wonder. ♪
He's just using me.
A customer is coming.
So hurry.
Huh?
You get students here, too?
Yeah.
Every day at six.
CLANG
CLANG

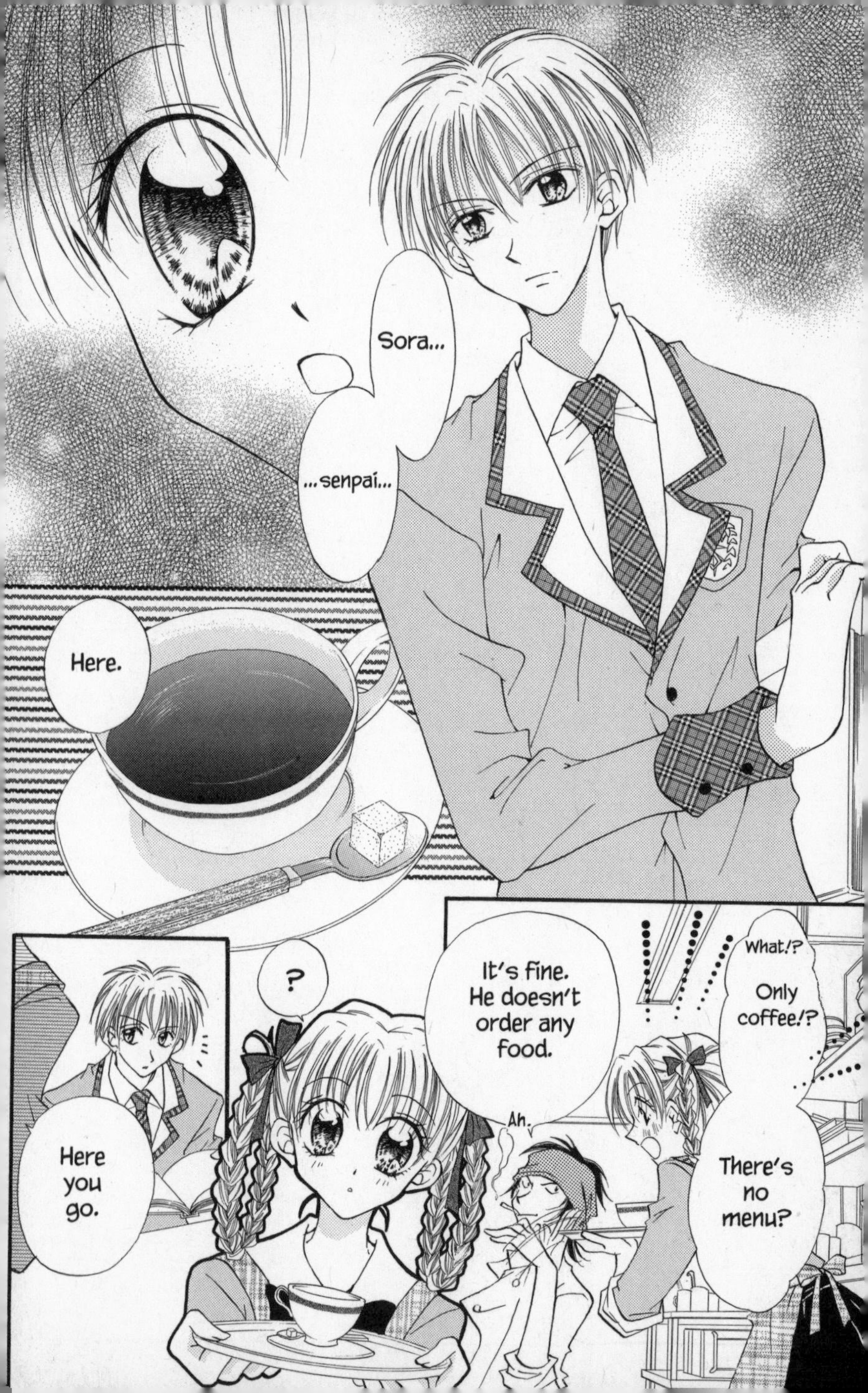
Sora...
...senpai...
Here.
What!?
Only coffee!?
There's no menu?
Ah.
It's fine. He doesn't order any food.
?
Here you go.

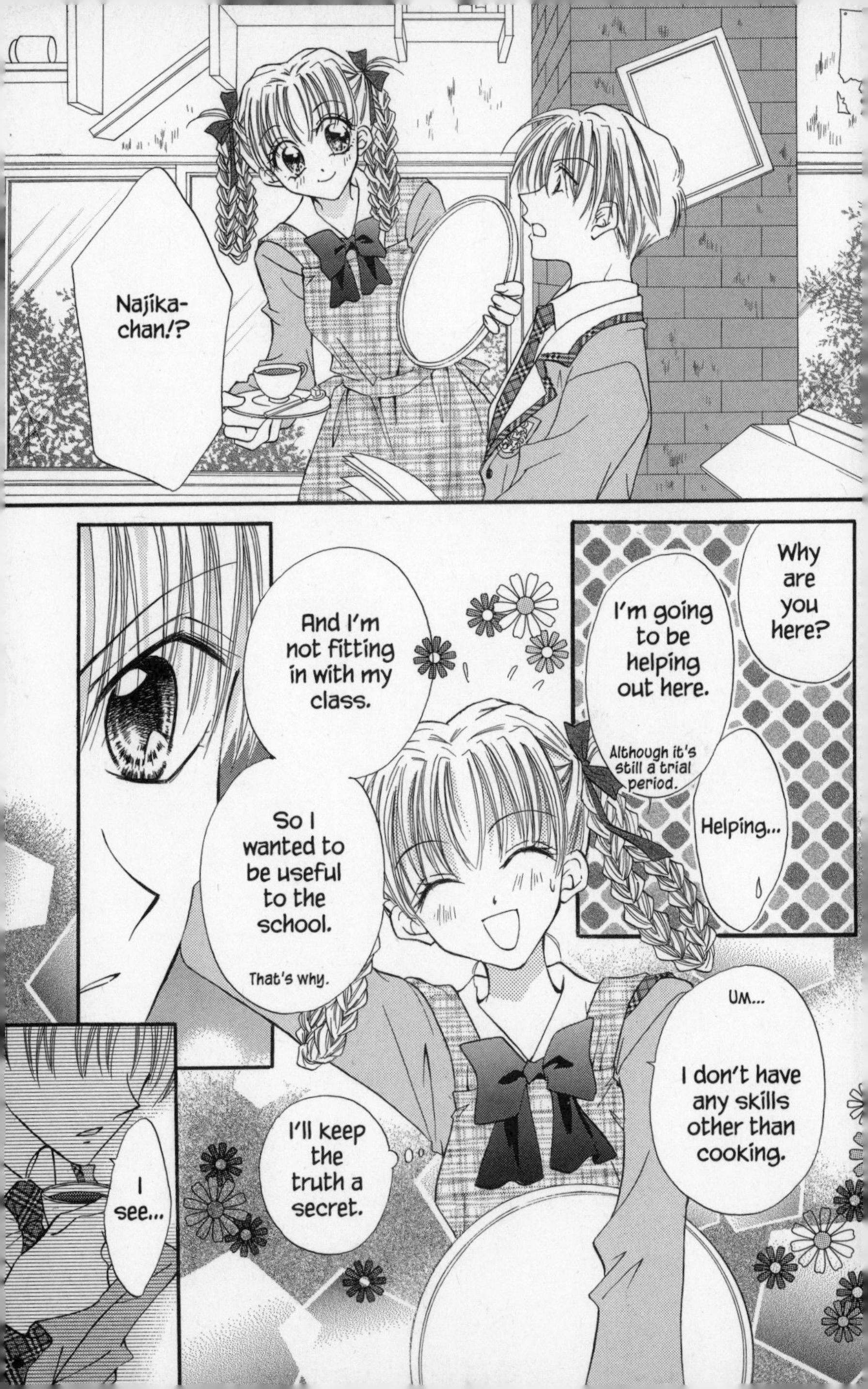
Najika-chan!?
Why are you here?
I'm going to be helping out here.
Although it's still a trial period.
Helping...
Um...
I don't have any skills other than cooking.
And I'm not fitting in with my class.
So I wanted to be useful to the school.
That's why.
I'll keep the truth a secret.
I see...

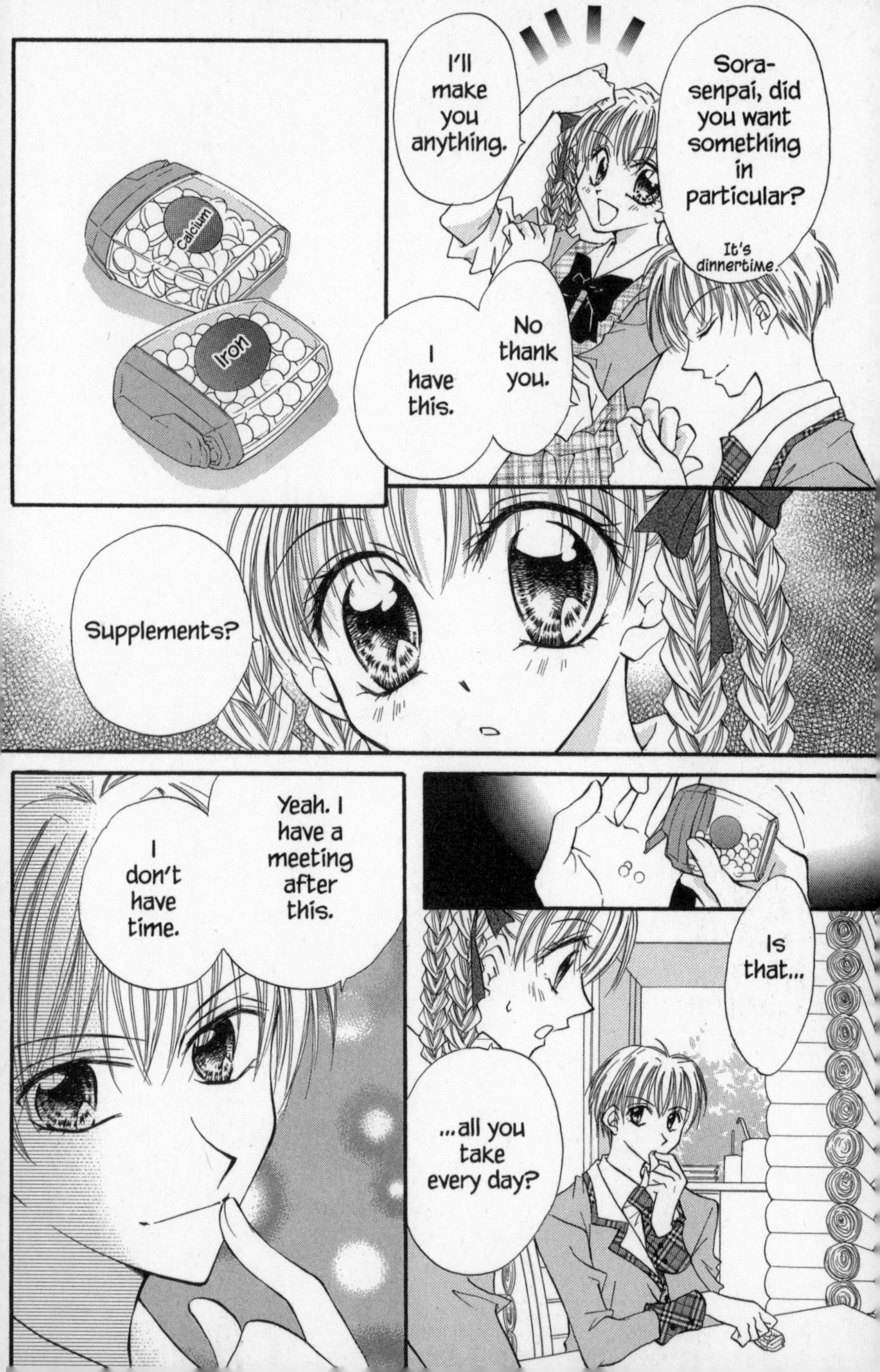

Sora-senpai, did you want something in particular?
It's dinnertime.
I'll make you anything.
No thank you.
I have this.
Calcium
Iron
Supplements?
Is that...
...all you take every day?
Yeah. I have a meeting after this.
I don't have time.

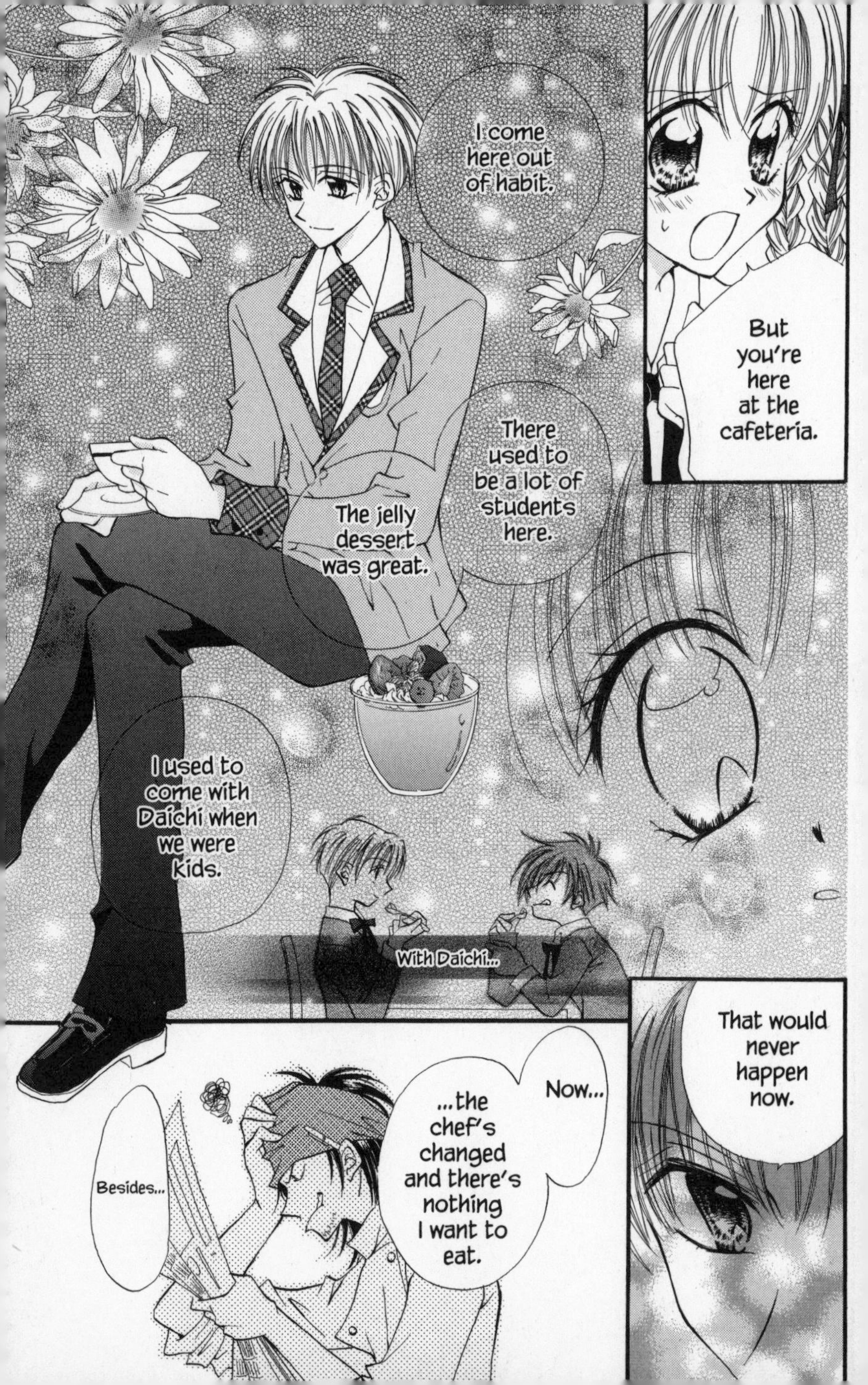
But you're here at the cafeteria.
I come here out of habit.
There used to be a lot of students here.
The jelly dessert was great.
I used to come with Daichi when we were kids.
With Daichi...
That would never happen now.
Now...
...the chef's changed and there's nothing I want to eat.
Besides...

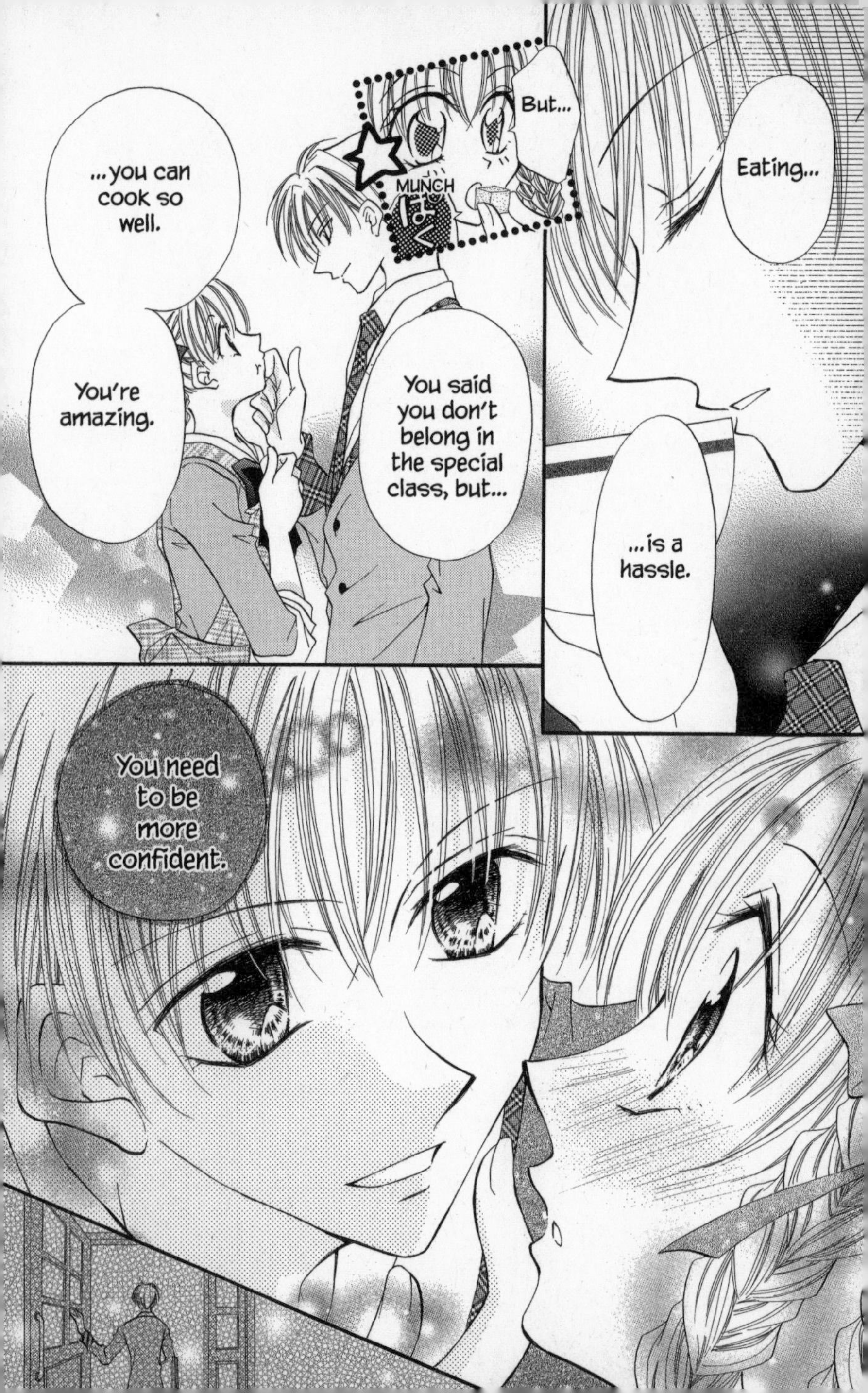
Eating...
...is a hassle.
But...
MUNCH
はぐ
You said you don't belong in the special class, but...
...you can cook so well.
You're amazing.
You need to be more confident.

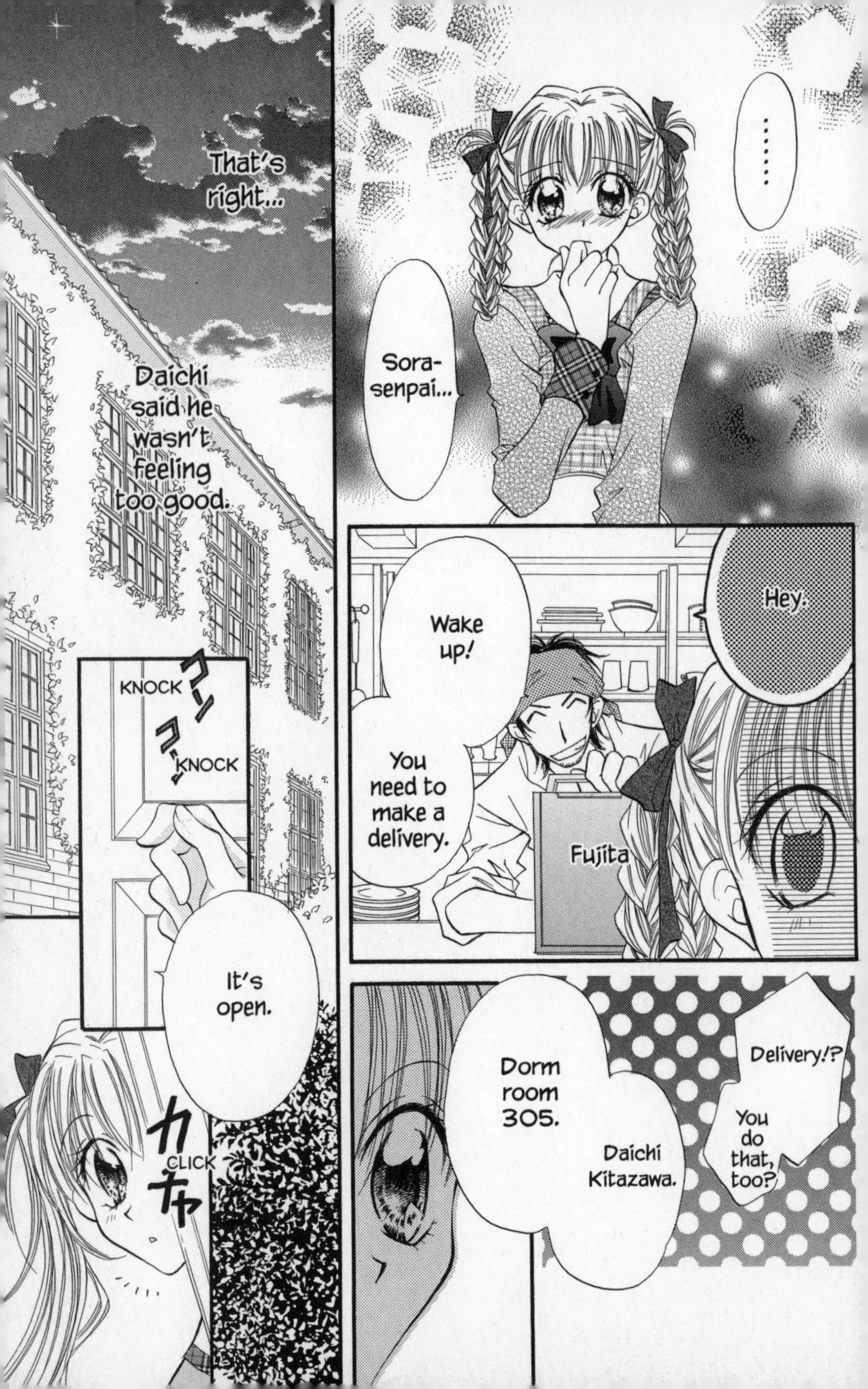
……
Sora-senpai…
Hey.
Wake up!
You need to make a delivery.
Fujita
Delivery!?
You do that, too?
Dorm room 305.
Daichi Kitazawa.
That's right…
Daichi said he wasn't feeling too good.
KNOCK
KNOCK
It's open.
CLICK

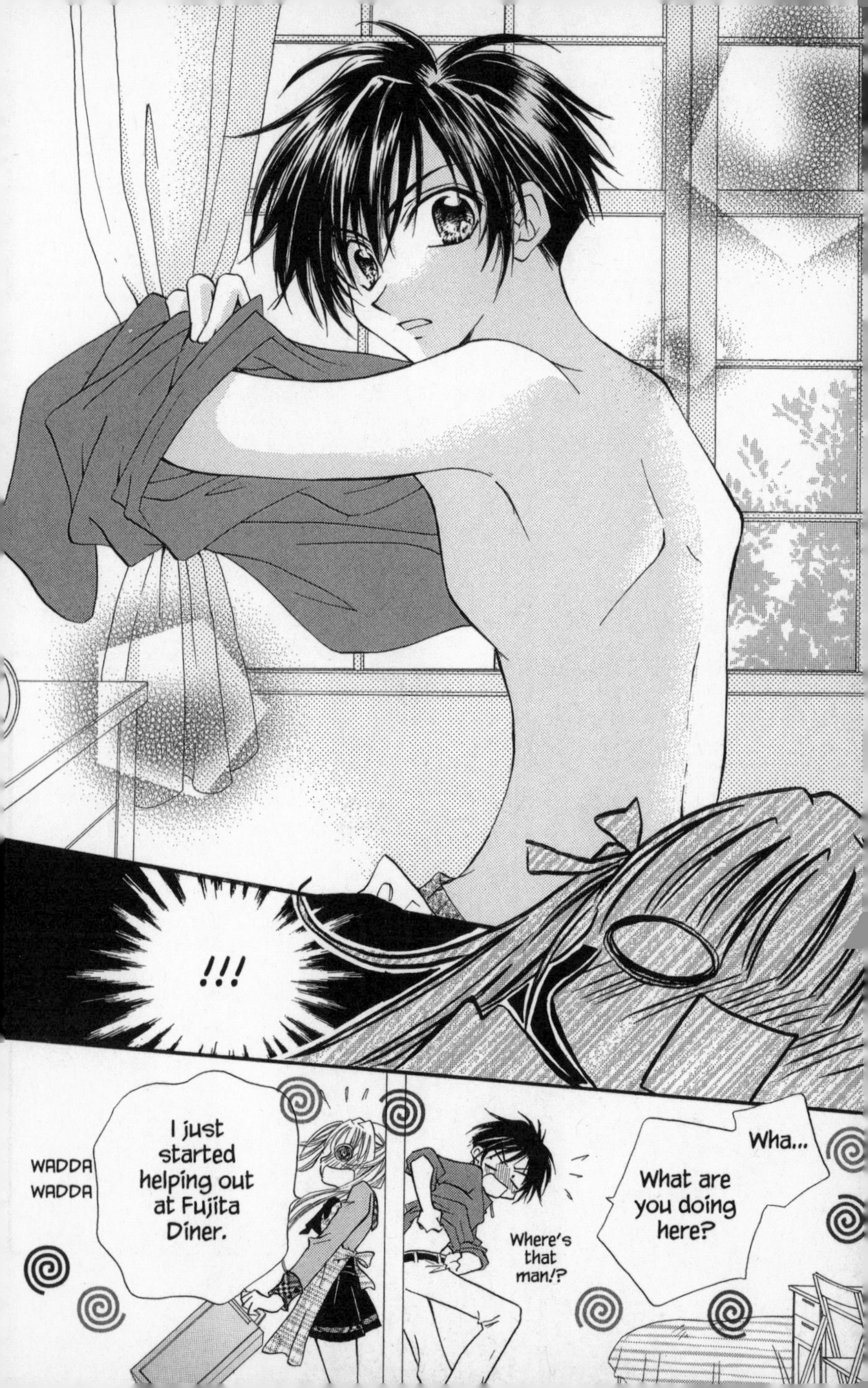
!!!
Wha...
What are you doing here?
Where's that man!?
I just started helping out at Fujita Diner.
WADDA WADDA

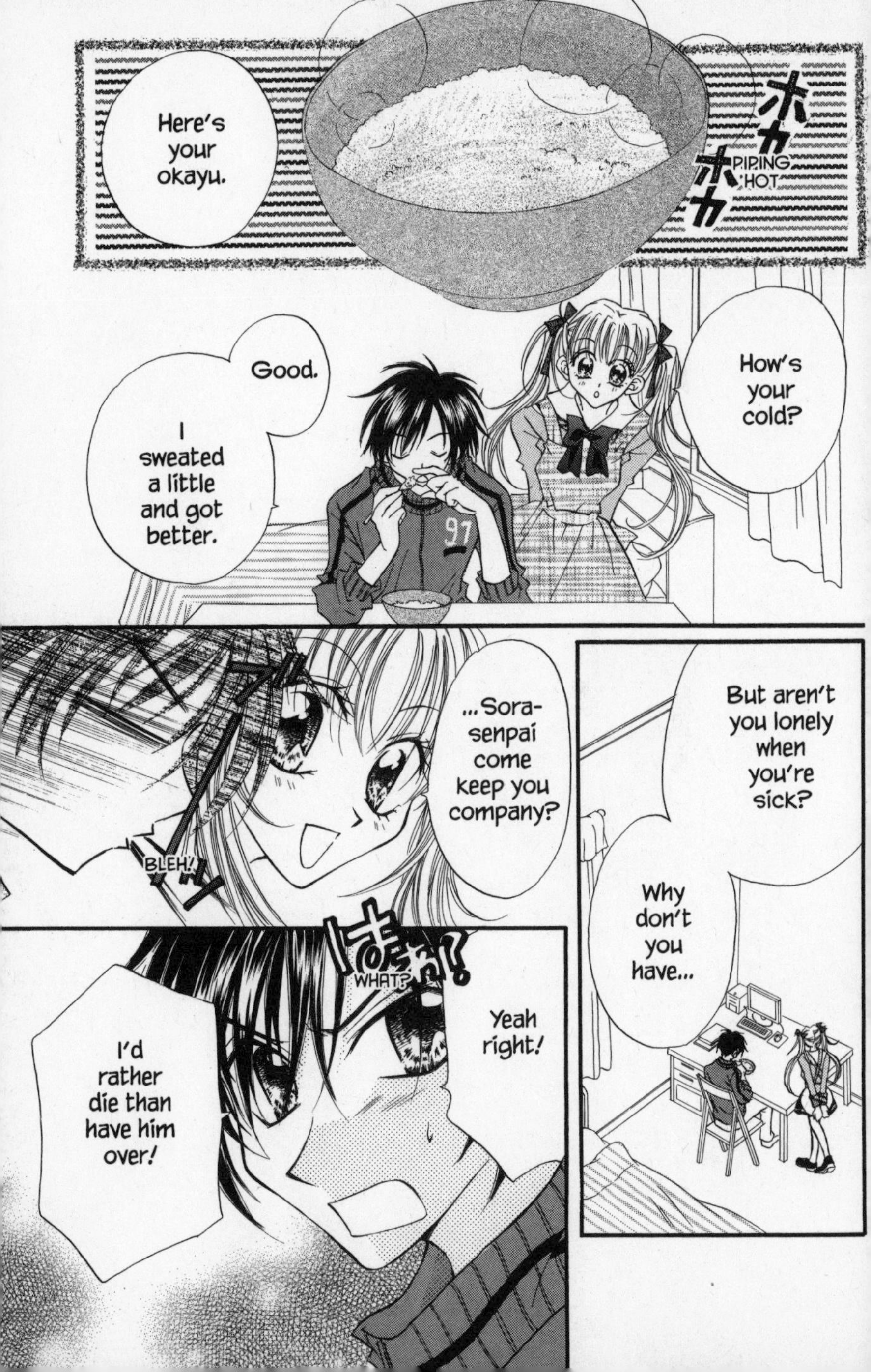

ホカホカ
PIPING HOT
Here's your okayu.
How's your cold?
Good.
I sweated a little and got better.
But aren't you lonely when you're sick?
Why don't you have...
...Sora-senpai come keep you company?
BLEH!
WHAT?
Yeah right!
I'd rather die than have him over!

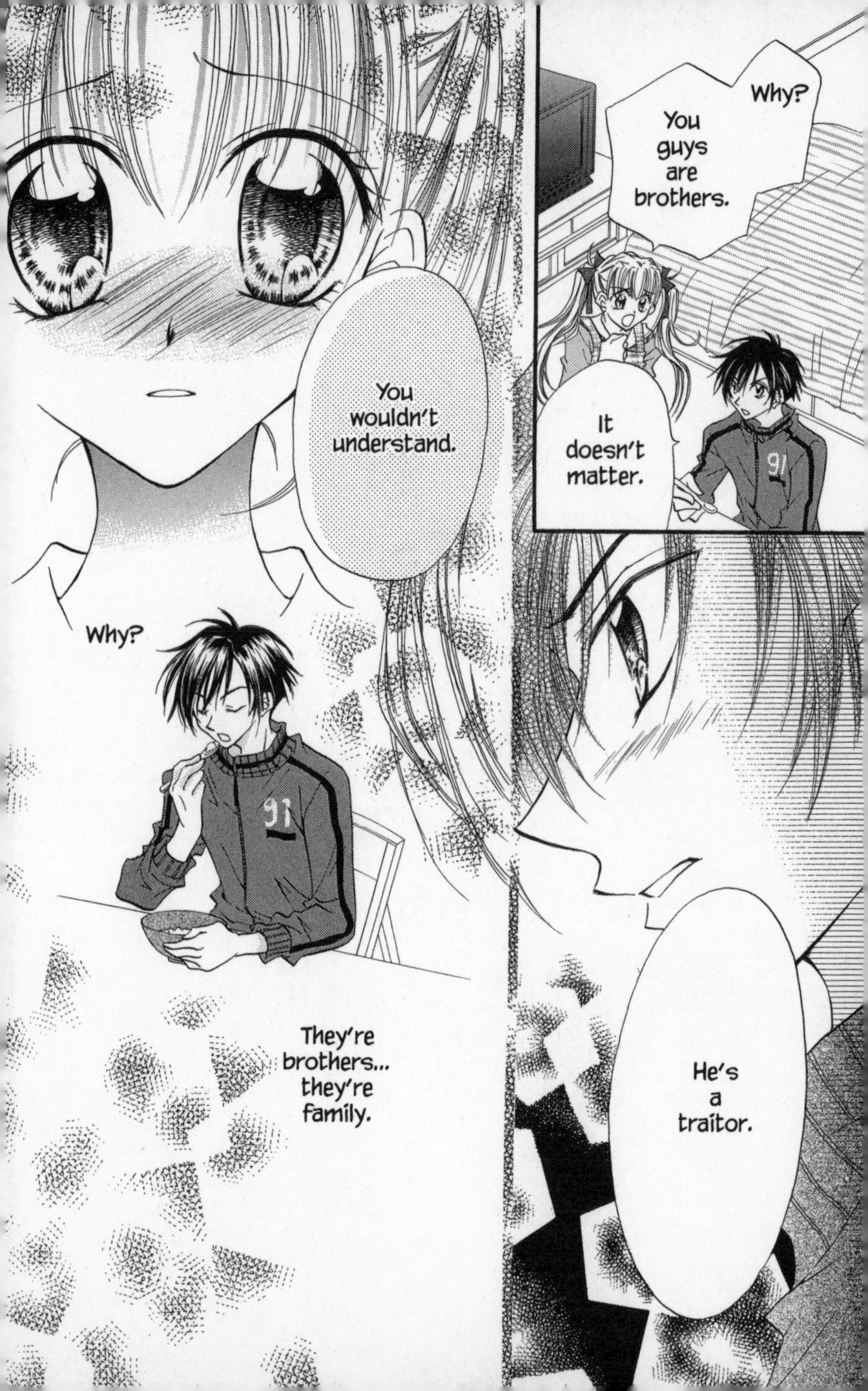
Why? You guys are brothers.
It doesn't matter.
He's a traitor.
You wouldn't understand.
Why?
They're brothers... they're family.

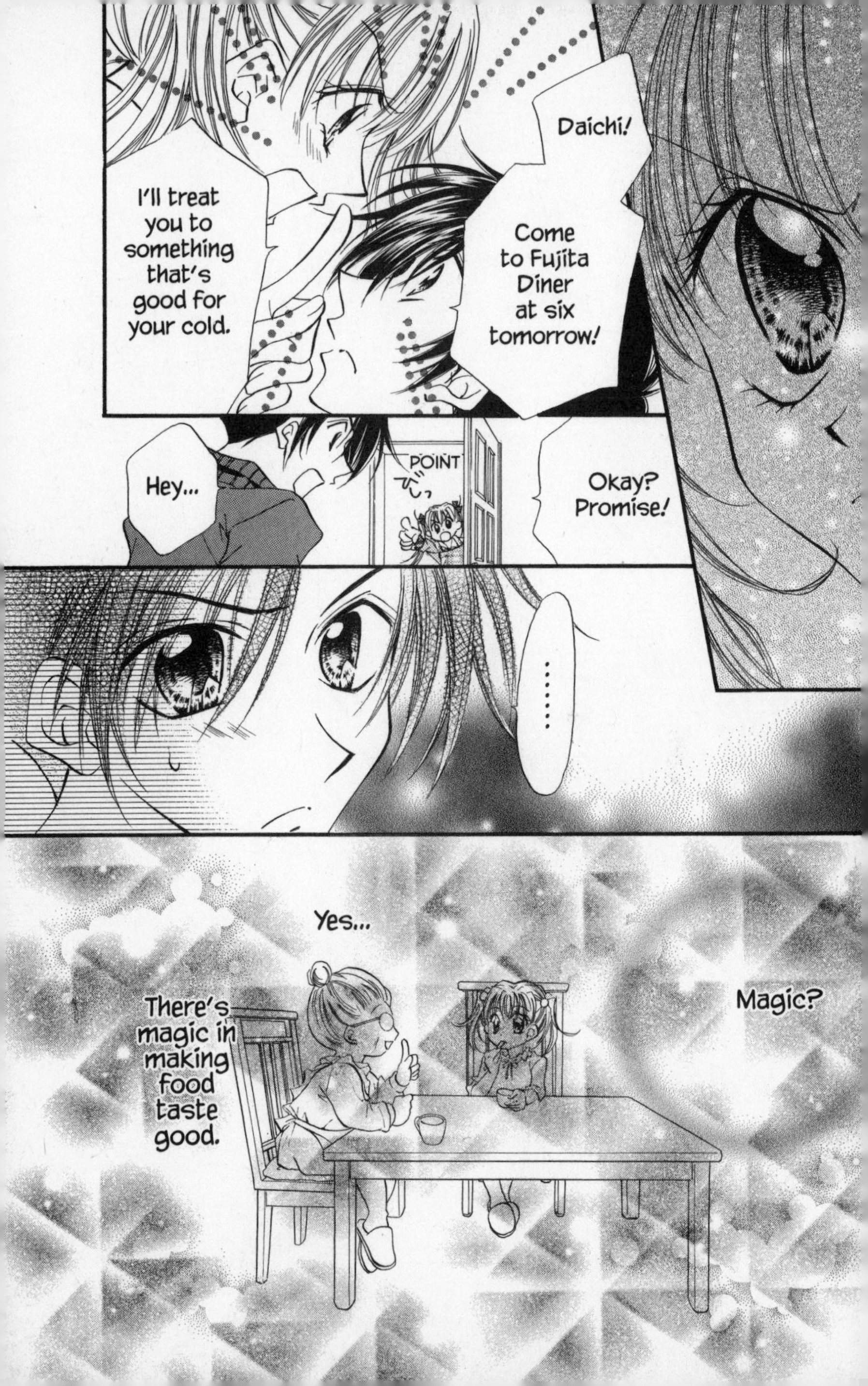

Daichi!
Come to Fujita Diner at six tomorrow!
I'll treat you to something that's good for your cold.
Okay? Promise!
POINT
びっ
Hey...
......
Magic?
Yes...
There's magic in making food taste good.

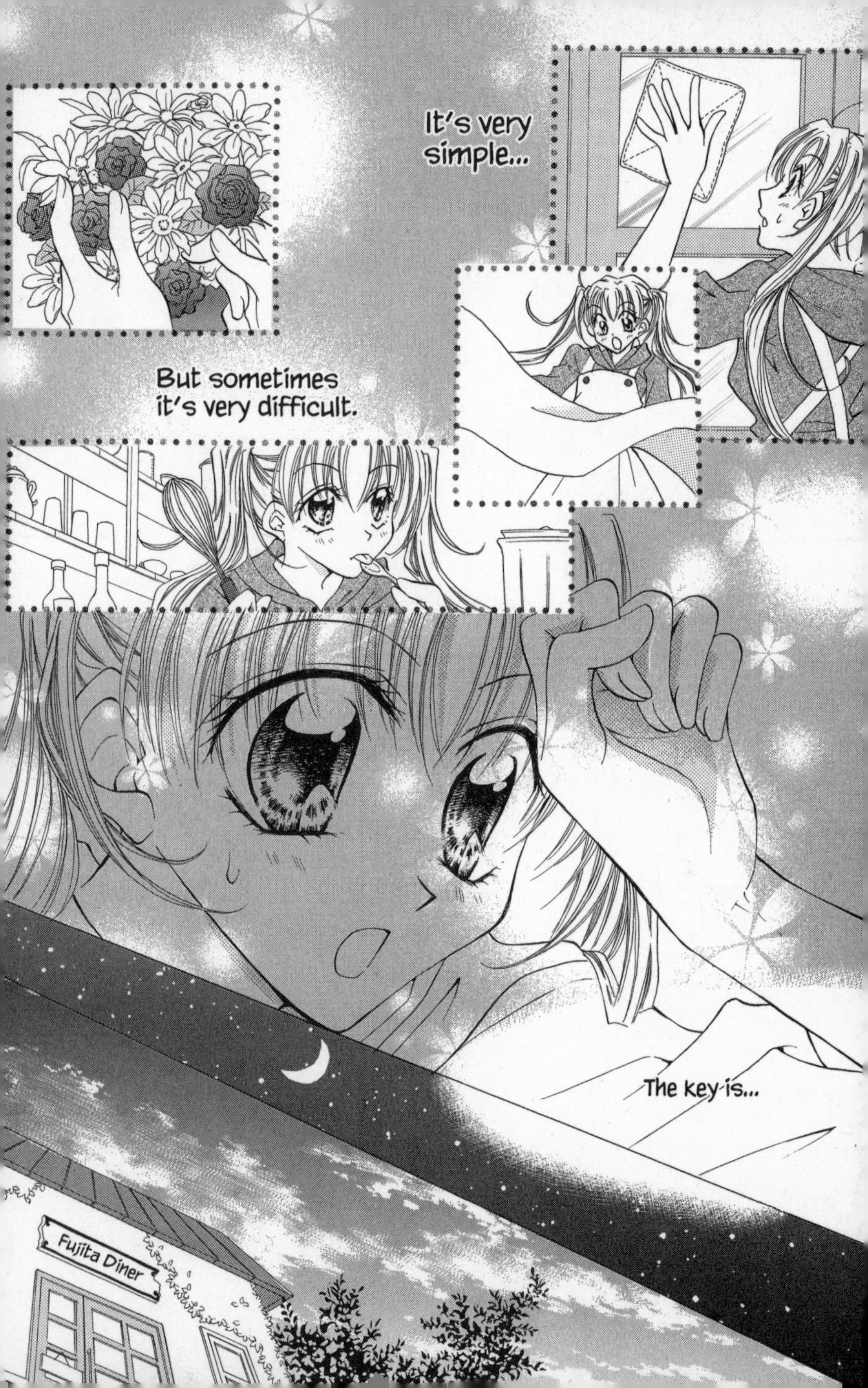
It's very simple...
But sometimes it's very difficult.
The key is...
Fujita Diner

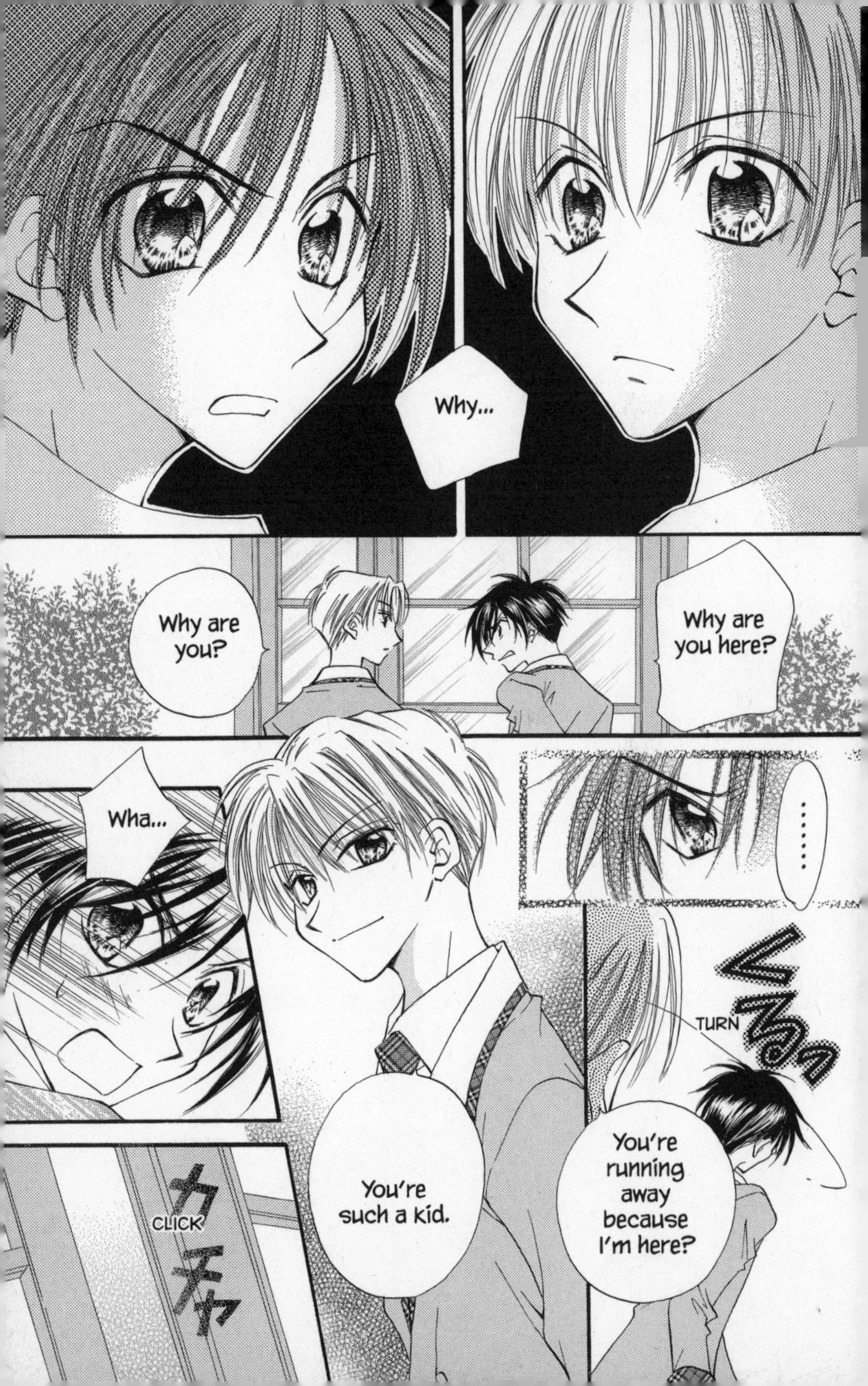
Why...
Why are you here?
Why are you?
......
TURN
You're running away because I'm here?
Wha...
You're such a kid.
カチャ
CLICK

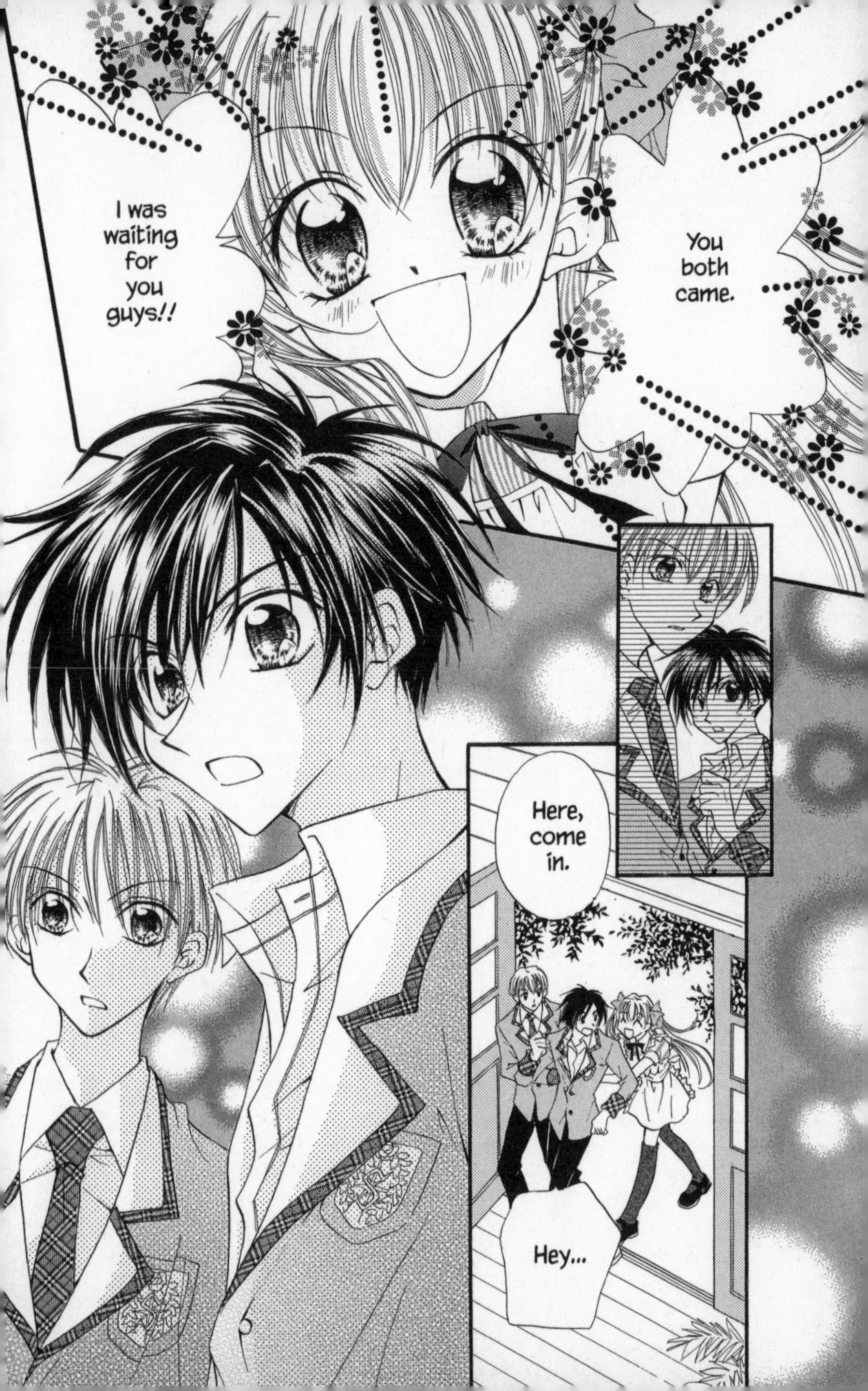
You both came.
I was waiting for you guys!!
Here, come in.
Hey...

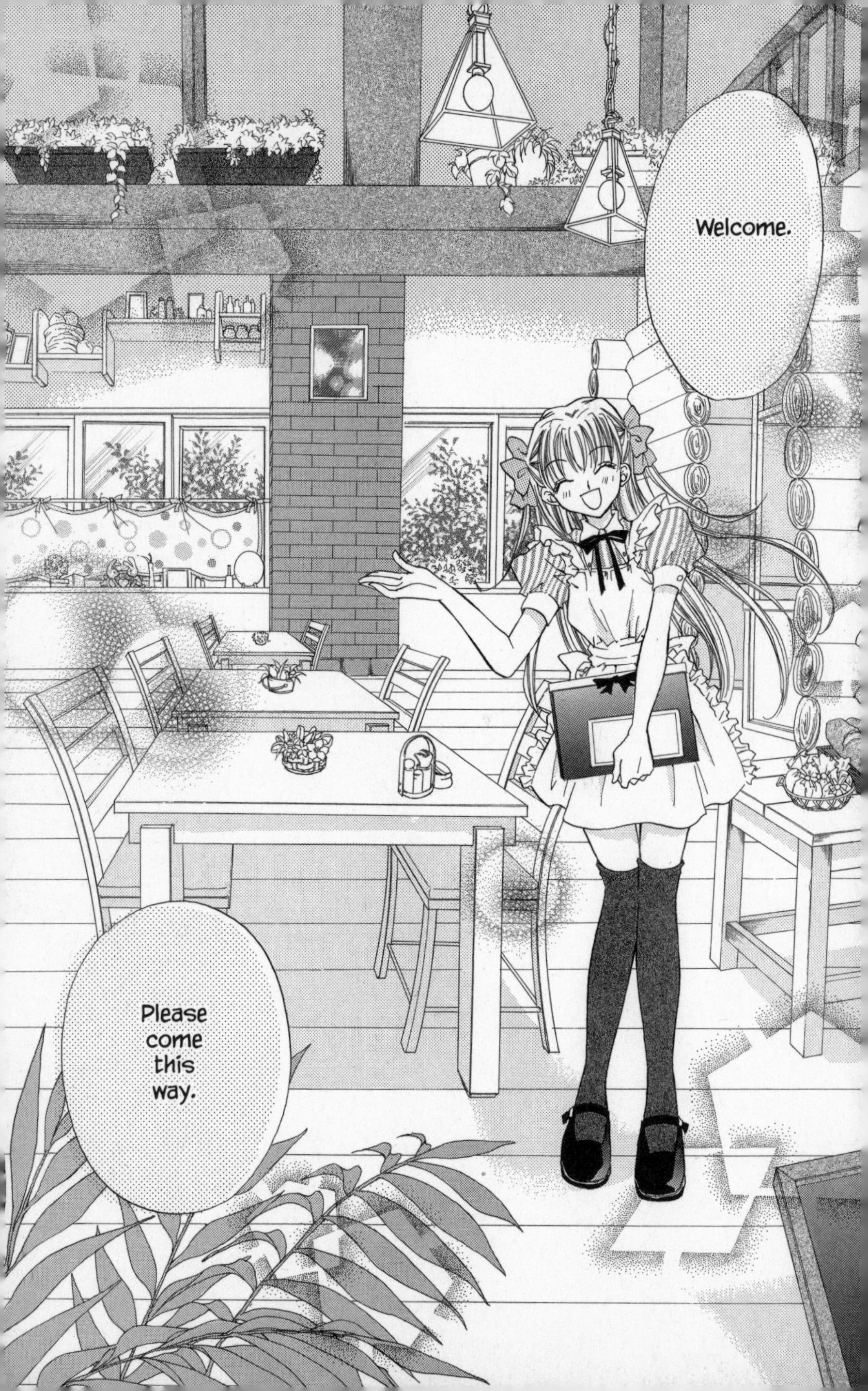
Welcome.
Please come this way.

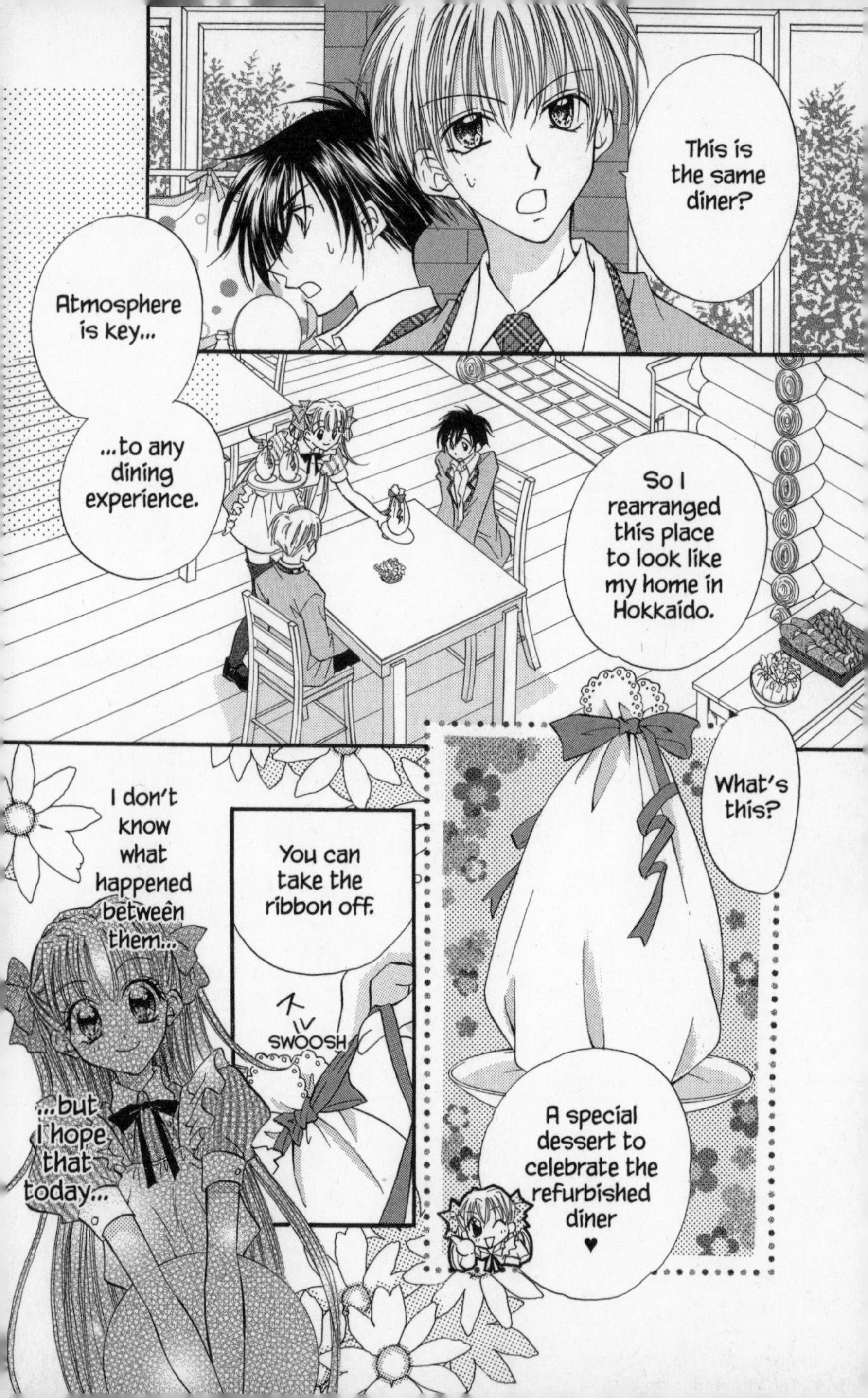
This is the same diner?
Atmosphere is key...
...to any dining experience.
So I rearranged this place to look like my home in Hokkaido.
What's this?
A special dessert to celebrate the refurbished diner ♥
You can take the ribbon off.
SWOOSH
I don't know what happened between them...
...but I hope that today...

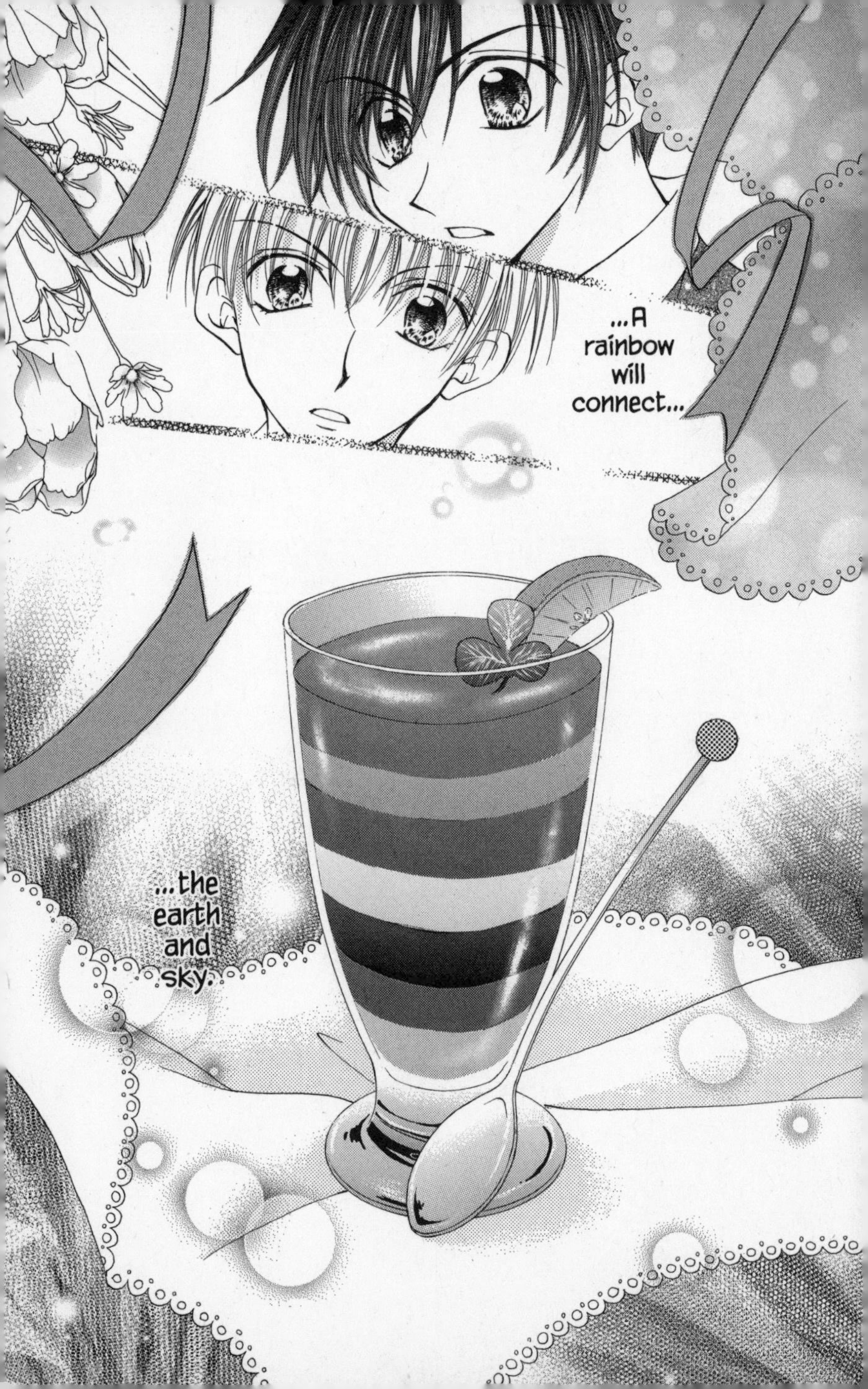
...A rainbow will connect...
...the earth and sky.

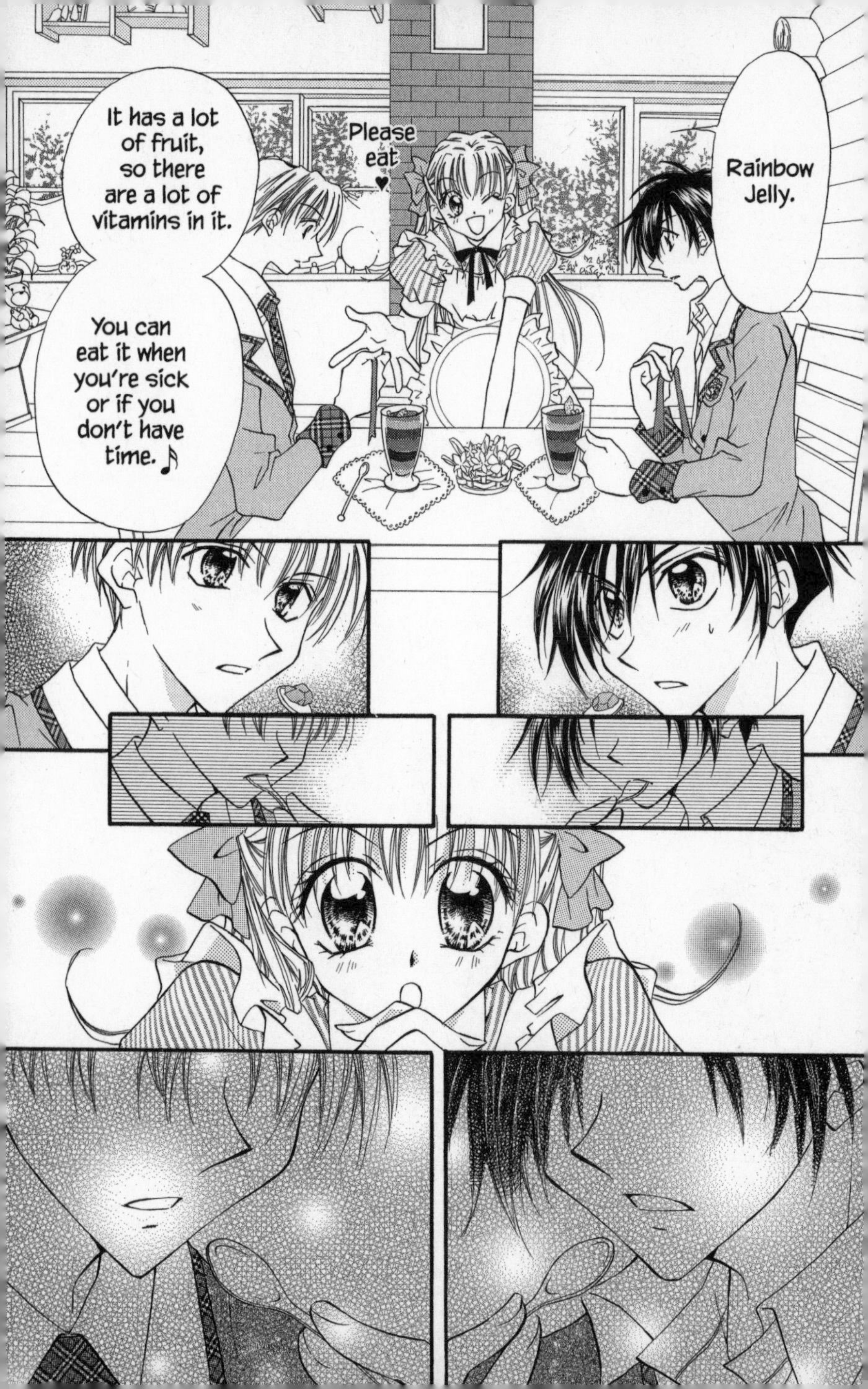
Rainbow Jelly.
Please eat ♥
It has a lot of fruit, so there are a lot of vitamins in it.
You can eat it when you're sick or if you don't have time. ♪

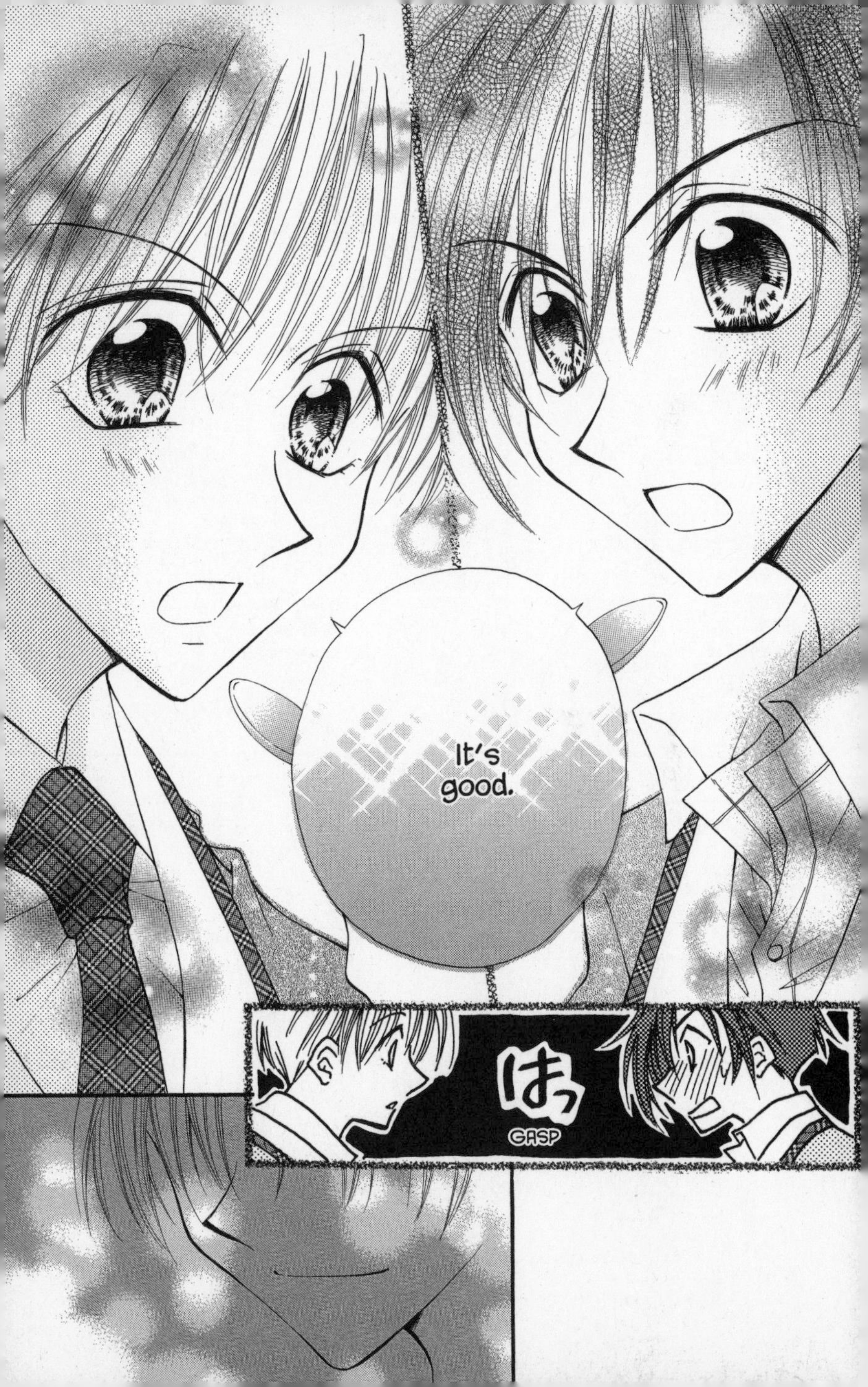
It's good.
はっ
GASP

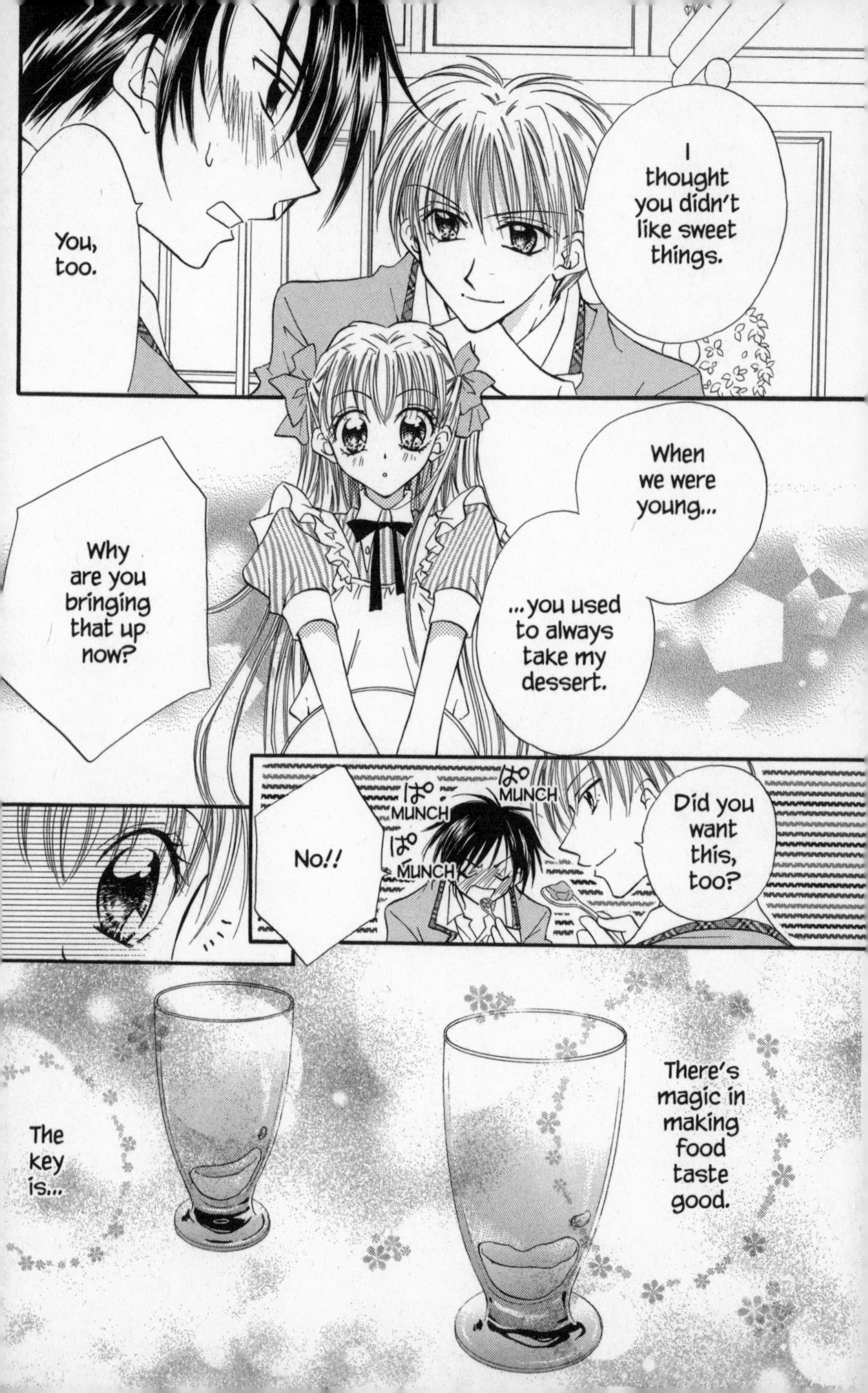
I thought you didn't like sweet things.
You, too.
When we were young...
...you used to always take my dessert.
Why are you bringing that up now?
Did you want this, too?
ぱ MUNCH
ぱ MUNCH
ぱ MUNCH
No!!
There's magic in making food taste good.
The key is...

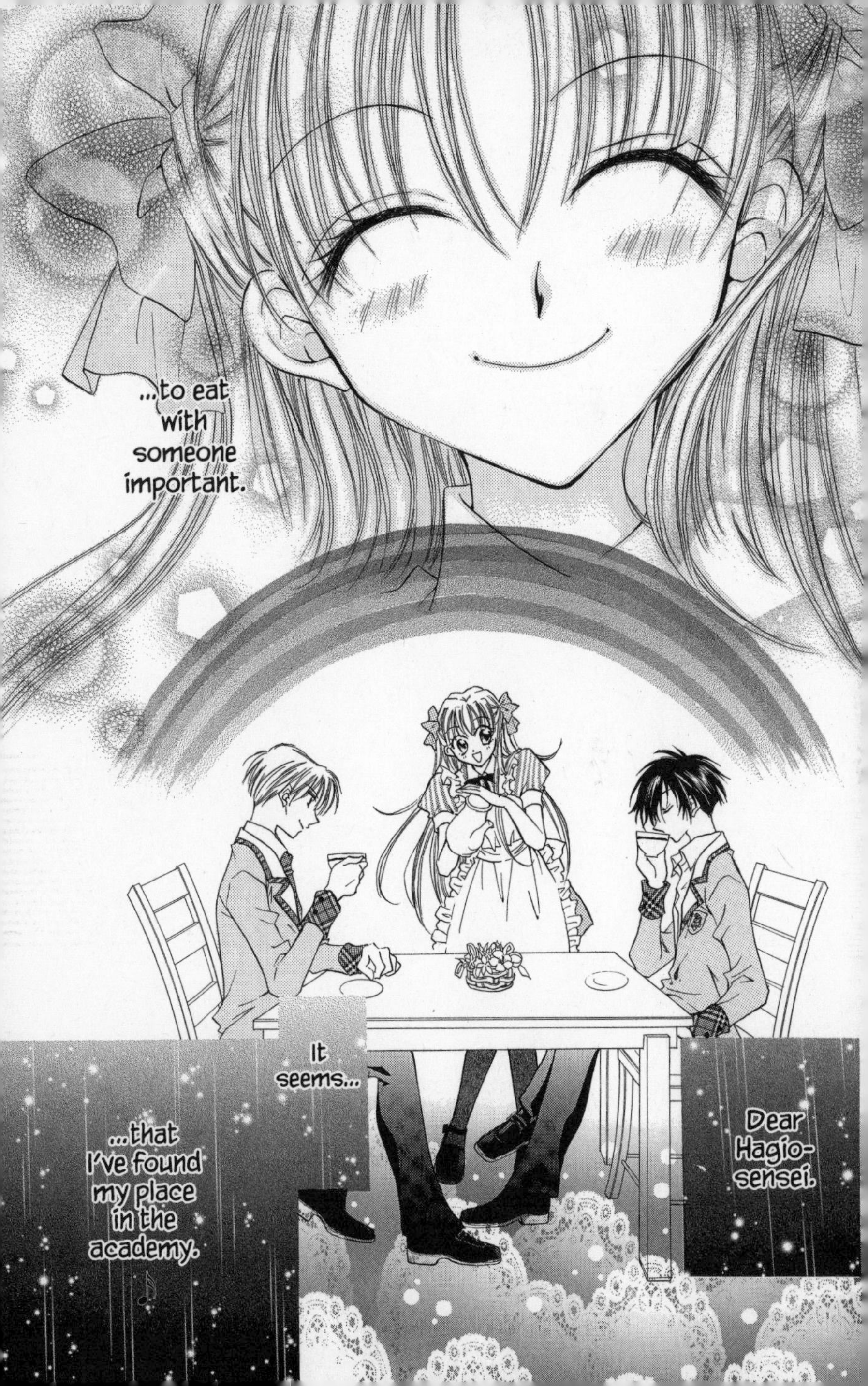
...to eat with someone important.
Dear Hagio-sensei.
It seems...
...that I've found my place in the academy.

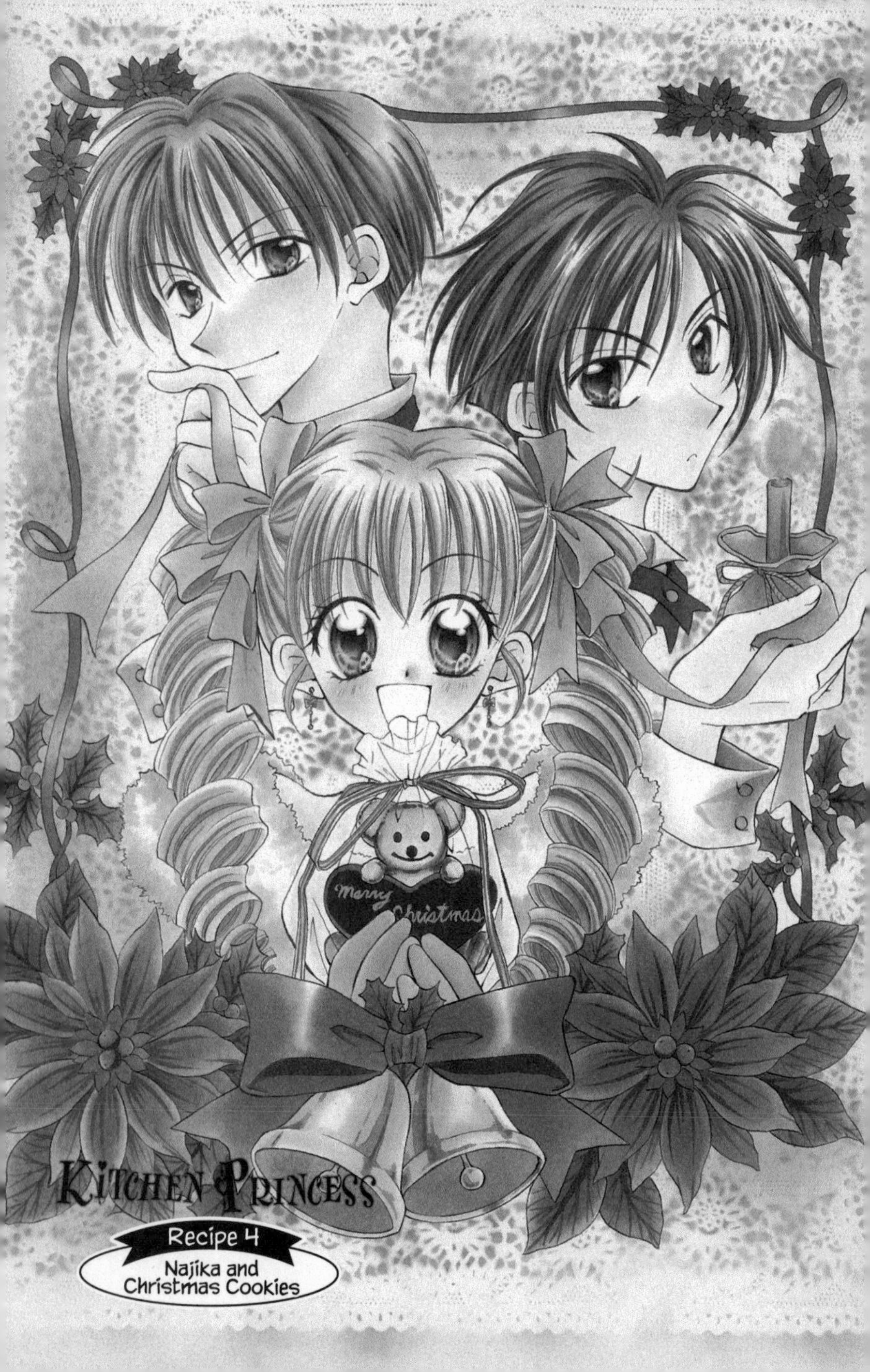

Merry Christmas
KITCHEN PRINCESS
Recipe 4
Najika and Christmas Cookies

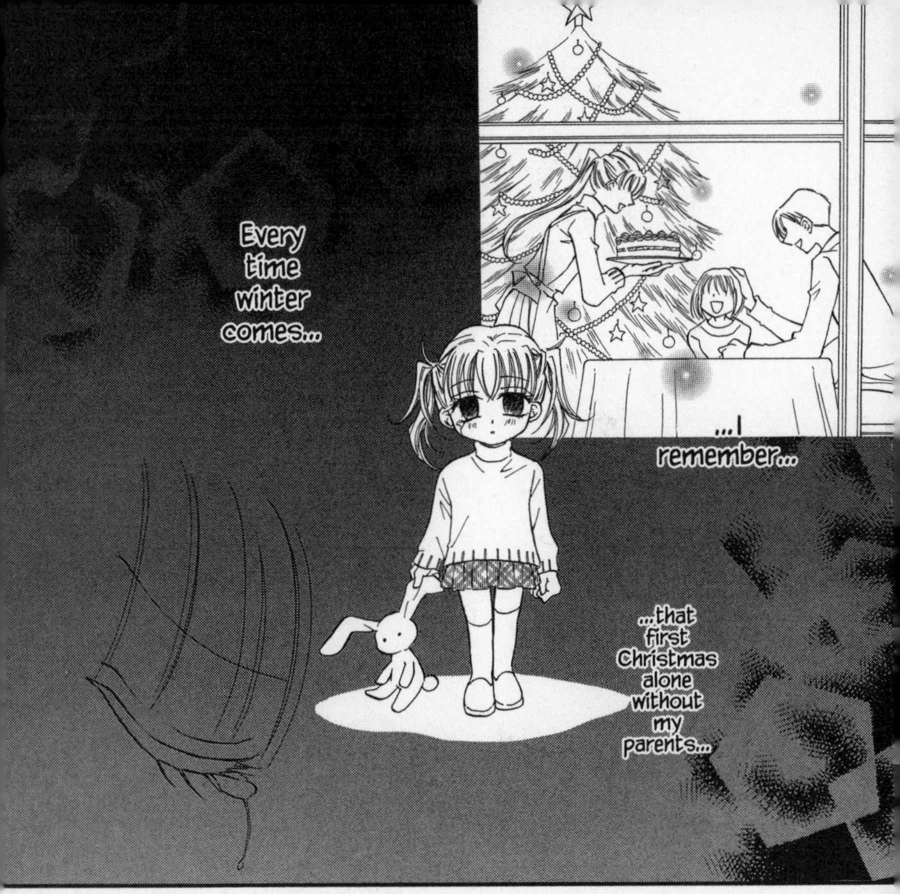
Every time winter comes...
...I remember...
...that first Christmas alone without my parents...

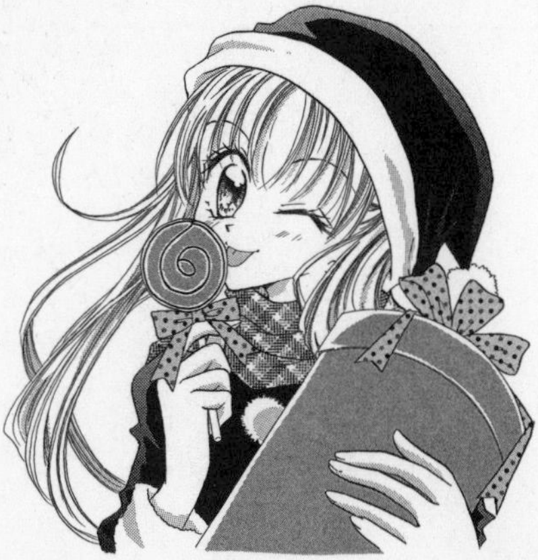

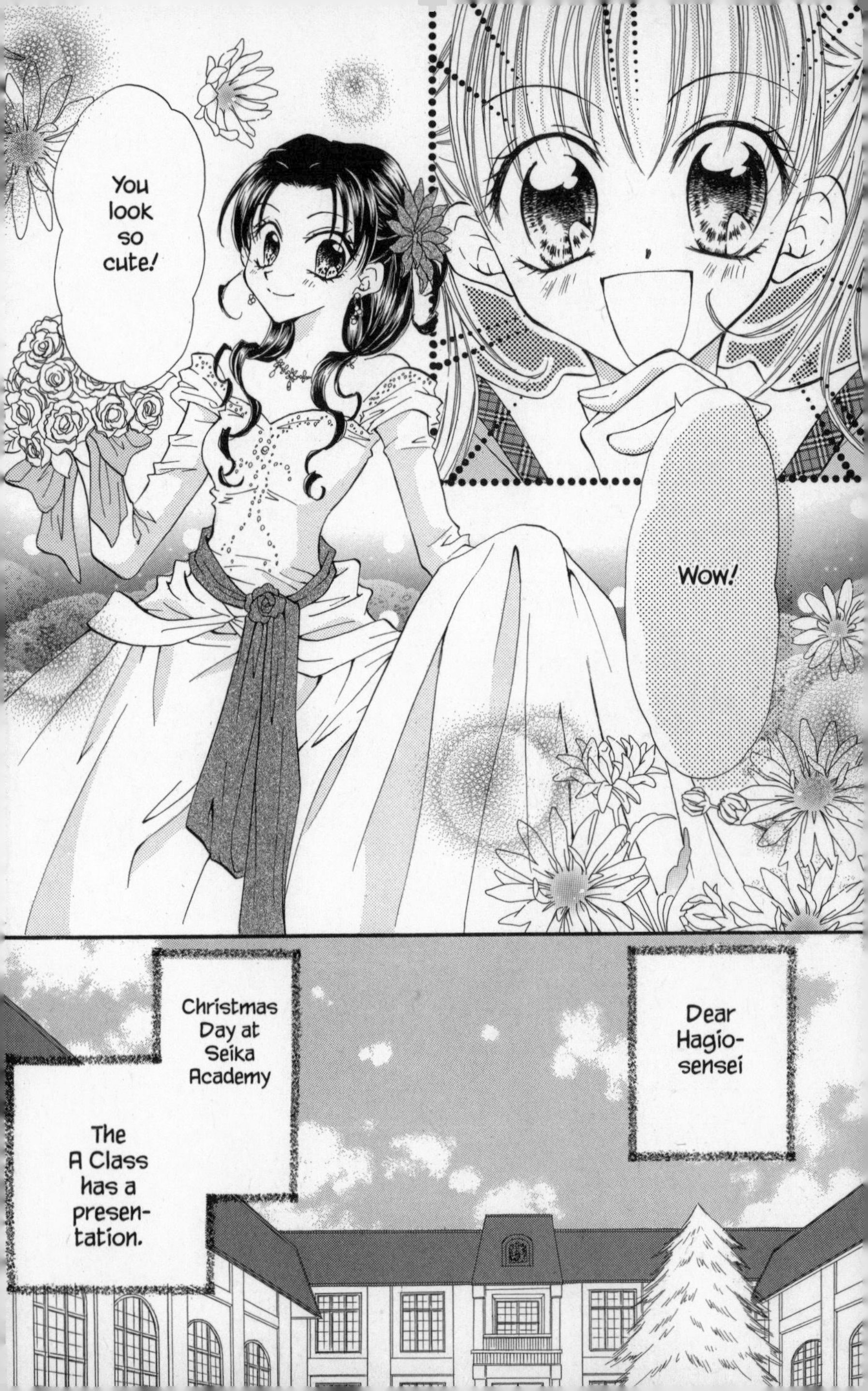
Wow!
You look so cute!
Dear Hagio-sensei
Christmas Day at Seika Academy
The A Class has a presentation.

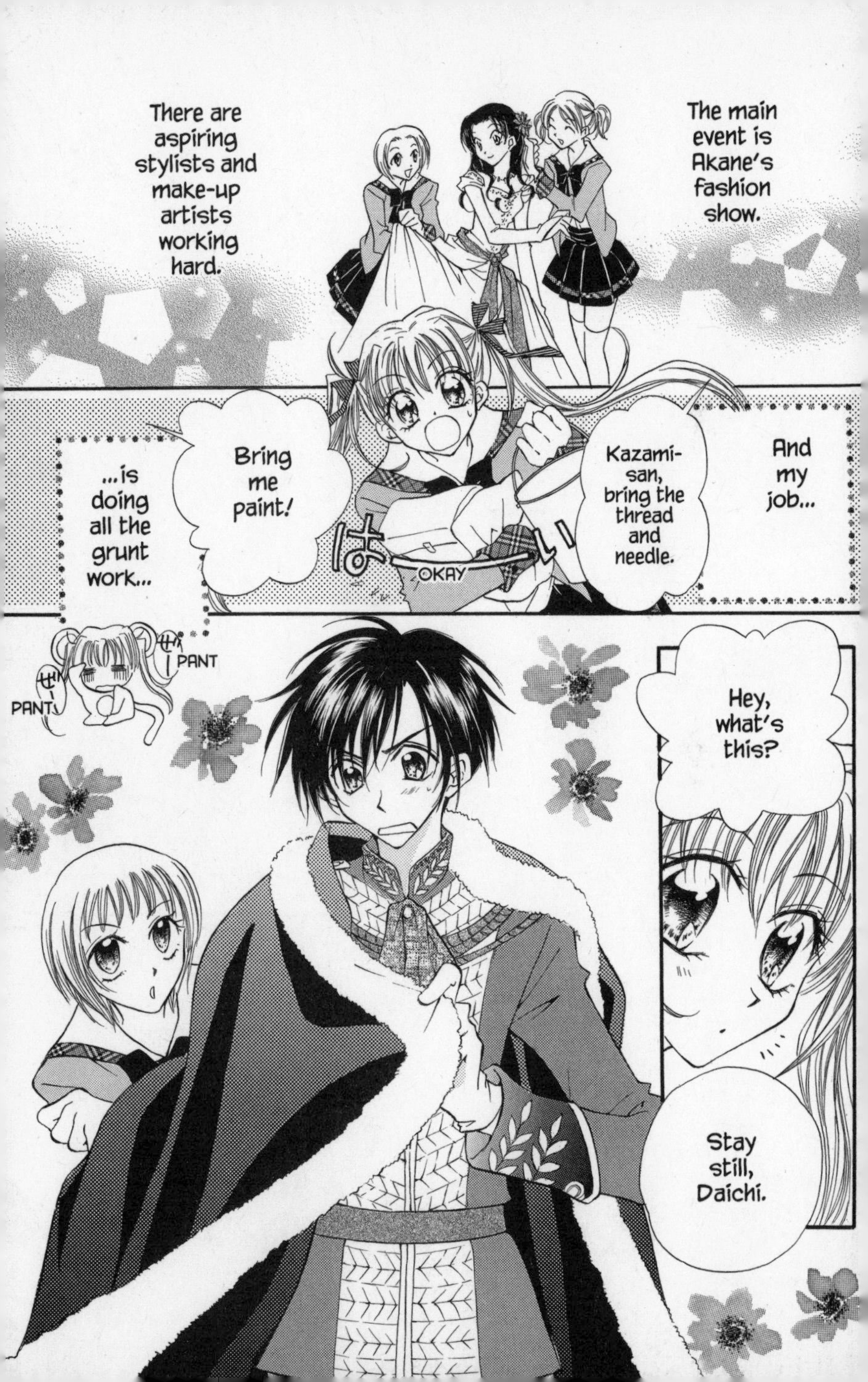
The main event is Akane's fashion show.
There are aspiring stylists and make-up artists working hard.
And my job...
Kazami-san, bring the thread and needle.
Bring me paint!
はーい
OKAY
...is doing all the grunt work...
PANT
PANT
Hey, what's this?
Stay still, Daichi.

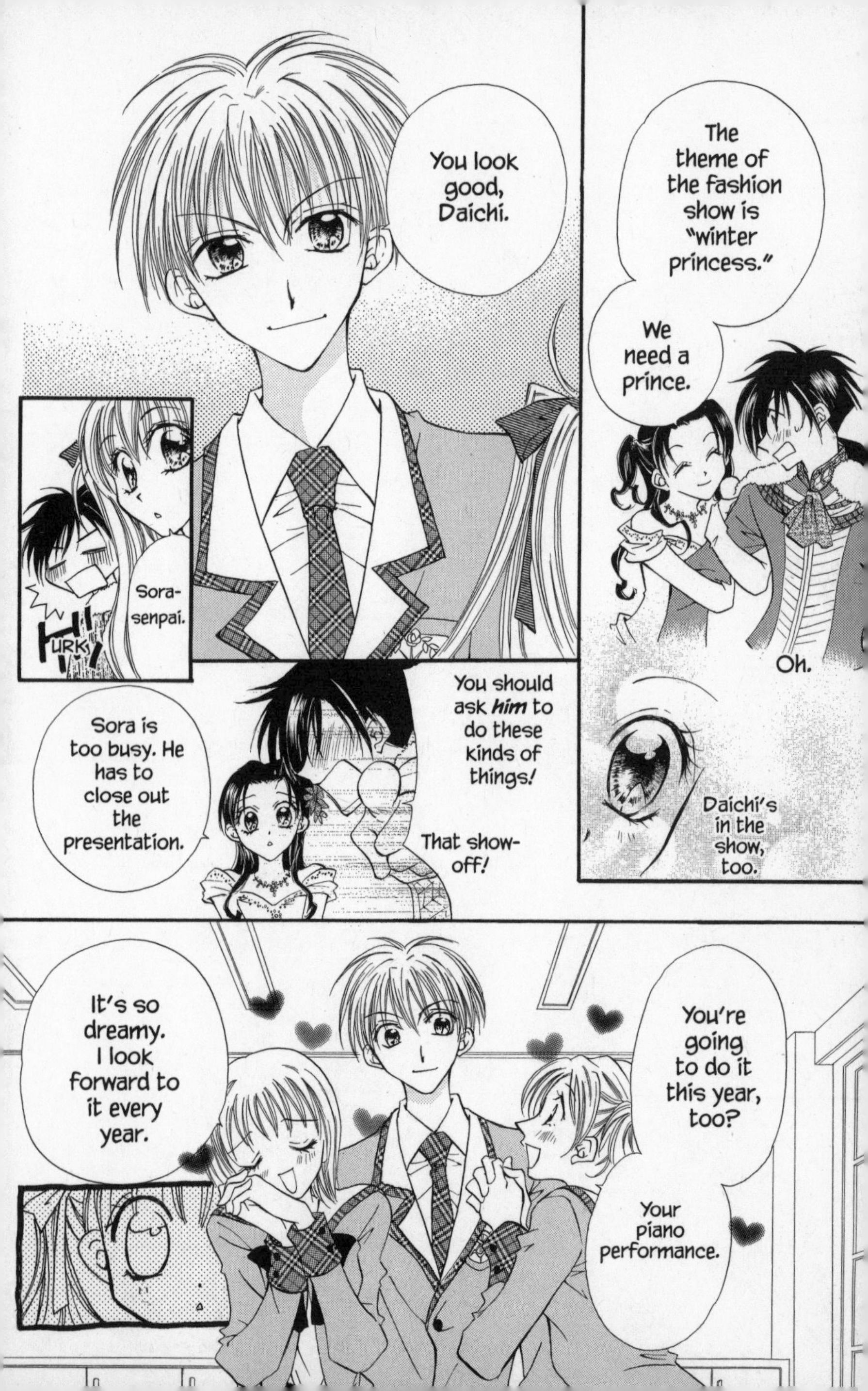

The theme of the fashion show is "winter princess."
We need a prince.
Oh.
Daichi's in the show, too.
You look good, Daichi.
Sora-senpai.
HURK
You should ask *him* to do these kinds of things!
That show-off!
Sora is too busy. He has to close out the presentation.
You're going to do it this year, too?
Your piano performance.
It's so dreamy. I look forward to it every year.

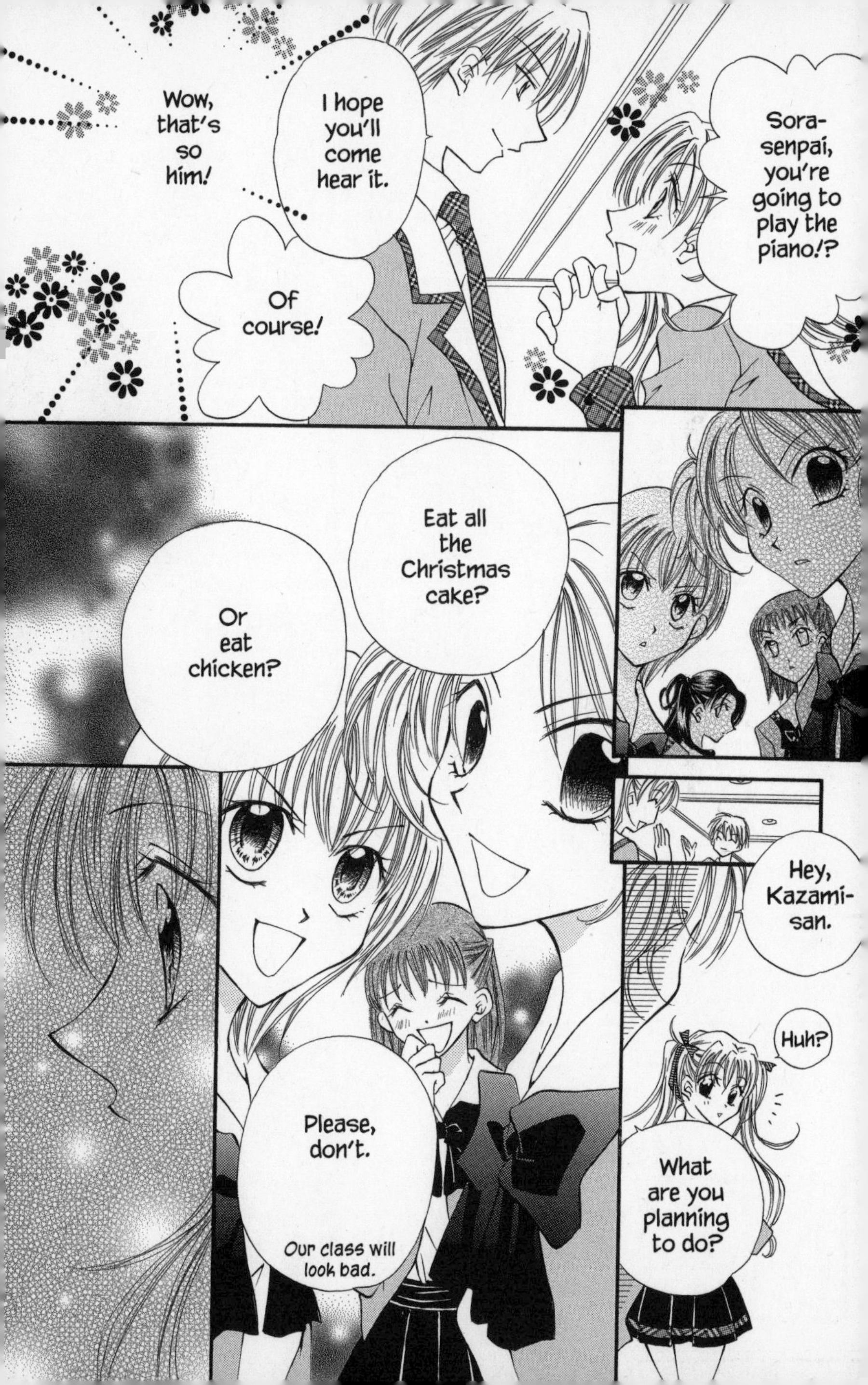
Sora-senpai, you're going to play the piano!?
I hope you'll come hear it.
Of course!
Wow, that's so him!
Hey, Kazami-san.
Huh?
What are you planning to do?
Eat all the Christmas cake?
Or eat chicken?
Please, don't.
Our class will look bad.

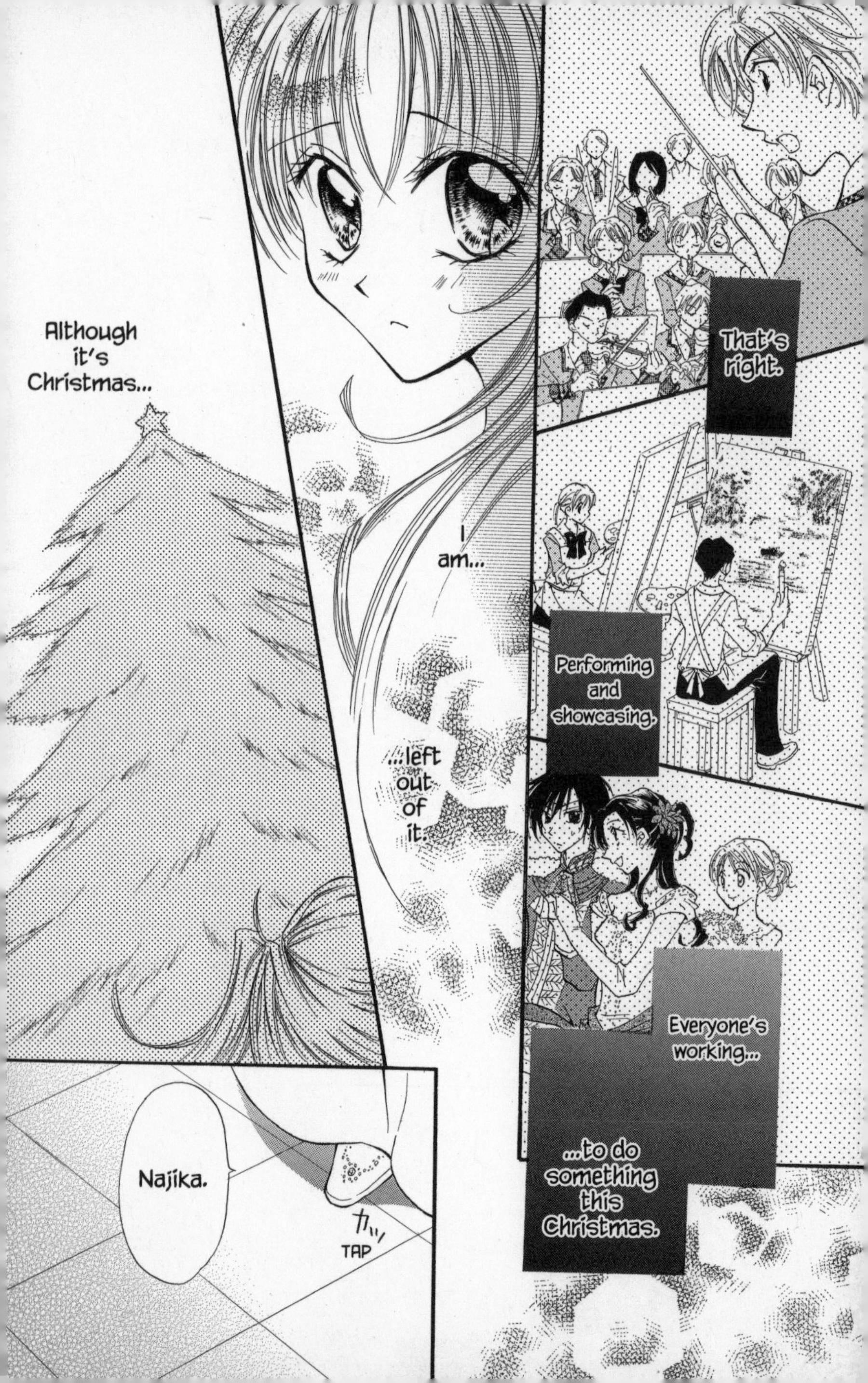
That's right.
Performing and showcasing.
Everyone's working...
...to do something this Christmas.
I am...
...left out of it.
Although it's Christmas...
Najika.
カッ
TAP

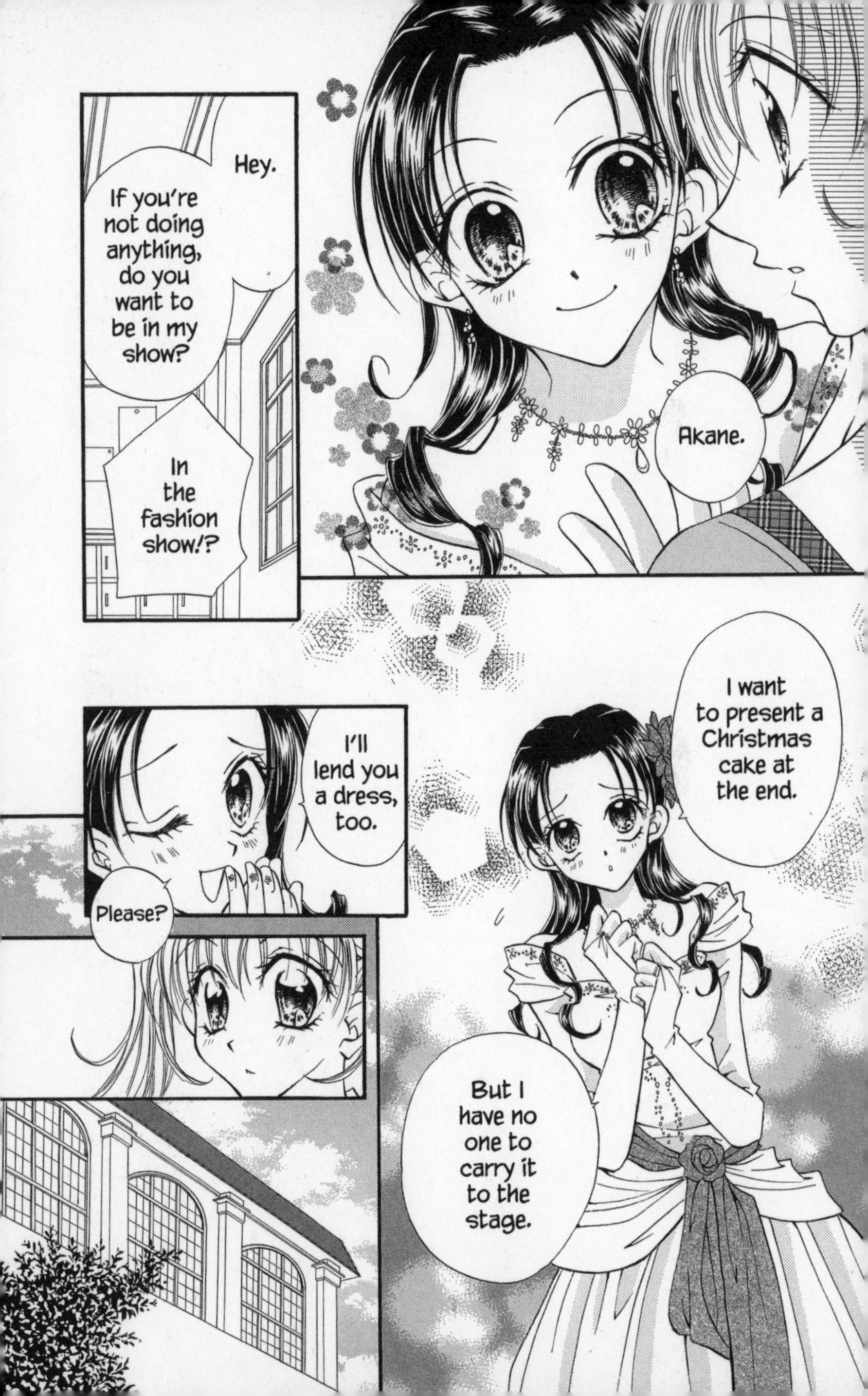
Akane.
Hey.
If you're not doing anything, do you want to be in my show?
In the fashion show!?
I want to present a Christmas cake at the end.
But I have no one to carry it to the stage.
I'll lend you a dress, too.
Please?

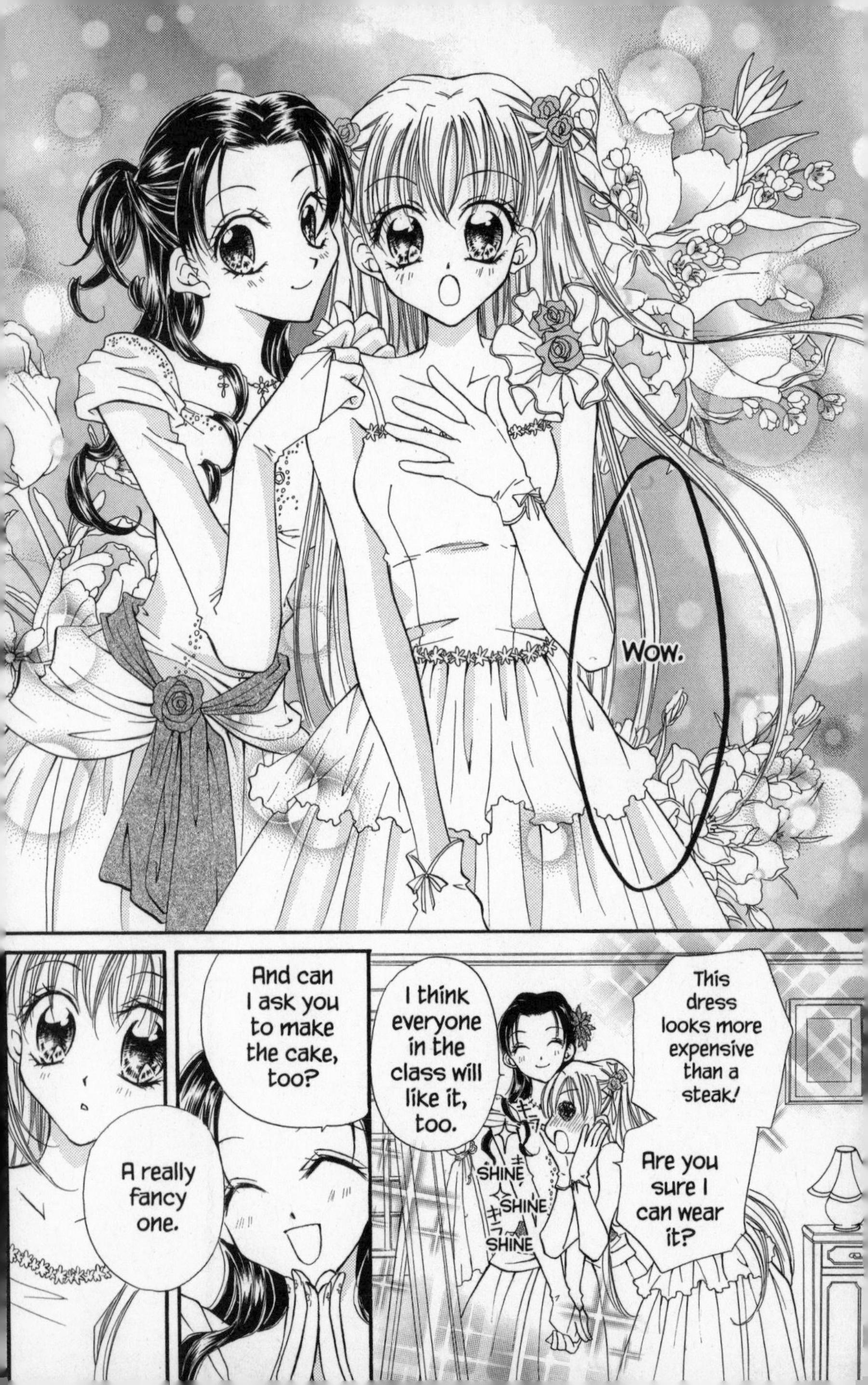
Wow.
This dress looks more expensive than a steak!
Are you sure I can wear it?
SHINE
SHINE
SHINE
I think everyone in the class will like it, too.
And can I ask you to make the cake, too?
A really fancy one.

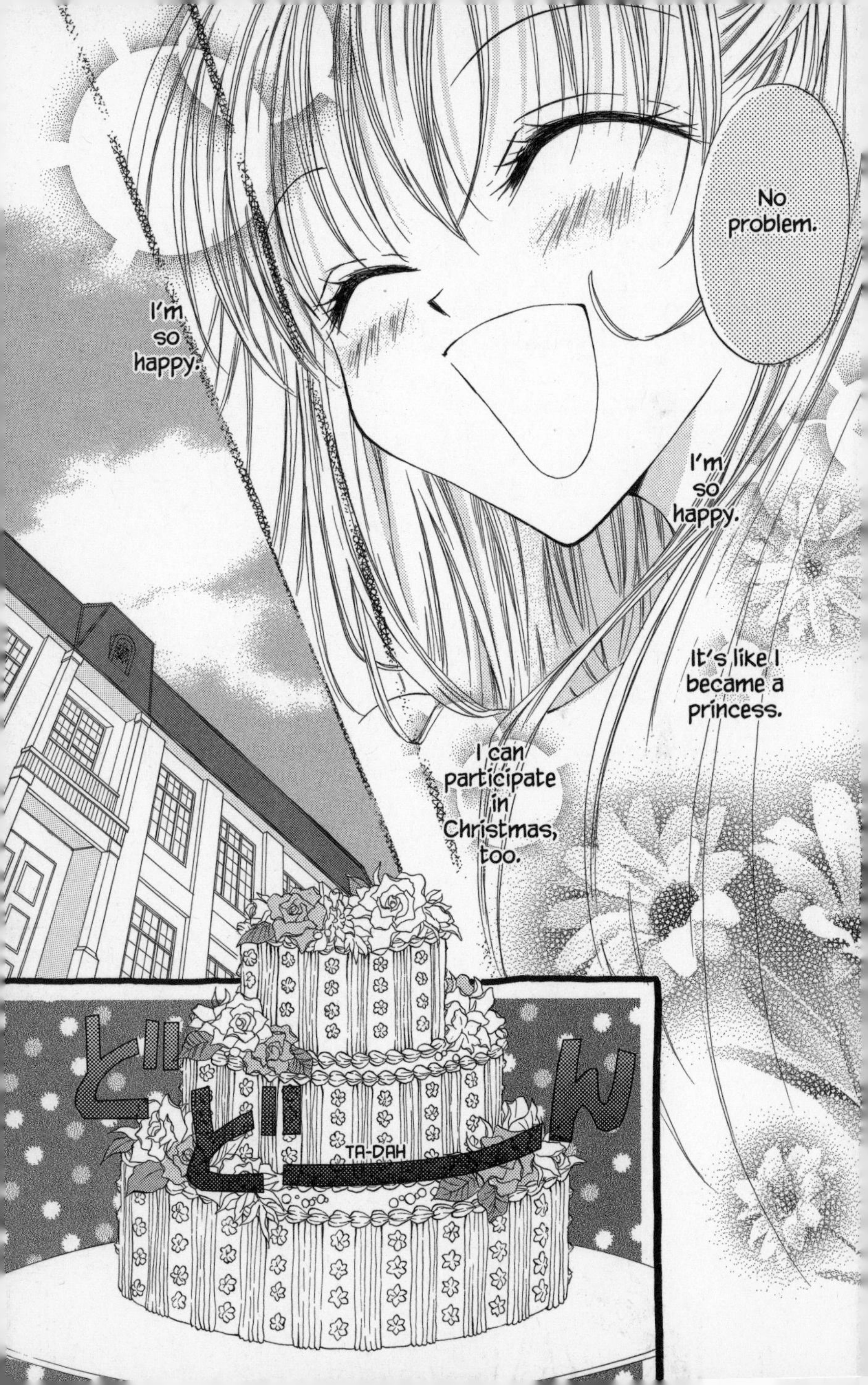
No problem.
I'm so happy.
I'm so happy.
It's like I became a princess.
I can participate in Christmas, too.
TA-DAH

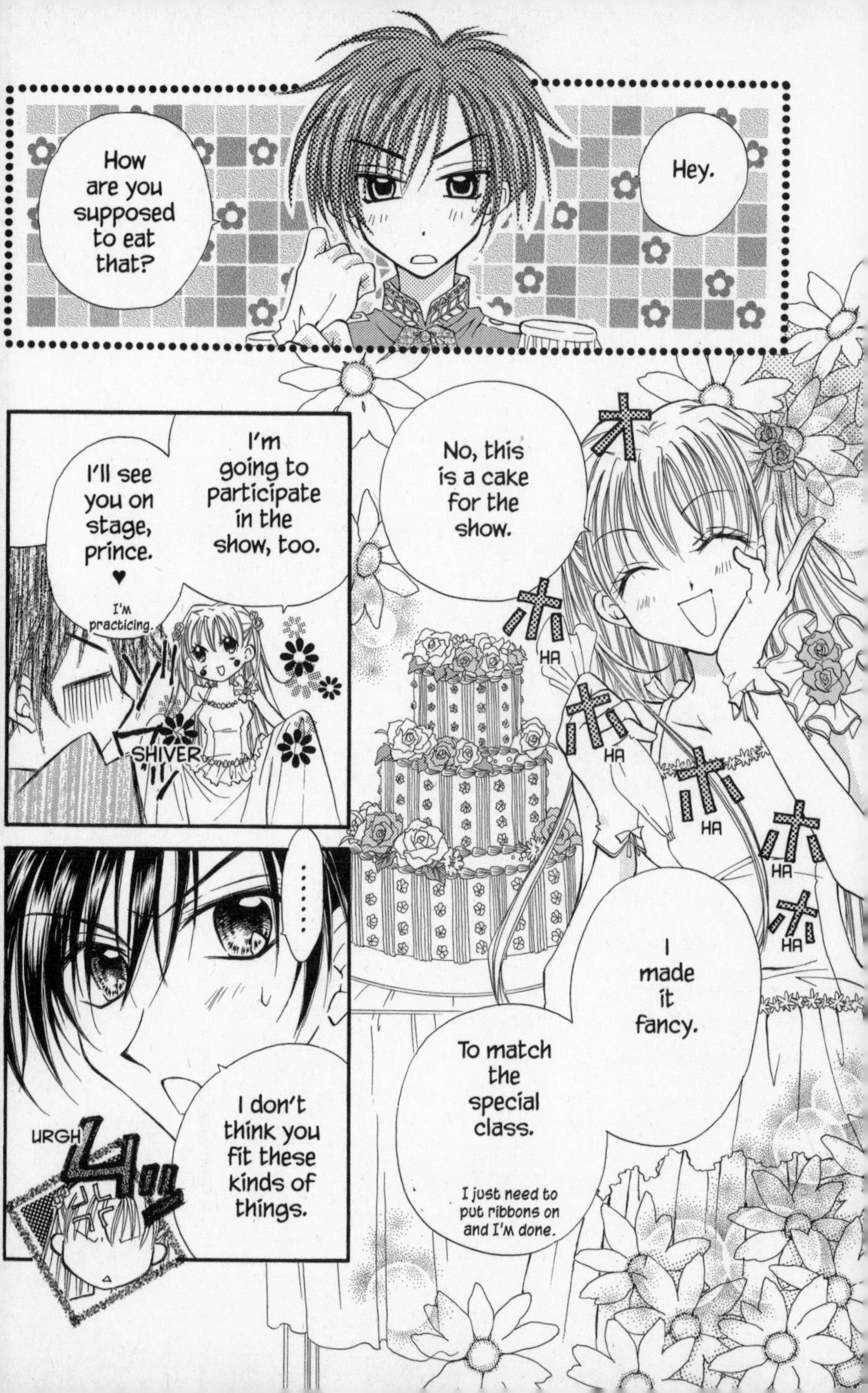

Hey.
How are you supposed to eat that?
No, this is a cake for the show.
HA HA HA HA HA
I made it fancy.
To match the special class.
I just need to put ribbons on and I'm done.
I'm going to participate in the show, too.
I'll see you on stage, prince. ♥
I'm practicing.
SHIVER
......
I don't think you fit these kinds of things.
URGH

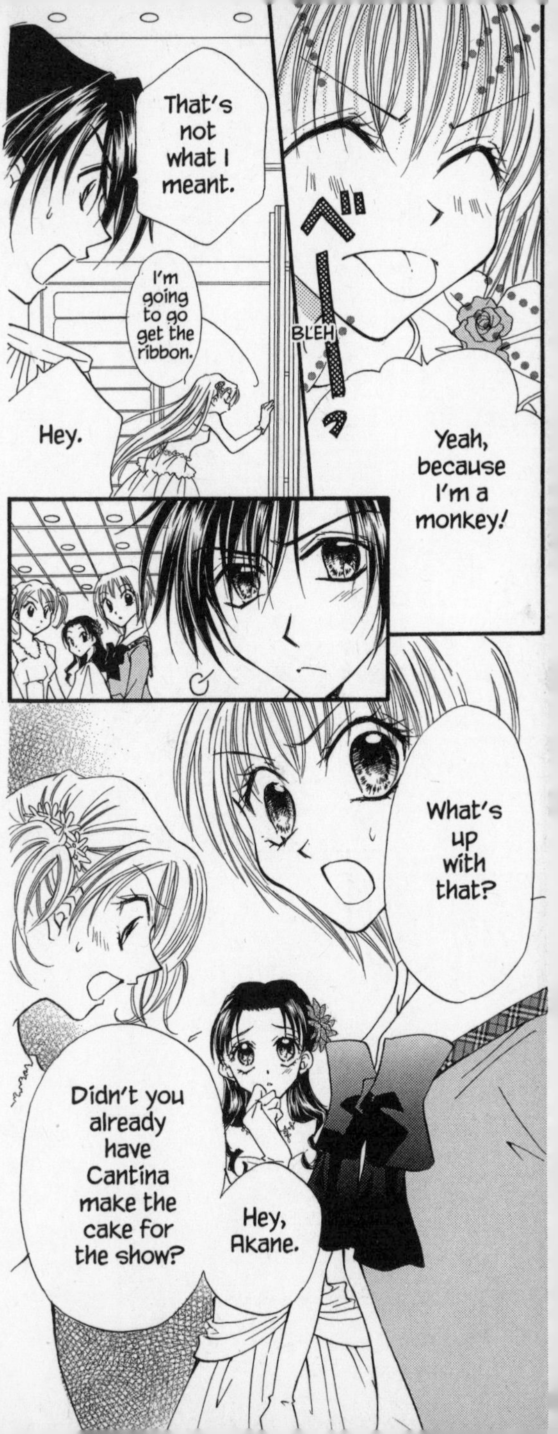
BLEH
Yeah, because I'm a monkey!
That's not what I meant.
I'm going to go get the ribbon.
Hey.
What's up with that?
Hey, Akane.
Didn't you already have Cantina make the cake for the show?

● All You Can Eat Buffet

I'm actually not good with this. I'm lazy, so I don't like to get up and go get the food. So what ends up happening is that I just sit around... I guess I'm a good customer for the restaurant!?

● A Popular Store with a Line Outside

The longest I waited to eat something was two and a half hours... It was at DisneySea, the curry buffet. When you get closer to the entrance, you can smell the curry and thirty minutes feels like an hour, and your empty stomach makes you only think of curry. It was torture. I was supposed to receive a pin, but by the time I got to my seat, I was so involved in eating that I lost the voucher...

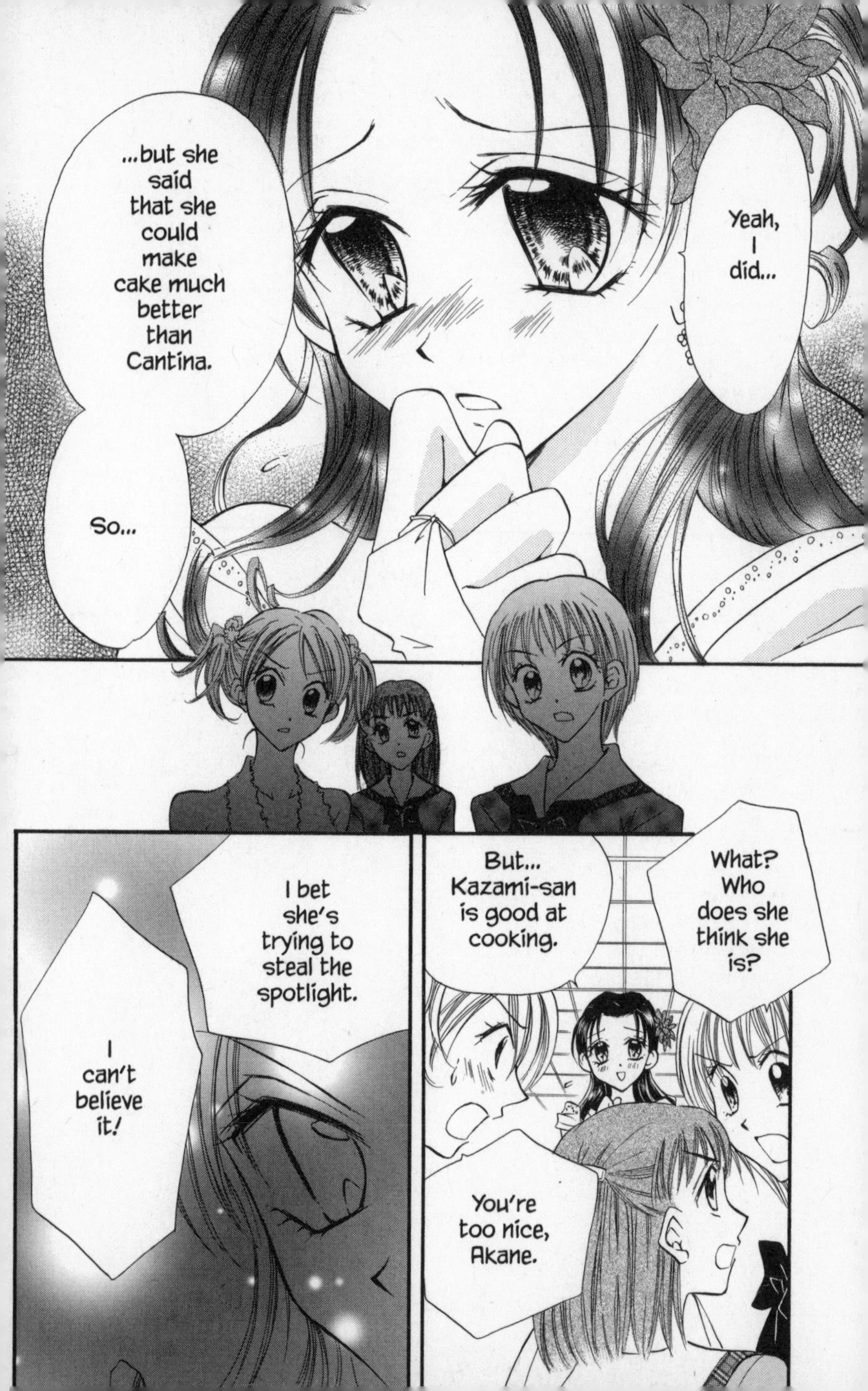
Yeah, I did...
...but she said that she could make cake much better than Cantina.
So...
What? Who does she think she is?
But... Kazami-san is good at cooking.
You're too nice, Akane.
I bet she's trying to steal the spotlight.
I can't believe it!

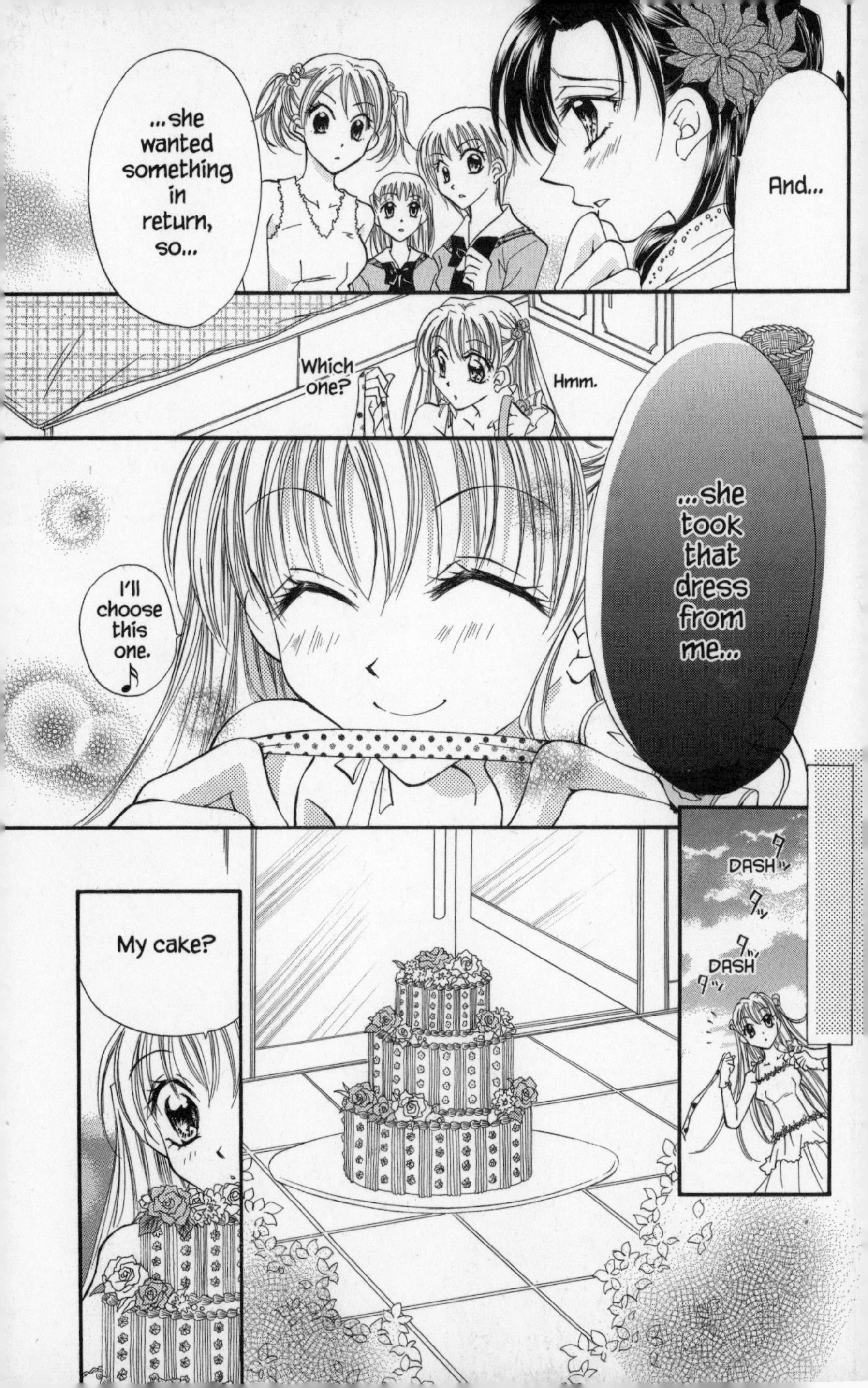
And...
...she wanted something in return, so...
Hmm.
Which one?
...she took that dress from me...
I'll choose this one. ♪
DASH
DASH
My cake?

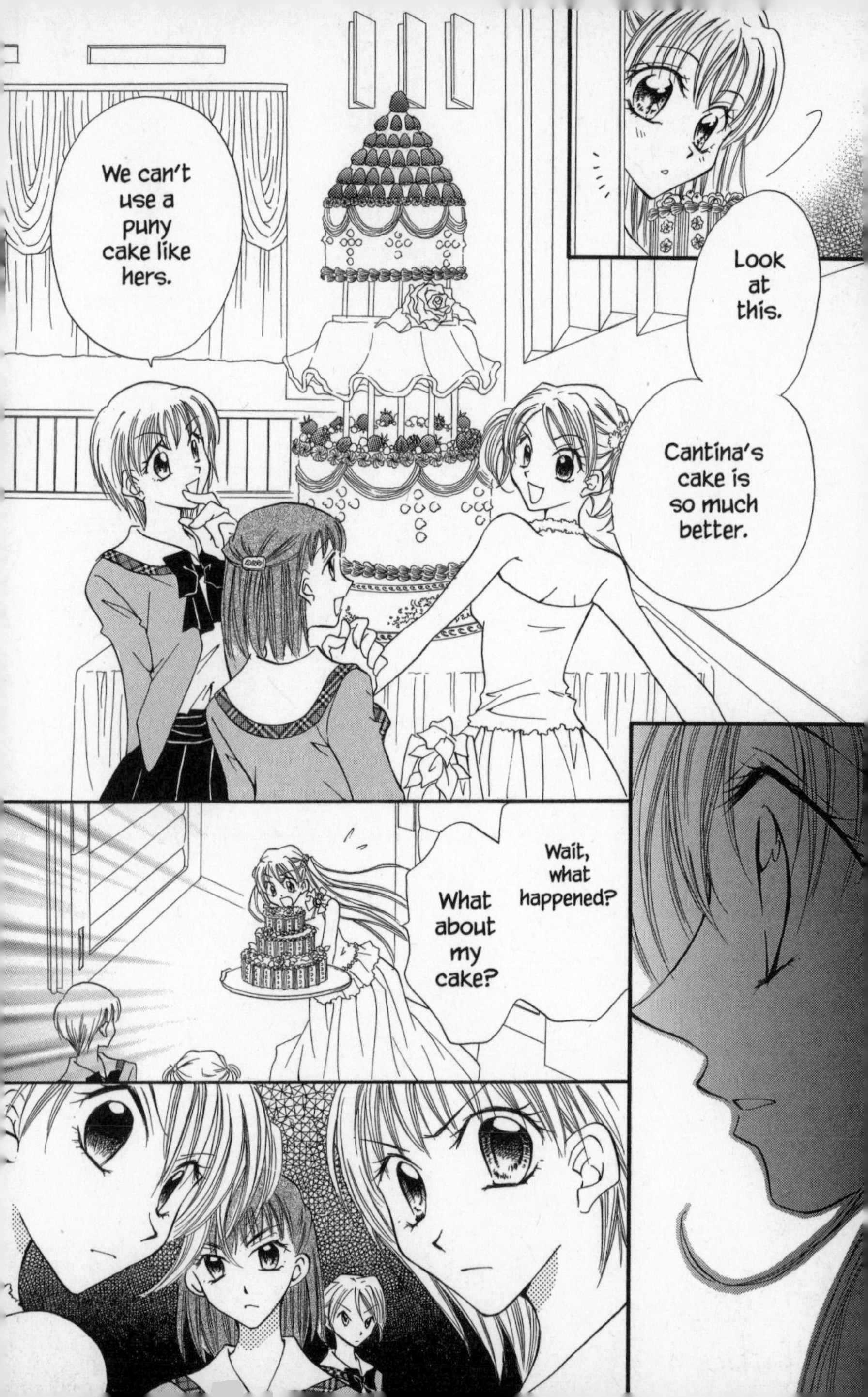
Look at this.
Cantina's cake is so much better.
We can't use a puny cake like hers.
Wait, what happened?
What about my cake?

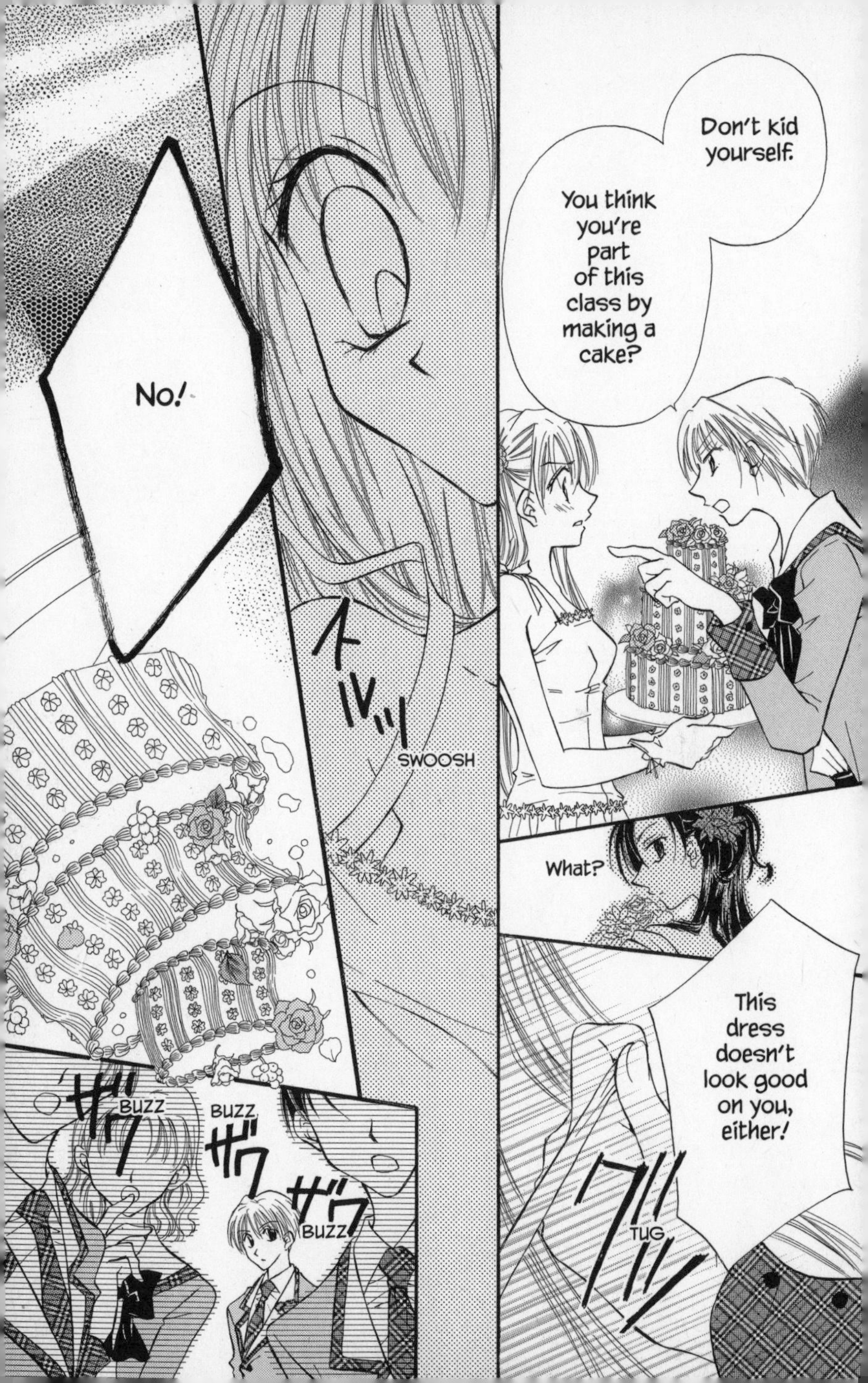
Don't kid yourself.
You think you're part of this class by making a cake?
What?
This dress doesn't look good on you, either!
TUG
SWOOSH
No!
BUZZ
BUZZ
BUZZ

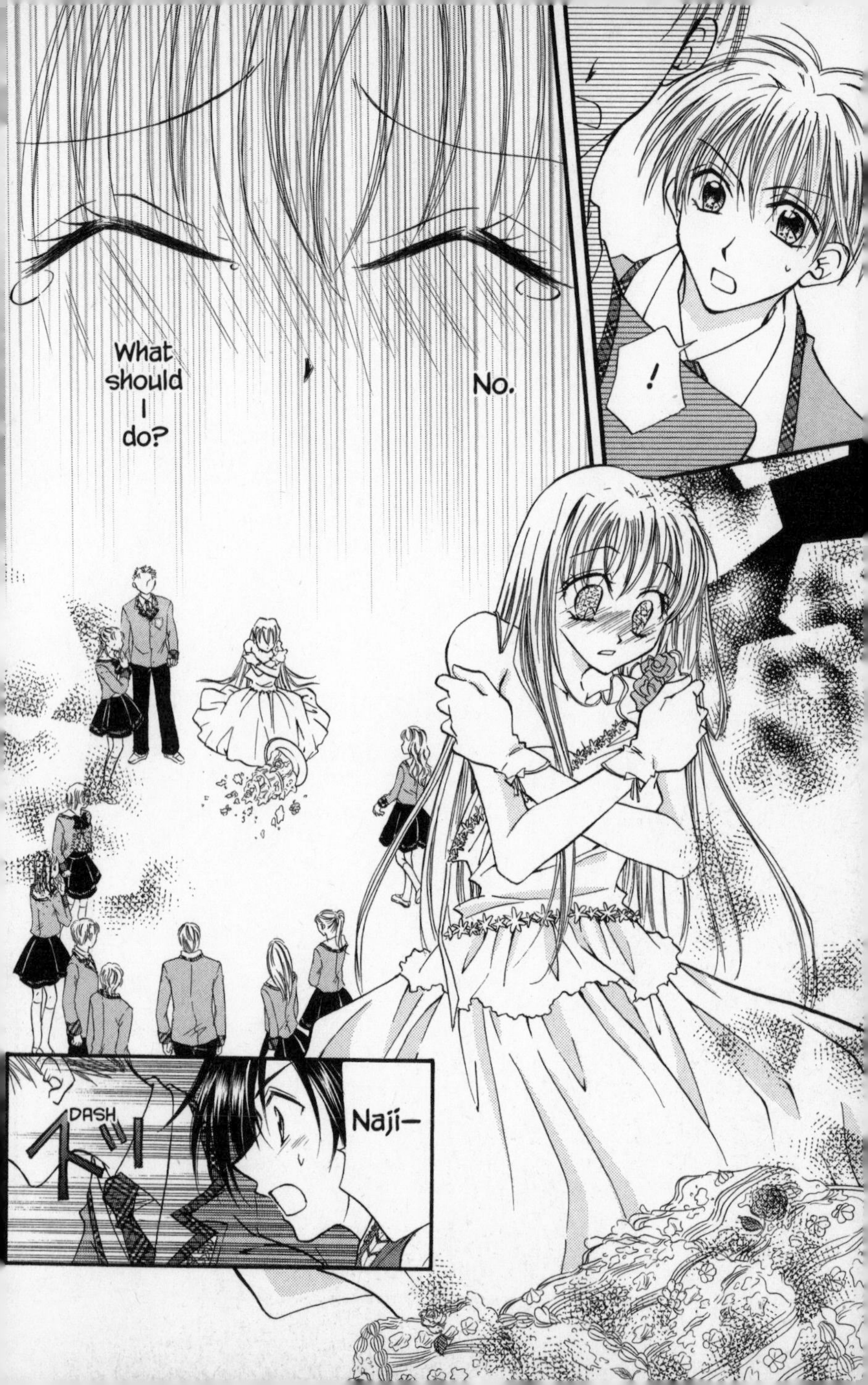
!
No.
What should I do?
DASH
Naji—

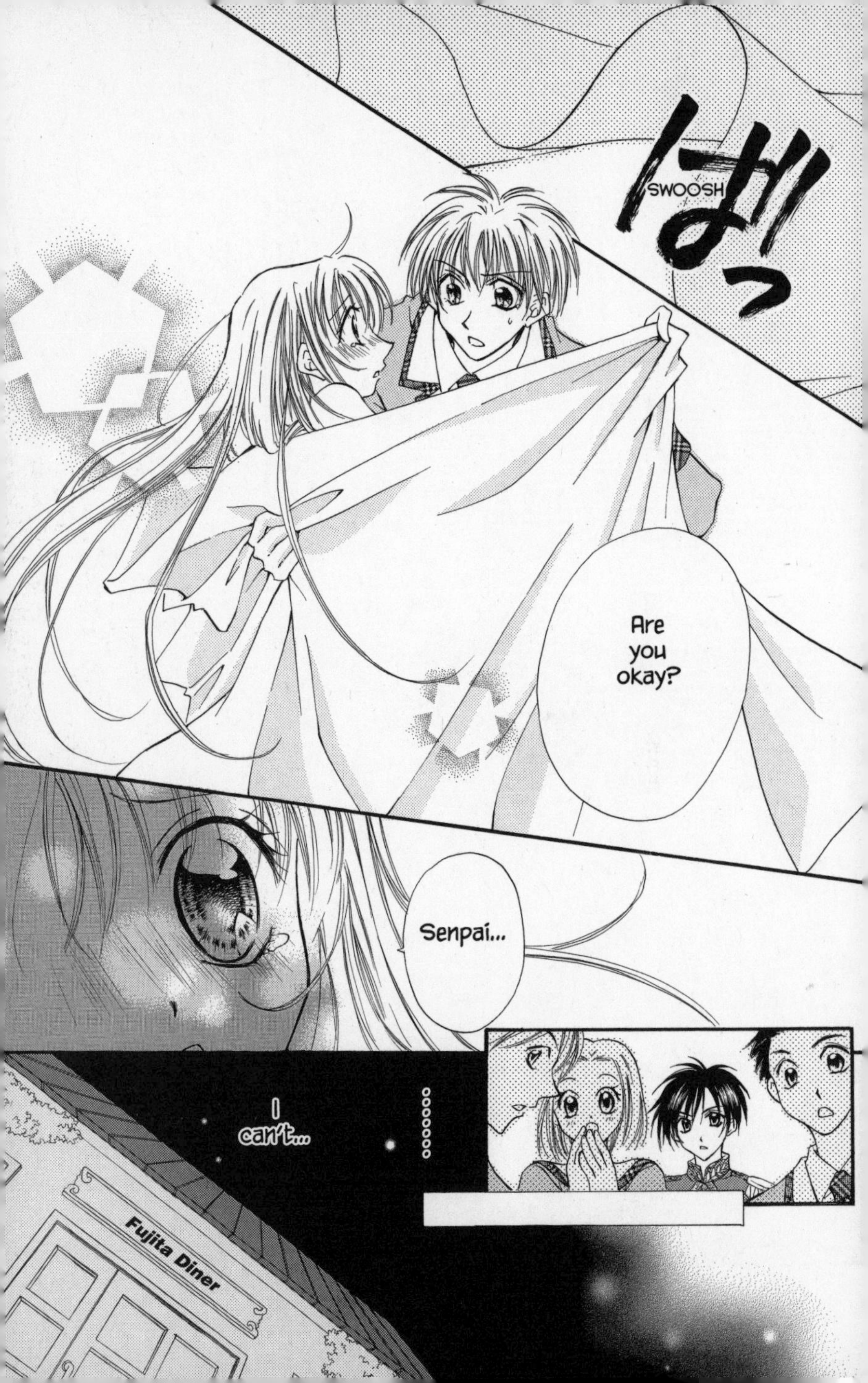
SWOOSH
Are you okay?
Senpai...
......
I can't...
Fujita Diner

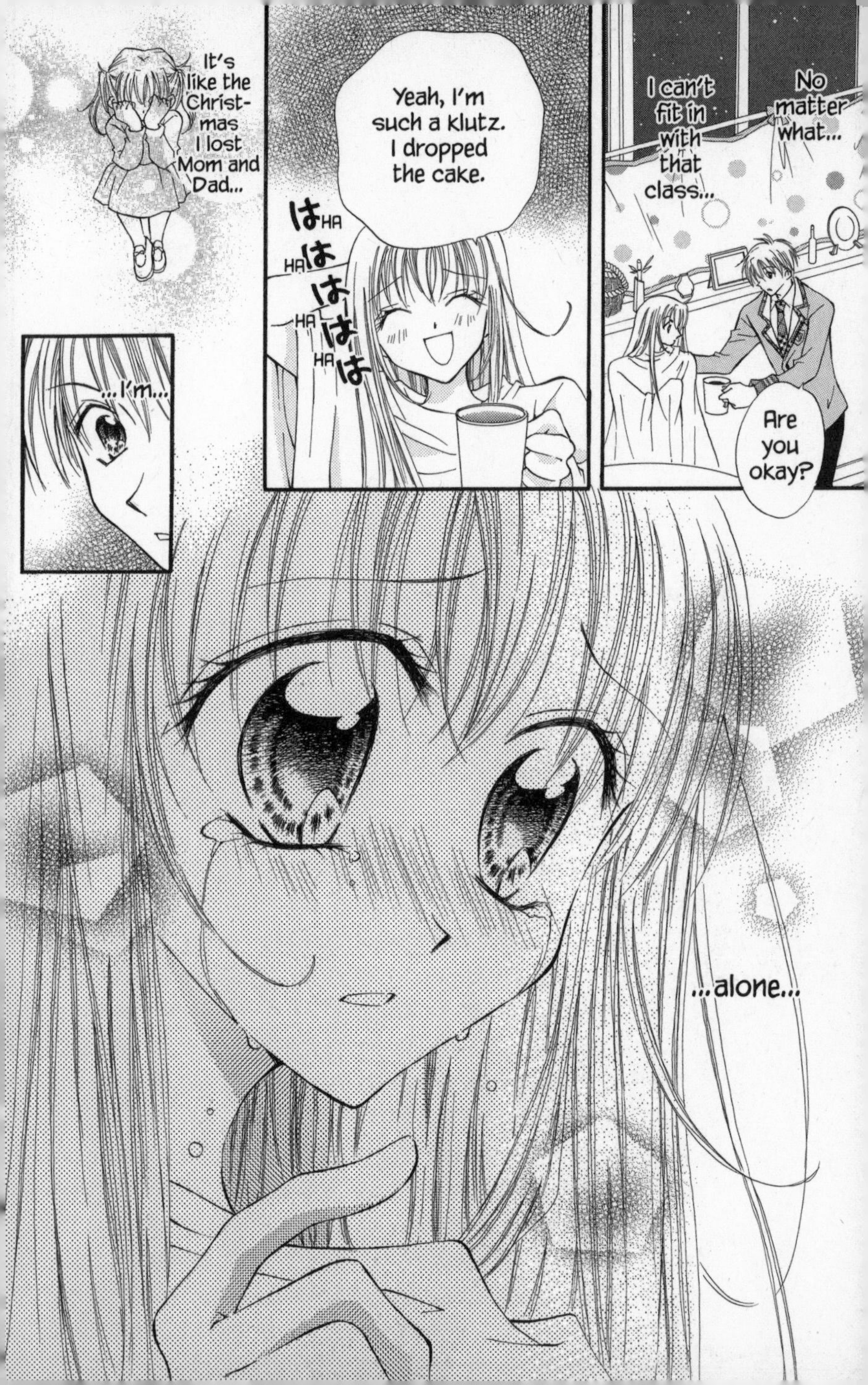

No matter what...
I can't fit in with that class...
Are you okay?
Yeah, I'm such a klutz. I dropped the cake.
はHA HAは は HAは HAは
It's like the Christmas I lost Mom and Dad...
...I'm...
...alone...

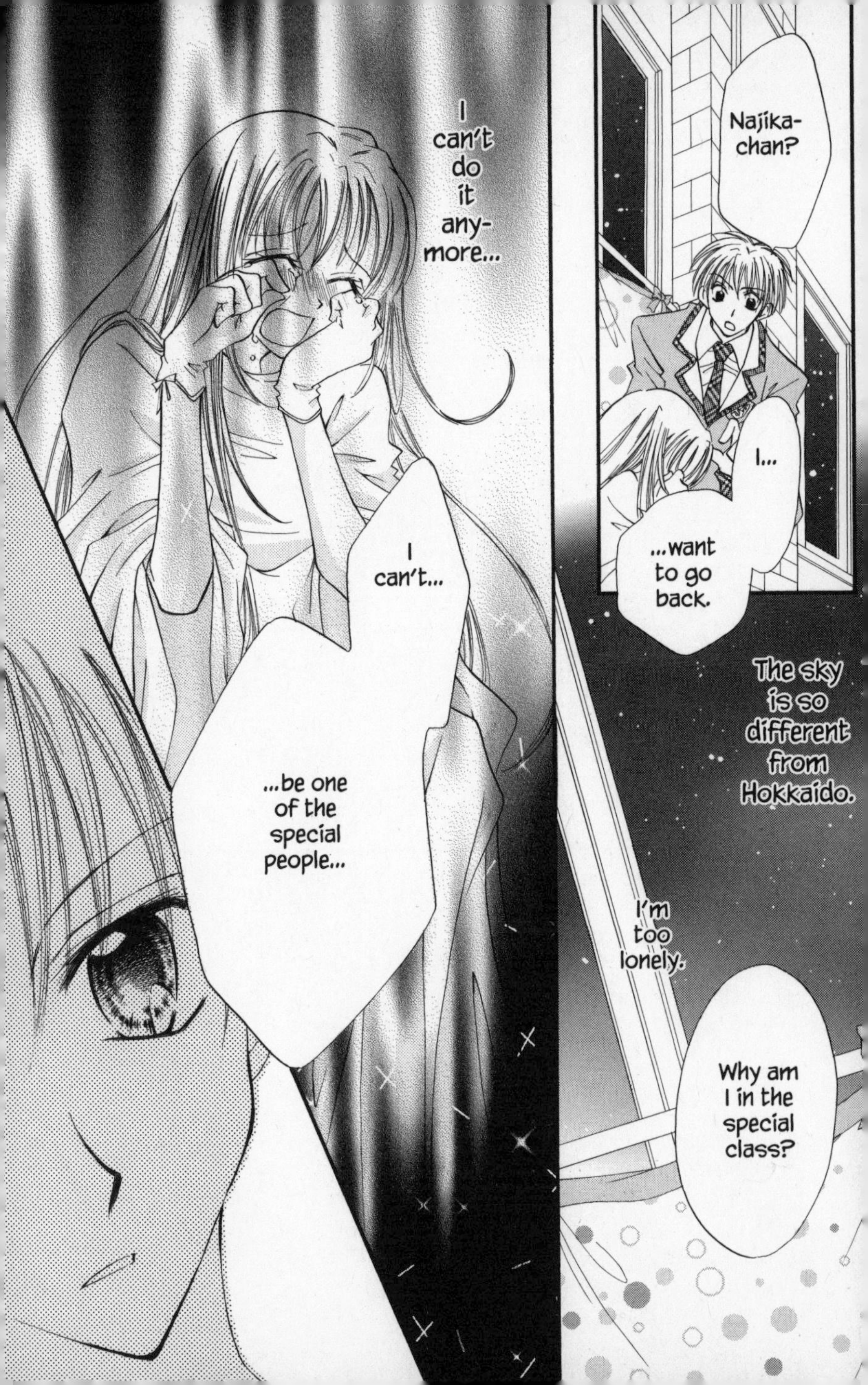
Najika-chan?
I...
...want to go back.
The sky is so different from Hokkaido.
I'm too lonely.
Why am I in the special class?
I can't do it anymore...
I can't...
...be one of the special people...

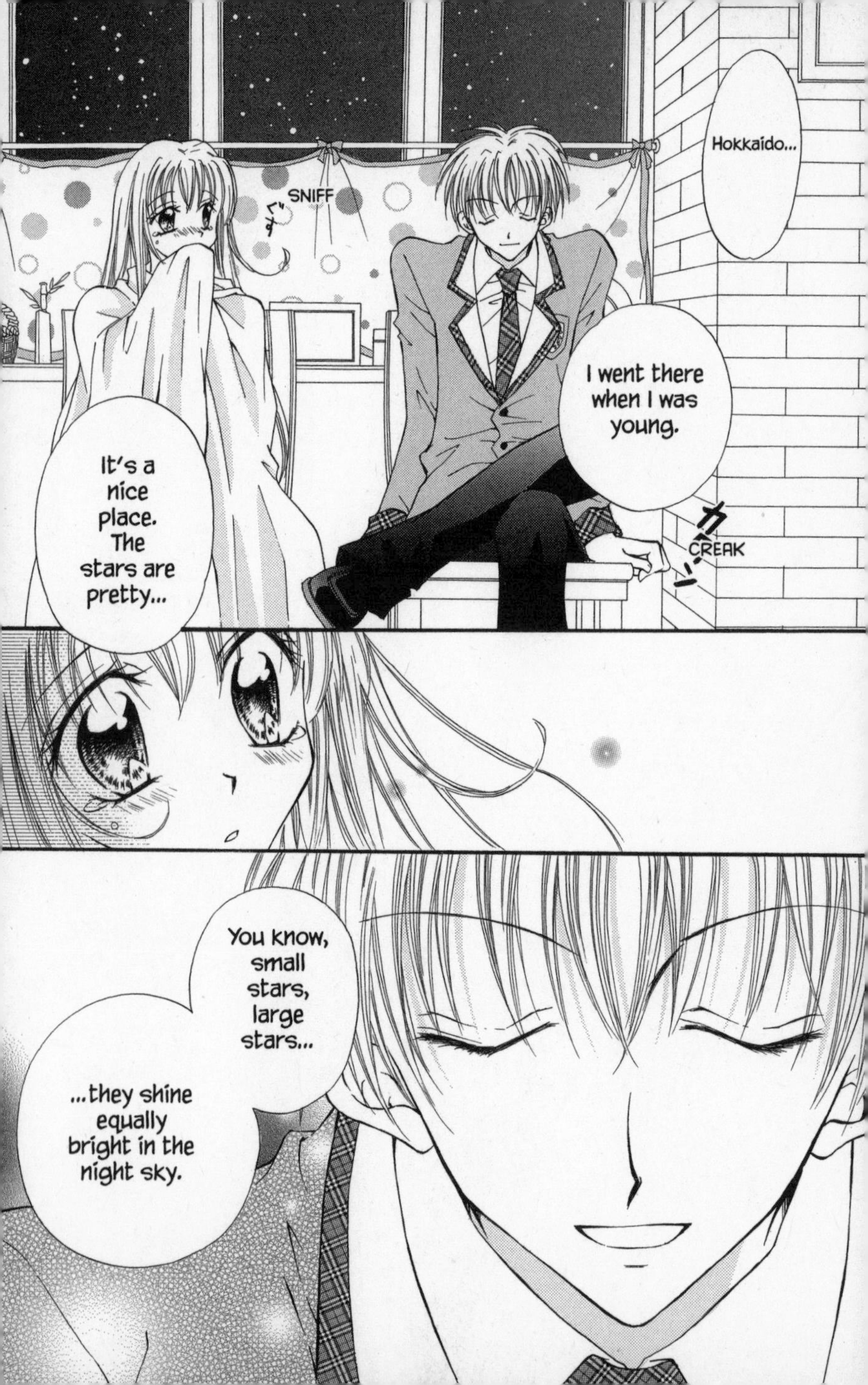
Hokkaido...
SNIFF
I went there when I was young.
CREAK
It's a nice place. The stars are pretty...
You know, small stars, large stars...
...they shine equally bright in the night sky.

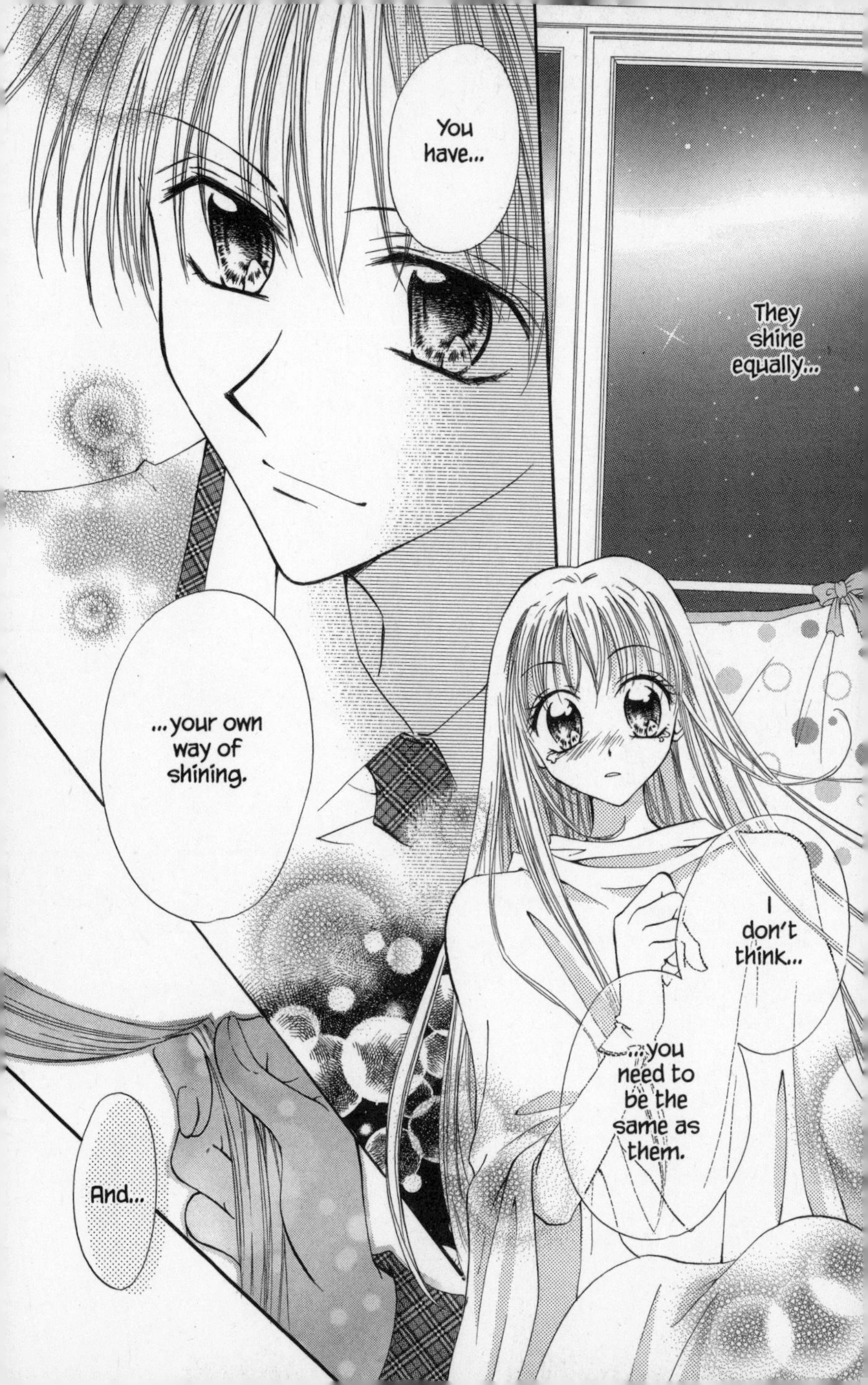
They shine equally...
I don't think...
...you need to be the same as them.
You have...
...your own way of shining.
And...

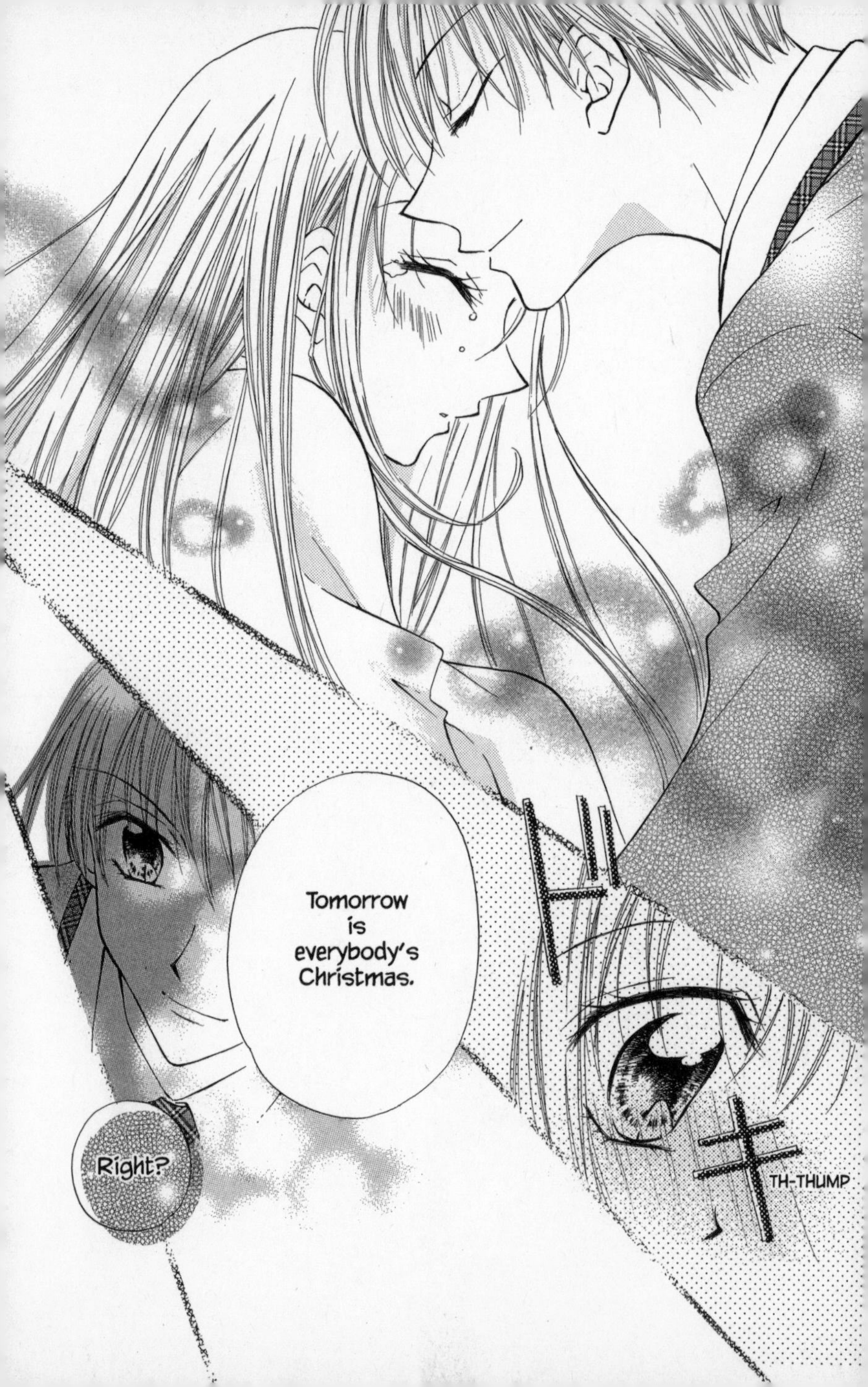
Tomorrow is everybody's Christmas.
Right?
TH-THUMP

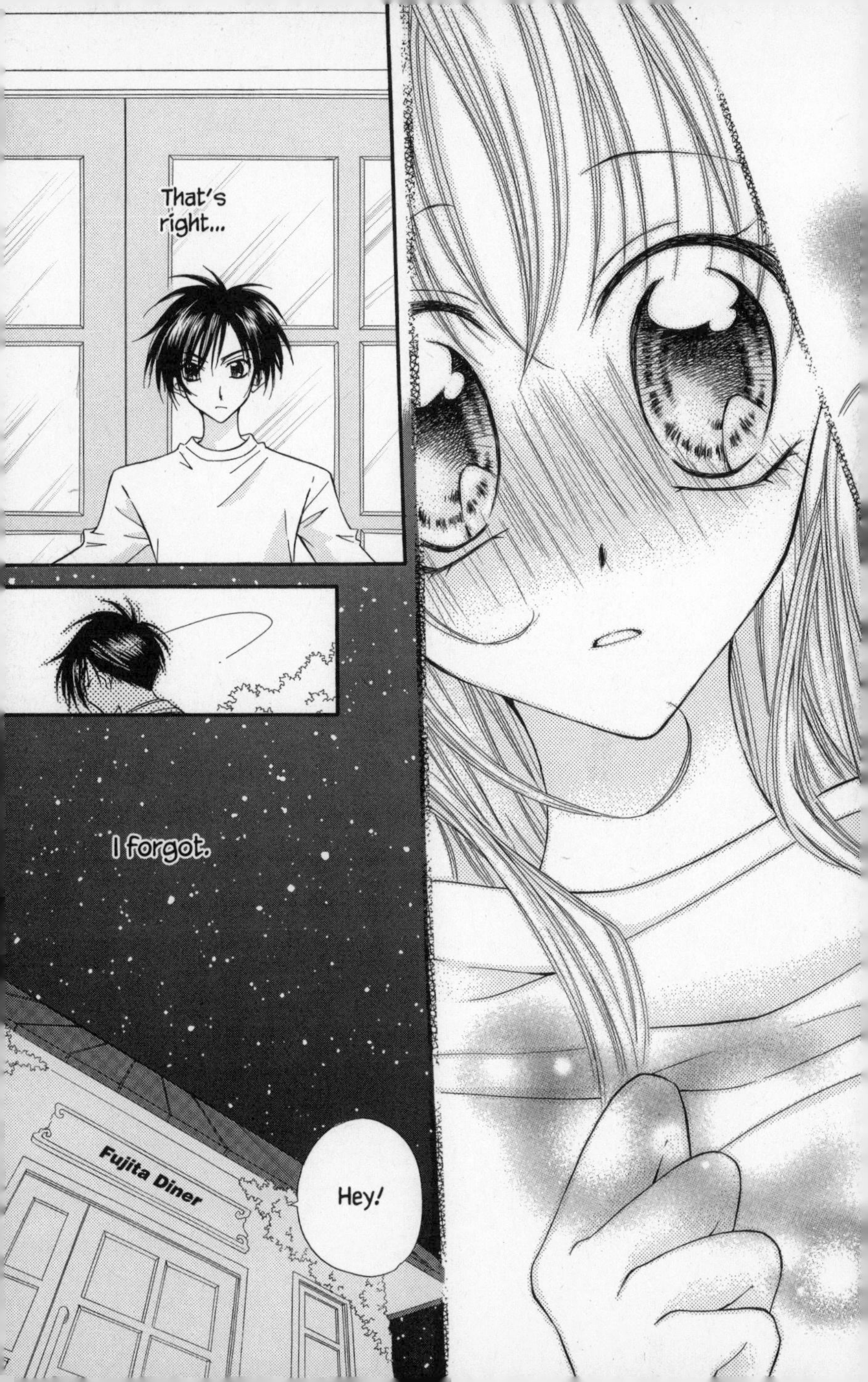
That's right...
I forgot.
Fujita Diner
Hey!

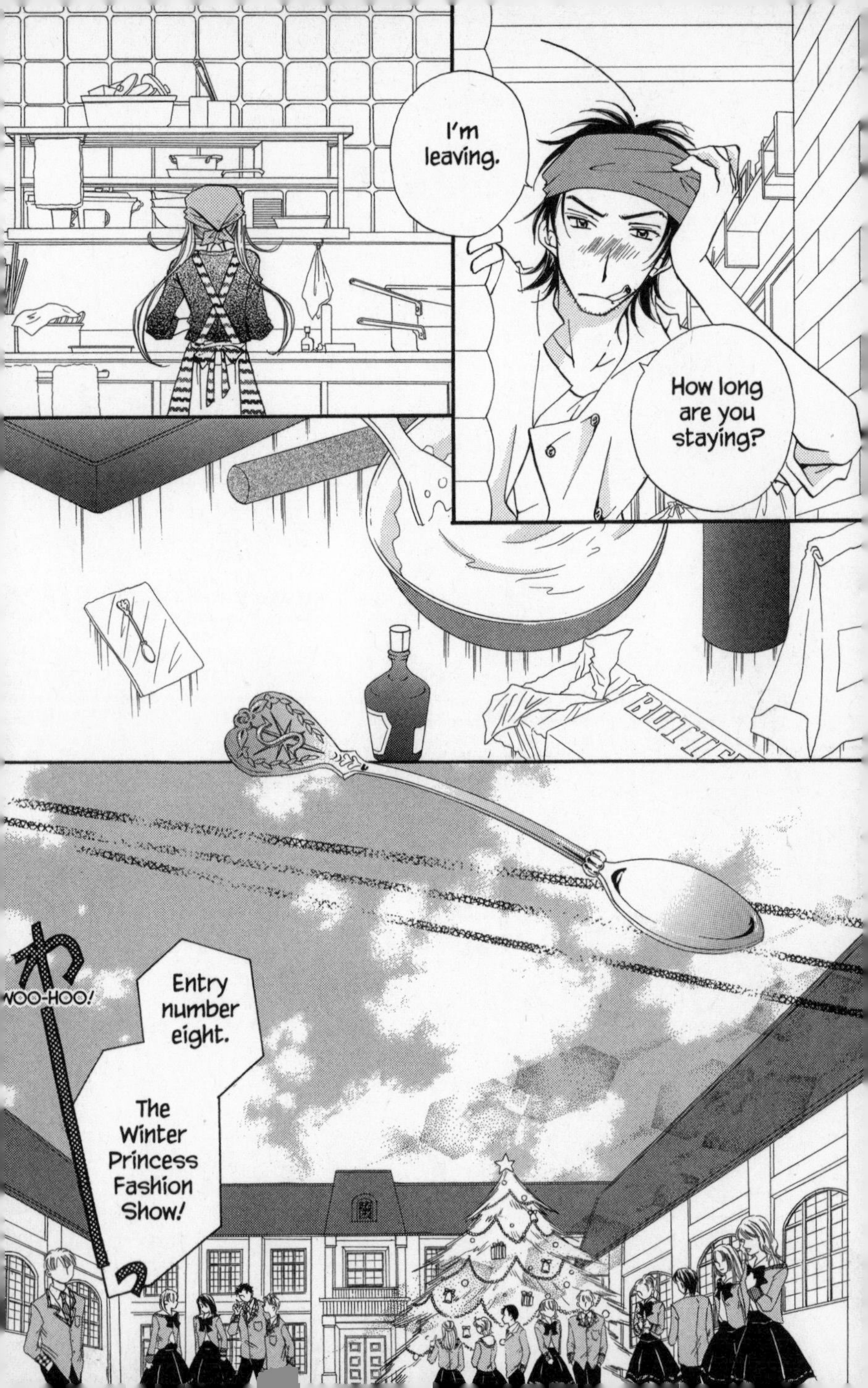
I'm leaving.
How long are you staying?
Entry number eight.
The Winter Princess Fashion Show!
WOO-HOO!

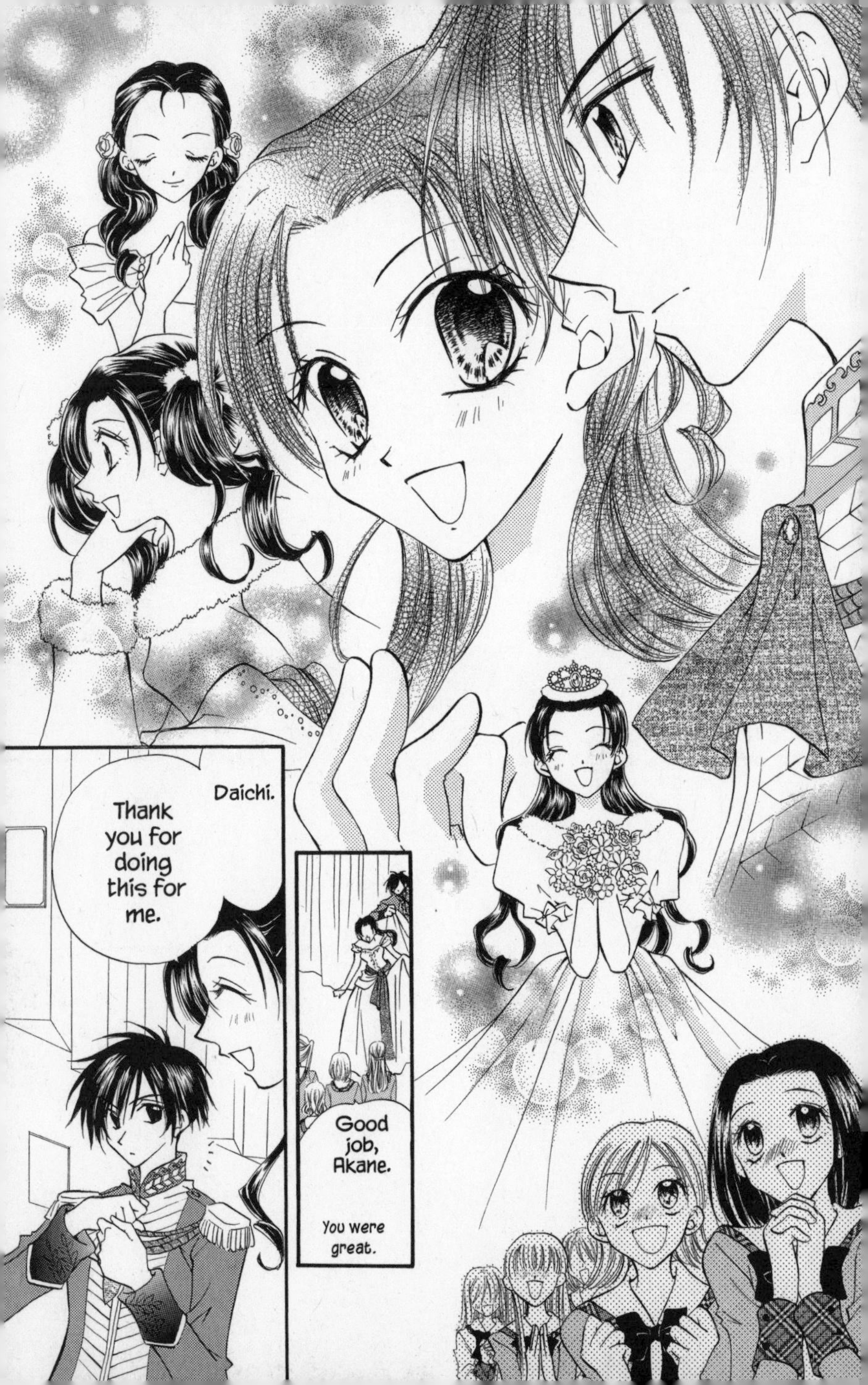
Good job, Akane.
You were great.
Daichi.
Thank you for doing this for me.

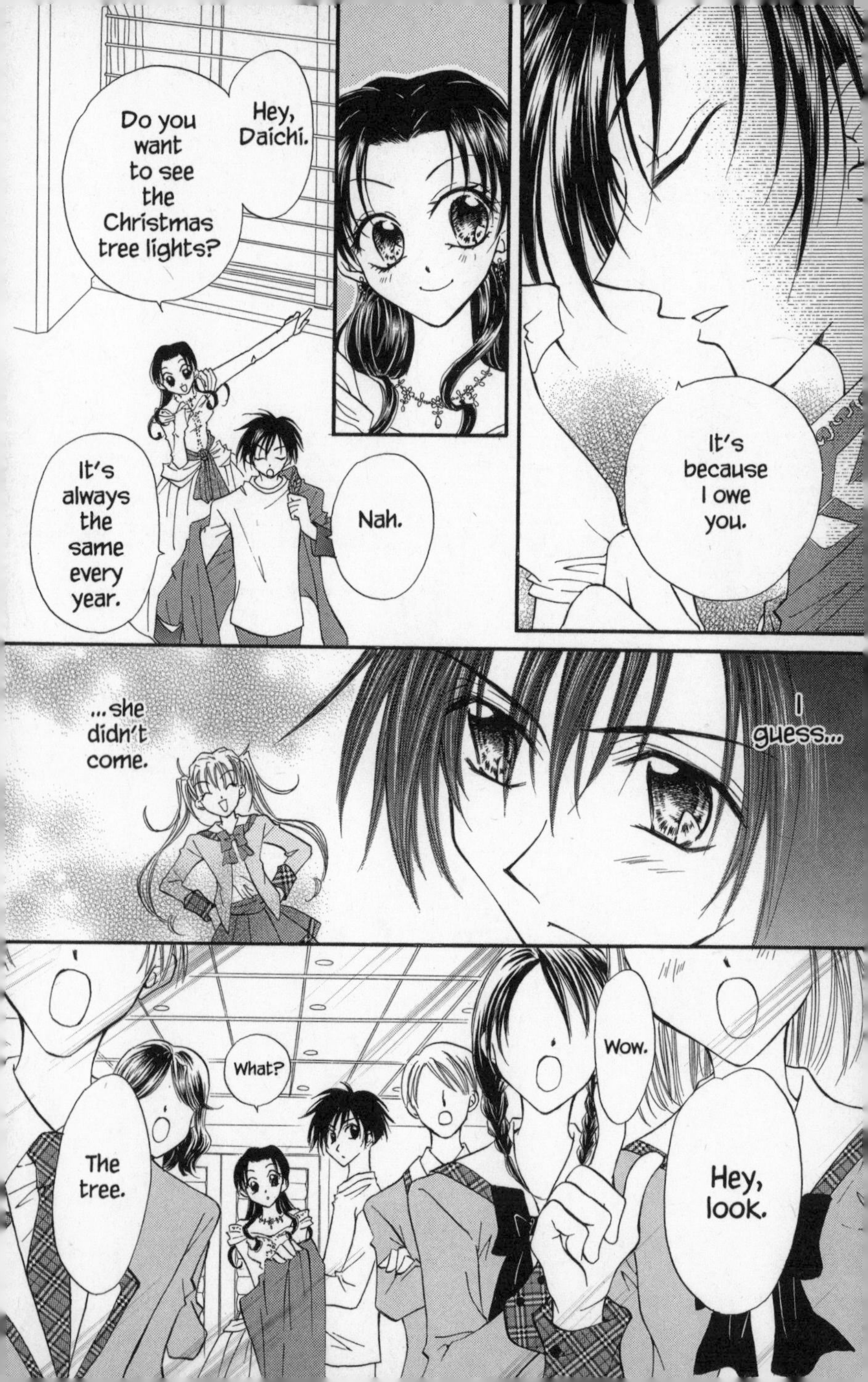
It's because I owe you.
Hey, Daichi.
Do you want to see the Christmas tree lights?
Nah.
It's always the same every year.
I guess...
...she didn't come.
Hey, look.
Wow.
What?
The tree.

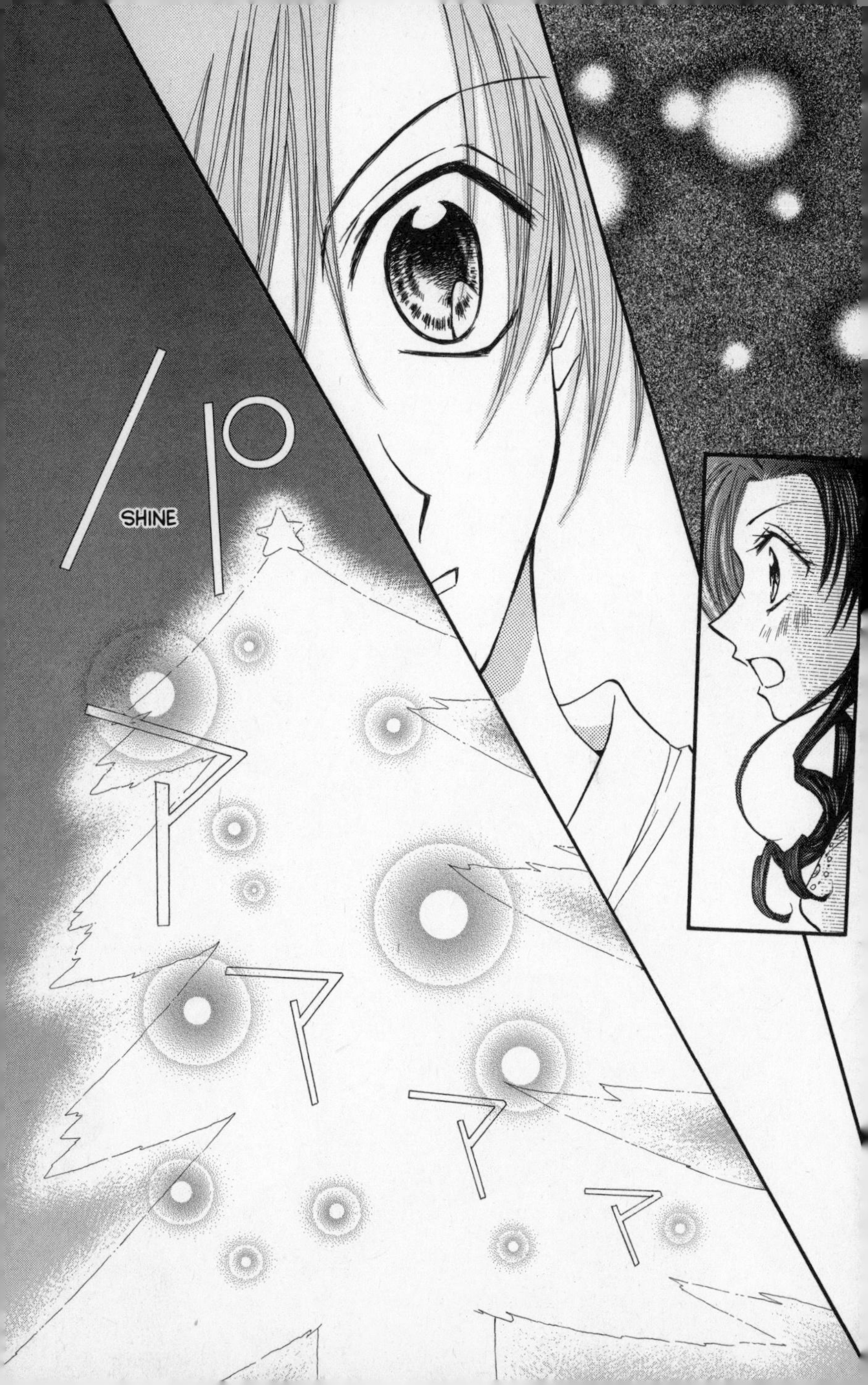
SHINE

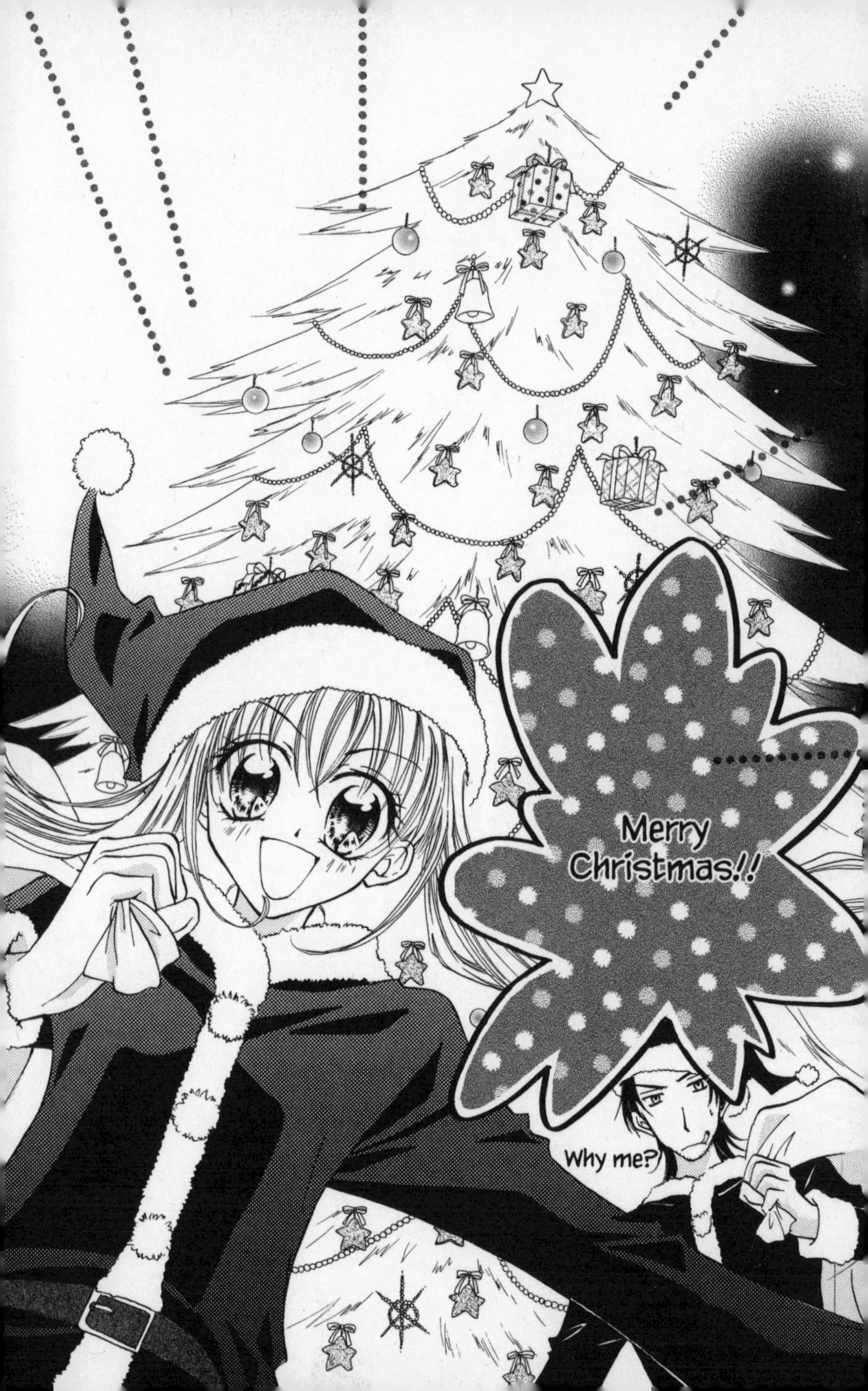
Merry Christmas!!
Why me?

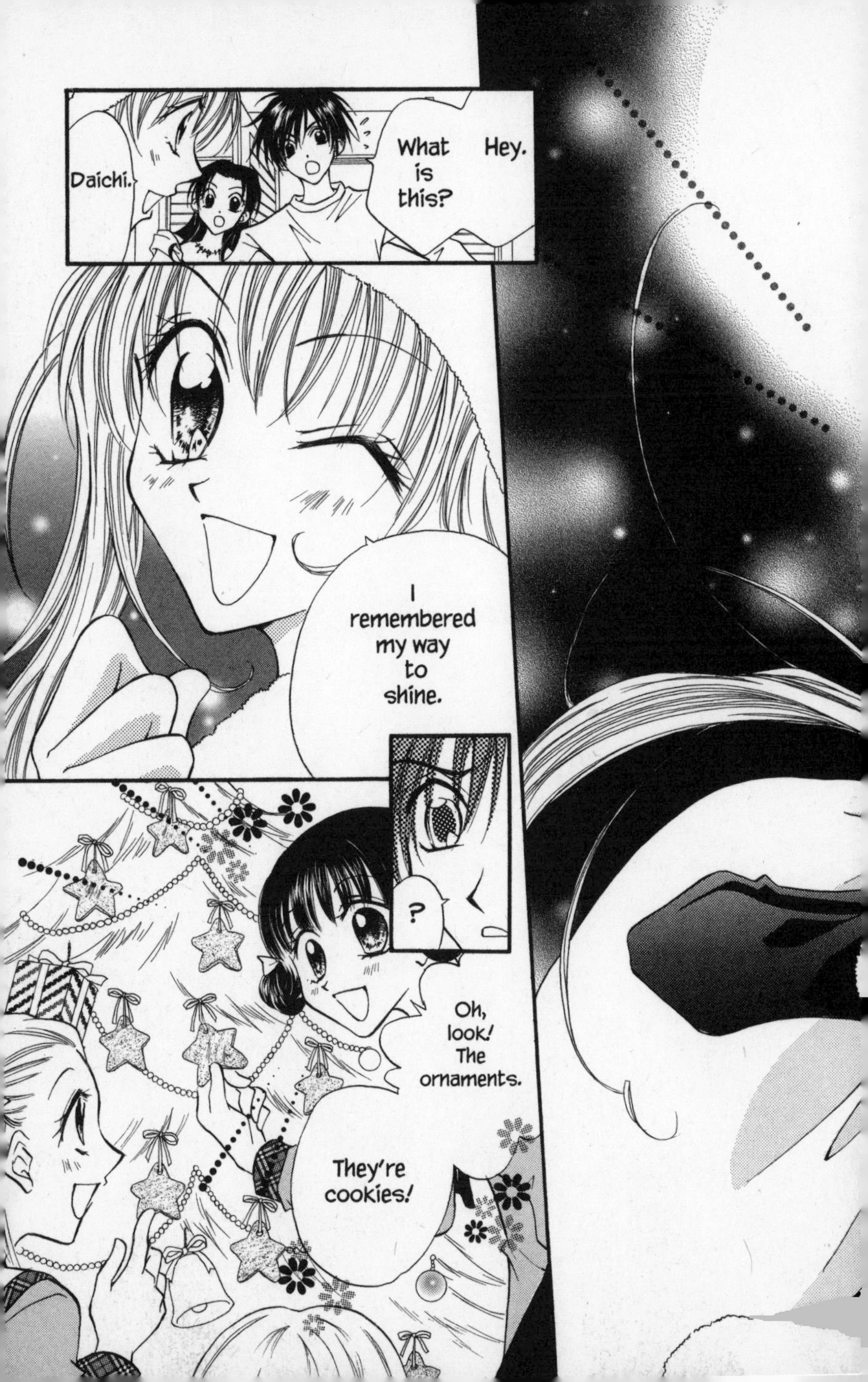
Hey.
What is this?
Daichi.
I remembered my way to shine.
?
Oh, look! The ornaments.
They're cookies!

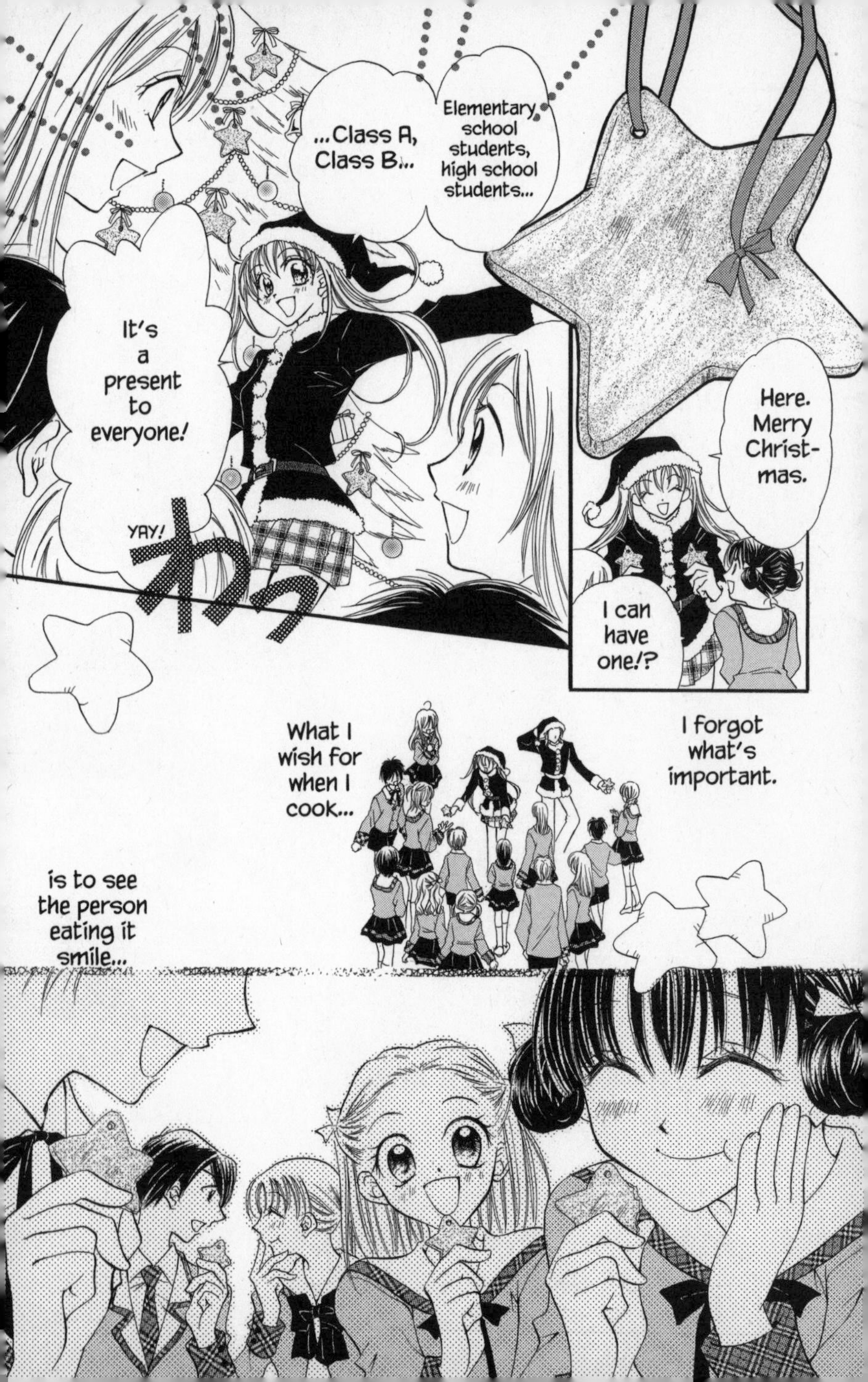
Elementary school students, high school students...
...Class A, Class B...
It's a present to everyone!
YAY!
Here. Merry Christmas.
I can have one!?
I forgot what's important.
What I wish for when I cook...
is to see the person eating it smile...

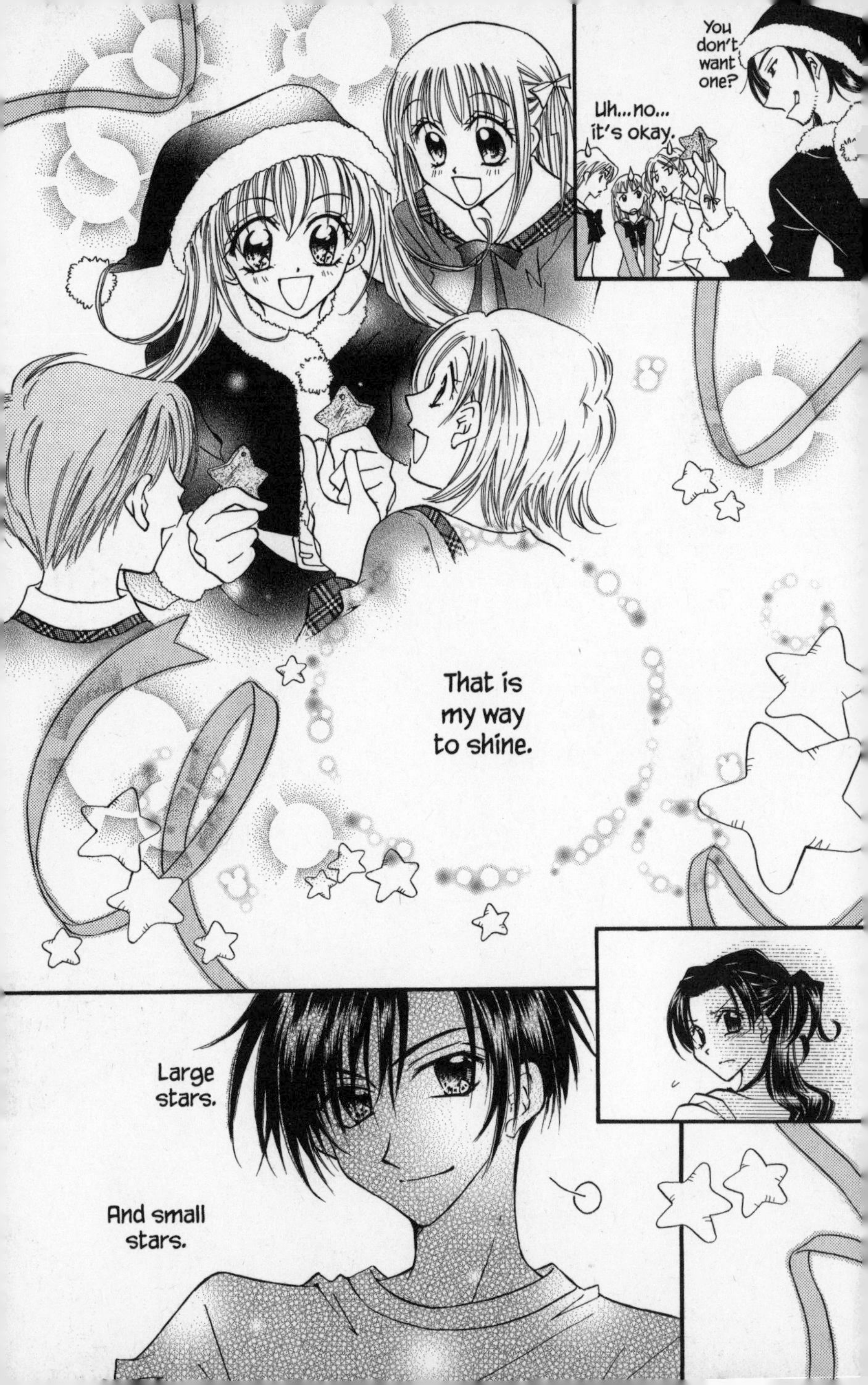
You don't want one?
Uh...no... it's okay.
That is my way to shine.
Large stars.
And small stars.

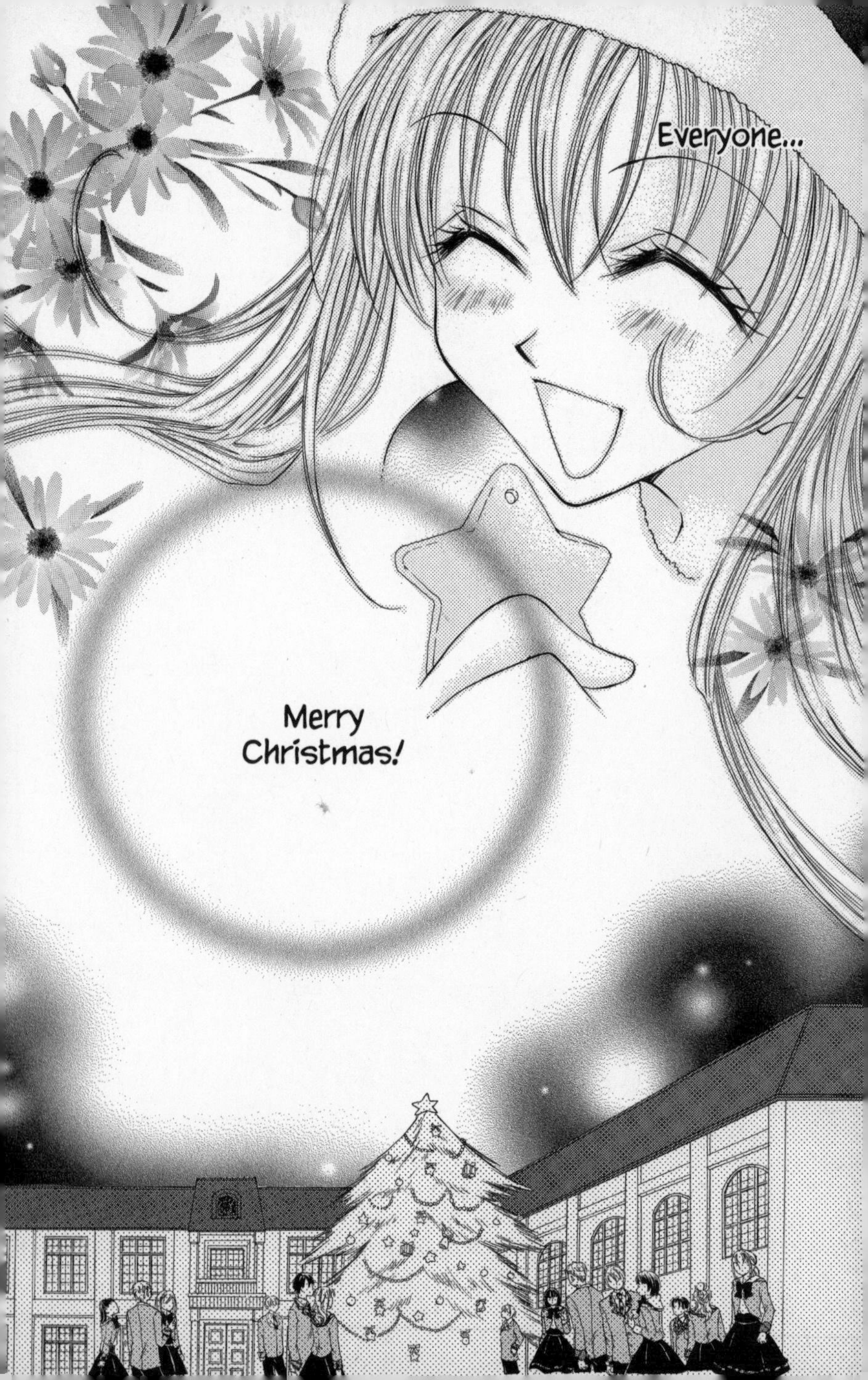
Everyone...
Merry Christmas!

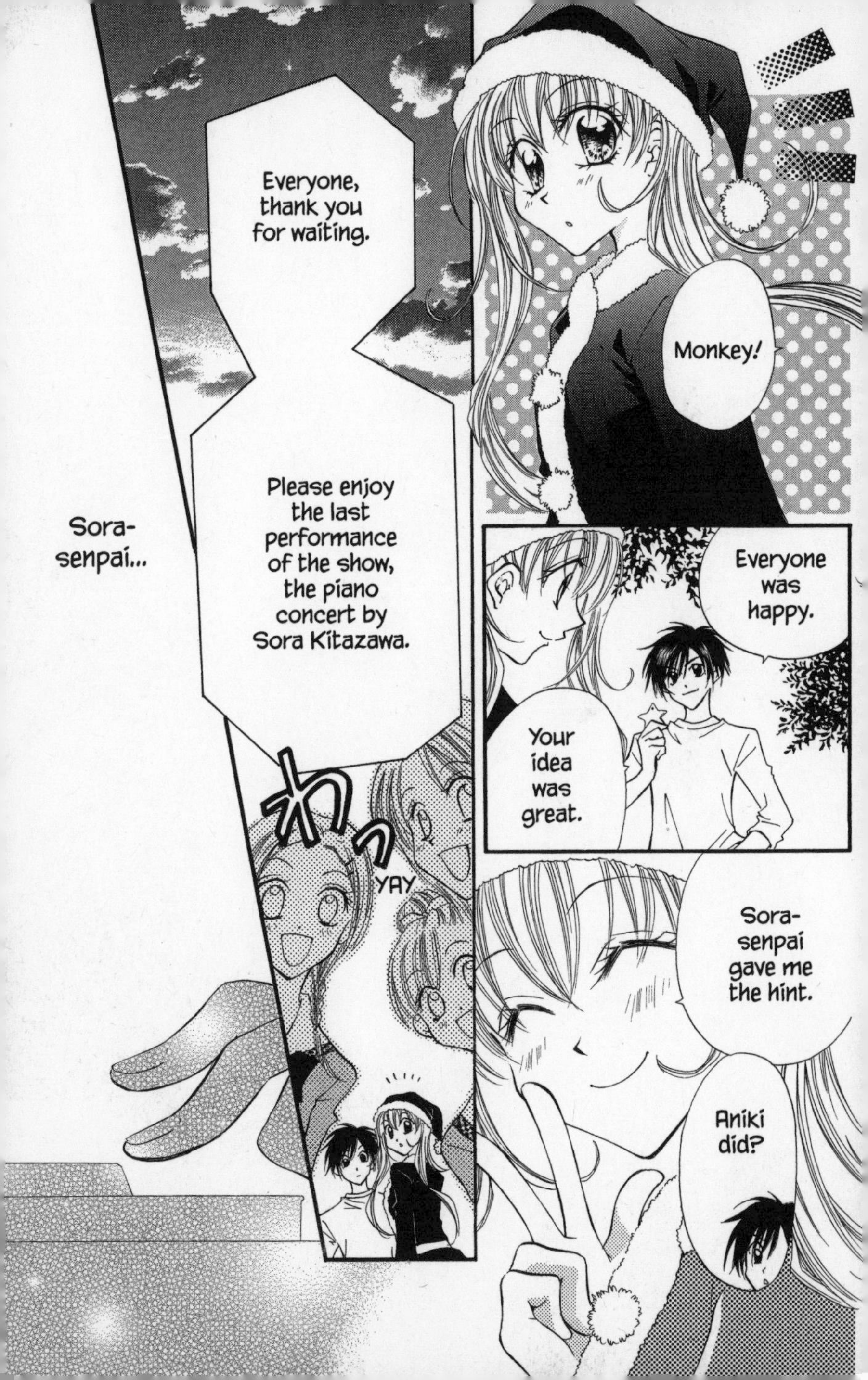
Monkey!
Everyone was happy.
Your idea was great.
Sora-senpai gave me the hint.
Aniki did?
Everyone, thank you for waiting.
Please enjoy the last performance of the show, the piano concert by Sora Kitazawa.
わっ
YAY
Sora-senpai...

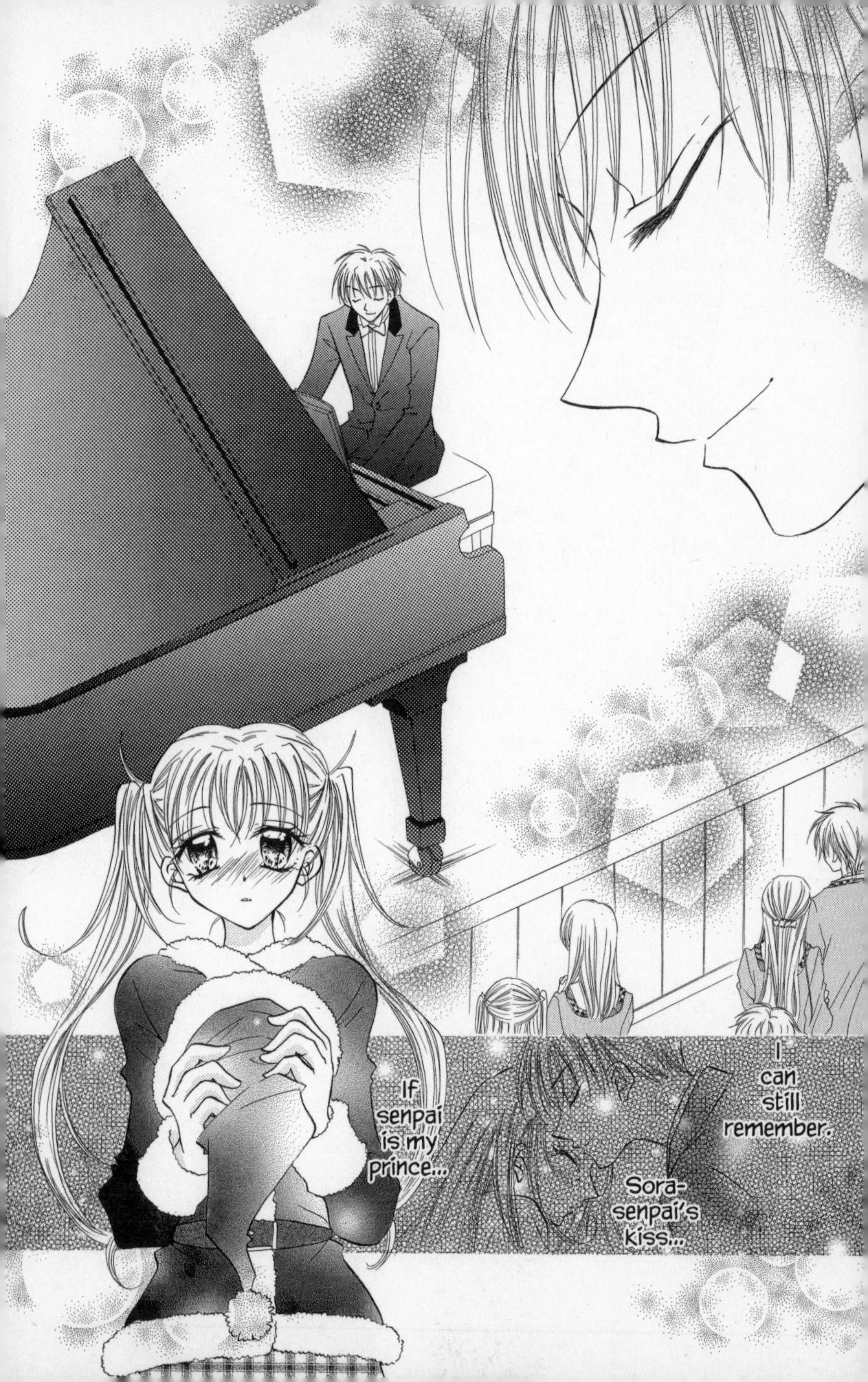
I can still remember.
Sora-senpai's kiss...
If senpai is my prince...

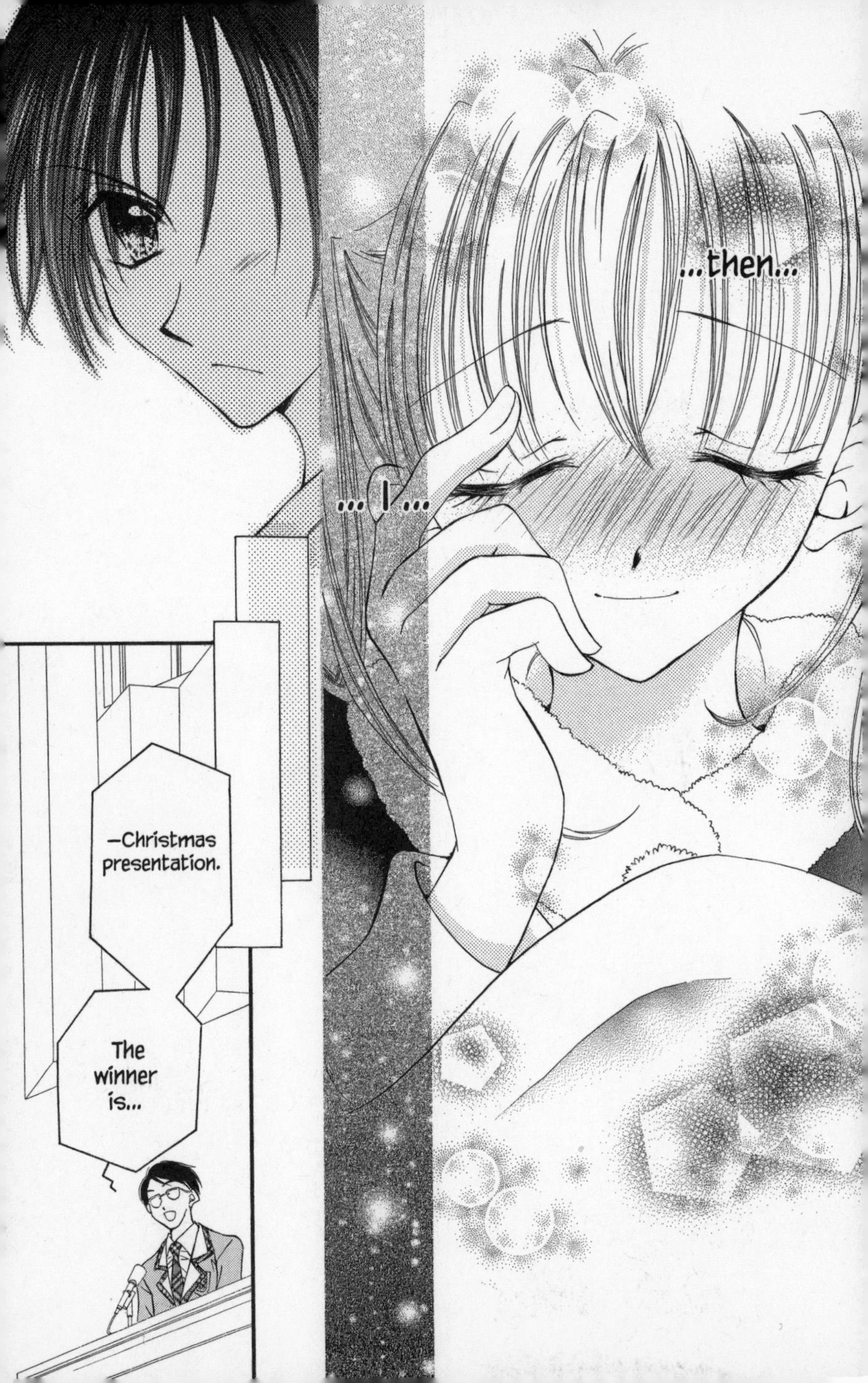
...then...
... I ...
—Christmas presentation.
The winner is...

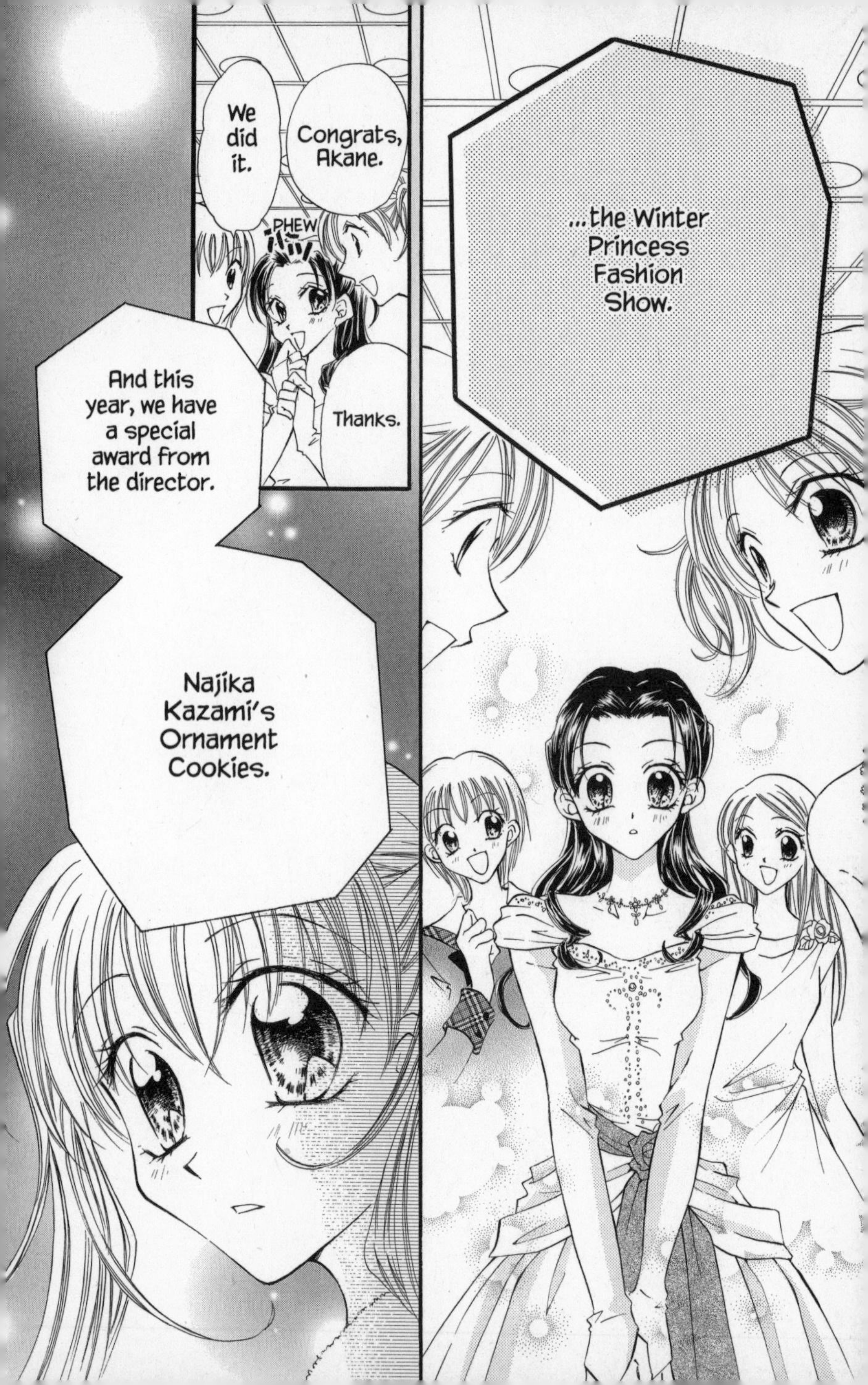
...the Winter Princess Fashion Show.
Congrats, Akane.
We did it.
PHEW
Thanks.
And this year, we have a special award from the director.
Najika Kazami's Ornament Cookies.

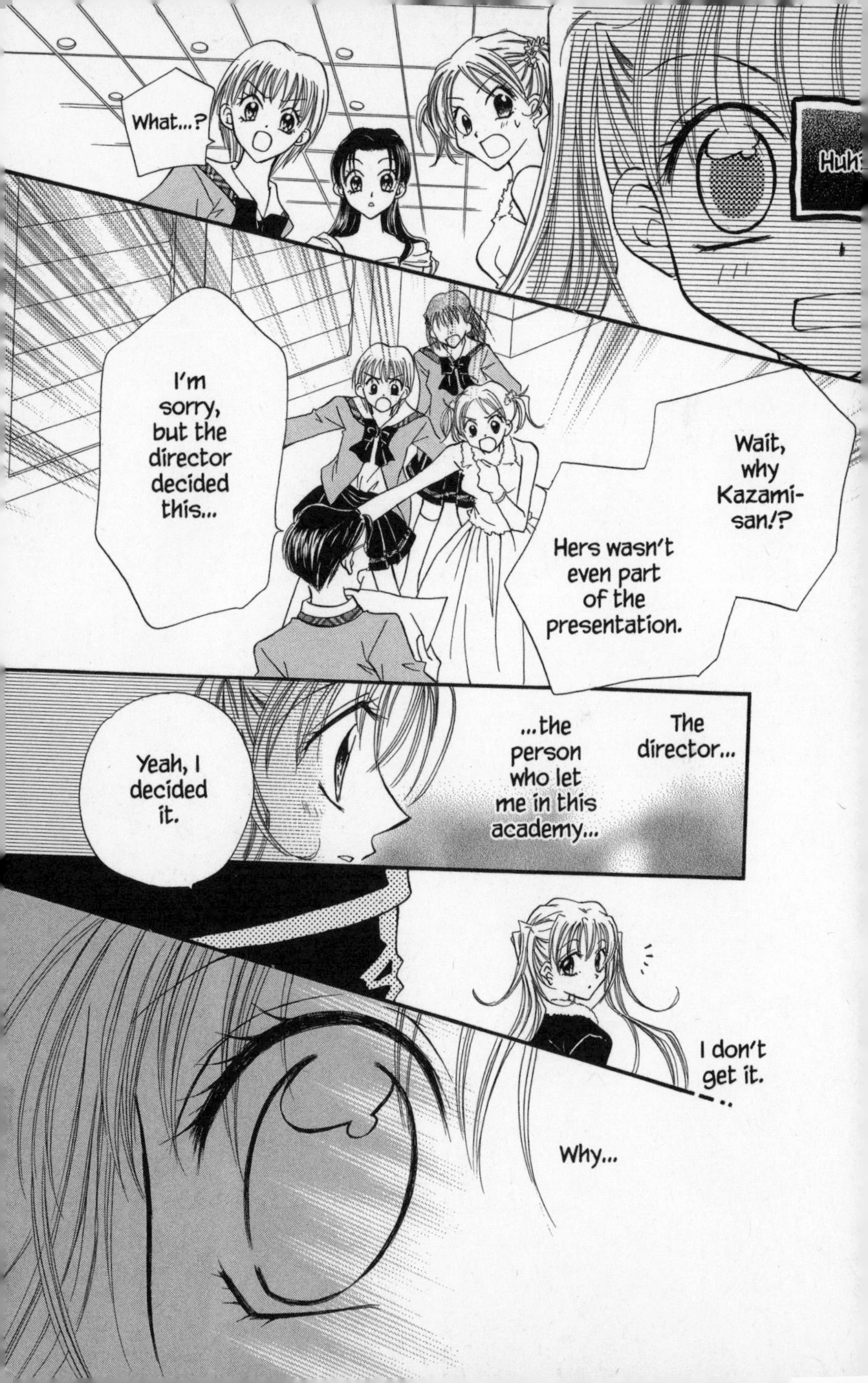
Huh
What...?
Wait, why Kazami-san!?
Hers wasn't even part of the presentation.
I'm sorry, but the director decided this...
The director...
...the person who let me in this academy...
Yeah, I decided it.
I don't get it.
Why...

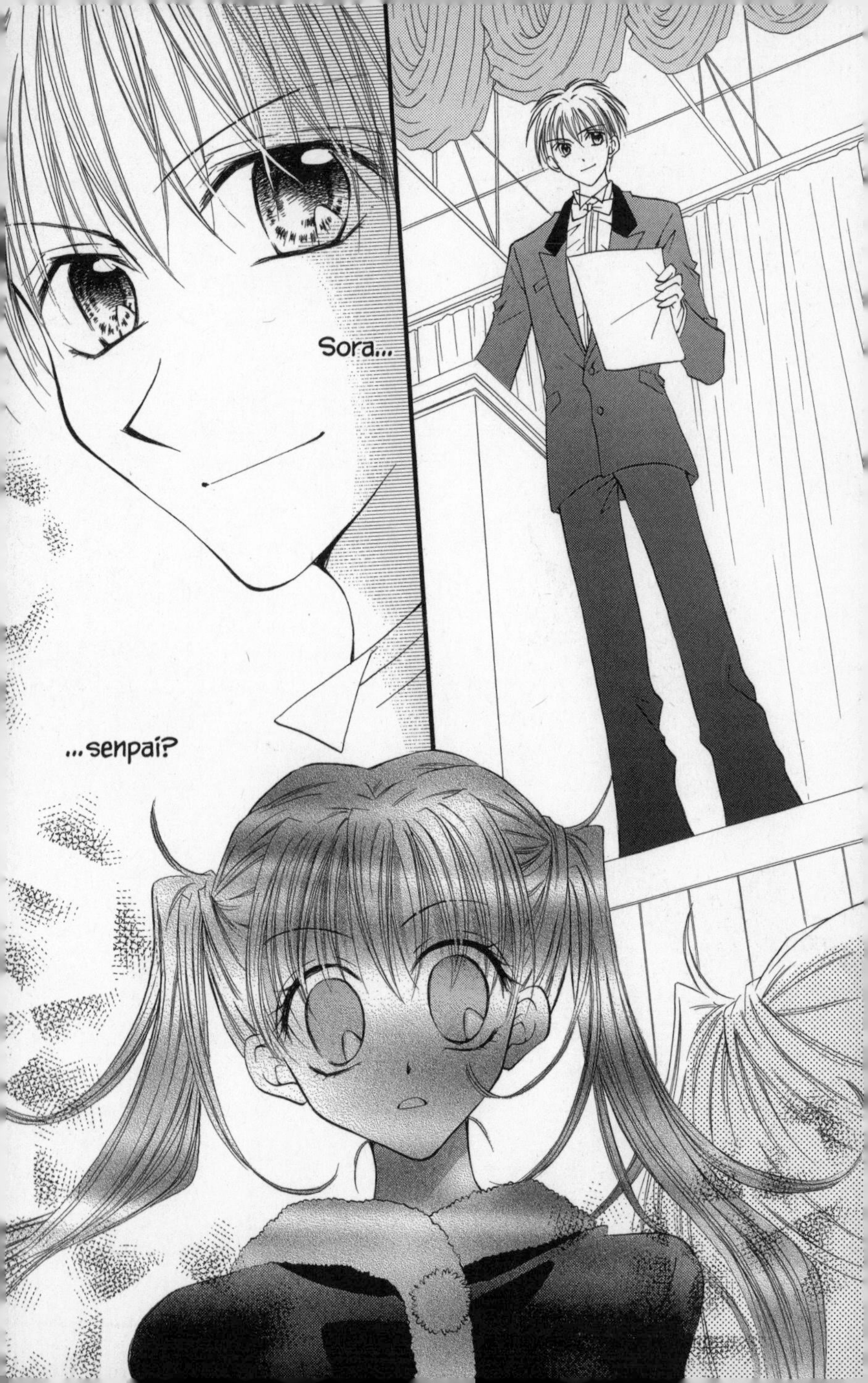
Sora...
...senpai?

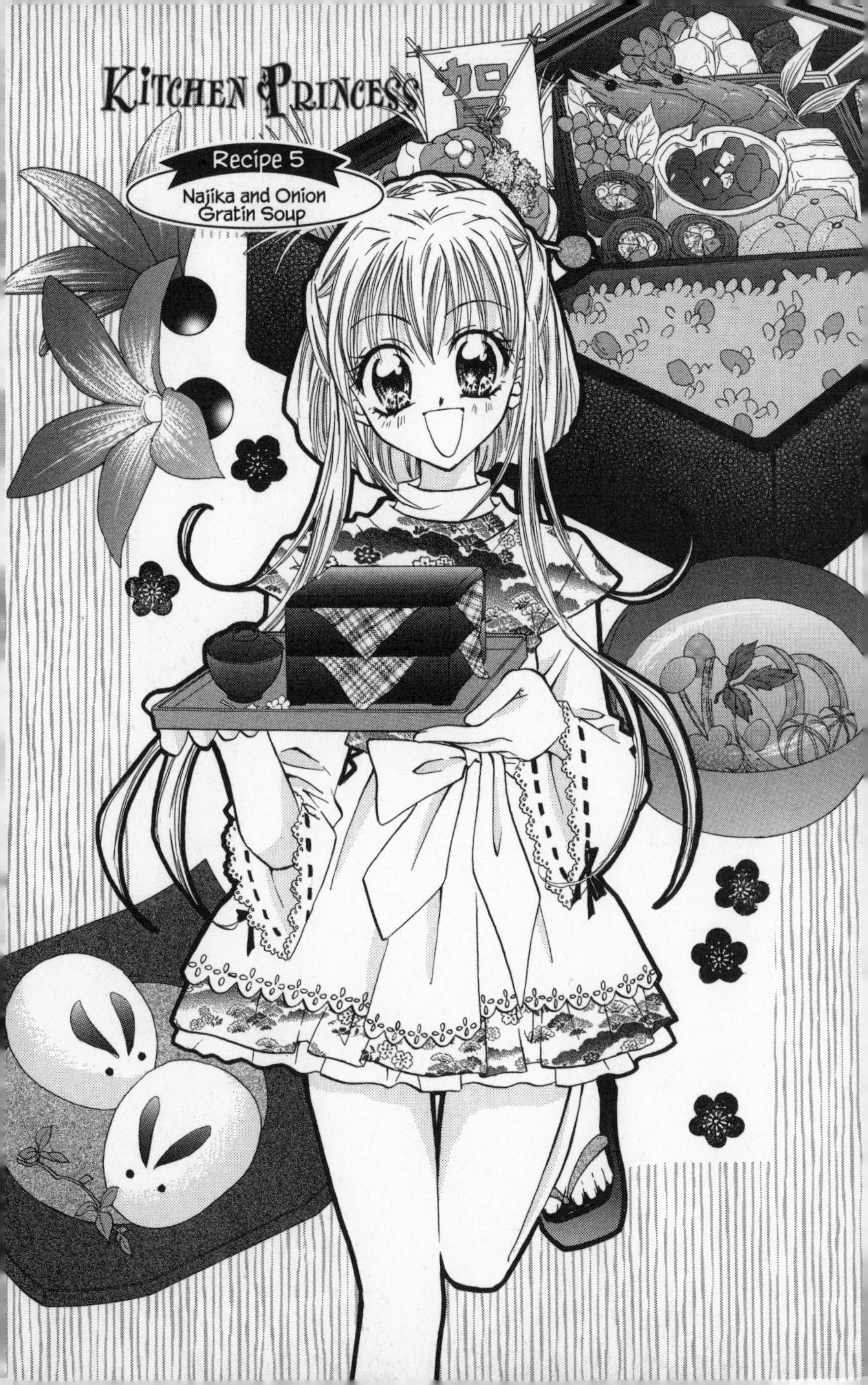

KITCHEN PRINCESS
Recipe 5
Najika and Onion Gratin Soup

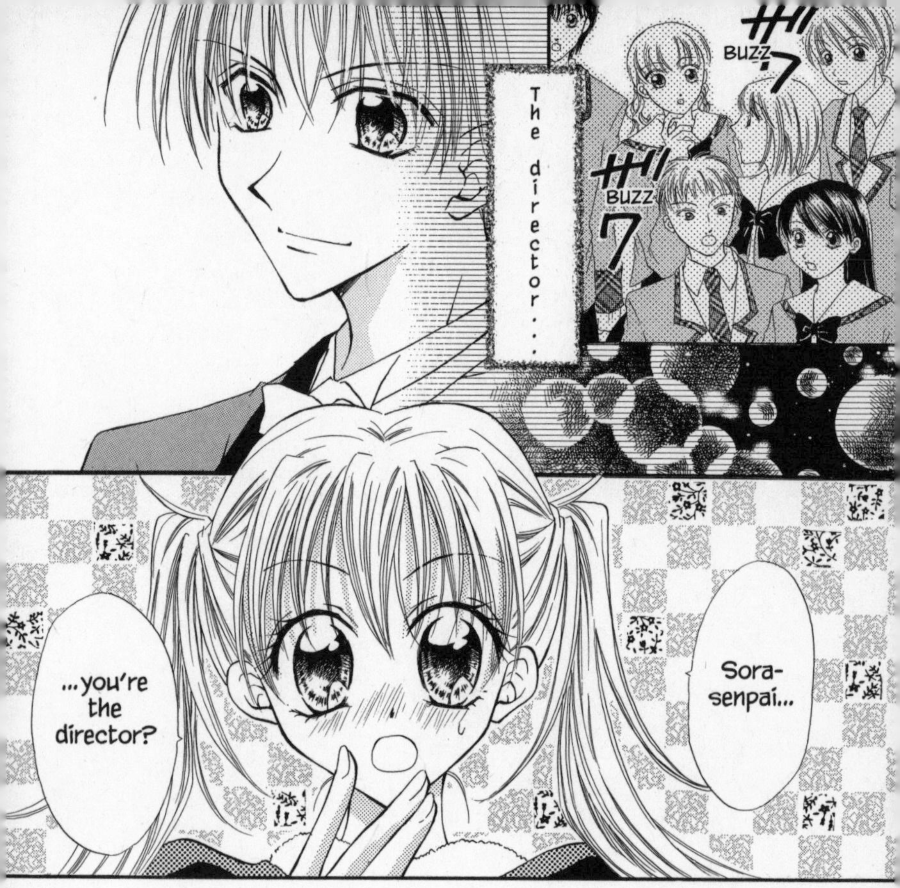
BUZZ
BUZZ
The director...
Sora-senpai...
...you're the director?

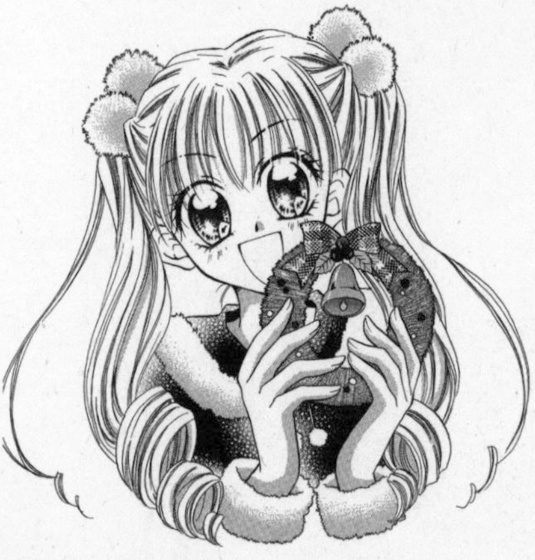

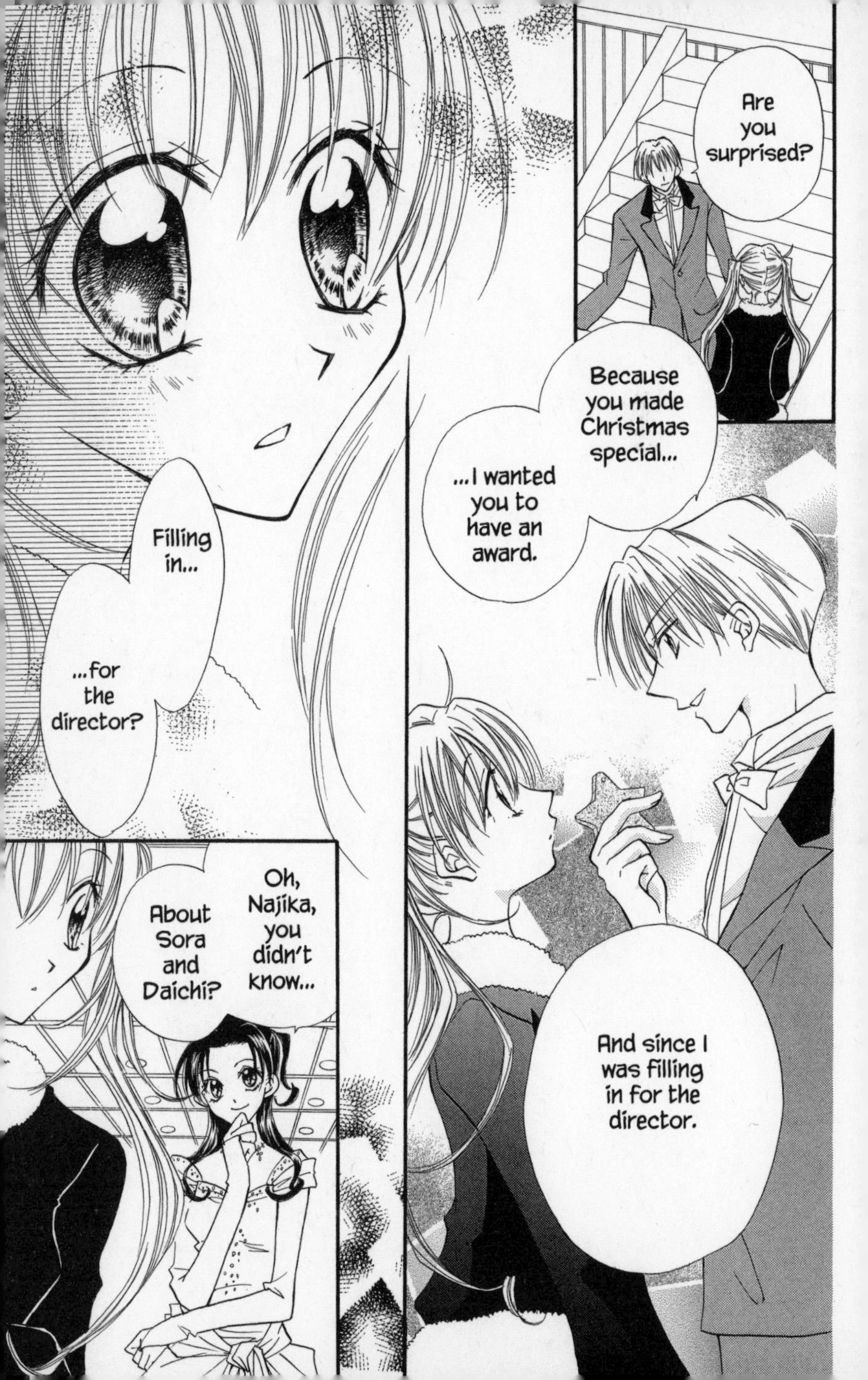
Are you surprised?
Because you made Christmas special...
...I wanted you to have an award.
And since I was filling in for the director.
Filling in...
...for the director?
Oh, Najika, you didn't know...
About Sora and Daichi?

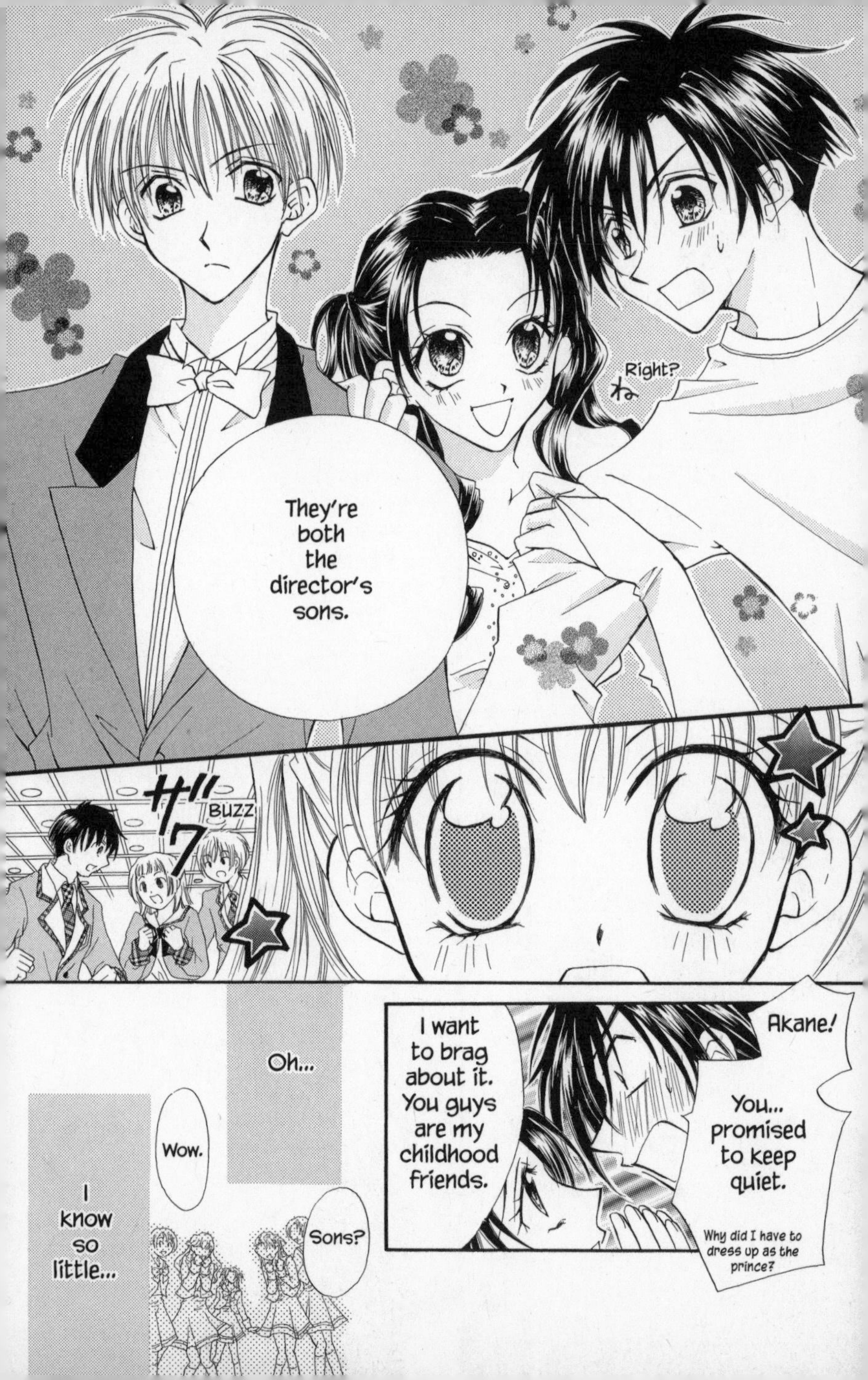
Right?
ね
They're both the director's sons.
ザワ
BUZZ
Akane!
I want to brag about it. You guys are my childhood friends.
You... promised to keep quiet.
Why did I have to dress up as the prince?
Oh...
Wow.
Sons?
I know so little...

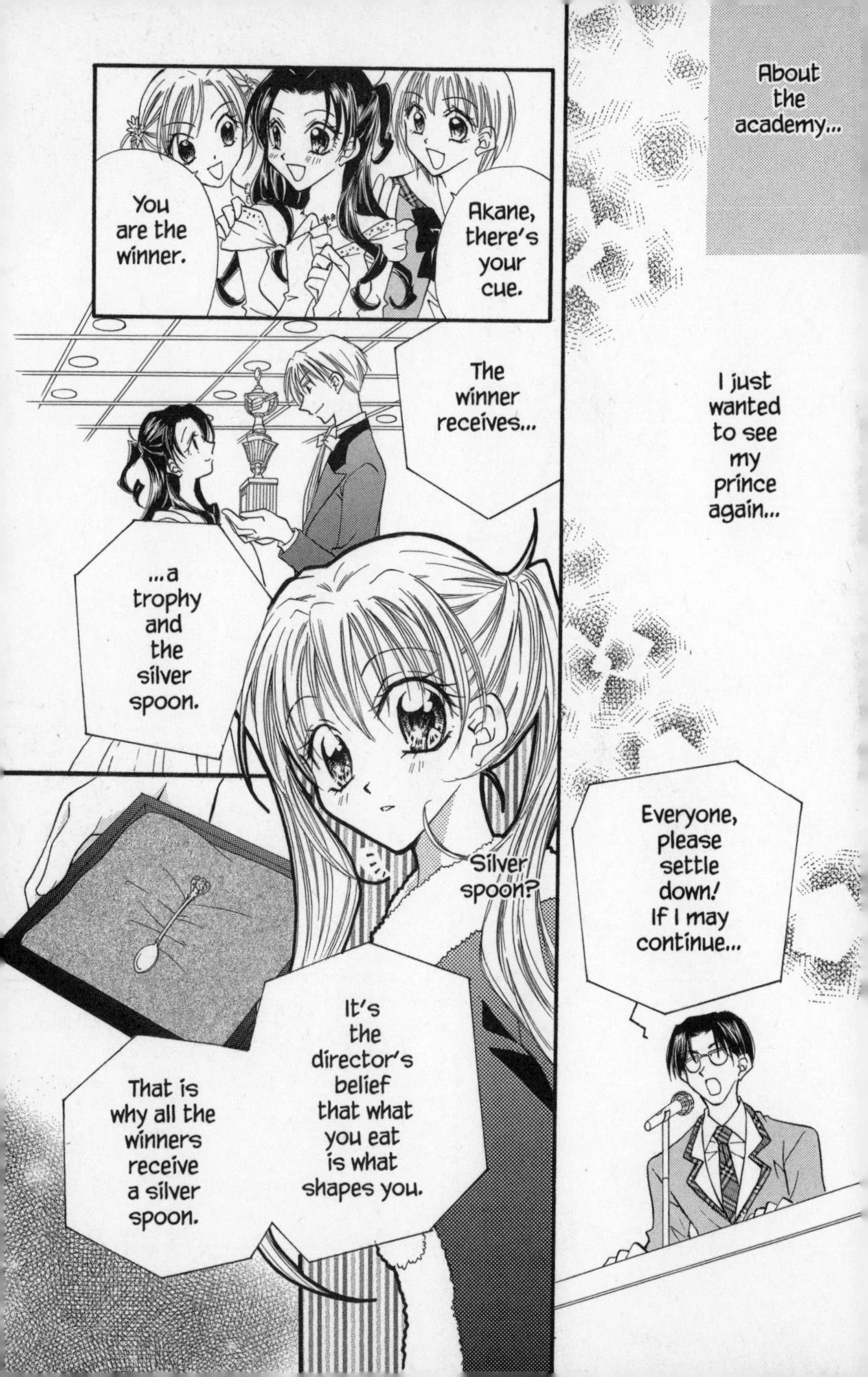
About the academy...
I just wanted to see my prince again...
Everyone, please settle down! If I may continue...
Akane, there's your cue.
You are the winner.
The winner receives...
...a trophy and the silver spoon.
Silver spoon?
It's the director's belief that what you eat is what shapes you.
That is why all the winners receive a silver spoon.

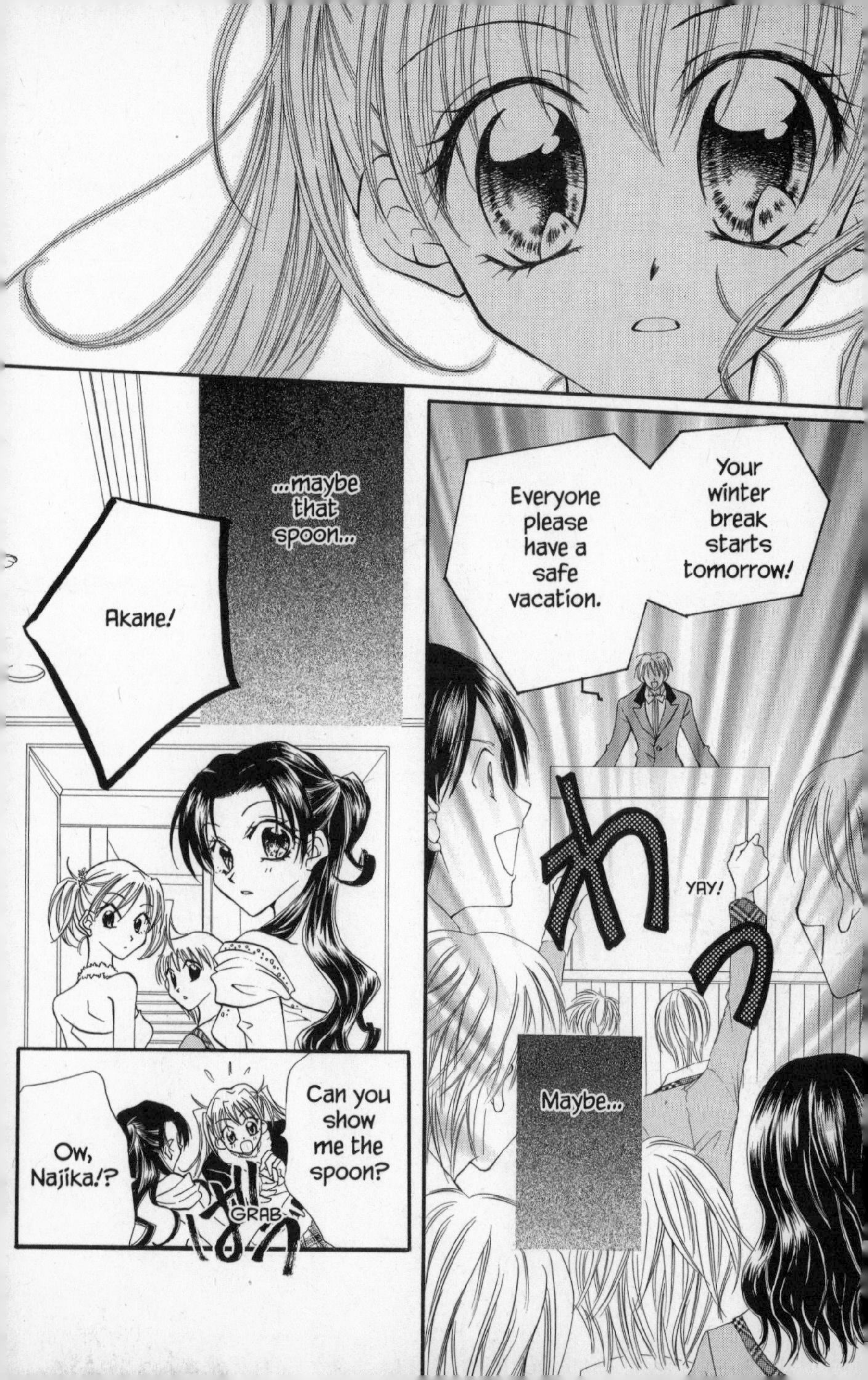
Your winter break starts tomorrow!
Everyone please have a safe vacation.
わっ
YAY!
Maybe...
...maybe that spoon...
Akane!
Can you show me the spoon?
Ow, Najika!?
GRAB

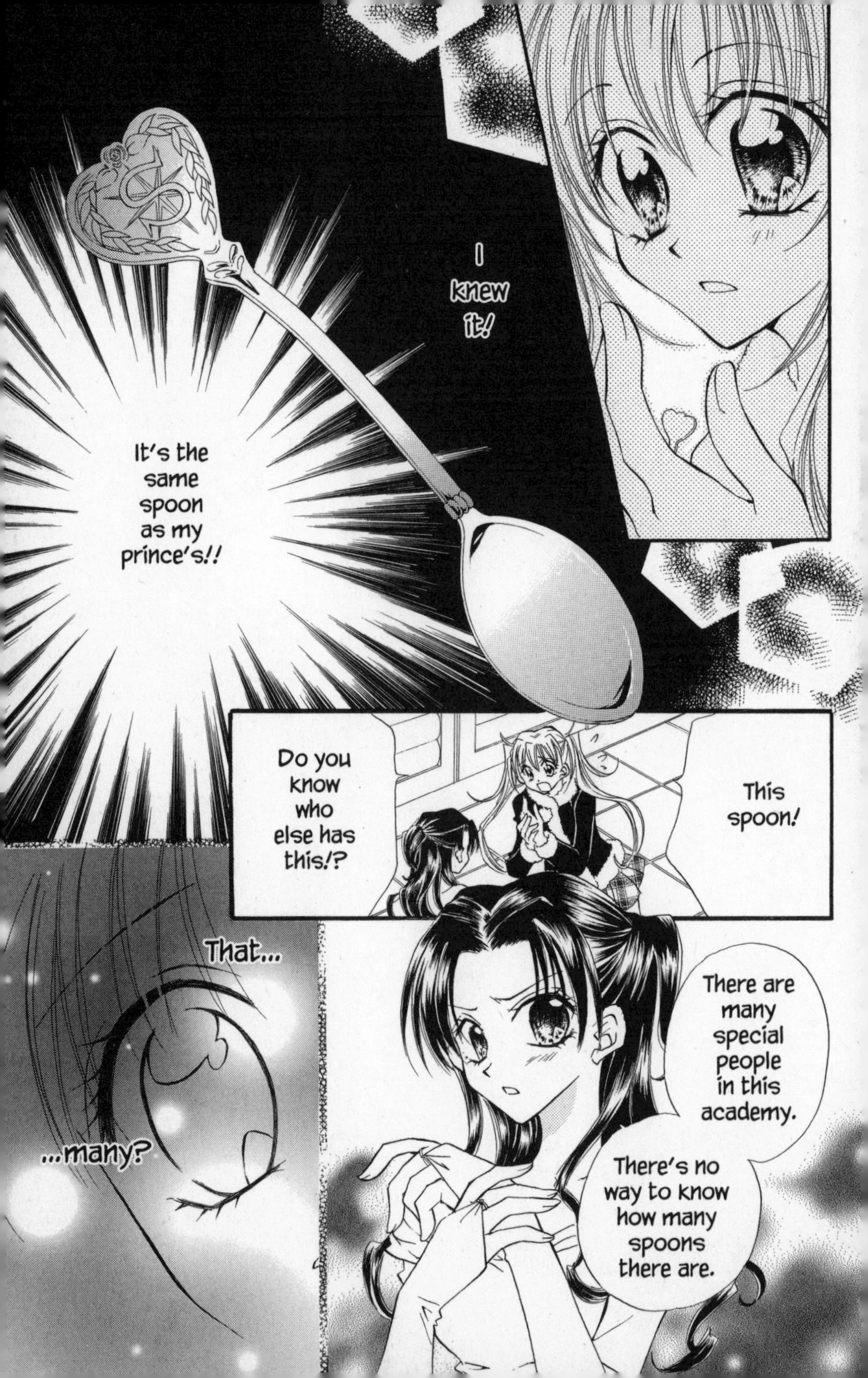
I knew it!
It's the same spoon as my prince's!!
This spoon!
Do you know who else has this!?
There are many special people in this academy.
There's no way to know how many spoons there are.
That...
...many?

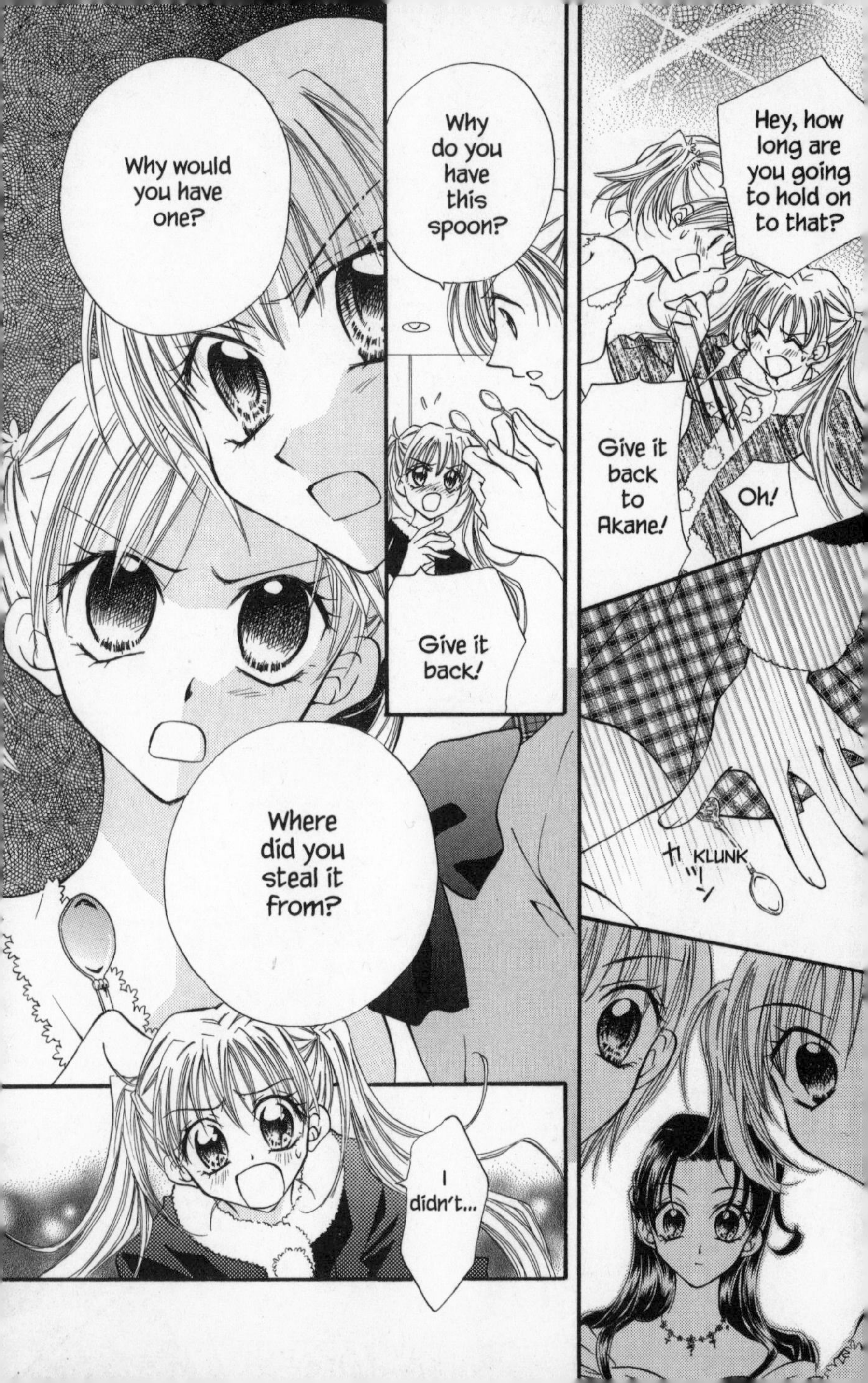
Hey, how long are you going to hold on to that?
Give it back to Akane!
Oh!
KLUNK
Why do you have this spoon?
Give it back!
Why would you have one?
Where did you steal it from?
I didn't...

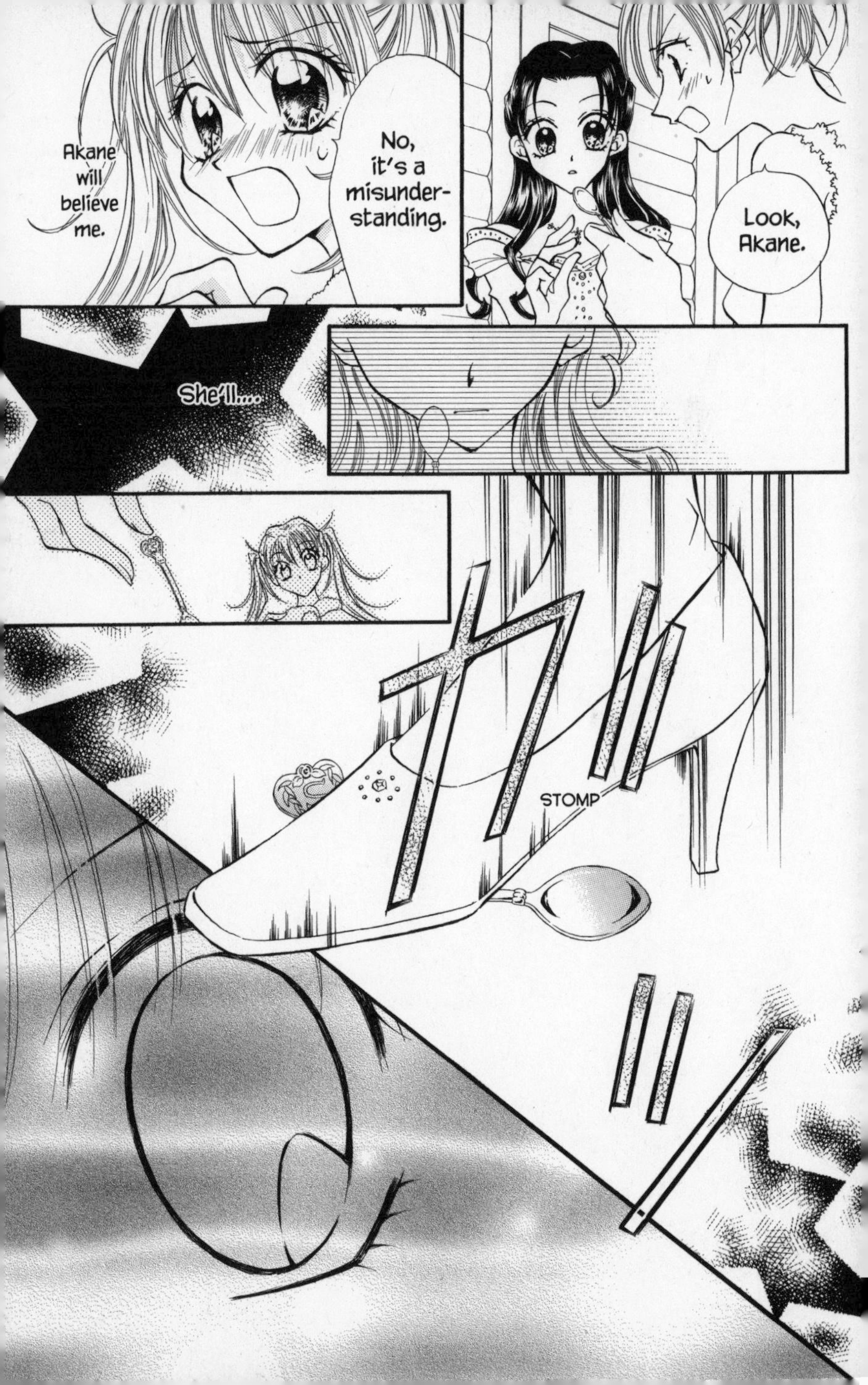

Look, Akane.
No, it's a misunderstanding.
Akane will believe me.
She'll...
STOMP

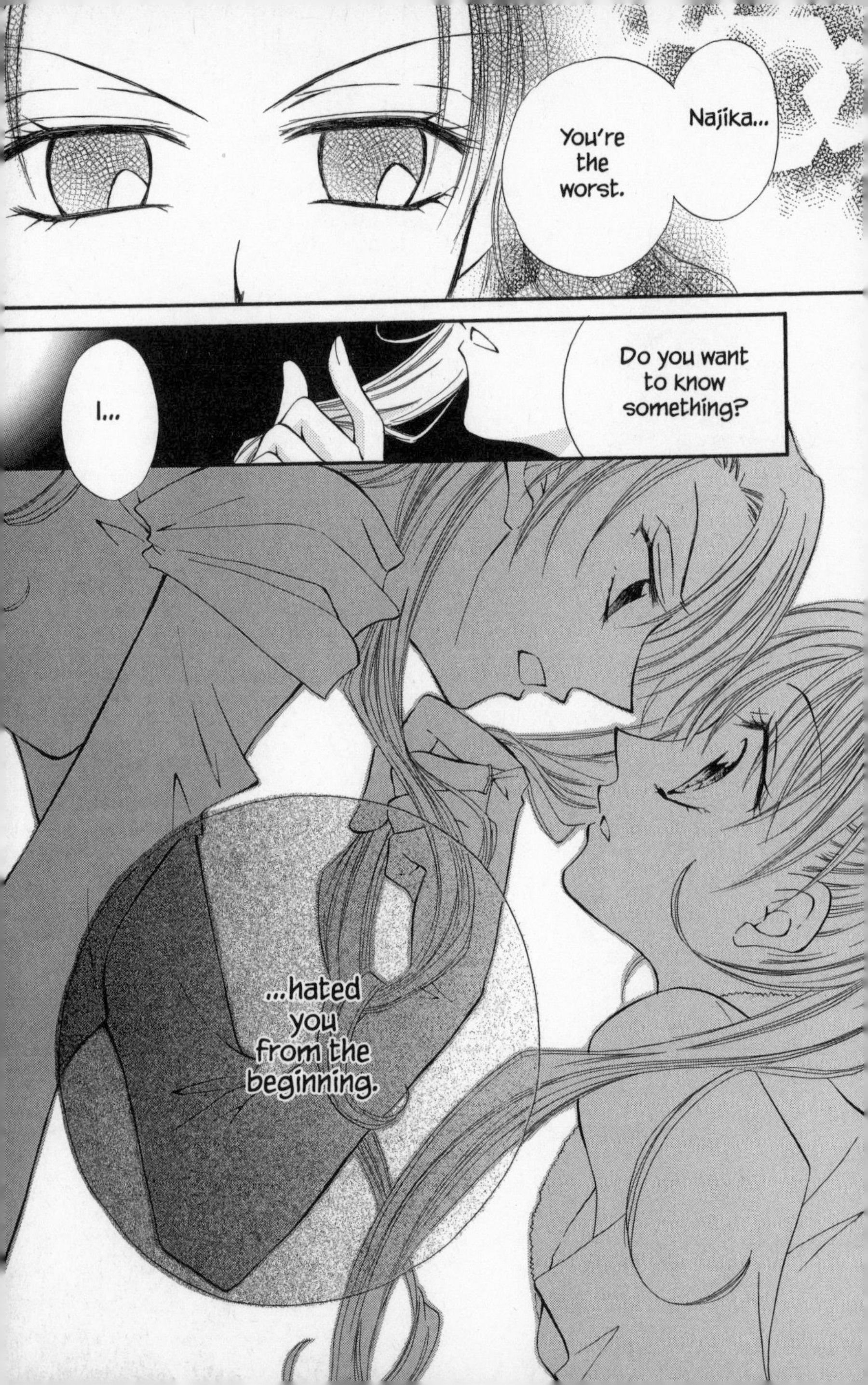
Najika...
You're the worst.
Do you want to know something?
I...
...hated you from the beginning.

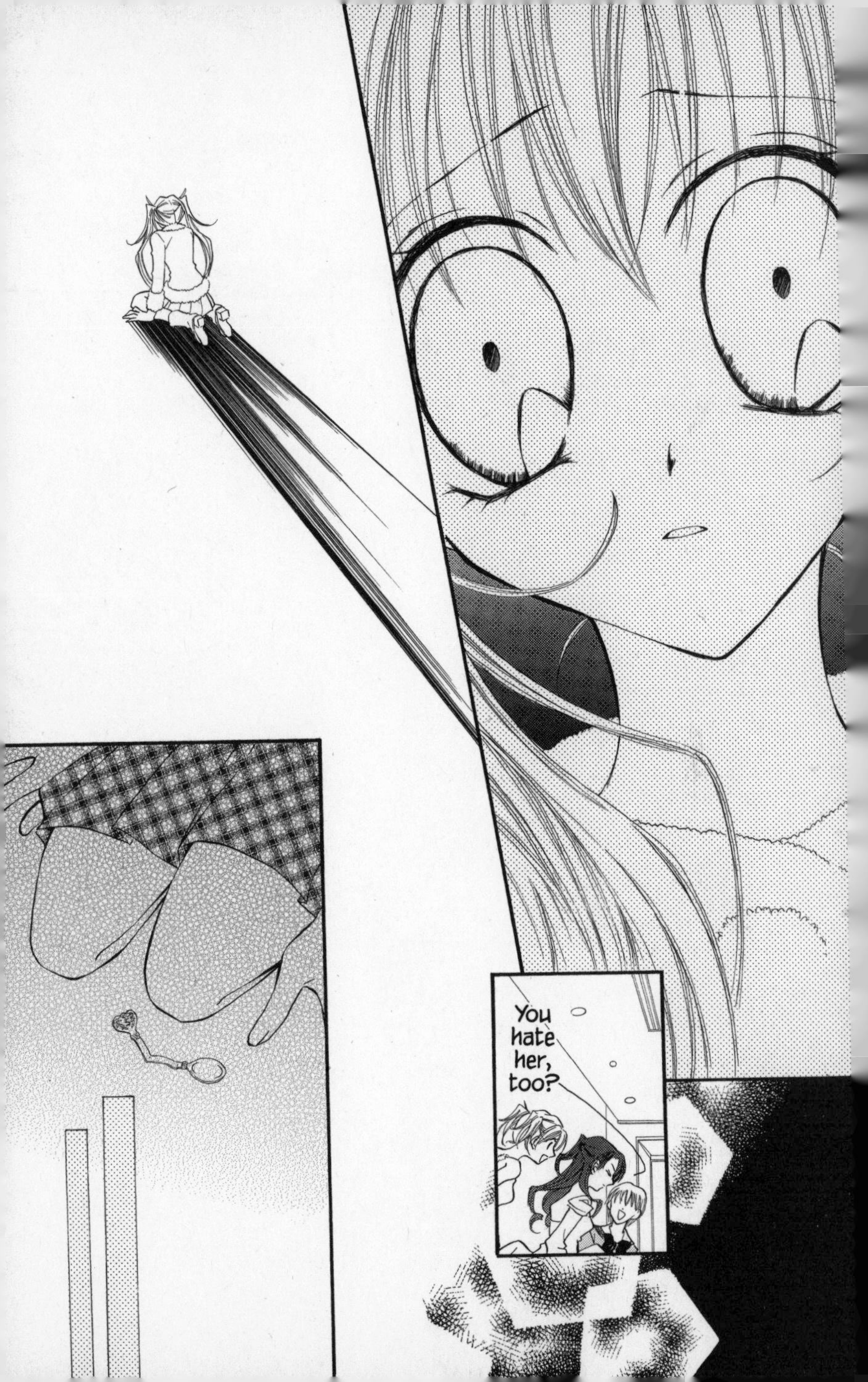
You hate her, too?

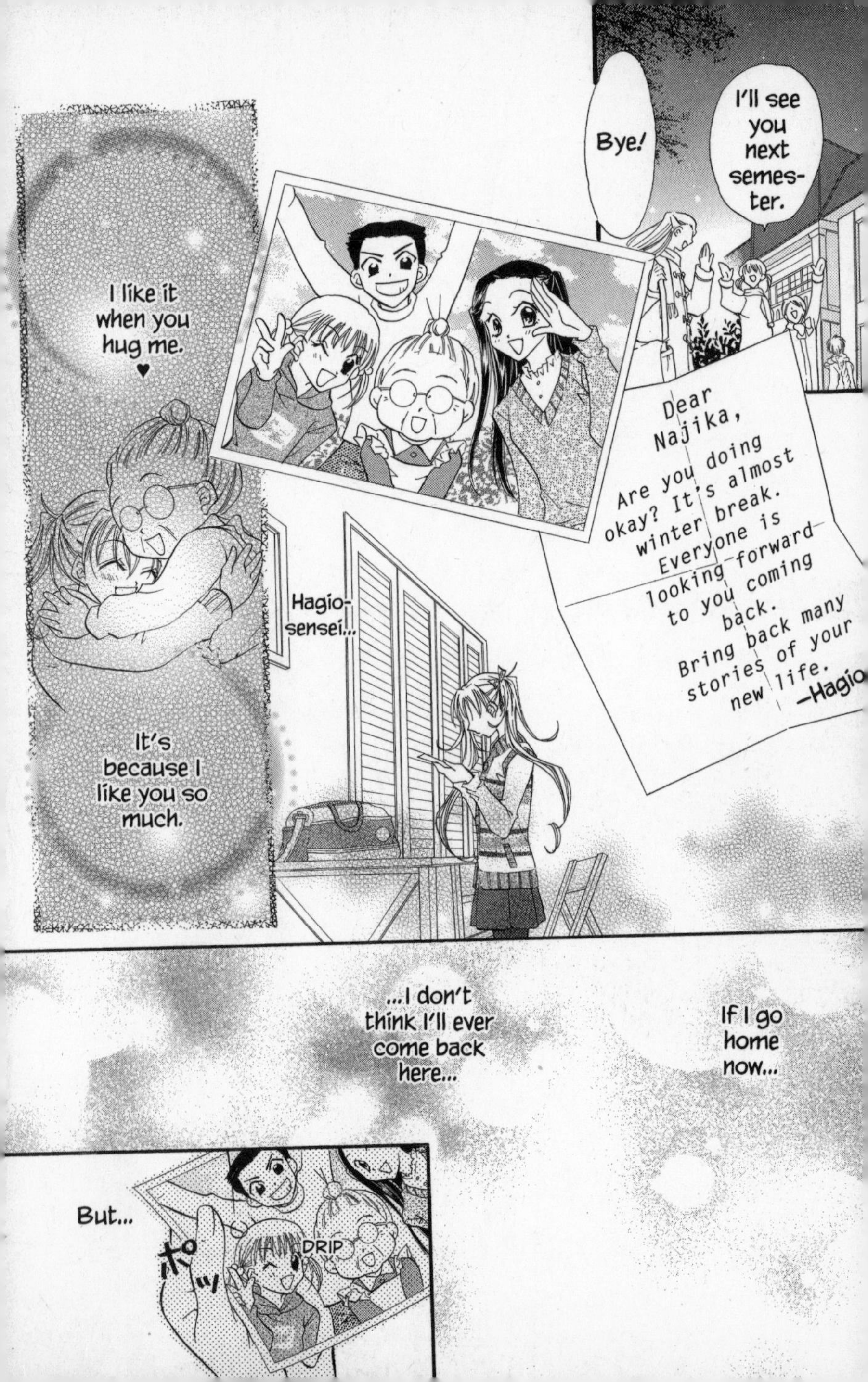

I'll see you next semester.
Bye!
Dear Najika,
Are you doing okay? It's almost winter break. Everyone is looking forward to you coming back.
Bring back many stories of your new life.
—Hagio
Hagio-sensei...
I like it when you hug me. ♥
It's because I like you so much.
If I go home now...
...I don't think I'll ever come back here...
DRIP
But...

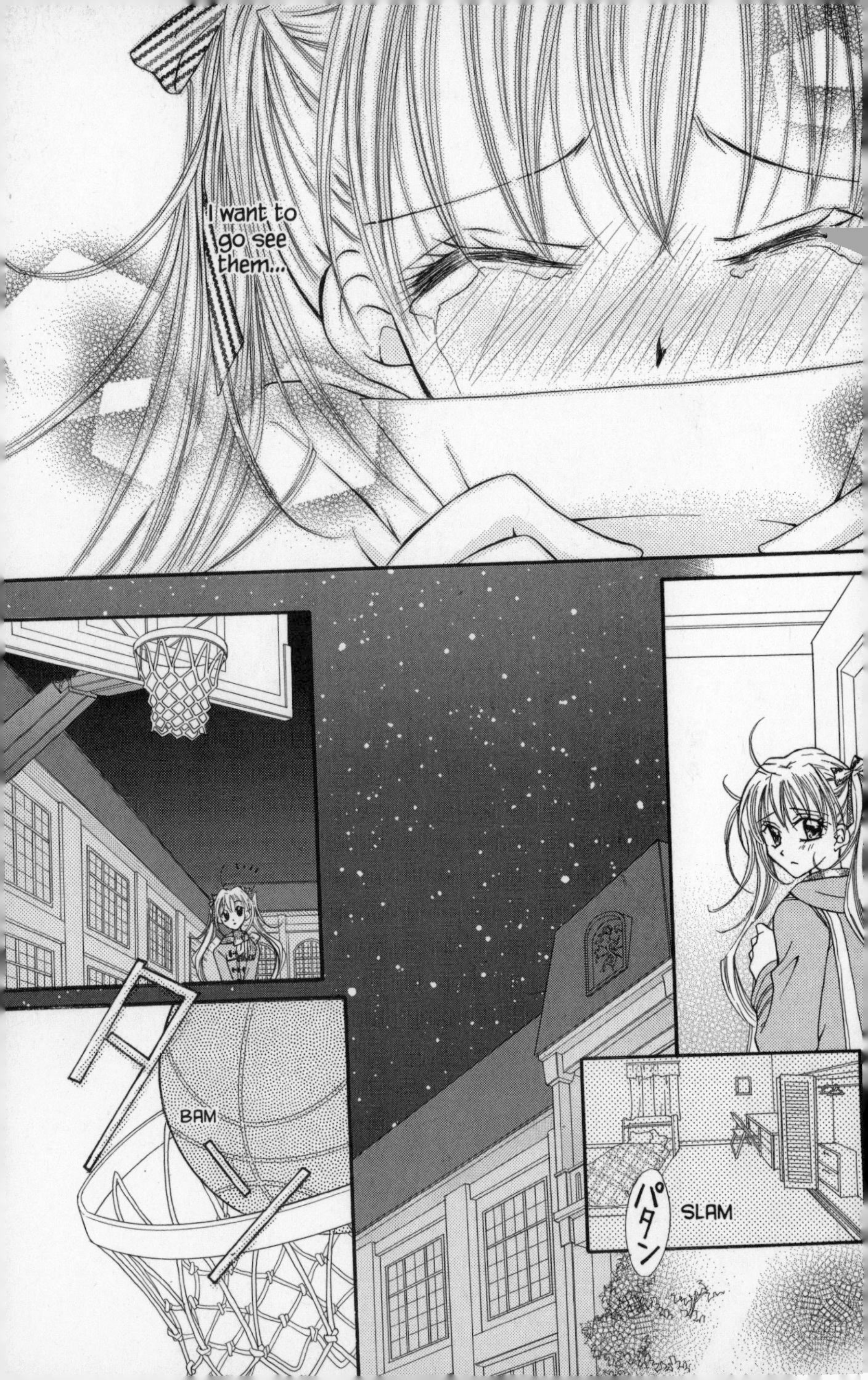
I want to go see them...
BAM
パタン
SLAM

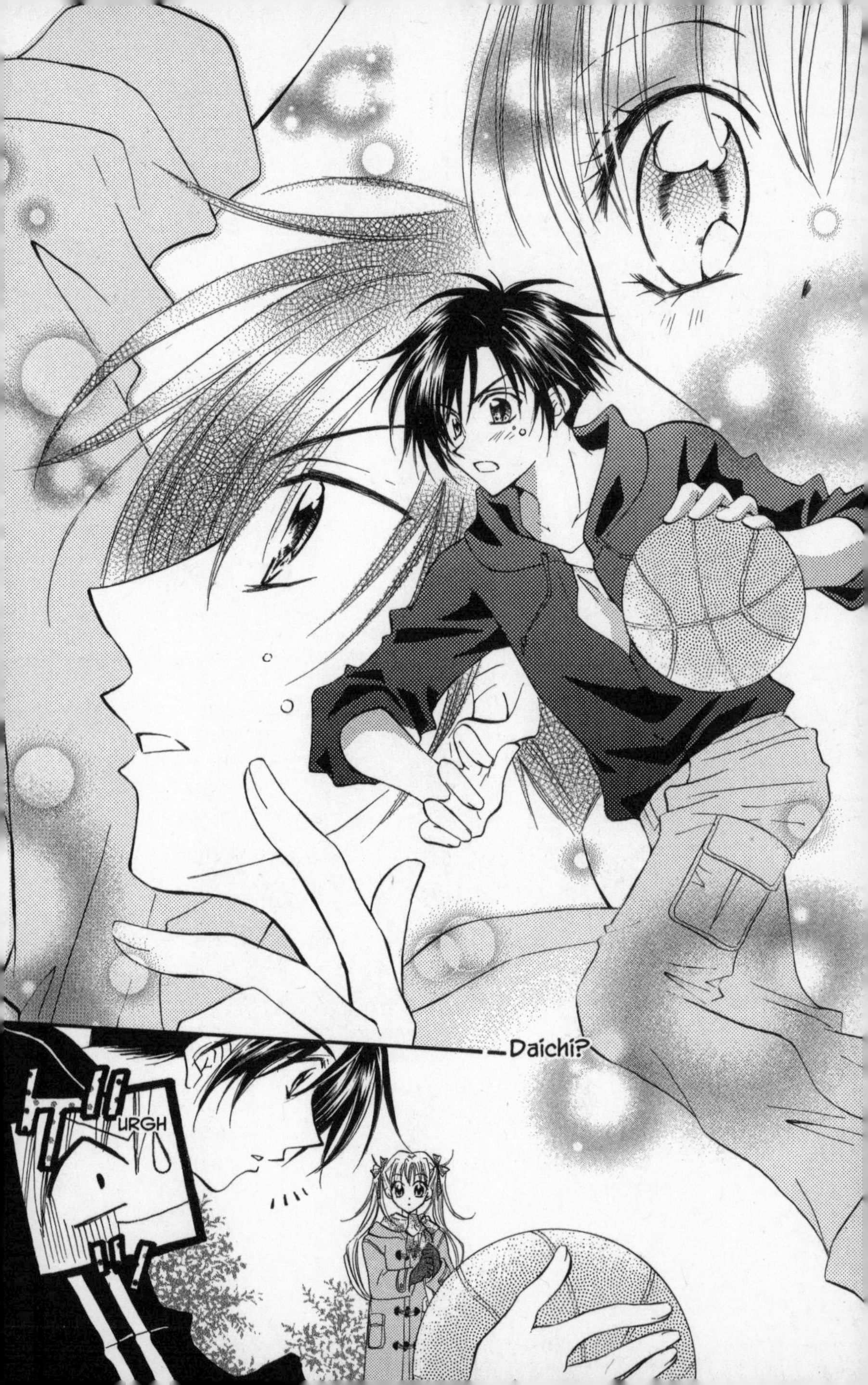
—Daichi?
URGH

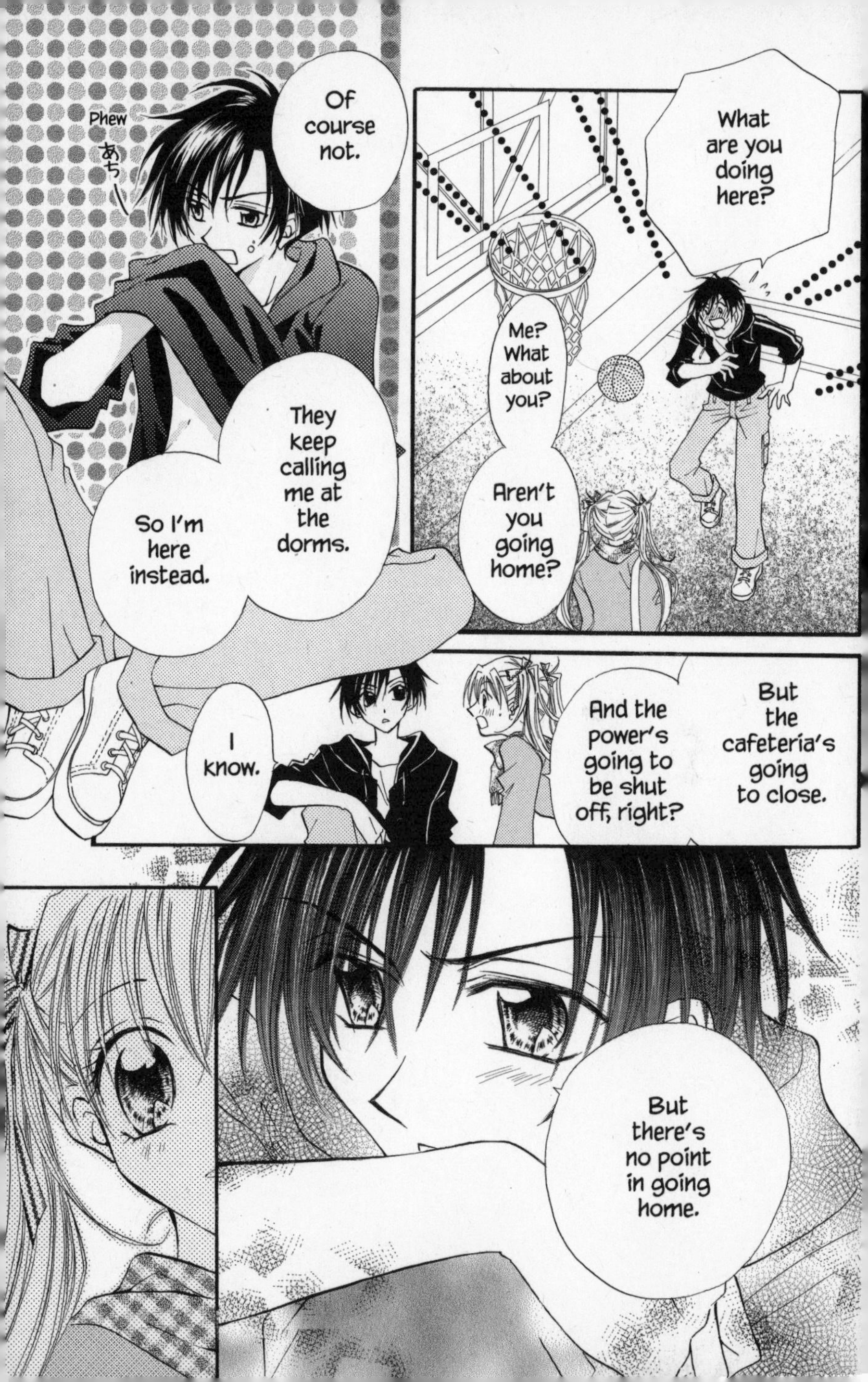
What are you doing here?
Me? What about you?
Aren't you going home?
Of course not.
Phew
あち
They keep calling me at the dorms.
So I'm here instead.
But the cafeteria's going to close.
And the power's going to be shut off, right?
I know.
But there's no point in going home.

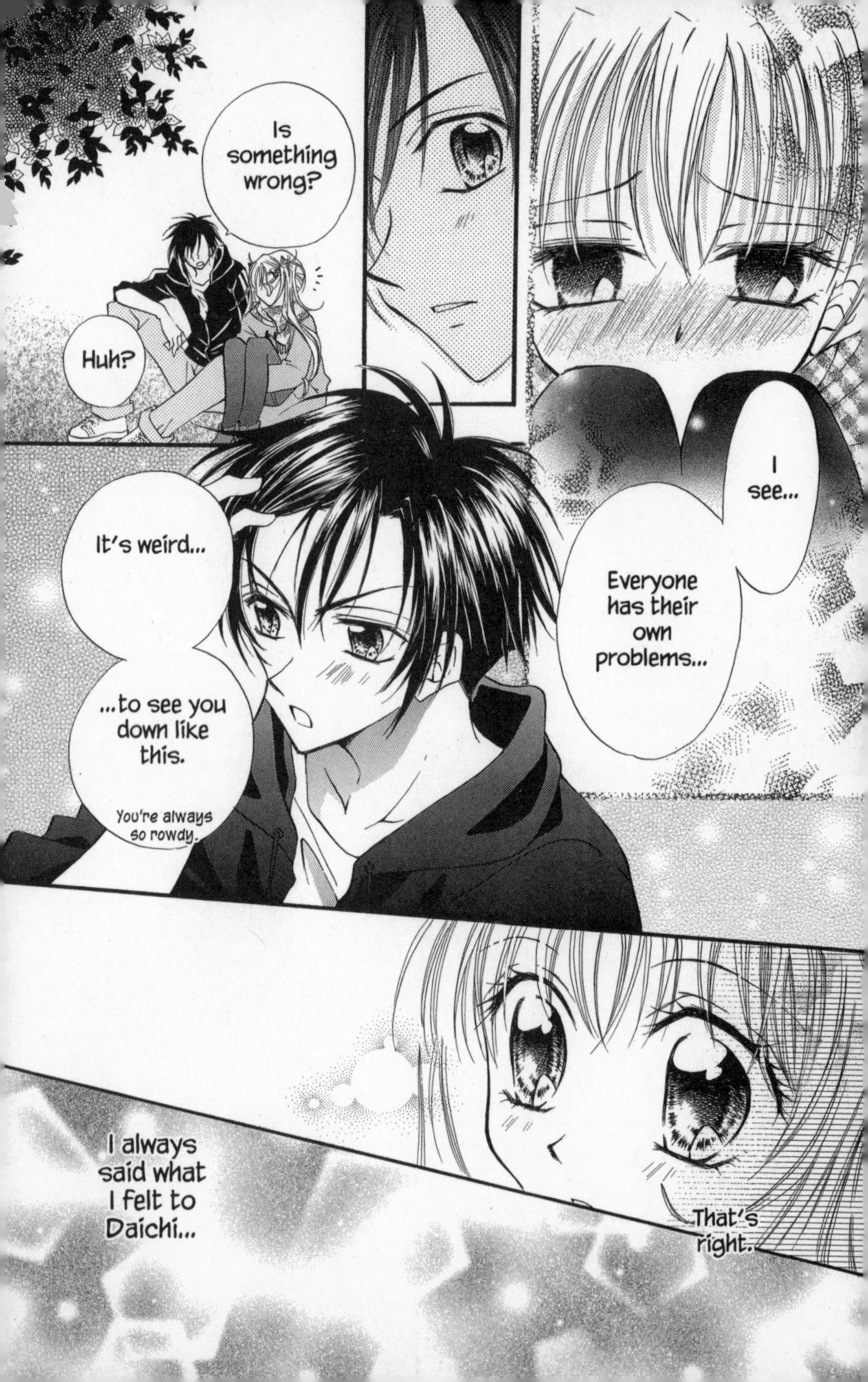
Is something wrong?
Huh?
It's weird...
...to see you down like this.
You're always so rowdy.
I see...
Everyone has their own problems...
That's right.
I always said what I felt to Daichi...

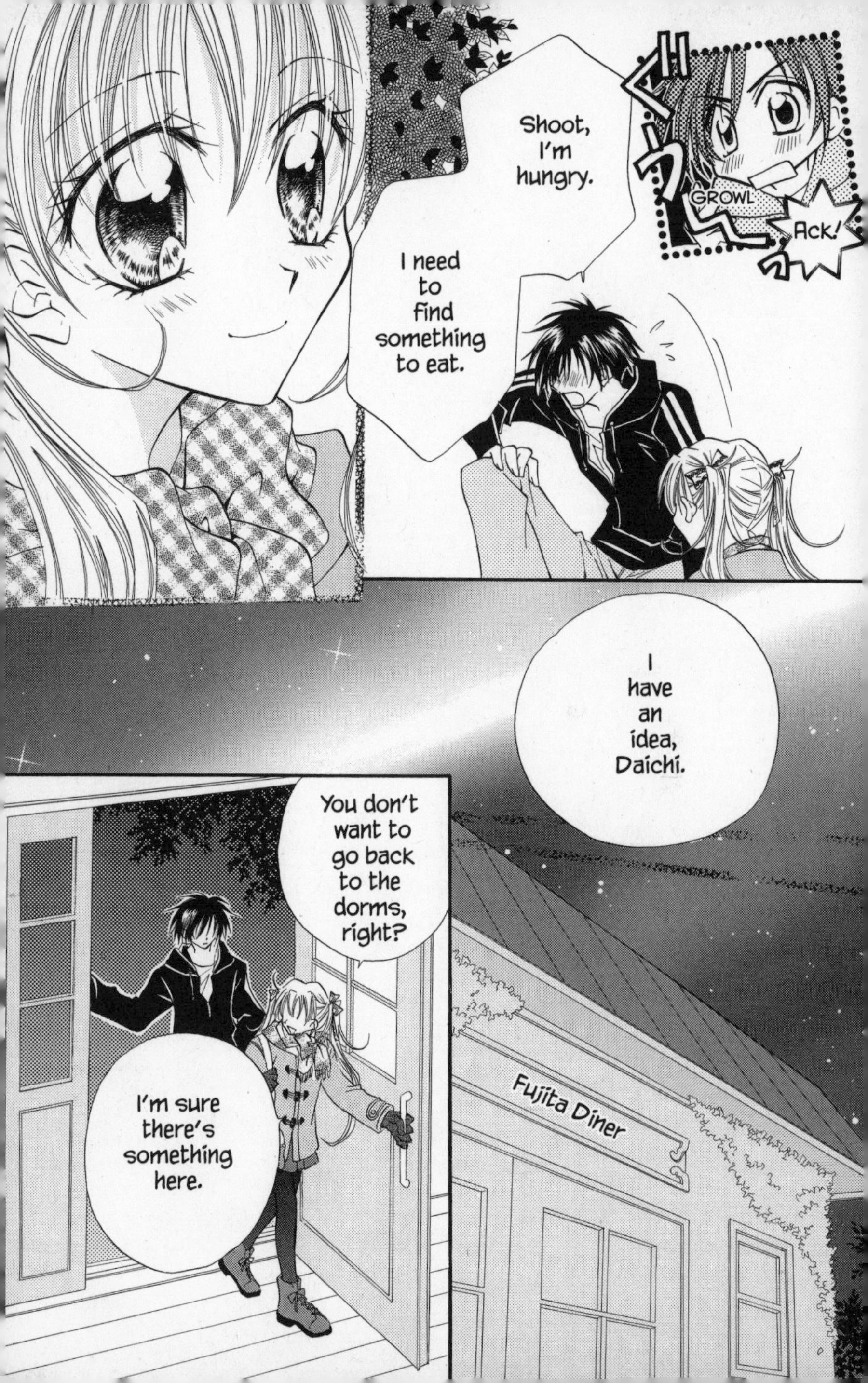
GROWL
Ack!
Shoot, I'm hungry.
I need to find something to eat.
I have an idea, Daichi.
Fujita Diner
You don't want to go back to the dorms, right?
I'm sure there's something here.

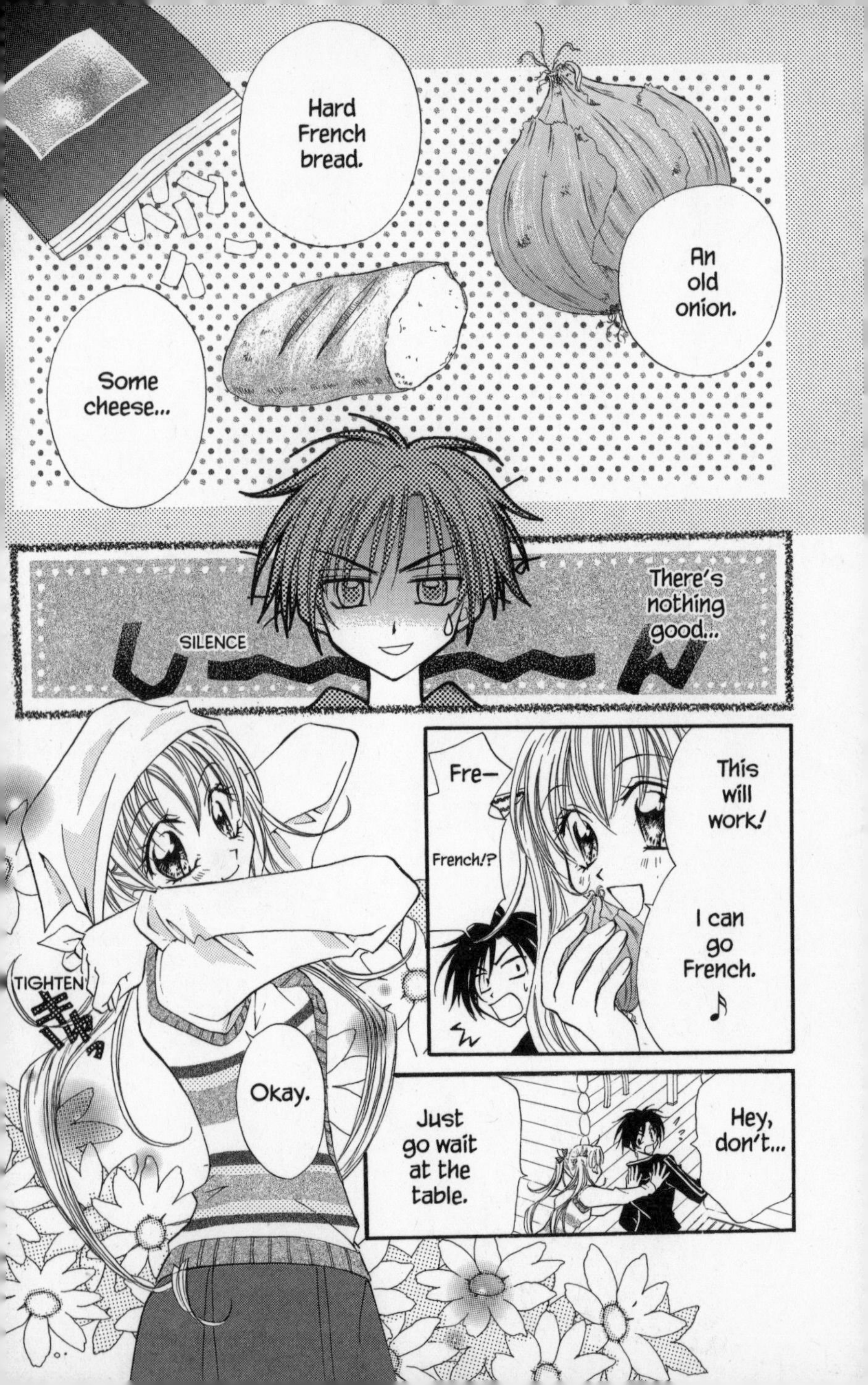
An old onion.
Hard French bread.
Some cheese...
There's nothing good...
SILENCE
This will work!
I can go French. ♪
Fre—
French!?
Hey, don't...
Just go wait at the table.
TIGHTEN
Okay.

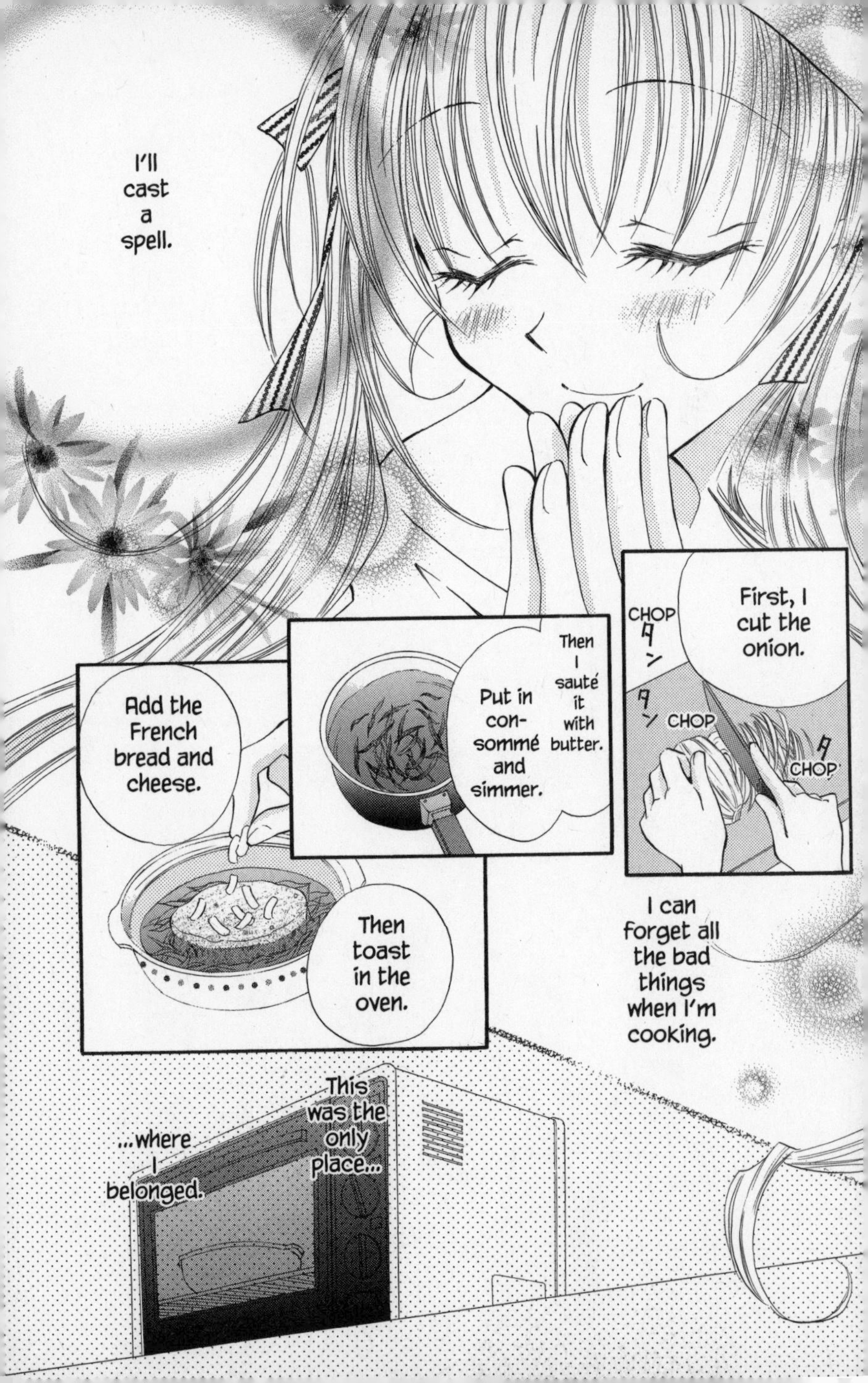
I'll cast a spell.
First, I cut the onion.
CHOP
CHOP
CHOP
Then I sauté it with butter.
Put in consommé and simmer.
Add the French bread and cheese.
Then toast in the oven.
I can forget all the bad things when I'm cooking.
This was the only place...
...where I belonged.

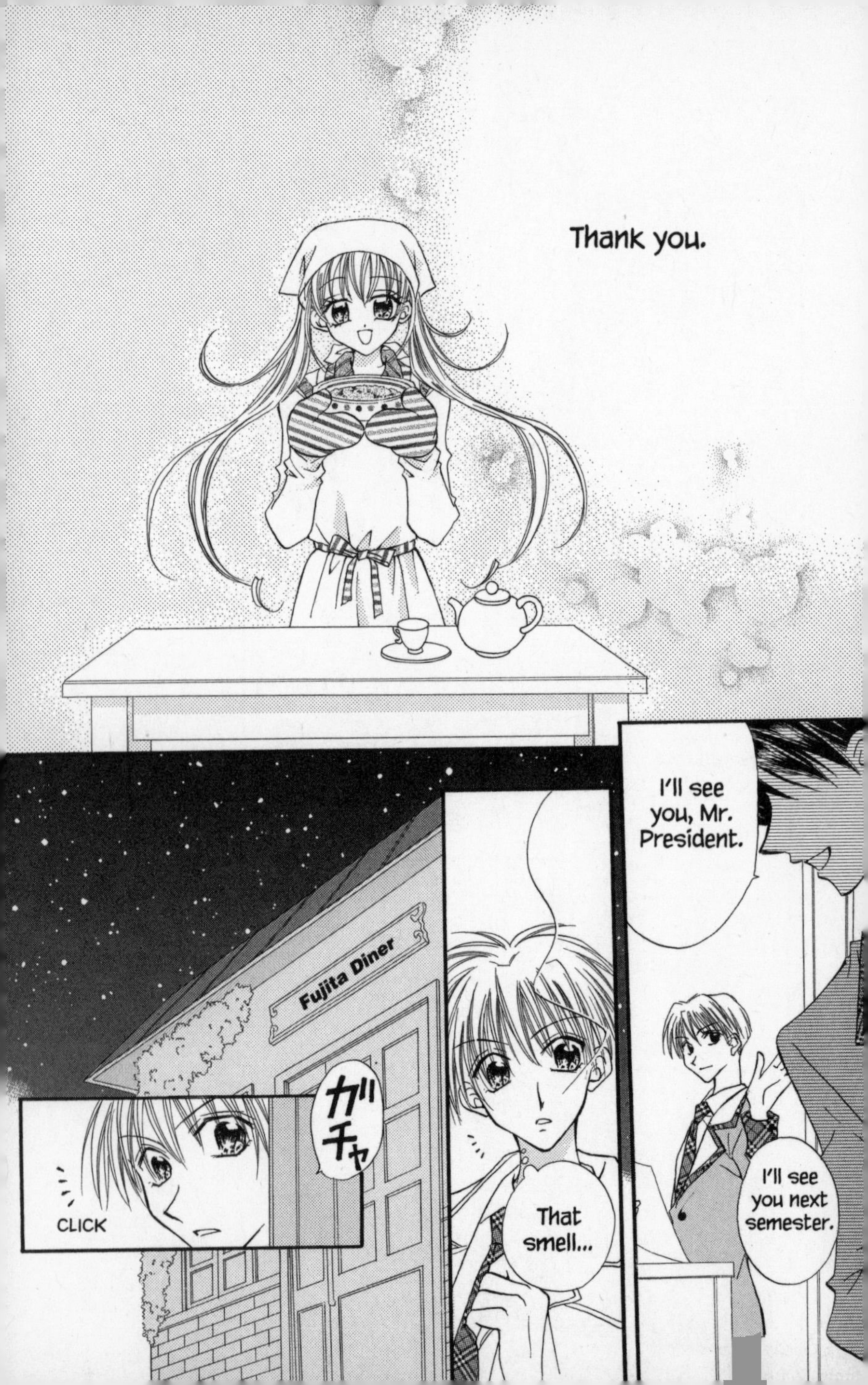
Thank you.
I'll see you, Mr. President.
I'll see you next semester.
That smell...
Fujita Diner
ガチャ
CLICK

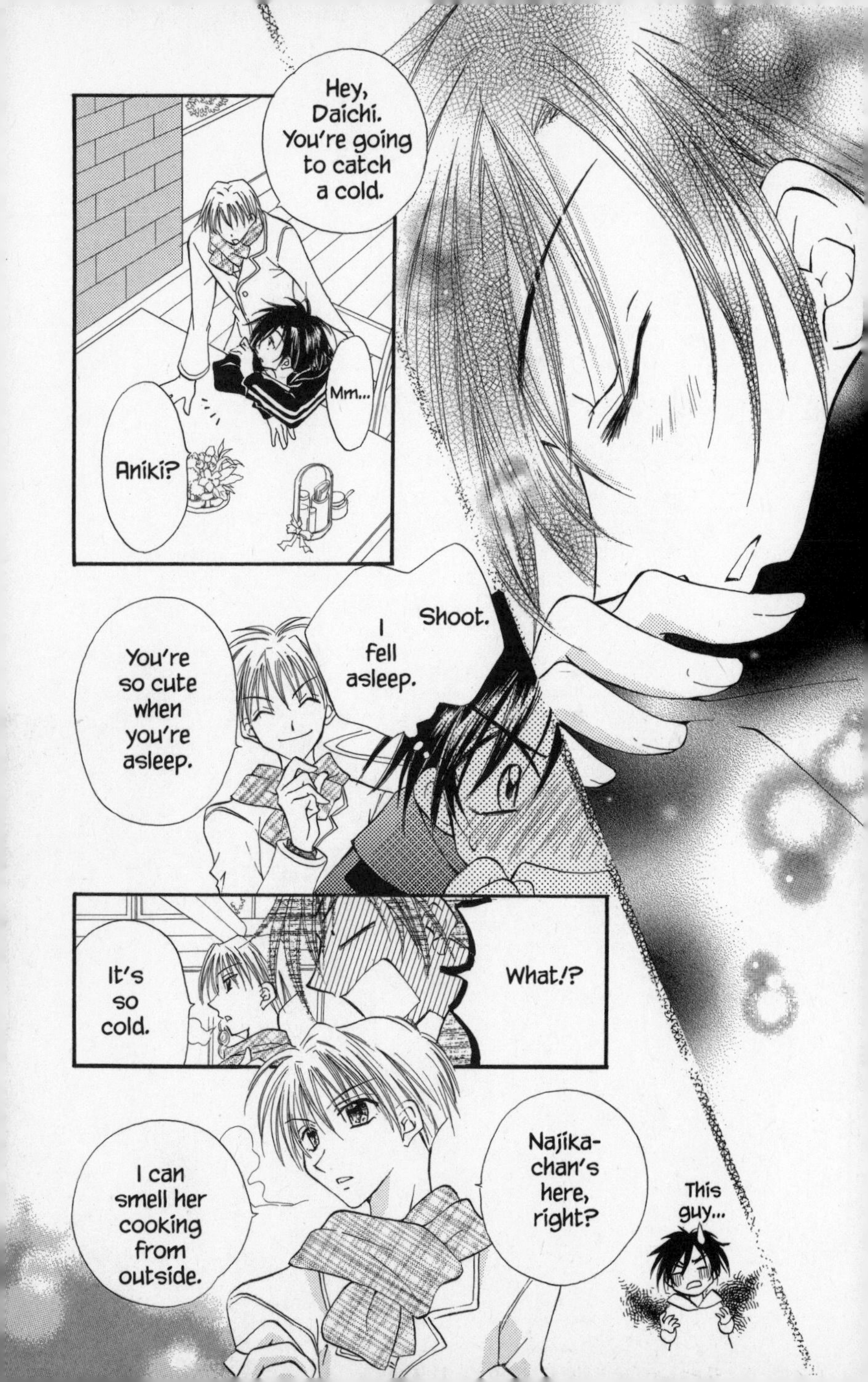
Hey, Daichi. You're going to catch a cold.
Mm...
Aniki?
Shoot. I fell asleep.
You're so cute when you're asleep.
What!?
It's so cold.
Najika-chan's here, right?
I can smell her cooking from outside.
This guy...

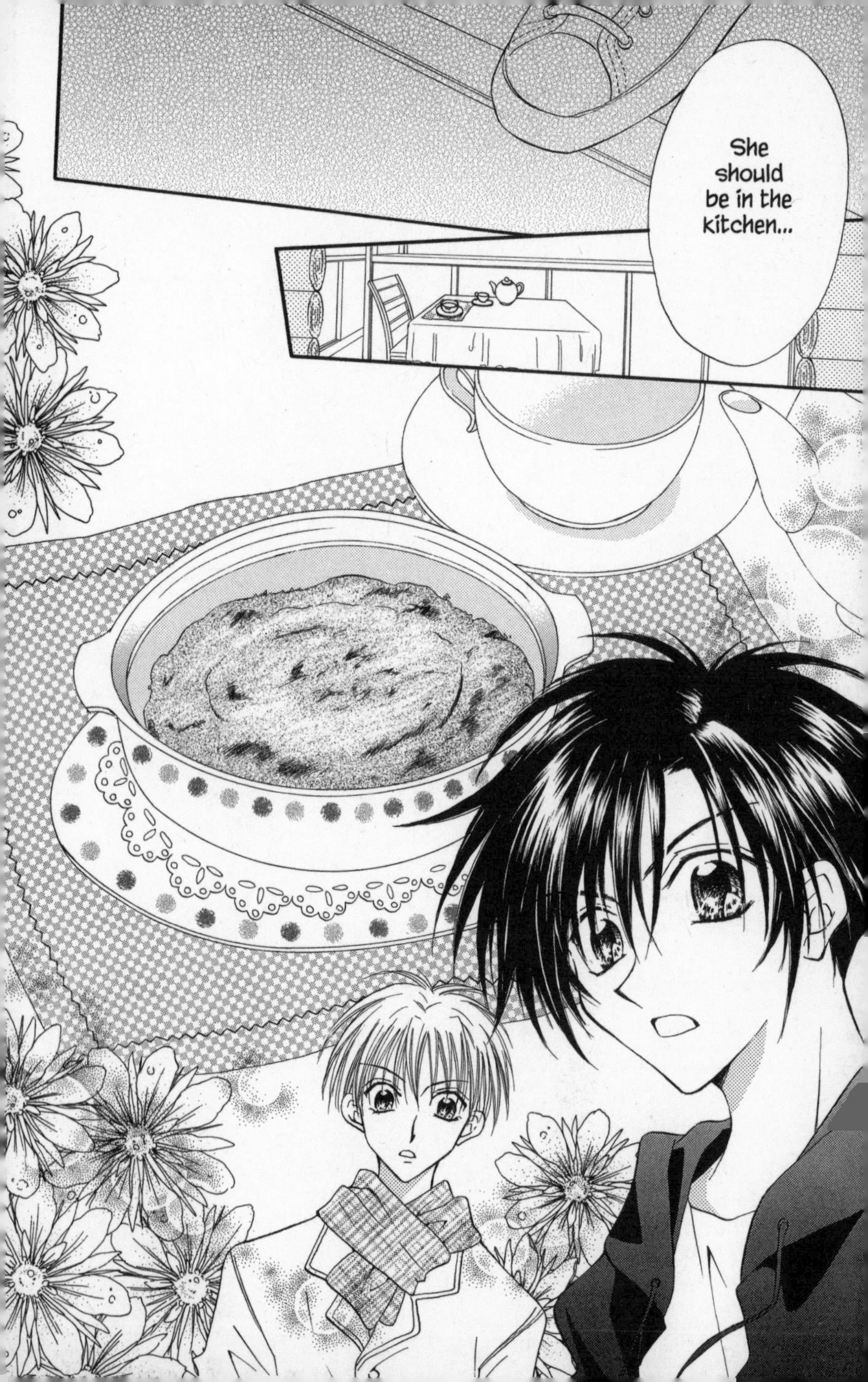
She should be in the kitchen...

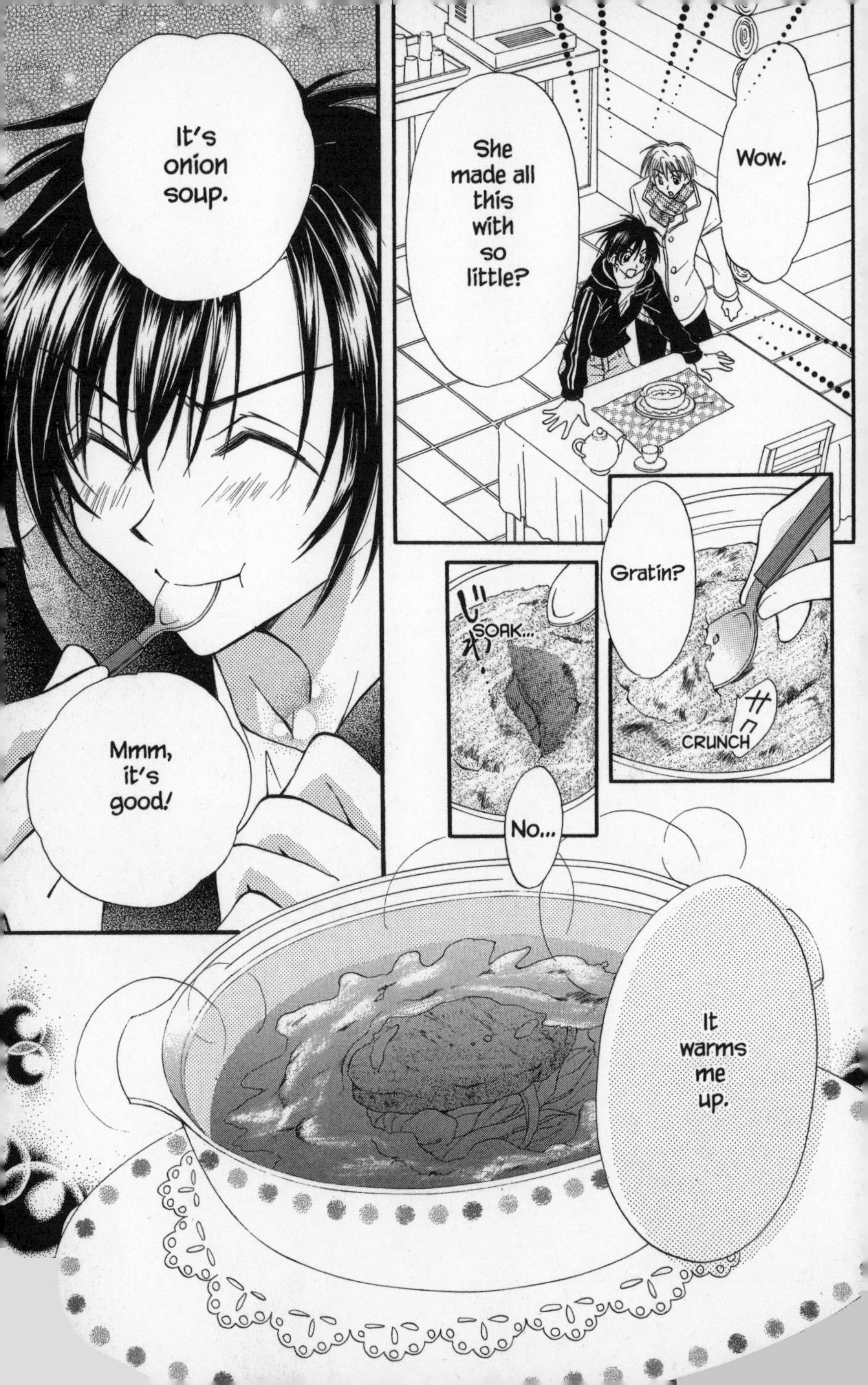
Wow.
She made all this with so little?
Gratin?
CRUNCH
SOAK...
It's onion soup.
Mmm, it's good!
No...
It warms me up.

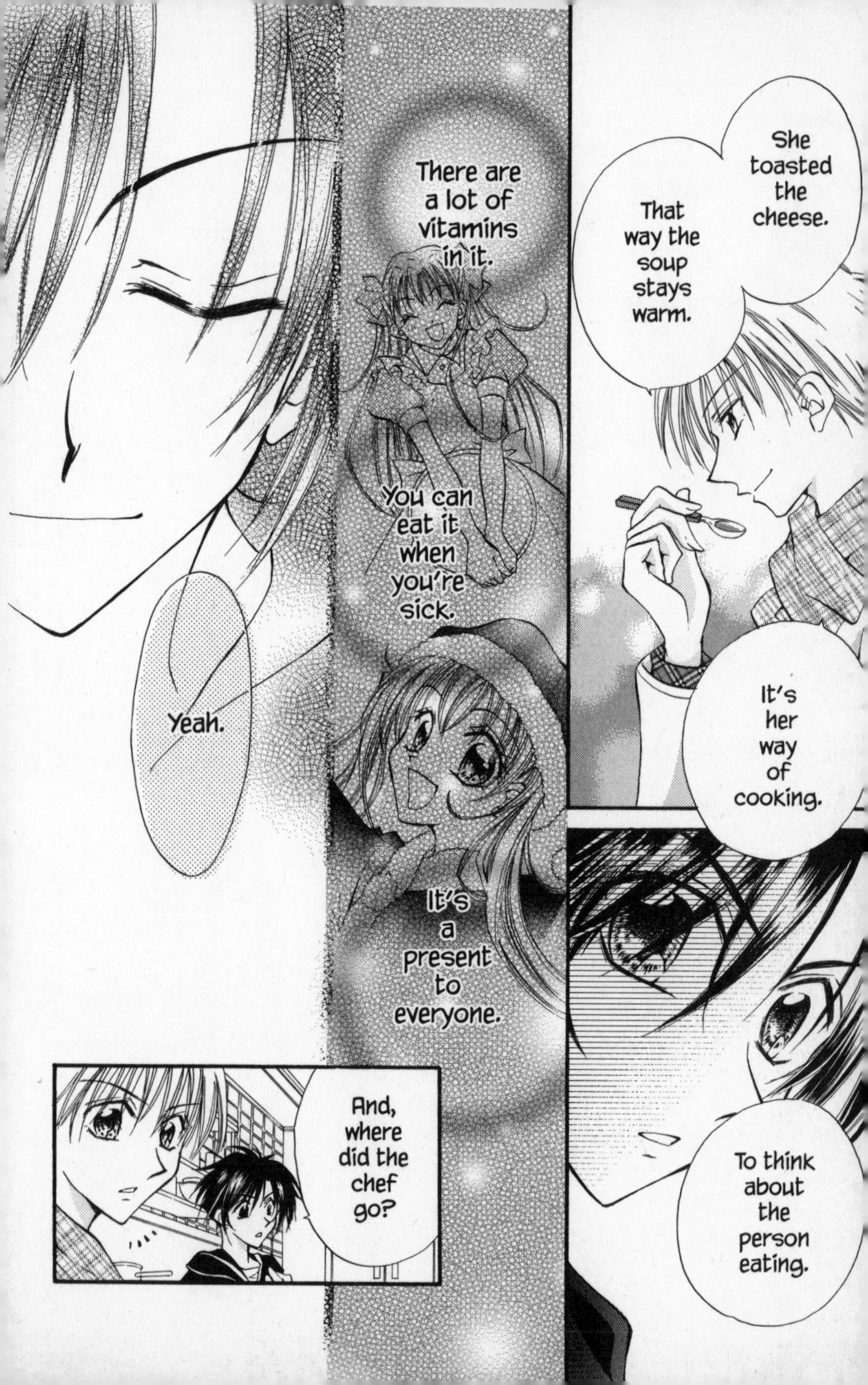
She toasted the cheese.
That way the soup stays warm.
It's her way of cooking.
To think about the person eating.
There are a lot of vitamins in it.
You can eat it when you're sick.
It's a present to everyone.
Yeah.
And, where did the chef go?

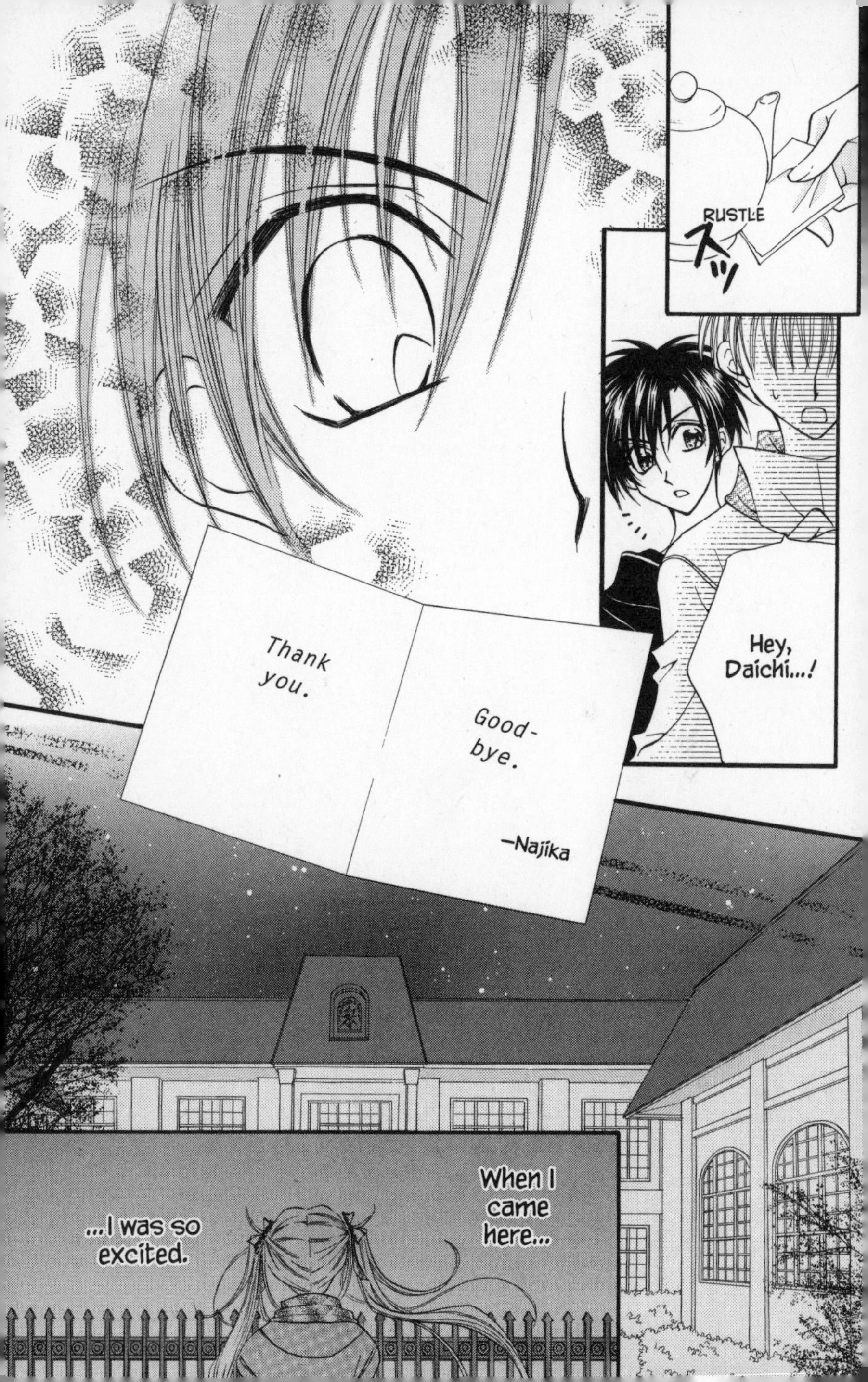
RUSTLE
スッ
Hey, Daichi...!
Thank you.
Good-bye.
—Najika
When I came here...
...I was so excited.

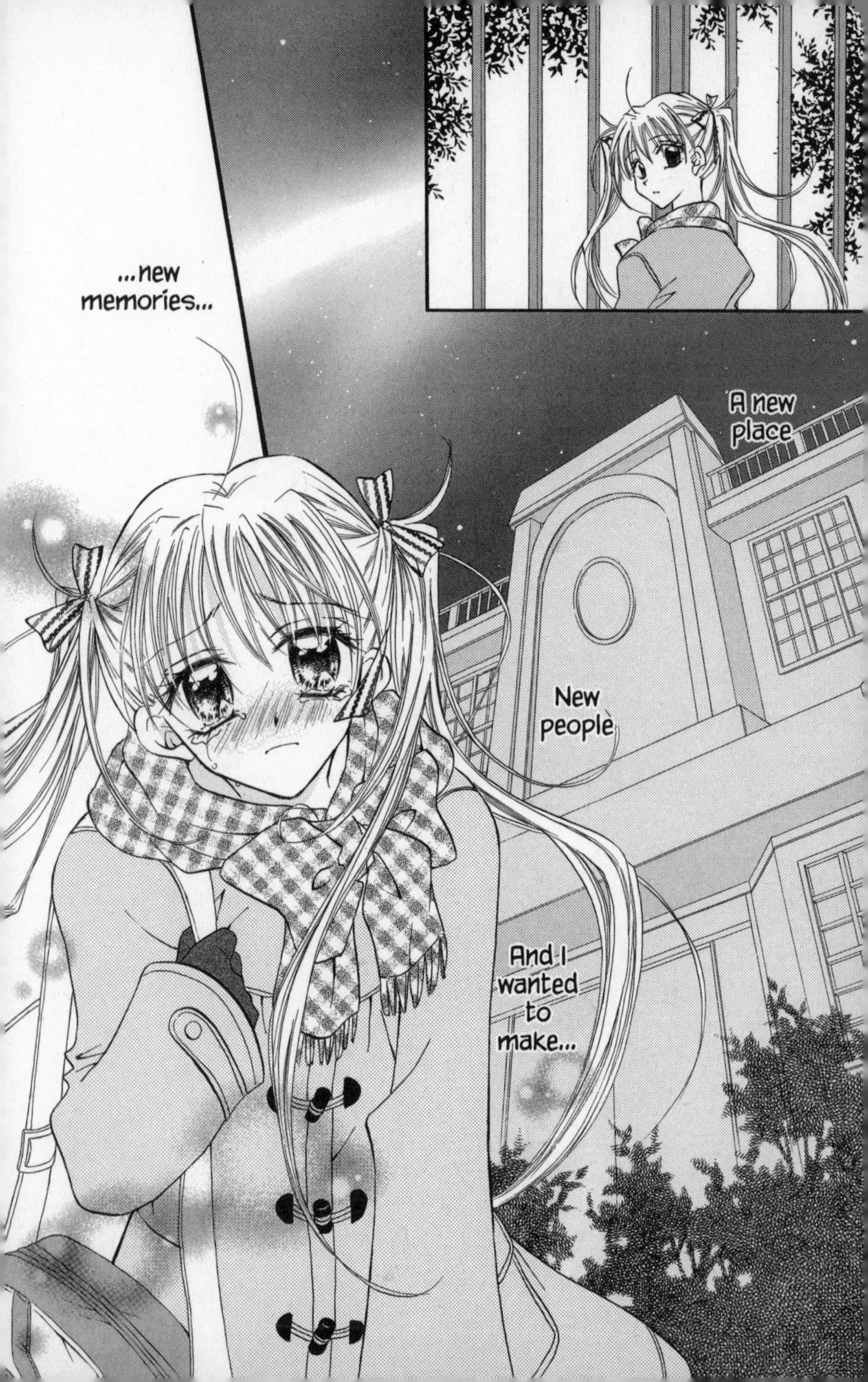
A new place
New people
And I wanted to make...
...new memories...

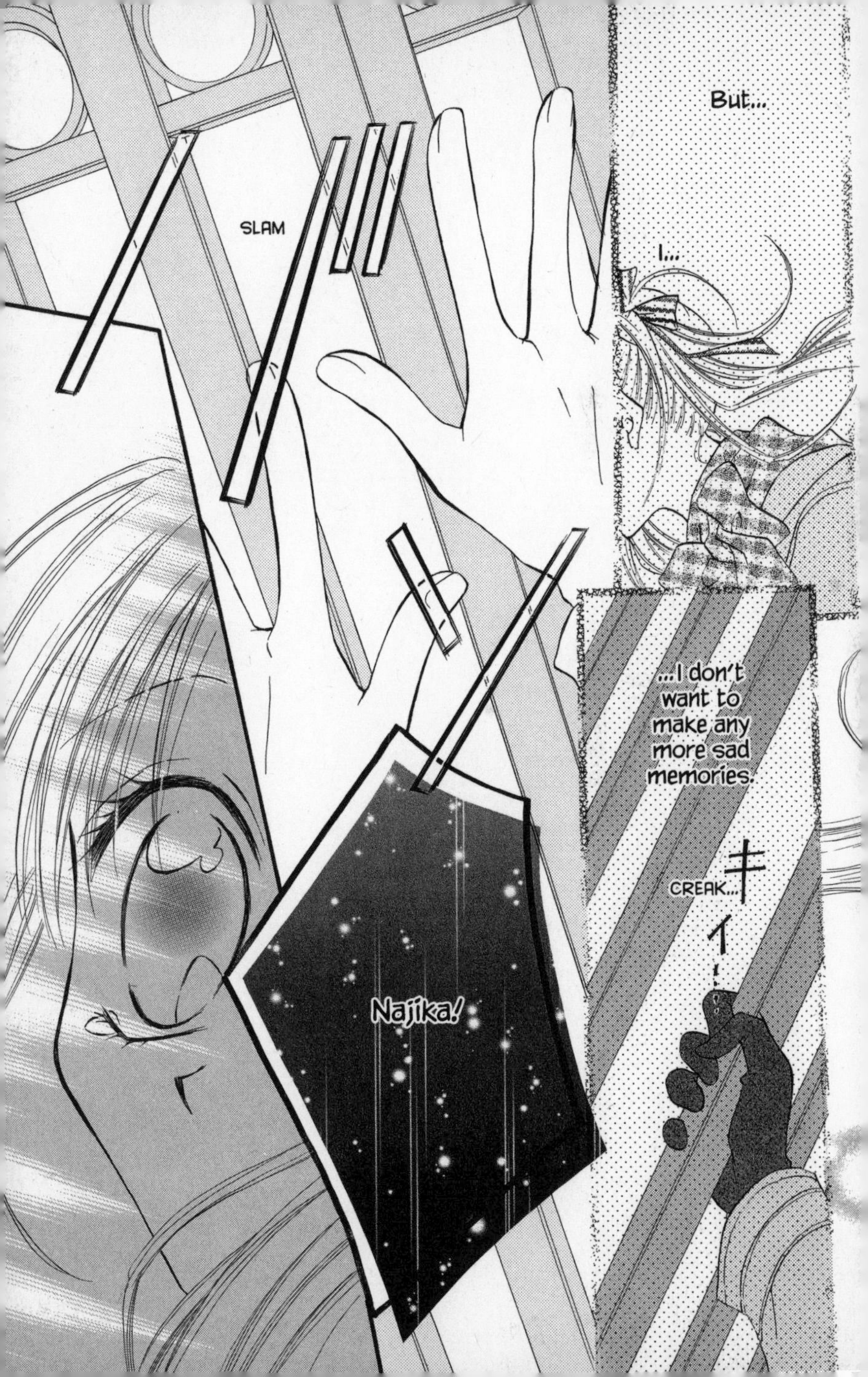
But...
I...
...I don't want to make any more sad memories.
キイ…
CREAK...
SLAM
Najika!

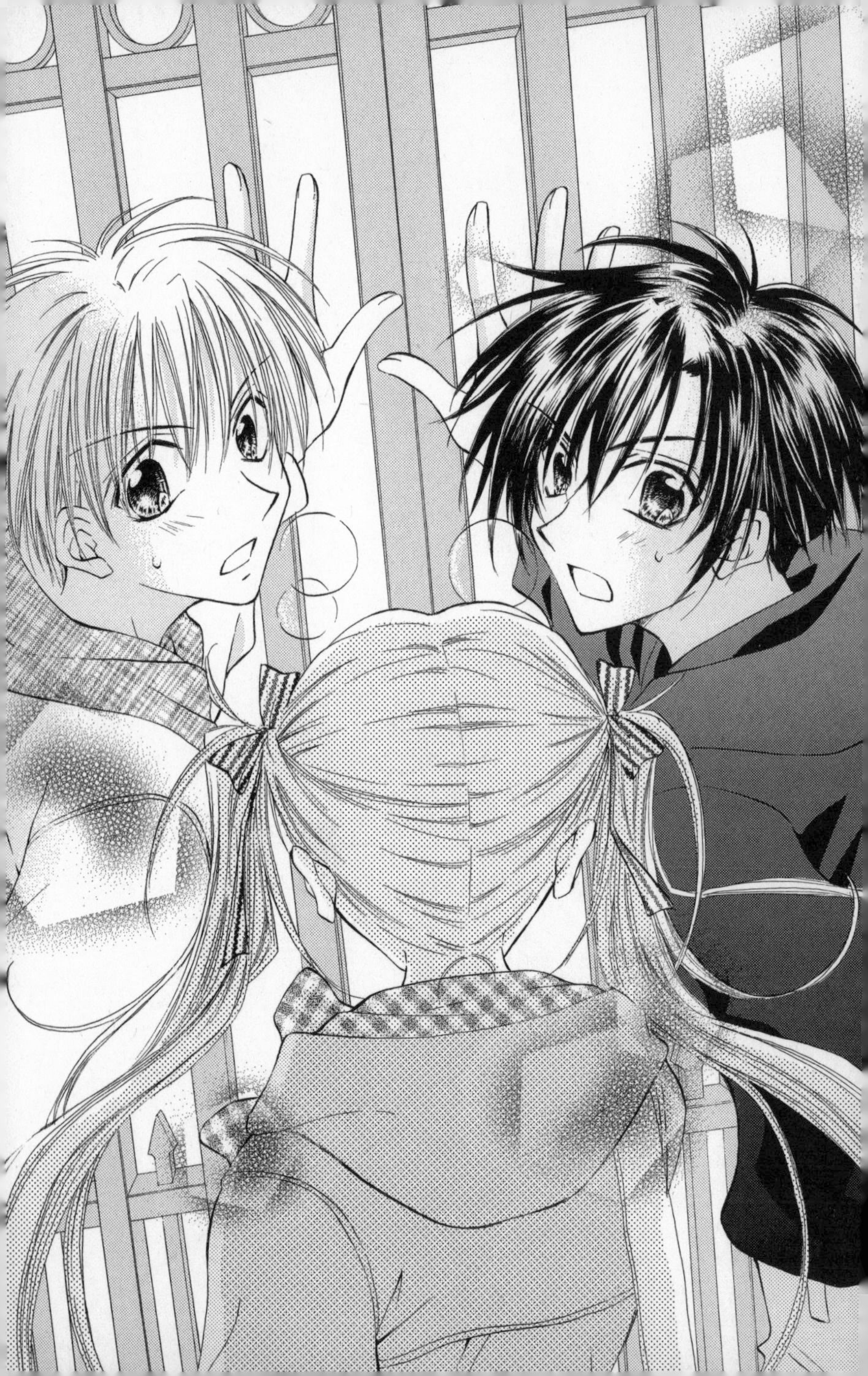

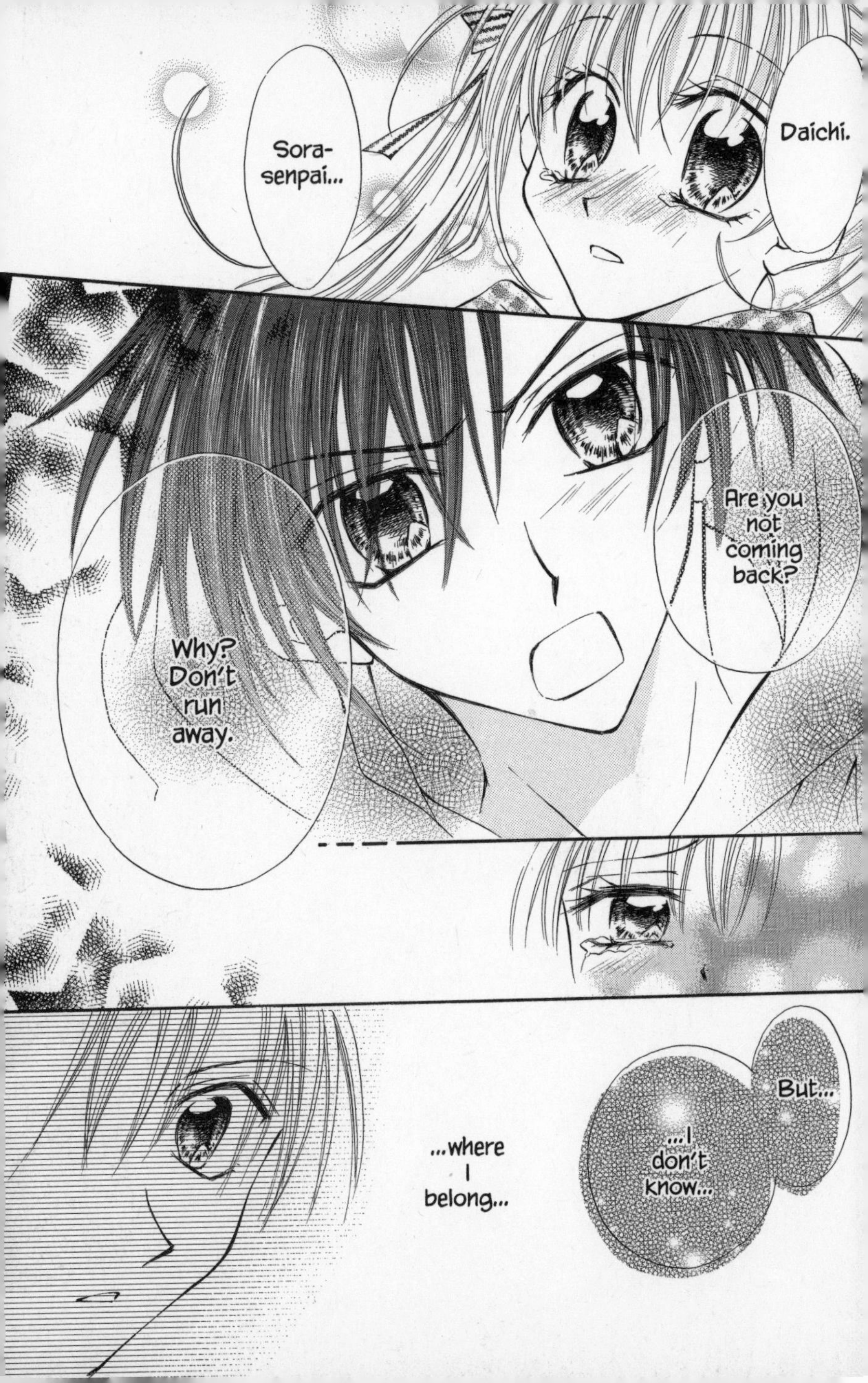
Daichi.
Sora-senpai...
Are you not coming back?
Why? Don't run away.
But...
...I don't know...
...where I belong...

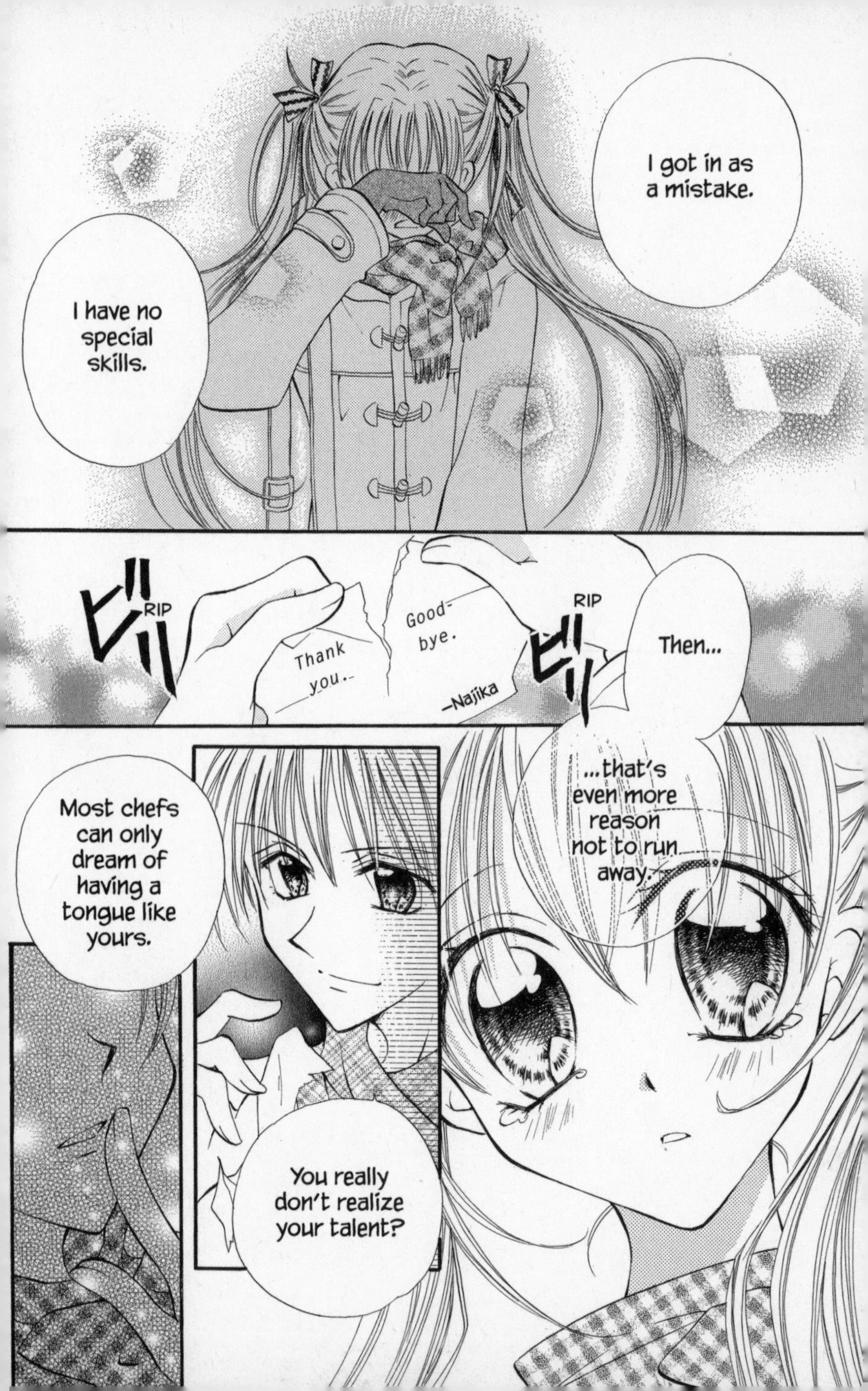
I got in as a mistake.
I have no special skills.
Then...
ビリ RIP
Good-bye.
Thank you...
—Najika
ビリ RIP
...that's even more reason not to run away.
Most chefs can only dream of having a tongue like yours.
You really don't realize your talent?

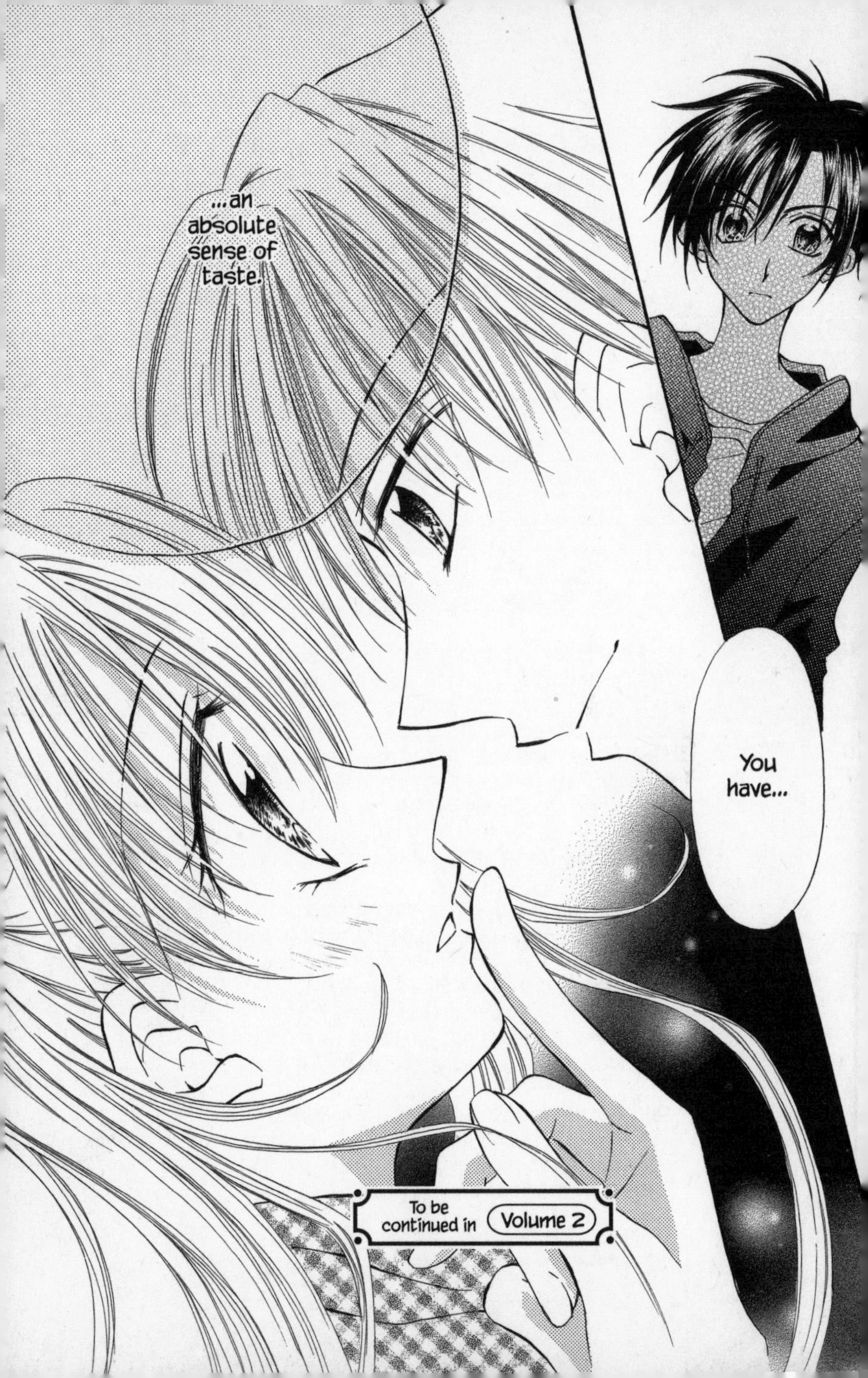
You have...
...an absolute sense of taste.
To be continued in Volume 2

Thank you
Maruyama-sama
Shobayashi-sama
Marimo-sama
Kishimoto-sama

Yay! Volume 1

All the food that appears in Kitchen
Princess comes from Miyuki-sensei, who
sends pictures. I use those to draw the good
food. It looks so delicious, I just want to run
to her house and eat! The other day, I guess
she heard my wishes, and I received the real
thing (it comes in Volume 2 ♥).

It was so good, I finished it immediately.

It's my first time doing manga with a script,
but Miyuki-sensei took my suggestions, too.
Hagio-sensei being an old lady, and the design
for the Diner chef (originally an old lady who
looked like Hagio-sensei, but I made it into a
rugged man) was all me. She was very open-
minded, and I am so grateful for that.

And I'm also grateful to all my readers!!
I am very, very behind in responding. But I will,
so please don't give up on me. ♥ I'll see you
again in Volume 2. ✿

Kitchen Palace

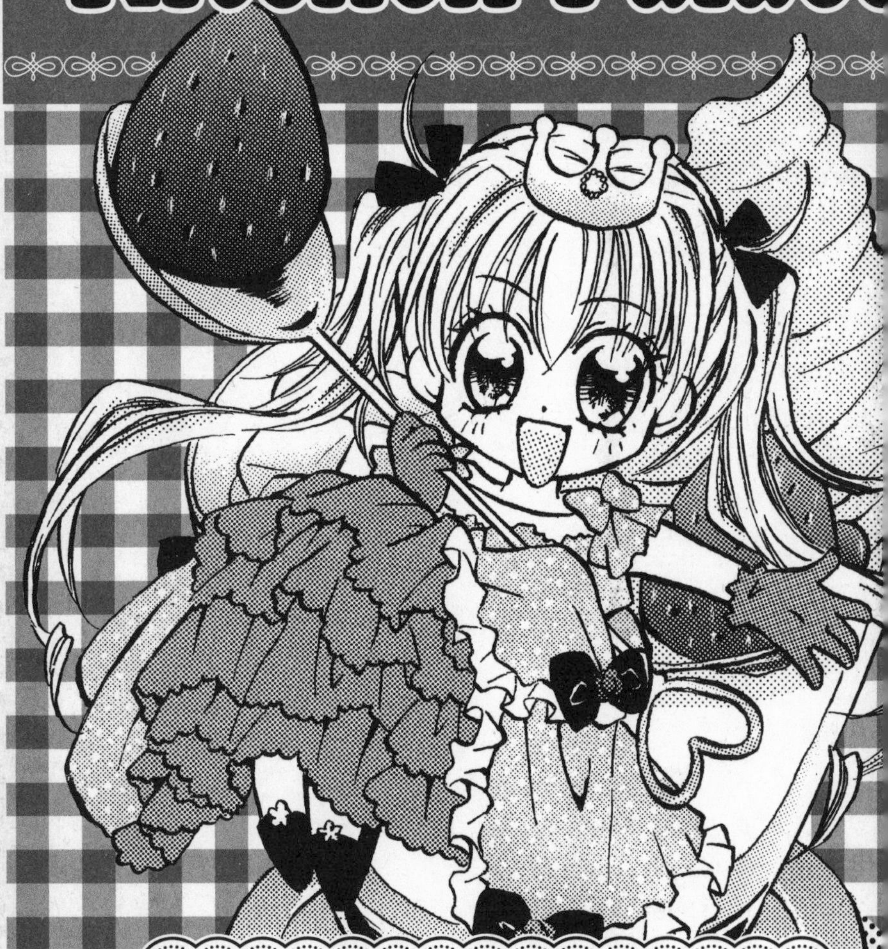

Did you enjoy Kitchen Princess?
In this section, we'll give you the recipes for the food that Najika makes in the story. Please try making them. ♥

Flan in a Cup

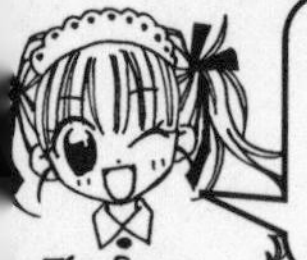

Tip from Najika.

Najika's special flan is made by pouring it in a teacup. Metal flan cups conduct heat and are hard to manage. Making the flan in plastic is easier and it will come out prettier!

Flan: Makes 4 cups of flan. 1¾ cups milk, 5 tablespoons sugar, 3 eggs, a little bit of vanilla. Caramel Sauce: 3 tablespoons sugar, 1 tablespoon water

How to make

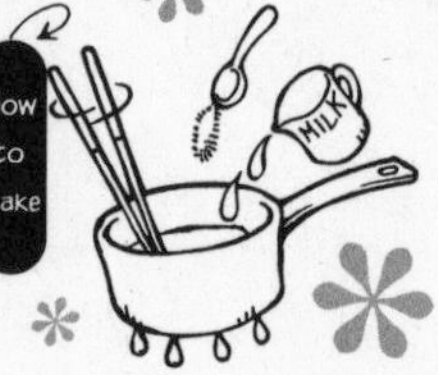

MILK

1. Put milk on low heat and add sugar. Stir well and when the sugar melts, stop the heat and cool for a minute. Make sure you don't let the milk boil.

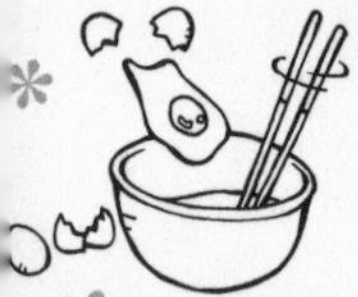

2. Break the eggs in a bowl and stir well.

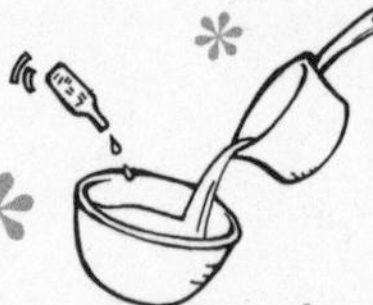

3. Slowly pour the milk from step 1 into the bowl from step 2 and stir. Add some vanilla.

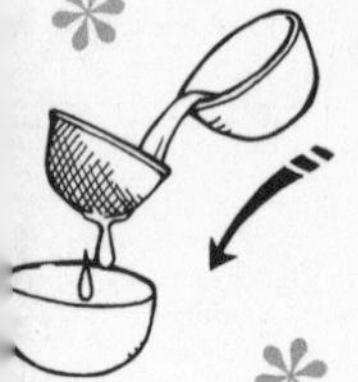

4. Pour the mix from step 3 through a strainer. This makes the flan smoother.

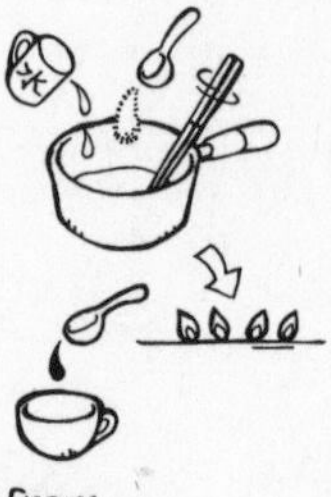

5. Make the caramel sauce in a small pot. Put the water and sugar in the pot and stir quickly over high heat. When it becomes brown, remove from heat and put it into four cups.

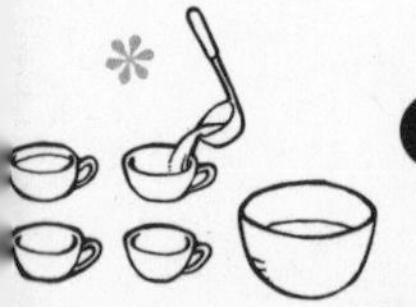

6. Pour the mix from step 4 into the cups over the caramel sauce.

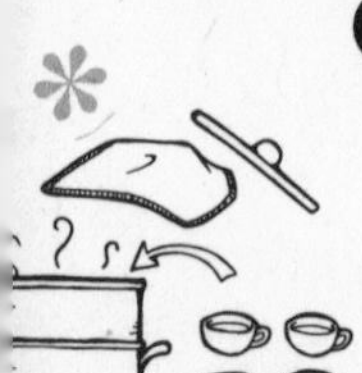

7. Fill a pot with water and put a steamer above it. When the water starts steaming, stop the heat and put the cups in the steamer. Please be careful not to burn yourself. After 2 to 3 minutes on high heat, lower the heat and steam for another 13 to 15 minutes. When you put it on low heat, move the lid a little so some of the steam will escape. The point is to maintain it on low heat. If you put a towel under the lid, water won't get into the flan.

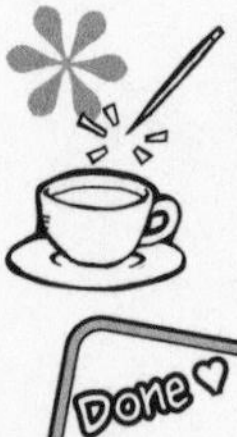

8. Poke a hole in the flan with a toothpick, and if juice doesn't come out, it's done. After it cools, put it in the refrigerator.

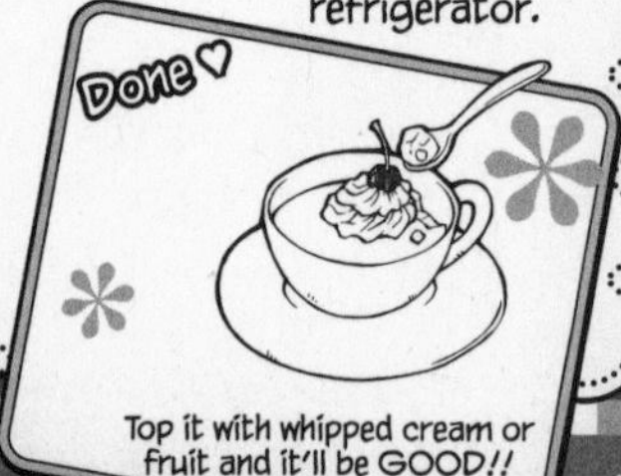

Done♡

Top it with whipped cream or fruit and it'll be GOOD!!

Taramasalata

Tip from Najika.

This time we're making one of Greece's finest dishes, the taramasalata. It's good on sliced French bread or crackers. Depending on the saltiness of the roe, you can adjust the amount of salt used.

Taramasalata Serves two people.
1 medium-sized potato, 1 roe, 2 tablespoons mayonnaise, 1 teaspoon olive oil, 1 teaspoon lemon juice, some salt and pepper

How to make

1. Wash the potato and wrap it in Saran Wrap. Microwave it for 5 minutes. It is ready when you can poke a bamboo stick through it.

2. Peel the potato while it's still hot. Make sure you don't burn yourself! Put the potato in a bowl and crush it with a fork.

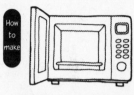

3. Cut a slit in the middle of the roe and scoop out the insides with a spoon. Pour lemon juice on it and throw away the roe skin. If you wra the cutting board with Saran Wrap it won't get dirty.

olive oil
mayonnaise

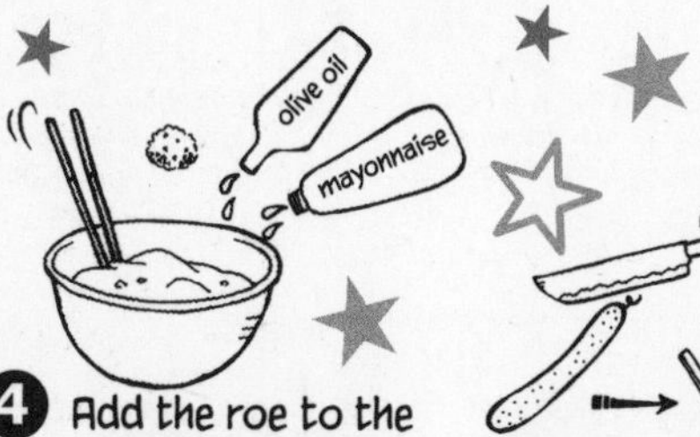

4. Add the roe to the bowl from step 2, along with the mayonnaise, olive oil, and pepper. Stir. Salt to taste, and then you're done!

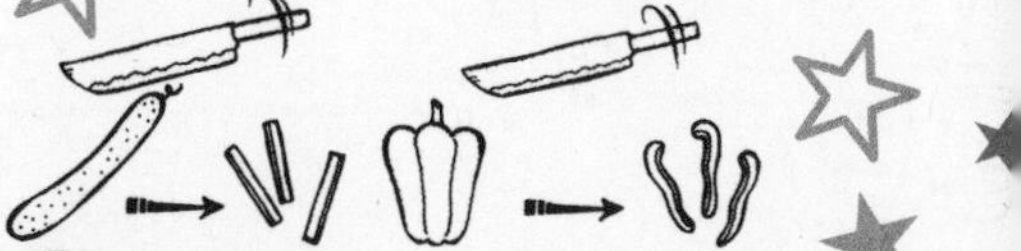

5. You can cut cucumbers or red peppers and lay them on a plate and put the taramasalata in the middle. Add basil or mint to make it pretty.

Taramasalata goes well with various vegetables. You can choose your favorite to eat with it!

Rainbow Jelly

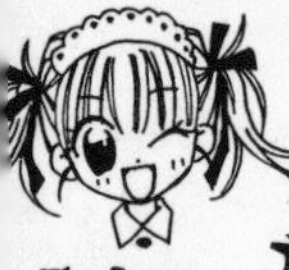

Tip from Najika.

This is jelly that you can enjoy in various flavors and colors. You can choose your favorite juices to use. It'll be delicious if you top it with fruit, too. ♥

Rainbow Jelly Makes eight glasses. 1 cup each of five different juices (grape, orange, melon, grapefruit, etc). *Try to choose different-colored juices. 5 bags gelatin, 2 teaspoons granulated sugar for each juice. *Adjust the sugar according to the sweetness of the juice

How to make

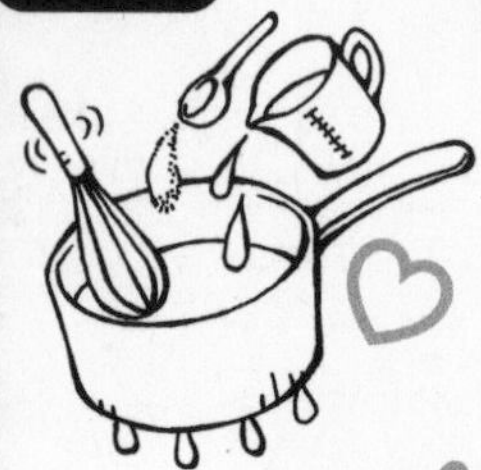

1. In a small pot, add 1 cup juice over low heat. When it warms up, add the granulated sugar and stir. When the sugar melts, stop the heat. Make sure you don't let the mix boil.

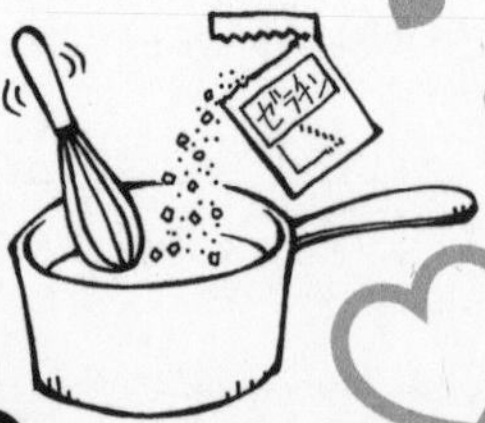
ゼラチン

2. Put gelatin in the pot and stir until it is completely melted.

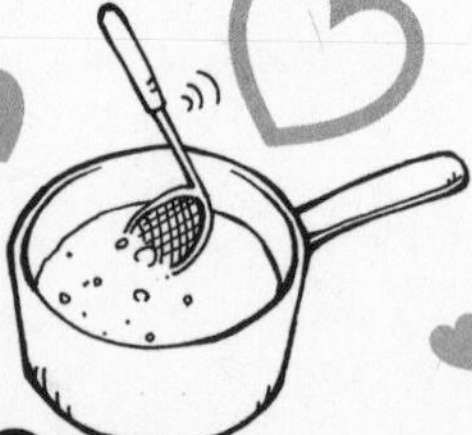

3. When you stir it, white foam will form, so remove it with a ladle. The jelly becomes smoother with this step.

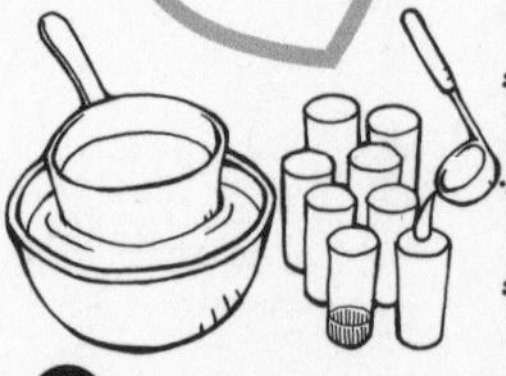

4. Put the pot from step 3 in a bowl filled with ice to cool. When the mix is cool, pour it into eight glasses.

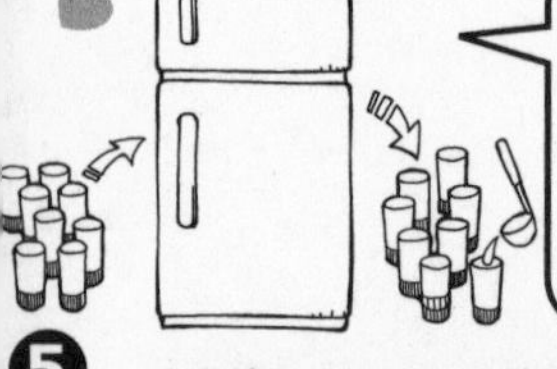

If you repeat the steps, you'll get a colorful jelly in your glass. If you want to make less, you can make each jelly with half the ingredients.

5. Put the glasses in the refrigerator and leave them in for about an hour. When the jelly hardens, you repeat the steps and add the different juices one at a time in the glass.

A rainbow is seven colors, but we made it with five colors this time for simplicity. If you get better at it, please try seven jelly colors!

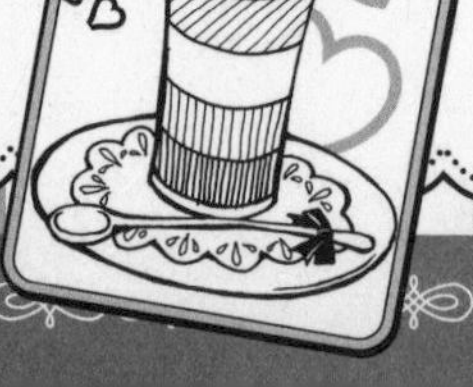
Done♡

Christmas Cookies

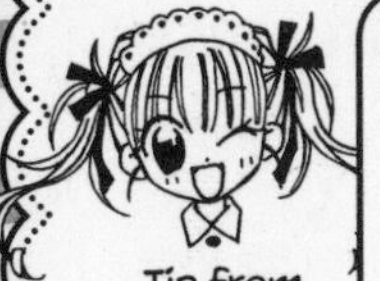

Tip from Najika.

Try making cookies! You can make them into ornaments like I did. If you put frosting on the cookies, they become colorful and pretty!

Christmas Cookies

Makes about 20 cookies.
½ cup soft flour,
½ cup sugar, 1 small egg,
7 tablespoons butter

How to make

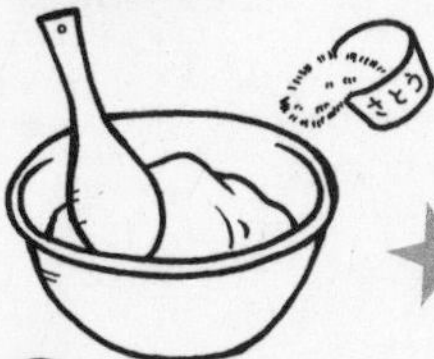

1. Soften the butter at room temperature and crush it in a bowl with a wooden spoon. Add sugar and stir more.

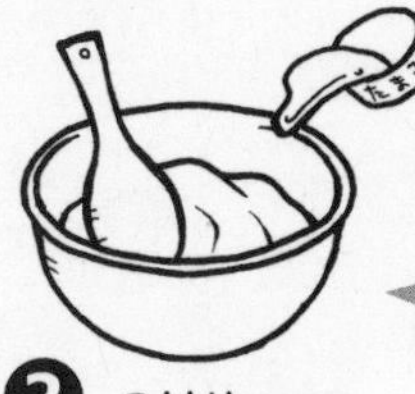

2. Add the egg and mix.

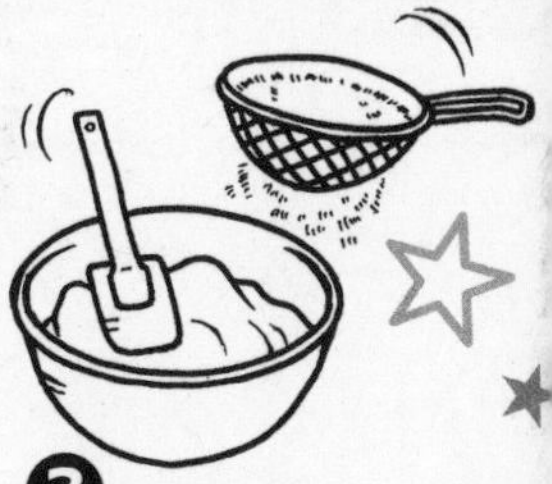

3. Sieve the flour into the mix and stir. It is ready when the white flour chunks are gone.

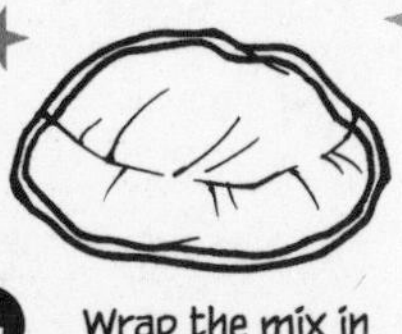

4. Wrap the mix in saran wrap and put it in the refrigerator for over 30 minutes.

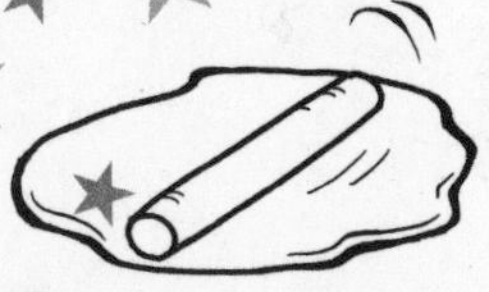

5. Pour some flour on the board and put the mix from step 4 onto it and flatten it with a rolling pin.

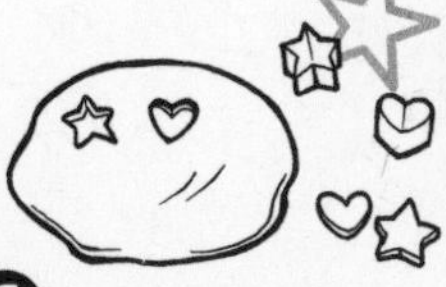

6. Cut out pieces using cookie cutters.

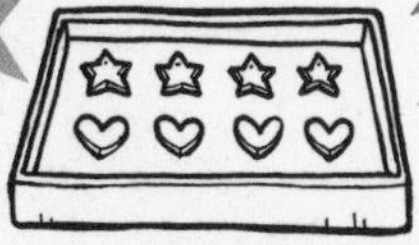

7. Lay out the pieces on a cookie sheet covered with wax paper and bake in the oven at 180 degrees Celsius (approx. 350 F) for 12 to 13 minutes. After it is baked, let cool.

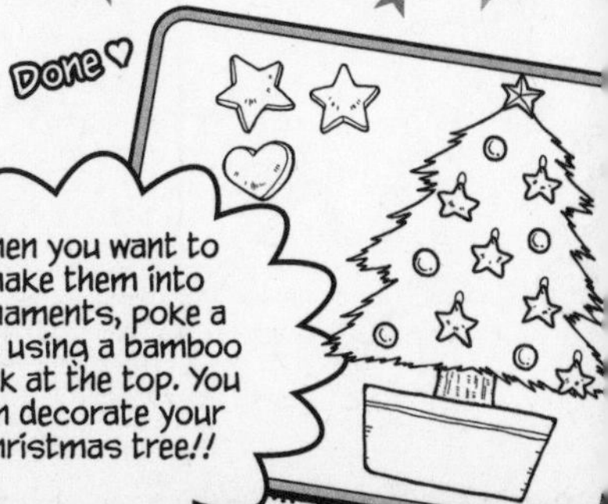
Done♡

When you want to make them into ornaments, poke a hole using a bamboo stick at the top. You can decorate your Christmas tree!!

Onion Gratin Soup

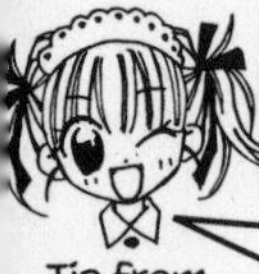

Tip from Najika.

You can make it Japanese style by using mochi instead of French bread. You can eat it New Year's Day.

Onion Gratin Soup

Serves two people. 1 large onion, 1 ½ tablespoons butter, 1¾ cups consommé soup (uses 1 block of consommé), ½ cup shredded cheese, 2 teaspoons grated cheese, 2 slices French bread, some salt and pepper

How to make

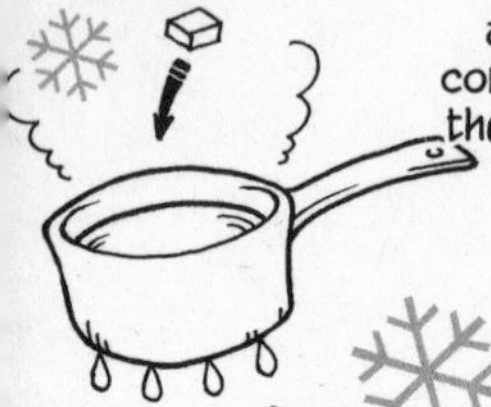

1. Boil 1¾ cups water and add 1 block consommé. Set the soup aside.

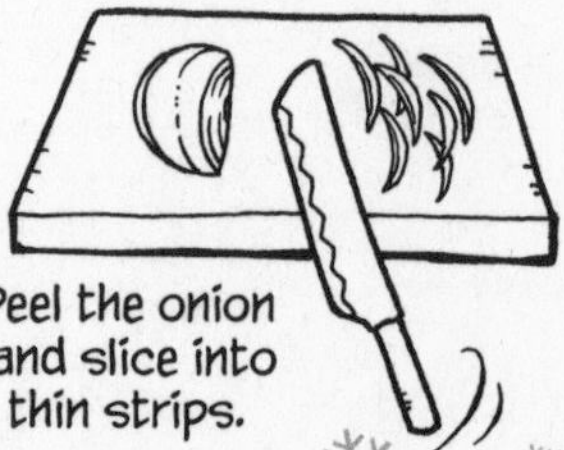

2. Peel the onion and slice into thin strips.

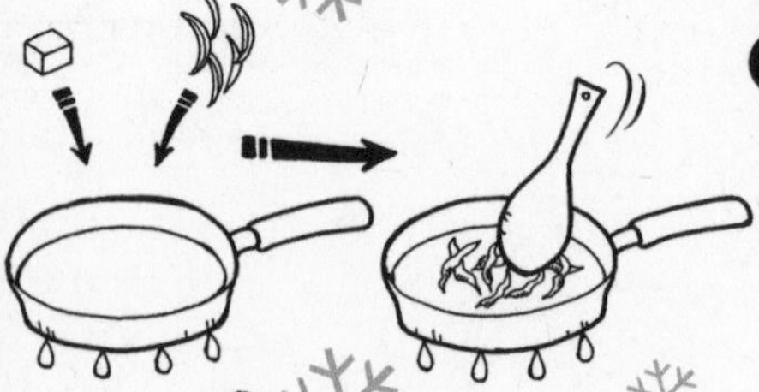

3. Heat the butter on medium in a frying pan. Be careful not to burn the butter. Put the onion in the butter and sauté until the onion turns a dark yellow color. Stir well with a wooden spoon so it won't burn. Sautéing it well here makes the sweetness come out of the onion!

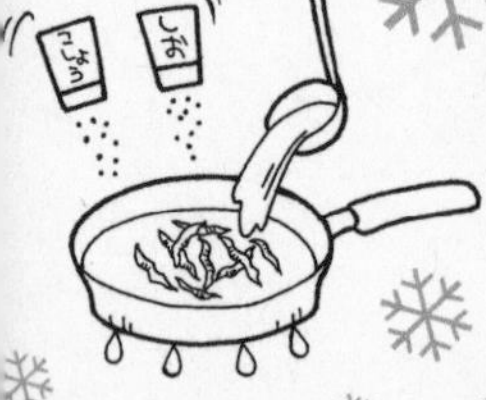

4. Add the consommé soup to the frying pan and stir. Add salt and pepper to taste.

This is a classic French dish that can be made out of simple ingredients. Eat it while it's hot!

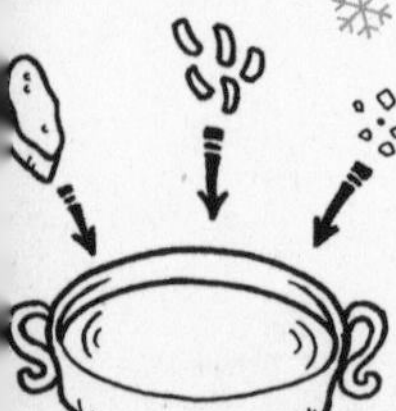

5. Put the soup into a heat-resistant bowl or cup. Put the French bread and shredded cheese on top, and shake some grated cheese on top of that. Put it in an oven toaster and toast for about 4 to 5 minutes. When it turns golden brown, it's done!

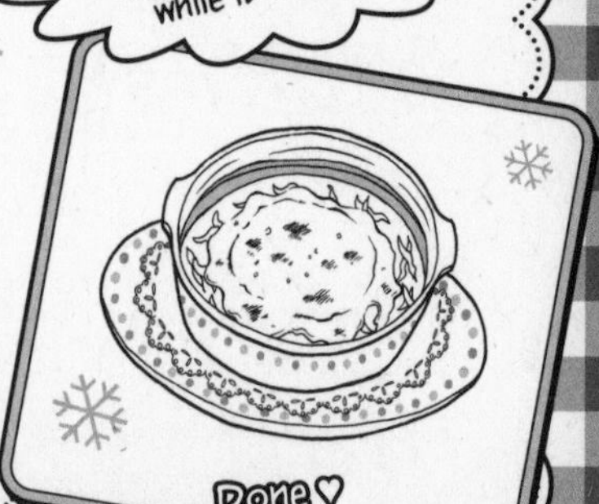
Done ♡

Kitchen Princess
From the Writer

Thank you for reading Volume 1 of Kitchen Princess! I am the writer, Miyuki Kobayashi. Usually I write novels for teen girls under the Kodansha X Bunko Teen's Heart label. There are over 100 volumes under this label, so please look for them in bookstores and the library! You might find something you like.

But back to *Kitchen Princess*. I usually think of the character's name first, and then the story. I really like Najika's name! It's ethnically ambiguous and the seven colors of the rainbow make it very nature-like. It's the perfect weird name for a mysterious new student. And then I made the two boys' names to match hers, by naming them "Daichi" and "Sora." I wanted Najika to connect the two boys. Please tell me which one you like...earth or sky? I'll be waiting for your letters!

Finally, I would like to thank Ando-sensei, my editor Kishimoto-san, and my publisher Nouchi-san. Thank you so much! I'll see you in Volume 2!

TIGHTEN

About the Creator

Natsumi Ando

She was born on January 27th in Aichi prefecture. She won the 19th Nakayoshi Rookie Award in 1994 and debuted as a manga artist. The title she drew was *Headstrong Cinderella*. Some of her other known works are Zodiac P.I. and Wild Heart. Her hobbies include reading, watching movies, and eating delicious food.

Translation Notes

Japanese is a tricky language for most Westerners, and translation is often more art than science. For your edification and reading pleasure, here are notes on some of the places where we could have gone in a different direction in our translation of the work, or where a Japanese cultural reference is used.

Hokkaido, page 6

Hokkaido is located in the northern part of Japan. It is the second largest island and the biggest prefecture.

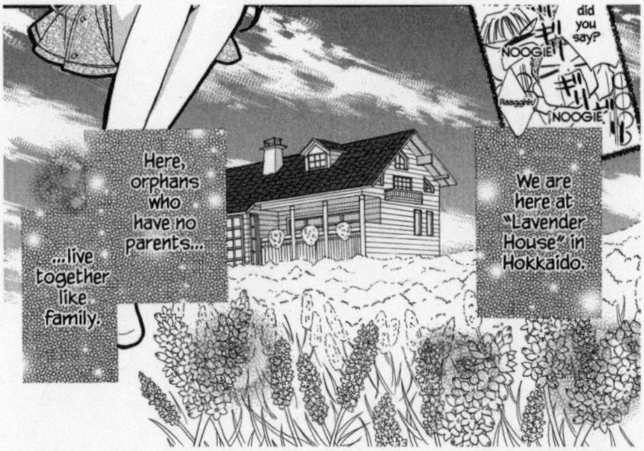
did you say?
NOOGIE
Raagghh!
NOOGIE
We are here at "Lavender House" in Hokkaido.
Here, orphans who have no parents...
...live together like family.

Hacchou Miso, page 33

Hacchou miso is a special type of red miso made with soybeans only, without using bacteria. It is manufactured in Aichi prefecture and is known for its rich taste. The name comes from the village, Hacchou, where it is manufactured.

Nagoya, page 33

Nagoya is the capital of Aichi prefecture, and one of the bigger cities in Japan. It is located just between Tokyo and Kyoto on the eastern side of Japan.

Tempura, page 33

Tempura is a Japanese dish that consists of seafood or vegetables dipped in a batter and deep-fried.

***Aniki*, page 75**

Aniki is a term for "older brother," usually used by boys (or girls who are tomboys) in their younger teens. It is less honorific than "onee-chan" and "onee-san."

Good.
Aniki.

***Okayu*, page 97**

Okayu is the Japanese word for "rice porridge." Because it is easy to digest and because it makes your body warm, it is a common thing to eat when one is sick.

ホカホカ
PIRING HOT
Here's your okayu.

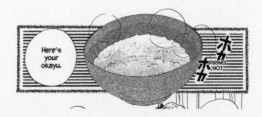

...A
rainbow
will
connect...

Rainbow, earth, and
sky, page 105

Najika's name, in Japanese characters, contains
the character for "rainbow." That is why there
are several references to rainbows in the manga.
Daichi's name means "earth," and Sora's name means
"sky." In this panel, Najika wants to be the rainbow
that connects the earth and sky.

DisneySea, page 121

DisneySea is part of the Tokyo
Disney Resort, located right
next to Tokyo Disneyland. It
is more adult-oriented than
Disney and has a water theme.

Mochi, page 186

Mochi is the Japanese word for "rice cake," and it is usually eaten on New Year's Day. It is very sticky and elderly people often choke on it.

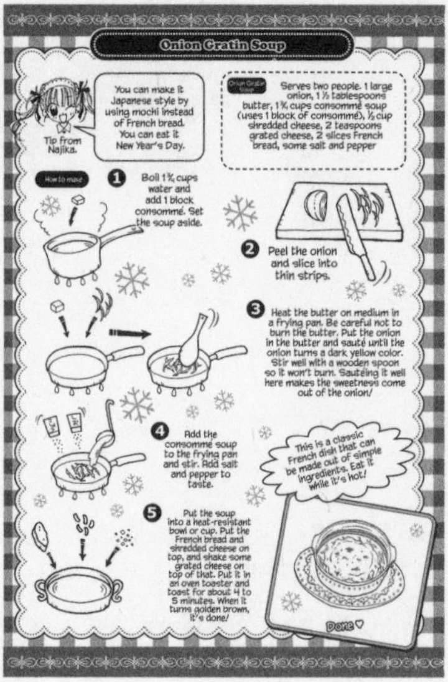
Onion Gratin Soup
You can make it Japanese style by using mochi instead of French bread. You can eat it New Year's Day.
Tip from Najika.
Serves two people. 1 large onion, 1 ½ tablespoons butter, 1 ¾ cups consommé soup (uses 1 block of consommé), ½ cup shredded cheese, 2 teaspoons grated cheese, 2 slices French bread, some salt and pepper
How to make
1 Boil 1 ¾ cups water and add 1 block consommé. Set the soup aside.
2 Peel the onion and slice into thin strips.
3 Heat the butter on medium in a frying pan. Be careful not to burn the butter. Put the onion in the butter and sauté until the onion turns a dark yellow color. Stir well with a wooden spoon so it won't burn. Sautéing it well here makes the sweetness come out of the onion!
4 Add the consommé soup to the frying pan and stir. Add salt and pepper to taste.
This is a classic French dish that can be made out of simple ingredients. Eat it while it's hot!
5 Put the soup into a heat-resistant bowl or cup. Put the French bread and shredded cheese on top, and shake some grated cheese on top of that. Put it in an oven toaster and toast for about 4 to 5 minutes. When it turns golden brown, it's done!
Done♡

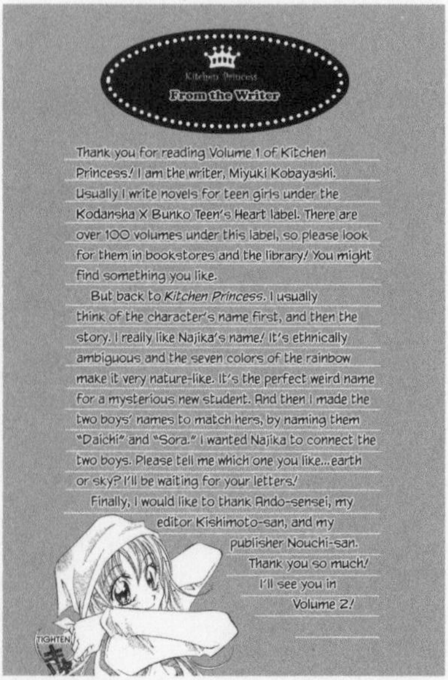
Kitchen Princess
From the Writer
Thank you for reading Volume 1 of Kitchen Princess! I am the writer, Miyuki Kobayashi. Usually I write novels for teen girls under the Kodansha X Bunko Teen's Heart label. There are over 100 volumes under this label, so please look for them in bookstores and the library! You might find something you like.
But back to *Kitchen Princess*. I usually think of the character's name first, and then the story. I really like Najika's name! It's ethnically ambiguous and the seven colors of the rainbow make it very nature-like. It's the perfect weird name for a mysterious new student. And then I made the two boys' names to match hers, by naming them "Daichi" and "Sora." I wanted Najika to connect the two boys. Please tell me which one you like...earth or sky? I'll be waiting for your letters!
Finally, I would like to thank Ando-sensei, my editor Kishimoto-san, and my publisher Nouchi-san. Thank you so much! I'll see you in Volume 2!
TIGHTEN

Najika's name, page 187

Najika's name is a combination of the characters for "seven," "rainbow," and "fragrance."

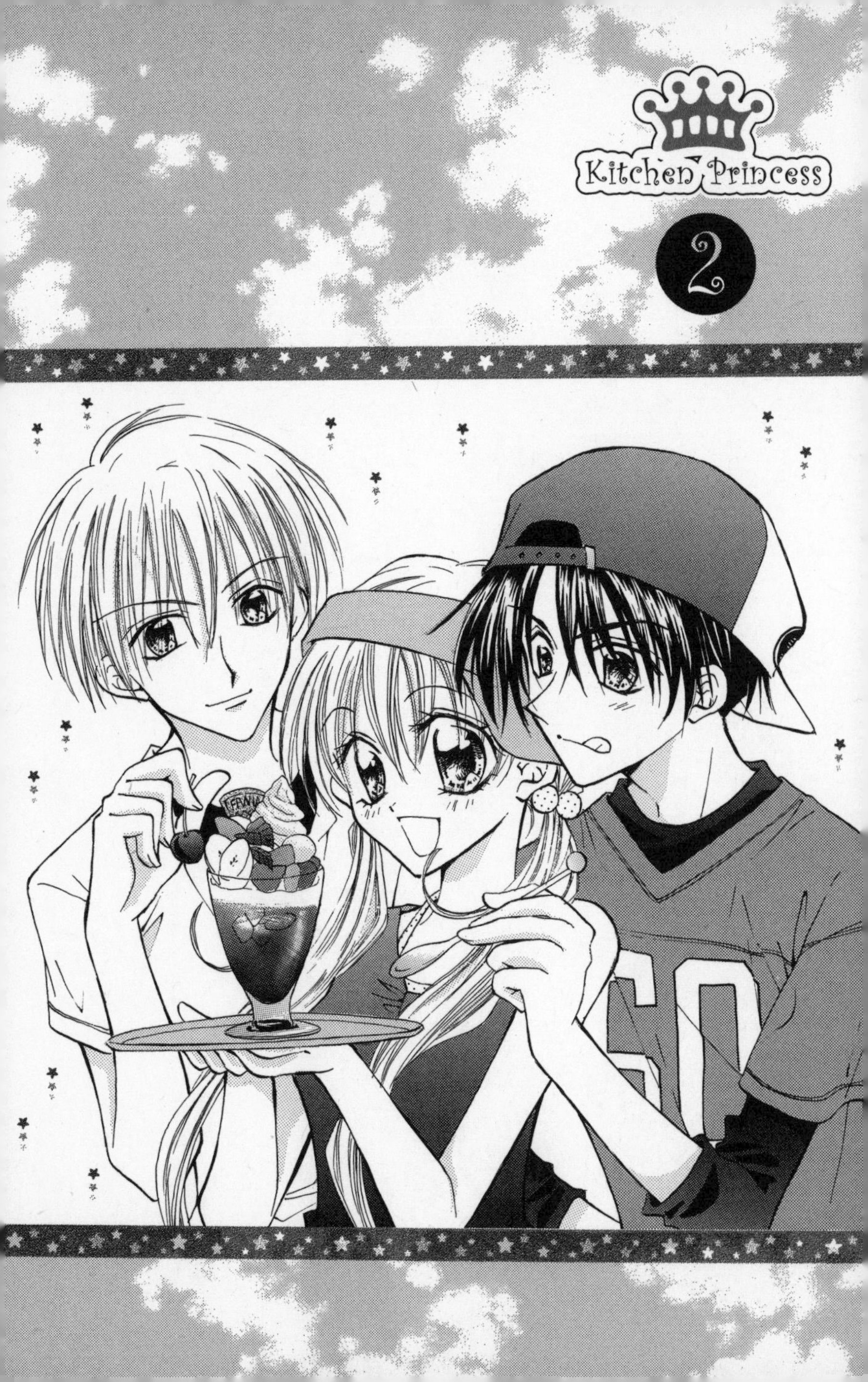
Kitchen Princess
2

Kitchen Princess

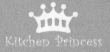

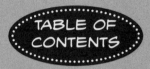

TABLE OF CONTENTS

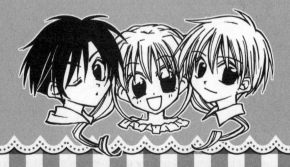

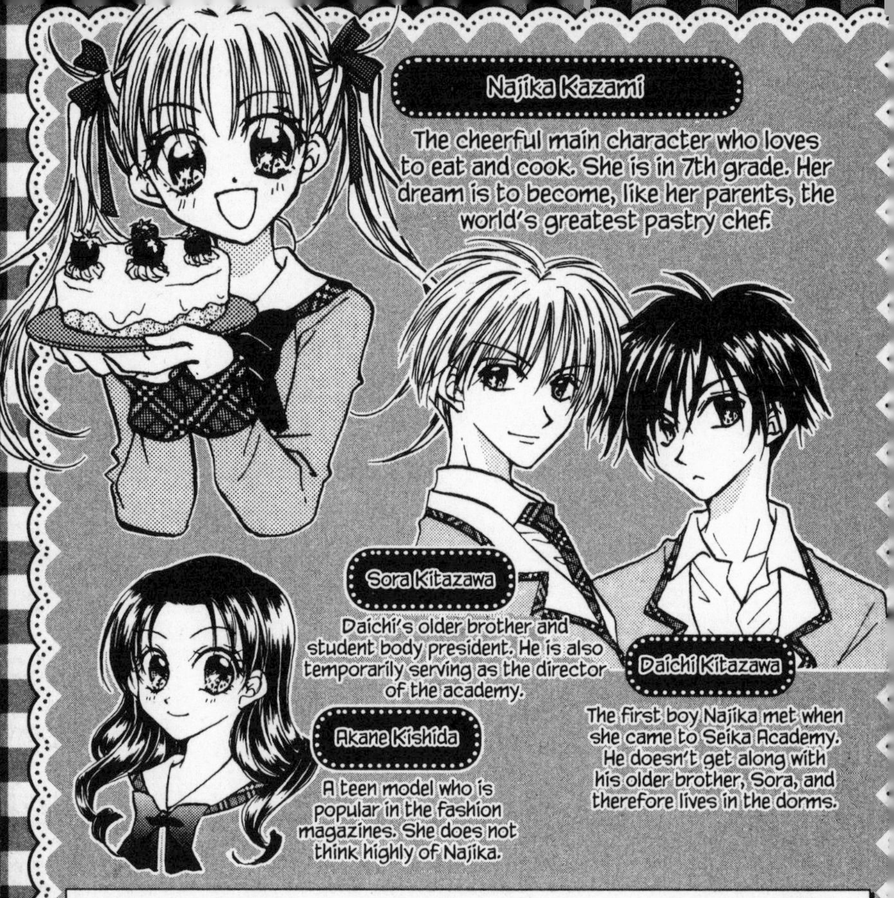
Najika Kazami
The cheerful main character who loves to eat and cook. She is in 7th grade. Her dream is to become, like her parents, the world's greatest pastry chef.
Sora Kitazawa
Daichi's older brother and student body president. He is also temporarily serving as the director of the academy.
Daichi Kitazawa
The first boy Najika met when she came to Seika Academy. He doesn't get along with his older brother, Sora, and therefore lives in the dorms.
Akane Kishida
A teen model who is popular in the fashion magazines. She does not think highly of Najika.

The Story So Far...

Kitchen Princess

Najika lost her parents when she was young and then moved to Lavender House, an orphanage in Hokkaido. She joined Seika Academy in Tokyo to find her Flan Prince, a boy who saved her from drowning when she was young. However, she failed to get along with her classmates because they saw her befriending Sora and Daichi, two popular boys at the academy. Even Akane, who had been nice to her, turned her back on Najika. Depressed, Najika tried to go back home, but Daichi and Sora stopped her.

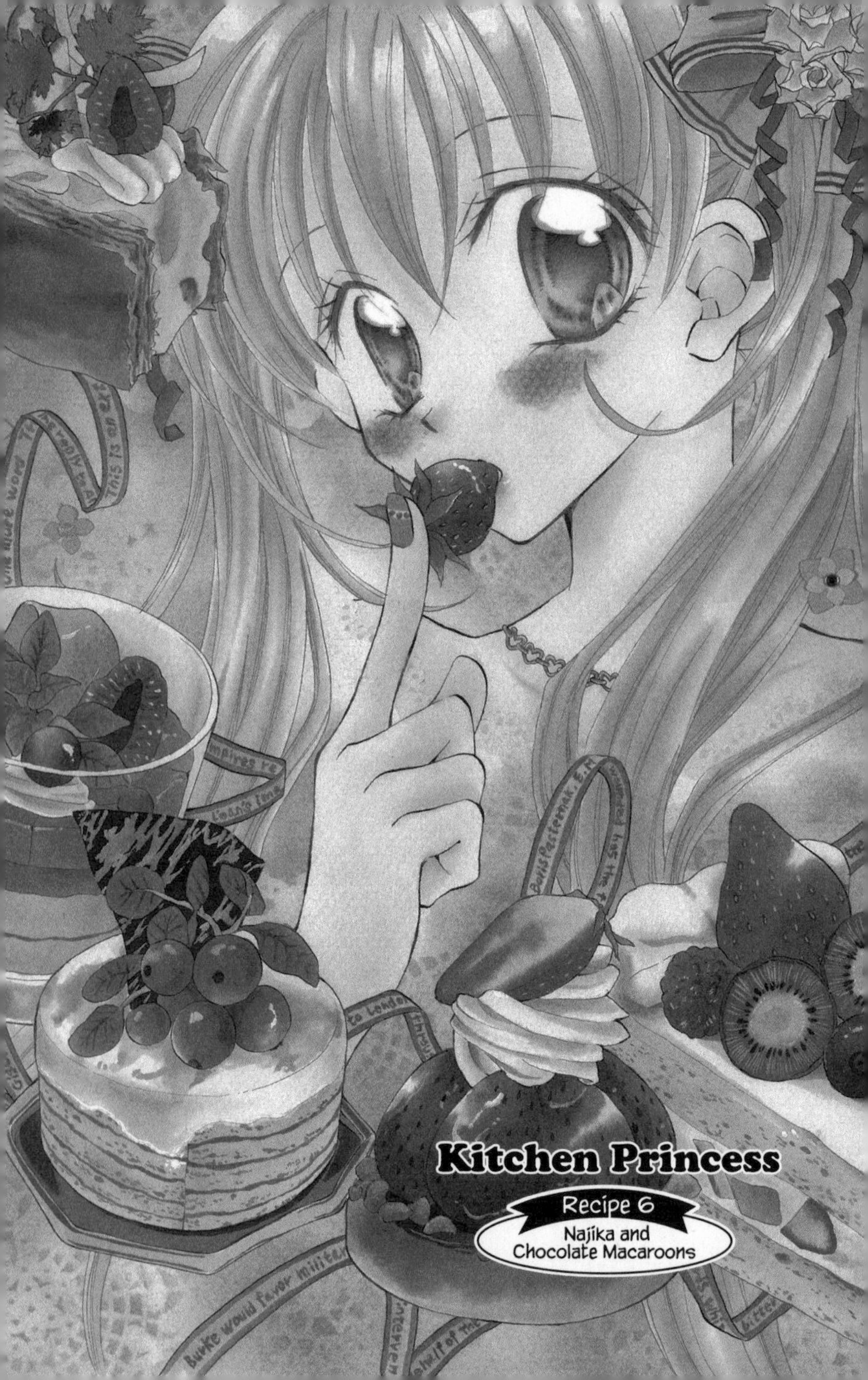
Kitchen Princess
Recipe 6
Najika and Chocolate Macaroons

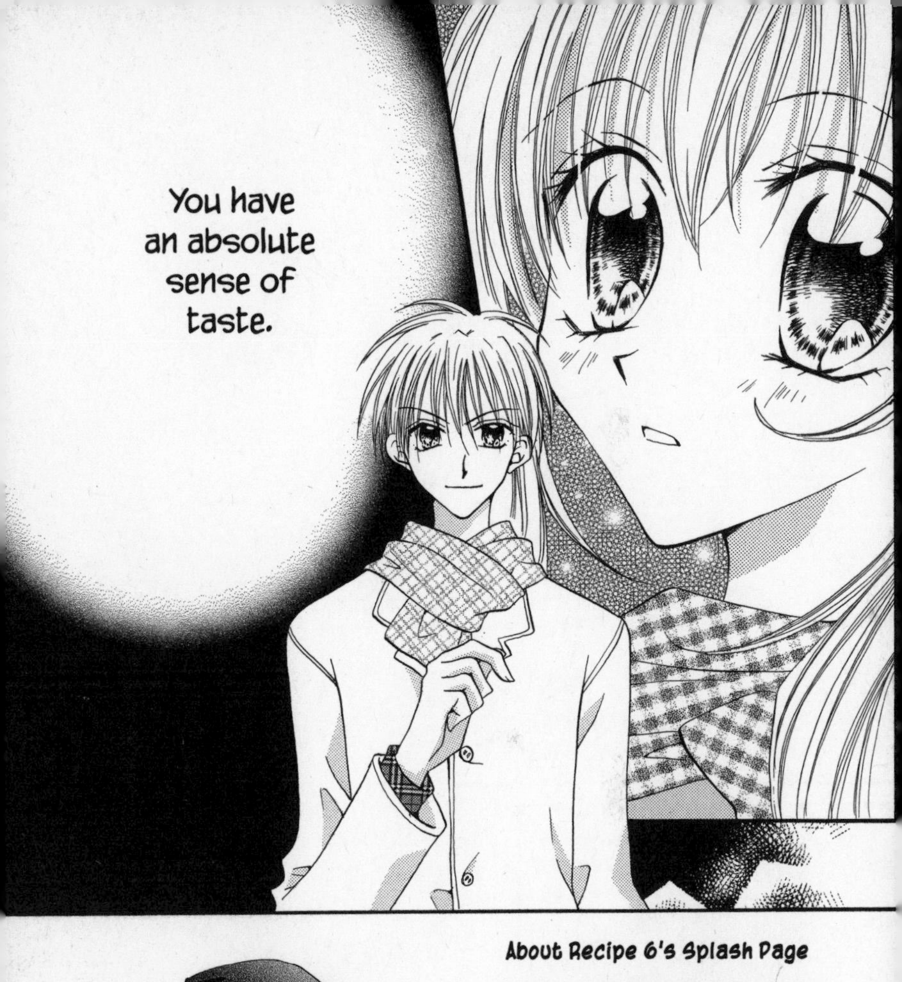
You have an absolute sense of taste.

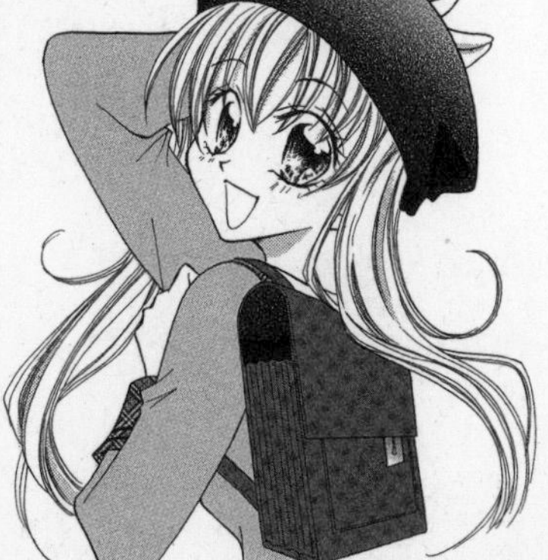

About Recipe 6's Splash Page

You can't tell because it's black and white in the comic, but I wanted to draw a lot of strawberries and used a lot of pink to draw a bunch of sweets ♪

Getting the right color for food is so hard... It usually takes longer than drawing the people.

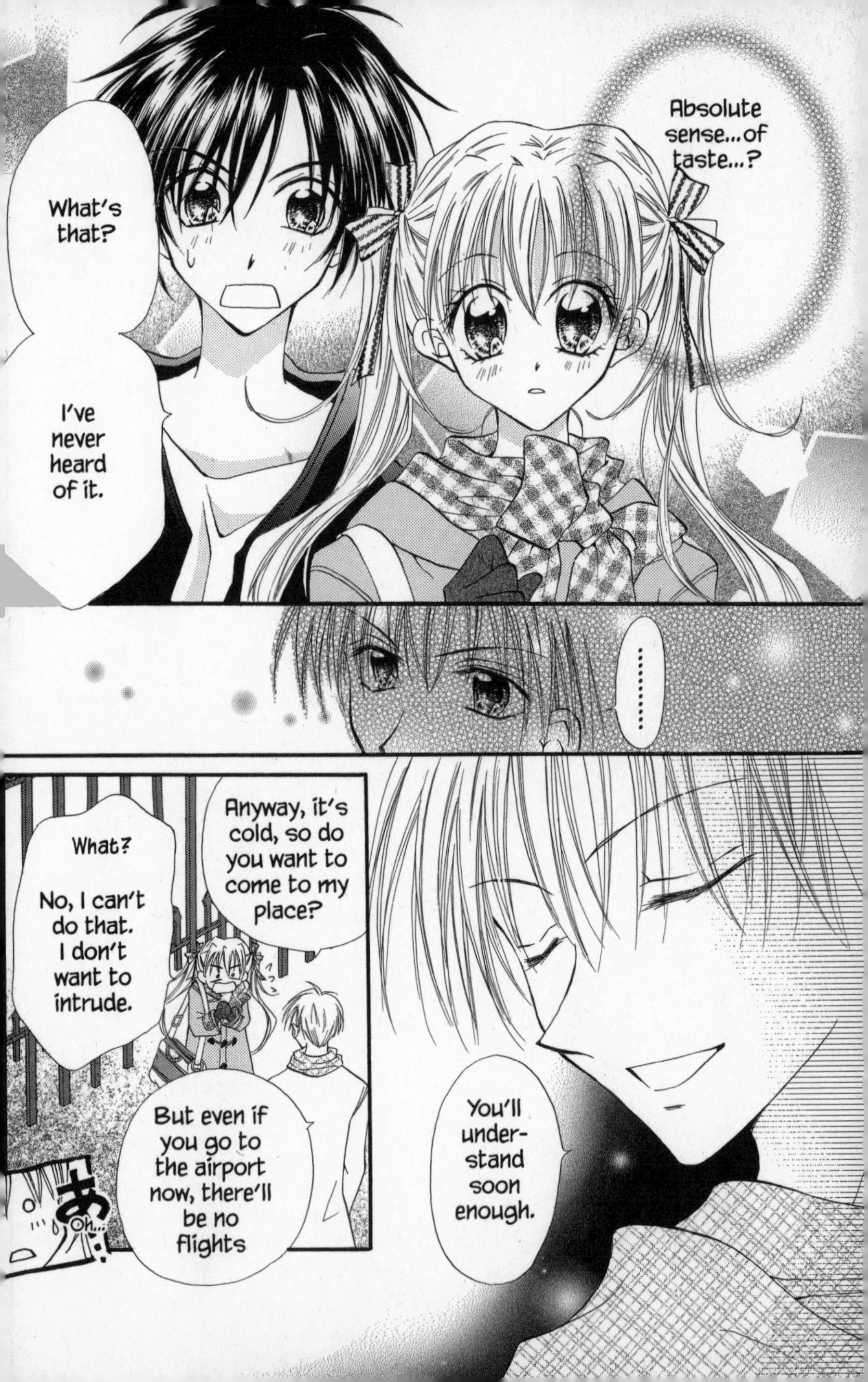
Absolute sense...of taste...?
What's that?
I've never heard of it.
......
You'll under-stand soon enough.
Anyway, it's cold, so do you want to come to my place?
What?
No, I can't do that. I don't want to intrude.
But even if you go to the airport now, there'll be no flights
あ
Oh...

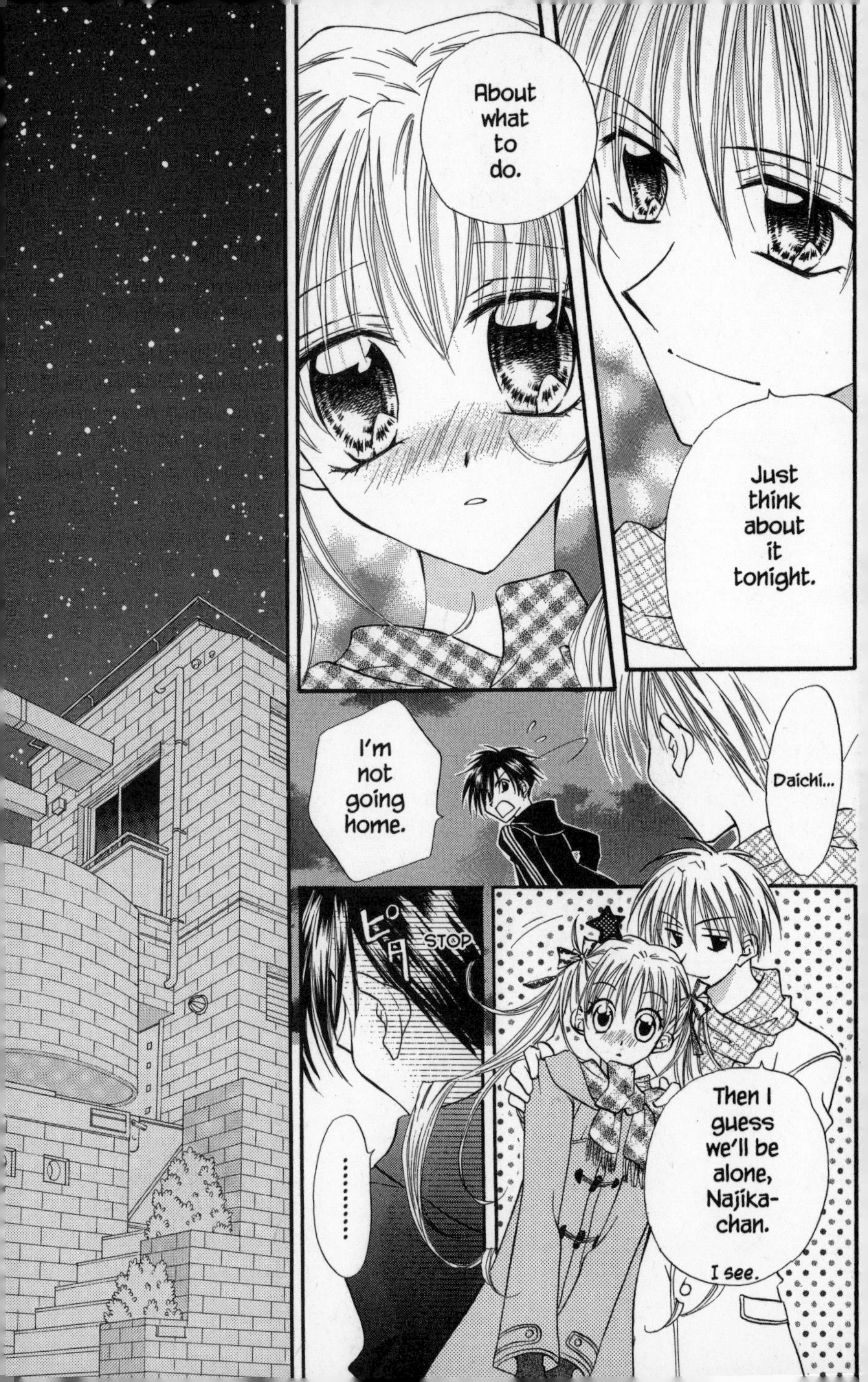
Just think about it tonight.
About what to do.
Daichi...
I'm not going home.
Then I guess we'll be alone, Najika-chan.
I see.
ピタ
STOP
......

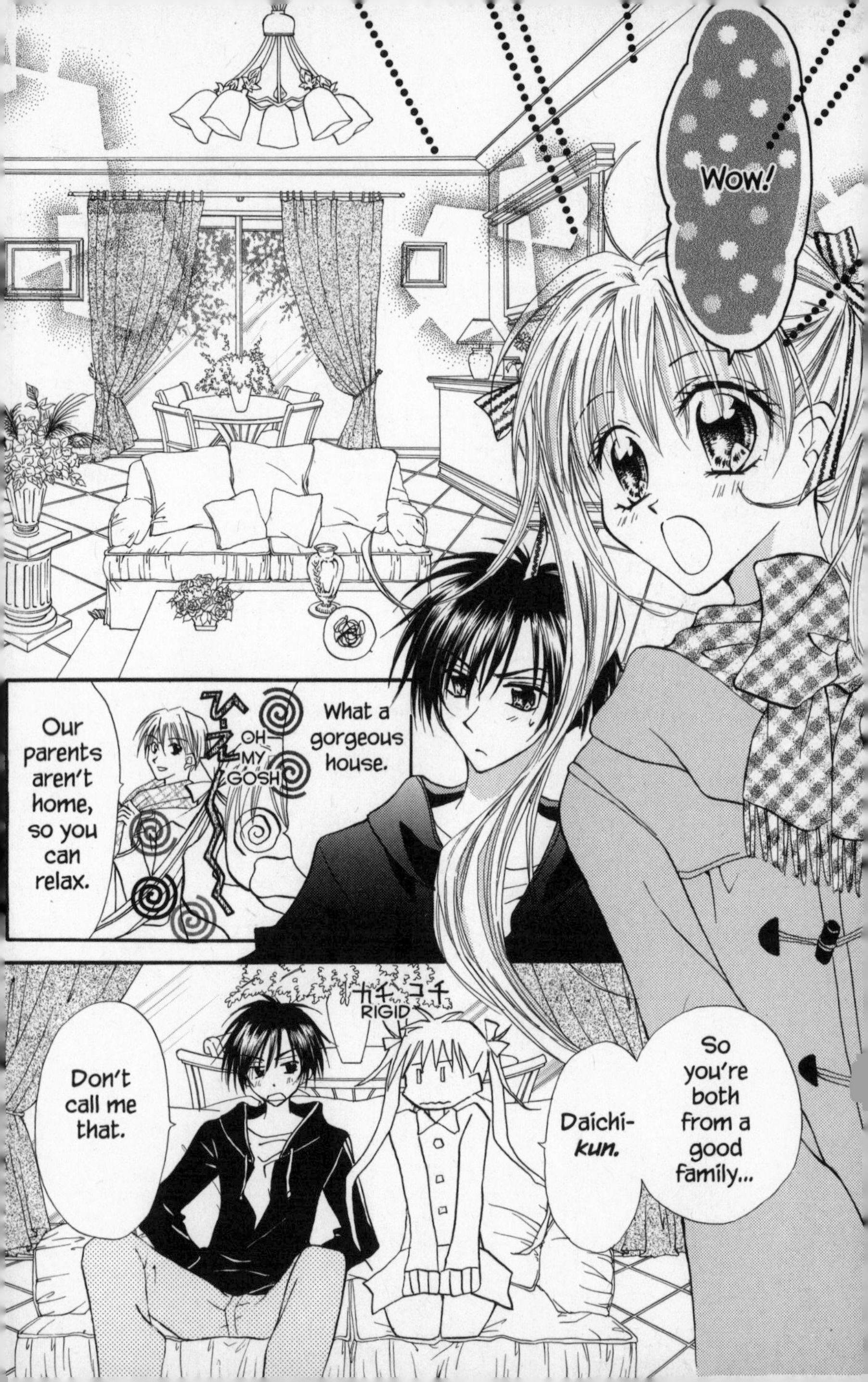
Wow!
What a gorgeous house.
OH-MY-GOSH
Our parents aren't home, so you can relax.
So you're both from a good family...
Daichi-*kun.*
カチコチ RIGID
Don't call me that.

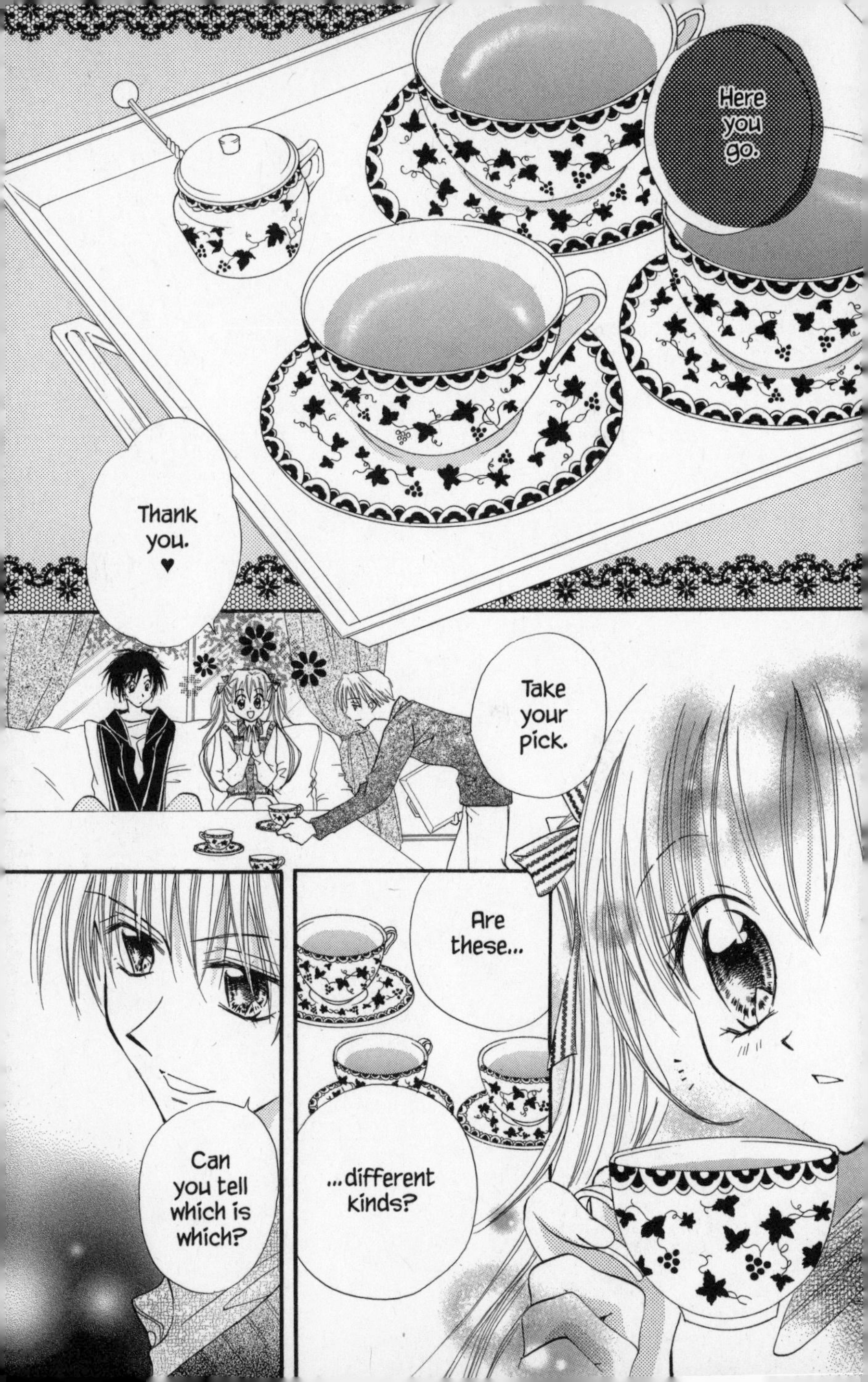
Here you go.
Thank you. ♥
Take your pick.
Are these...
...different kinds?
Can you tell which is which?

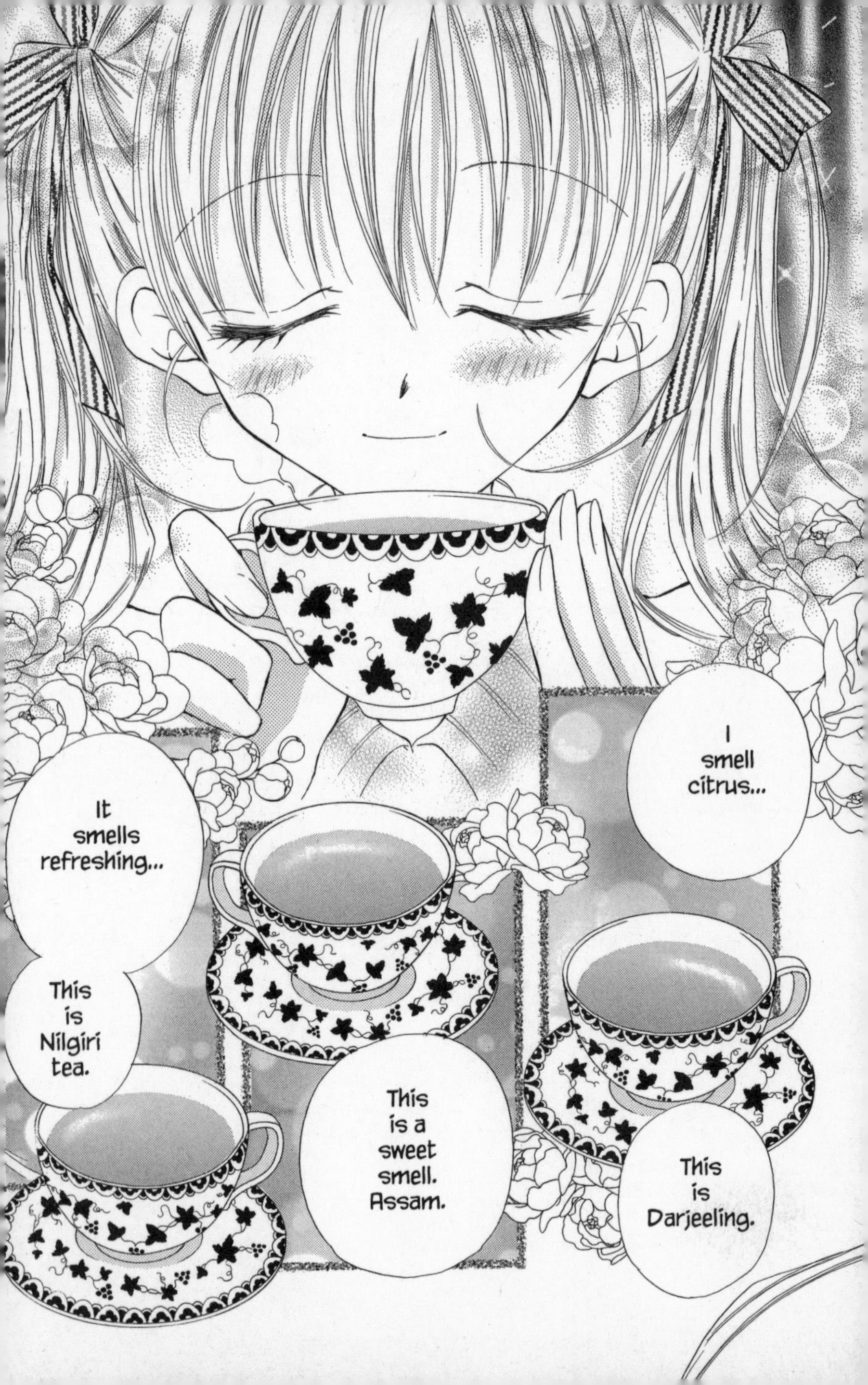
I smell citrus...
It smells refreshing...
This is Nilgiri tea.
This is Darjeeling.
This is a sweet smell. Assam.

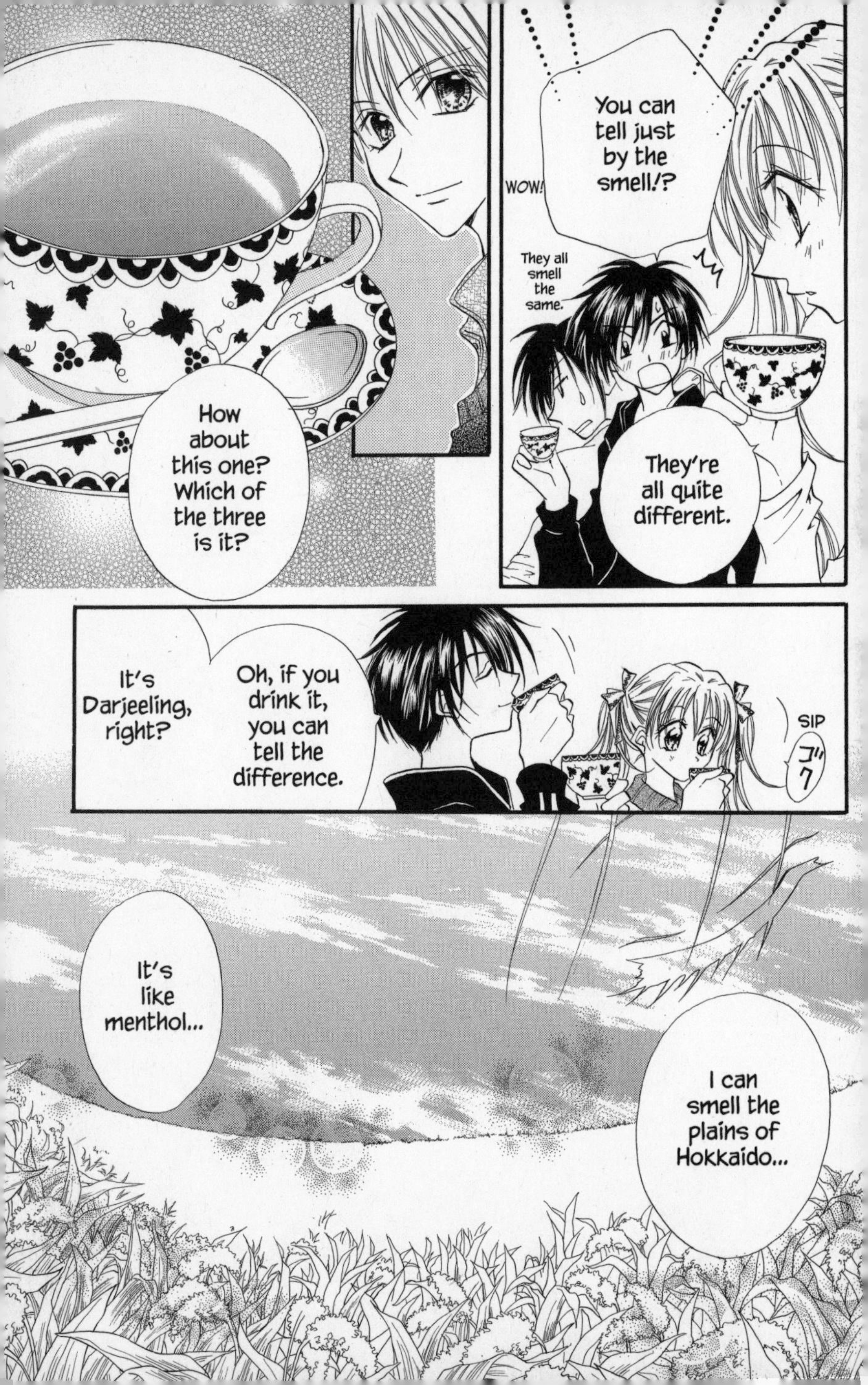
You can tell just by the smell!?
WOW!
They all smell the same.
They're all quite different.
How about this one? Which of the three is it?
SIP
ゴク
Oh, if you drink it, you can tell the difference.
It's Darjeeling, right?
I can smell the plains of Hokkaido...
It's like menthol...

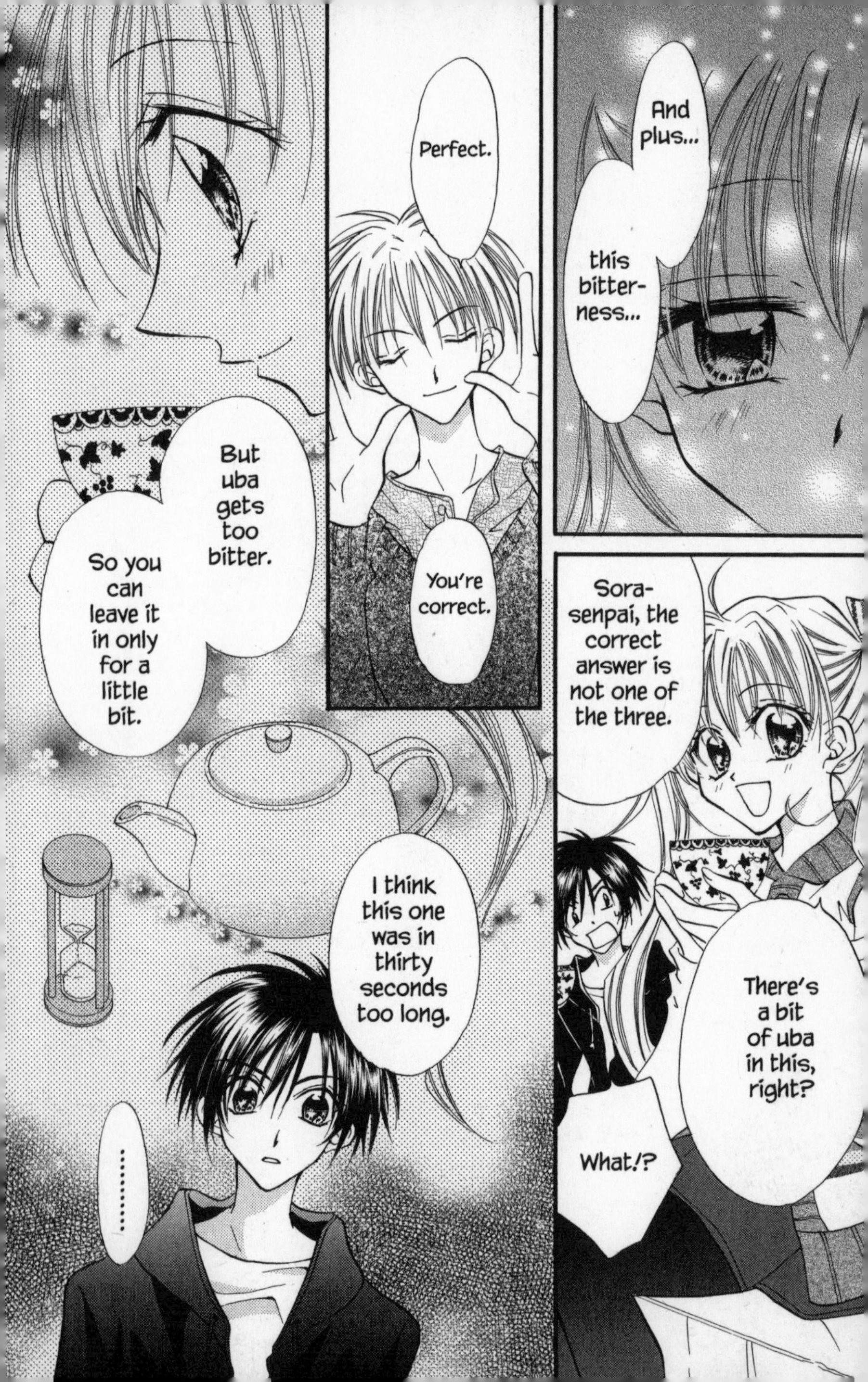
And plus...
this bitterness...
Sora-senpai, the correct answer is not one of the three.
There's a bit of uba in this, right?
What!?
Perfect.
You're correct.
But uba gets too bitter.
So you can leave it in only for a little bit.
I think this one was in thirty seconds too long.
....

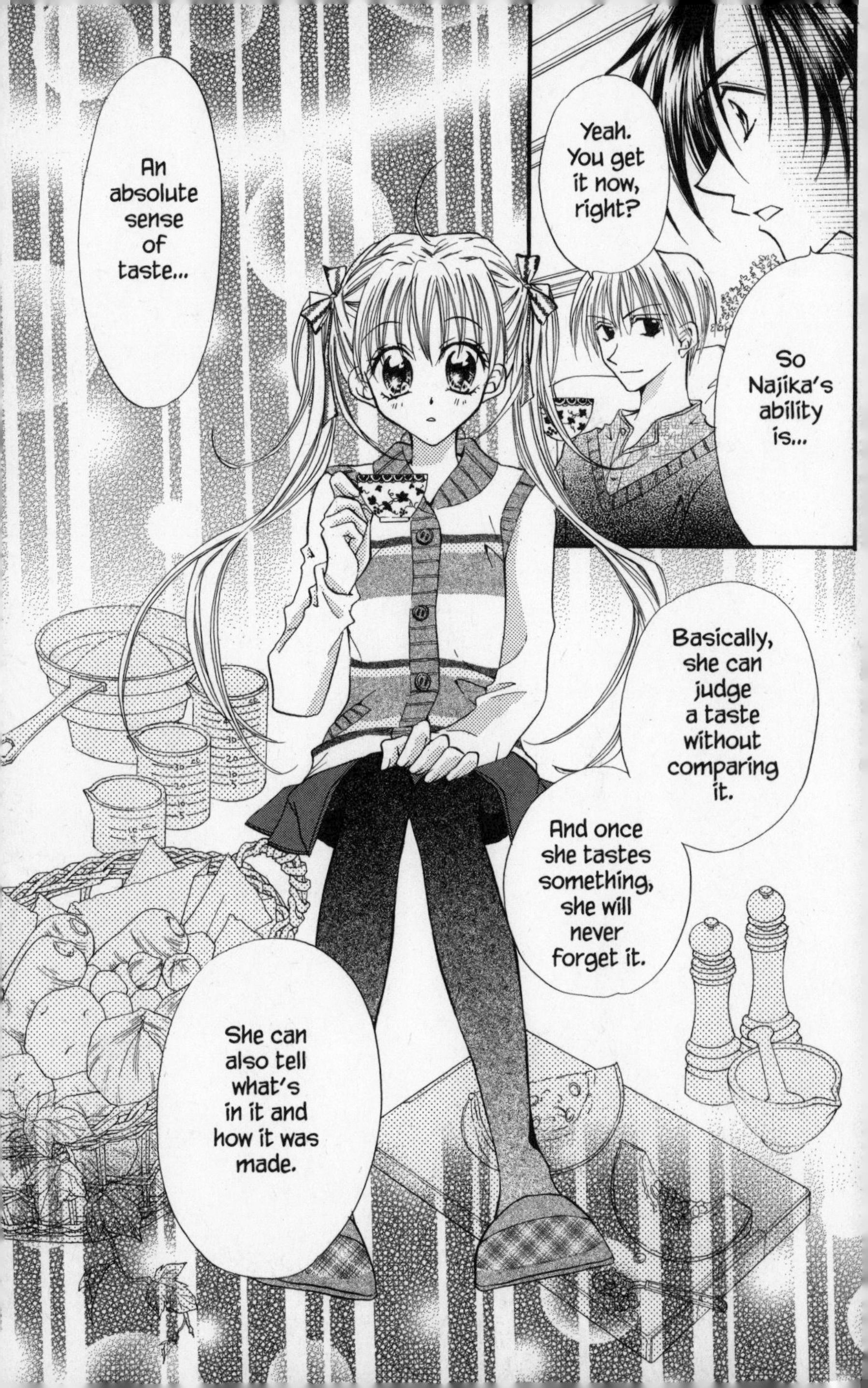
So Najika's ability is...
Yeah. You get it now, right?
An absolute sense of taste...
Basically, she can judge a taste without comparing it.
And once she tastes something, she will never forget it.
She can also tell what's in it and how it was made.

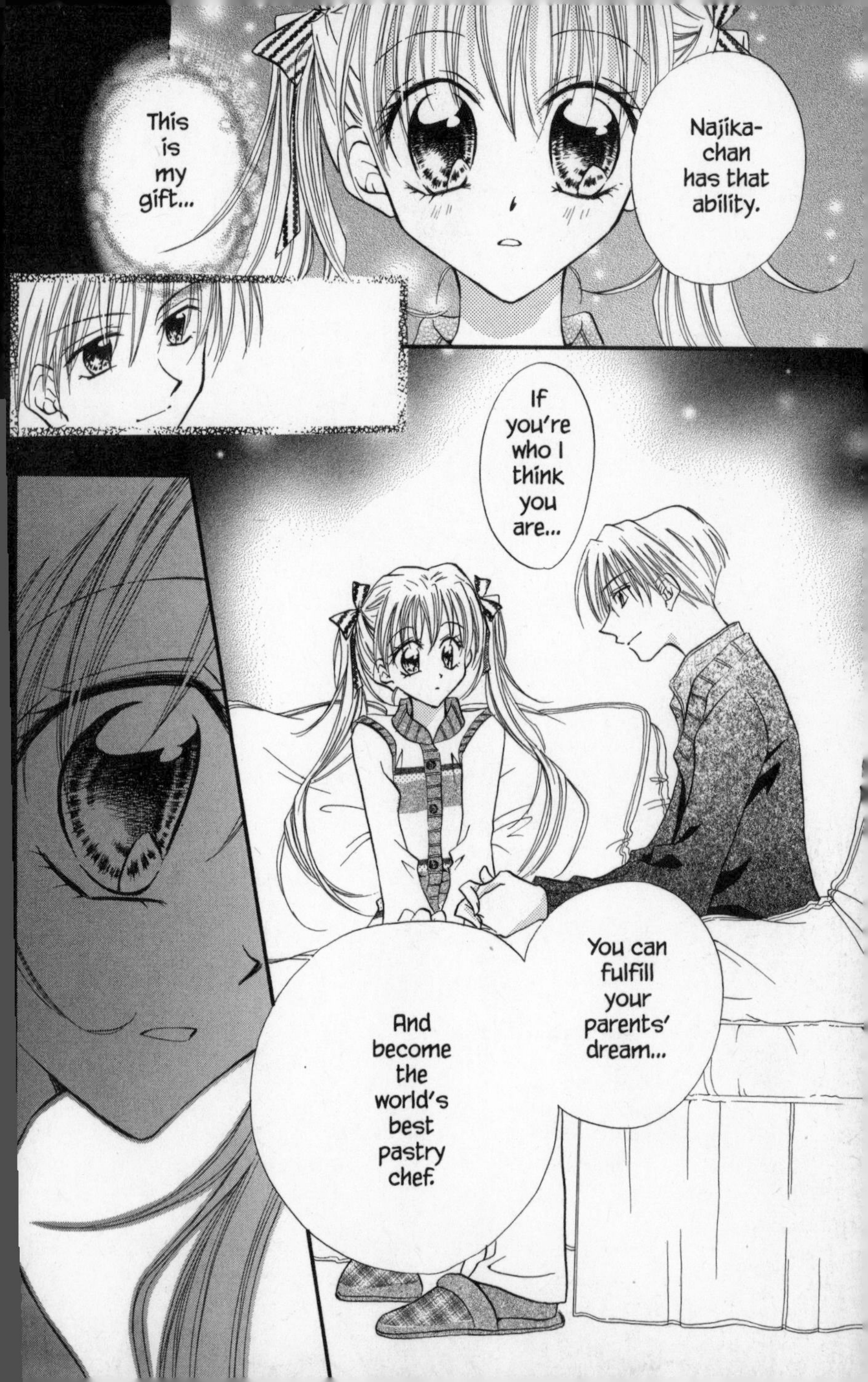
Najika-chan has that ability.
This is my gift...
If you're who I think you are...
You can fulfill your parents' dream...
And become the world's best pastry chef.

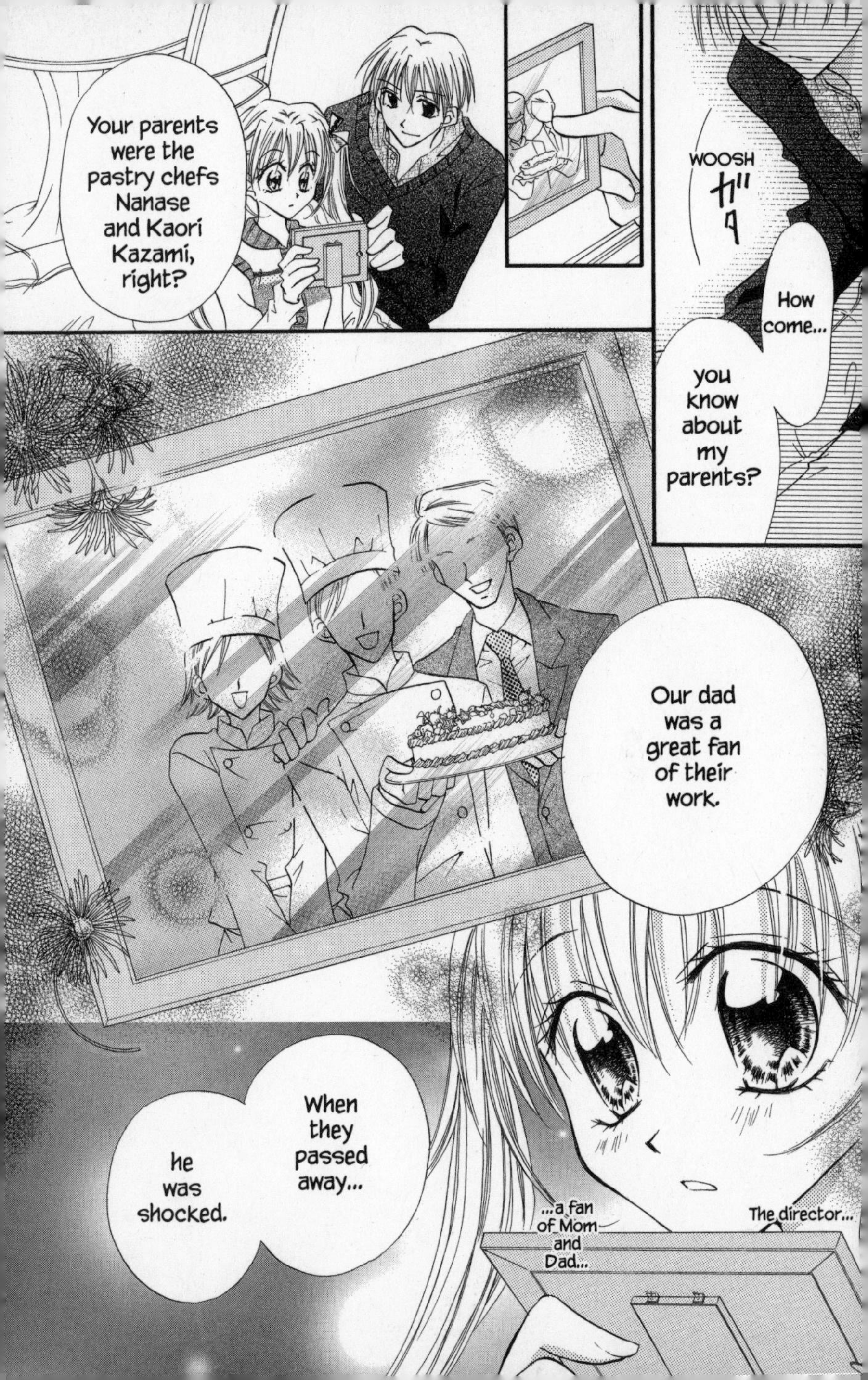
WOOSH
ガバ
How come...
you know about my parents?
Your parents were the pastry chefs Nanase and Kaori Kazami, right?
Our dad was a great fan of their work.
The director...
...a fan of Mom and Dad...
When they passed away...
he was shocked.

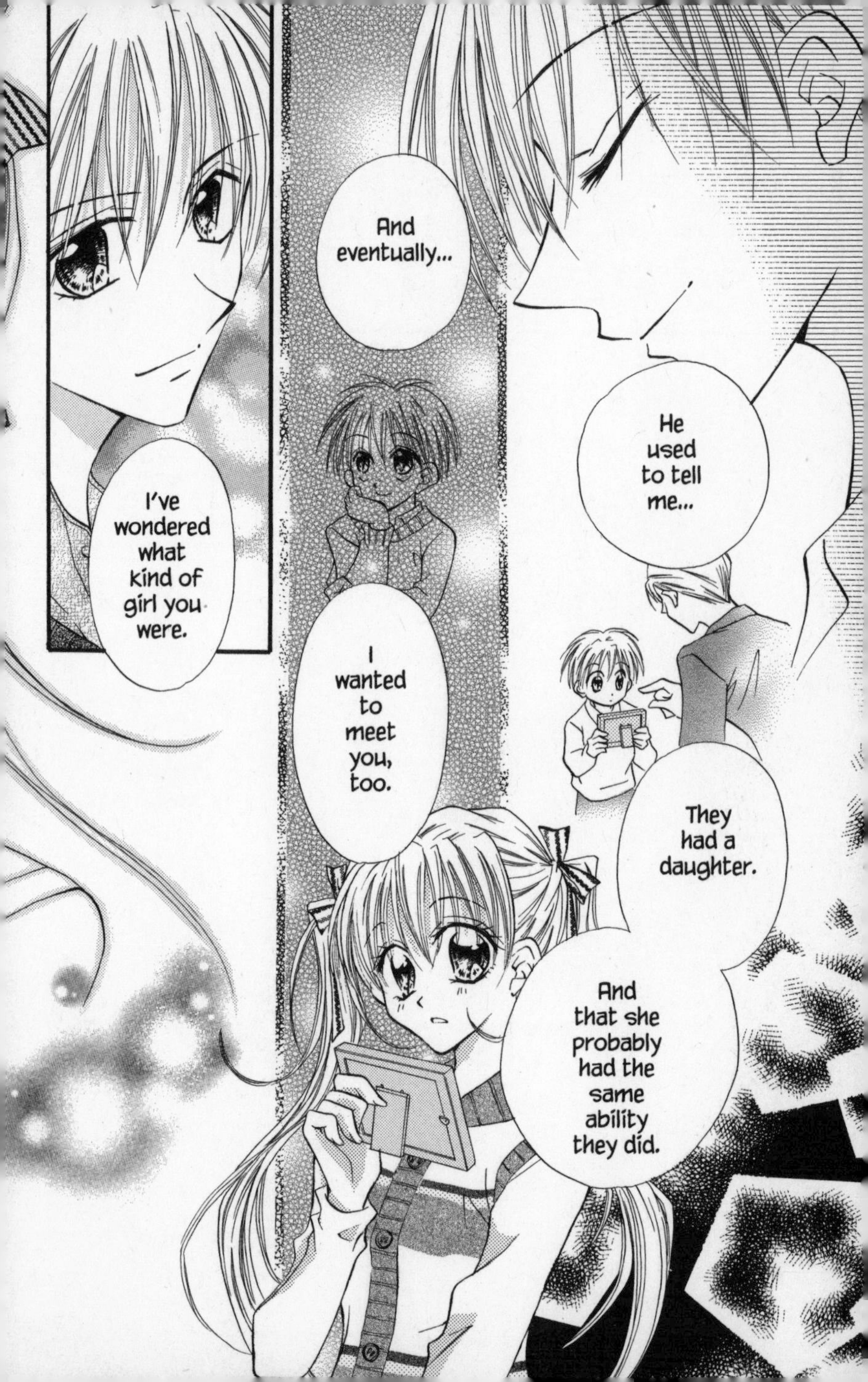
He used to tell me...
They had a daughter.
And that she probably had the same ability they did.
And eventually...
I wanted to meet you, too.
I've wondered what kind of girl you were.

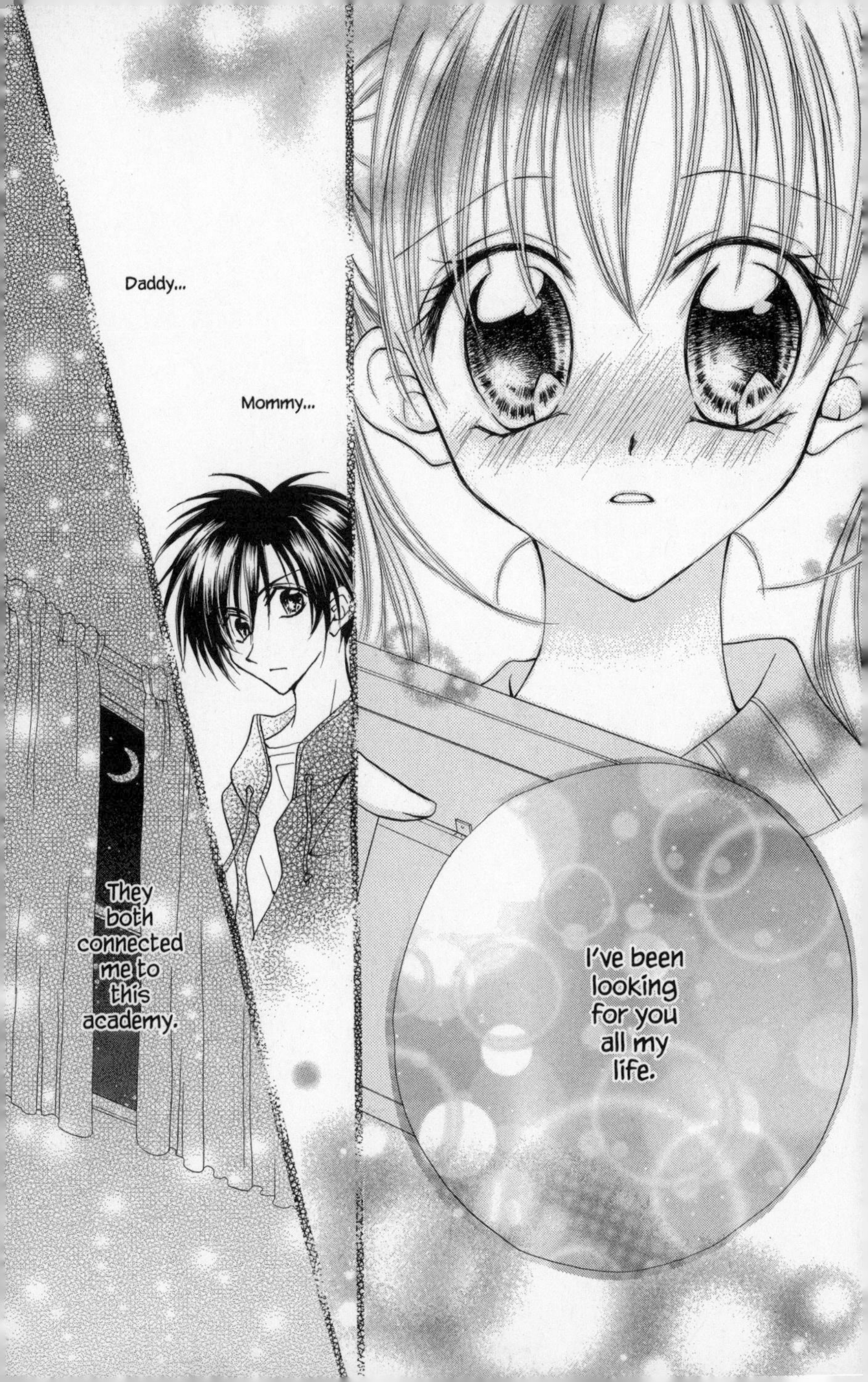
I've been looking for you all my life.
Daddy...
Mommy...
They both connected me to this academy.

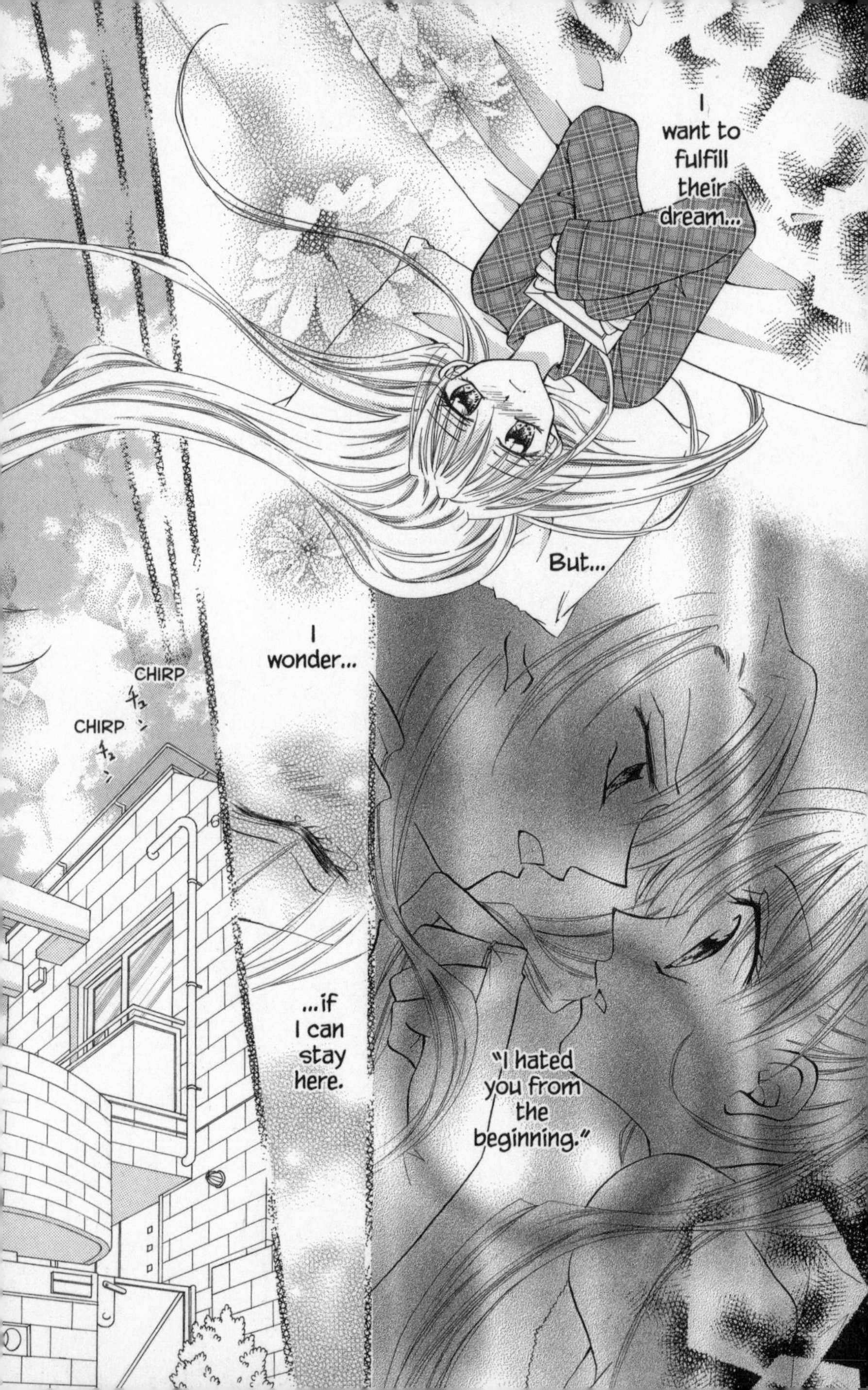
I want to fulfill their dream...
But...
"I hated you from the beginning."
I wonder...
CHIRP
CHIRP
...if I can stay here.

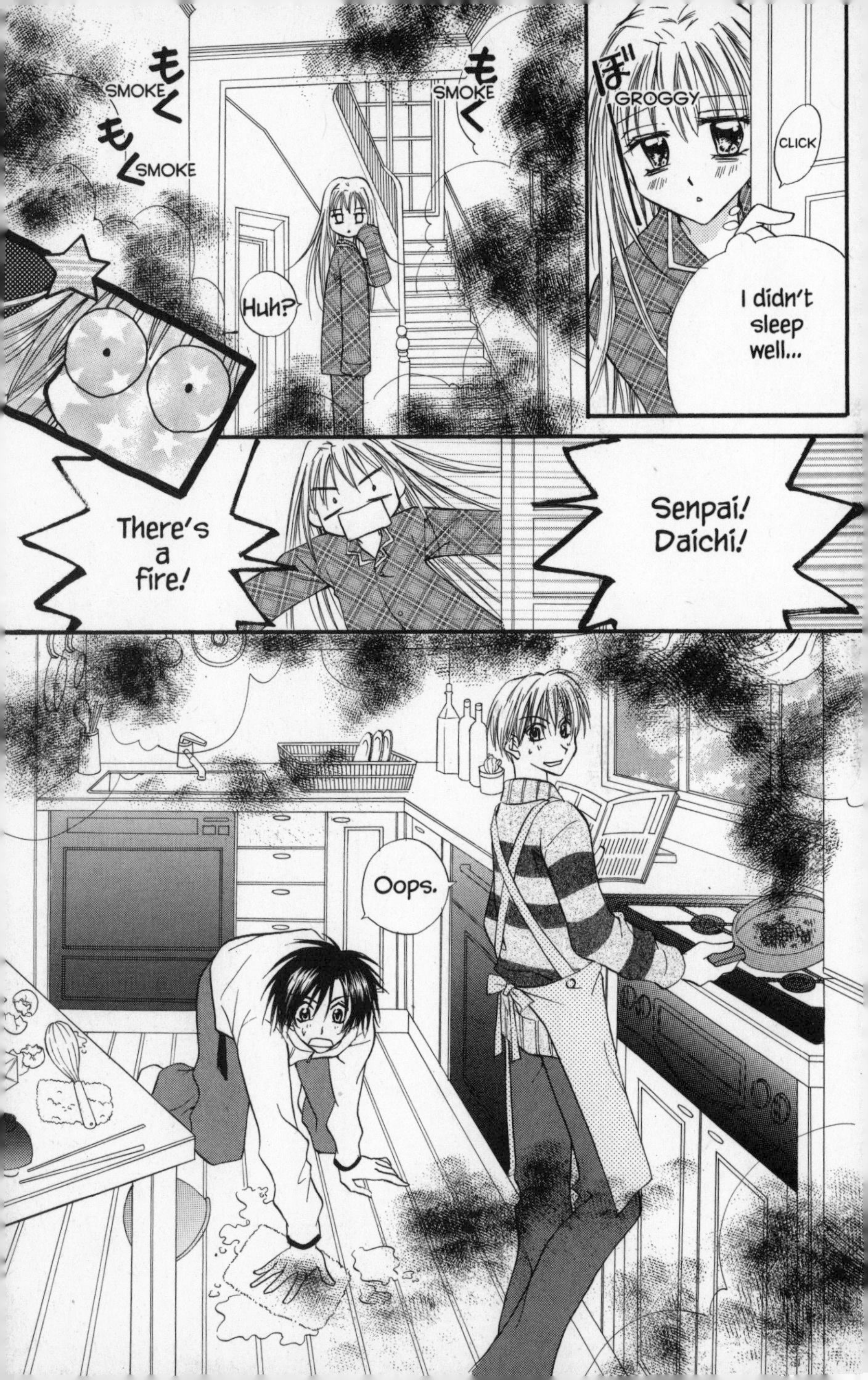
ぼ
GROGGY
CLICK
I didn't sleep well...
もく
SMOKE
もく
SMOKE
もく
SMOKE
Huh?
Senpai! Daichi!
There's a fire!
Oops.

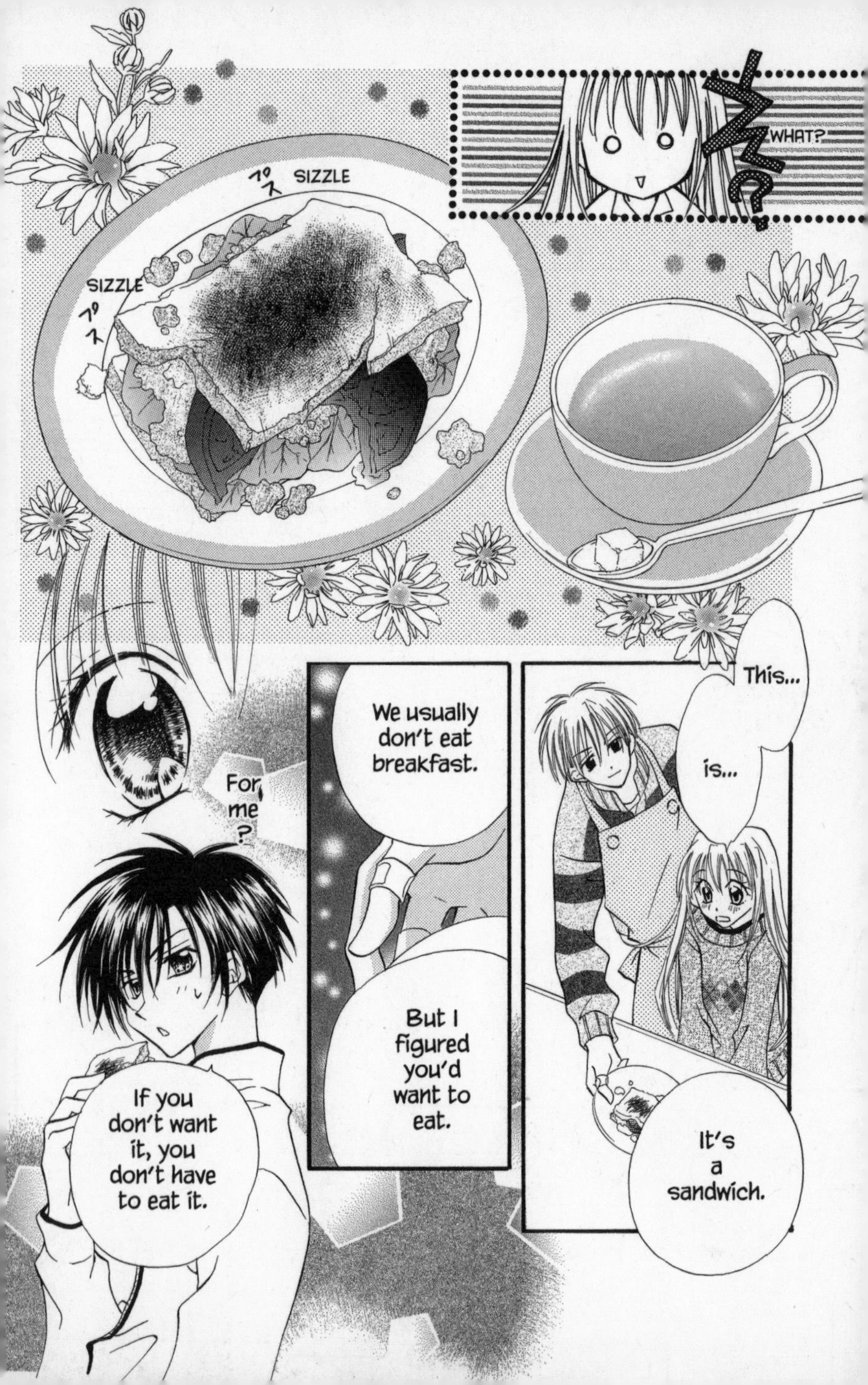
WHAT?
SIZZLE
SIZZLE
This...
is...
It's a sandwich.
We usually don't eat breakfast.
But I figured you'd want to eat.
For me?
If you don't want it, you don't have to eat it.

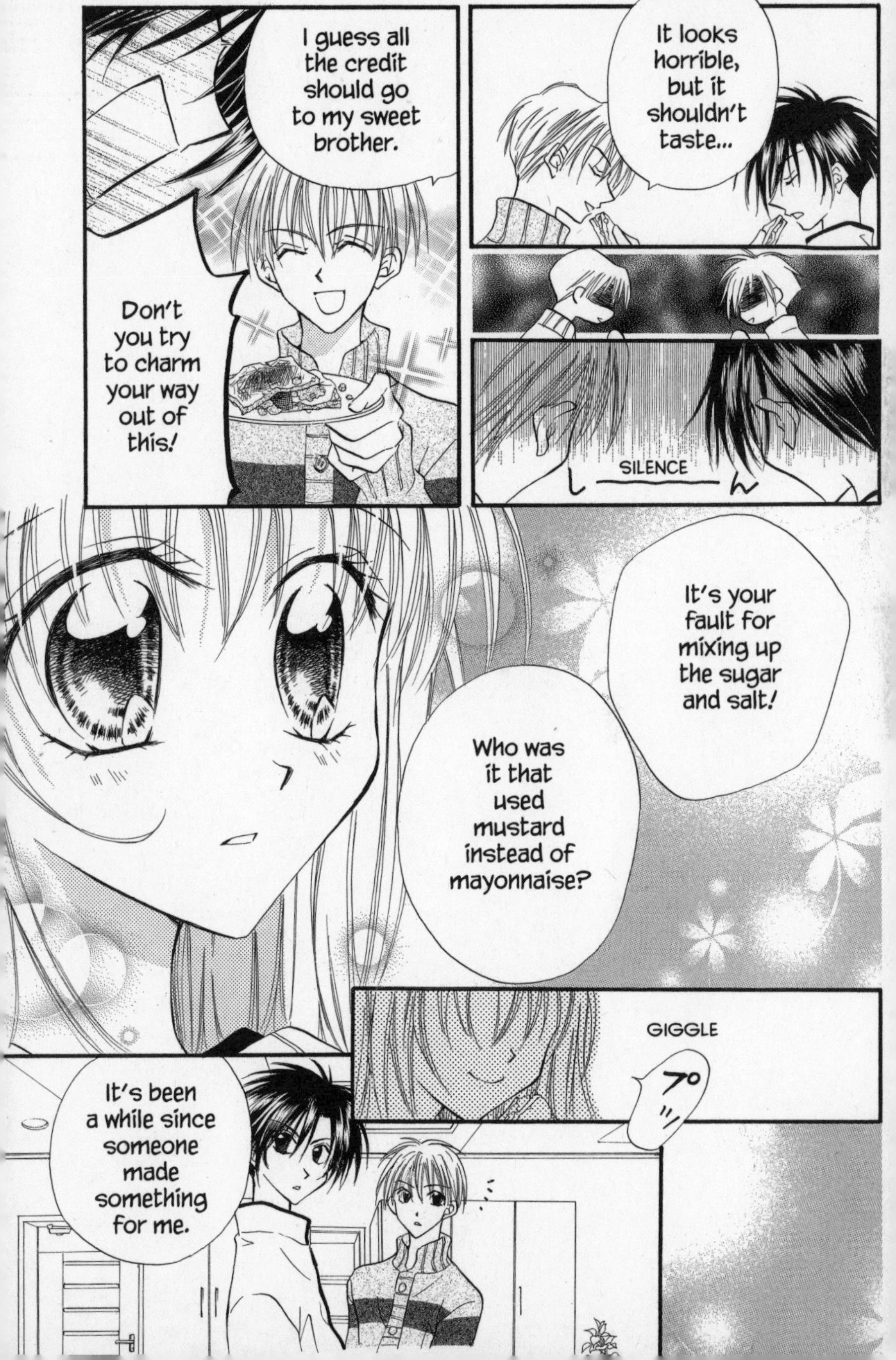
It looks horrible, but it shouldn't taste...
SILENCE
I guess all the credit should go to my sweet brother.
Don't you try to charm your way out of this!
It's your fault for mixing up the sugar and salt!
Who was it that used mustard instead of mayonnaise?
GIGGLE
It's been a while since someone made something for me.

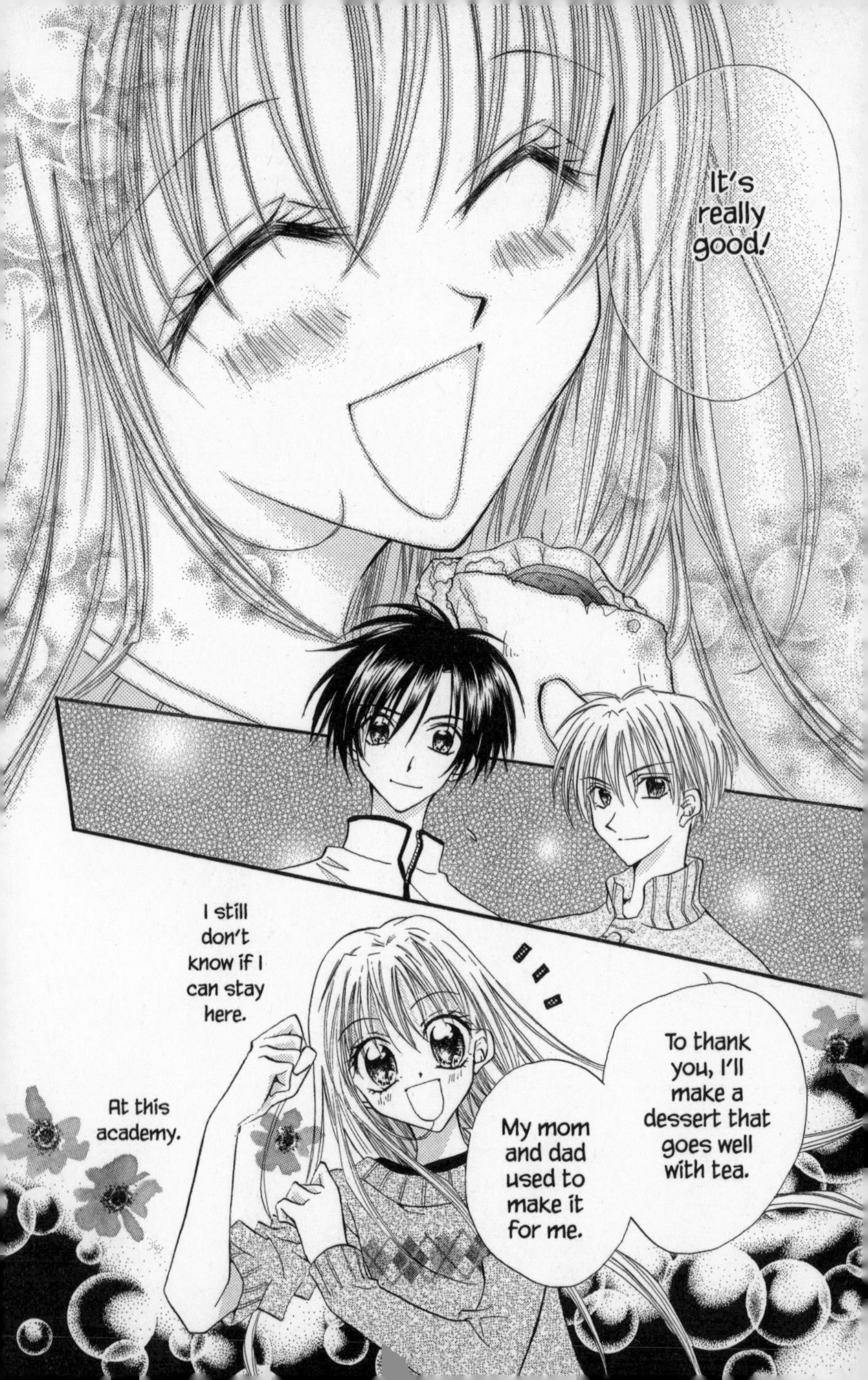
It's really good!
To thank you, I'll make a dessert that goes well with tea.
My mom and dad used to make it for me.
I still don't know if I can stay here.
At this academy.

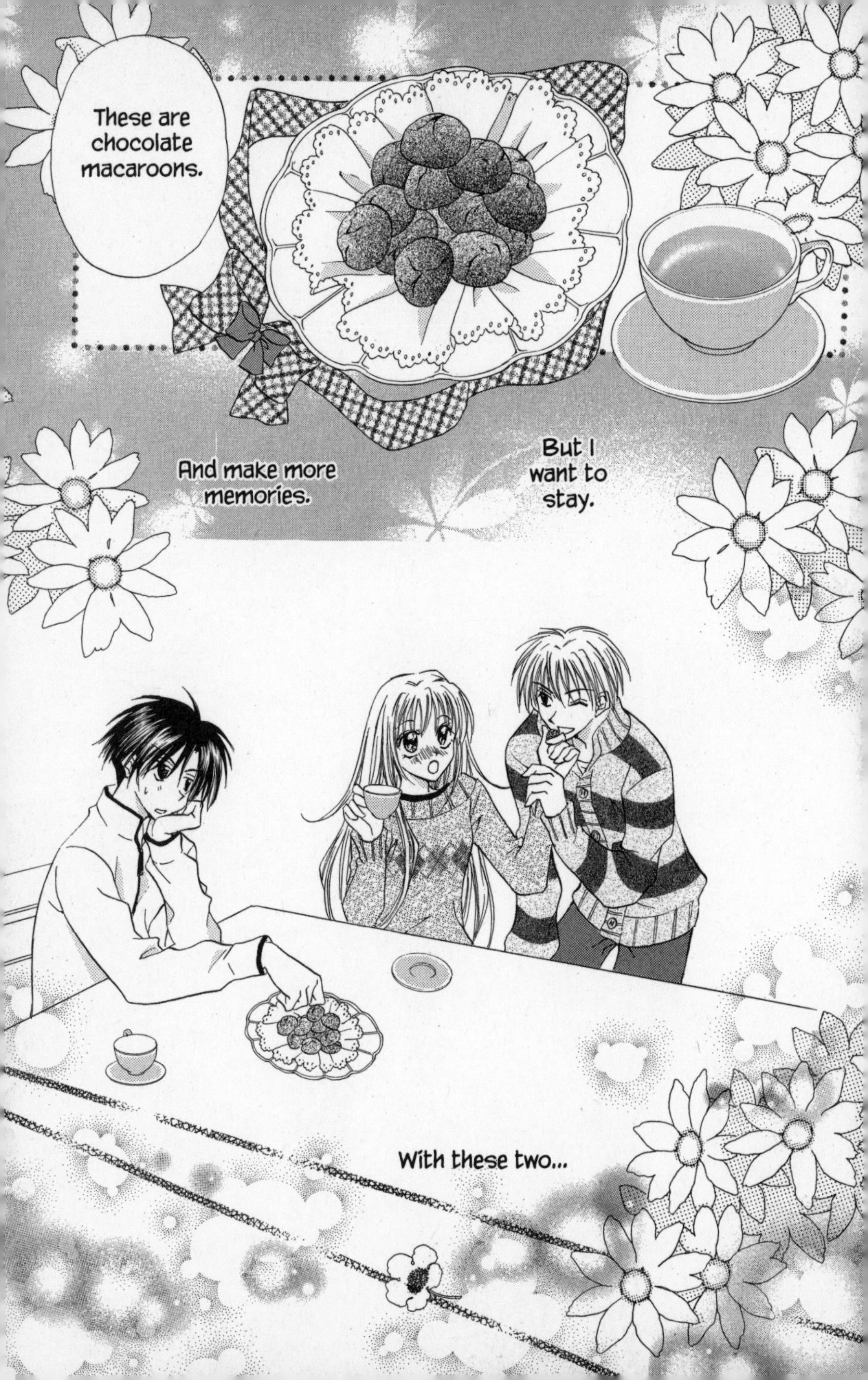
These are chocolate macaroons.
But I want to stay.
And make more memories.
With these two...

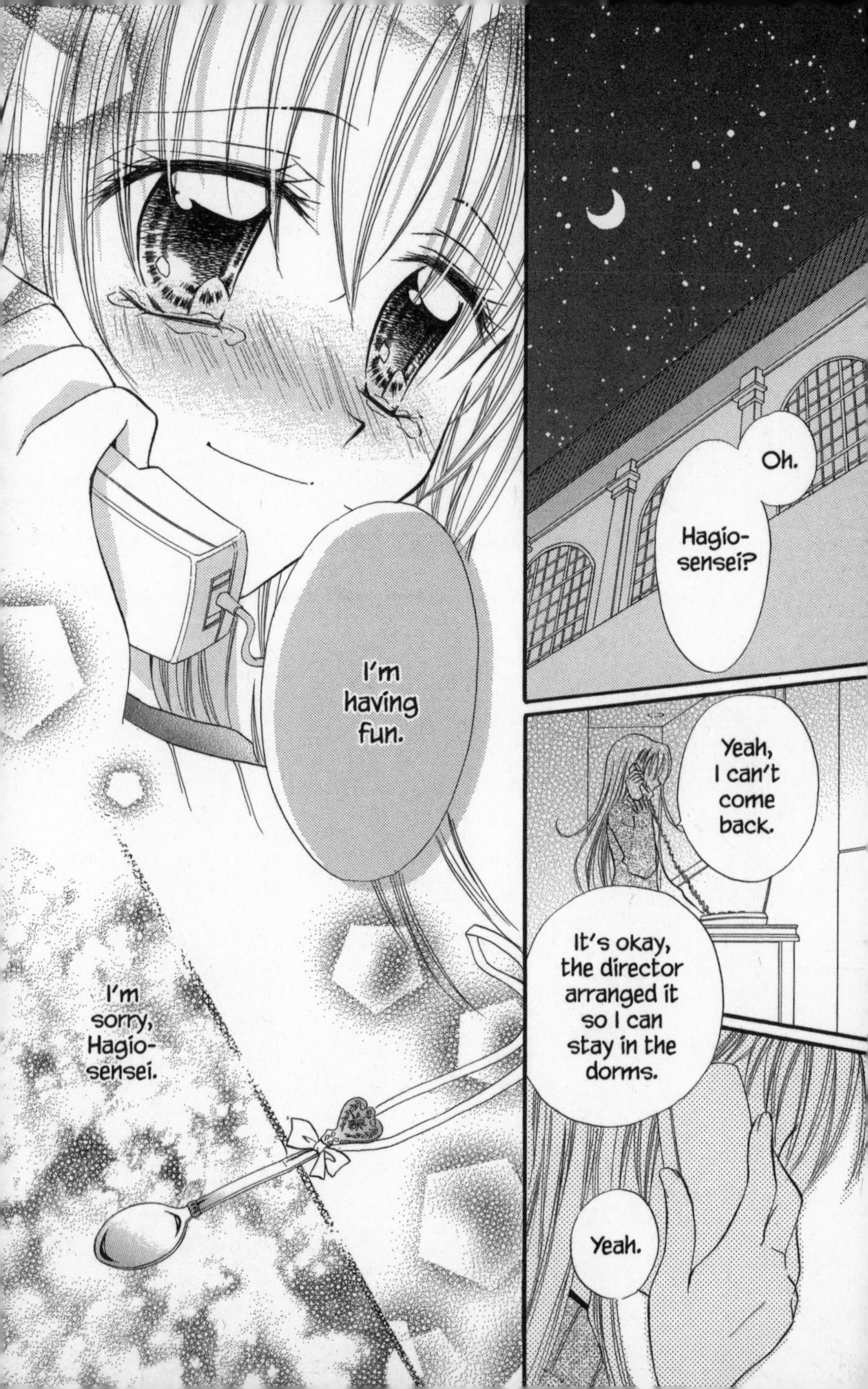
Oh.
Hagio-sensei?
Yeah, I can't come back.
It's okay, the director arranged it so I can stay in the dorms.
Yeah.
I'm having fun.
I'm sorry, Hagio-sensei.

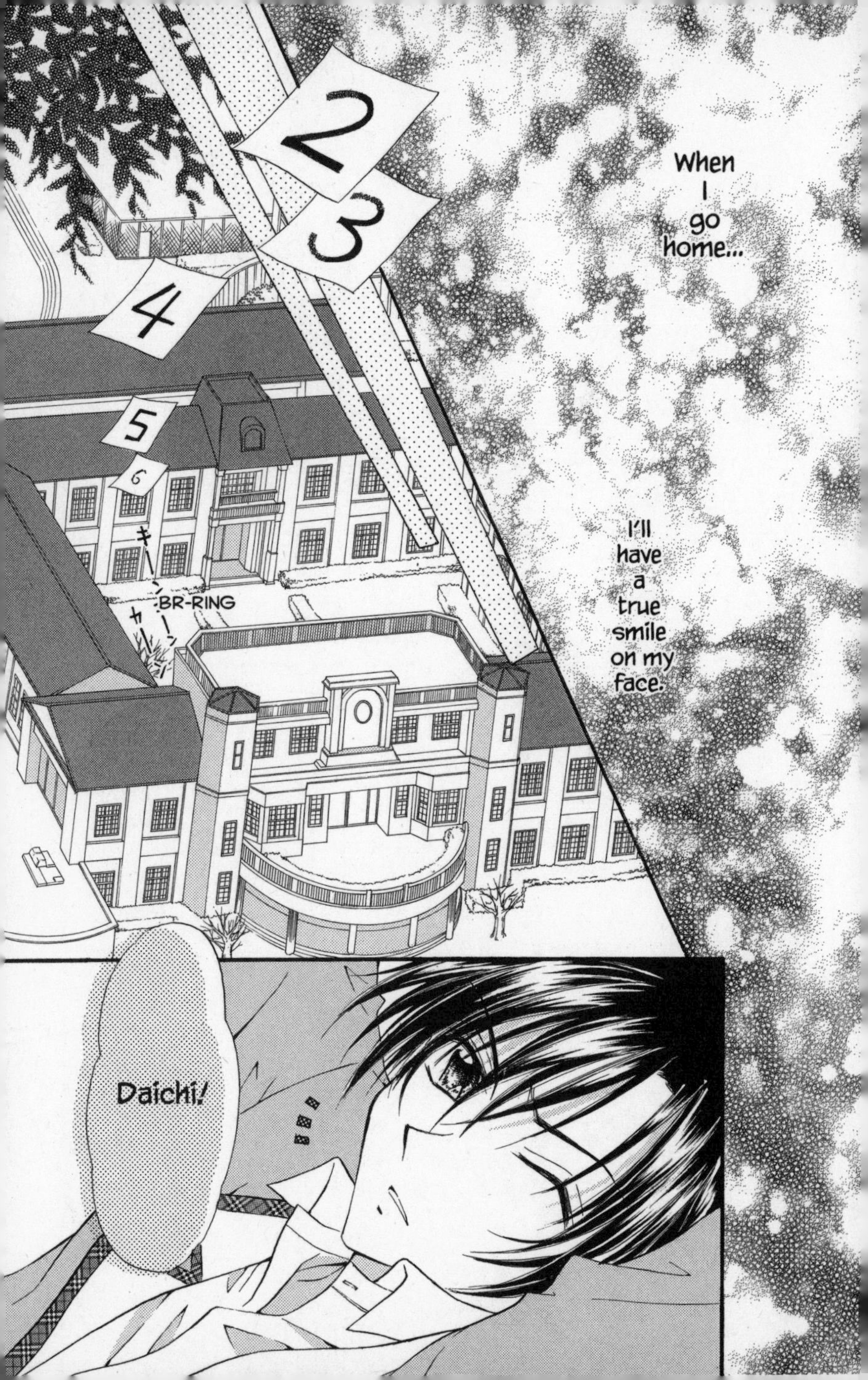
When I go home...
I'll have a true smile on my face.
2
3
4
5
6
BR-RING
Daichi!
...

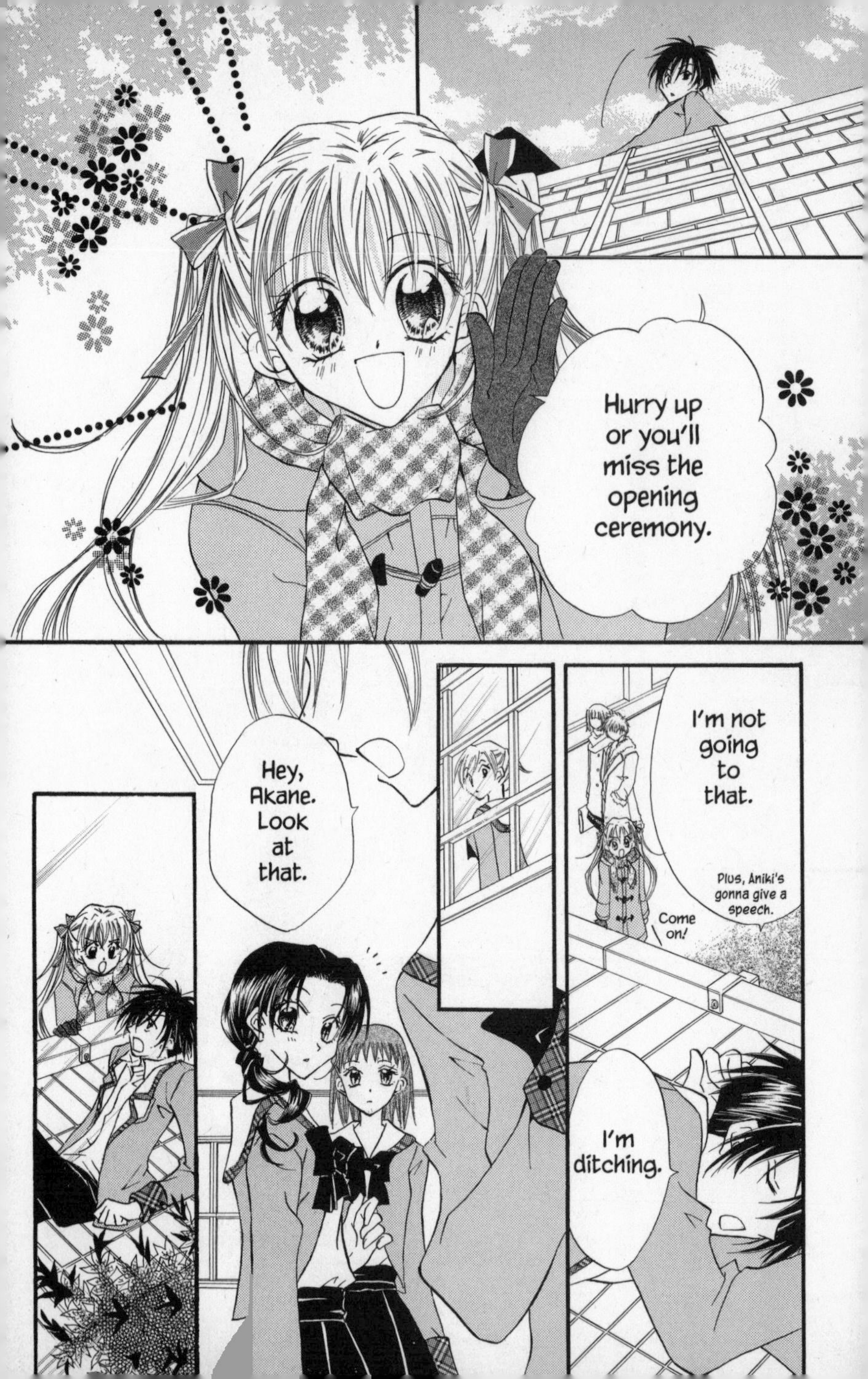
Hurry up or you'll miss the opening ceremony.
I'm not going to that.
Plus, Aniki's gonna give a speech.
Come on!
I'm ditching.
Hey, Akane. Look at that.

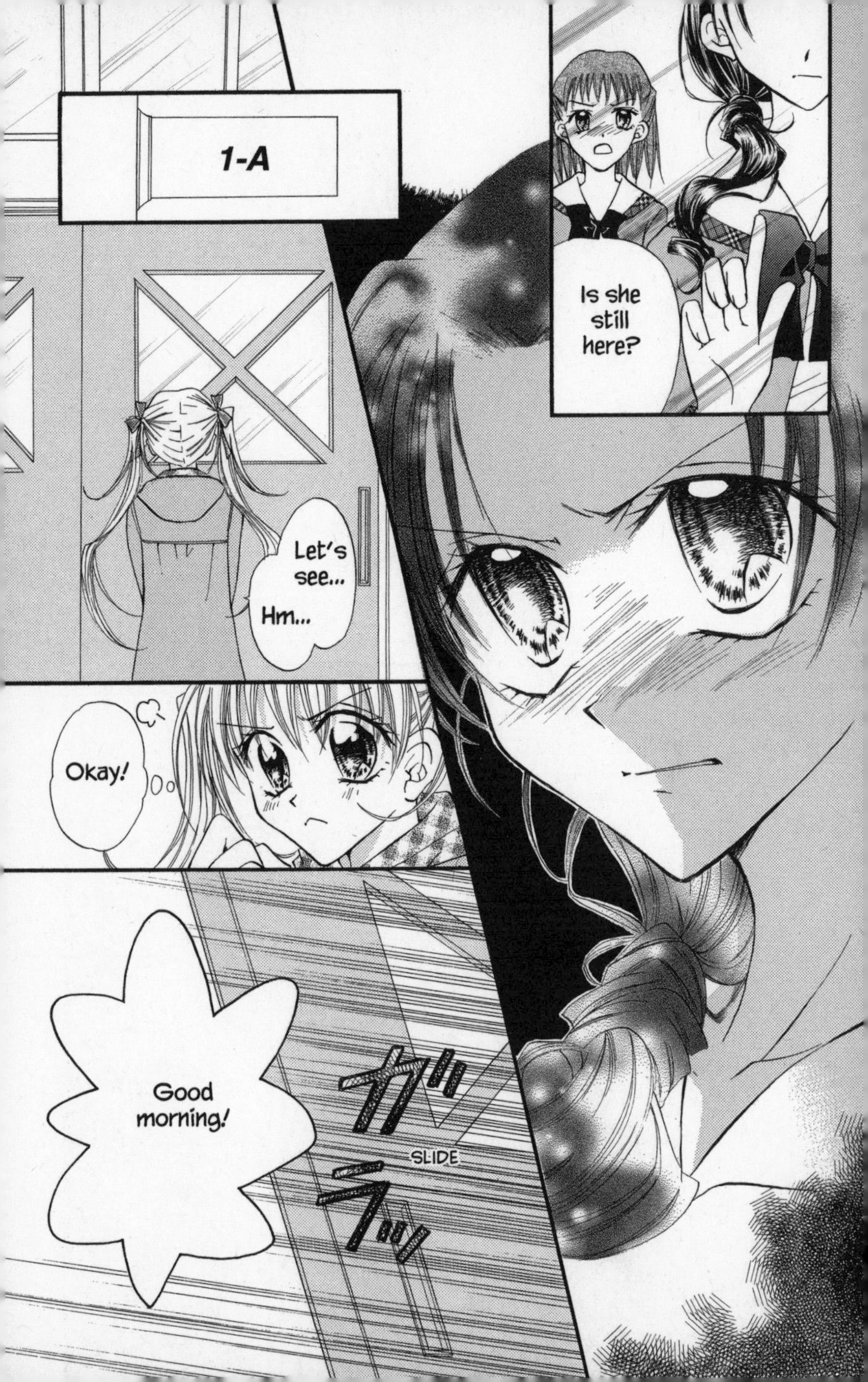
Is she still here?
1-A
Let's see...
Hm...
Okay!
Good morning!
ガラッ
SLIDE

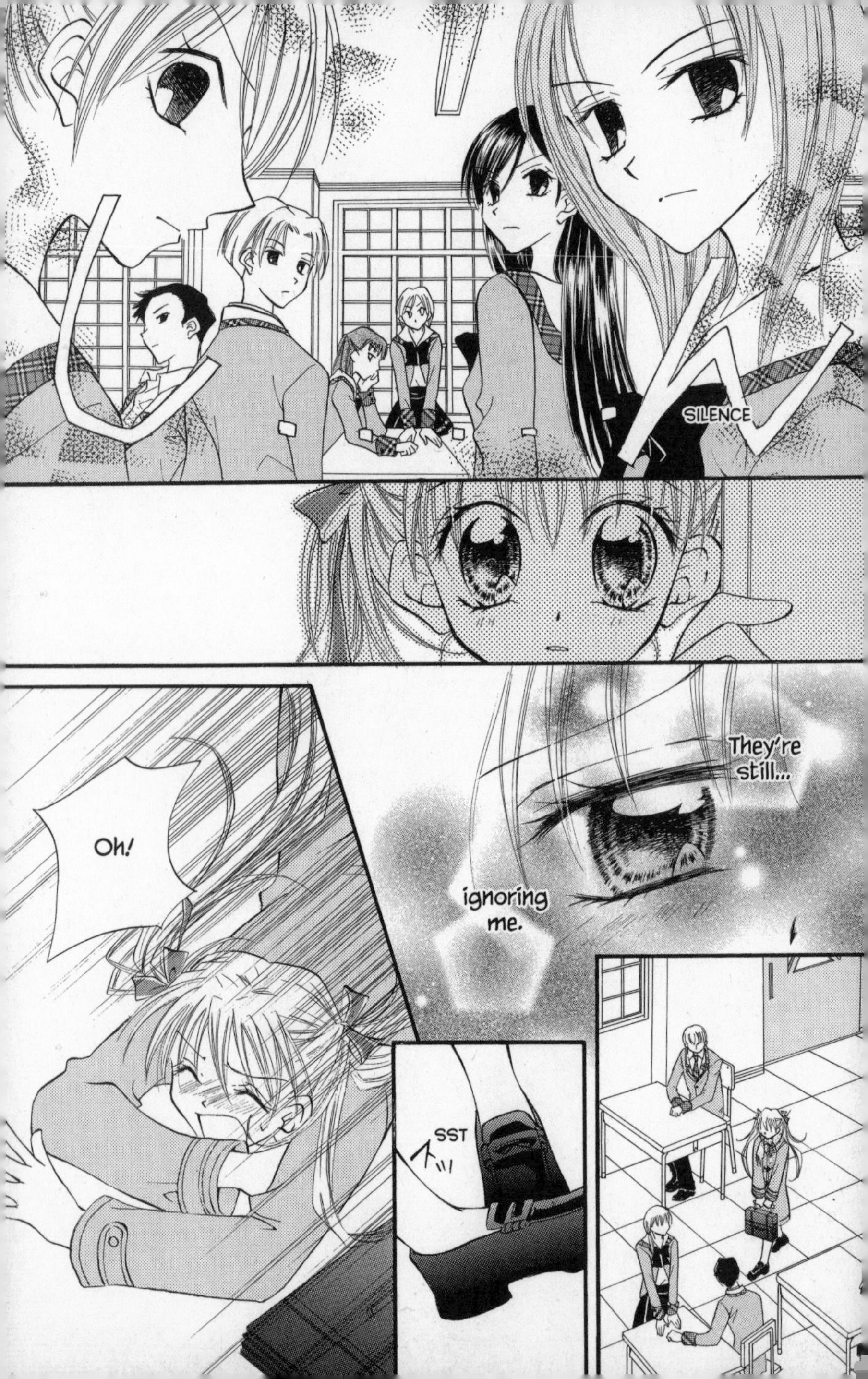
SILENCE
They're still...
ignoring me.
SST
Oh!

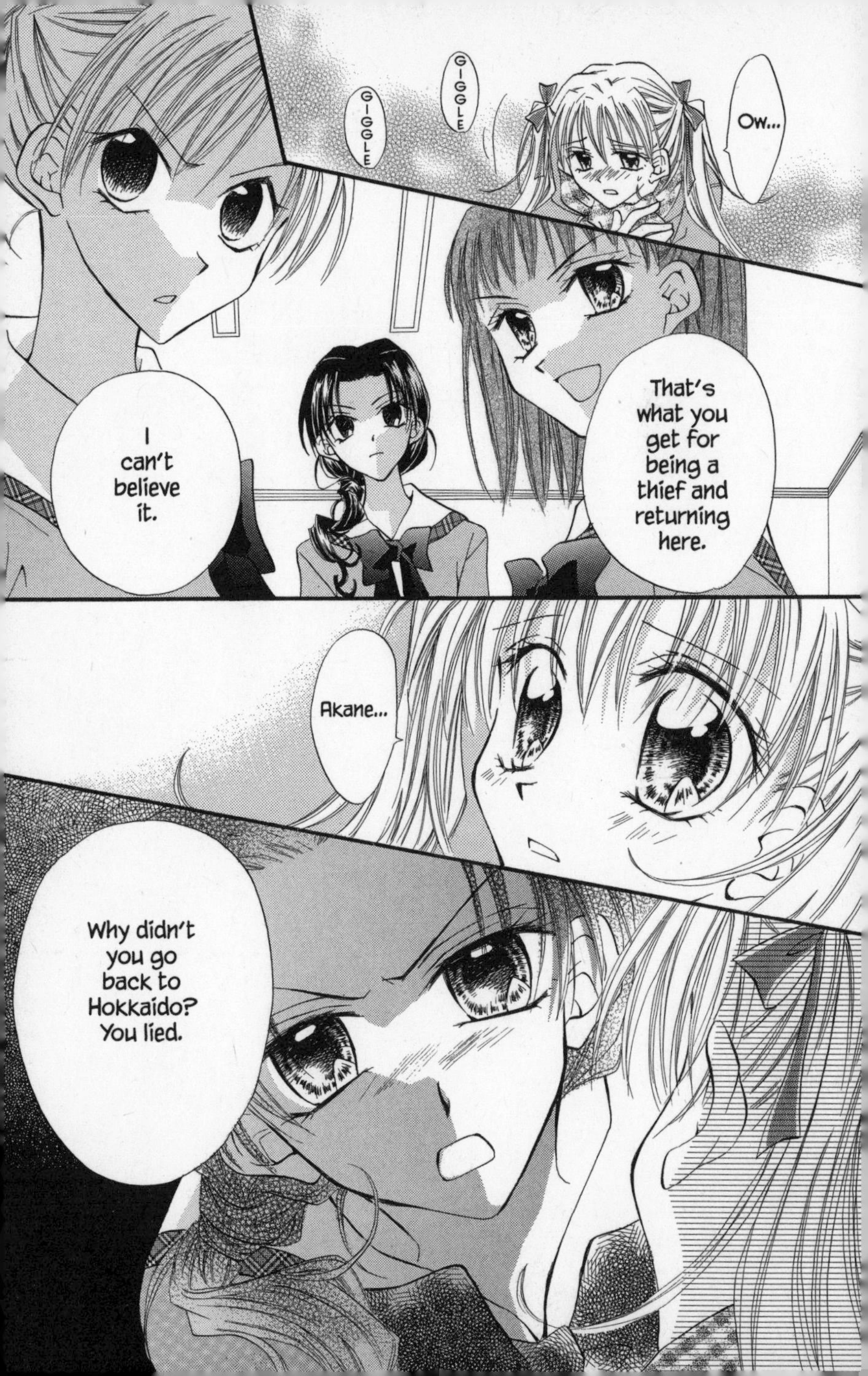
Ow...
GIGGLE
GIGGLE
That's what you get for being a thief and returning here.
I can't believe it.
Akane...
Why didn't you go back to Hokkaido? You lied.

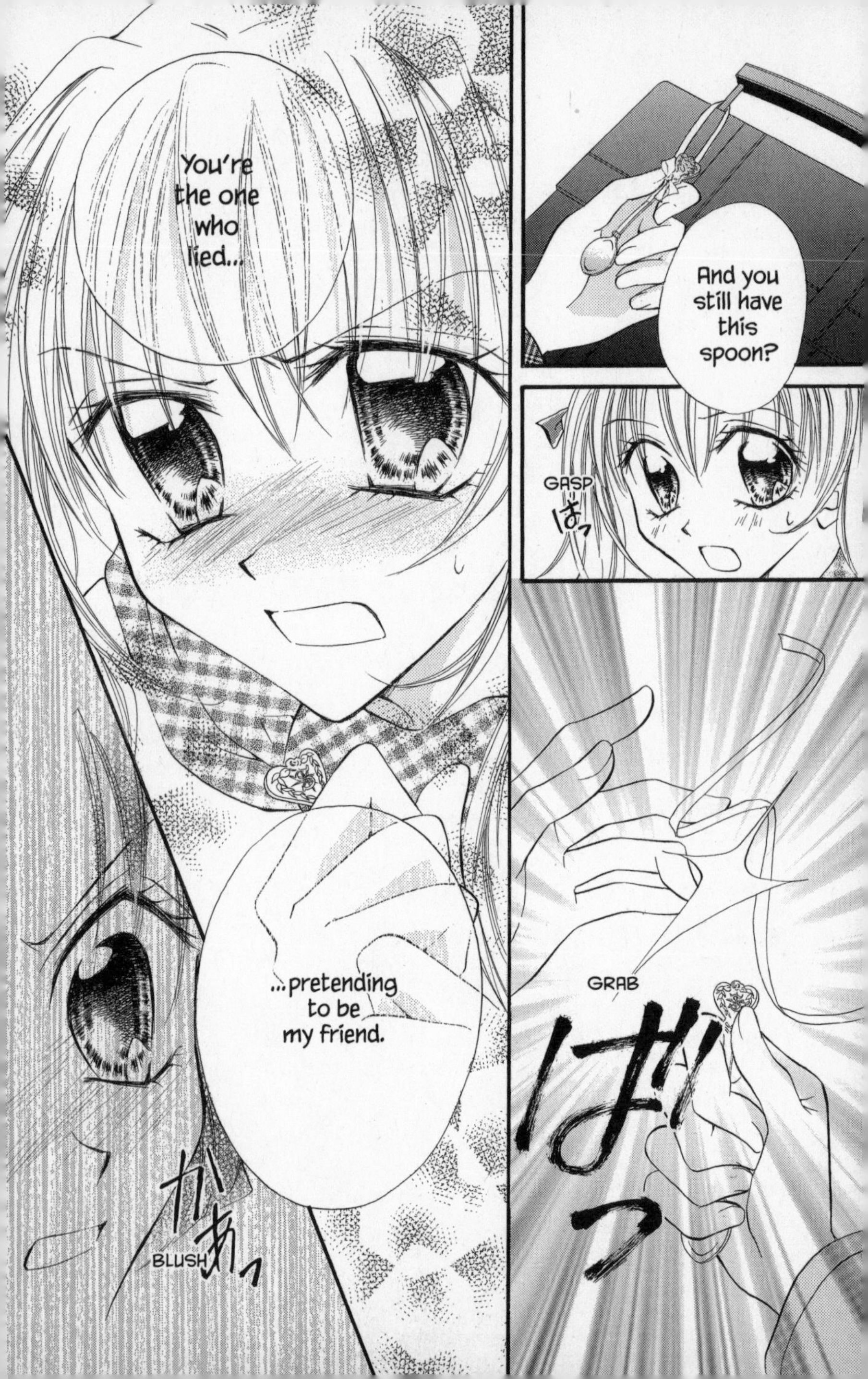
And you still have this spoon?
GASP
はっ
GRAB
You're the one who lied...
...pretending to be my friend.
BLUSH
かあっ

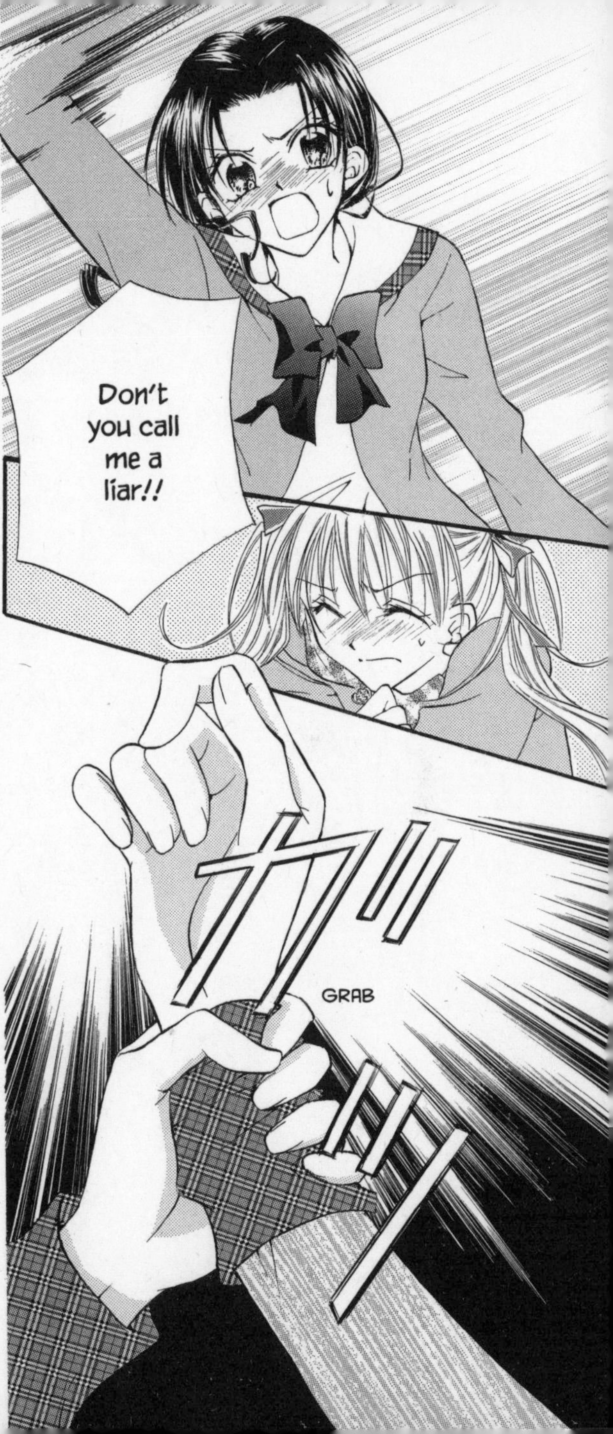
Don't you call me a liar!!
GRAB

Hello

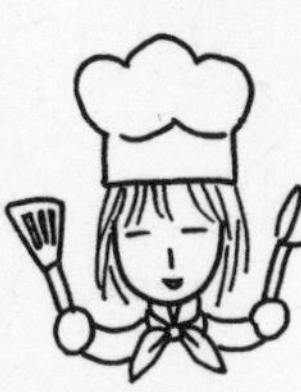

Hi there!
This is Ando, who's been drawing a manga about cooking when she hardly cooks herself. Lately during work I've been sucking on "Milkies." I love these!! I can eat a whole bag in a day. ♥
I even go through withdrawal when I run out. ♥
There are seasonal flavors, too. Strawberry, chocolate, and banana. But I like the original kind.
♥

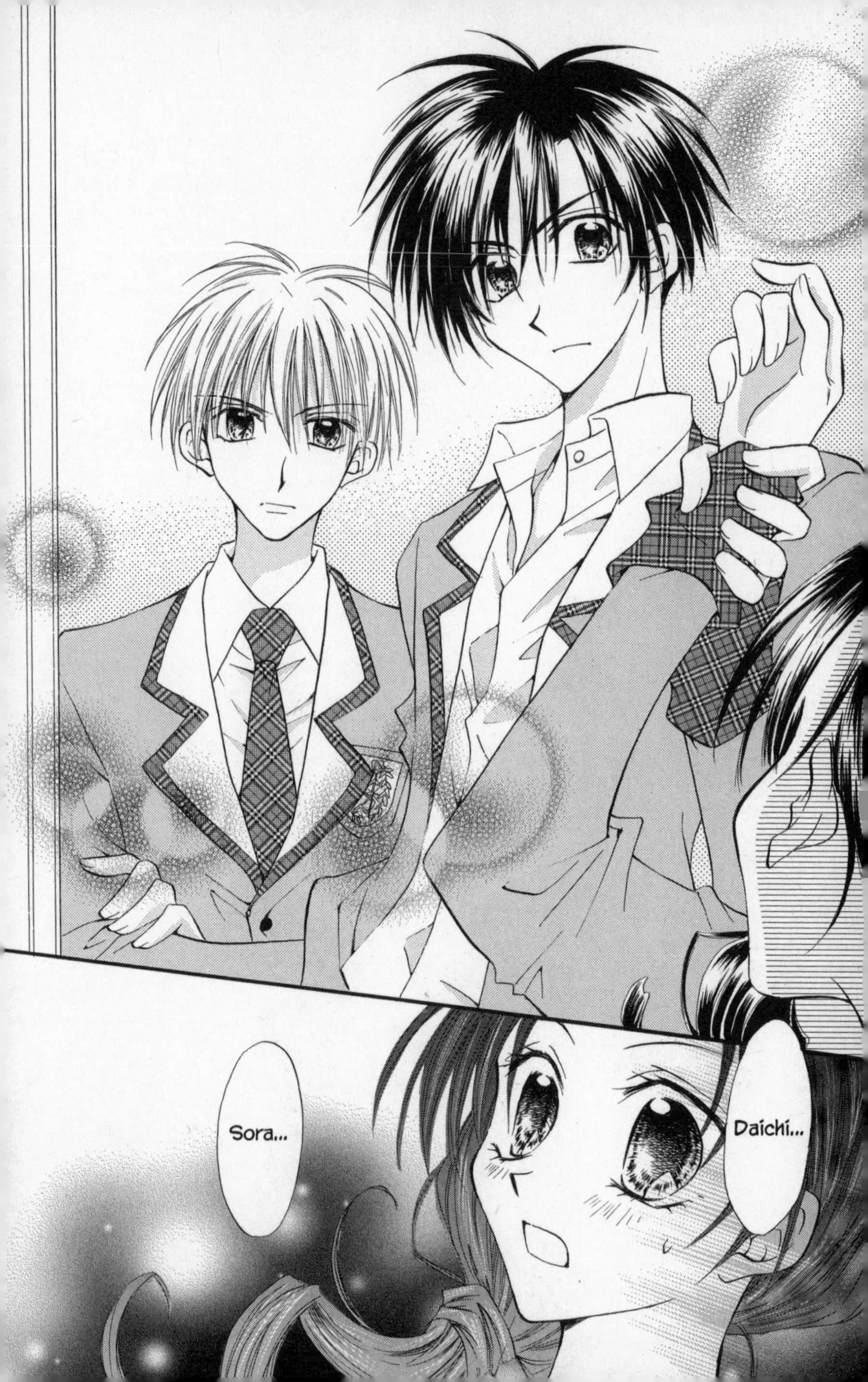
Daichi...
Sora...

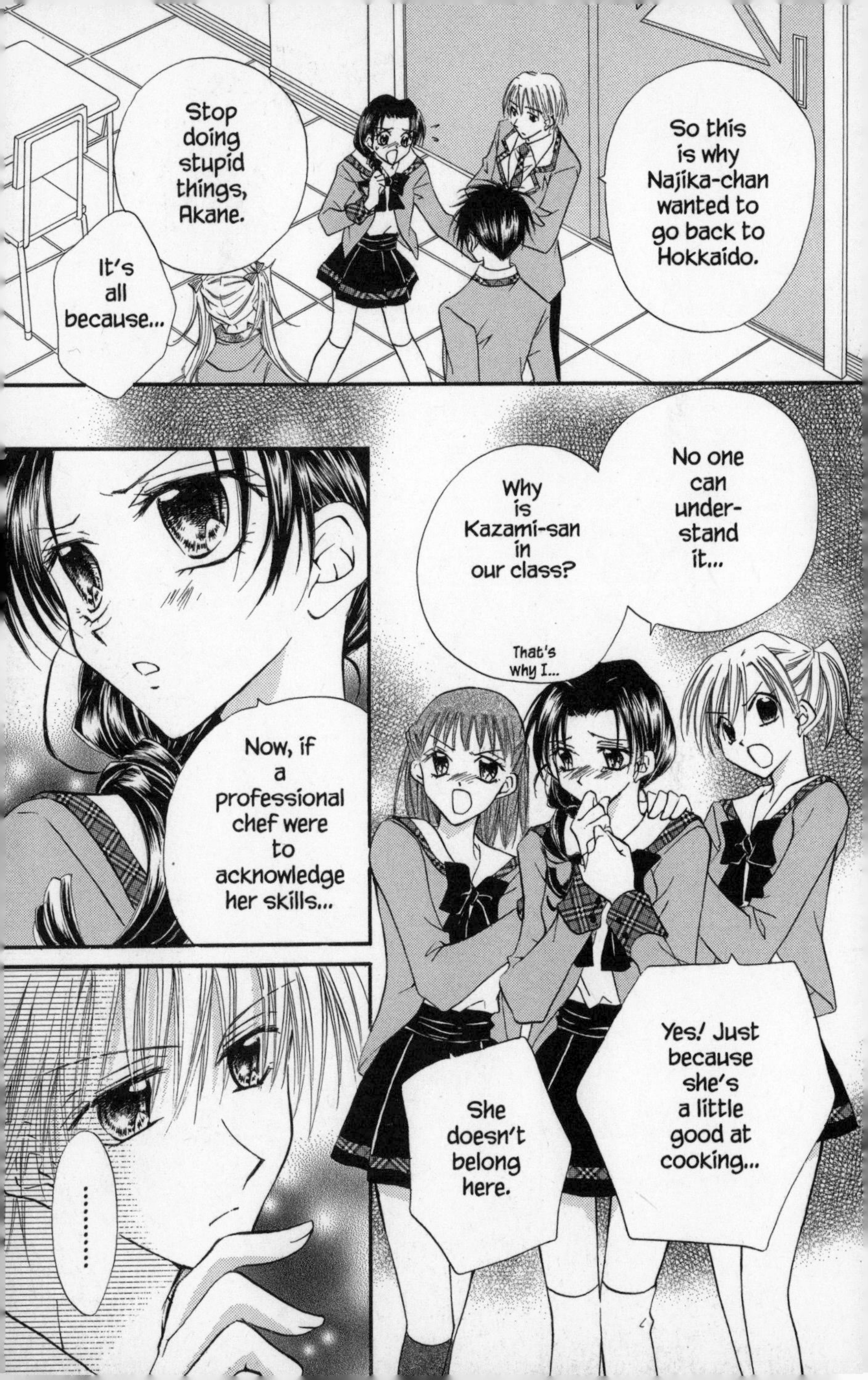
So this is why Najika-chan wanted to go back to Hokkaido.
Stop doing stupid things, Akane.
It's all because...
No one can under-stand it...
Why is Kazami-san in our class?
That's why I...
Yes! Just because she's a little good at cooking...
She doesn't belong here.
Now, if a professional chef were to acknowledge her skills...
....

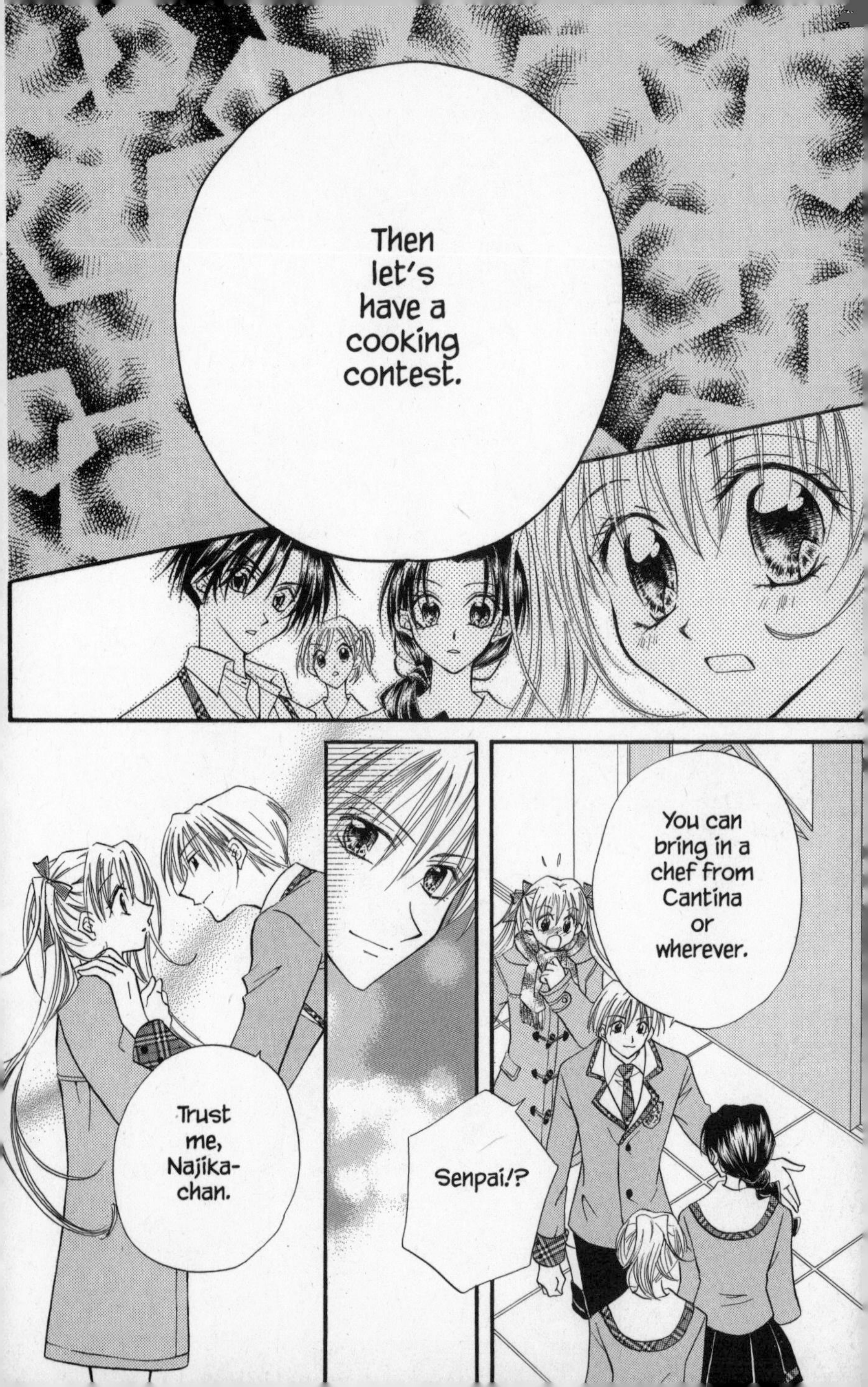
Then let's have a cooking contest.
You can bring in a chef from Cantina or wherever.
Senpai!?
Trust me, Najika-chan.

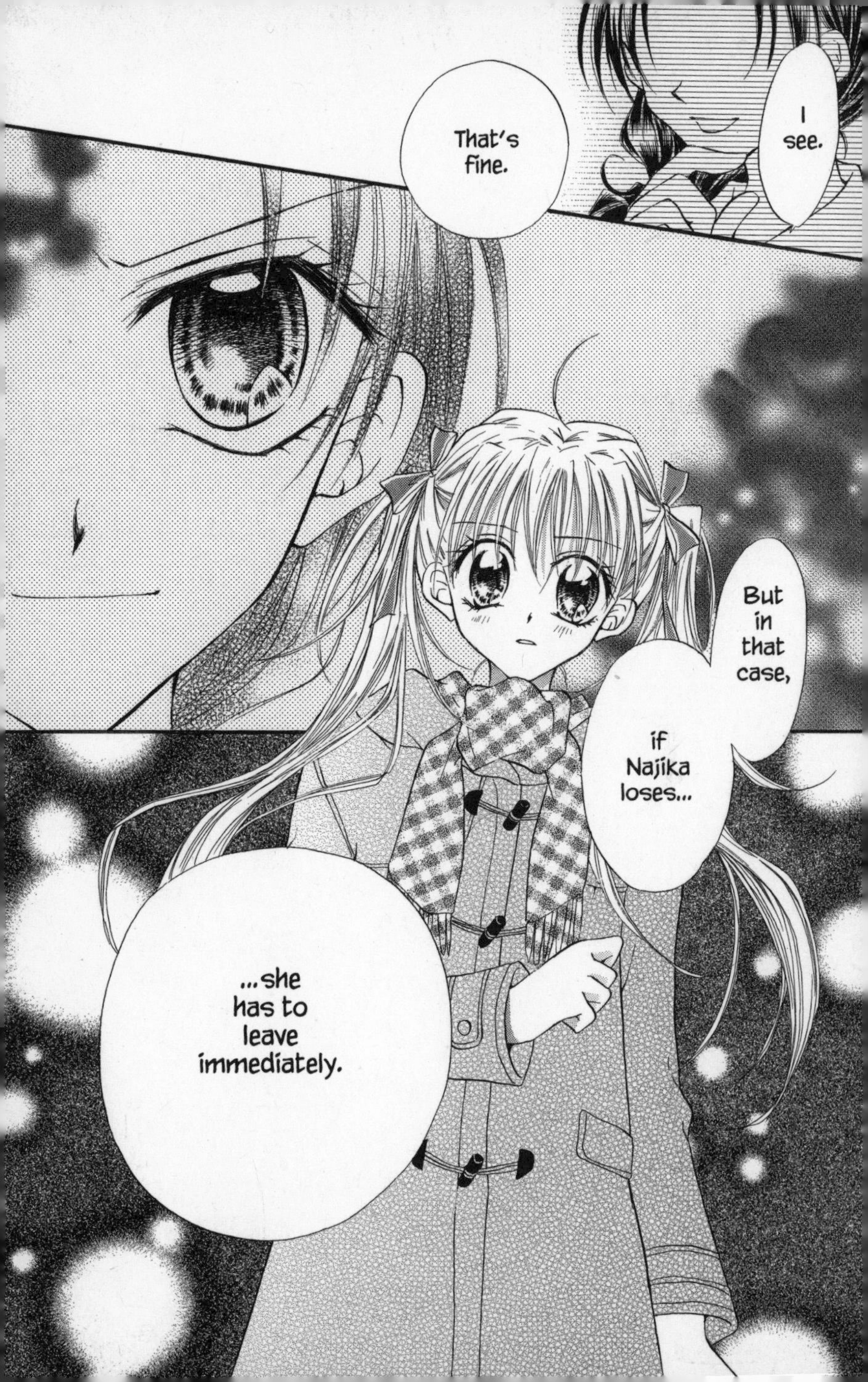
I see.
That's fine.
But in that case,
if Najika loses...
...she has to leave immediately.

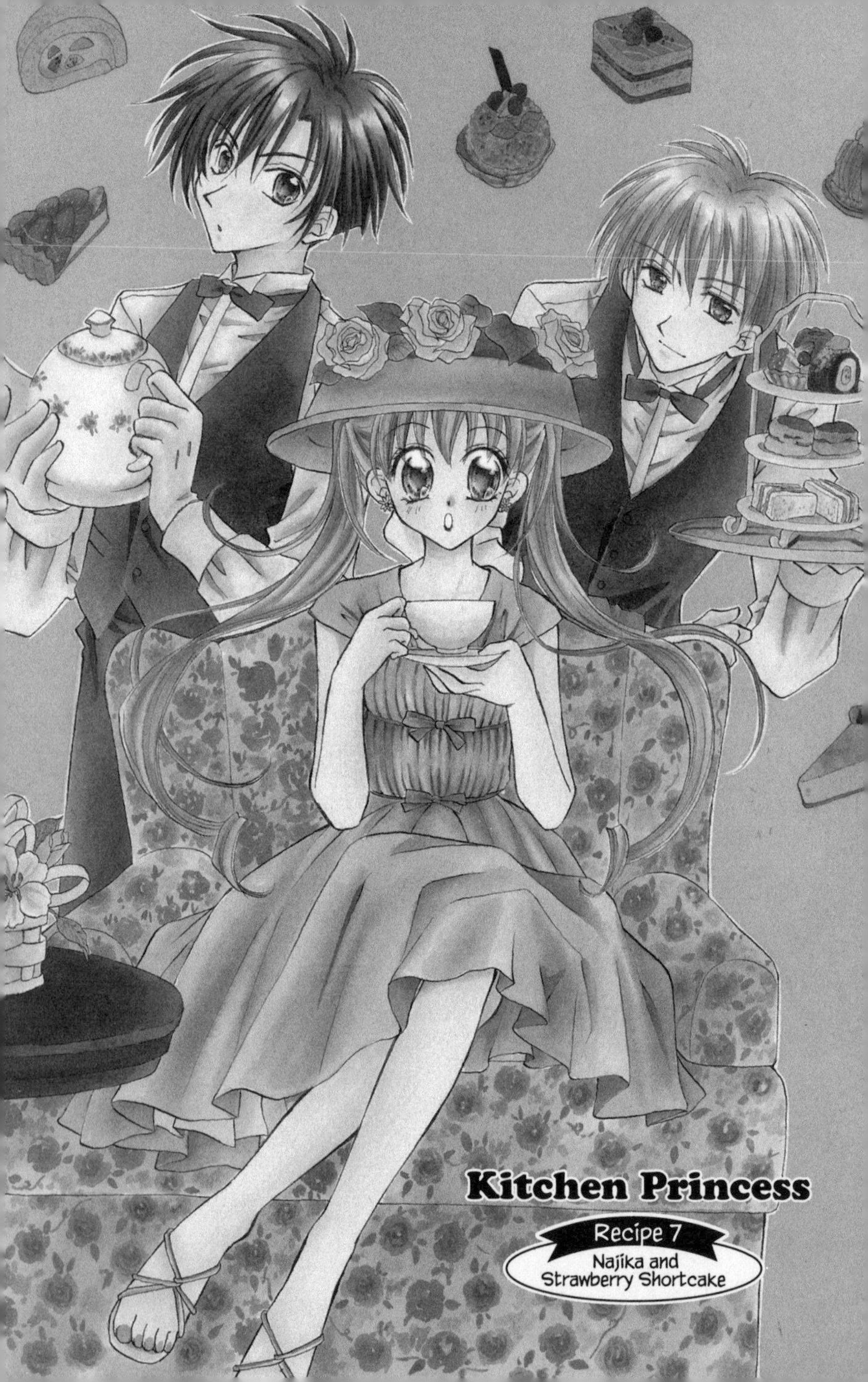
Kitchen Princess
Recipe 7
Najika and
Strawberry Shortcake

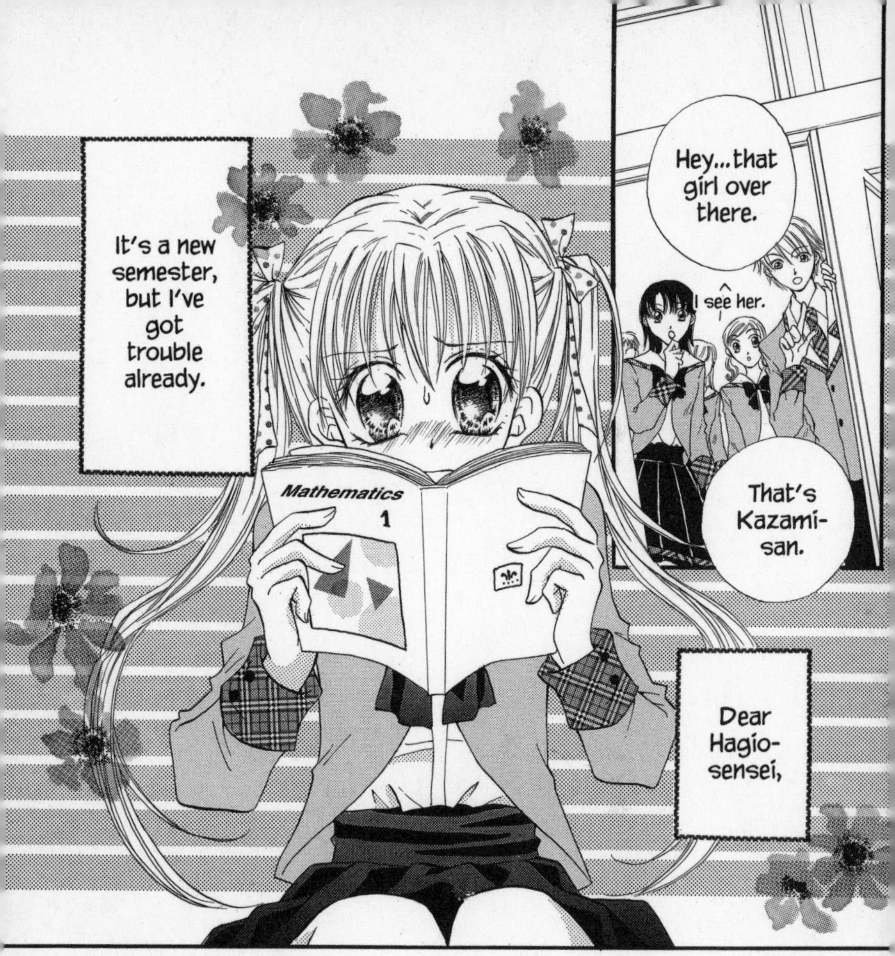
Hey...that girl over there.
I see her.
That's Kazami-san.
It's a new semester, but I've got trouble already.
Mathematics 1
Dear Hagio-sensei,

About Recipe 7's Splash Pag

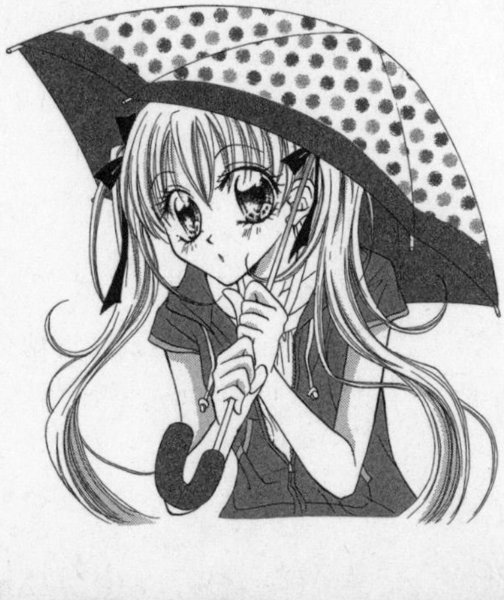

This is Najika chilling in a hotel lounge. The couch pattern was really difficult, and I regretted drawing it so many times while filling it in. Her clothes have a 1950s American feel.

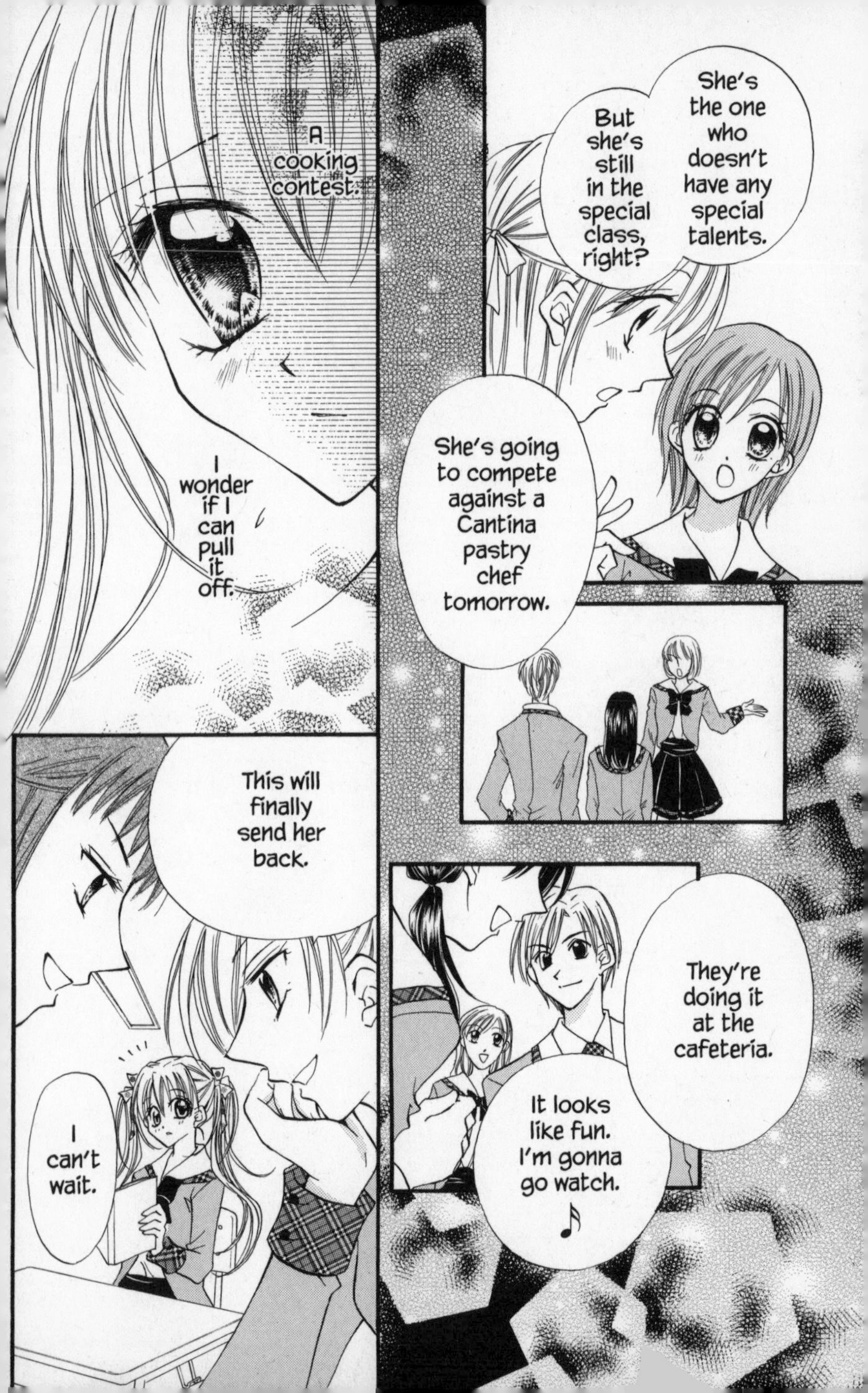

She's the one who doesn't have any special talents.
But she's still in the special class, right?
She's going to compete against a Cantina pastry chef tomorrow.
They're doing it at the cafeteria.
It looks like fun. I'm gonna go watch. ♪
A cooking contest.
I wonder if I can pull it off.
This will finally send her back.
I can't wait.

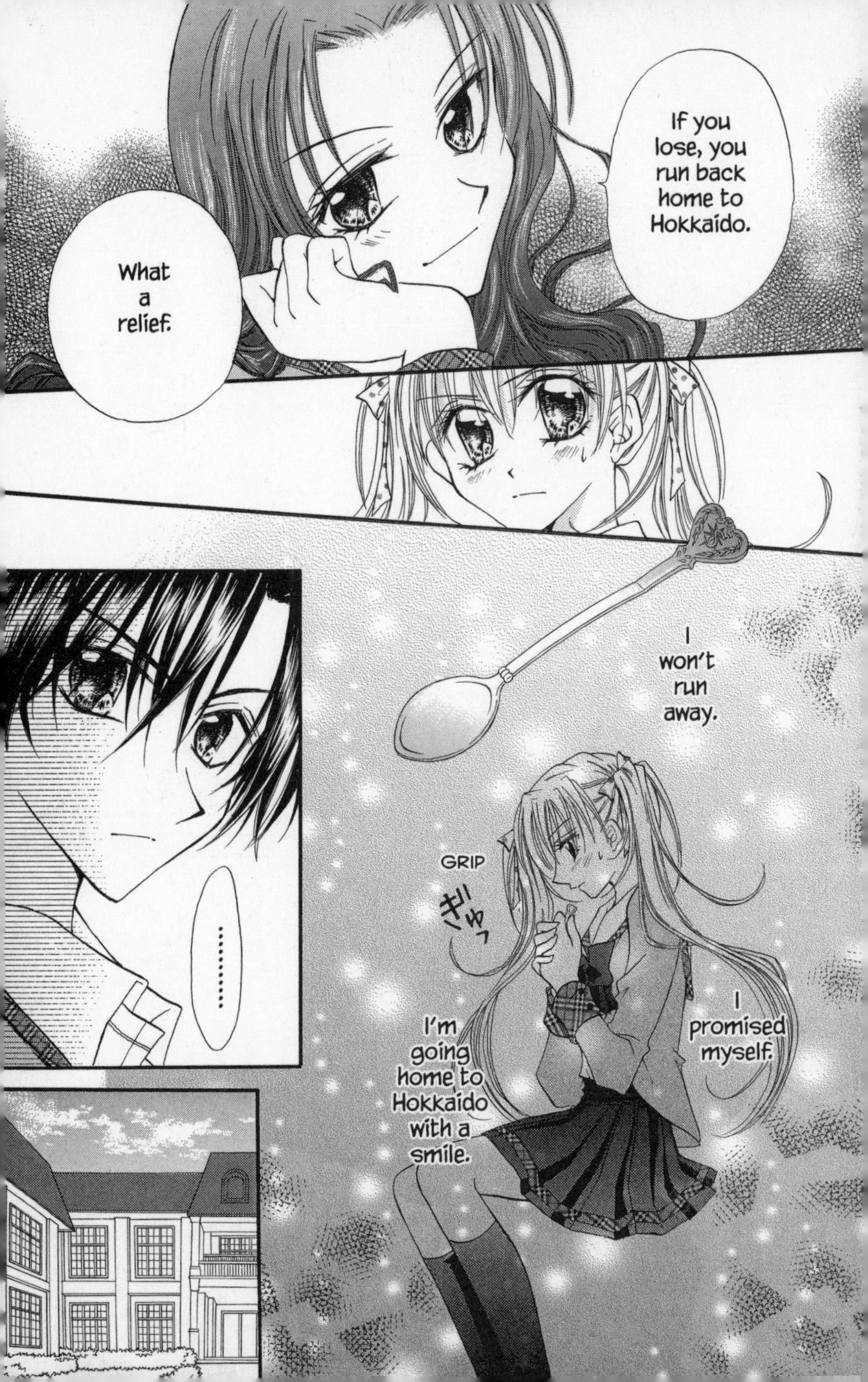
If you lose, you run back home to Hokkaido.
What a relief.
I won't run away.
GRIP
ぎゅっ
I promised myself.
I'm going home to Hokkaido with a smile.
......

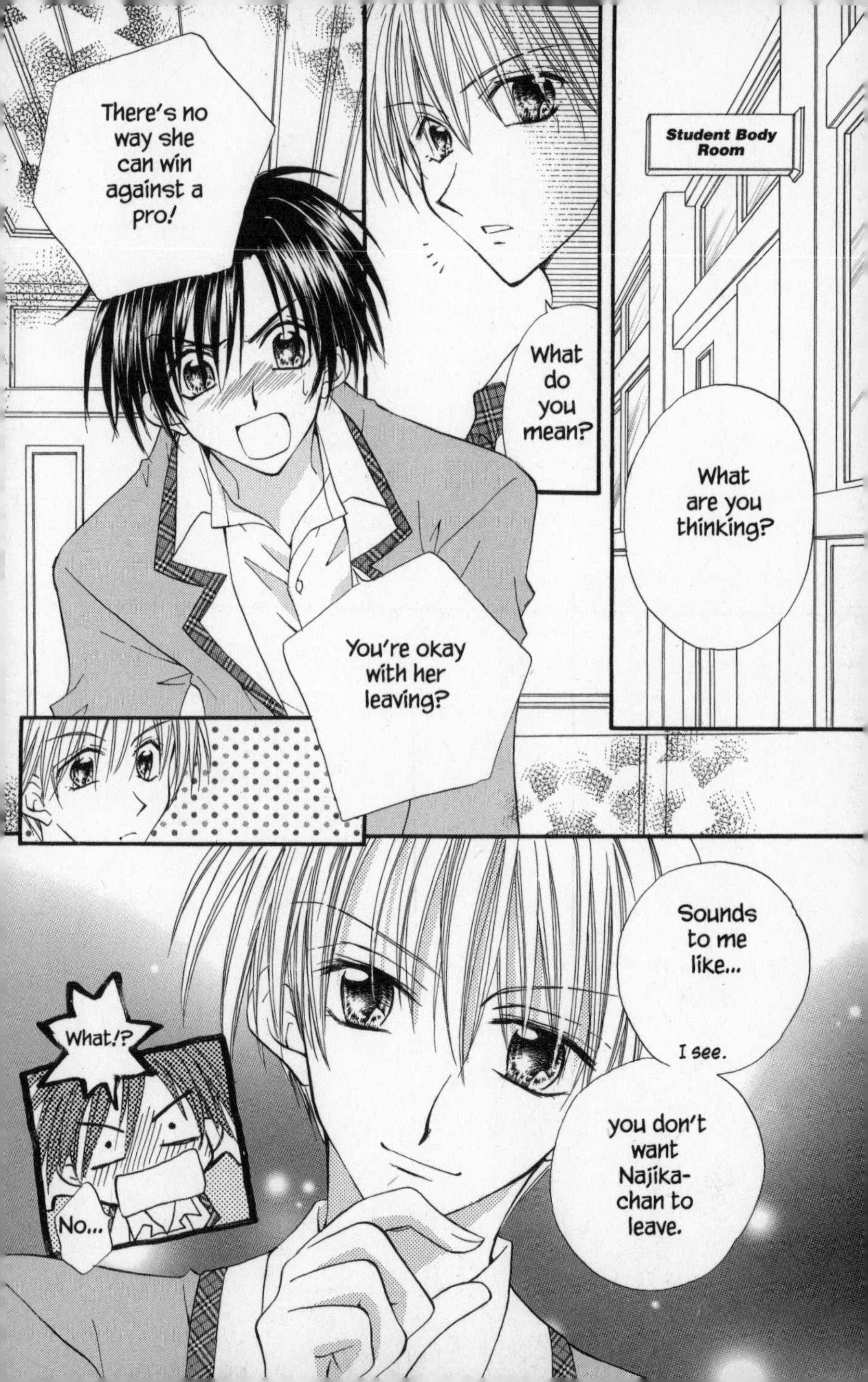
Student Body Room
What are you thinking?
What do you mean?
There's no way she can win against a pro!
You're okay with her leaving?
Sounds to me like...
I see.
you don't want Najika-chan to leave.
What!?
No...

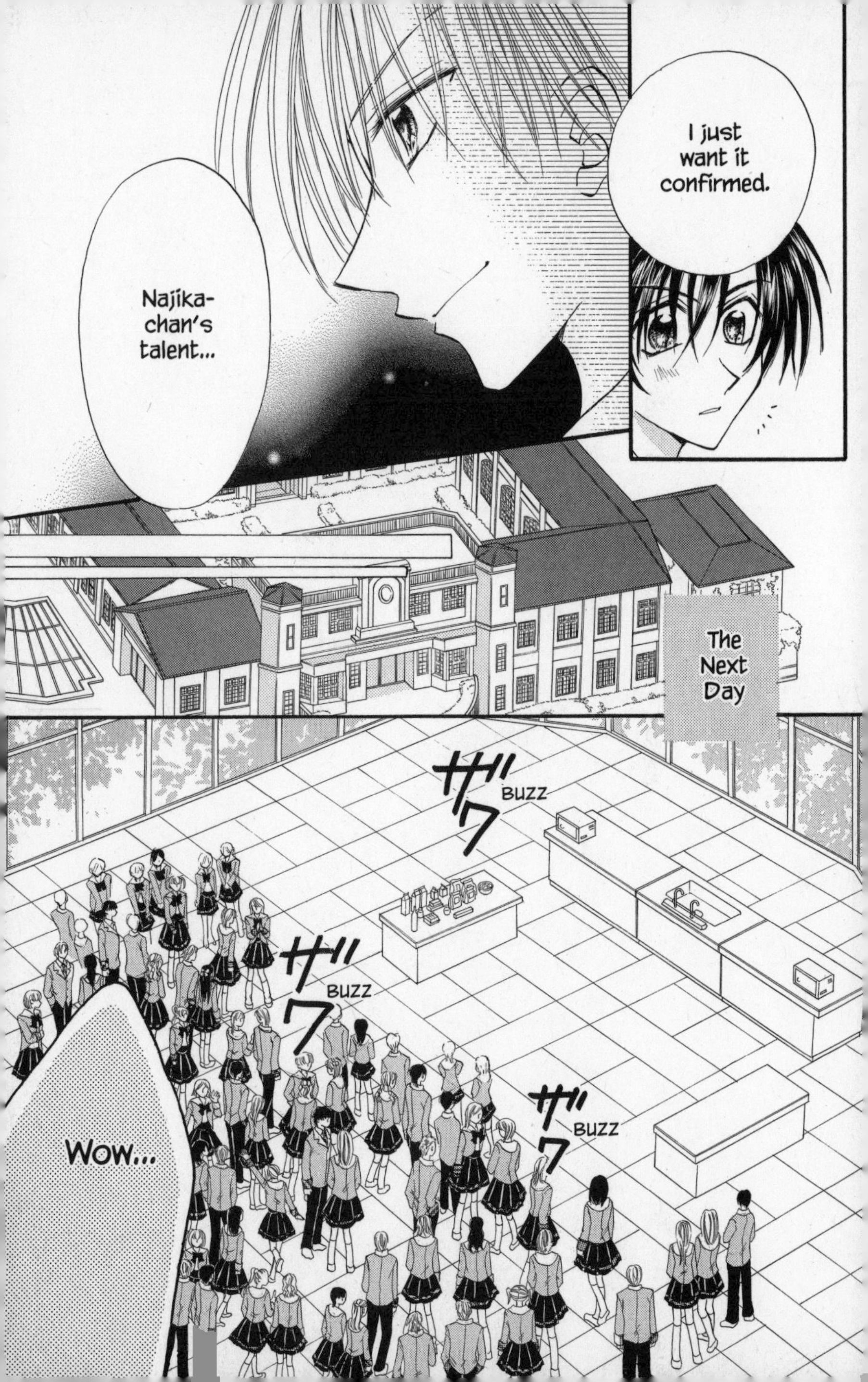
I just want it confirmed.
Najika-chan's talent...
The Next Day
ザワ
BUZZ
ザワ
BUZZ
ザワ
BUZZ
Wow...

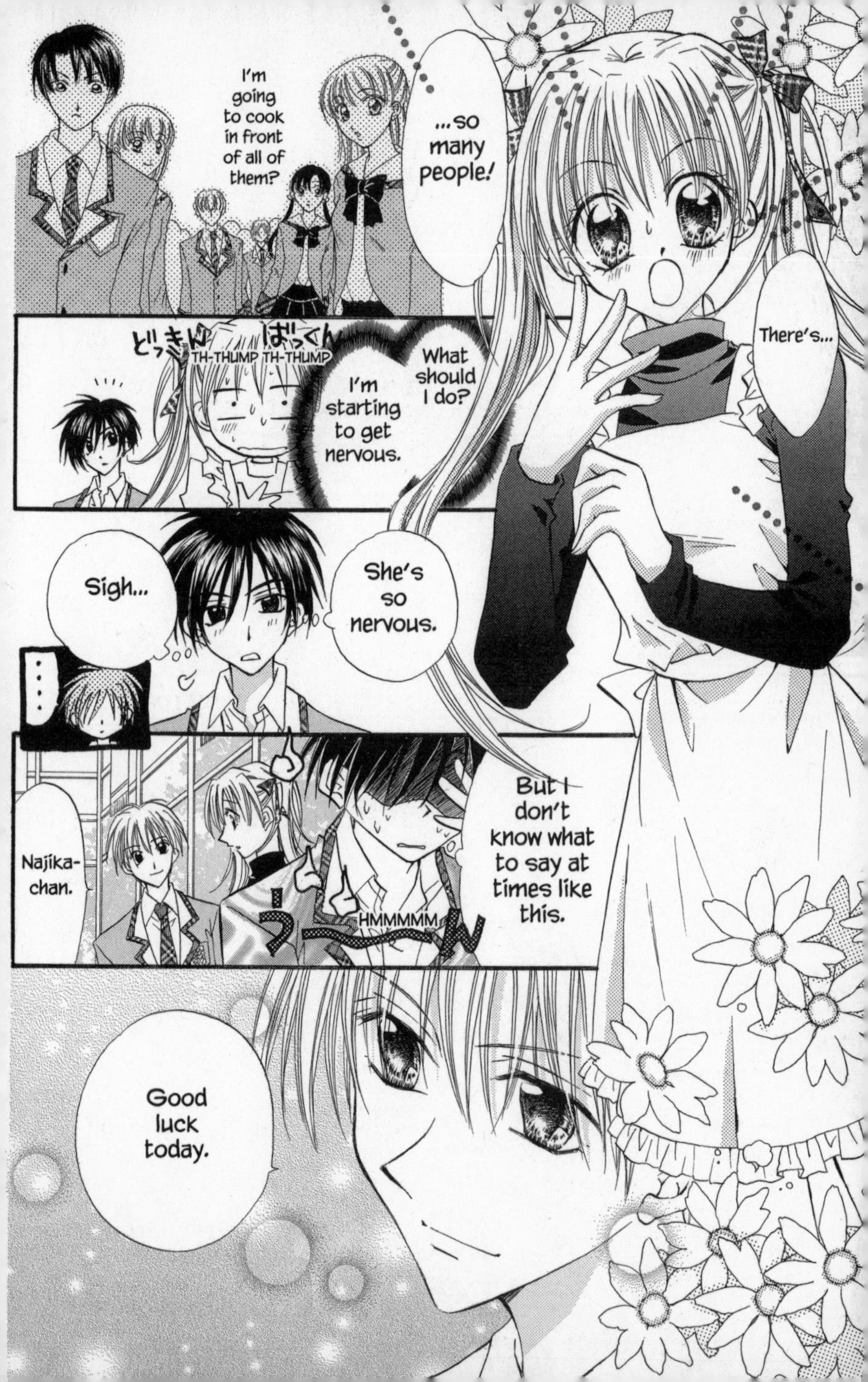
There's...
...so many people!
I'm going to cook in front of all of them?
ばっくん TH-THUMP
どっきん TH-THUMP
What should I do?
I'm starting to get nervous.
She's so nervous.
Sigh...
...
But I don't know what to say at times like this.
うーーん HMMMMM
Najika-chan.
Good luck today.

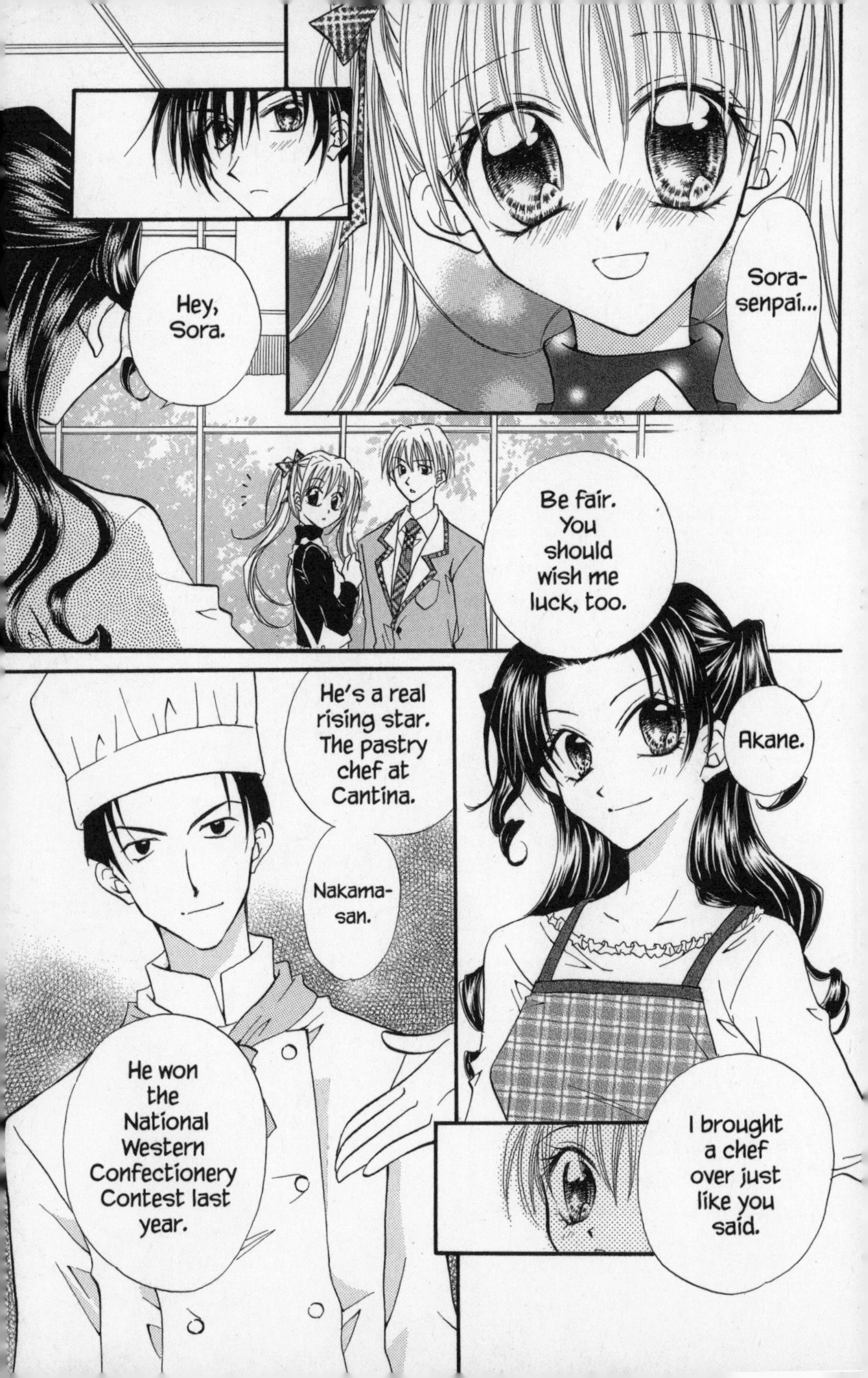
Sora-senpai...
Hey, Sora.
Be fair. You should wish me luck, too.
Akane.
I brought a chef over just like you said.
He's a real rising star. The pastry chef at Cantina.
Nakama-san.
He won the National Western Confectionery Contest last year.

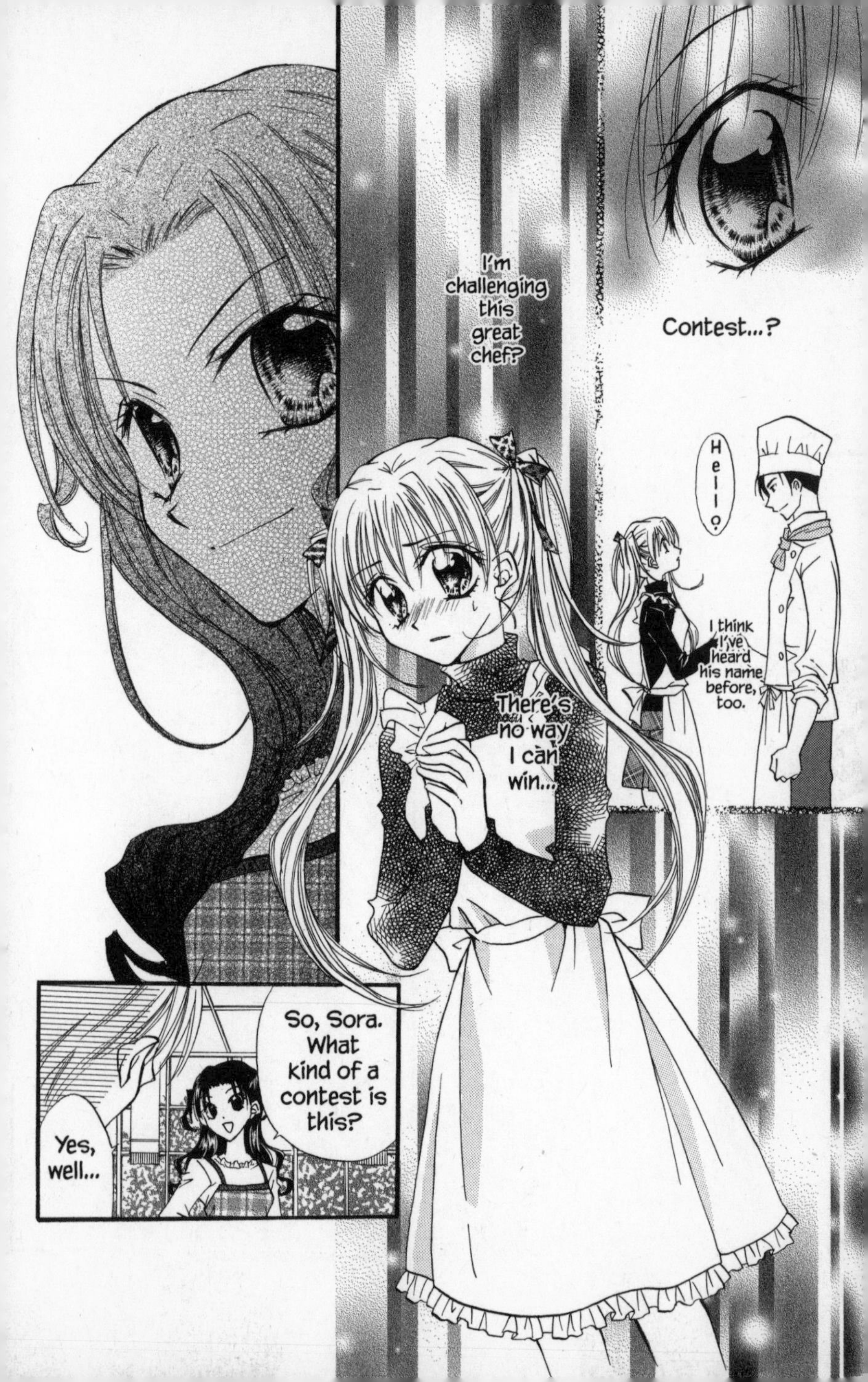
Contest...?
Hello.
I think I've heard his name before, too.
I'm challenging this great chef?
There's no way I can win...
So, Sora. What kind of a contest is this?
Yes, well...

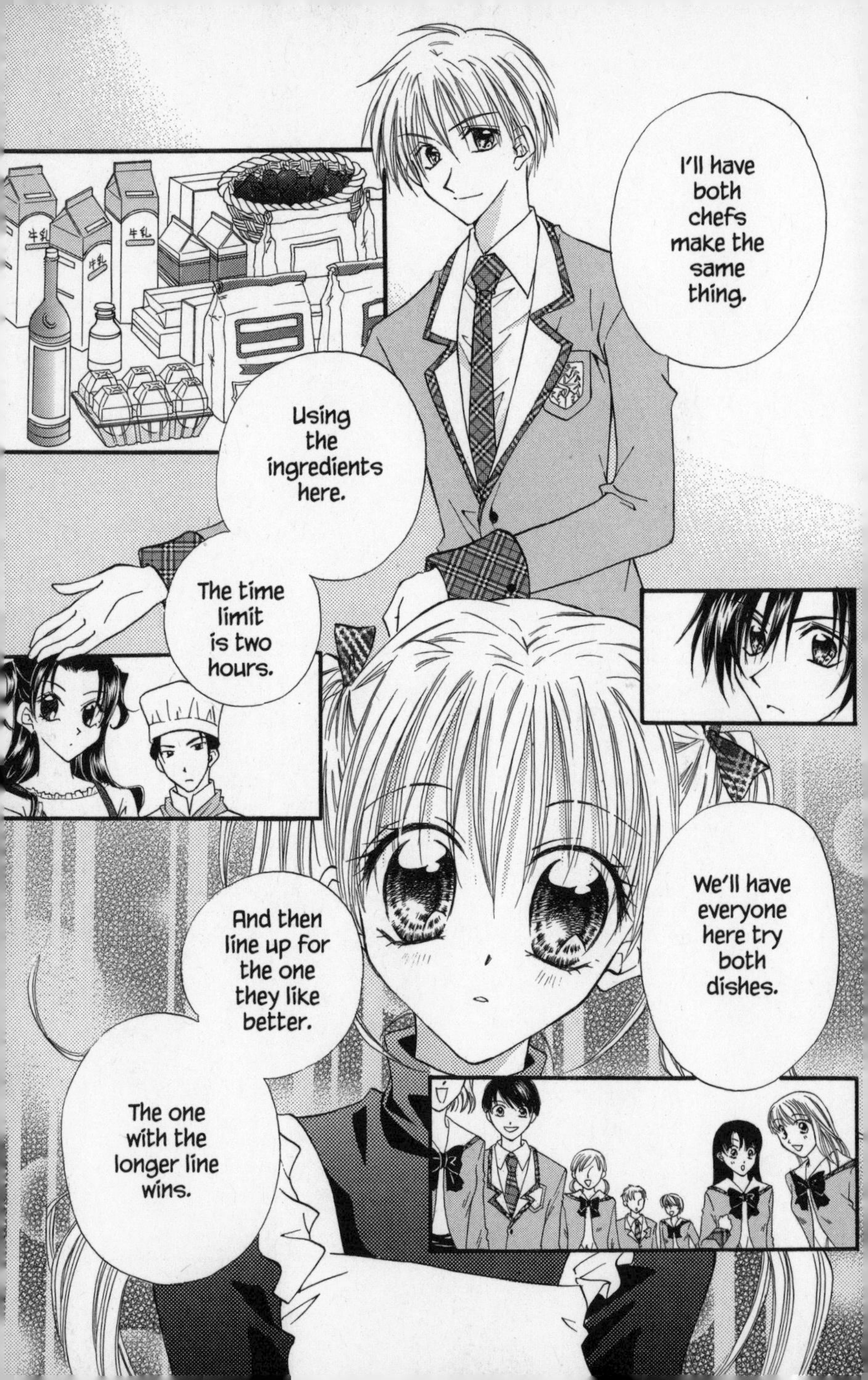
I'll have both chefs make the same thing.
Using the ingredients here.
The time limit is two hours.
We'll have everyone here try both dishes.
And then line up for the one they like better.
The one with the longer line wins.

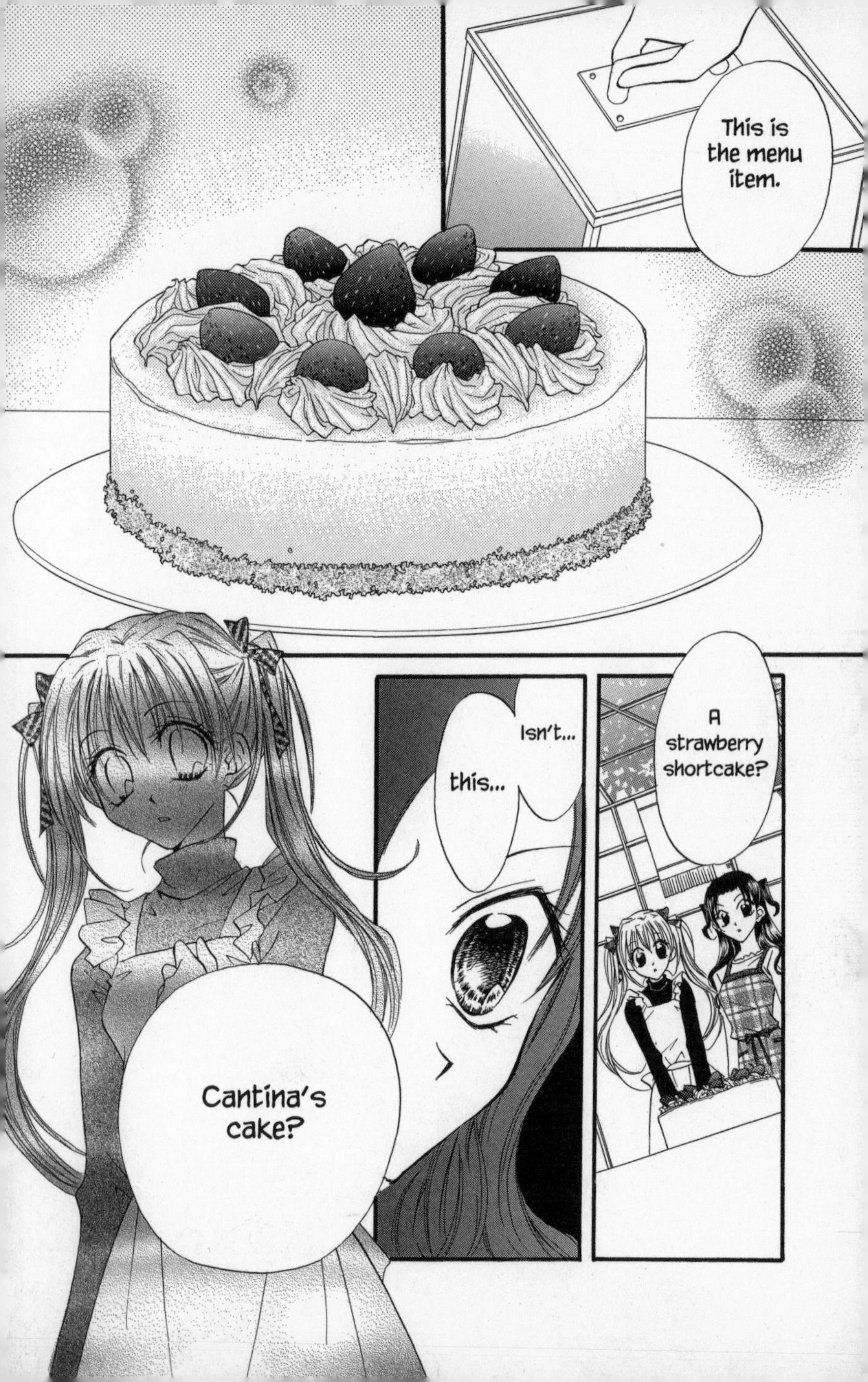
This is the menu item.
A strawberry shortcake?
Isn't... this...
Cantina's cake?

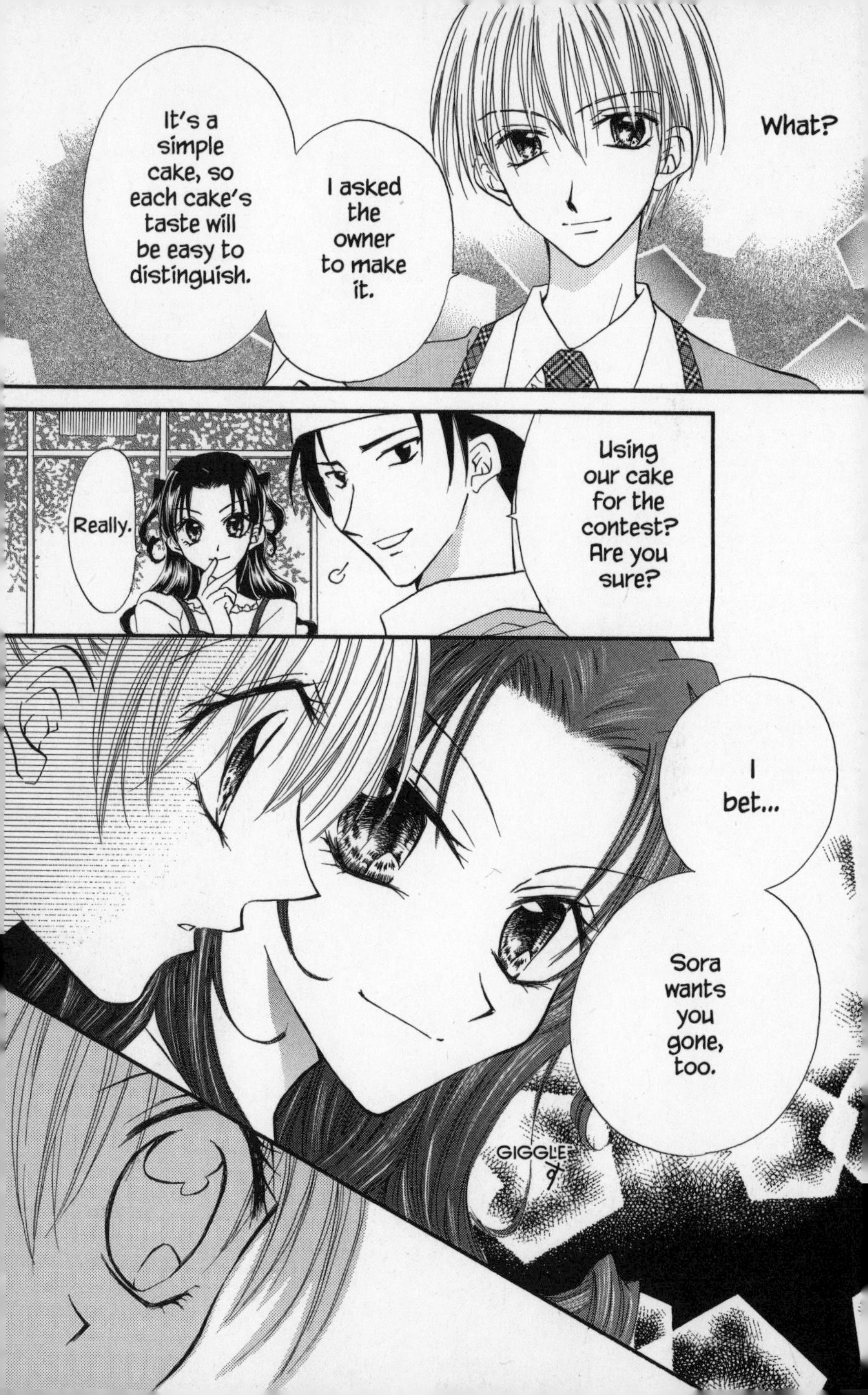
What?
I asked the owner to make it.
It's a simple cake, so each cake's taste will be easy to distinguish.
Using our cake for the contest? Are you sure?
Really.
I bet...
Sora wants you gone, too.
GIGGLE

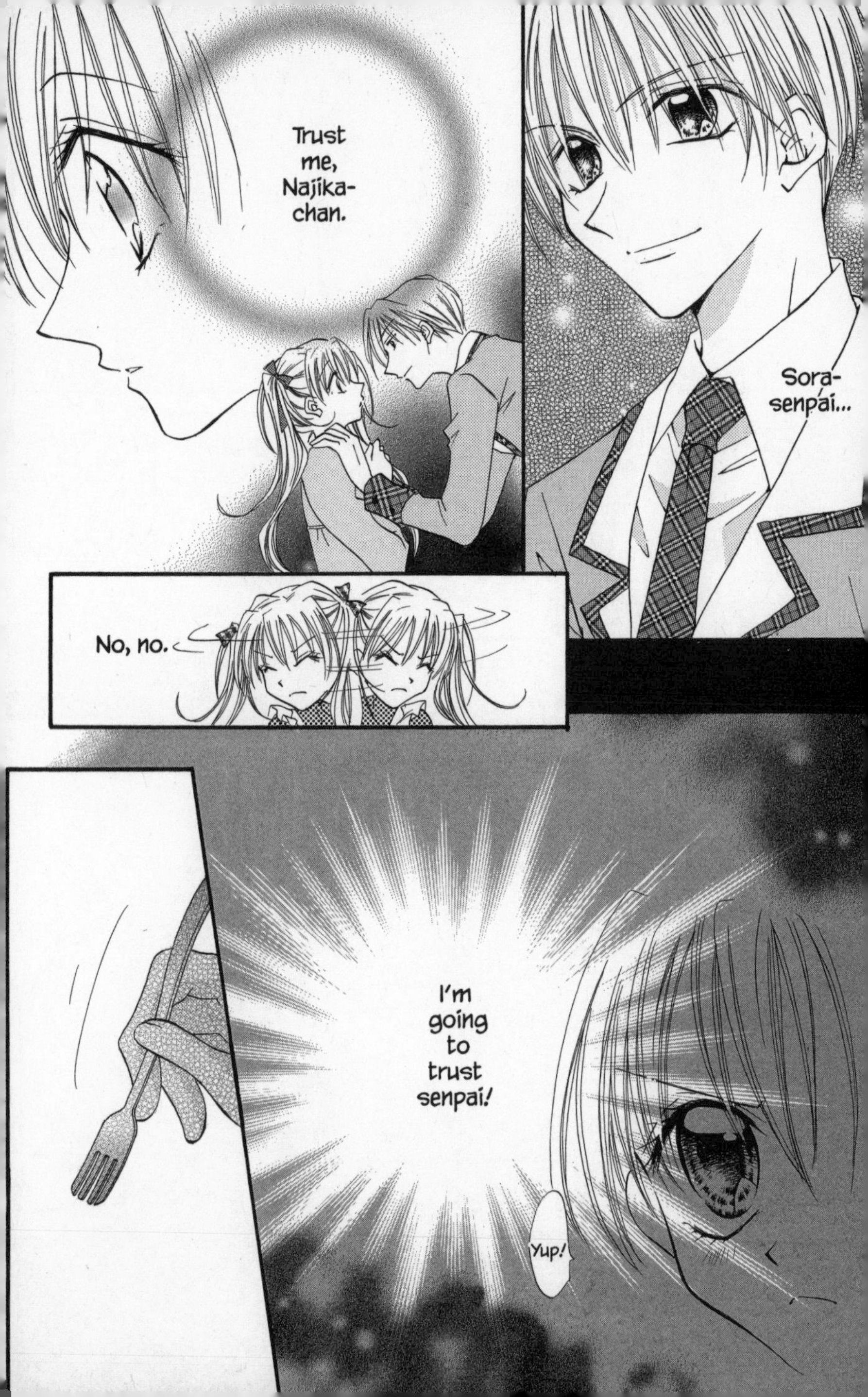
Sora-senpai...
Trust me, Najika-chan.
No, no.
I'm going to trust senpai!
Yup!

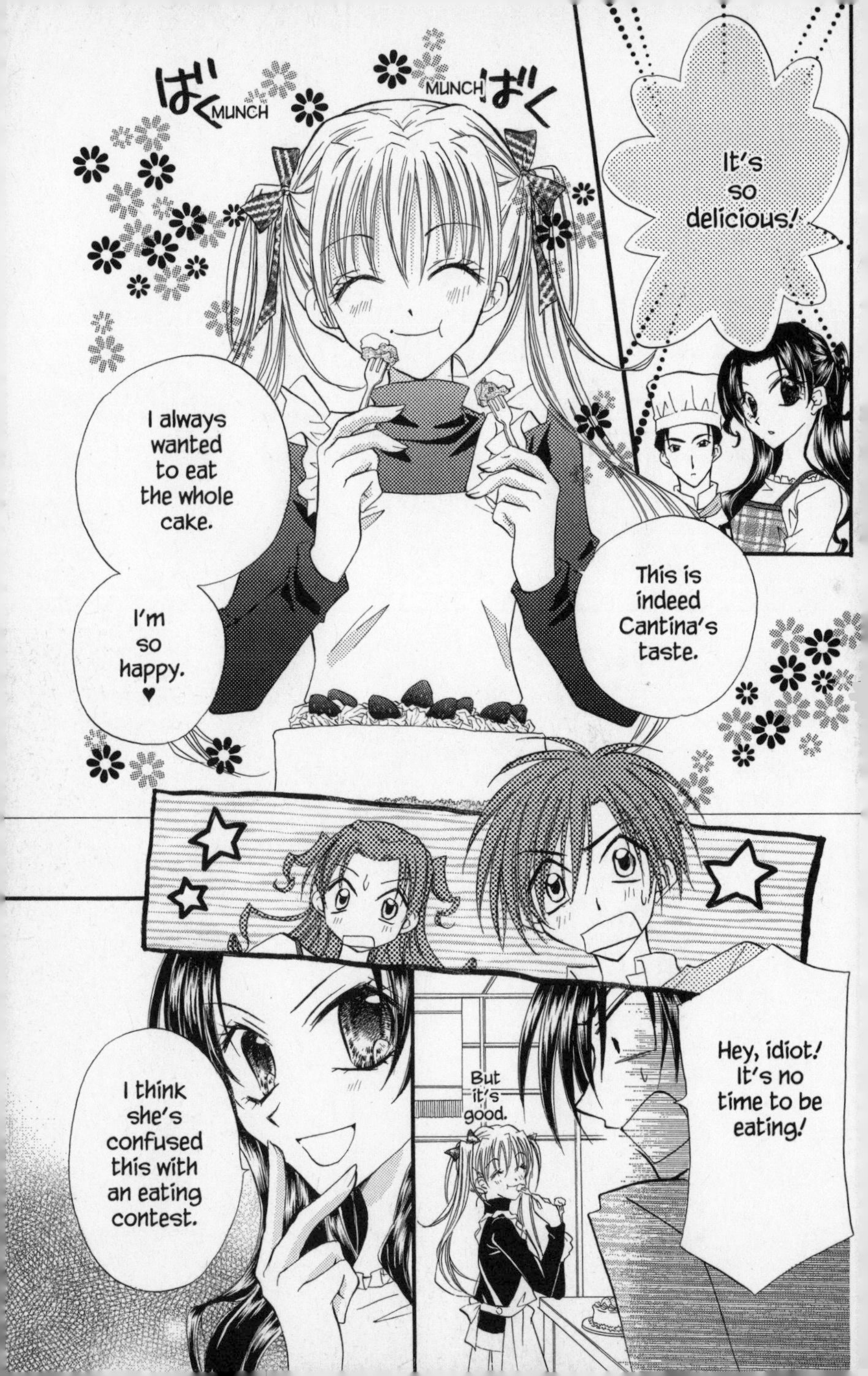
It's so delicious!
MUNCH ぱく
ぱく MUNCH
I always wanted to eat the whole cake.
I'm so happy. ♥
This is indeed Cantina's taste.
Hey, idiot! It's no time to be eating!
But it's good.
I think she's confused this with an eating contest.

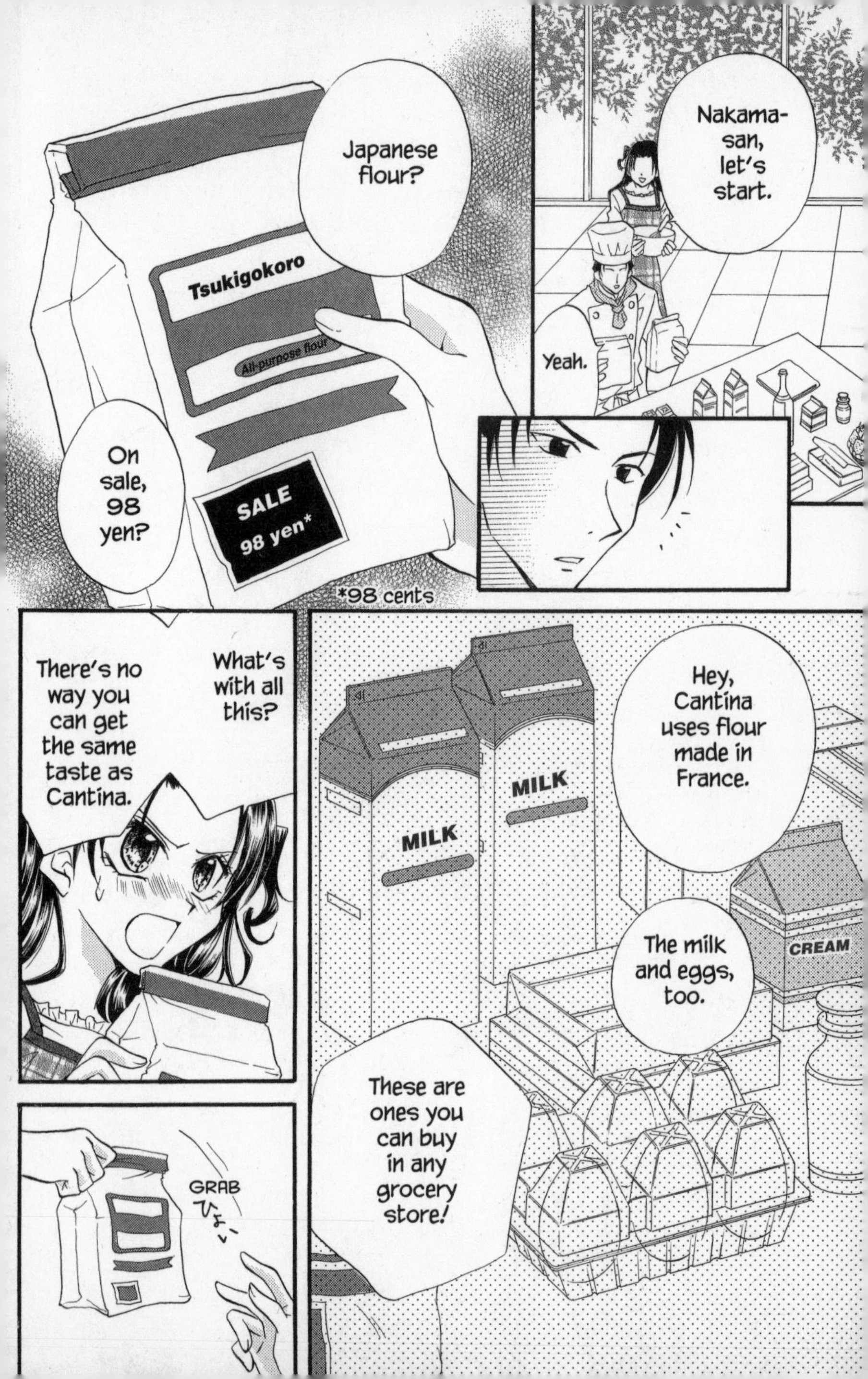
Nakama-san, let's start.
Yeah.
Japanese flour?
Tsukigokoro
All-purpose flour
On sale, 98 yen?
SALE 98 yen*
*98 cents
Hey, Cantina uses flour made in France.
MILK
MILK
CREAM
The milk and eggs, too.
These are ones you can buy in any grocery store!
What's with all this?
There's no way you can get the same taste as Cantina.
GRAB
ひょい

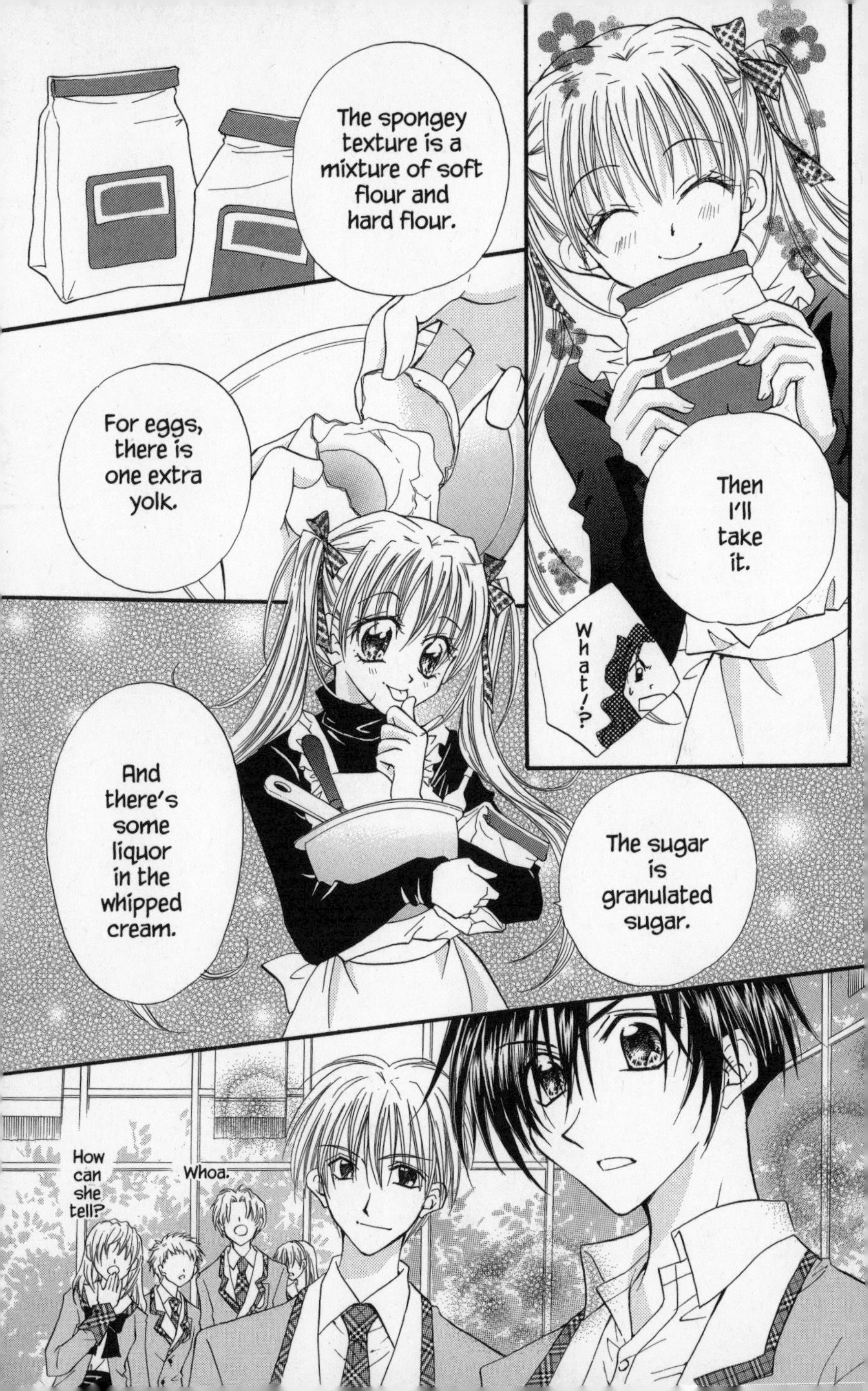
Then I'll take it.
What!?
The spongey texture is a mixture of soft flour and hard flour.
For eggs, there is one extra yolk.
The sugar is granulated sugar.
And there's some liquor in the whipped cream.
Whoa.
How can she tell?

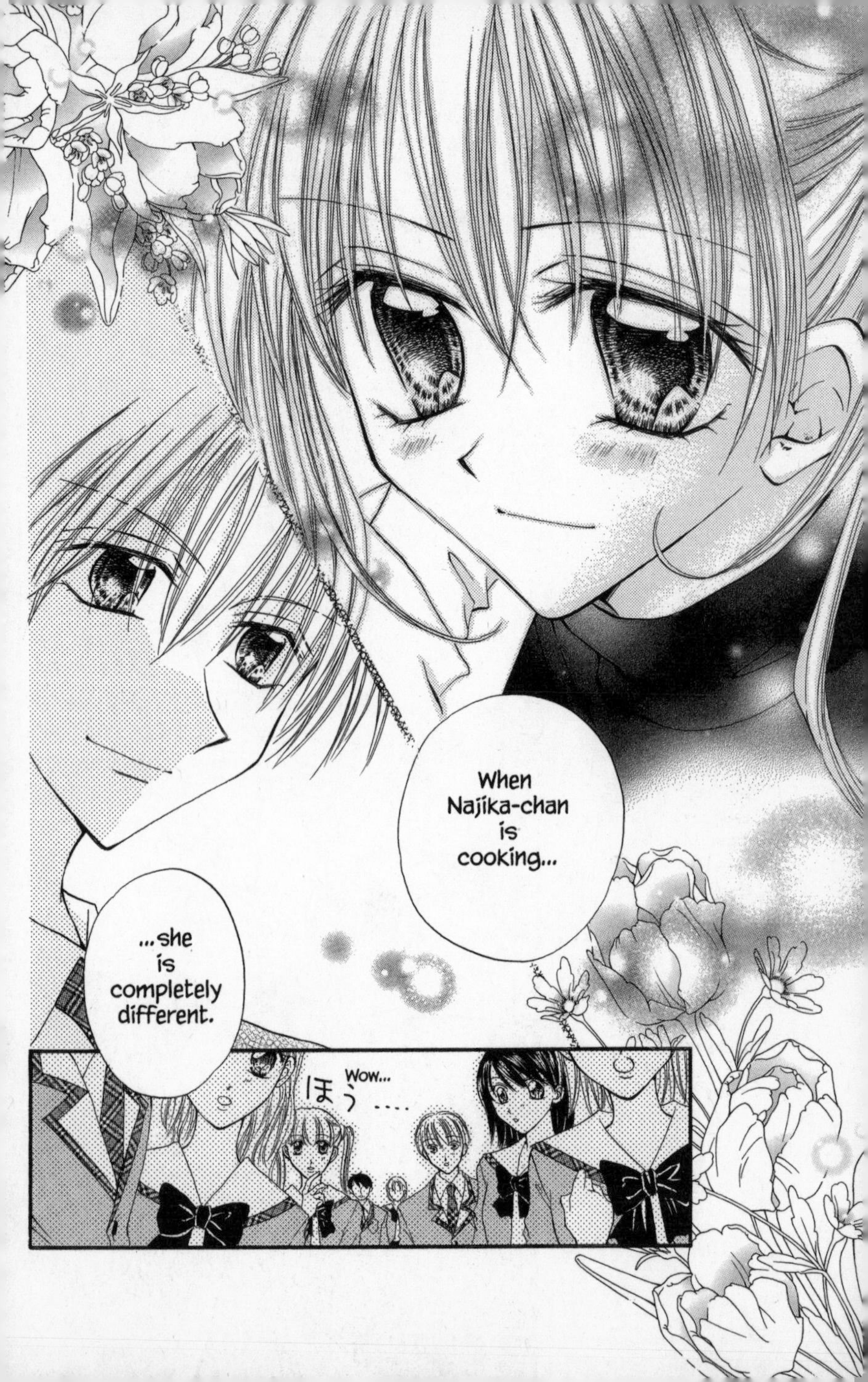
When Najika-chan is cooking...
...she is completely different.
ほう....
Wow...

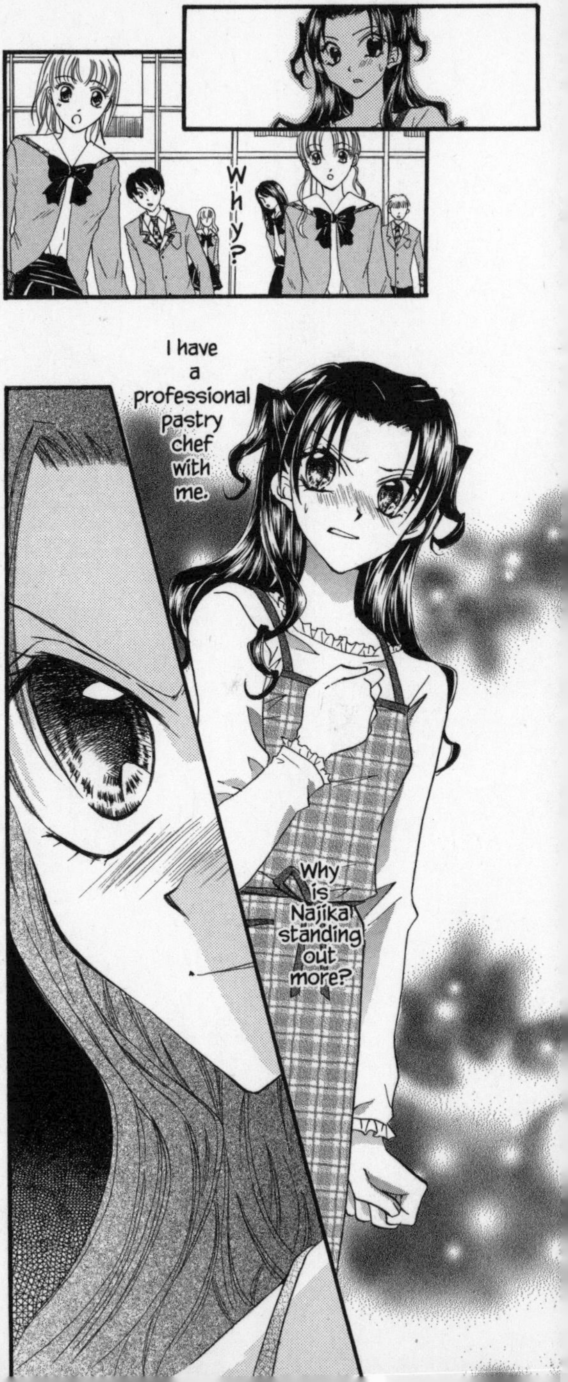
Why?
I have a professional pastry chef with me.
Why is Najika standing out more?

This is a first for me. I would like to talk about memories from each chapter. There may be spoilers, so please read it after you read the story. ♥

Recipe 6

In this chapter, Najika makes the chocolate macaroons. Miyuki-sensei actually sent some, so I got to eat them. Since they were so good, I decided to make them. But it was impossible. Why? Because I don't have an oven...

Recipe 7

When I was younger, I remember making something where I had to whisk the eggs really hard. And I imagined how I would feel if someone dropped it, so I let Akane do that to Najika (laugh). A store that has good strawberry shortcake has good everything else, don't you think? ♥

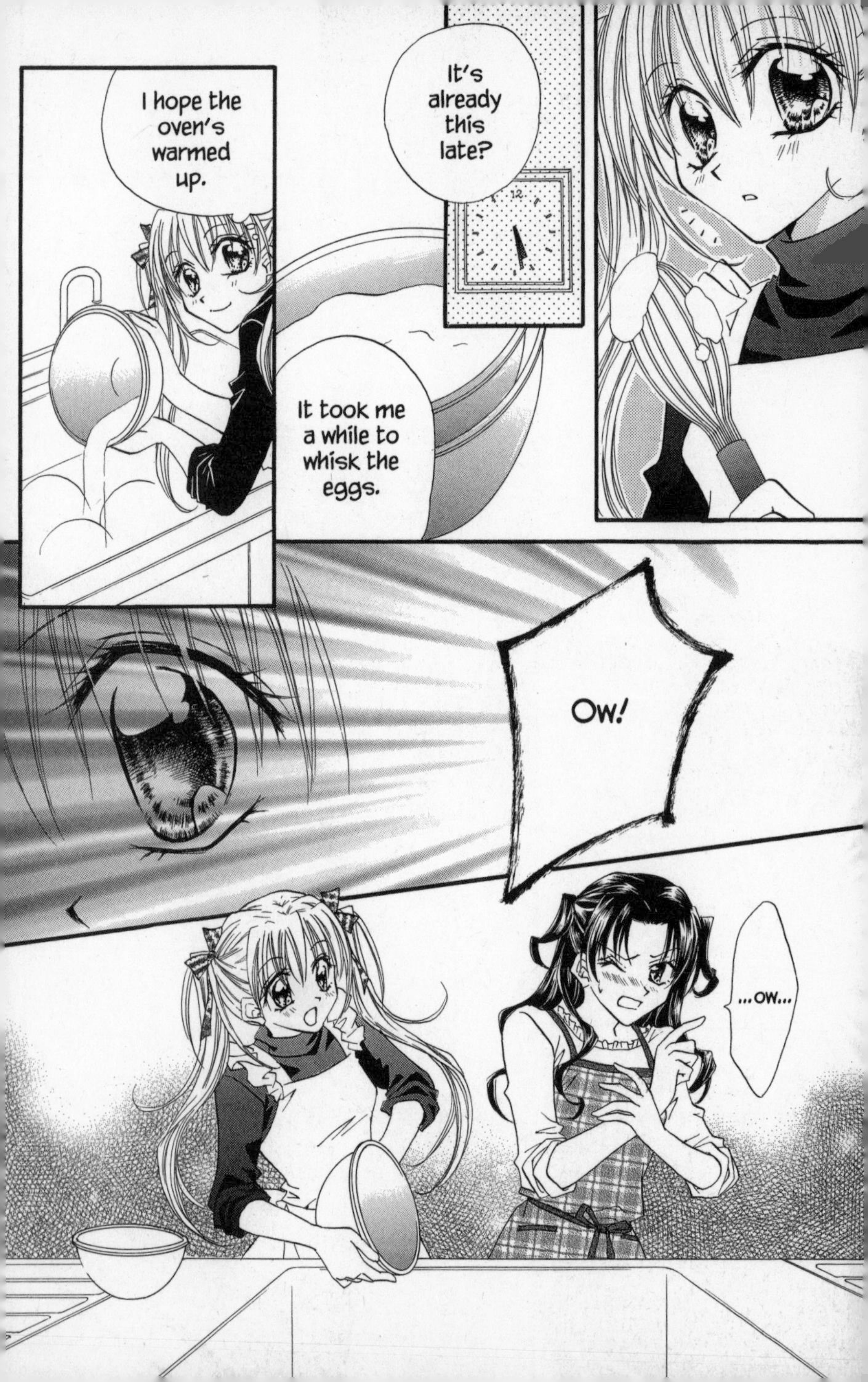
It took me a while to whisk the eggs.
It's already this late?
I hope the oven's warmed up.
Ow!
...ow...

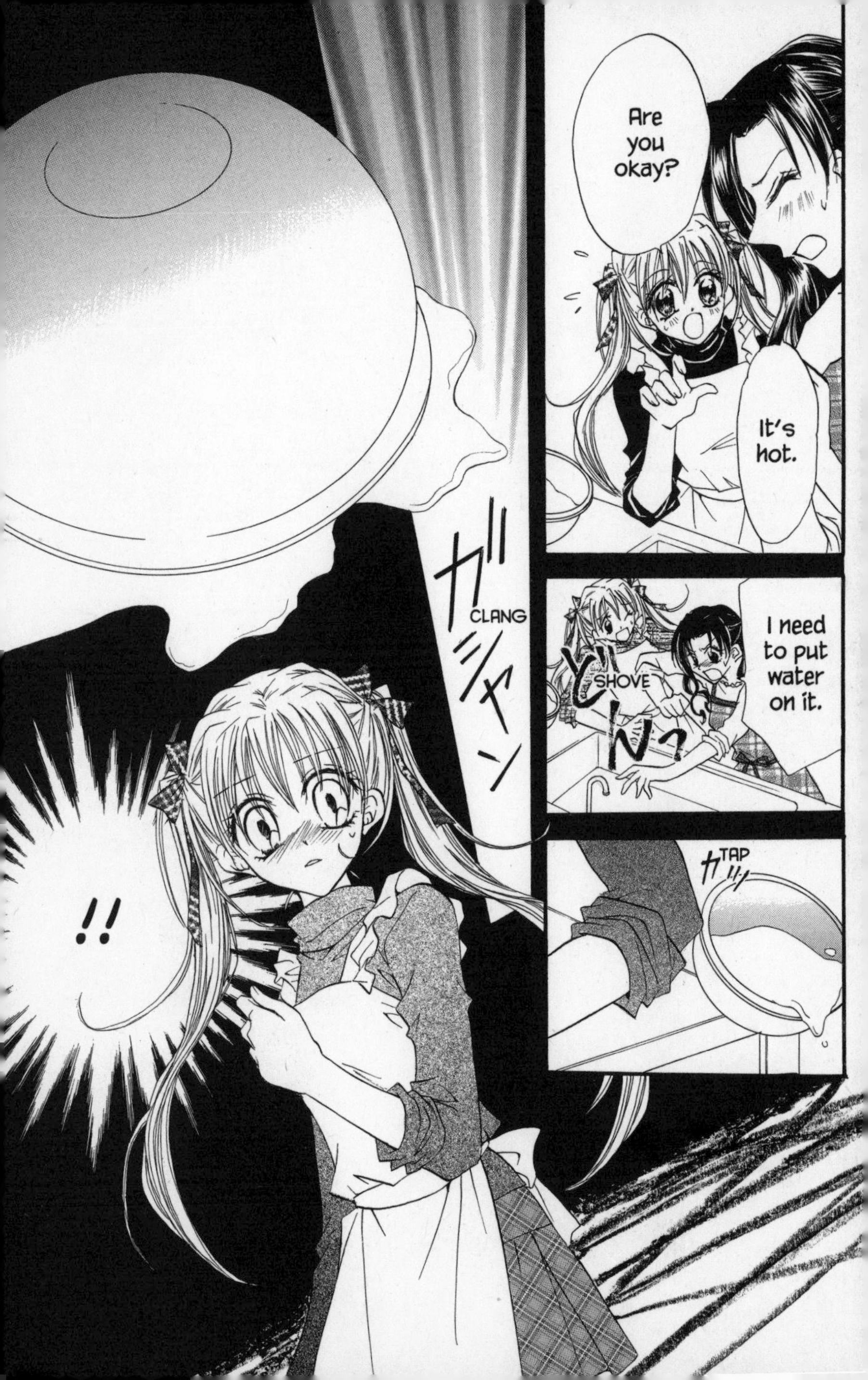
Are you okay?
It's hot.
I need to put water on it.
SHOVE
TAP
ガシャン
CLANG
!!

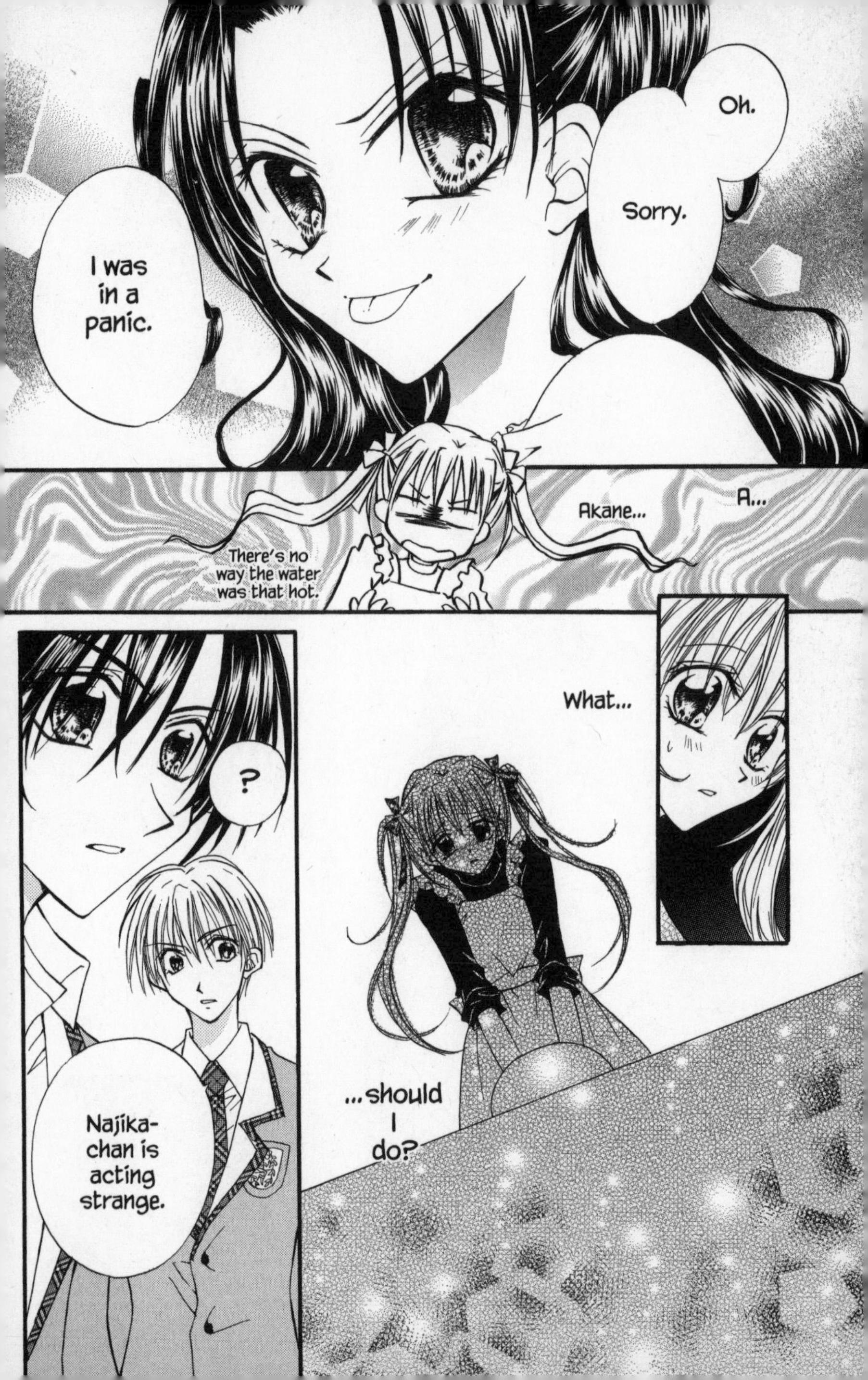
Oh.
Sorry.
I was in a panic.
A...
Akane...
There's no way the water was that hot.
What...
...should I do?
?
Najika-chan is acting strange.

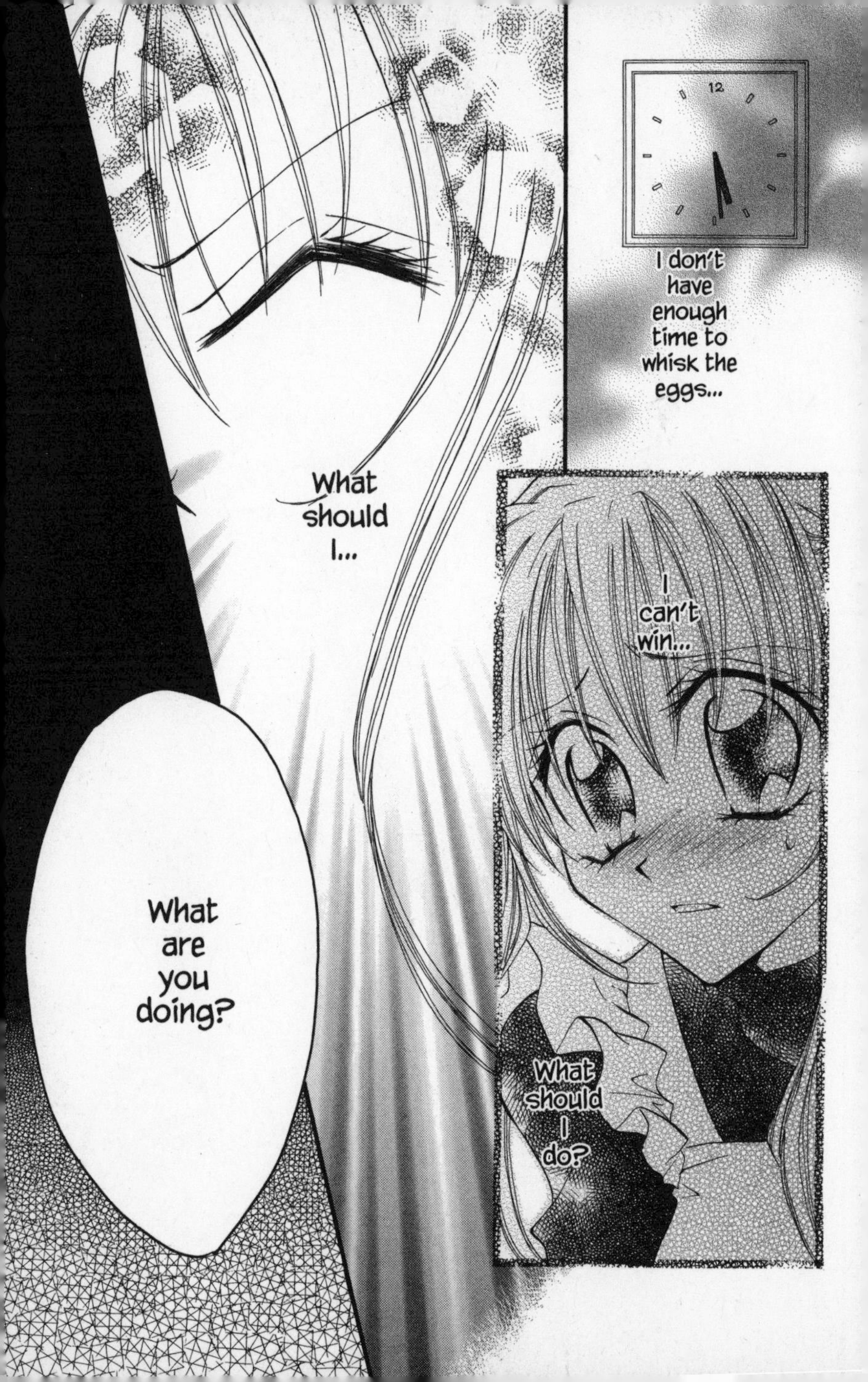
I don't have enough time to whisk the eggs...
I can't win...
What should I do?
What should I...
What are you doing?

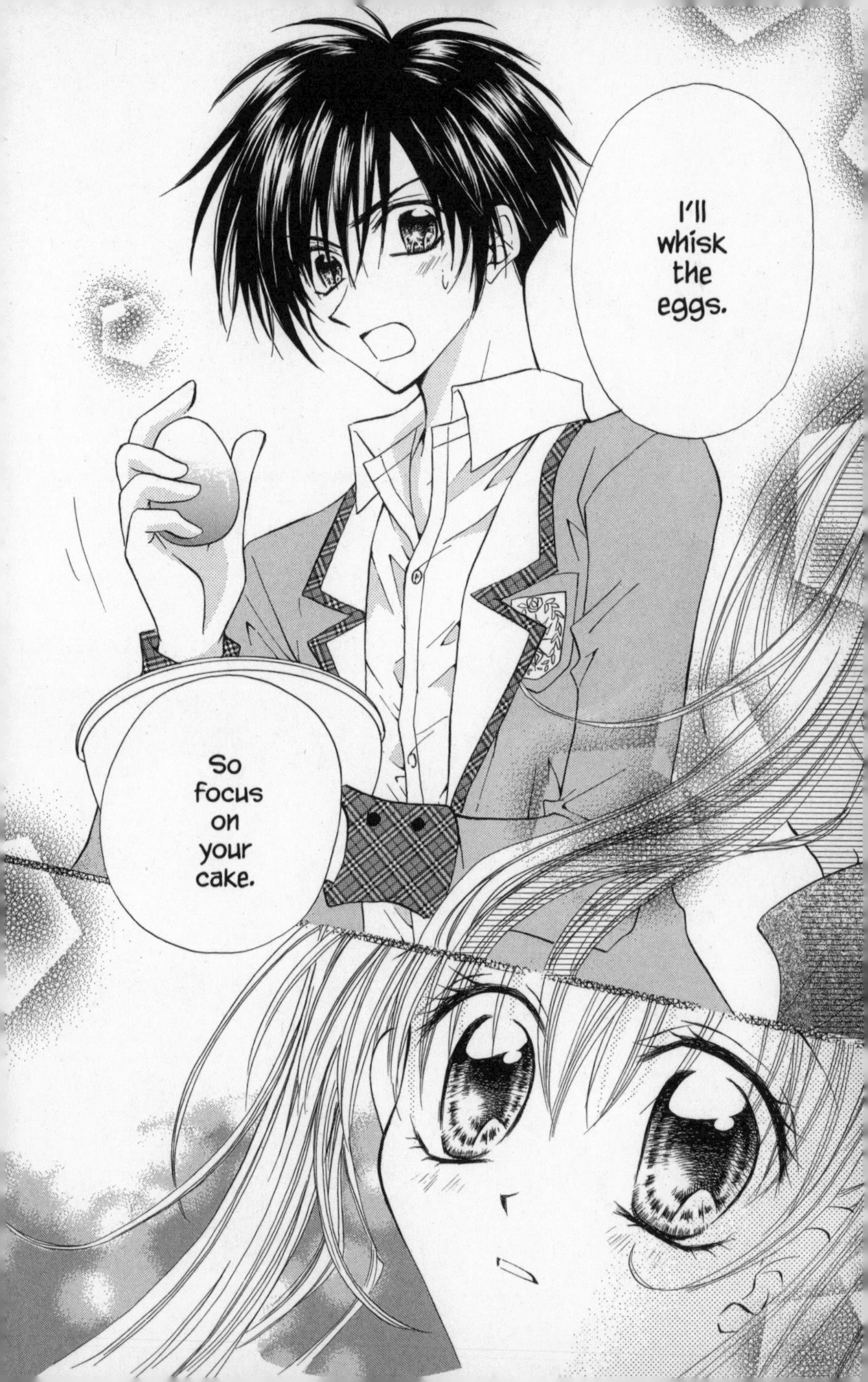
I'll whisk the eggs.
So focus on your cake.

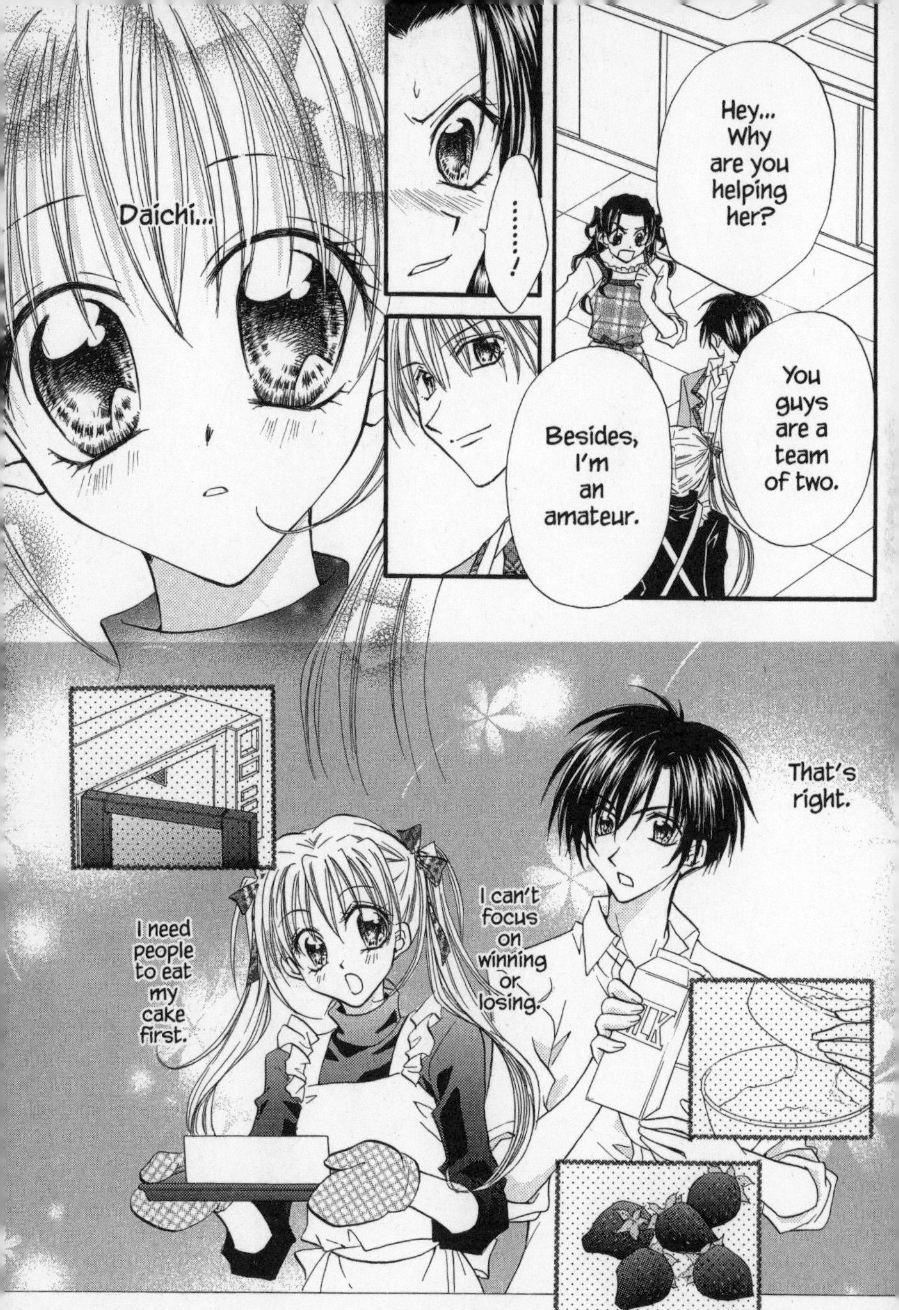
Hey... Why are you helping her?
You guys are a team of two.
Besides, I'm an amateur.
......!
Daichi...
That's right.
I can't focus on winning or losing.
I need people to eat my cake first.

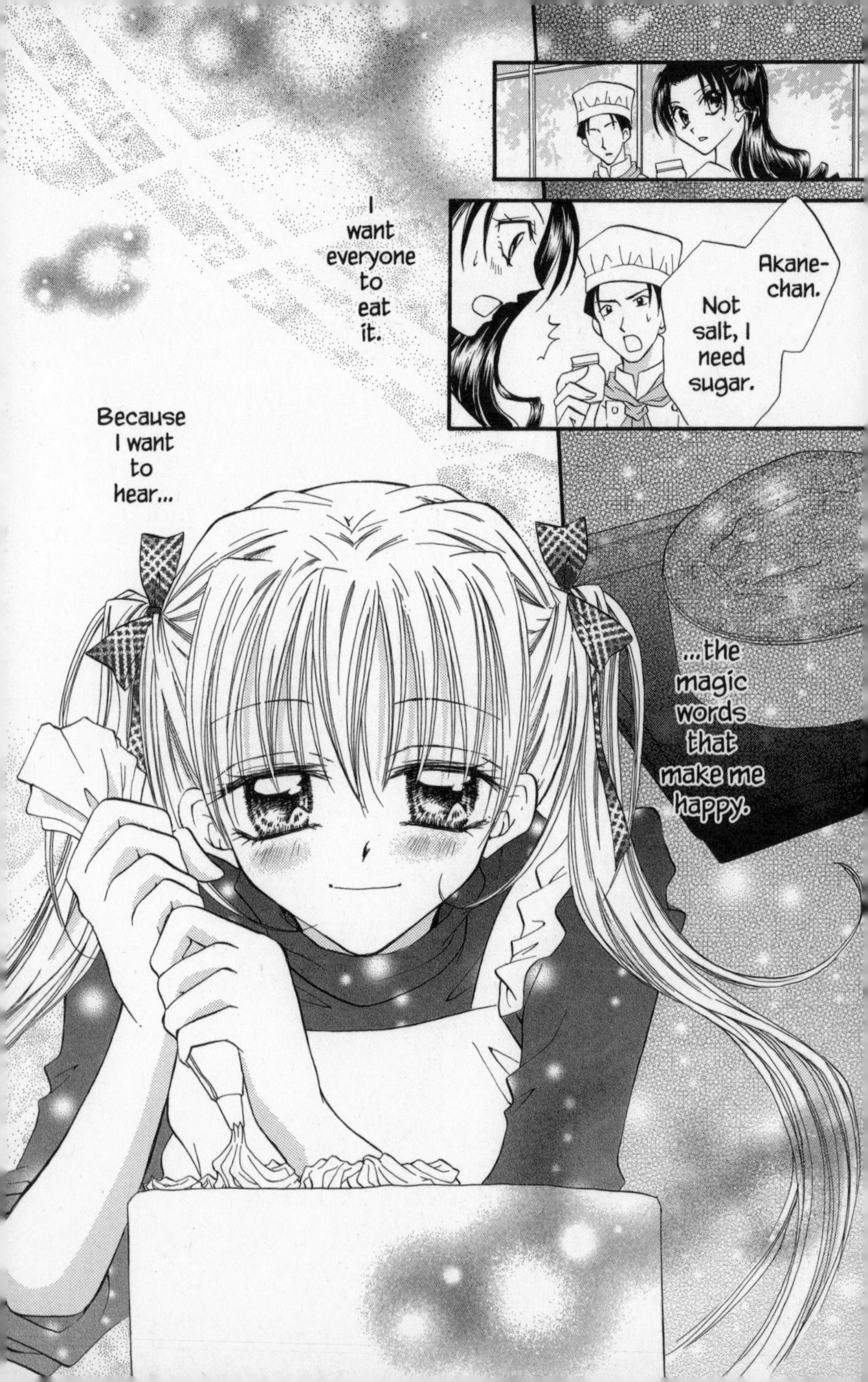
Akane-chan.
Not salt, I need sugar.
I want everyone to eat it.
Because I want to hear...
...the magic words that make me happy.

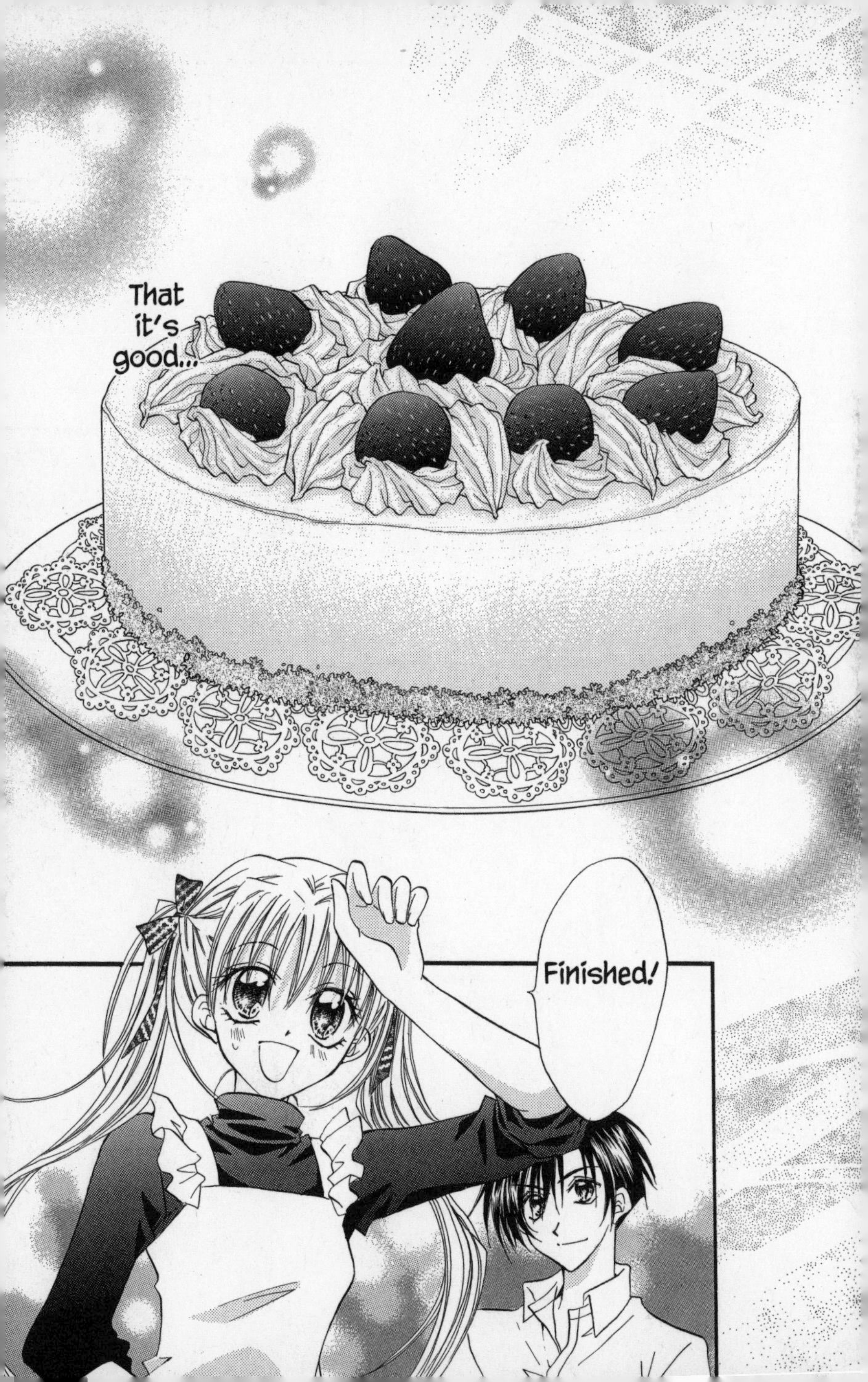
That it's good...
Finished!

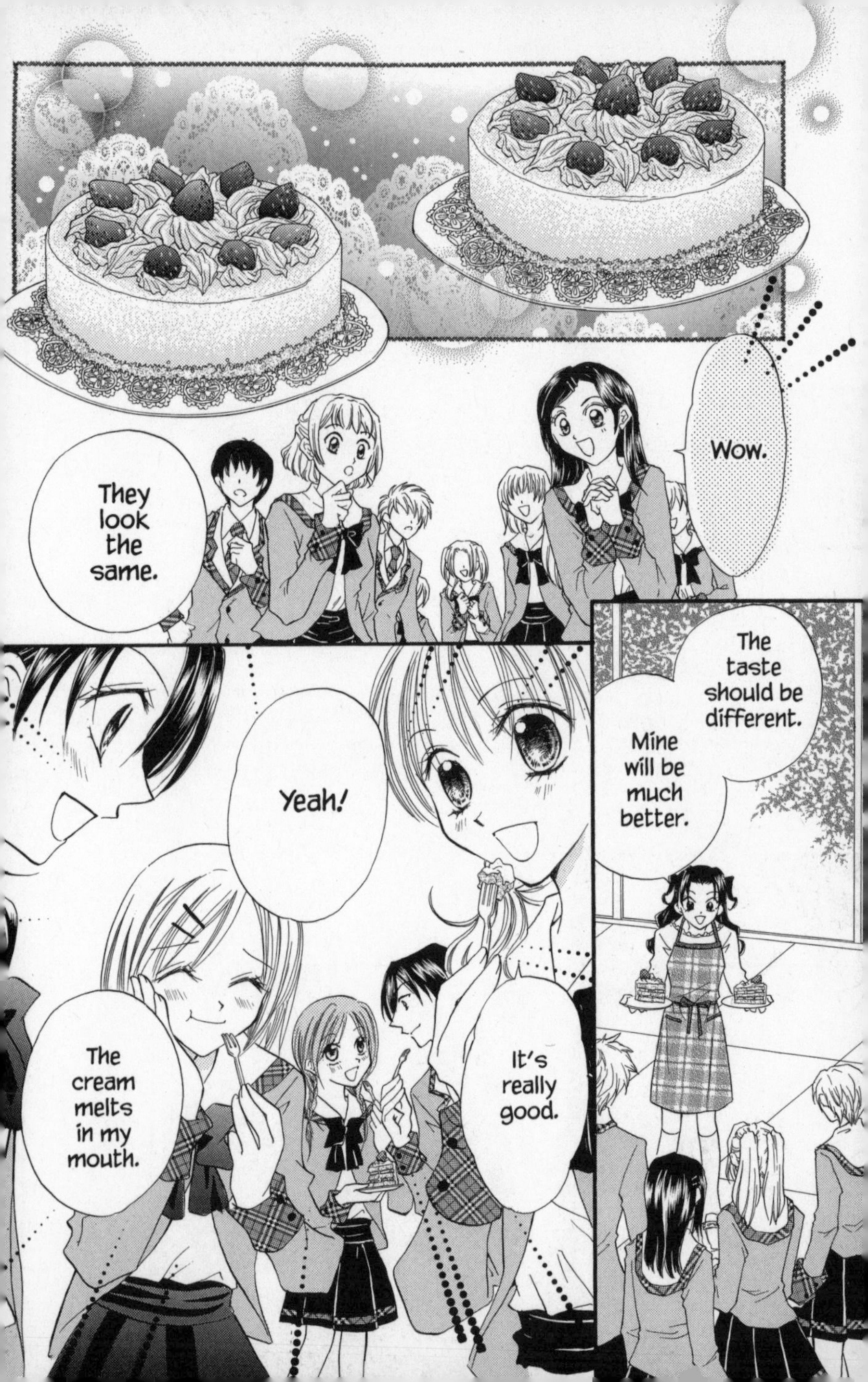
Wow.
They look the same.
The taste should be different.
Mine will be much better.
Yeah!
It's really good.
The cream melts in my mouth.

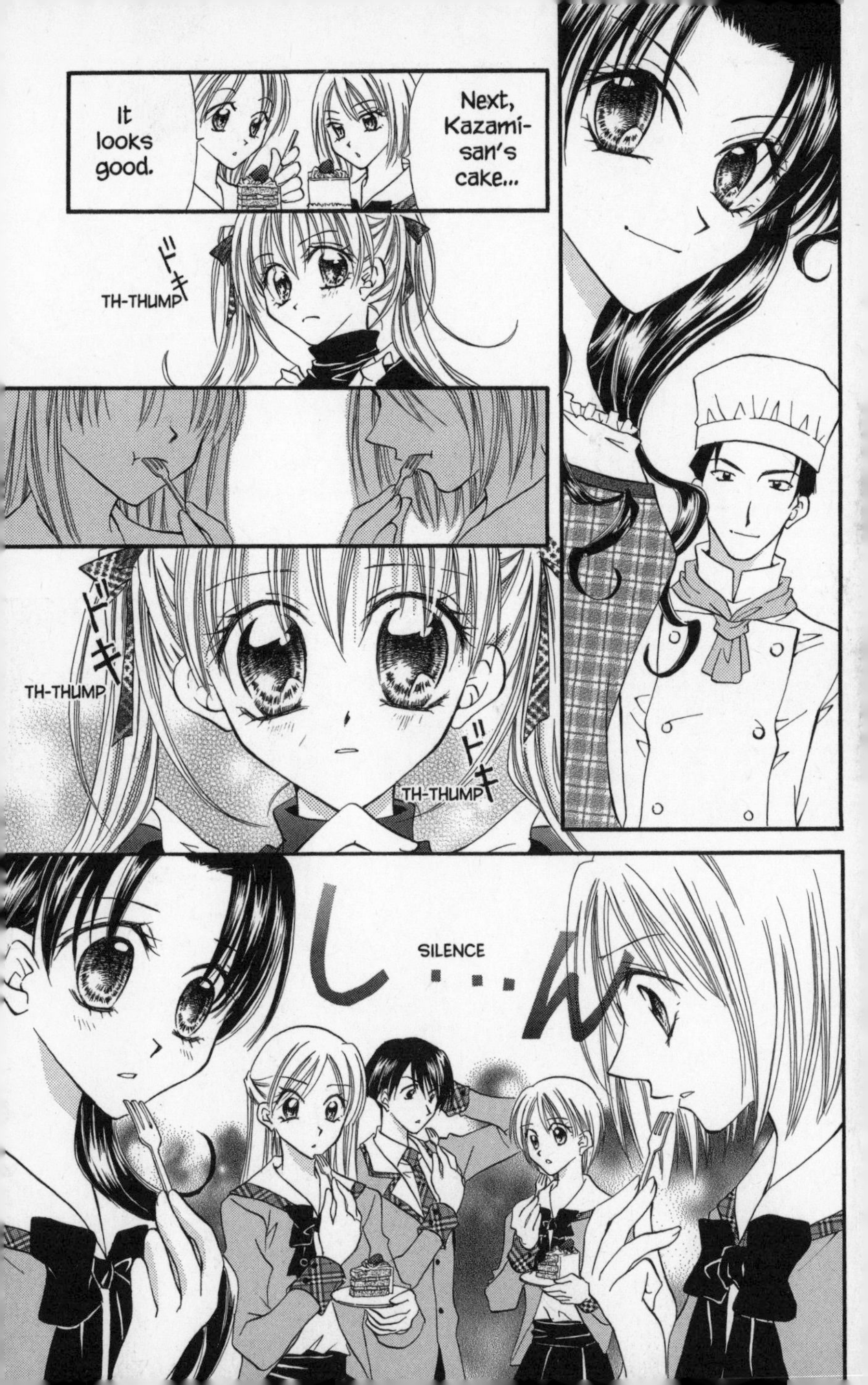
Next, Kazami-san's cake...
It looks good.
ドキ
TH-THUMP
ドキ
TH-THUMP
ドキ
TH-THUMP
し…ん
SILENCE

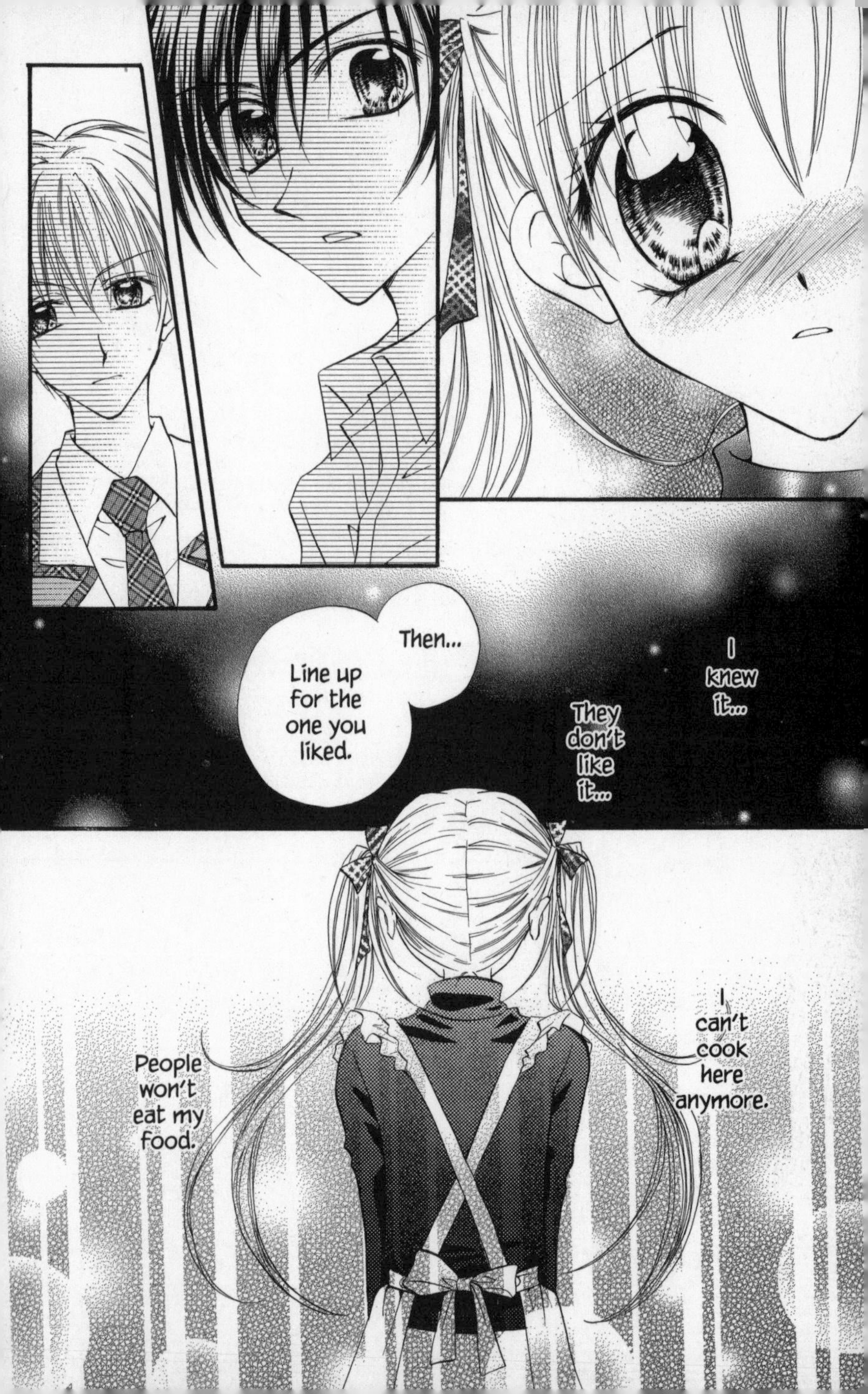
I knew it...
They don't like it...
Then... Line up for the one you liked.
I can't cook here anymore.
People won't eat my food.

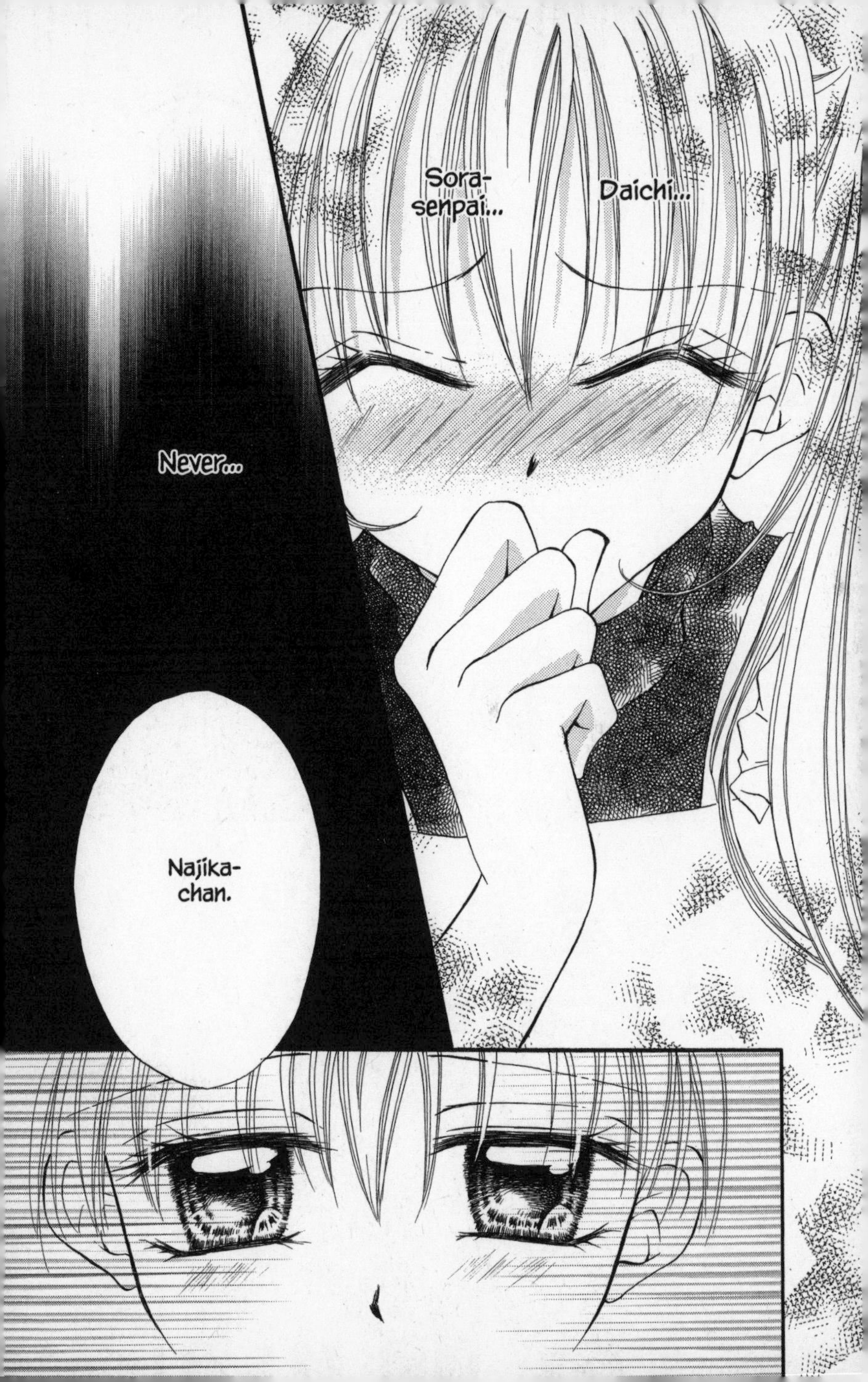
Daichi...
Sora-senpai...
Never...
Najika-chan.

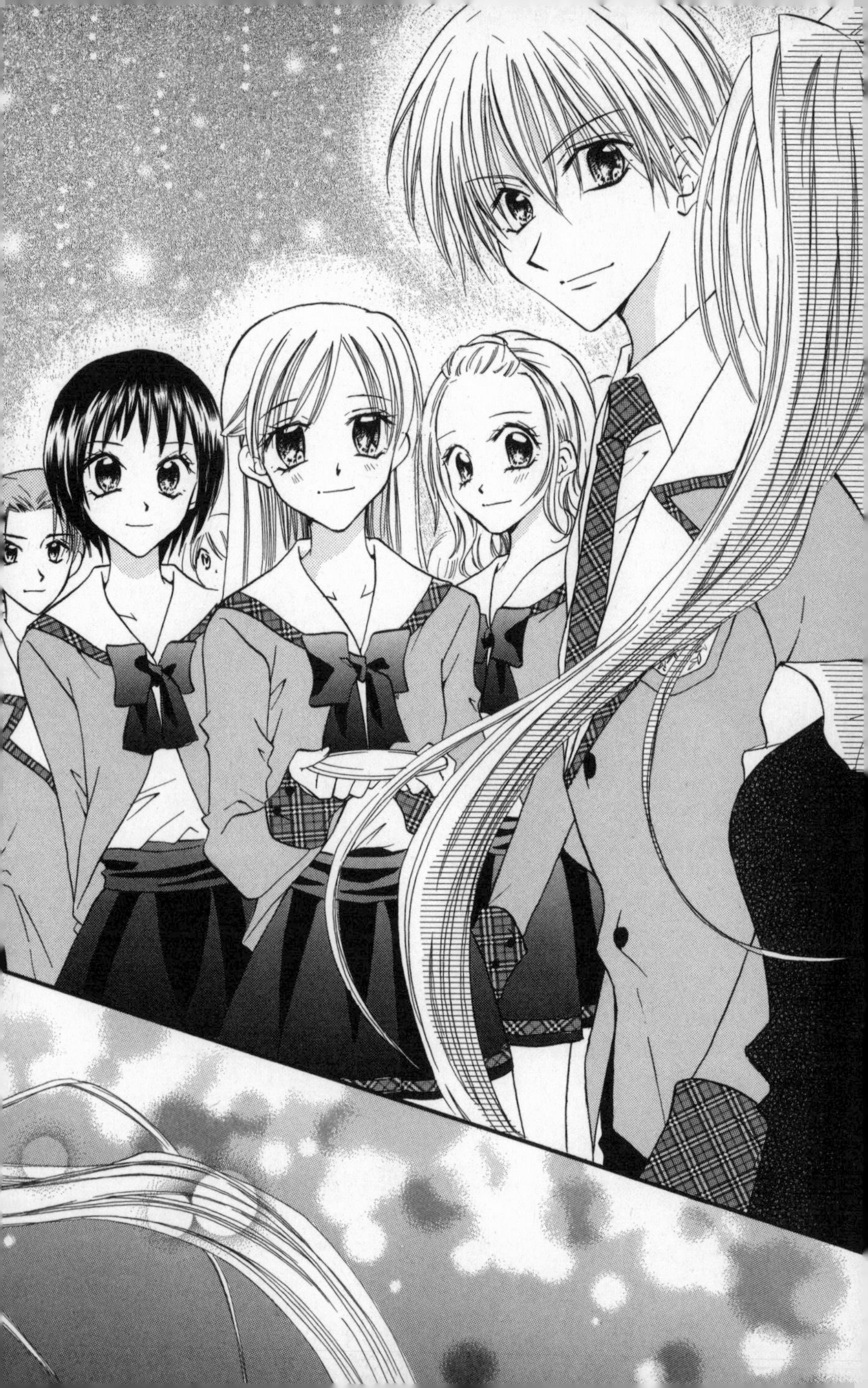

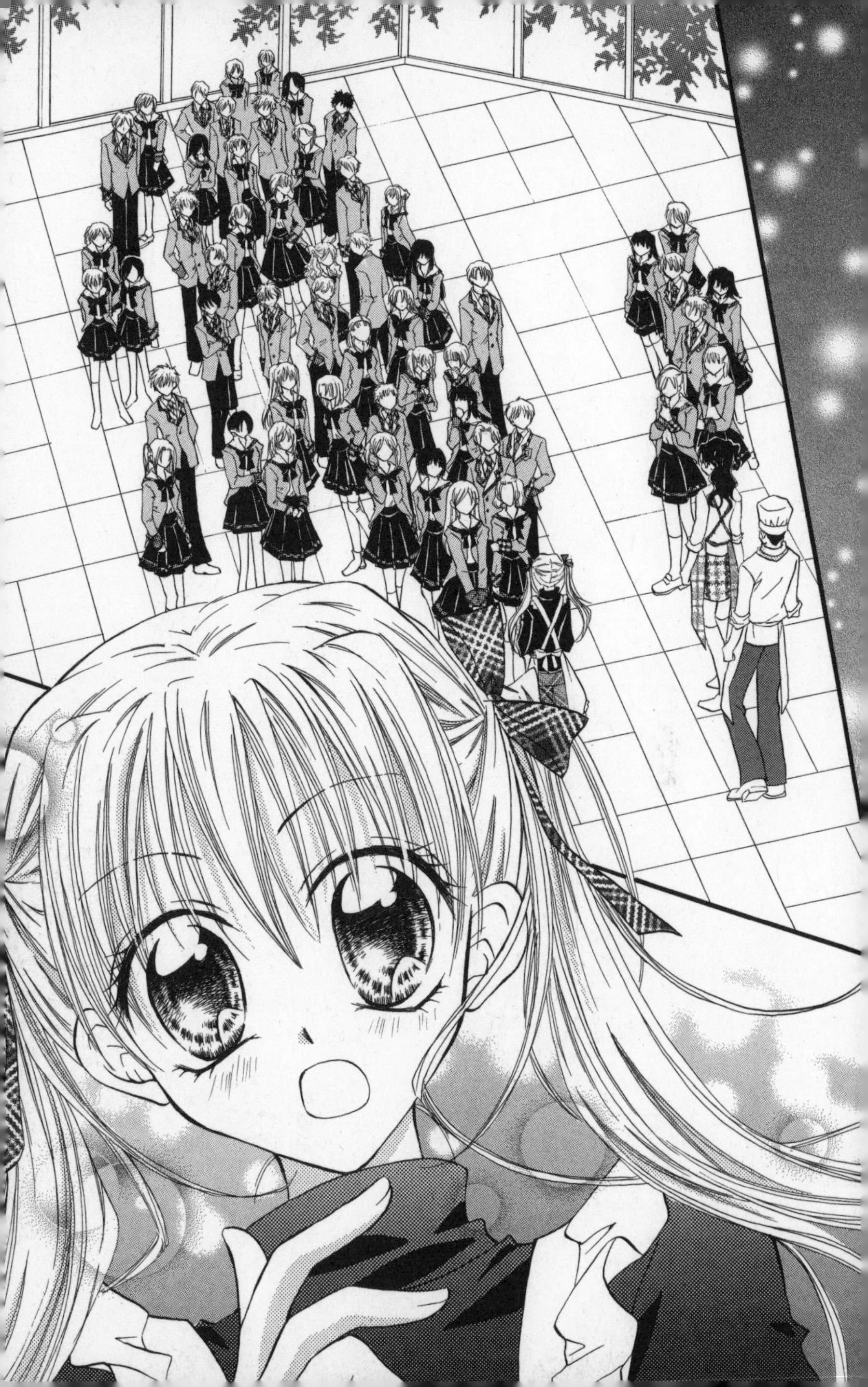

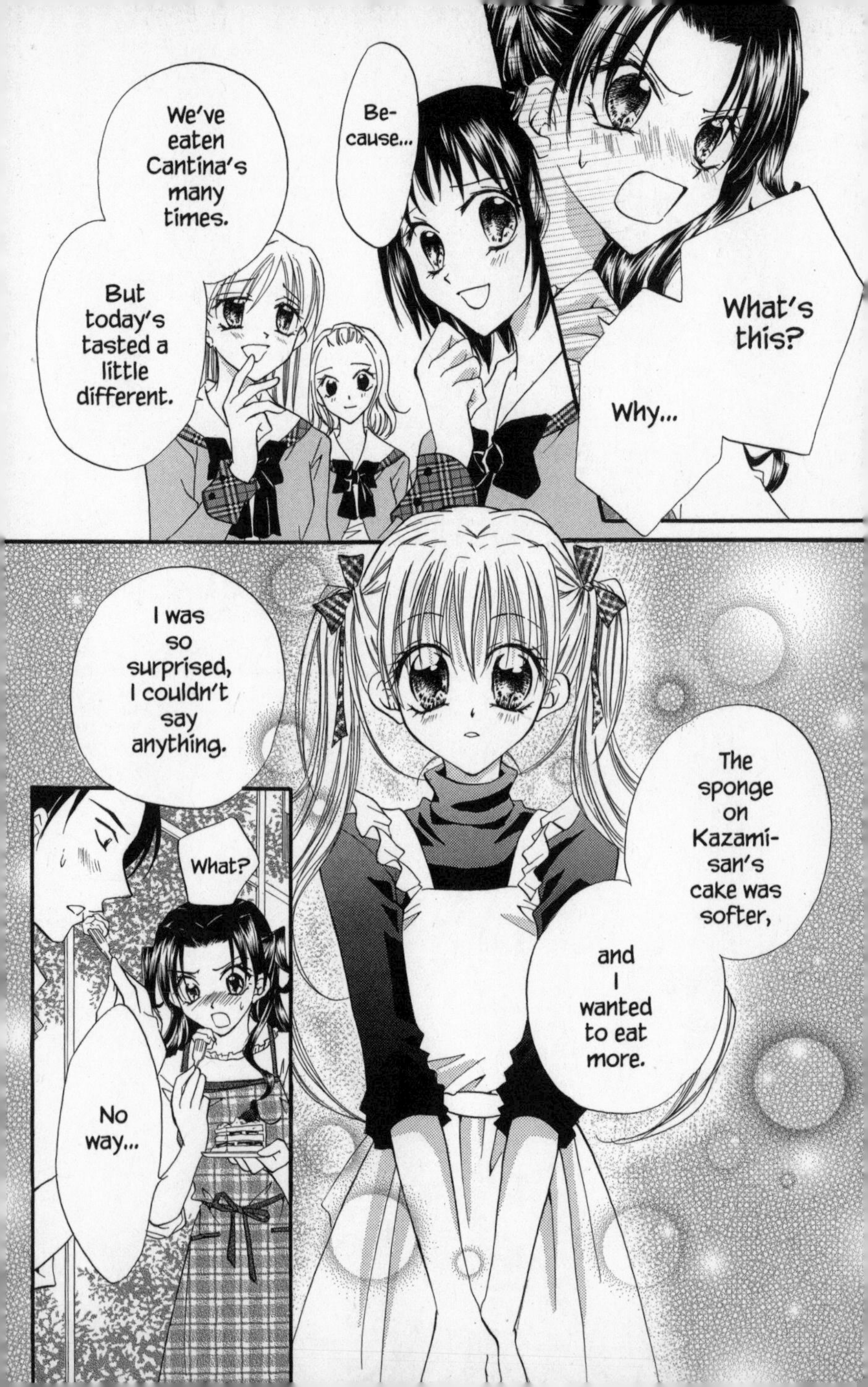
What's this?
Why...
Be-cause...
We've eaten Cantina's many times.
But today's tasted a little different.
The sponge on Kazami-san's cake was softer,
and I wanted to eat more.
I was so surprised, I couldn't say anything.
What?
No way...

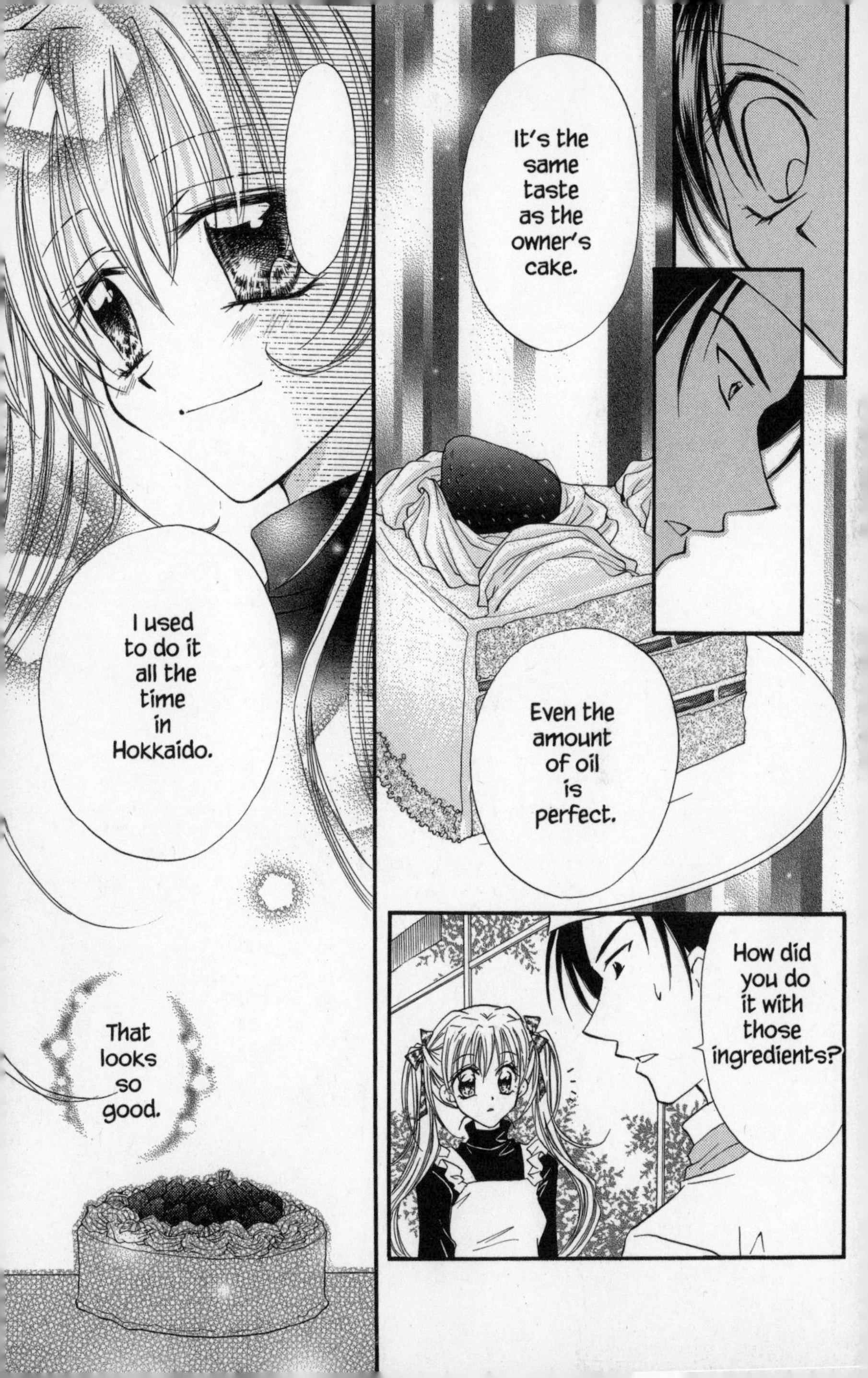
It's the same taste as the owner's cake.
Even the amount of oil is perfect.
How did you do it with those ingredients?
I used to do it all the time in Hokkaido.
That looks so good.

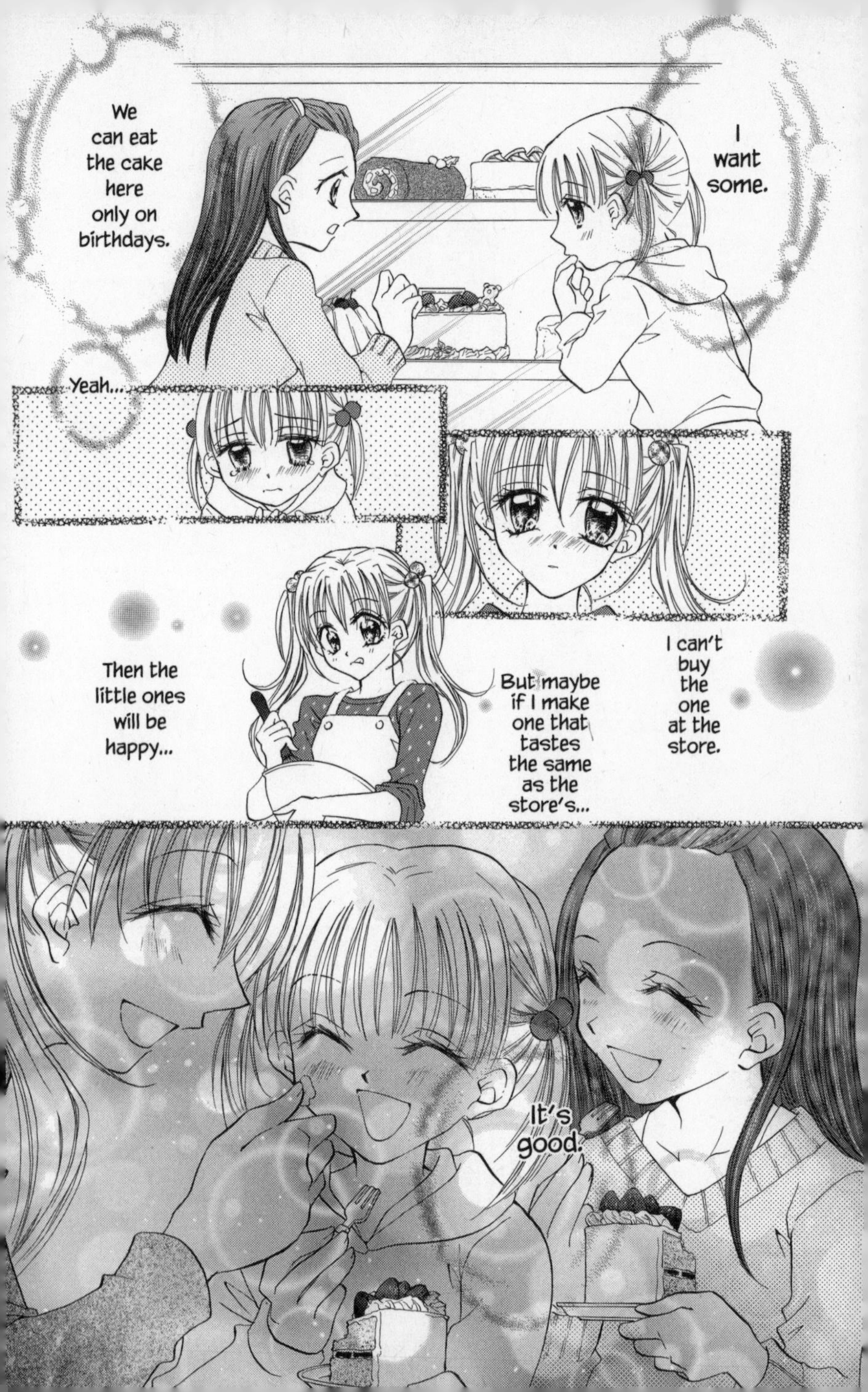

I want some.
We can eat the cake here only on birthdays.
Yeah...
I can't buy the one at the store.
But maybe if I make one that tastes the same as the store's...
Then the little ones will be happy...
It's good.

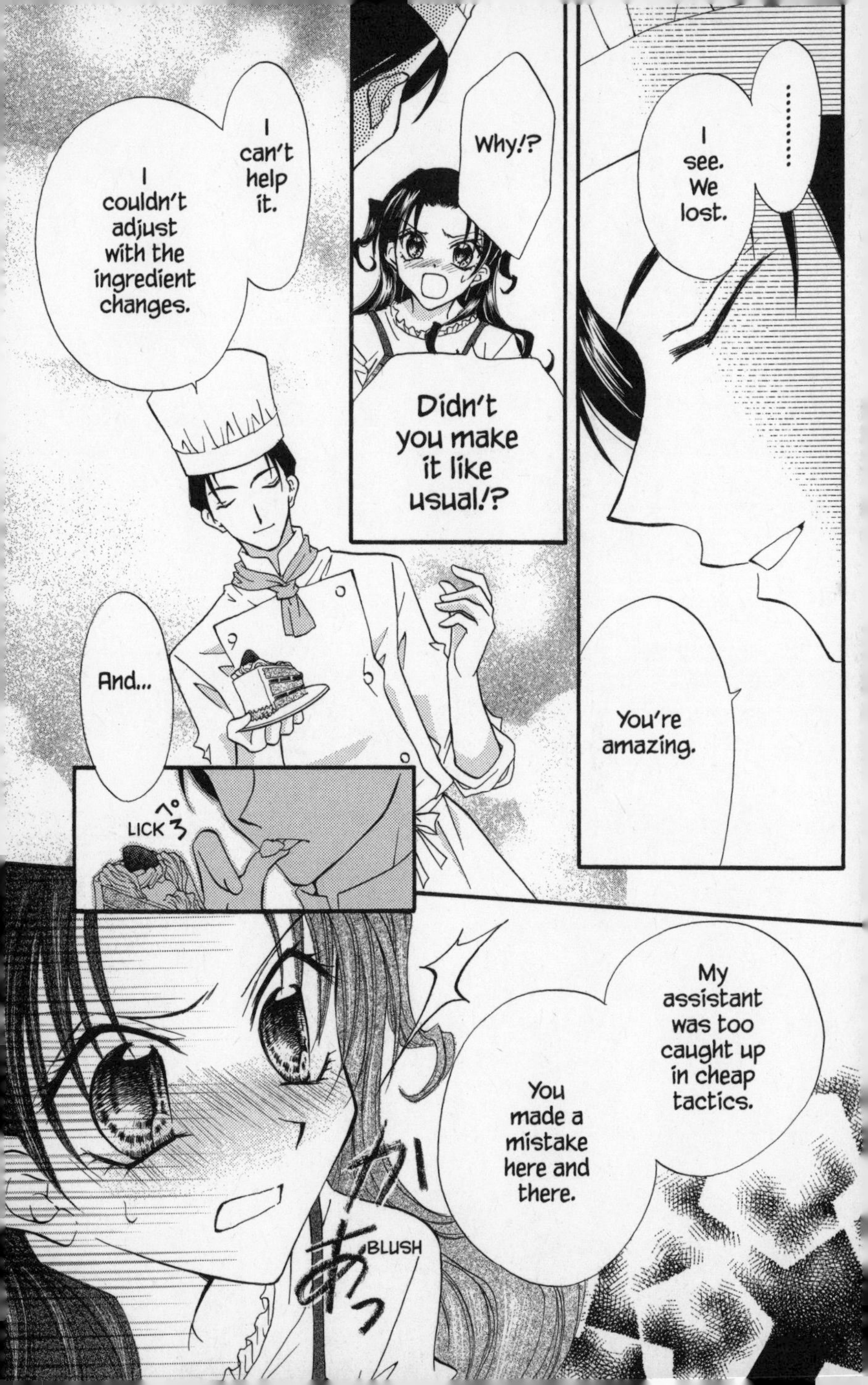
……
I see. We lost.
You're amazing.
Why!?
Didn't you make it like usual!?
I can't help it.
I couldn't adjust with the ingredient changes.
And...
LICK
ぺろ
My assistant was too caught up in cheap tactics.
You made a mistake here and there.
BLUSH

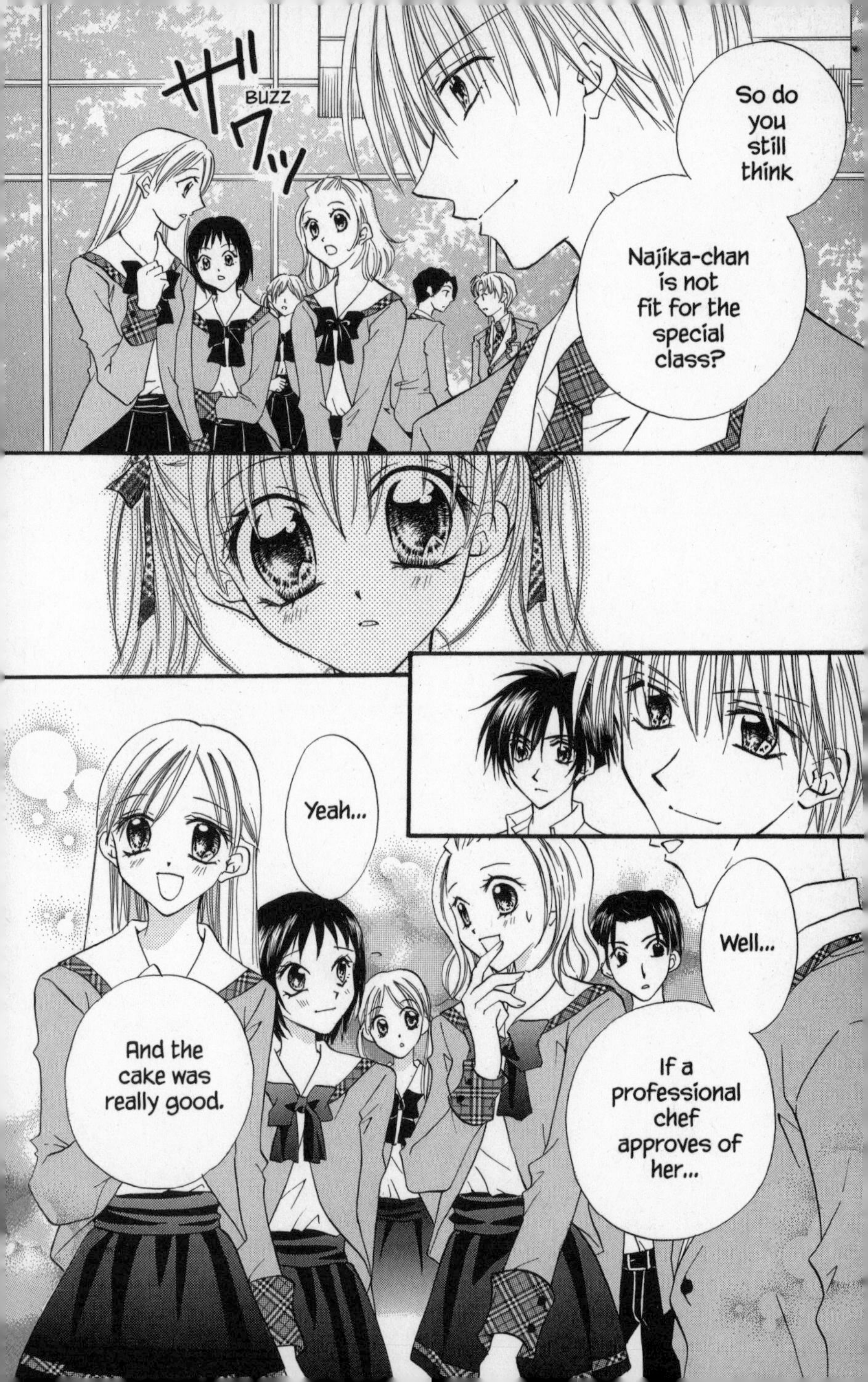
So do you still think
Najika-chan is not fit for the special class?
ザワッ
BUZZ
Well...
If a professional chef approves of her...
Yeah...
And the cake was really good.

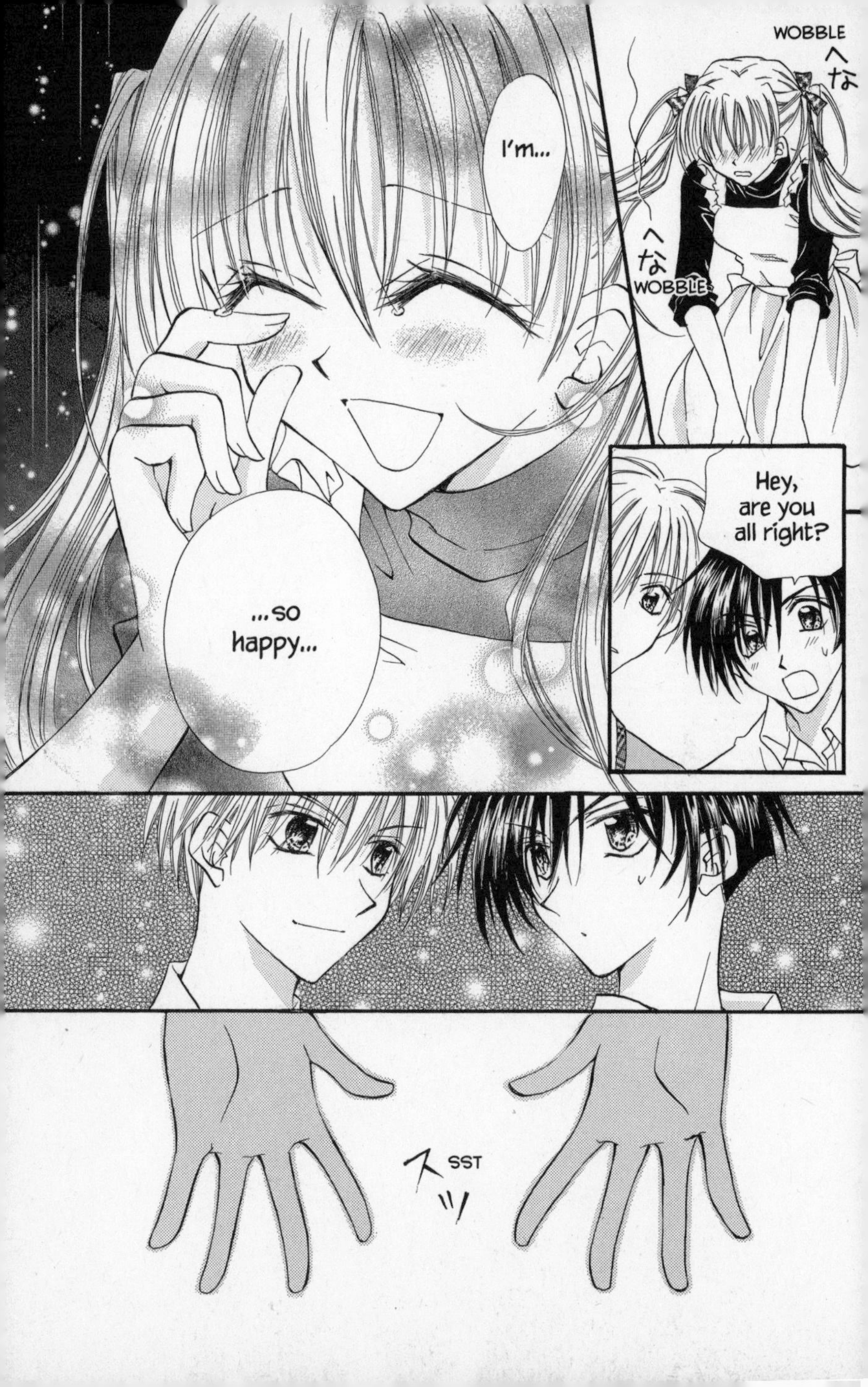
WOBBLE
へな
へな
WOBBLE
Hey, are you all right?
I'm...
...so happy...
ス SST
ッ

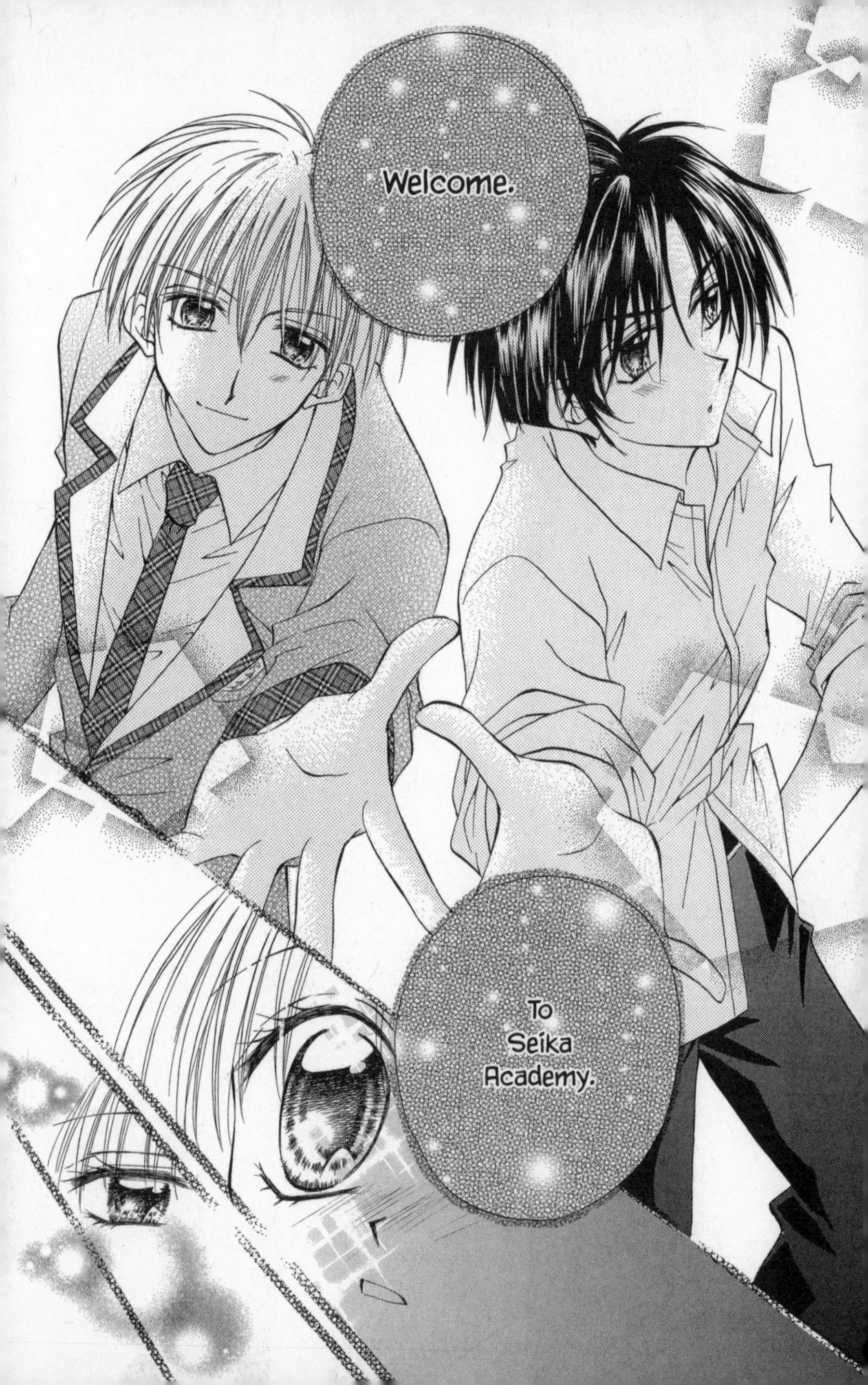
Welcome.
To Seika Academy.

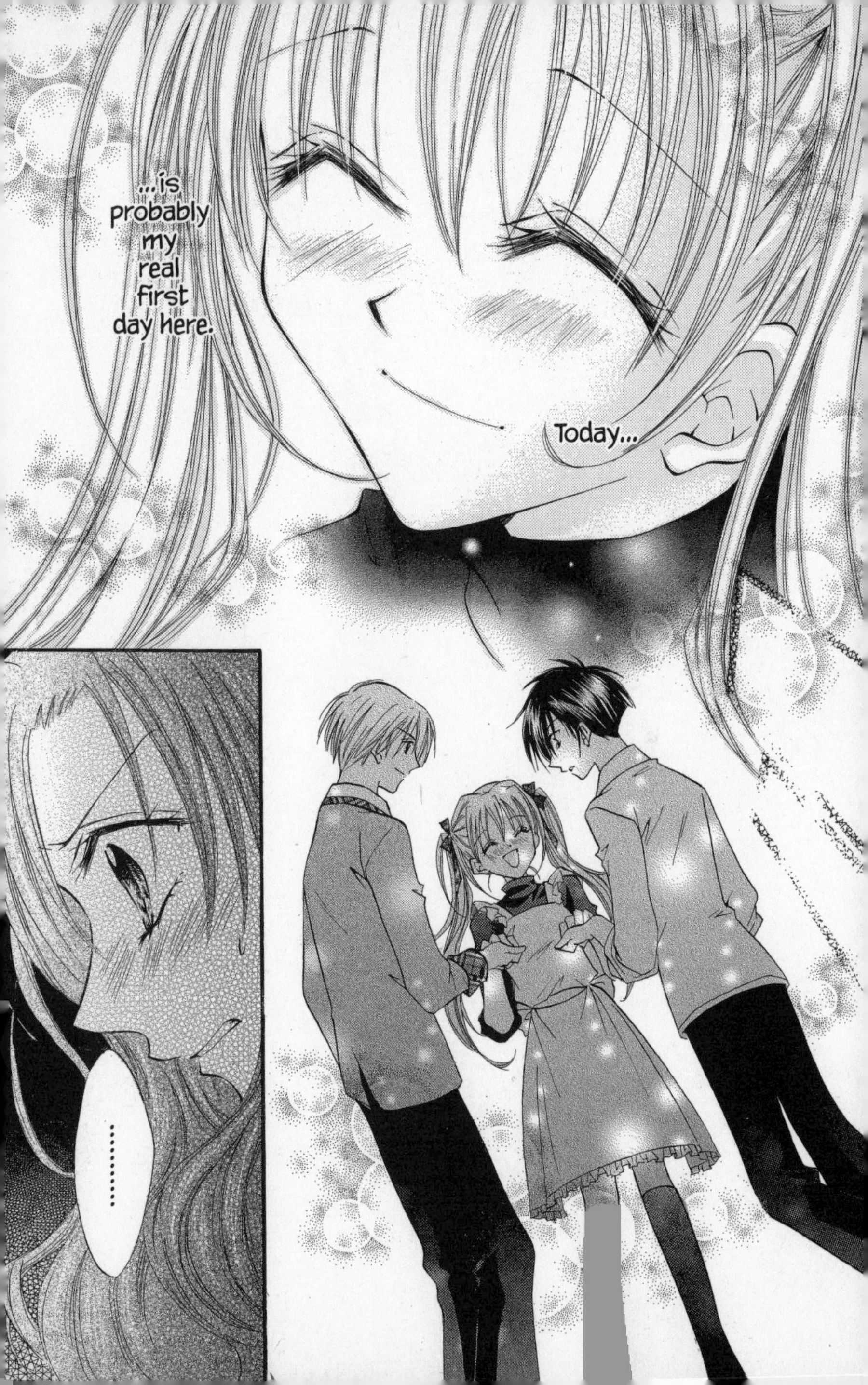
Today...
...is probably my real first day here.
......

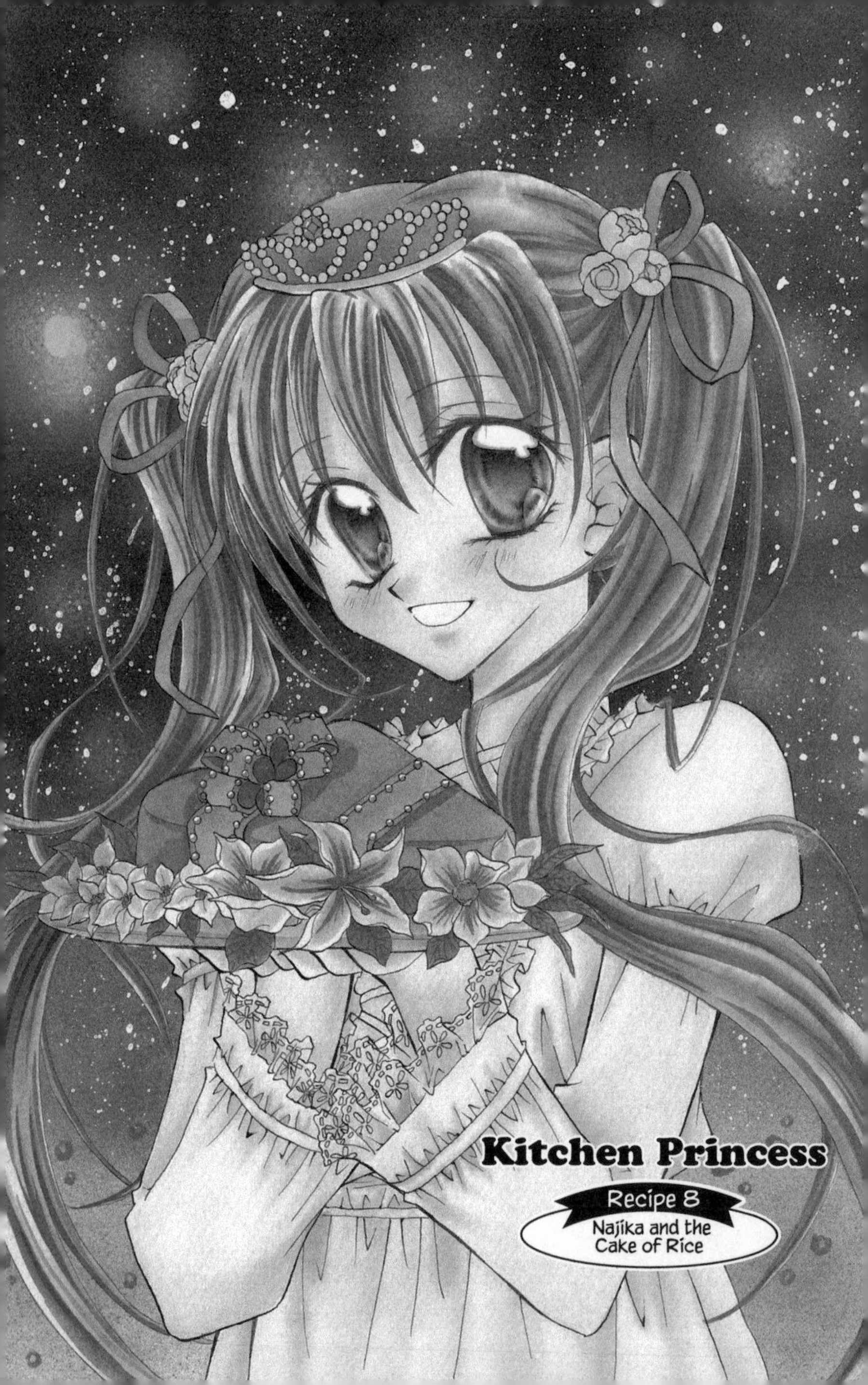
Kitchen Princess
Recipe 8
Najika and the Cake of Rice

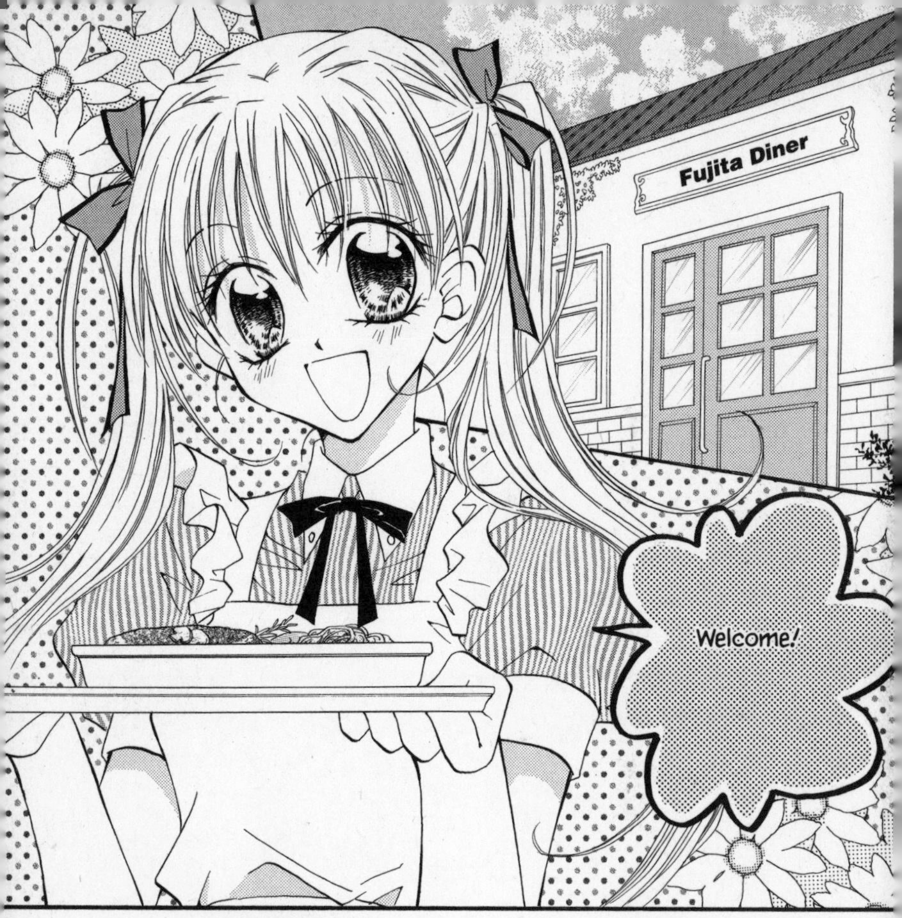
Fujita Diner
Welcome!

About Recipe 8's Splash Pag

I had a really hard time getting the color right on the cake Najika is holding. And I didn't like the art as much until I put in the background. The background finished it off nicely. I think it was my first time drawing an expression like this, too...

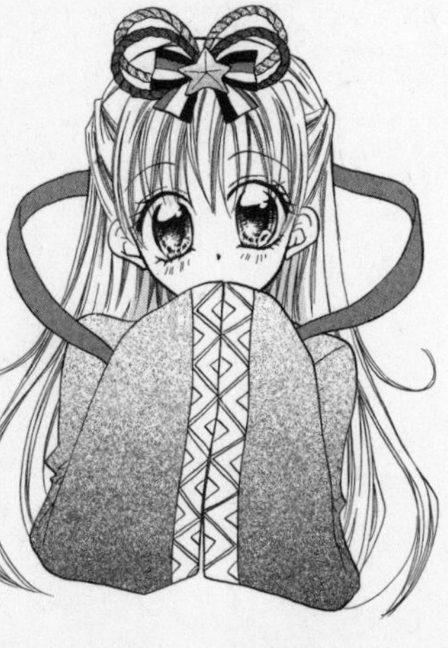

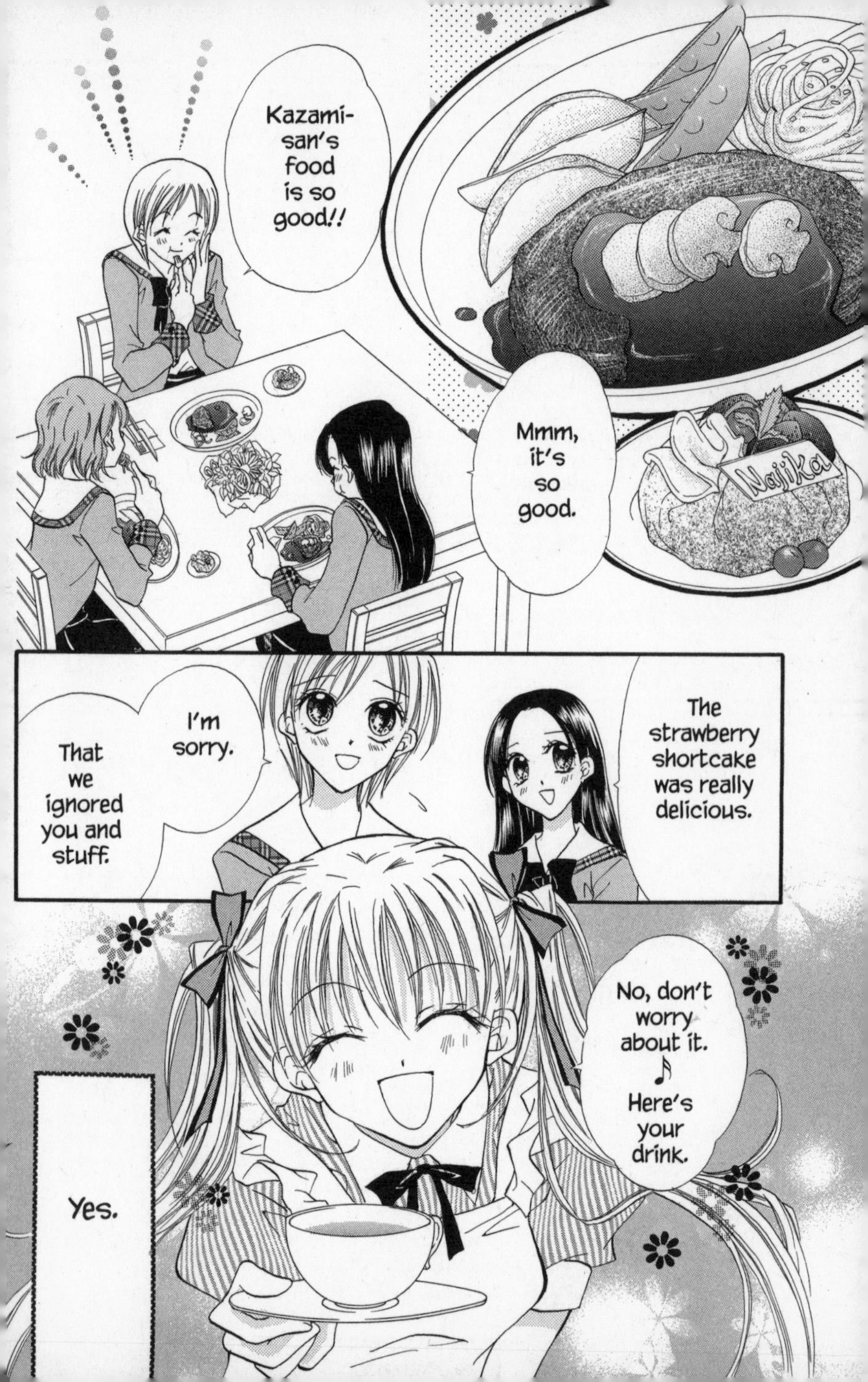
Kazami-san's food is so good!!
Mmm, it's so good.
Najika
The strawberry shortcake was really delicious.
I'm sorry.
That we ignored you and stuff.
No, don't worry about it. ♪ Here's your drink.
Yes.

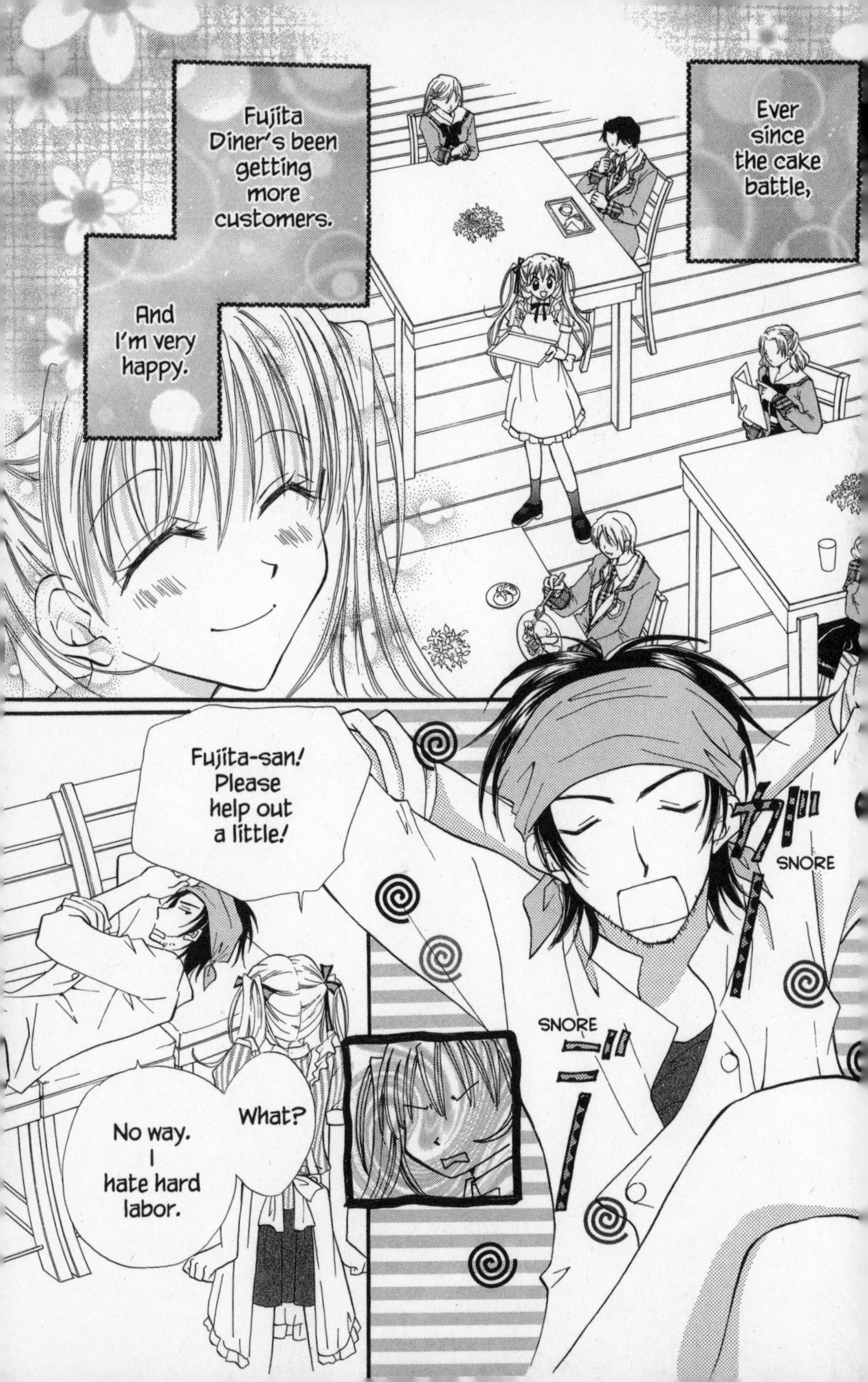
Ever since the cake battle,
Fujita Diner's been getting more customers.
And I'm very happy.
Fujita-san! Please help out a little!
SNORE
SNORE
What?
No way. I hate hard labor.

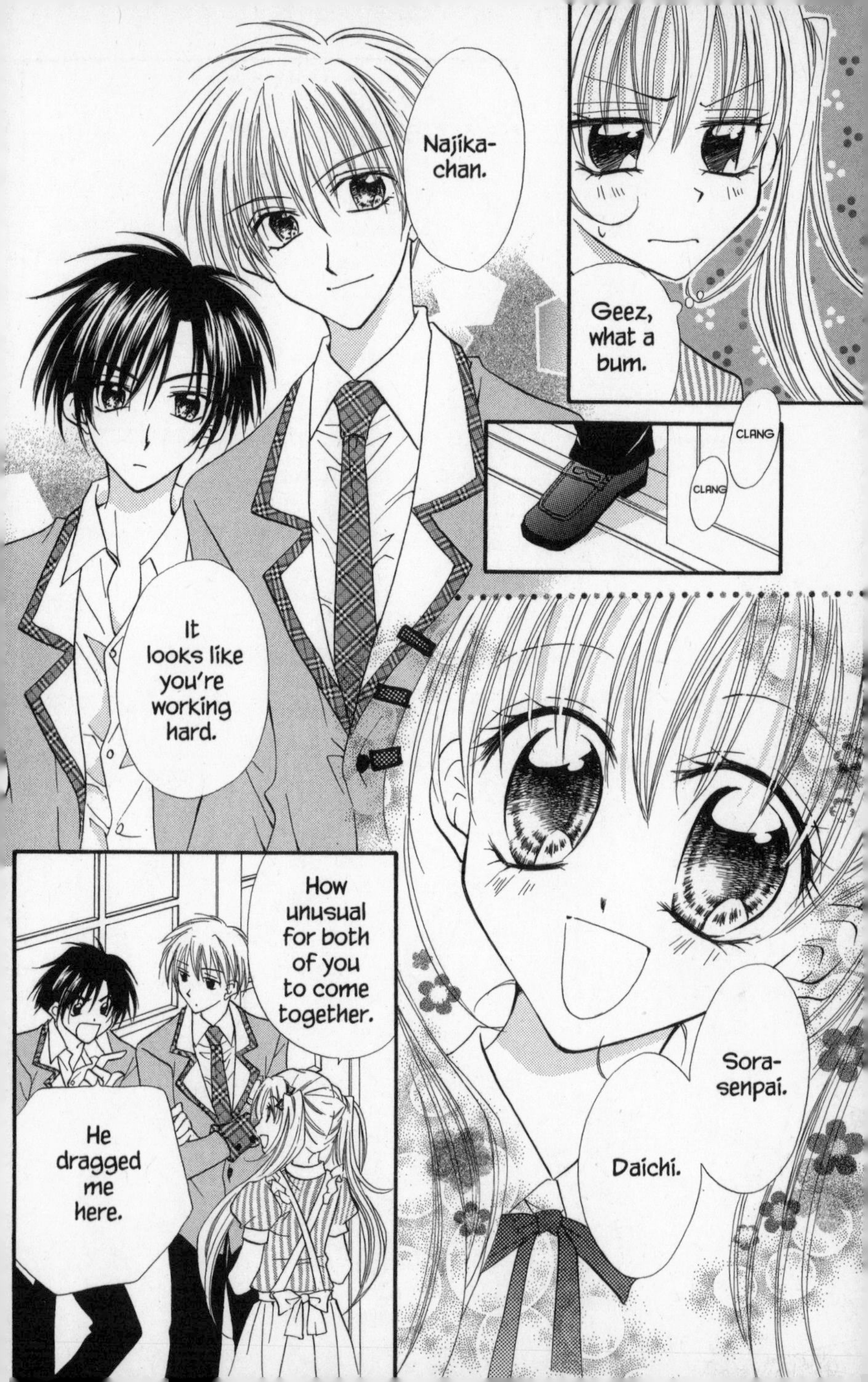
Geez, what a bum.
CLANG
CLANG
Sora-senpai.
Daichi.
Najika-chan.
It looks like you're working hard.
How unusual for both of you to come together.
He dragged me here.

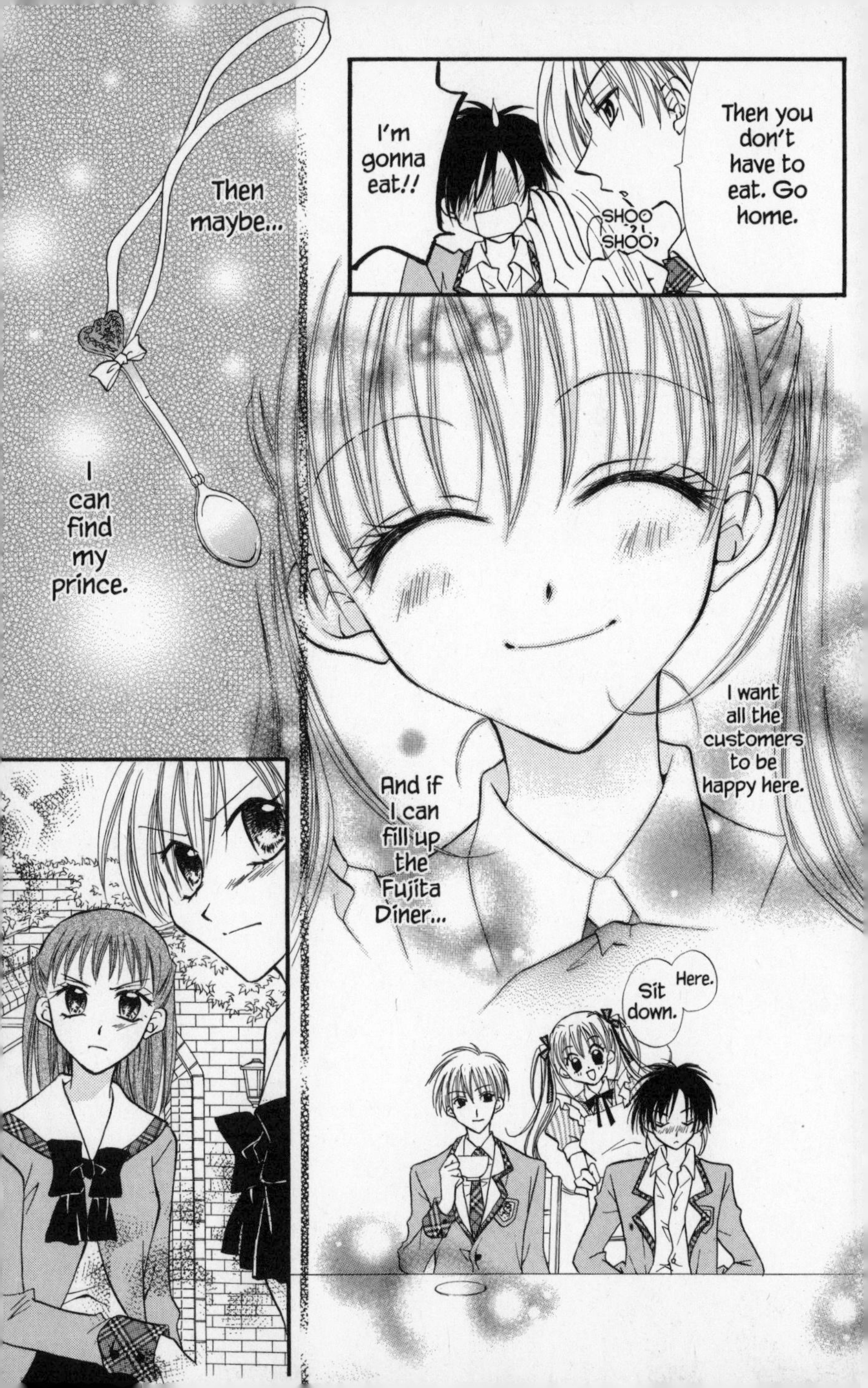
Then you don't have to eat. Go home.
SHOO SHOO
I'm gonna eat!!
I want all the customers to be happy here.
And if I can fill up the Fujita Diner...
Here.
Sit down.
Then maybe...
I can find my prince.

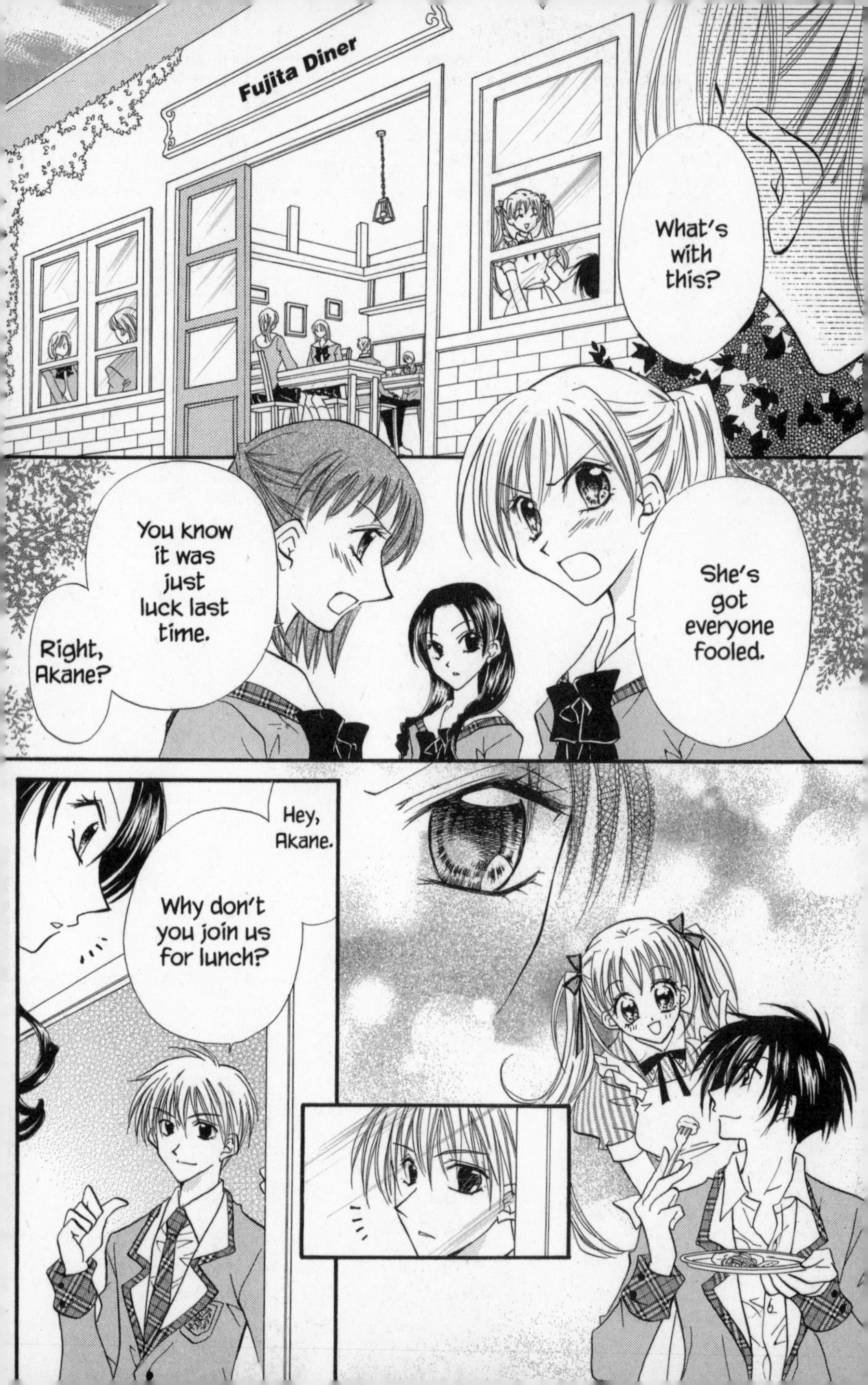
Fujita Diner
What's with this?
She's got everyone fooled.
You know it was just luck last time.
Right, Akane?
Hey, Akane.
Why don't you join us for lunch?

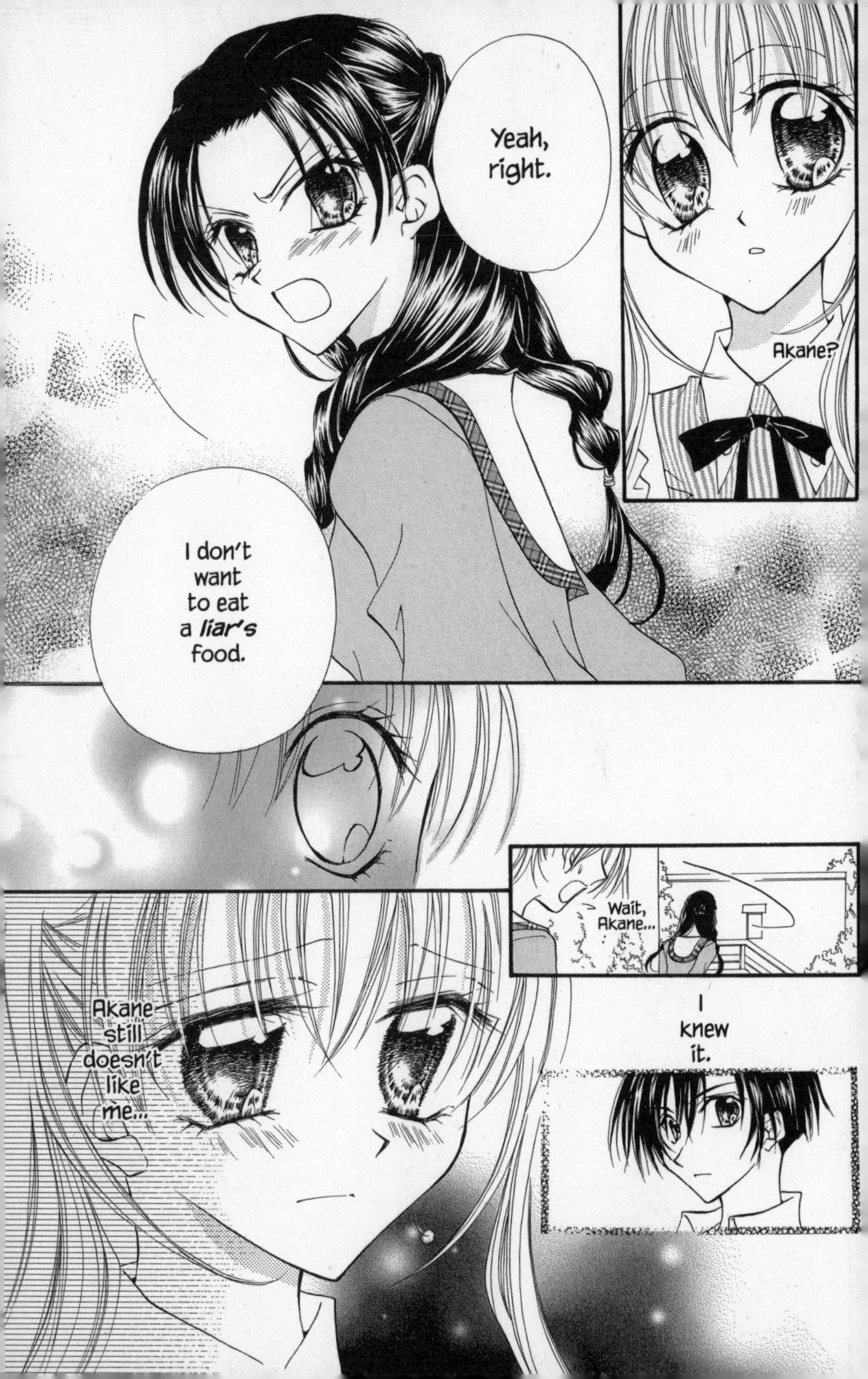
Akane?
Yeah, right.
I don't want to eat a *liar's* food.
Wait, Akane...
I knew it.
Akane still doesn't like me...

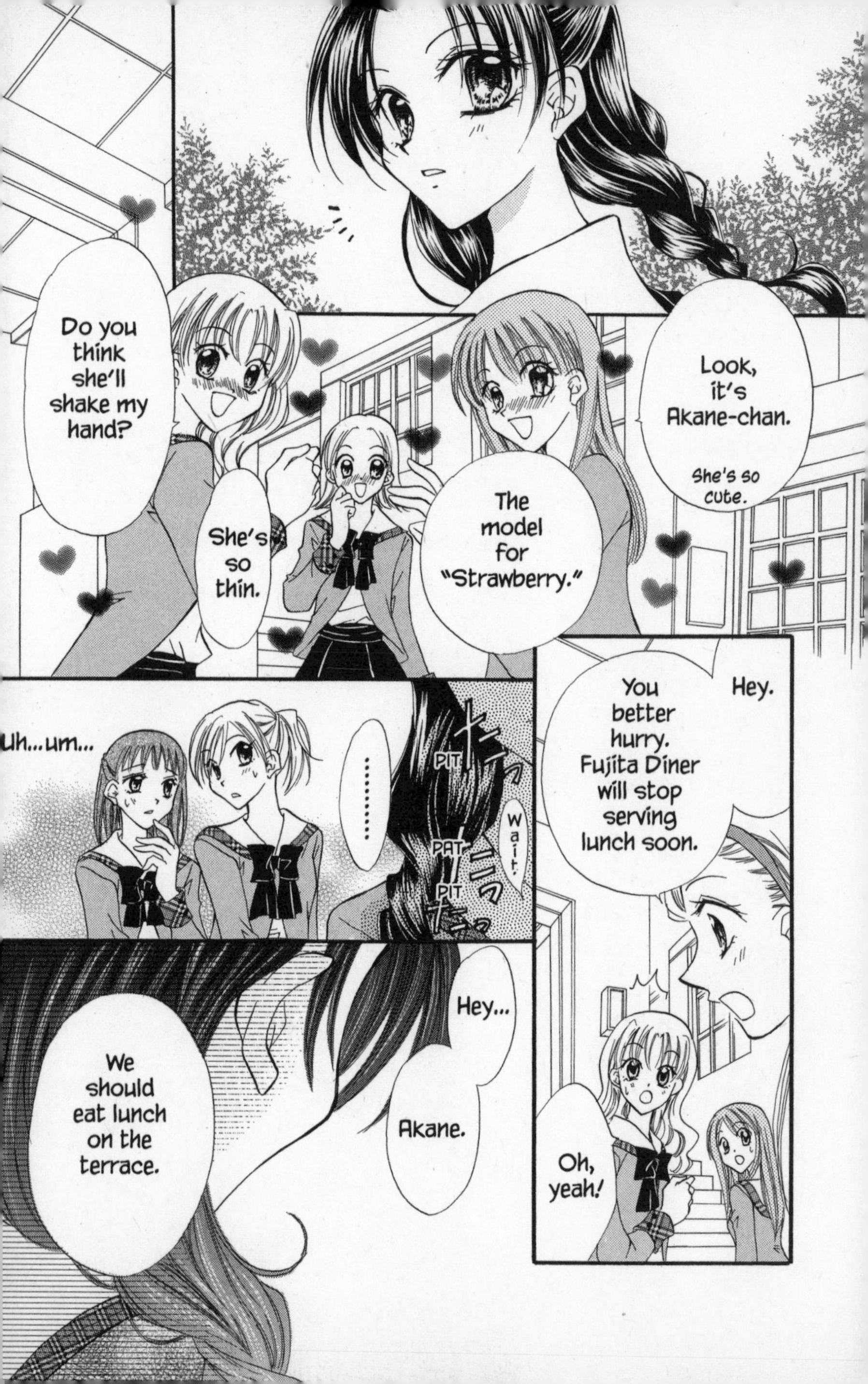
Look, it's Akane-chan.
She's so cute.
The model for "Strawberry."
She's so thin.
Do you think she'll shake my hand?
Hey.
You better hurry. Fujita Diner will stop serving lunch soon.
Oh, yeah!
......
Wait!
PIT
PAT
PIT
uh...um...
Hey...
Akane.
We should eat lunch on the terrace.

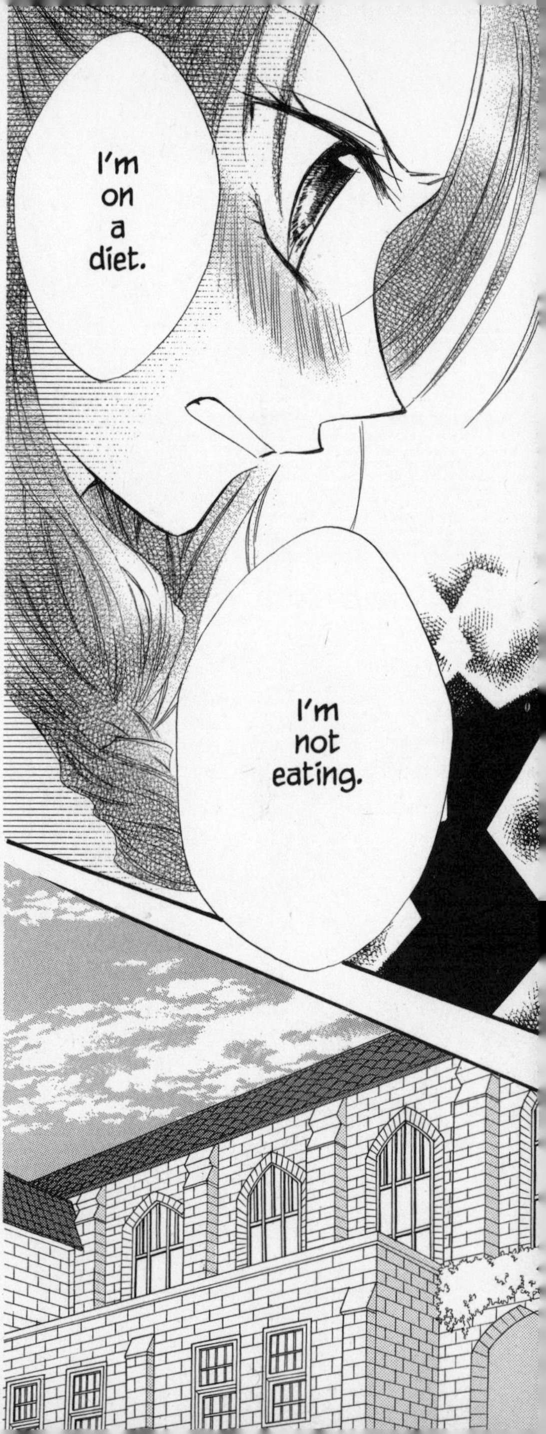

I'm on a diet.
I'm not eating.

Recipe 8

For this chapter, I got to observe the *Nakayoshi* photo shoot for Nami Uehara. Sigh... She's so cute and has a great figure. I was very shocked.

Recipe 9

For dieting, it's best to lose 2.5kg (about 5 1/2 lbs.) in a month... It's best to make your body burn more fat, but that's easier said than done... Anyway, I hear it's good to drink 2 liters (a little over a half gallon) of water every day!

Recipe 10

I have to admit, I didn't know there was such a thing as a frozen pie sheet!! So I tried buying one. But as I mentioned before, I don't have an oven, so it's still sitting in my freezer... What should I do with it?

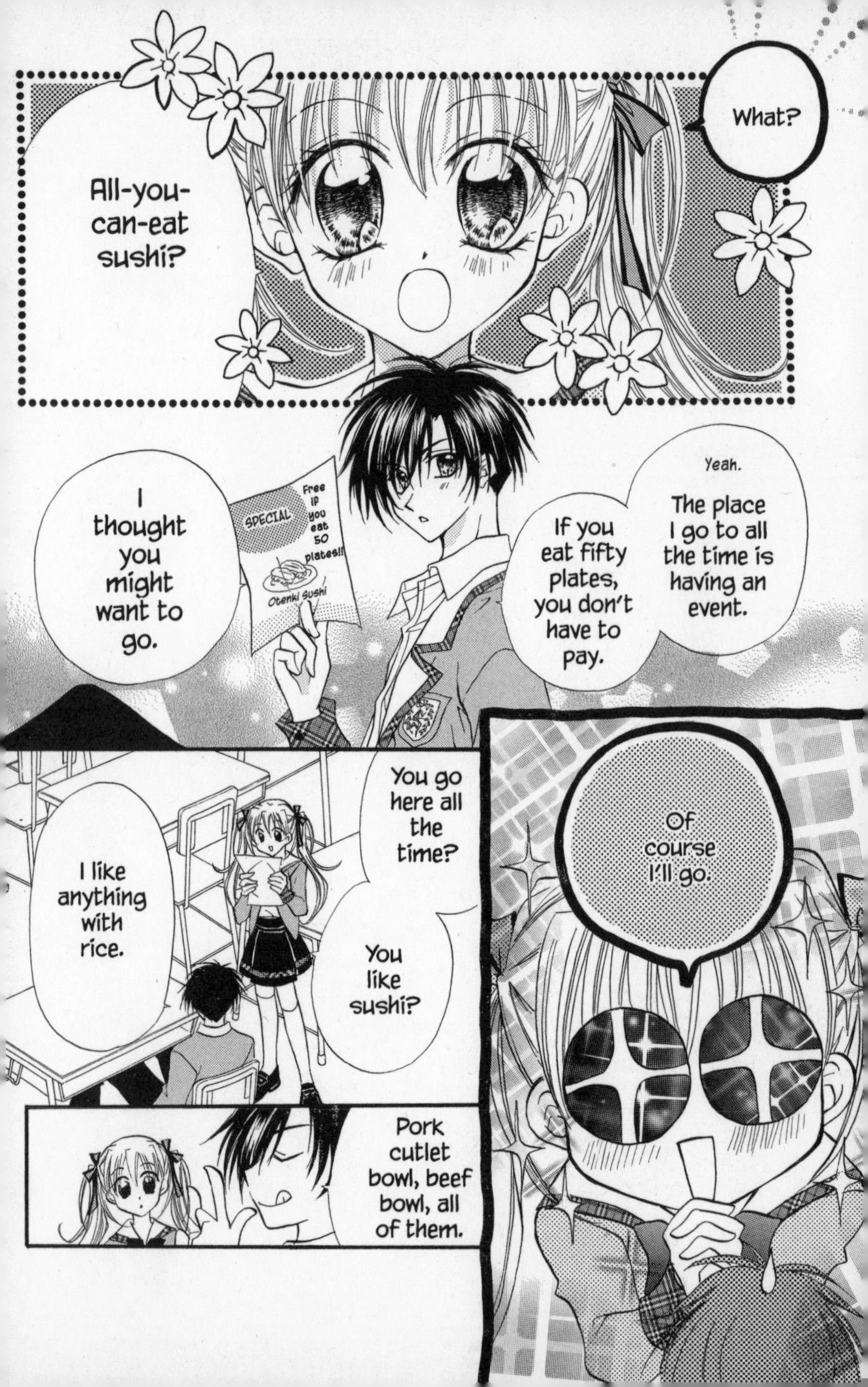
What?
All-you-can-eat sushi?
Yeah.
The place I go to all the time is having an event.
If you eat fifty plates, you don't have to pay.
Free if you eat 50 plates!!
SPECIAL
Otenki Sushi
I thought you might want to go.
Of course I'll go.
You go here all the time?
You like sushi?
I like anything with rice.
Pork cutlet bowl, beef bowl, all of them.

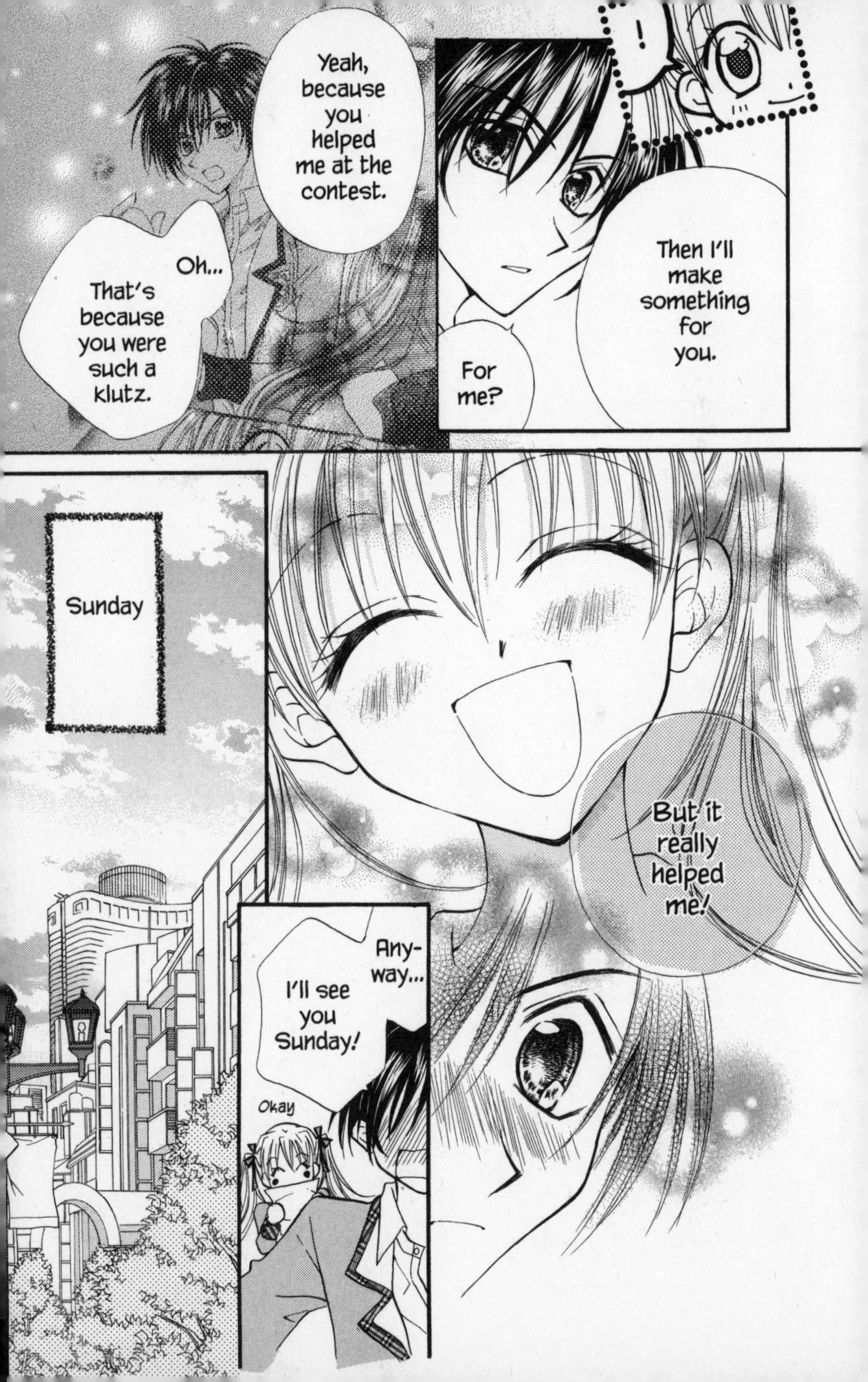
!
Then I'll make something for you.
For me?
Yeah, because you helped me at the contest.
Oh...
That's because you were such a klutz.
But it really helped me!
Any-way...
I'll see you Sunday!
Okay
Sunday

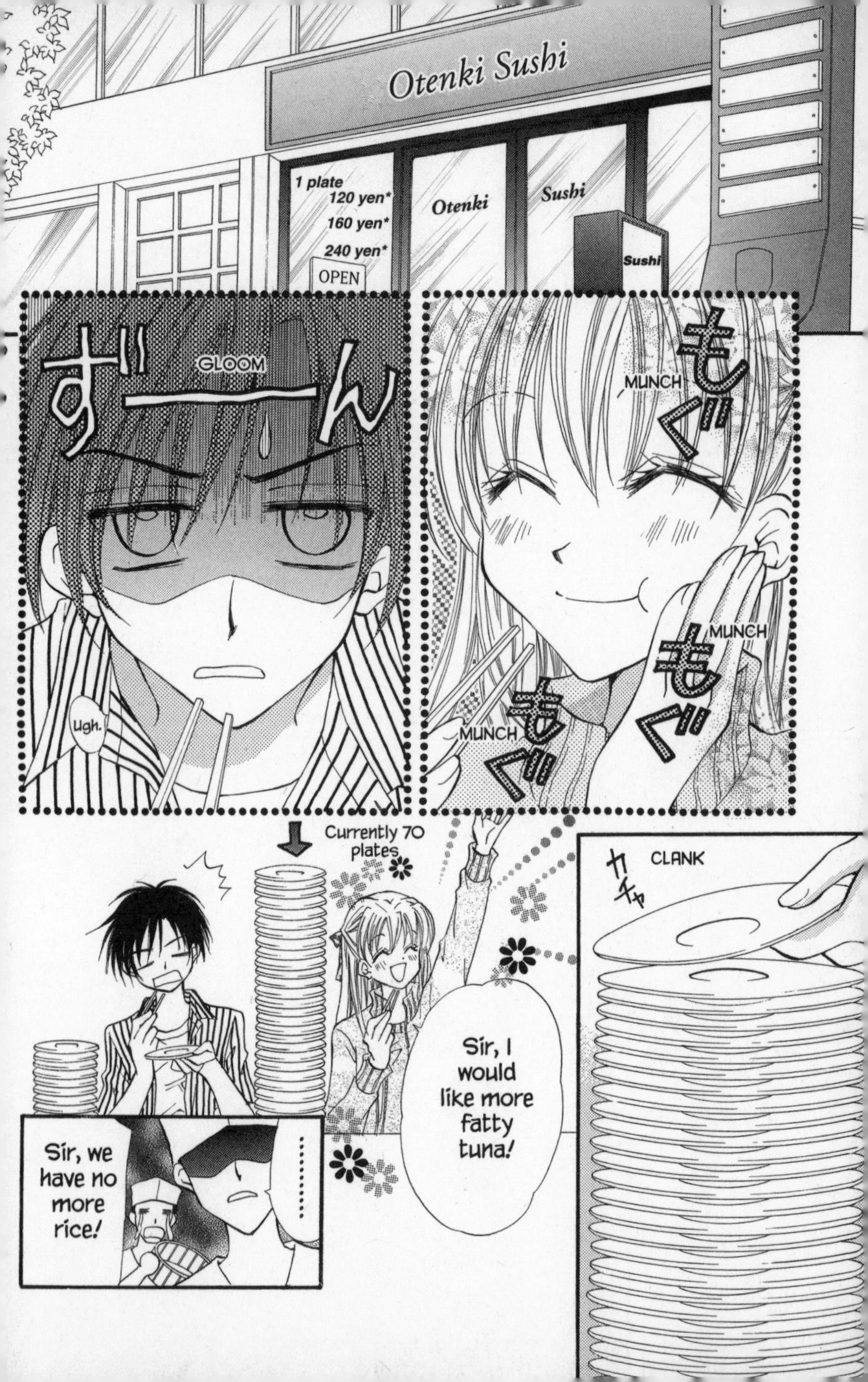
Otenki Sushi
1 plate
120 yen*
160 yen*
240 yen*
Otenki
Sushi
OPEN
Sushi
もぐ
MUNCH
もぐ
MUNCH
もぐ
MUNCH
ずーん
GLOOM
Ugh.
カチャ
CLANK
Sir, I would like more fatty tuna!
Currently 70 plates
......
Sir, we have no more rice!

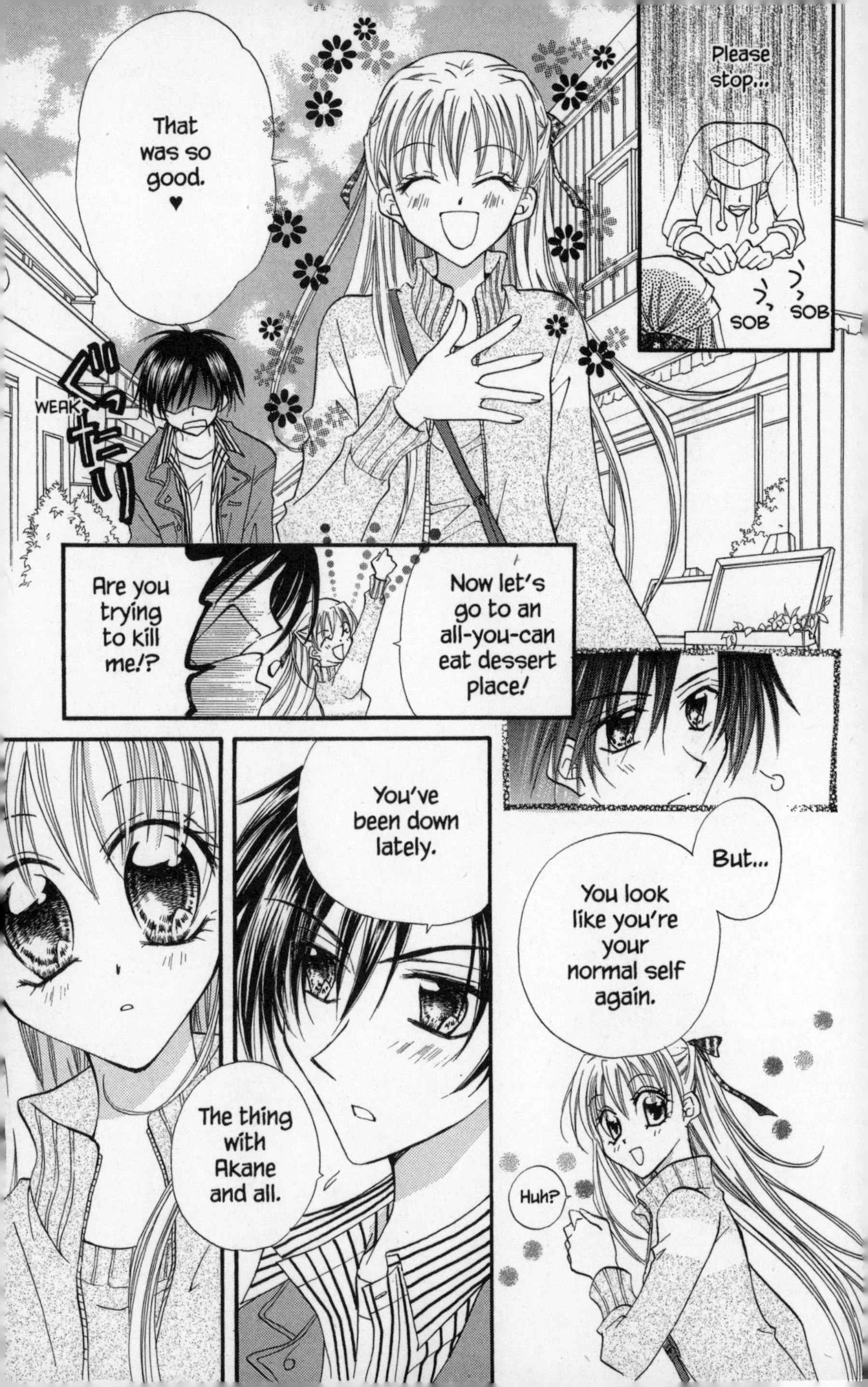
Please stop...
SOB SOB
That was so good. ♥
WEAK
Now let's go to an all-you-can eat dessert place!
Are you trying to kill me!?
But...
You look like you're your normal self again.
Huh?
You've been down lately.
The thing with Akane and all.

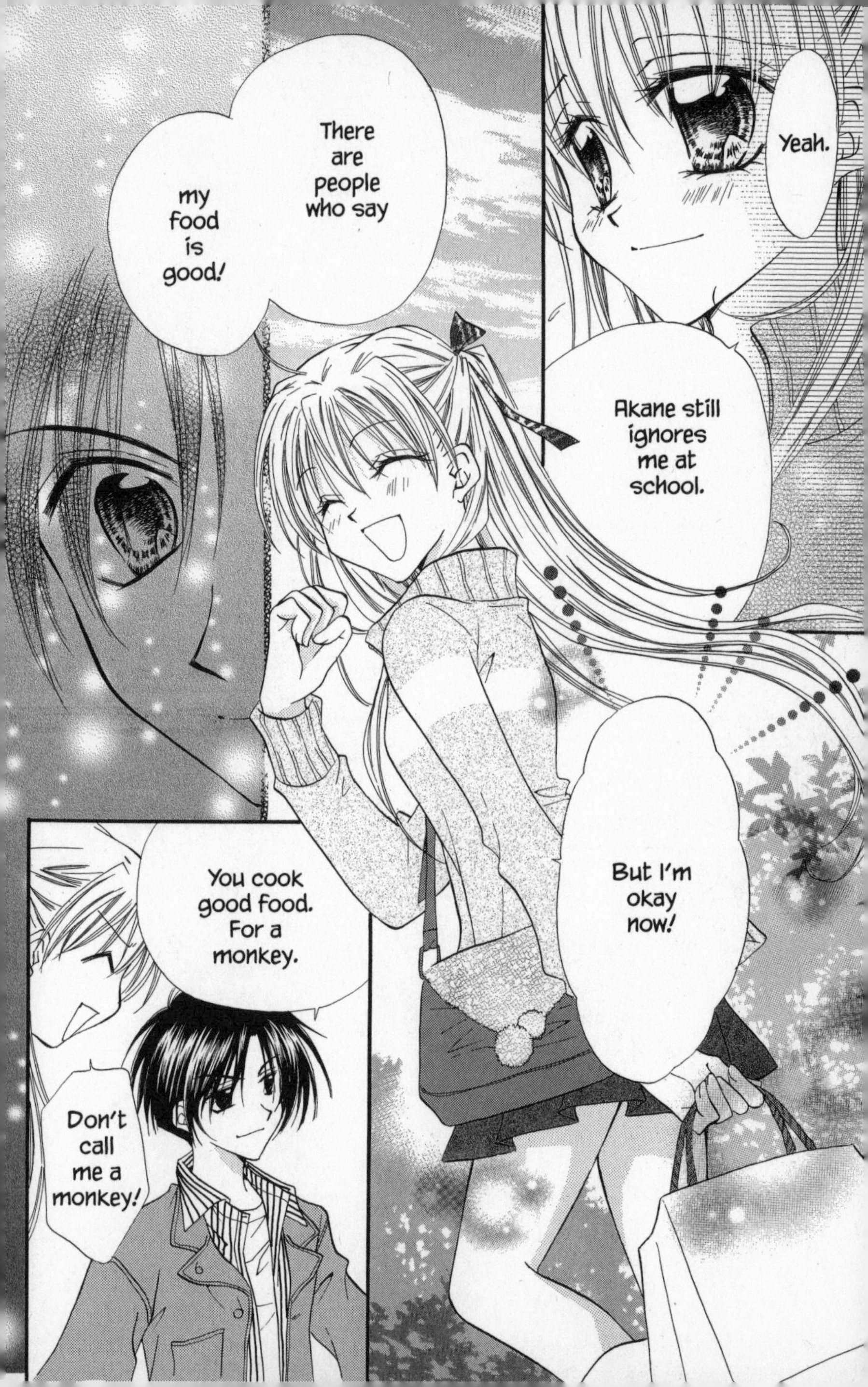
Yeah.
Akane still ignores me at school.
But I'm okay now!
There are people who say my food is good!
You cook good food. For a monkey.
Don't call me a monkey!

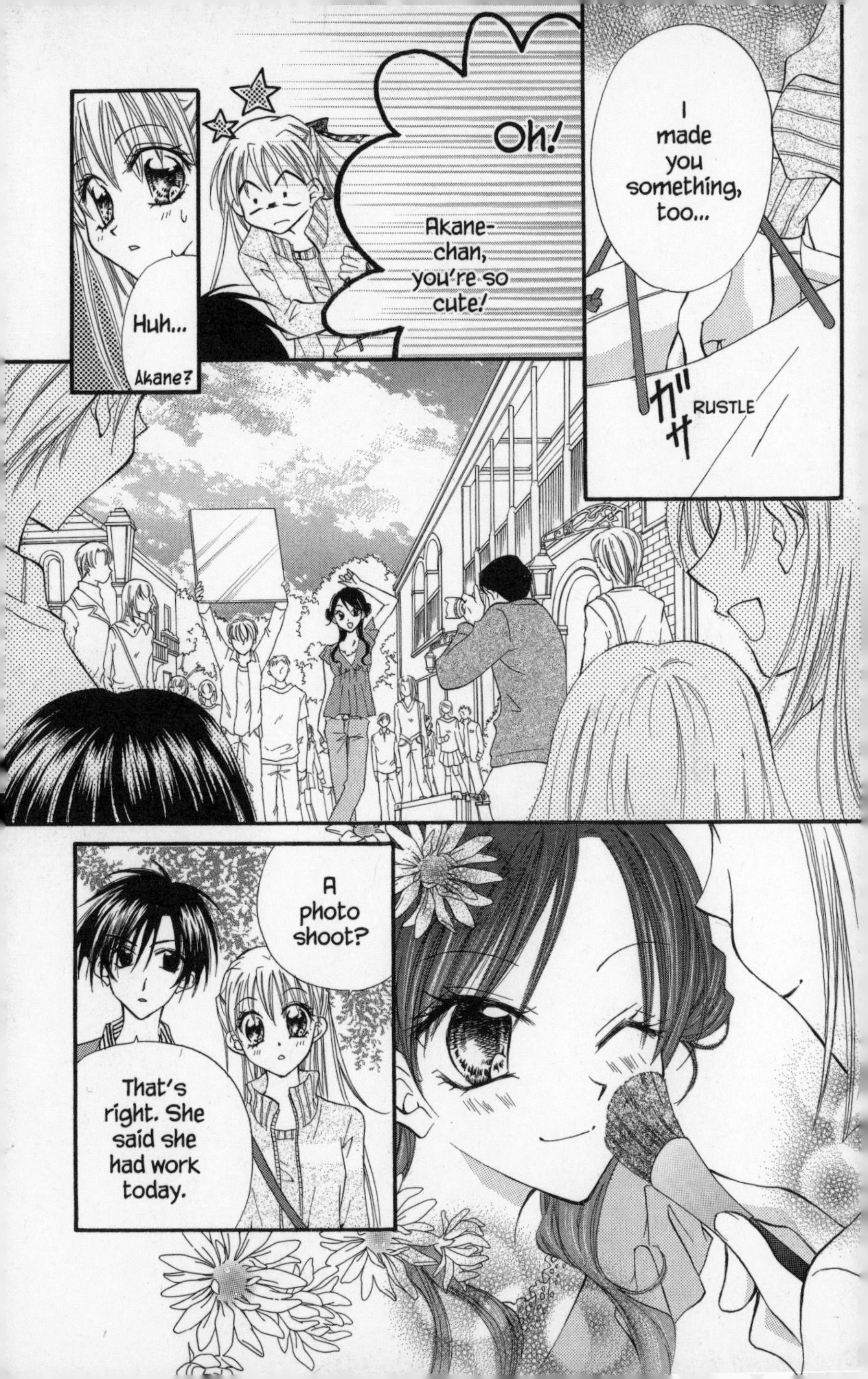
I made you something, too...
ガサ
RUSTLE
Oh!
Akane-chan, you're so cute!
Huh...
Akane?
A photo shoot?
That's right. She said she had work today.

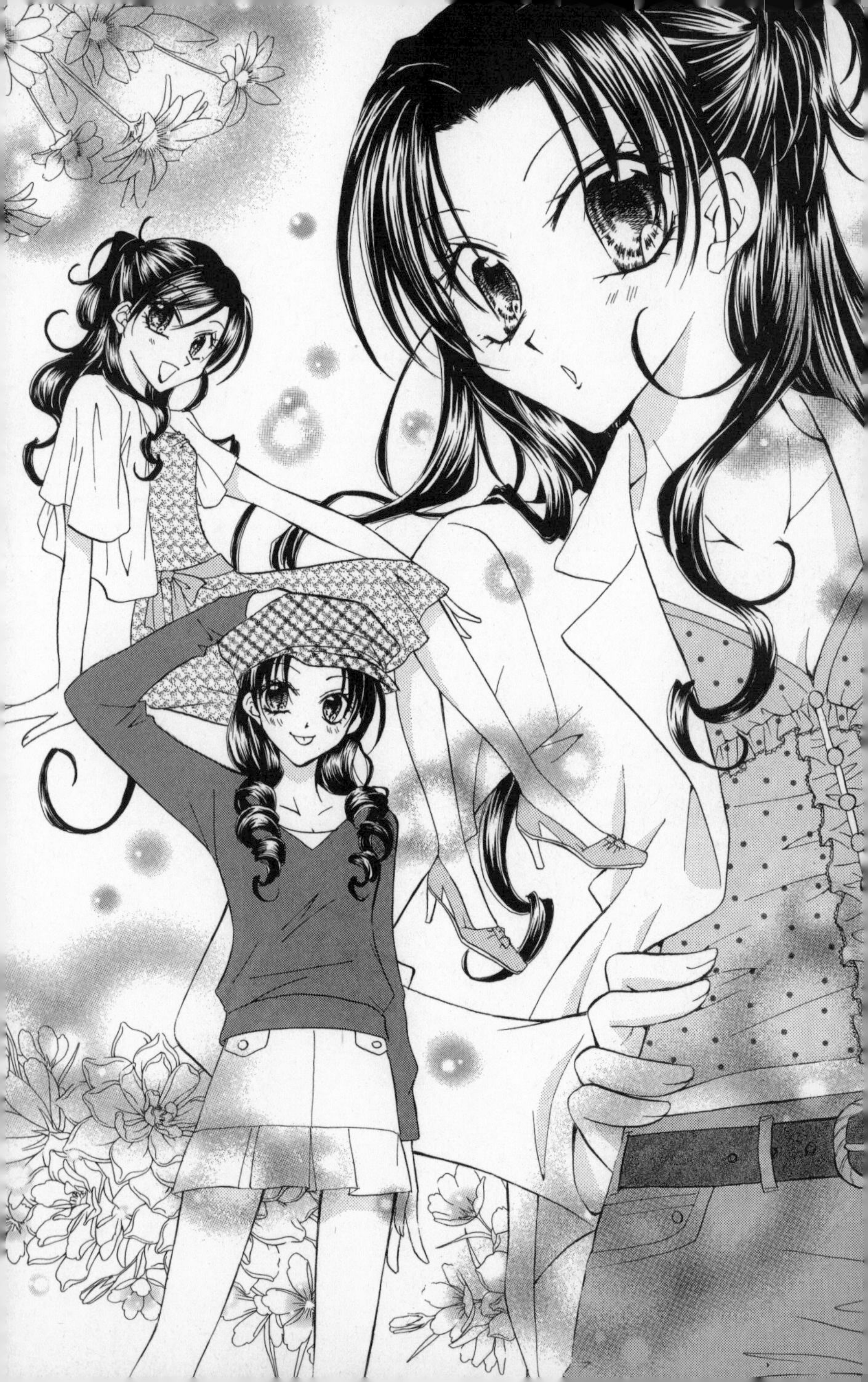

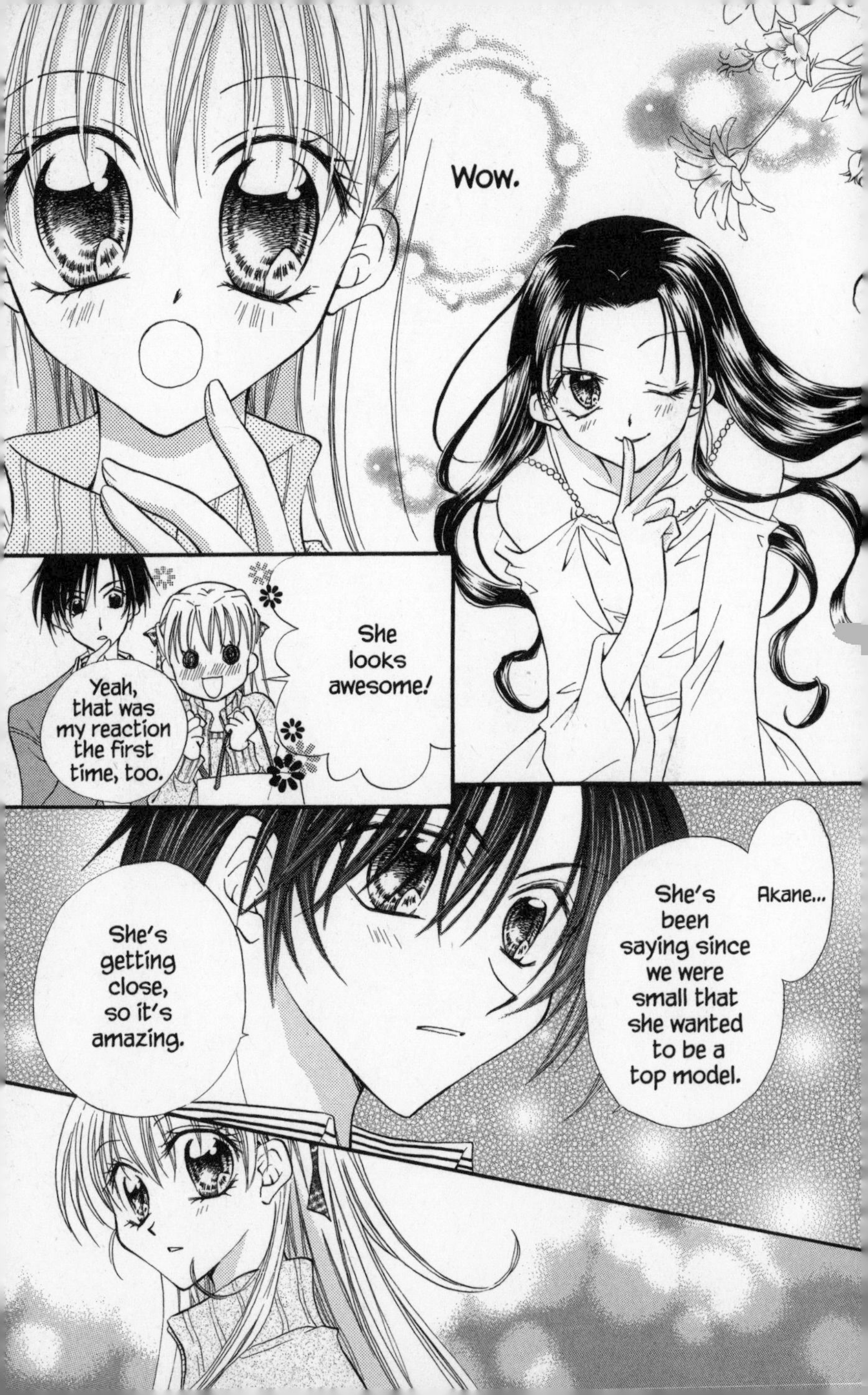
Wow.
She looks awesome!
Yeah, that was my reaction the first time, too.
Akane...
She's been saying since we were small that she wanted to be a top model.
She's getting close, so it's amazing.

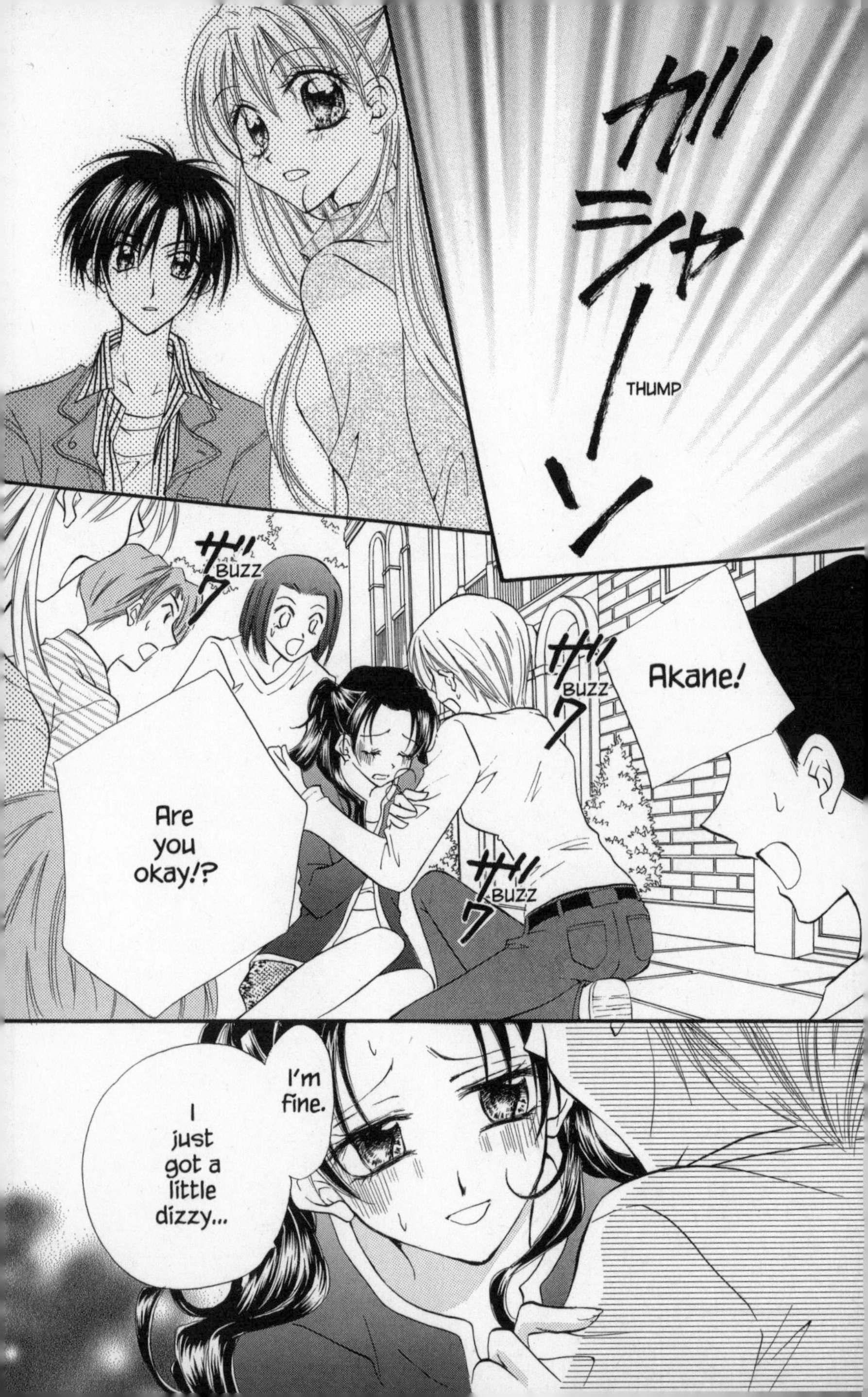

ガシャーーン
THUMP
ザワ
BUZZ
Akane!
ザワ
BUZZ
ザワ
BUZZ
Are you okay!?
I'm fine.
I just got a little dizzy...

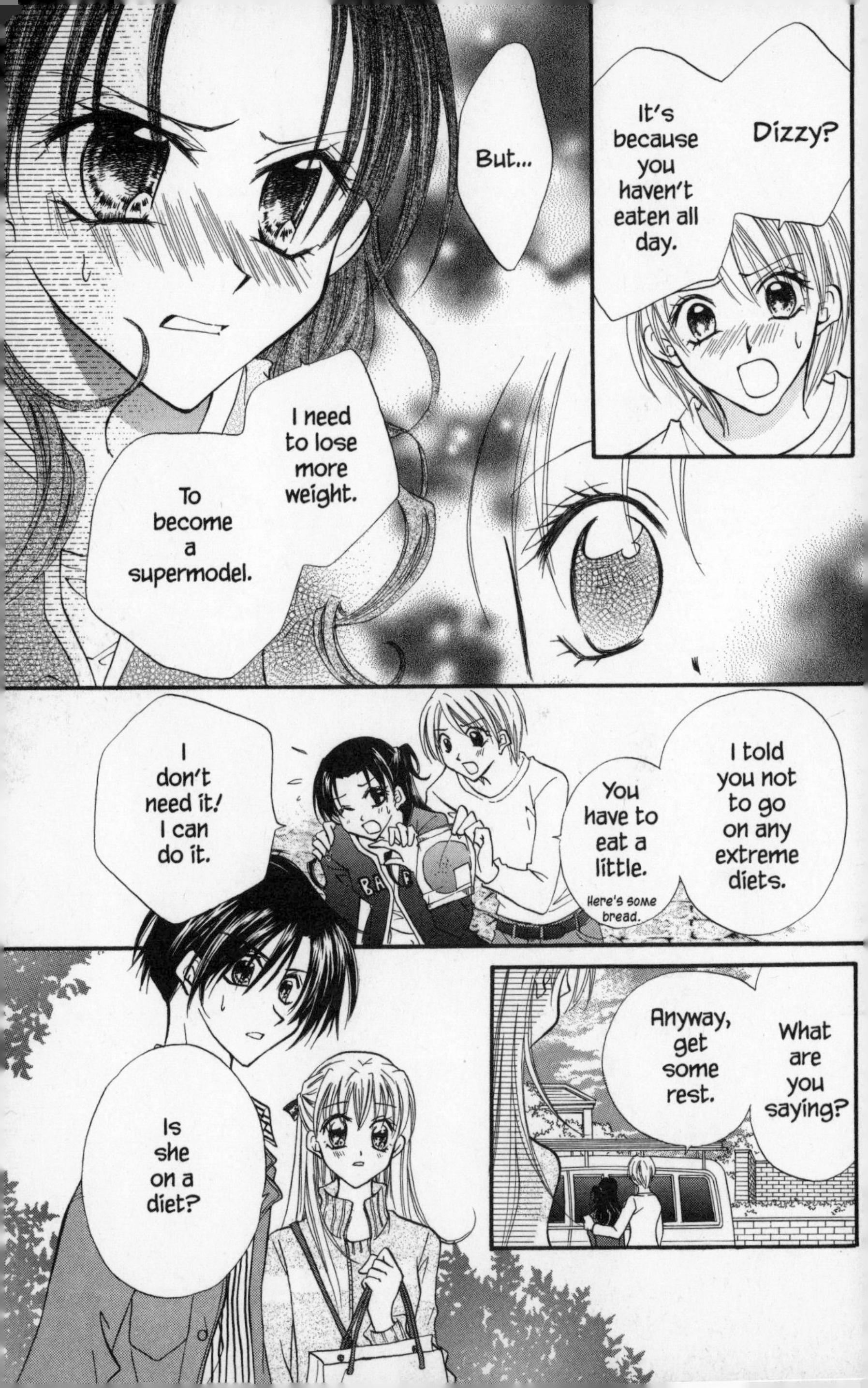
Dizzy?
It's because you haven't eaten all day.
But...
I need to lose more weight.
To become a supermodel.
I told you not to go on any extreme diets.
You have to eat a little.
Here's some bread.
I don't need it! I can do it.
What are you saying?
Anyway, get some rest.
Is she on a diet?

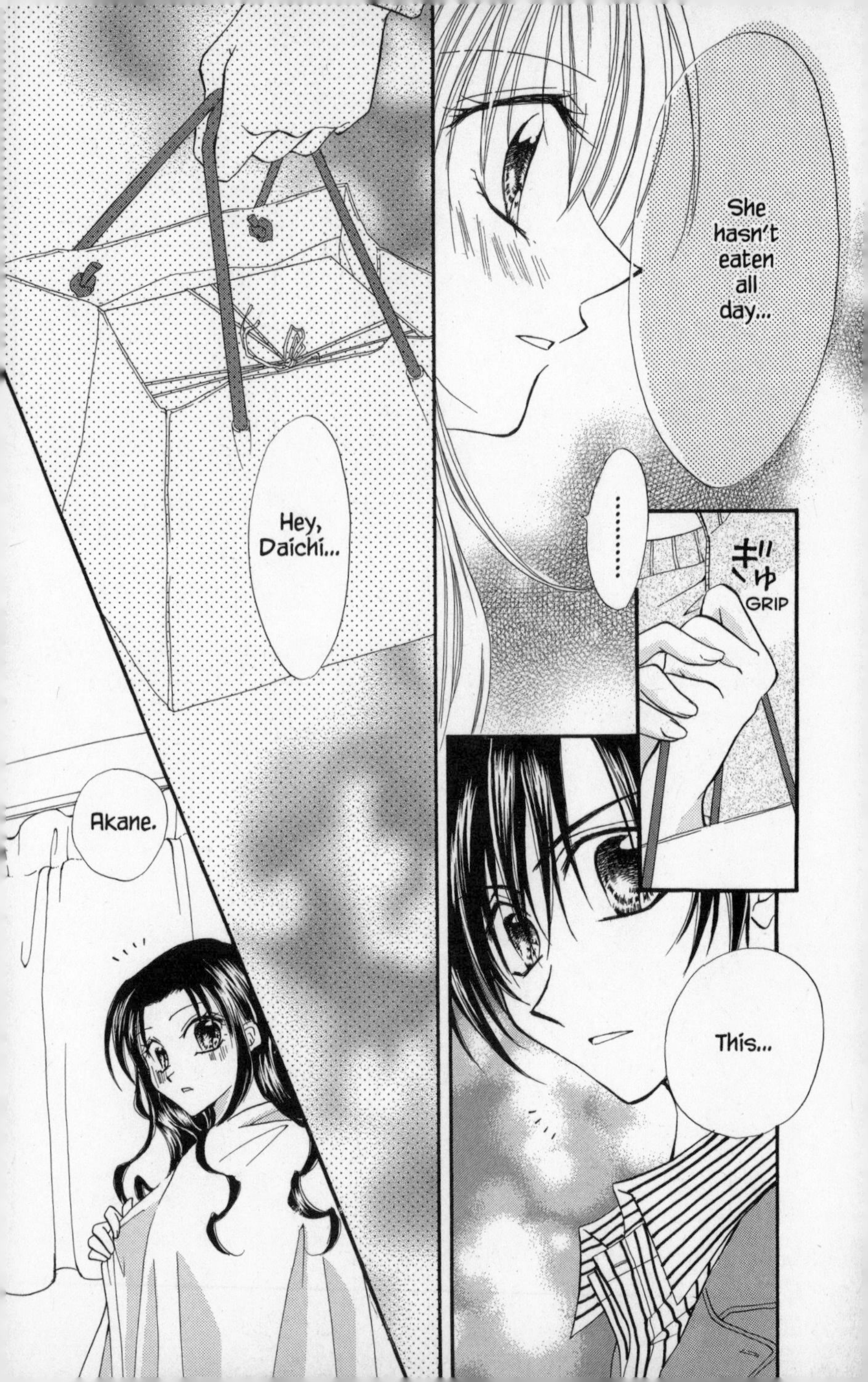
She hasn't eaten all day...
......
ぎゅ
GRIP
This...
Hey, Daichi...
Akane.

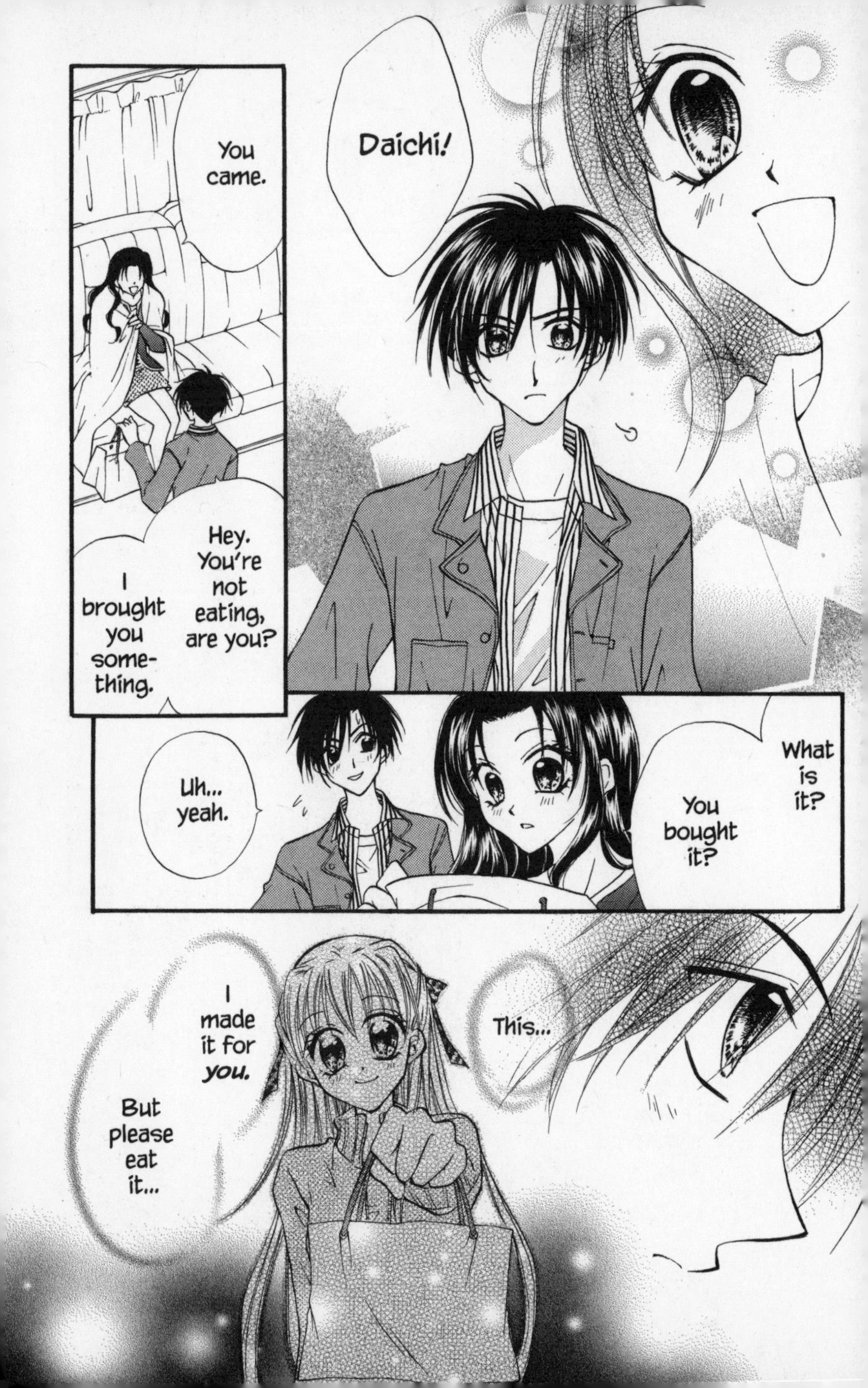
Daichi!
You came.
Hey. You're not eating, are you?
I brought you some-thing.
What is it?
You bought it?
Uh... yeah.
This...
I made it for *you.*
But please eat it...

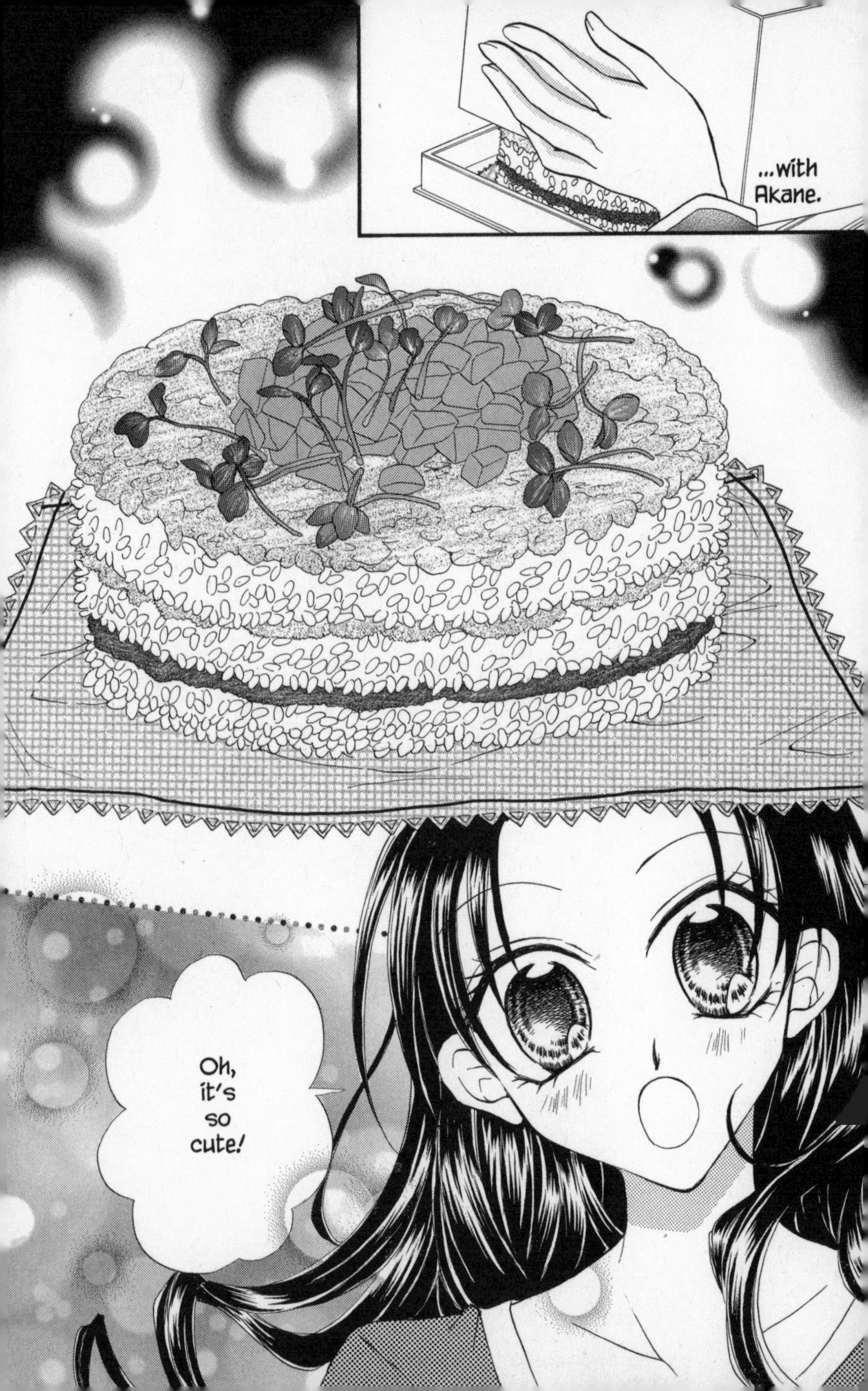
...with Akane.
Oh, it's so cute!

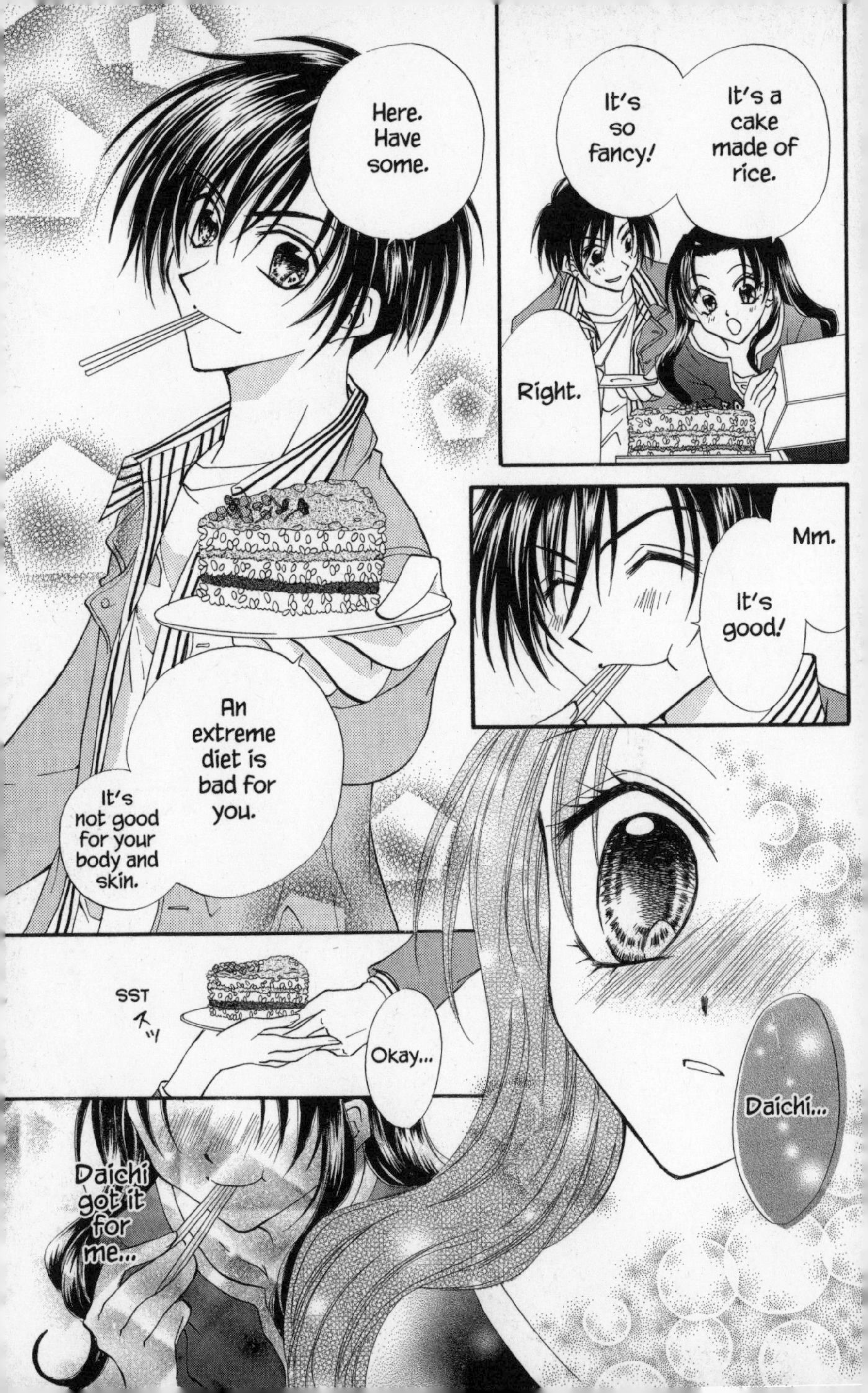
It's a cake made of rice.
It's so fancy!
Right.
Mm.
It's good!
Here. Have some.
An extreme diet is bad for you.
It's not good for your body and skin.
Okay...
SST
スッ
Daichi...
Daichi got it for me...

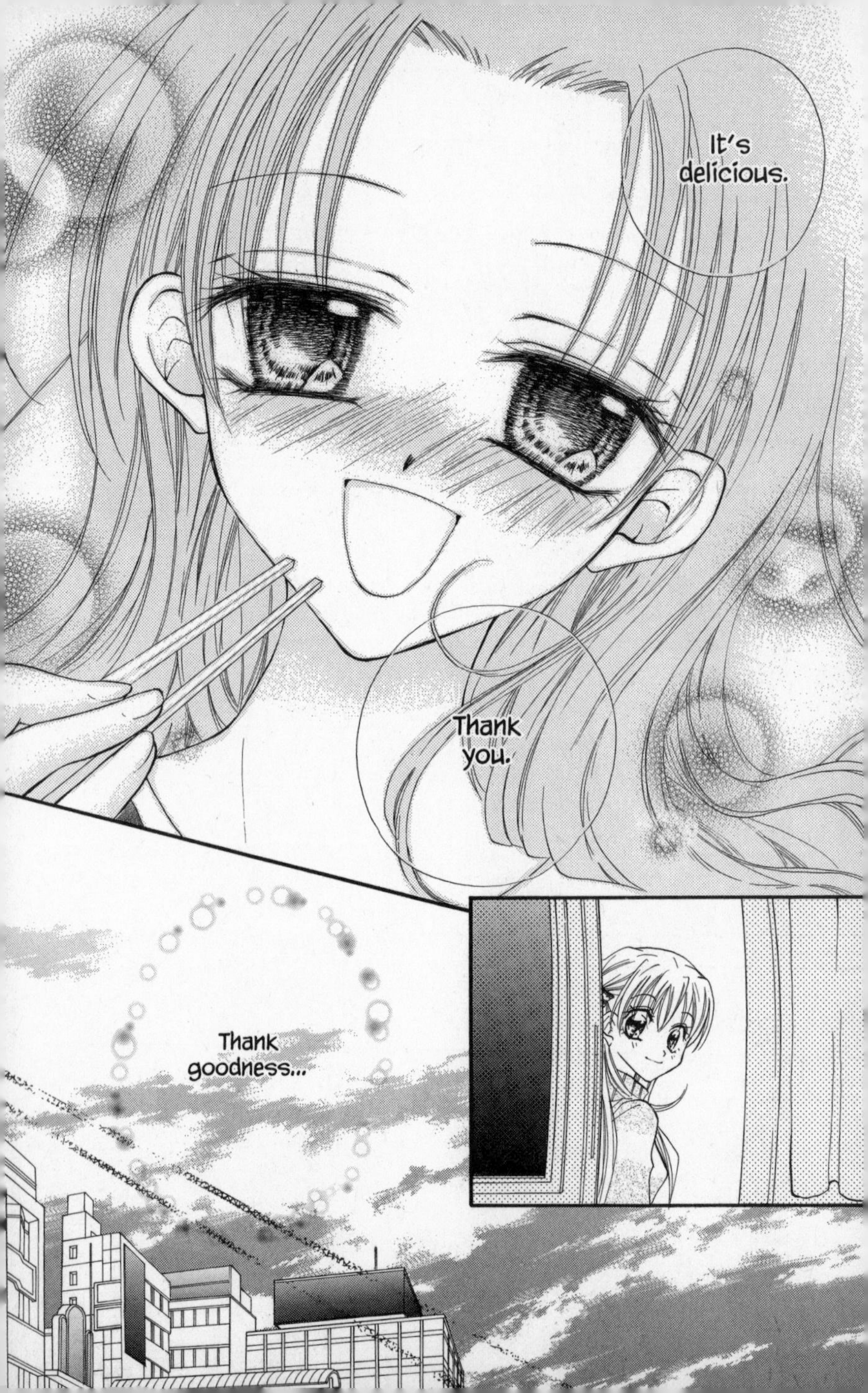
It's delicious.
Thank you.
Thank goodness...

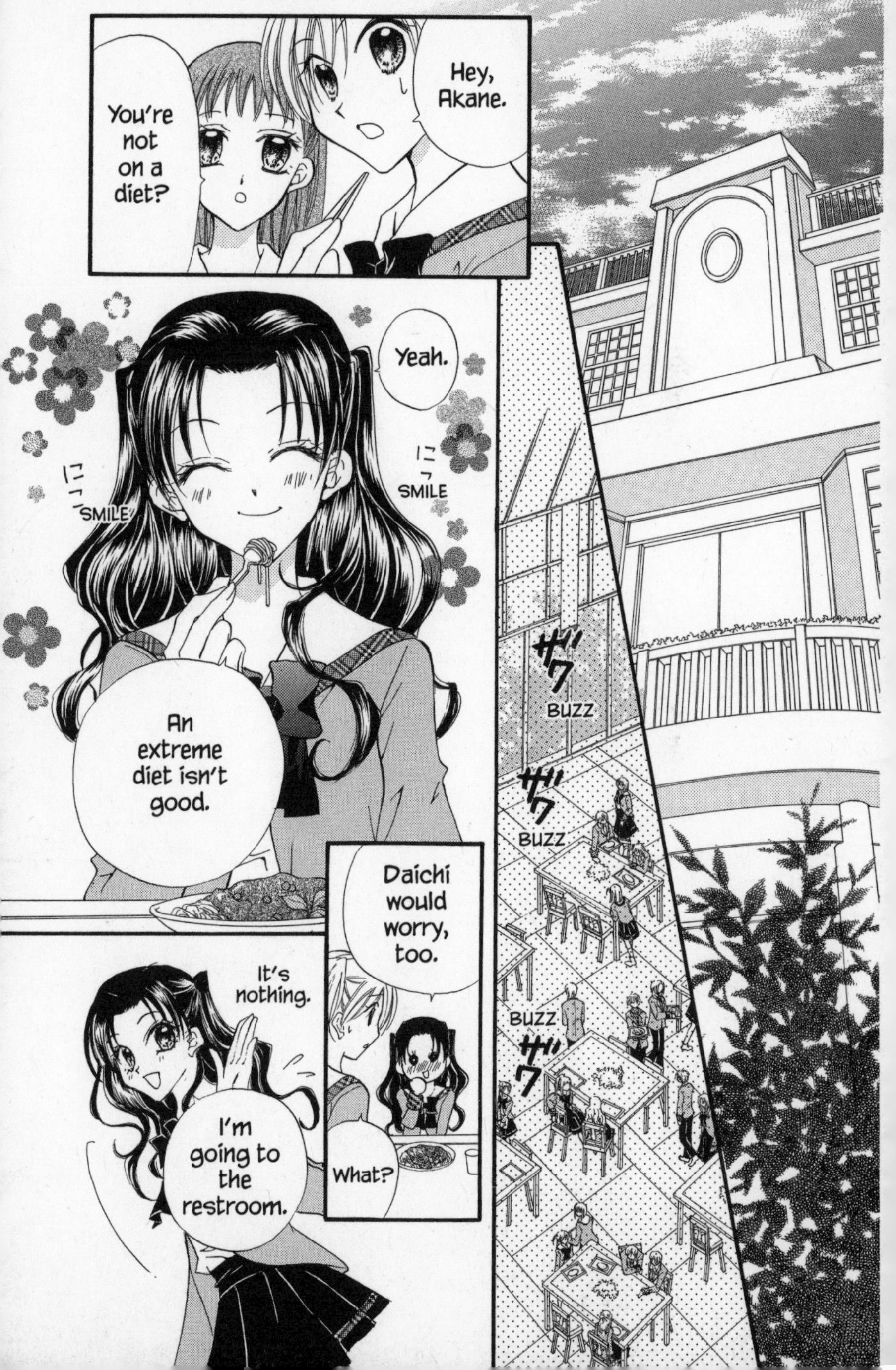
ザワ
BUZZ
ザワ
BUZZ
BUZZ
ザワ
Hey, Akane.
You're not on a diet?
Yeah.
にこ
SMILE
にこ
SMILE
An extreme diet isn't good.
Daichi would worry, too.
What?
It's nothing.
I'm going to the restroom.

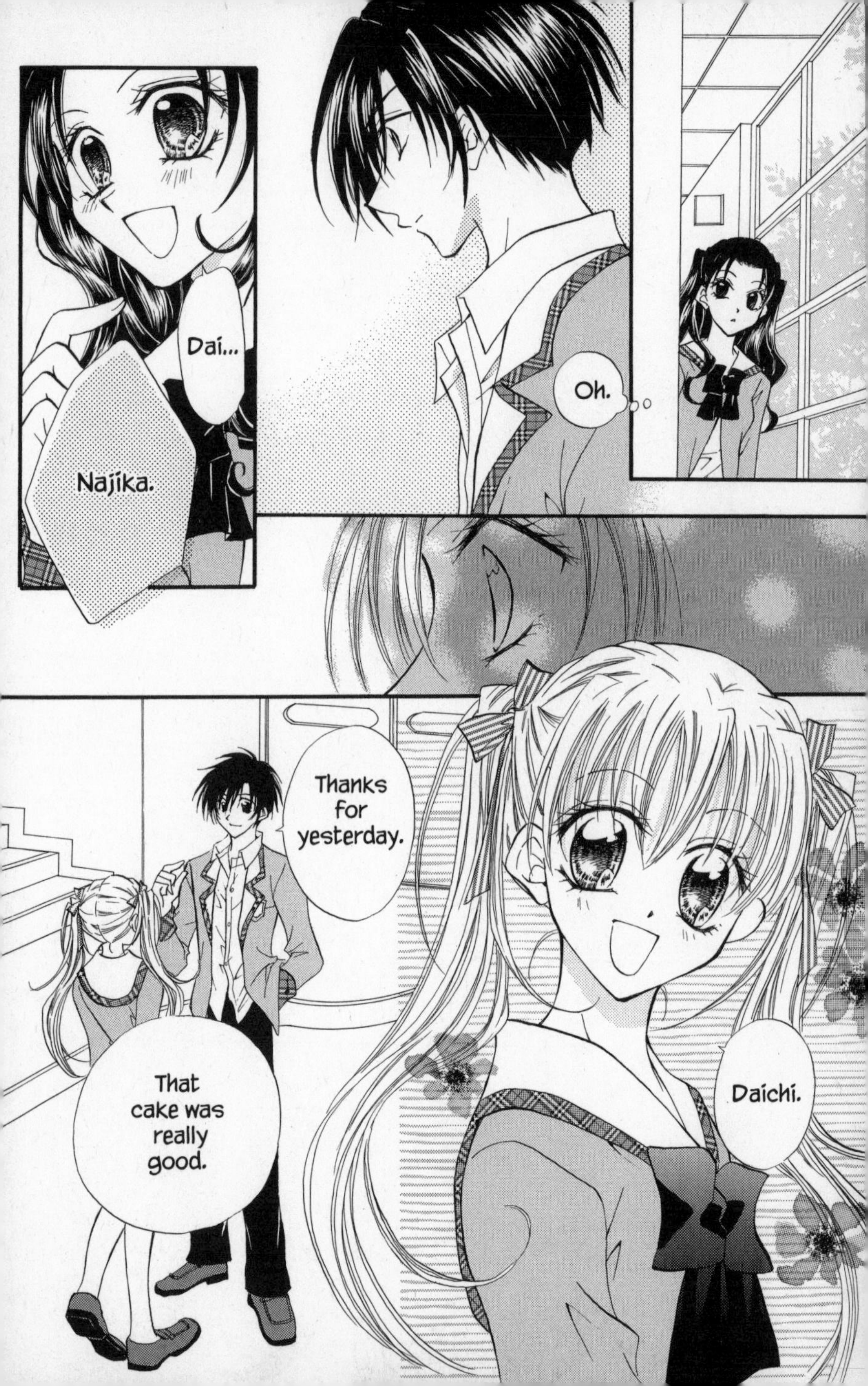
Oh.
Dai...
Najika.
Daichi.
Thanks for yesterday.
That cake was really good.

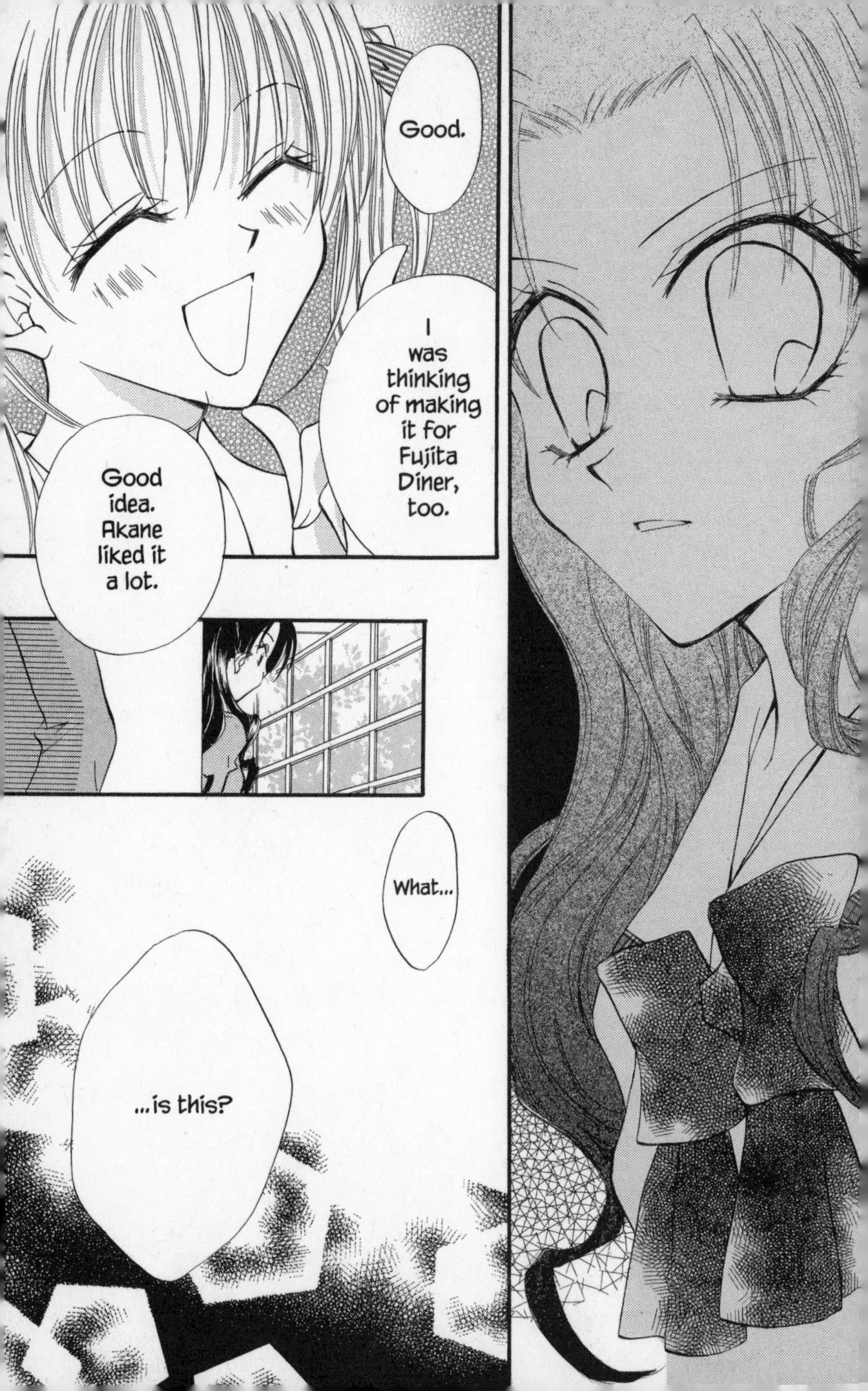
Good.
I was thinking of making it for Fujita Diner, too.
Good idea. Akane liked it a lot.
What...
...is this?

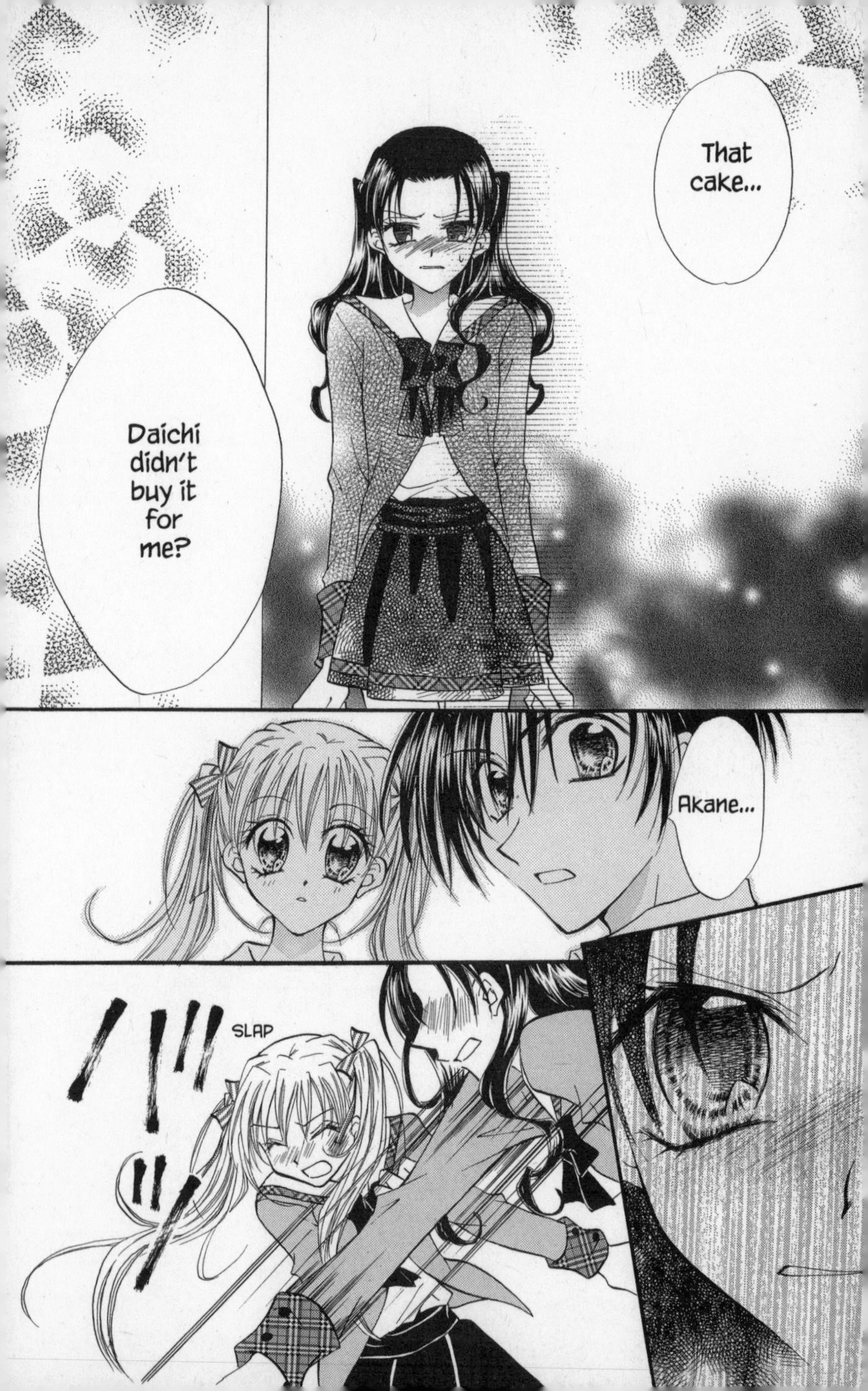
That cake...
Daichi didn't buy it for me?
Akane...
SLAP

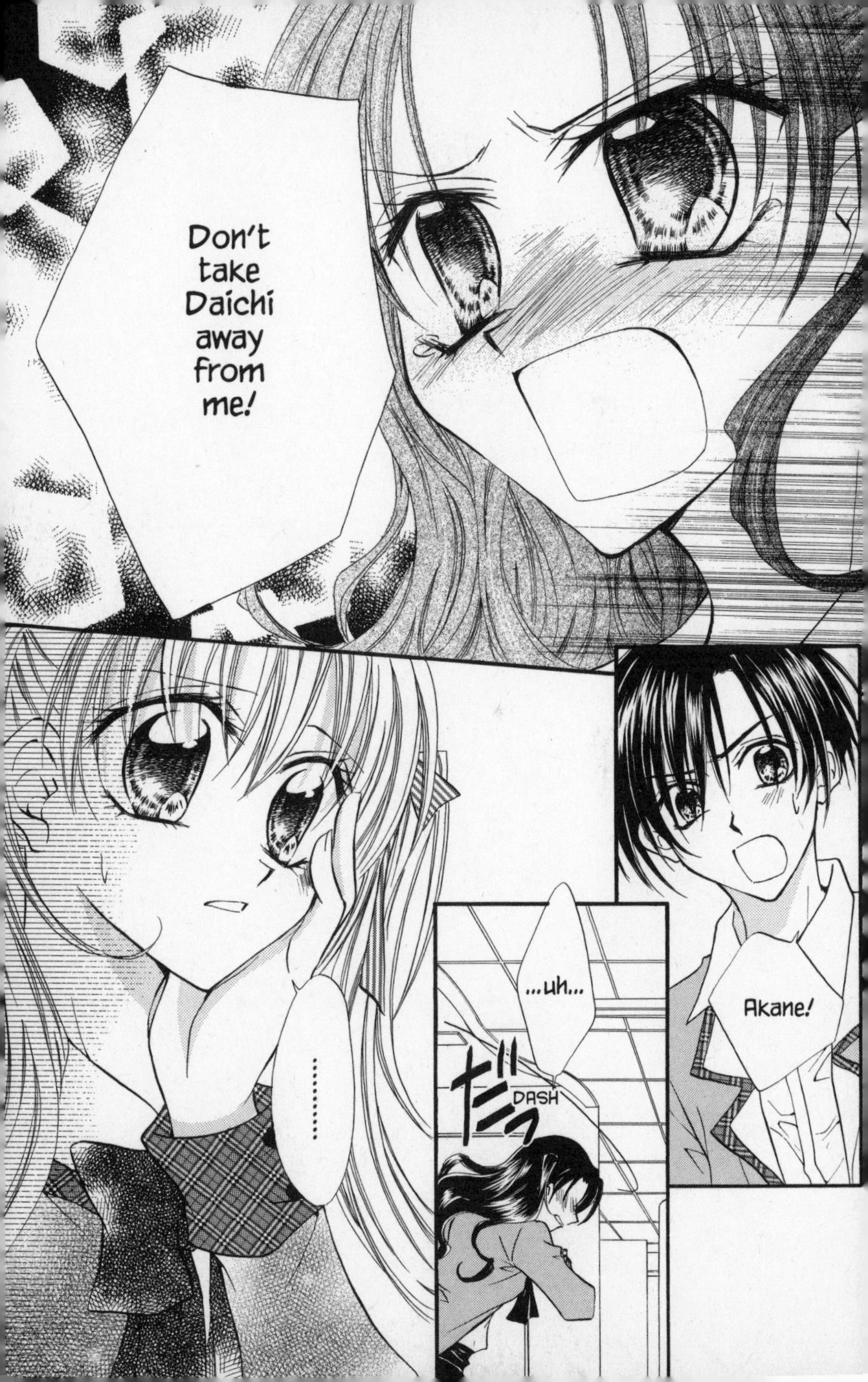
Don't take Daichi away from me!
Akane!
...uh...
DASH
....

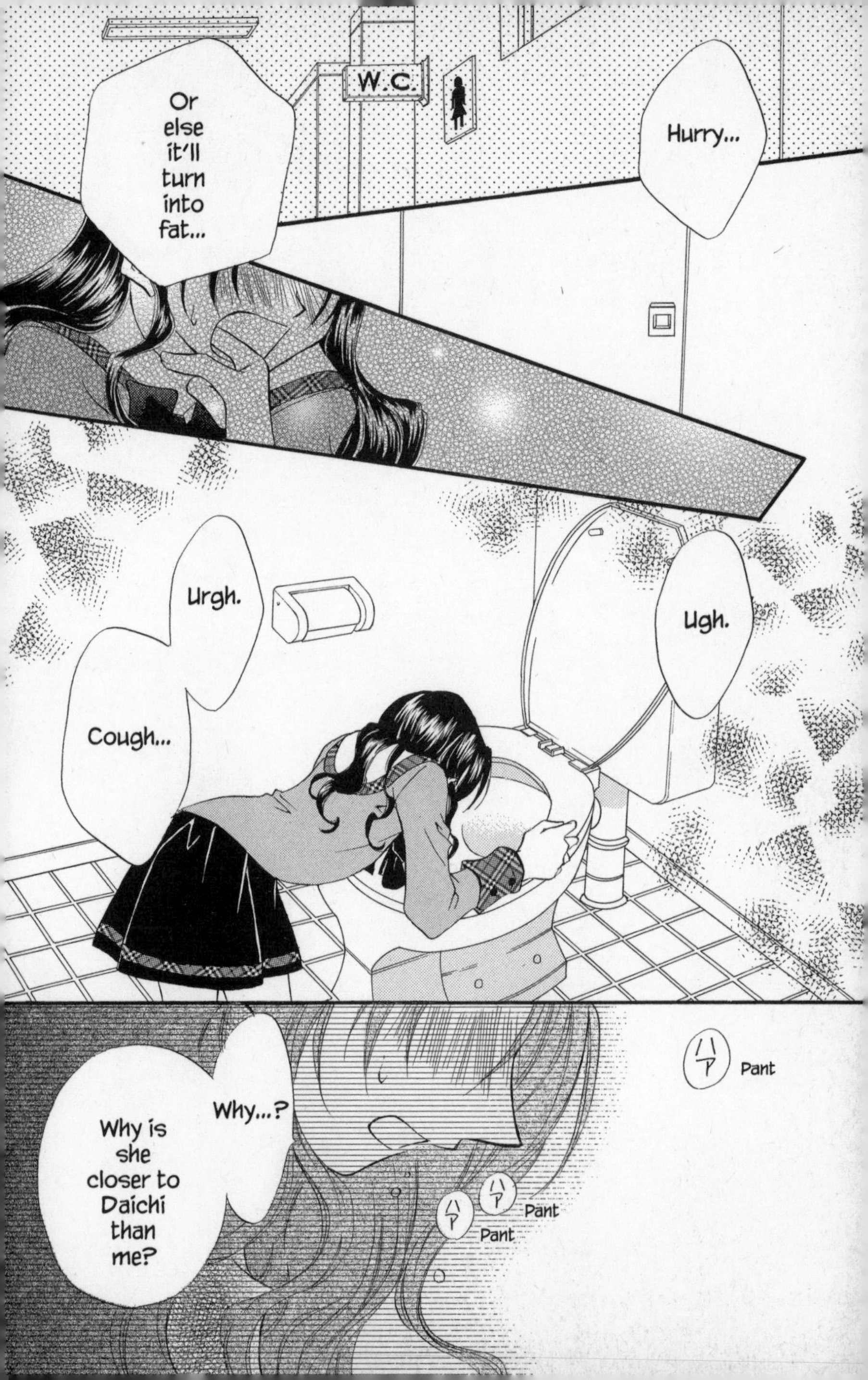
W.C.
Hurry...
Or else it'll turn into fat...
Ugh.
Urgh.
Cough...
Pant
Pant
Pant
Why...?
Why is she closer to Daichi than me?

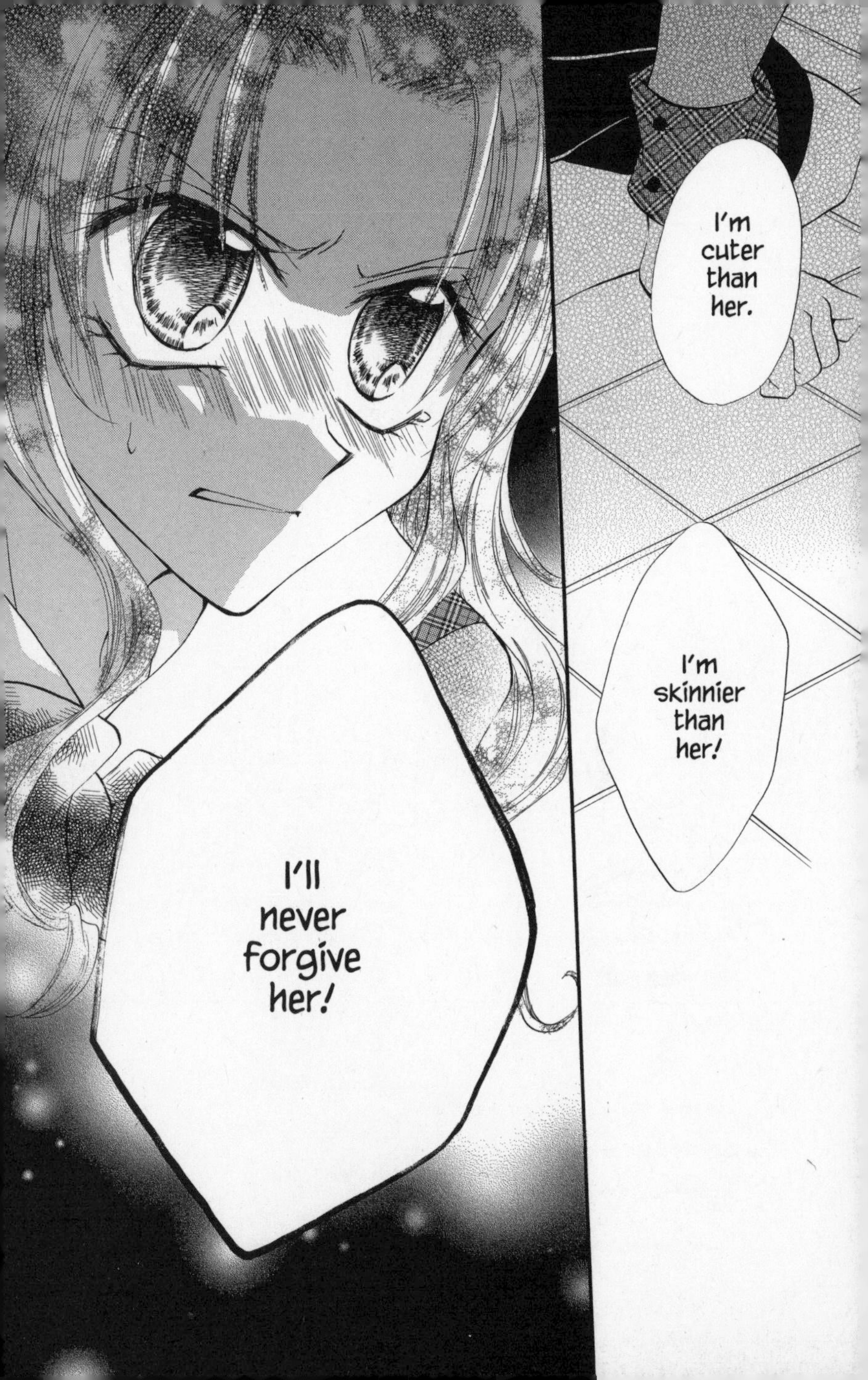
I'm cuter than her.
I'm skinnier than her!
I'll never forgive her!

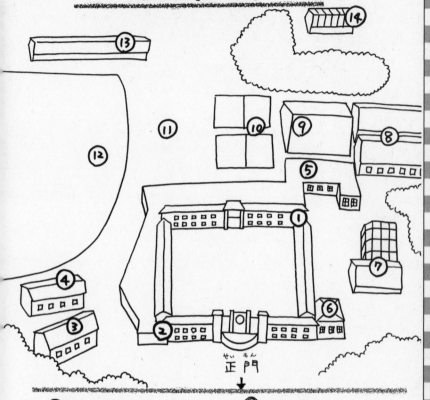

A Map of Seika Academy
(at least part of it)

せい もん
正 門

1. The Junior High Section. Najika attends this.
2. High School Section
3. Girls' Dorm
4. Boys' Dorm
5. Building with Nurse's Office and Music Room
6. Hall where they had the Christmas presentation
7. Terrace and Cafeteria
8. Elementary School Section
9. Gym
10. Tennis Courts
11. Yard (big)
12. Field (really big)
13. Rooms for clubs
14. Fujita Diner

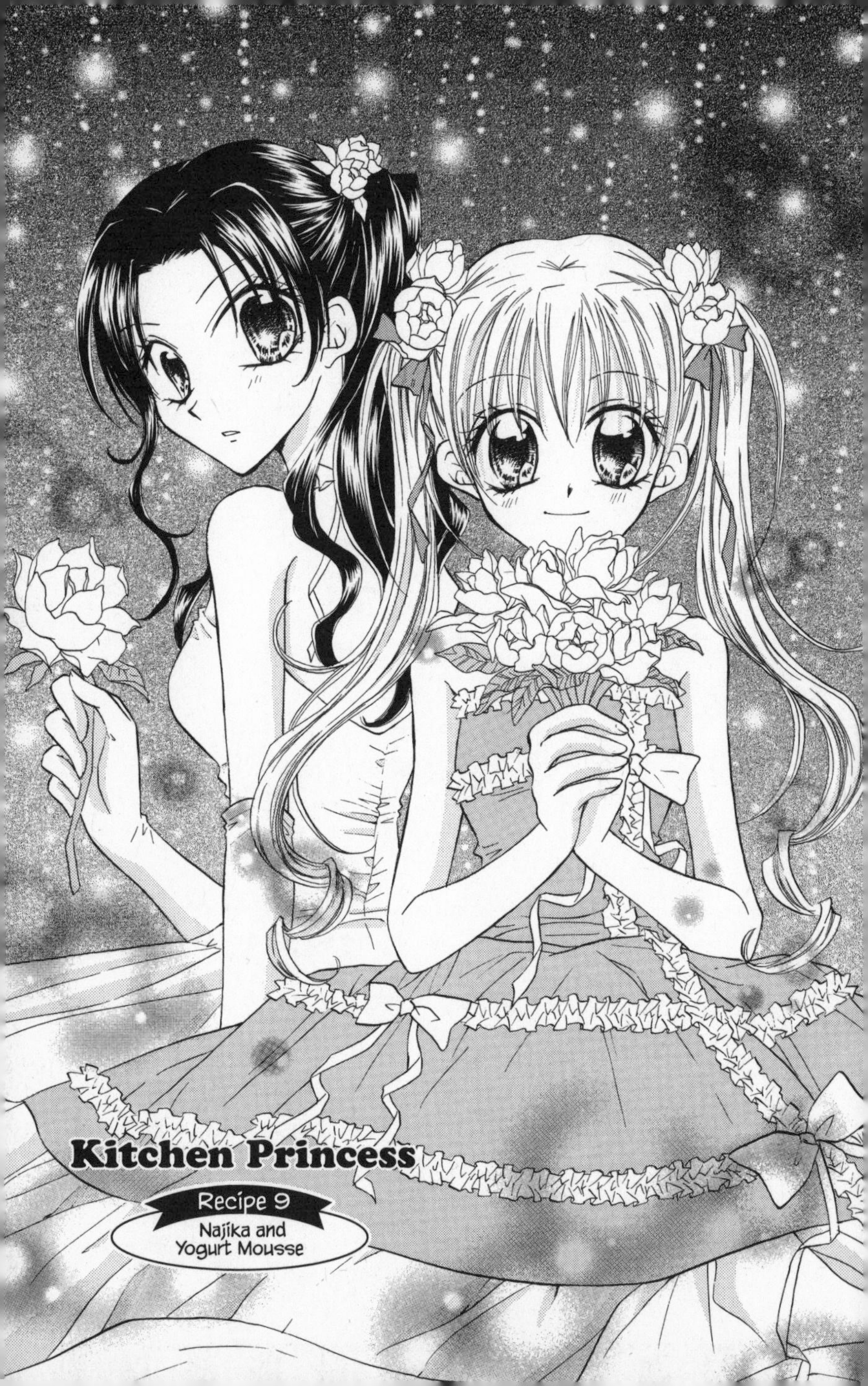
Kitchen Princess
Recipe 9
Najika and
Yogurt Mousse

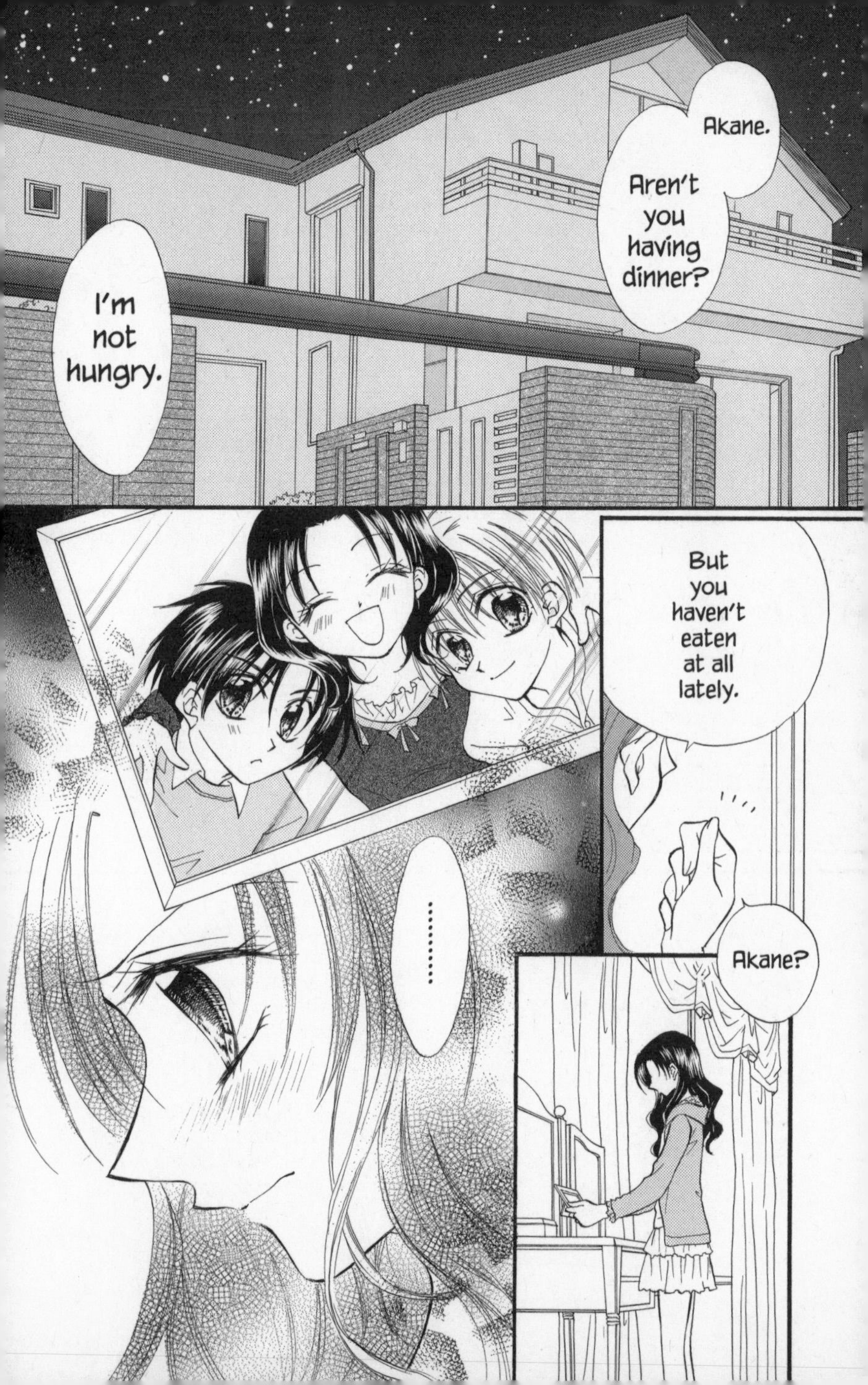
Akane.
Aren't you having dinner?
I'm not hungry.
But you haven't eaten at all lately.
Akane?
......

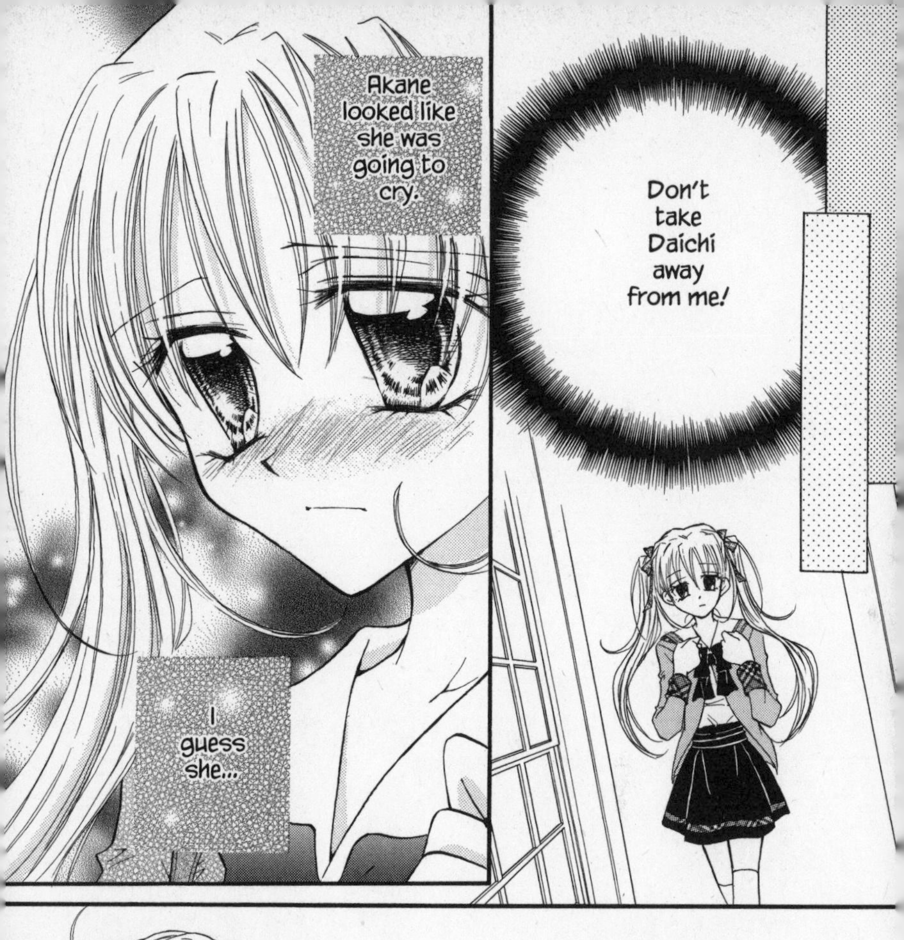
Don't take Daichi away from me!
Akane looked like she was going to cry.
I guess she...

About Recipe 9's Splash Page

I always wanted to do a splash page with the two girls. And since the story was revolving around Akane, I decided to do it for this chapter. Akane's hair is fun to draw. ♪ Although coloring it in is hard work...

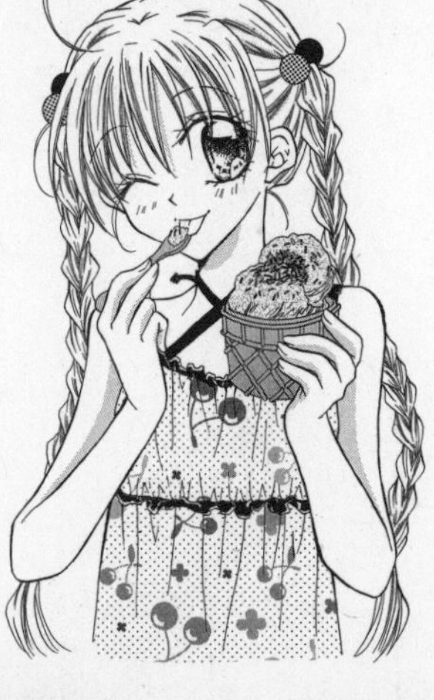

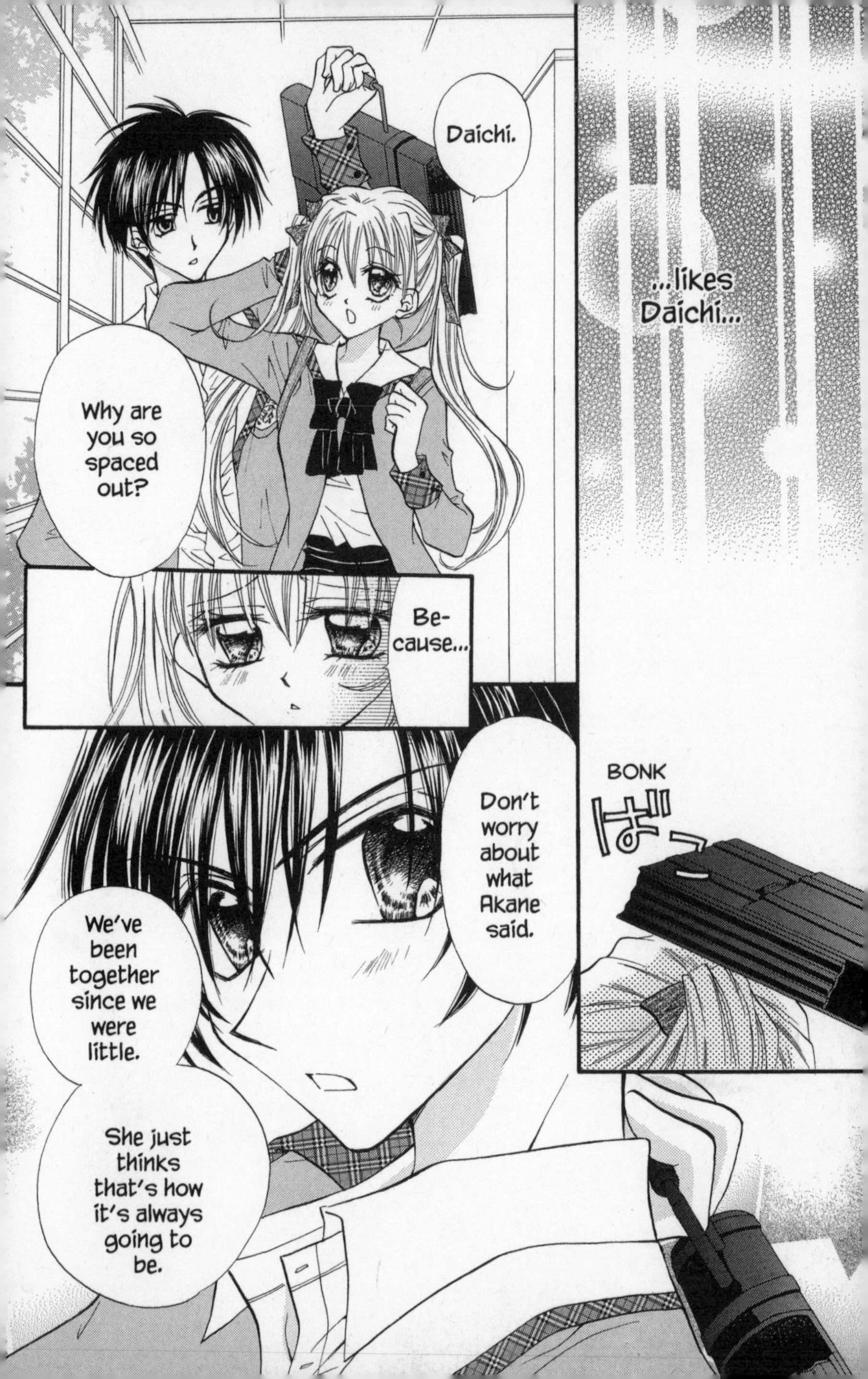
...likes Daichi...
Daichi.
Why are you so spaced out?
Be-cause...
BONK
Don't worry about what Akane said.
We've been together since we were little.
She just thinks that's how it's always going to be.

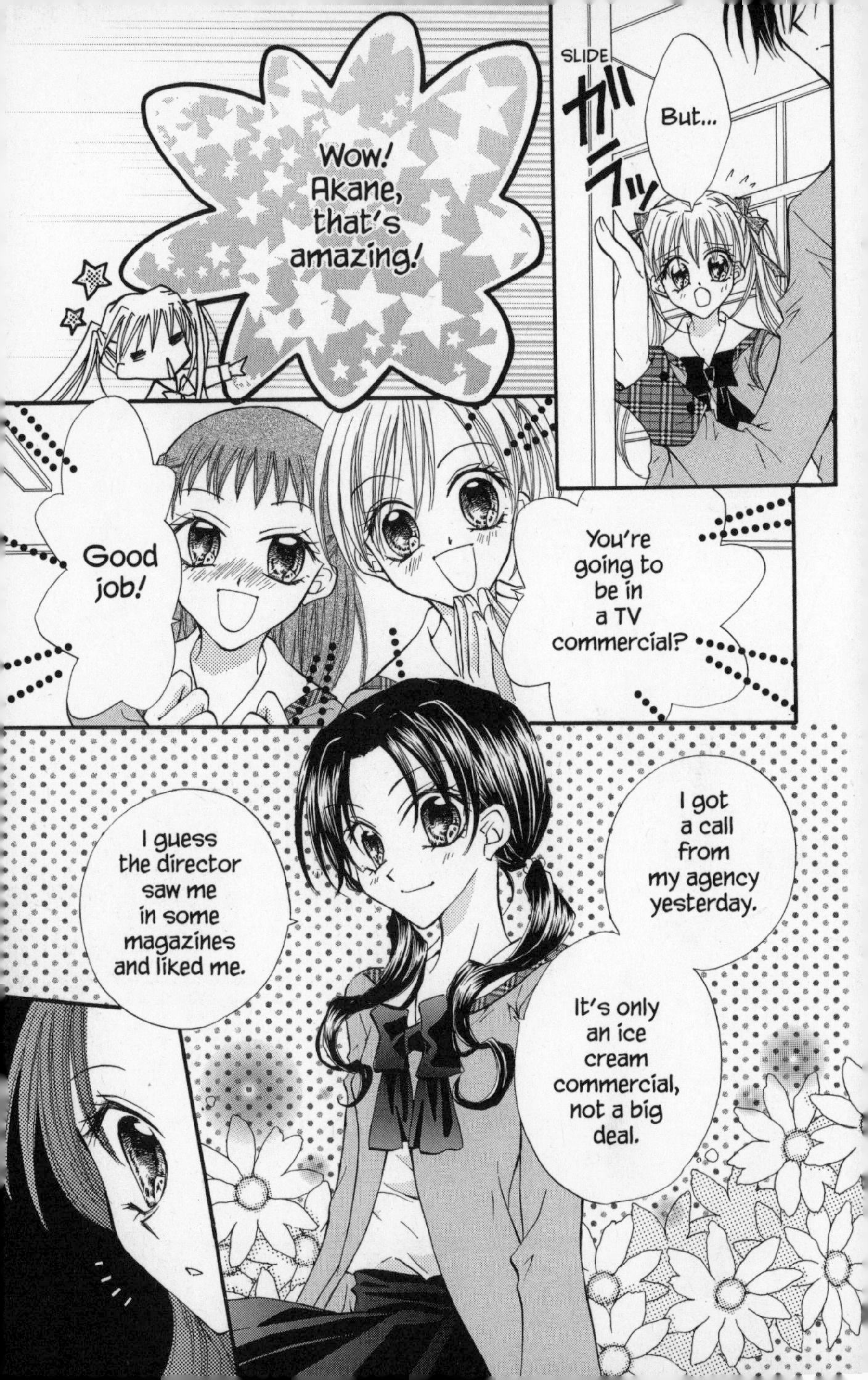
SLIDE
ガラッ
But...
Wow! Akane, that's amazing!
You're going to be in a TV commercial?
Good job!
I got a call from my agency yesterday.
I guess the director saw me in some magazines and liked me.
It's only an ice cream commercial, not a big deal.

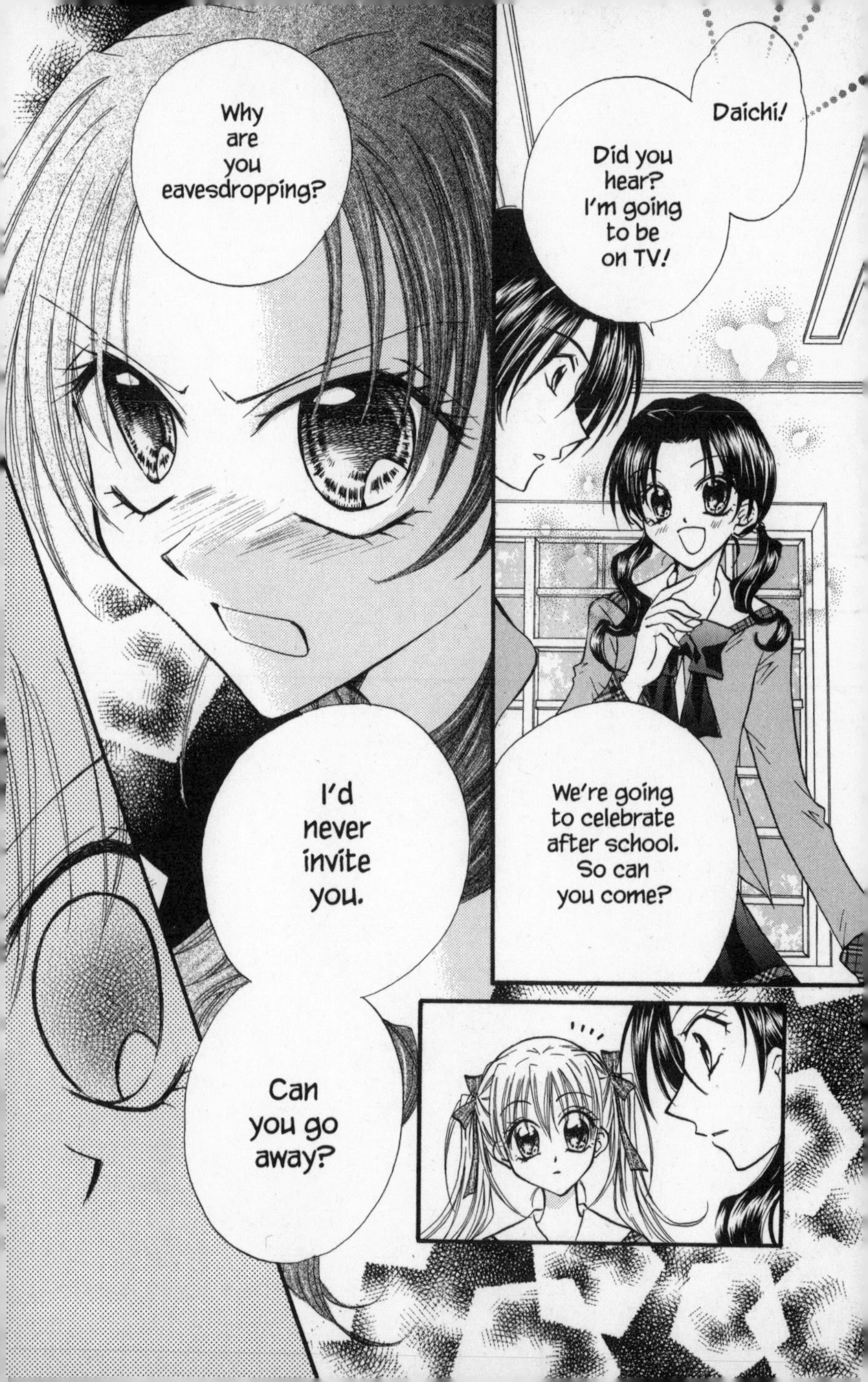
Daichi!
Did you hear? I'm going to be on TV!
We're going to celebrate after school. So can you come?
Why are you eavesdropping?
I'd never invite you.
Can you go away?

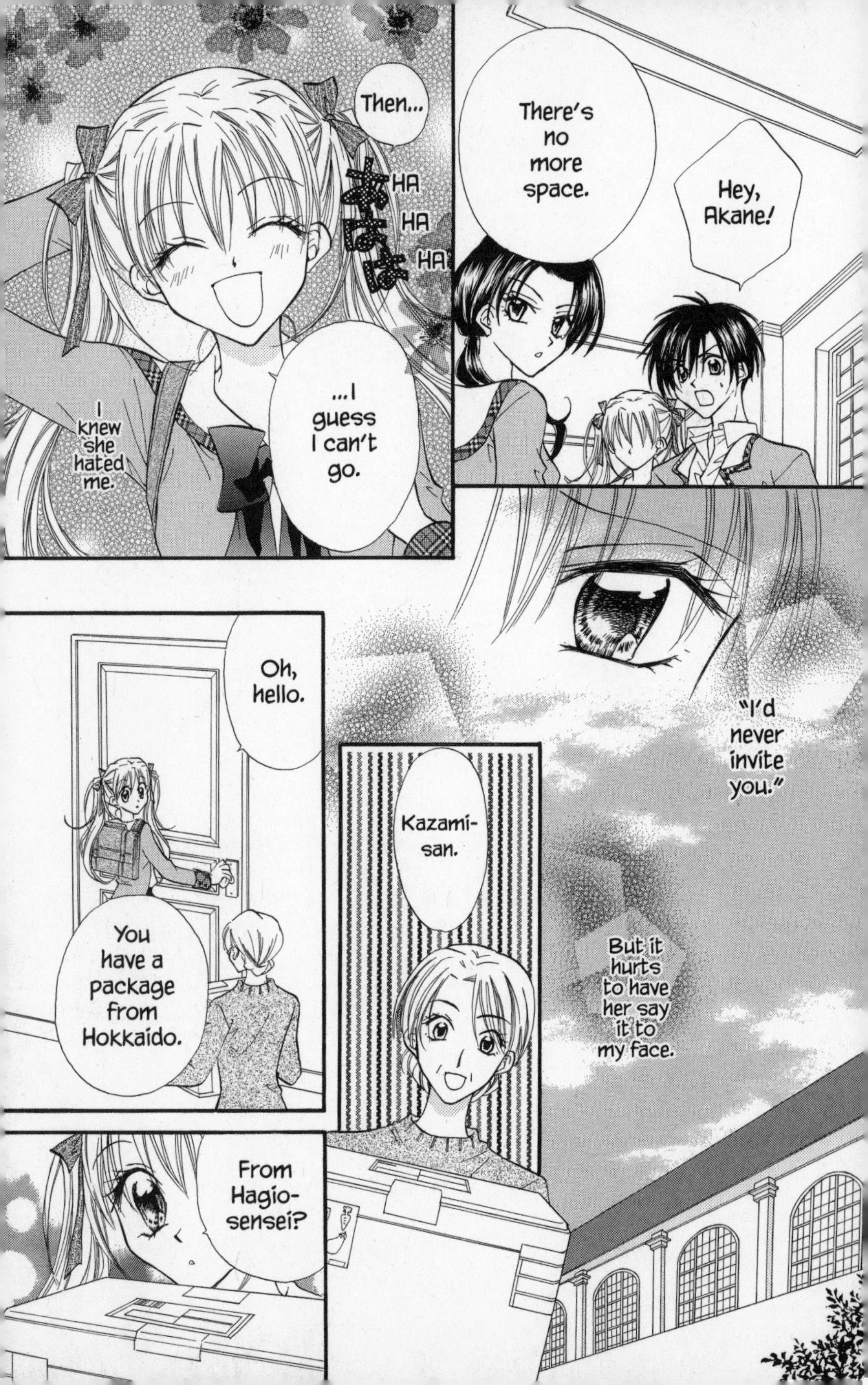
There's no more space.
Hey, Akane!
Then...
あはは HA HA HA
...I guess I can't go.
I knew she hated me.
"I'd never invite you."
But it hurts to have her say it to my face.
Kazami-san.
Oh, hello.
You have a package from Hokkaido.
From Hagio-sensei?

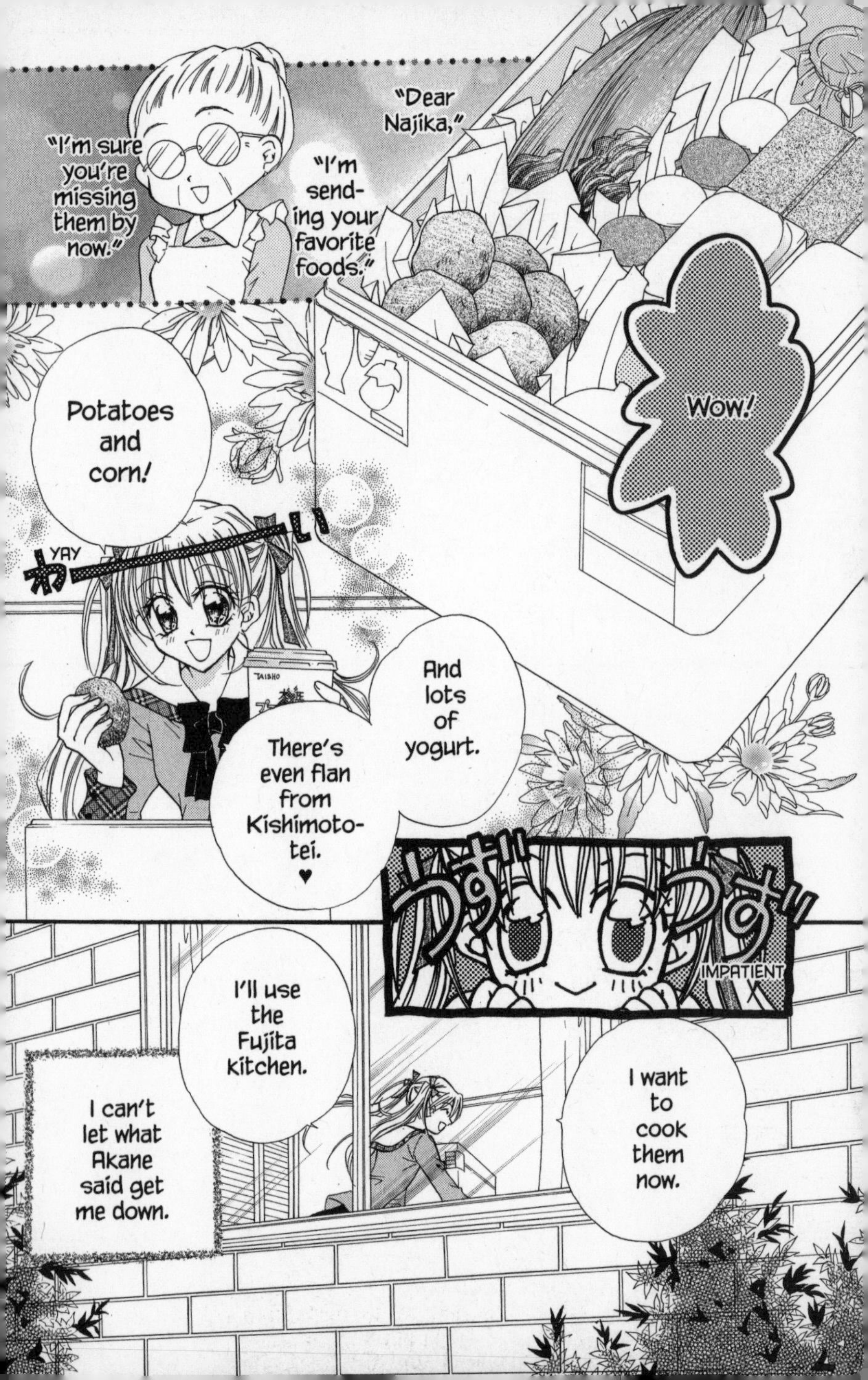
"Dear Najika,"
"I'm sending your favorite foods."
"I'm sure you're missing them by now."
Wow!
わーい
YAY
Potatoes and corn!
And lots of yogurt.
There's even flan from Kishimoto-tei. ♥
うずうず
IMPATIENT
I want to cook them now.
I'll use the Fujita kitchen.
I can't let what Akane said get me down.

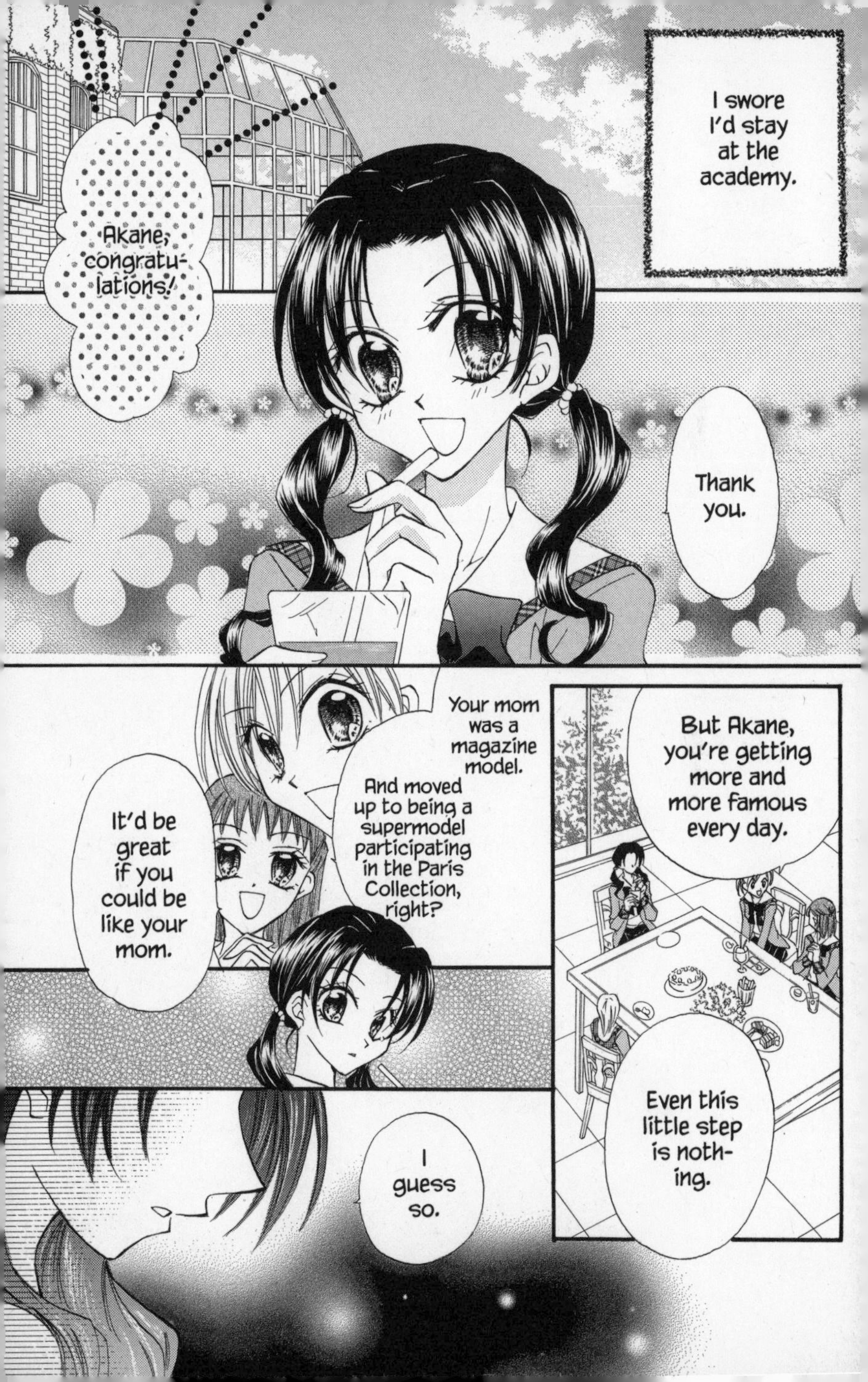
I swore I'd stay at the academy.
Akane, congratulations!
Thank you.
But Akane, you're getting more and more famous every day.
Even this little step is nothing.
Your mom was a magazine model.
And moved up to being a supermodel participating in the Paris Collection, right?
It'd be great if you could be like your mom.
I guess so.

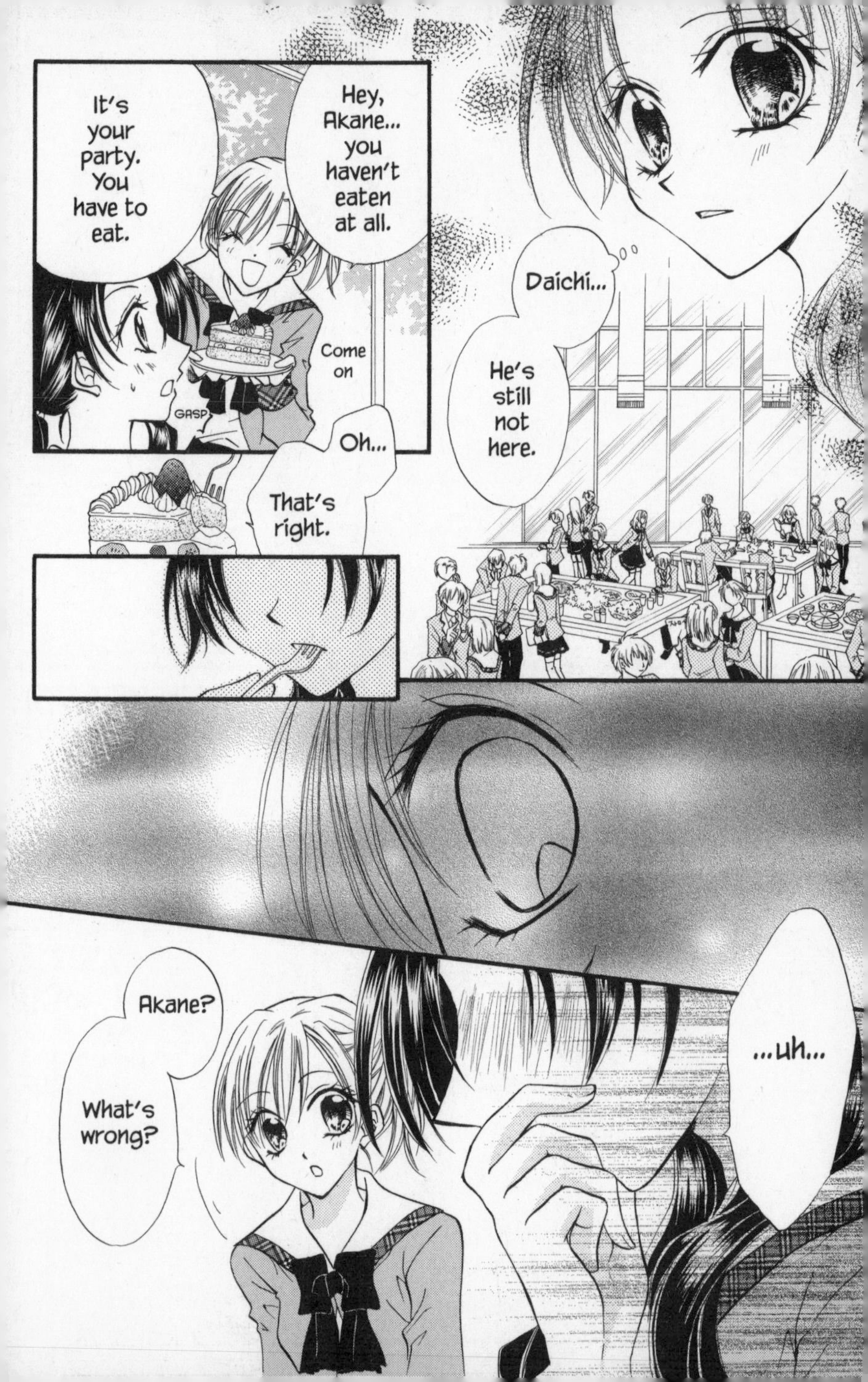
Daichi...
He's still not here.
Hey, Akane... you haven't eaten at all.
It's your party. You have to eat.
Come on
GASP
Oh...
That's right.
Akane?
What's wrong?
...uh...

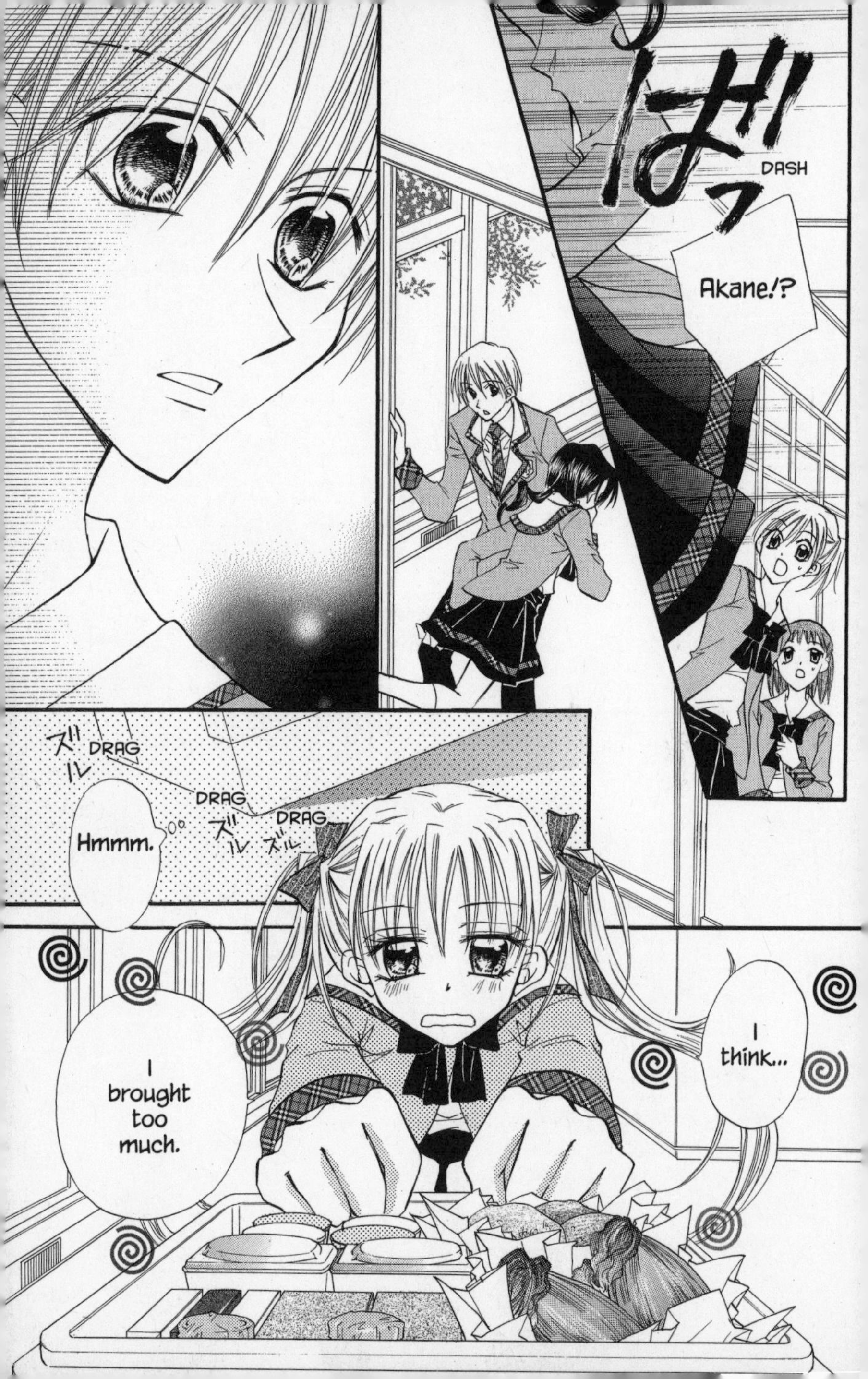
はっ
DASH
Akane!?
ズル DRAG
DRAG
ズル DRAG
ズル
Hmmm.
I think...
I brought too much.

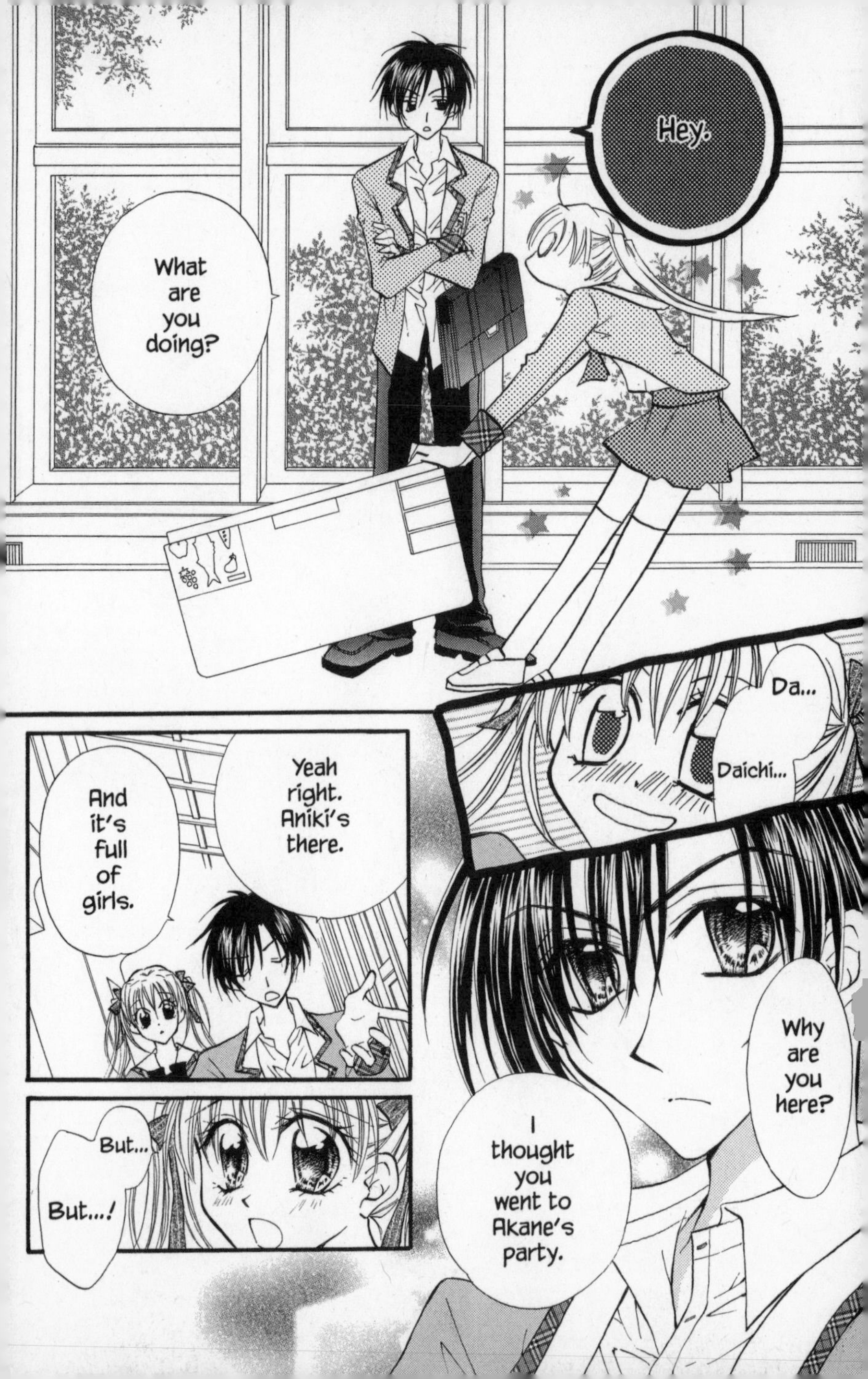
Hey.
What are you doing?
Da...
Daichi...
Why are you here?
I thought you went to Akane's party.
Yeah right. Aniki's there.
And it's full of girls.
But...
But...!

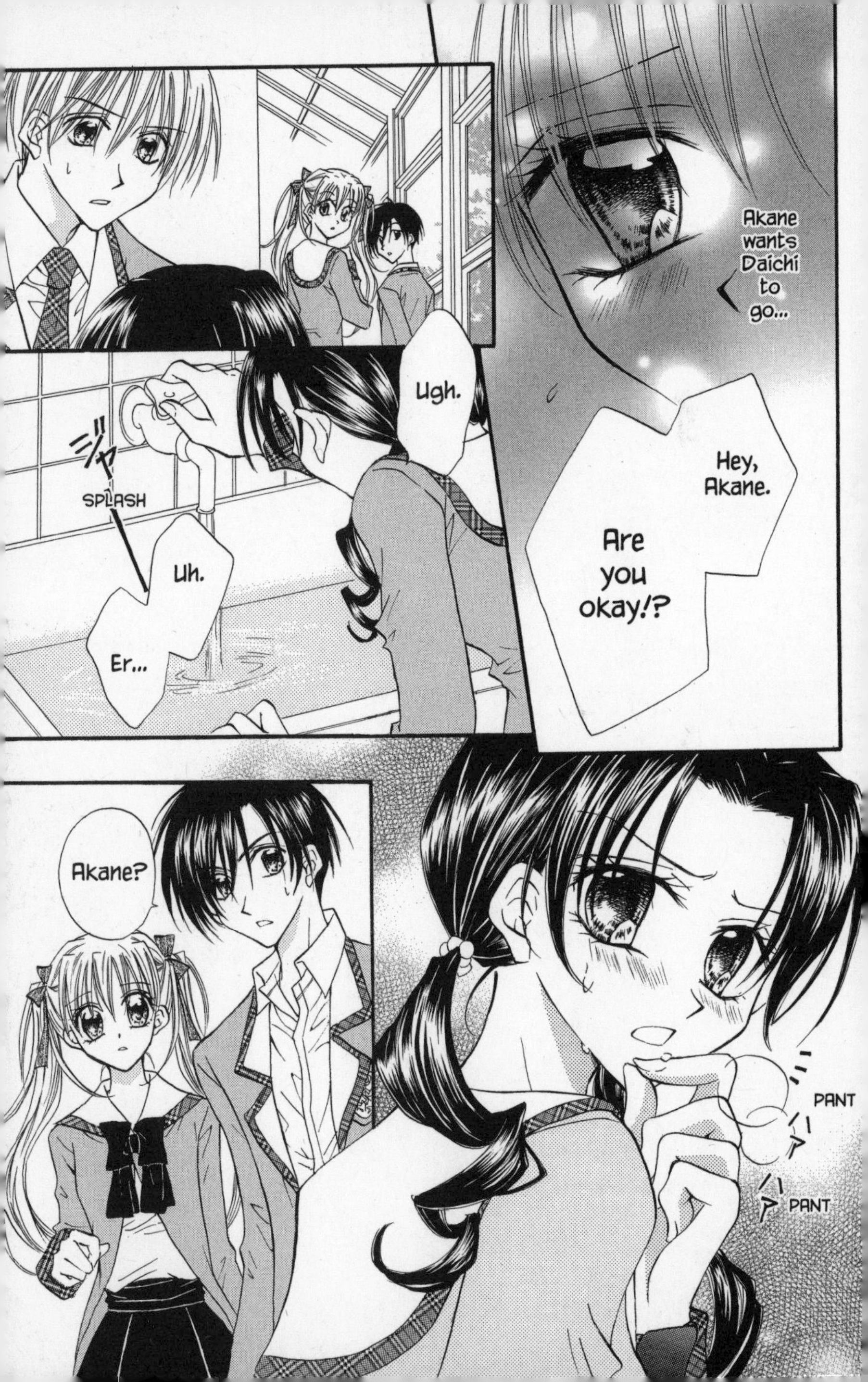

Akane wants Daichi to go...
Hey, Akane.
Are you okay!?
Ugh.
ジャ
SPLASH
Uh.
Er...
PANT
PANT
Akane?

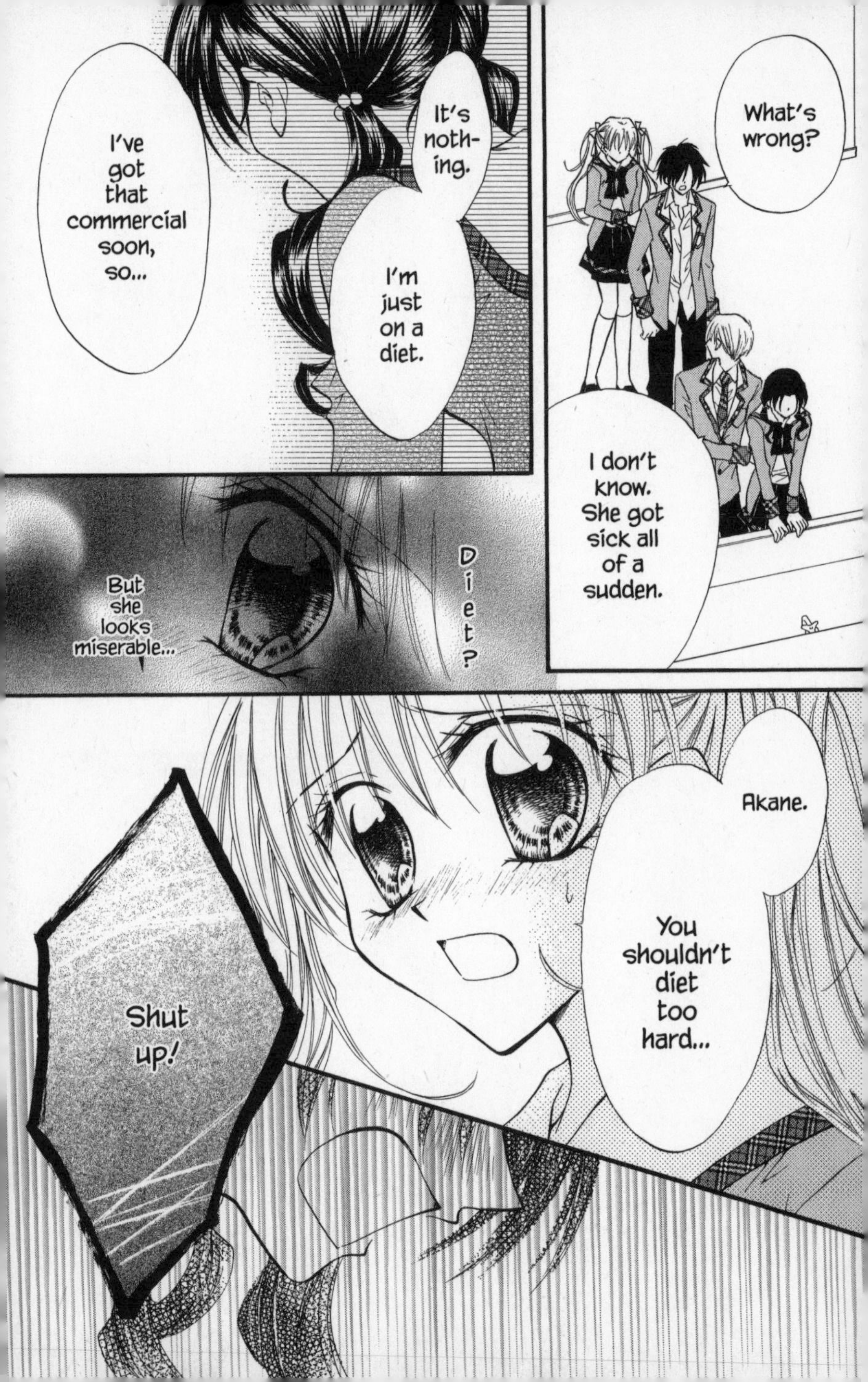
What's wrong?
I don't know. She got sick all of a sudden.
It's nothing.
I'm just on a diet.
I've got that commercial soon, so...
Diet?
But she looks miserable...
Akane.
You shouldn't diet too hard...
Shut up!

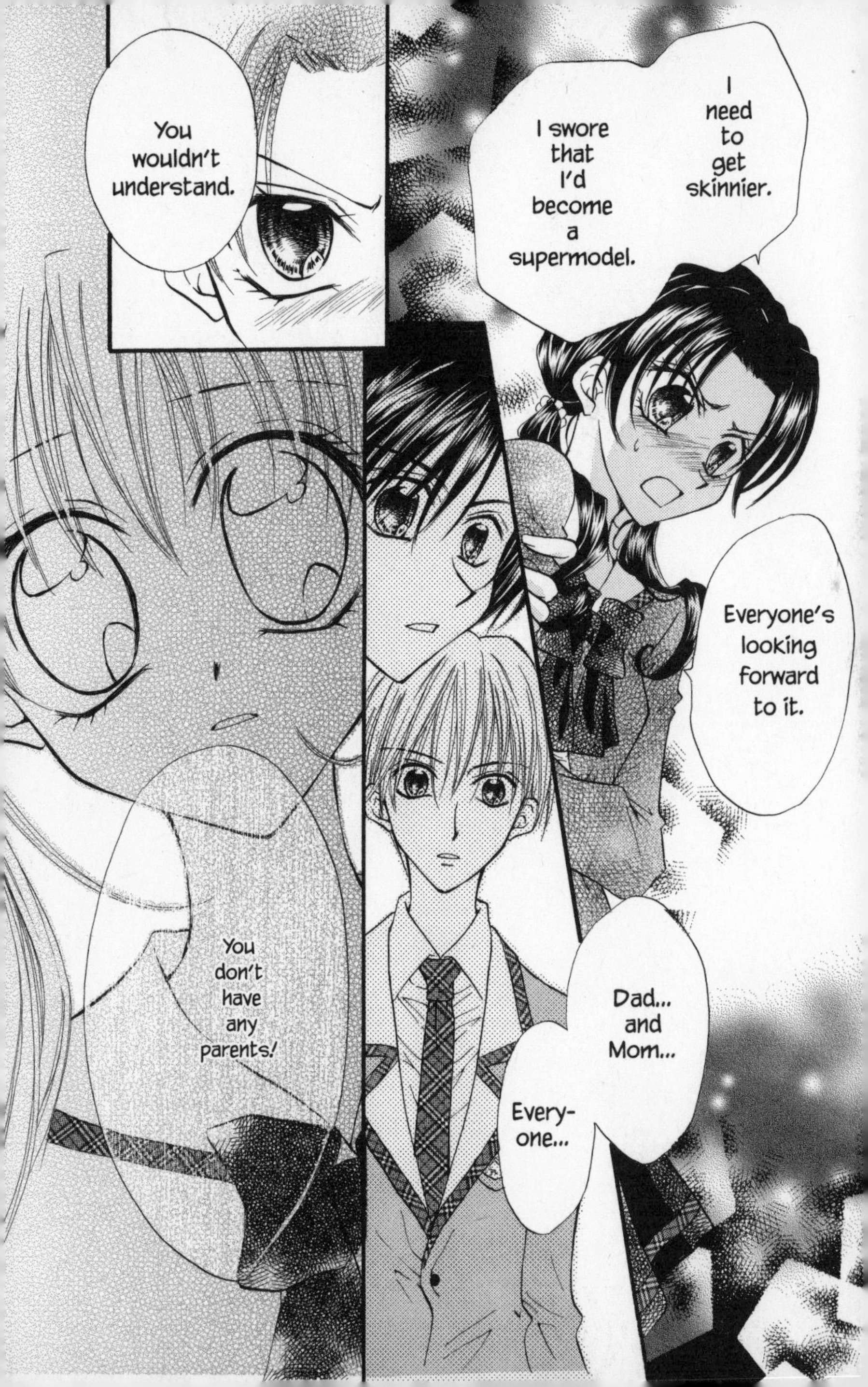
I need to get skinnier.
I swore that I'd become a supermodel.
You wouldn't understand.
Everyone's looking forward to it.
Dad... and Mom...
Every-one...
You don't have any parents!

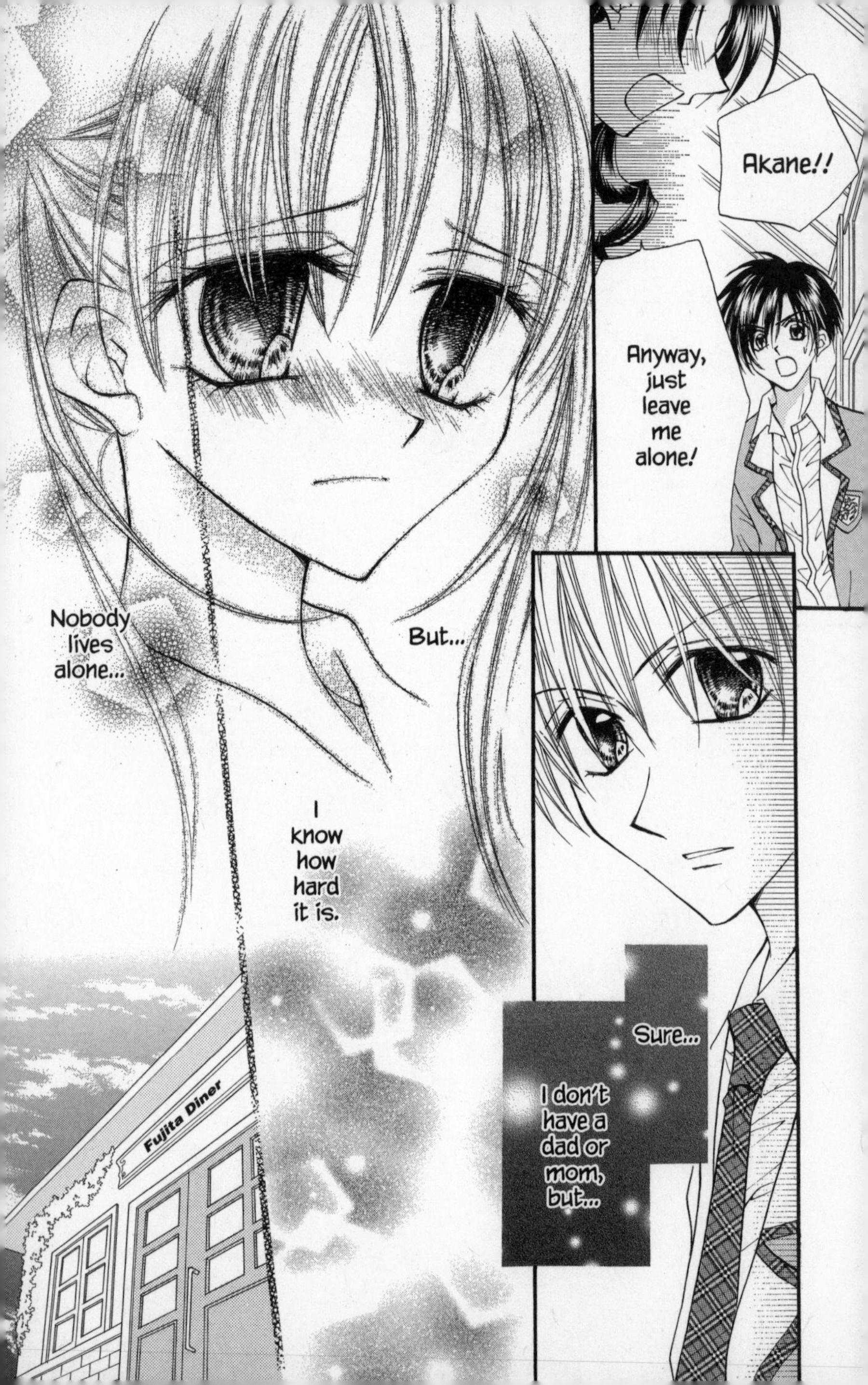
Akane!!
Anyway, just leave me alone!
Sure...
I don't have a dad or mom, but...
But...
Nobody lives alone...
I know how hard it is.
Fujita Diner

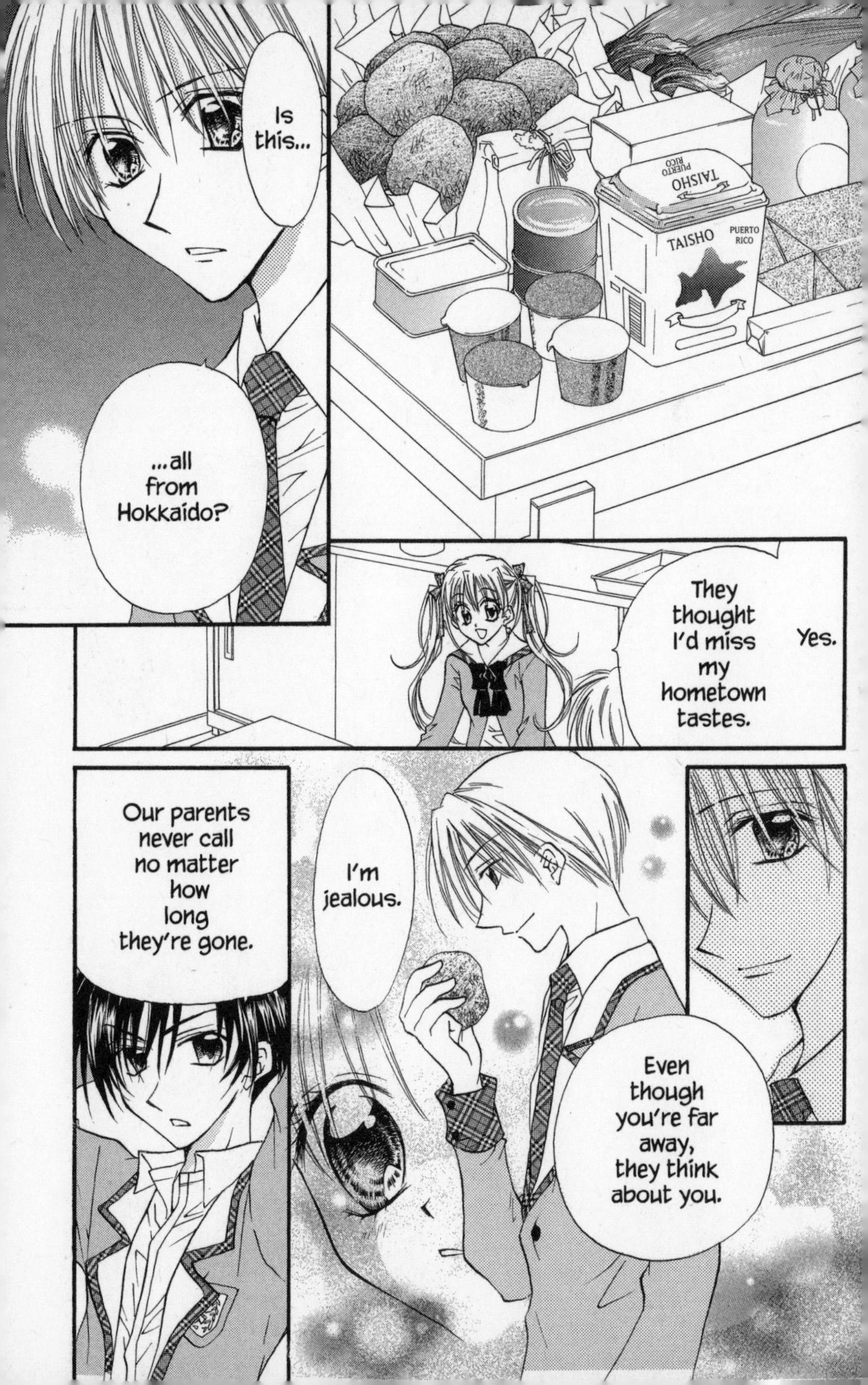
TAISHO
PUERTO RICO
Is this...
...all from Hokkaido?
Yes.
They thought I'd miss my hometown tastes.
Even though you're far away, they think about you.
I'm jealous.
Our parents never call no matter how long they're gone.

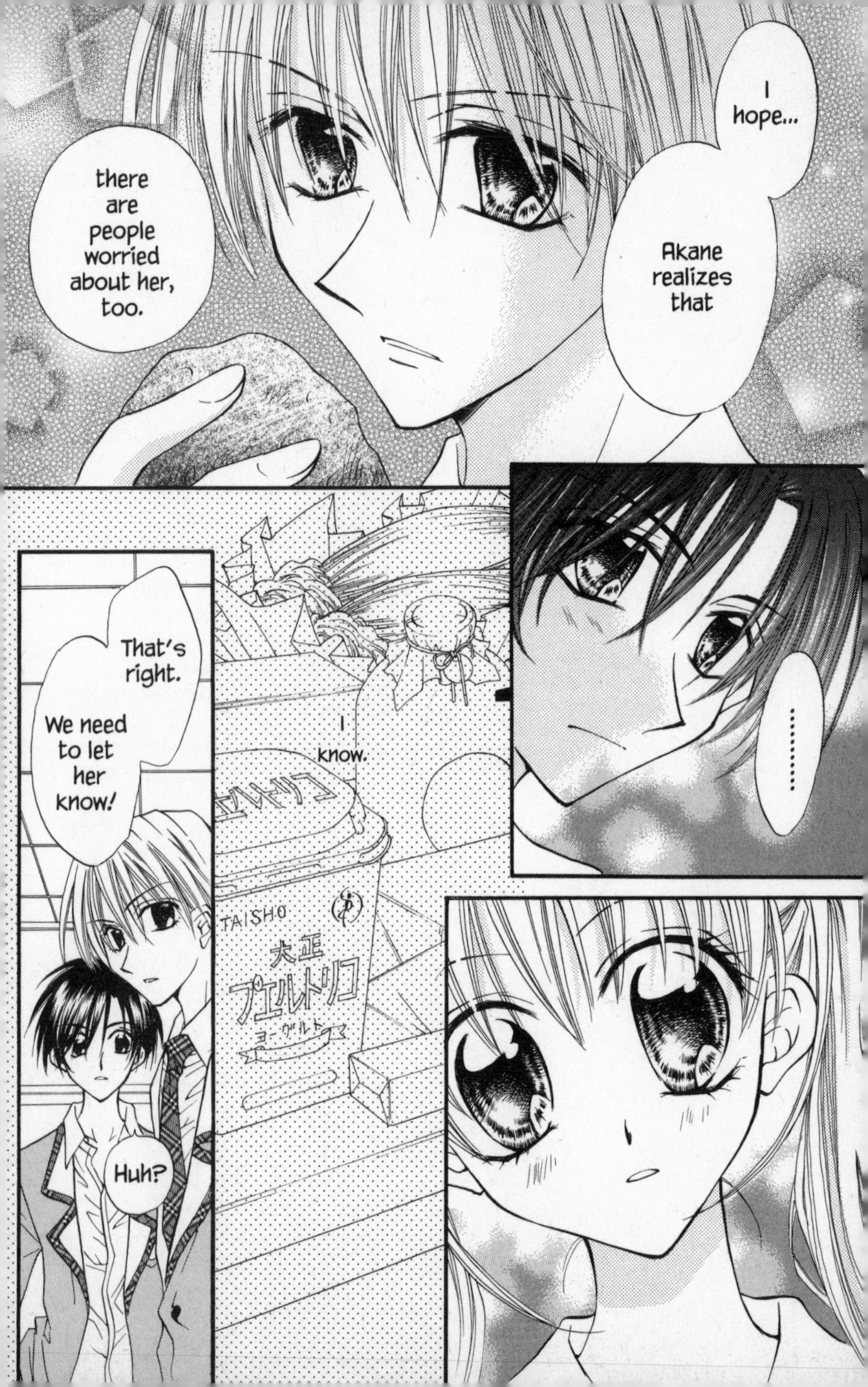
I hope...
Akane realizes that
there are people worried about her, too.
......
I know.
TAISHO
大正
プエルトリコ
ヨーグルト
That's right.
We need to let her know!
Huh?

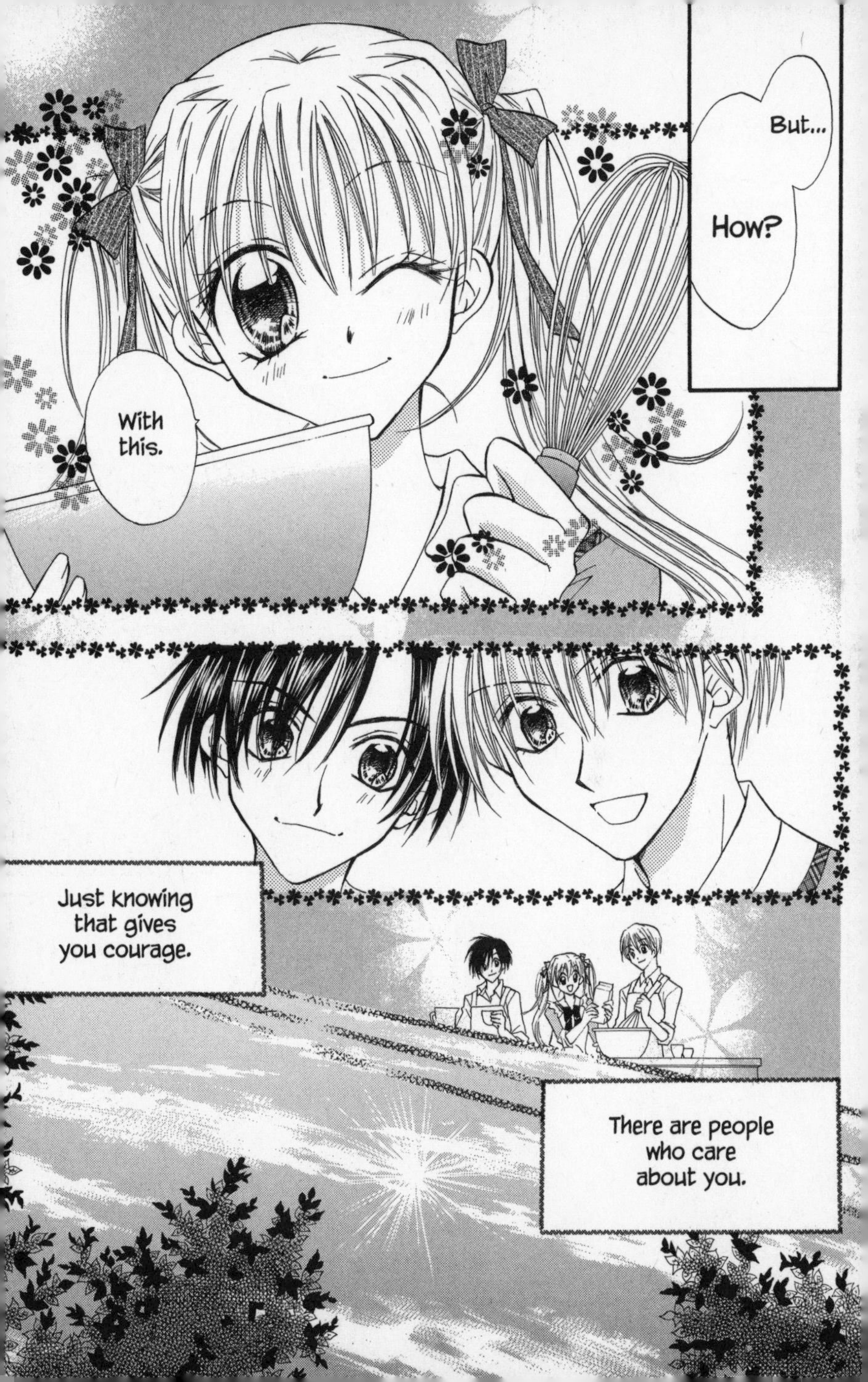
But...
How?
With this.
There are people who care about you.
Just knowing that gives you courage.

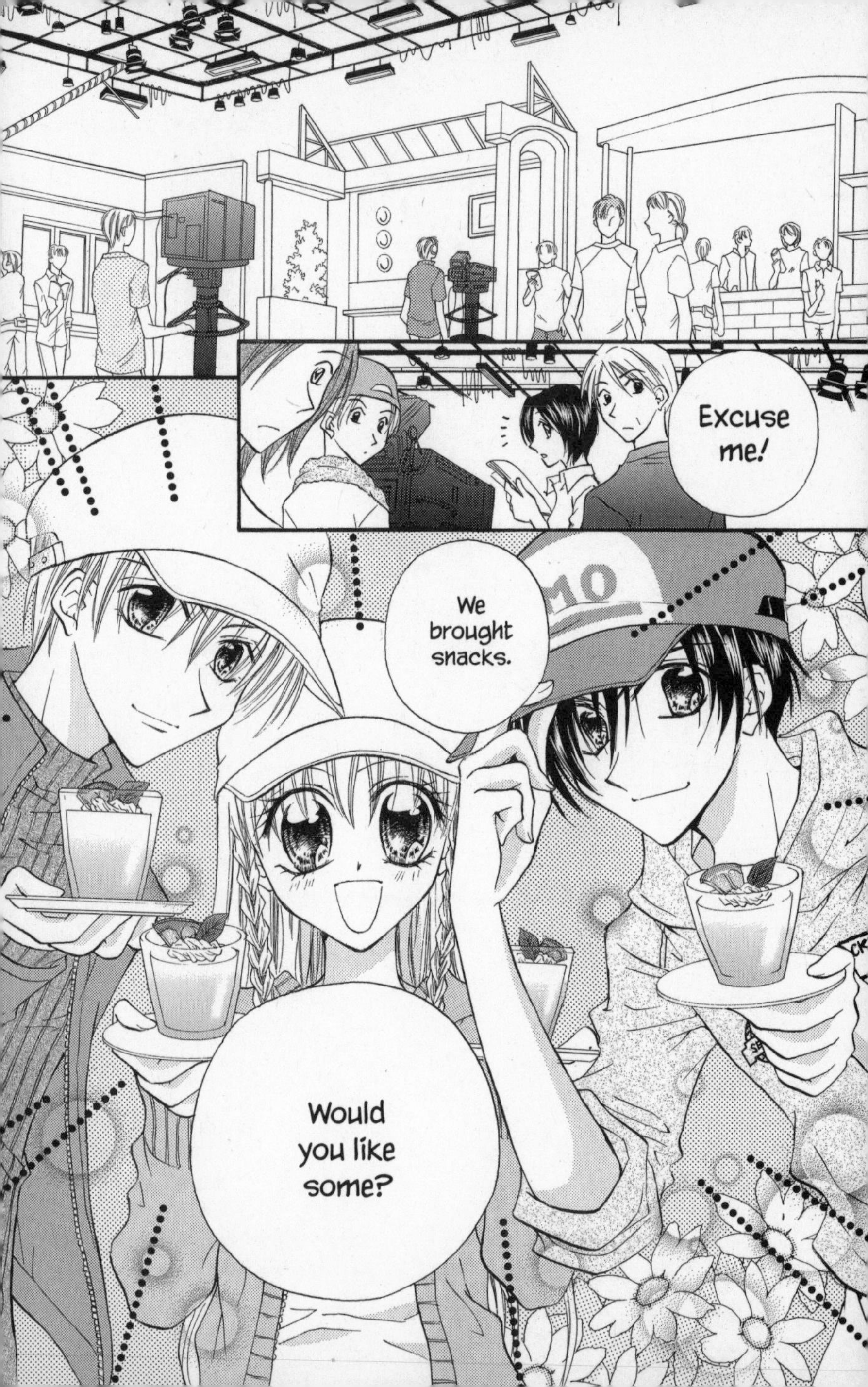
Excuse me!
We brought snacks.
Would you like some?

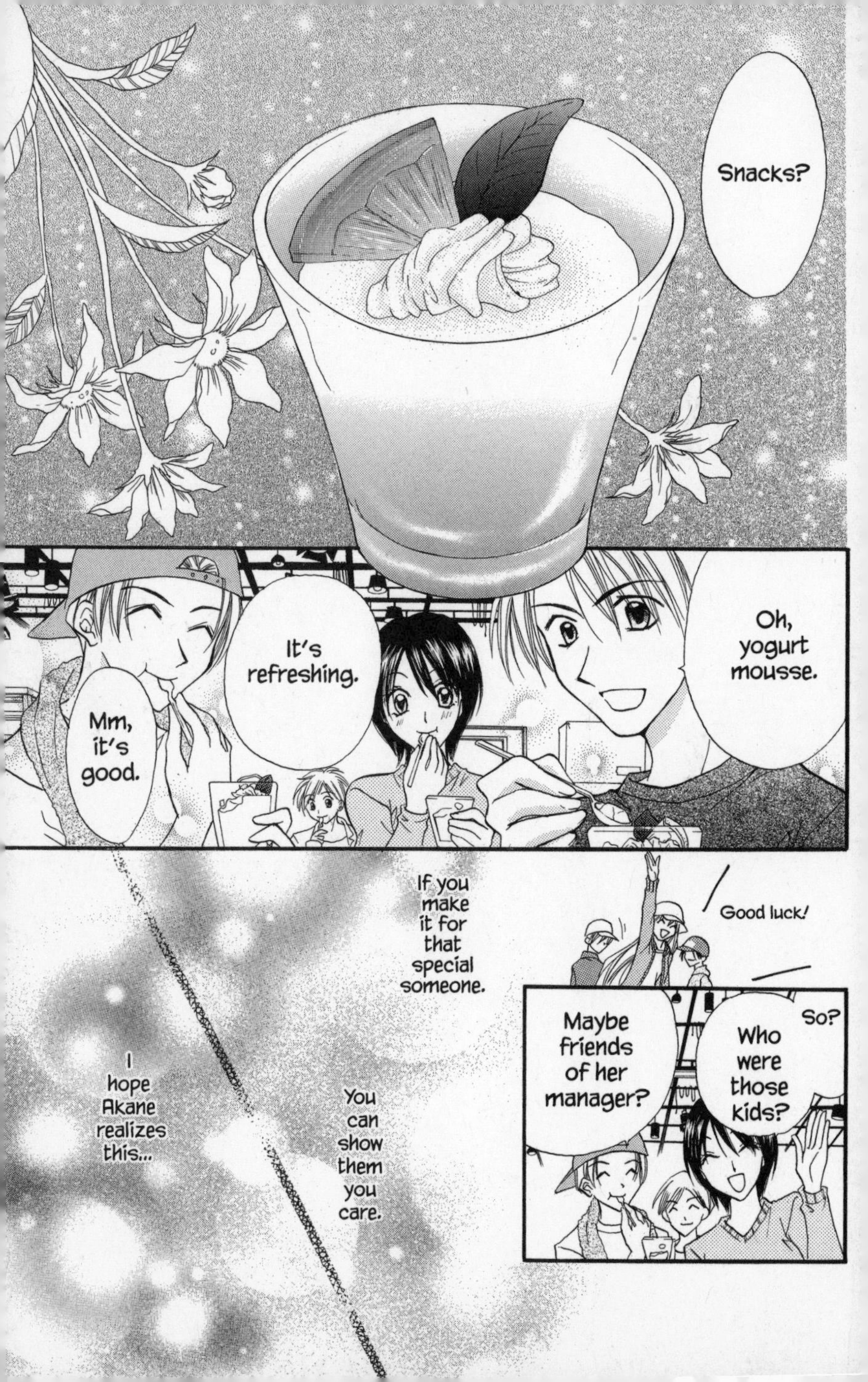
Snacks?
Oh, yogurt mousse.
It's refreshing.
Mm, it's good.
Good luck!
So?
Who were those kids?
Maybe friends of her manager?
If you make it for that special someone.
You can show them you care.
I hope Akane realizes this...

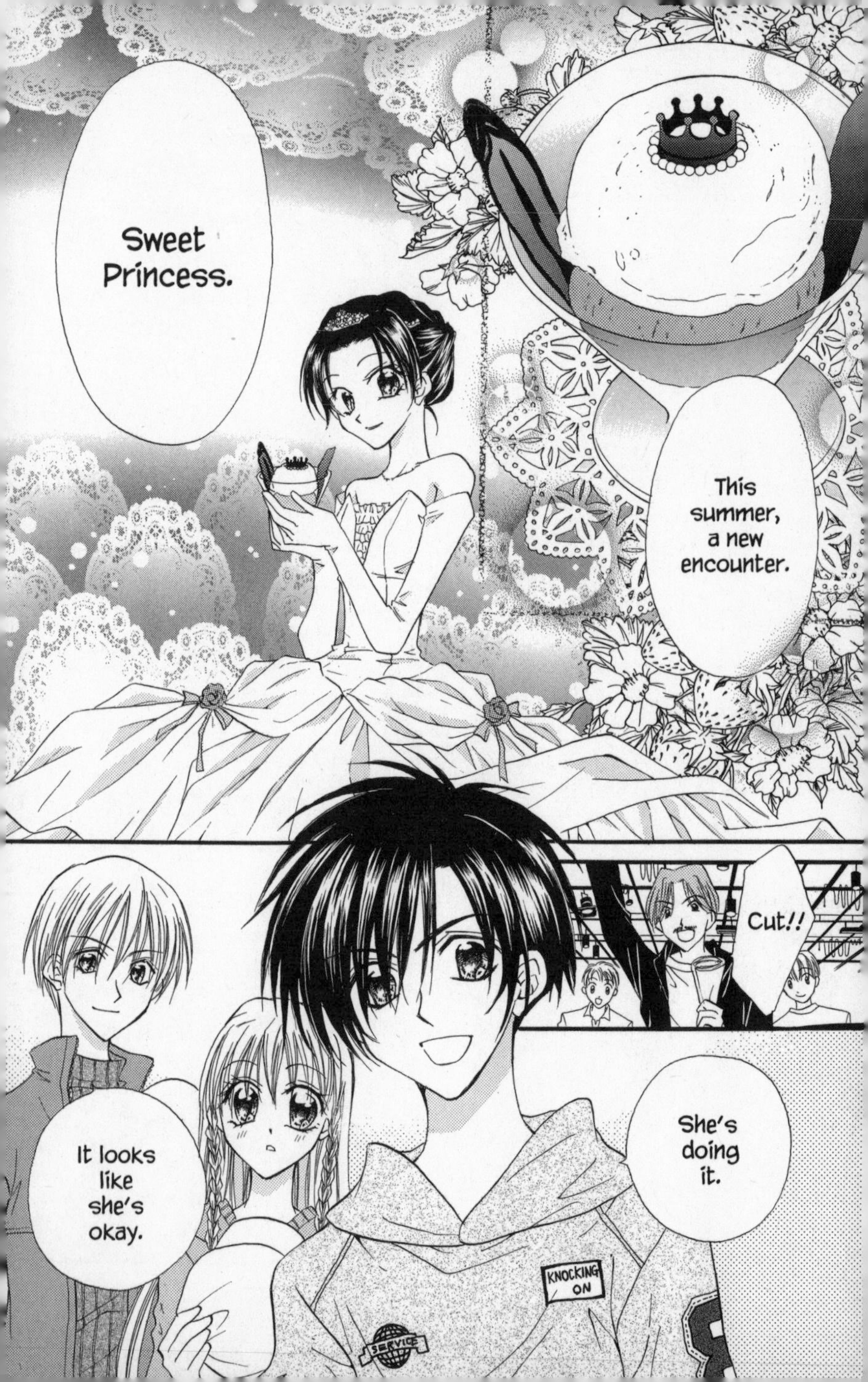
This summer, a new encounter.
Sweet Princess.
Cut!!
She's doing it.
It looks like she's okay.
KNOCKING ON
SERVICE

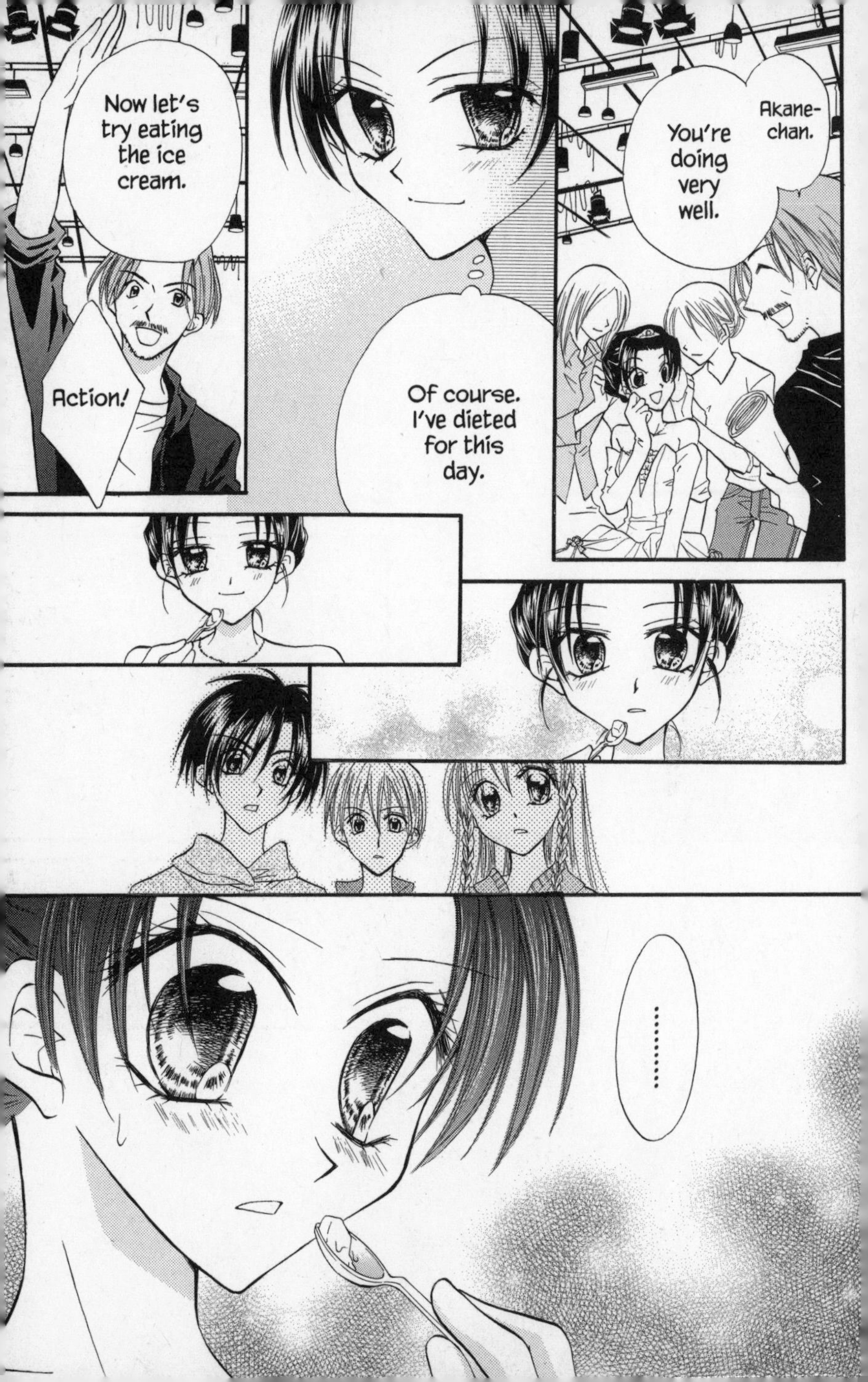
Akane-chan.
You're doing very well.
Of course. I've dieted for this day.
Now let's try eating the ice cream.
Action!
......

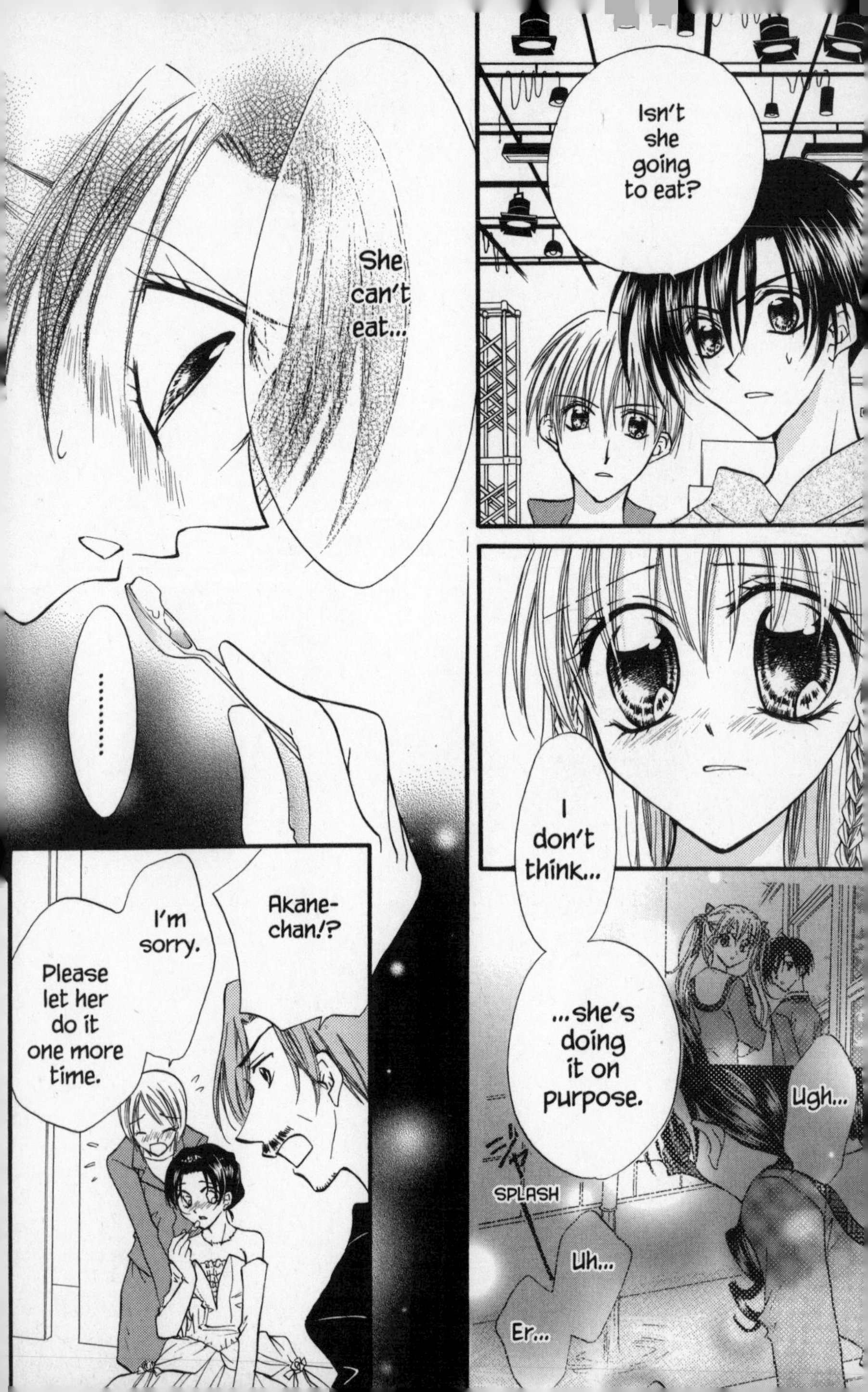
Isn't she going to eat?
She can't eat...
......
I don't think...
...she's doing it on purpose.
Ugh...
ジャ
SPLASH
Uh...
Er...
Akane-chan!?
I'm sorry.
Please let her do it one more time.

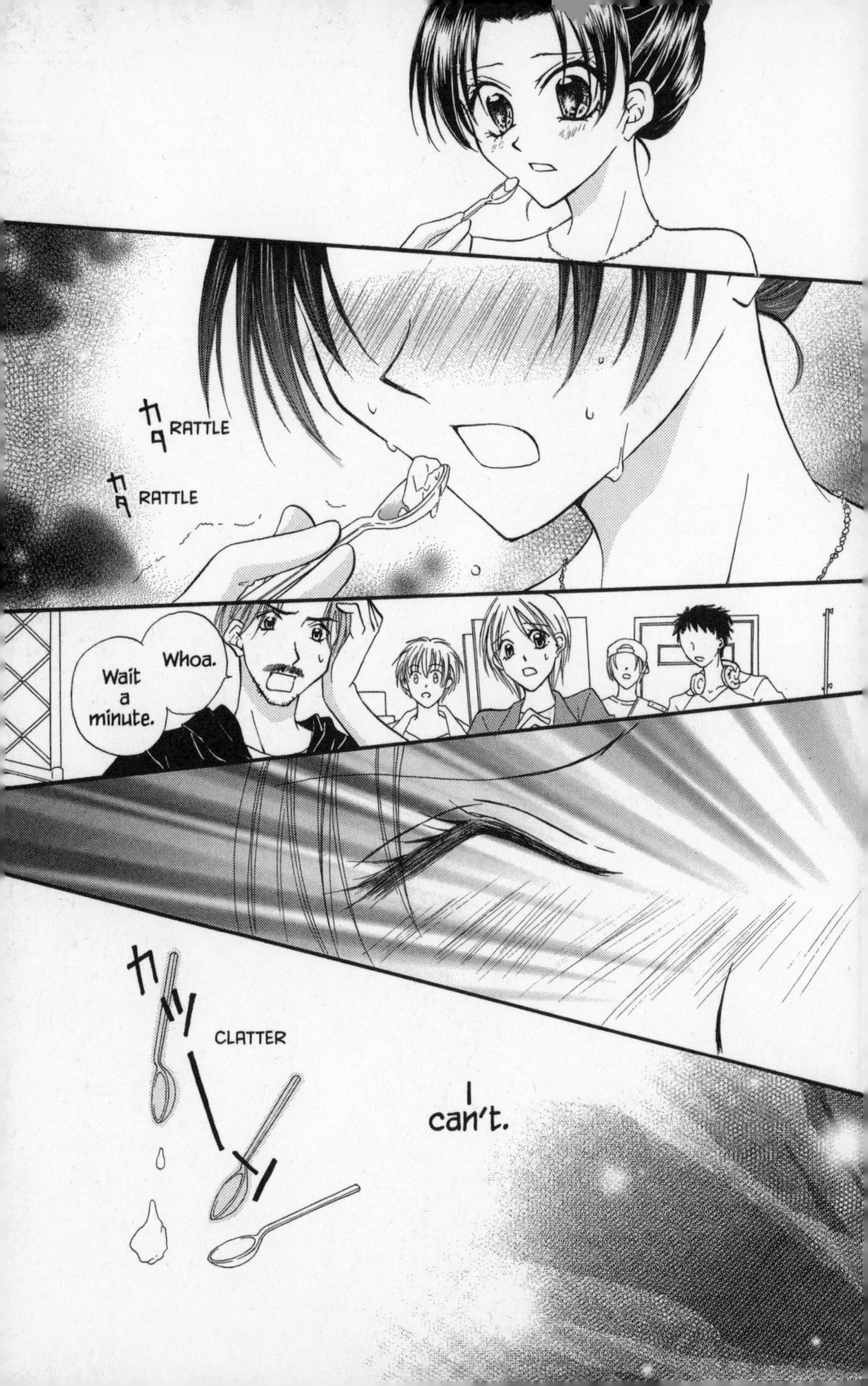
カタ RATTLE
カタ RATTLE
Whoa.
Wait a minute.
カツーン
CLATTER
I can't.

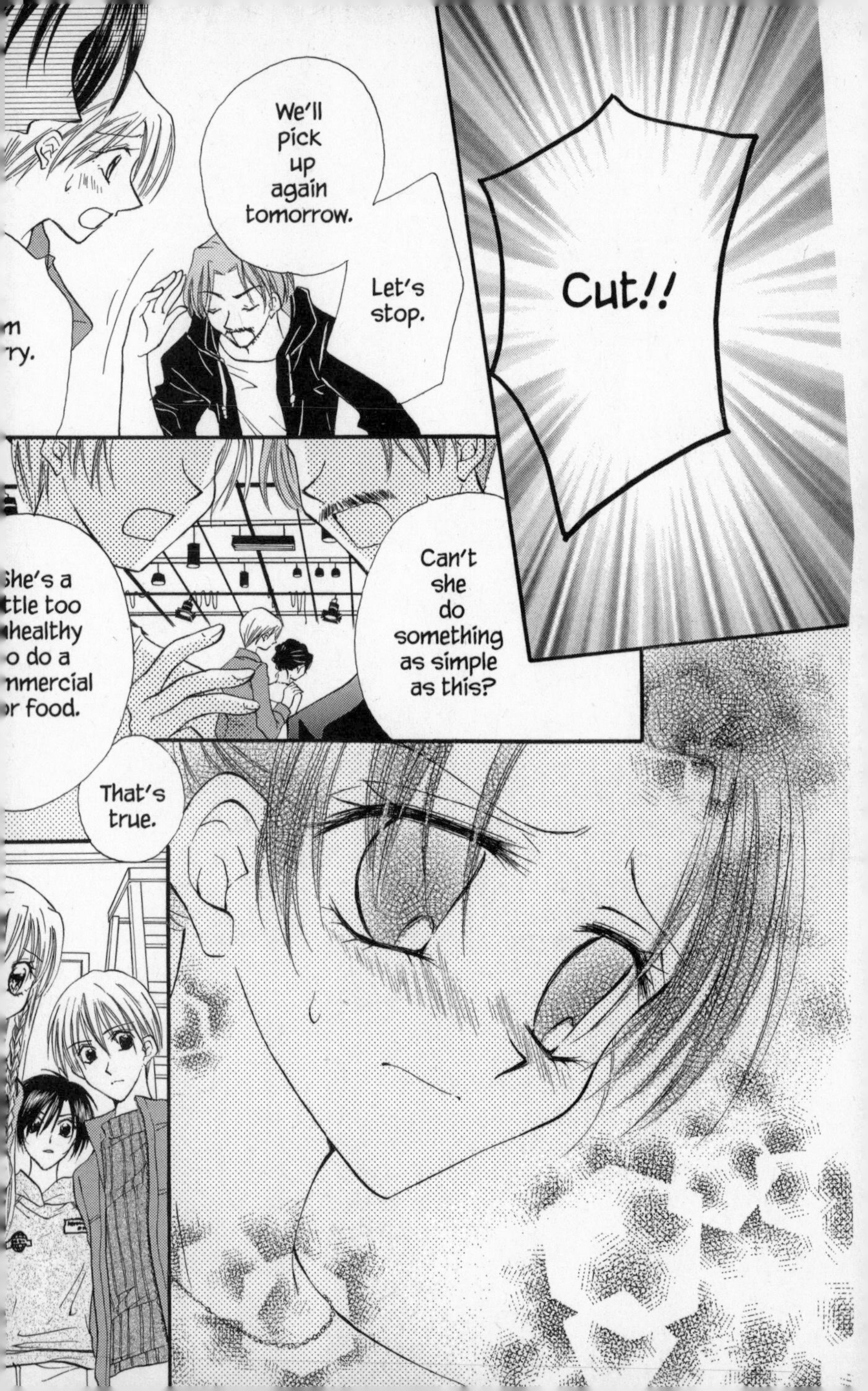

Cut!!
Let's stop.
We'll pick up again tomorrow.
ry.
Can't she do something as simple as this?
he's a ttle too healthy o do a nmercial r food.
That's true.

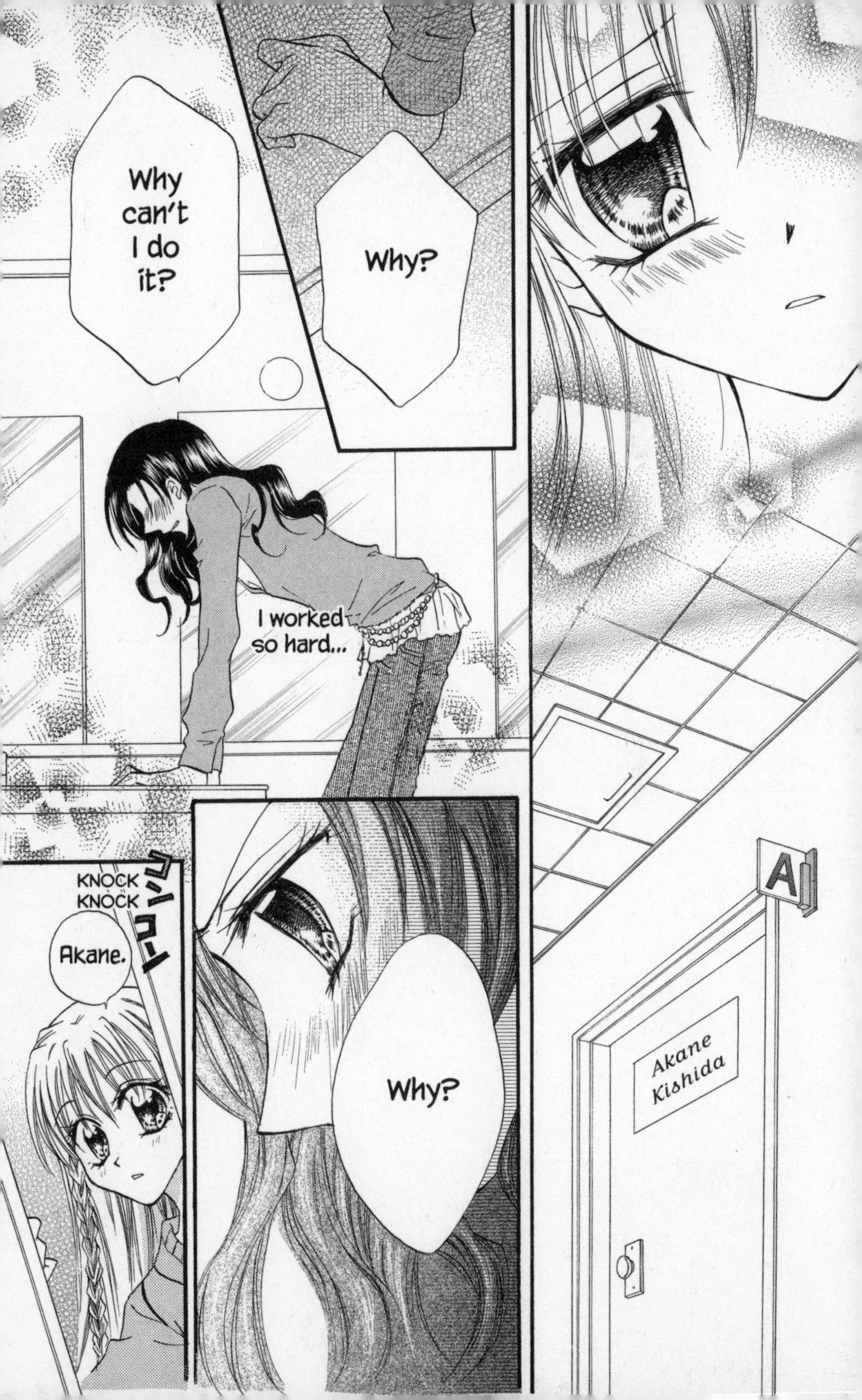
A
Akane Kishida
Why?
Why can't I do it?
I worked so hard...
Why?
KNOCK KNOCK
Akane.

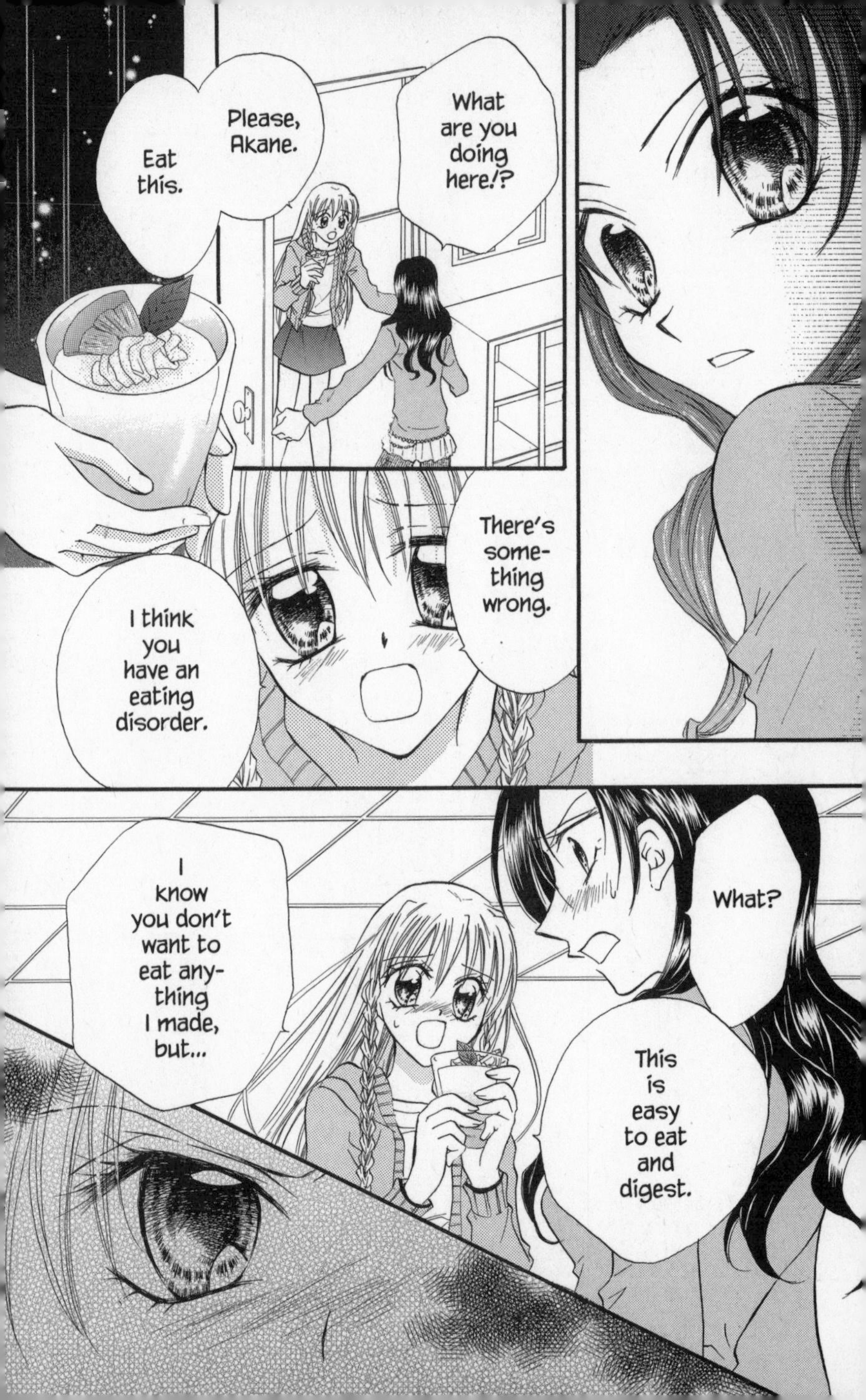
What are you doing here!?
Please, Akane.
Eat this.
There's some-thing wrong.
I think you have an eating disorder.
What?
I know you don't want to eat any-thing I made, but...
This is easy to eat and digest.

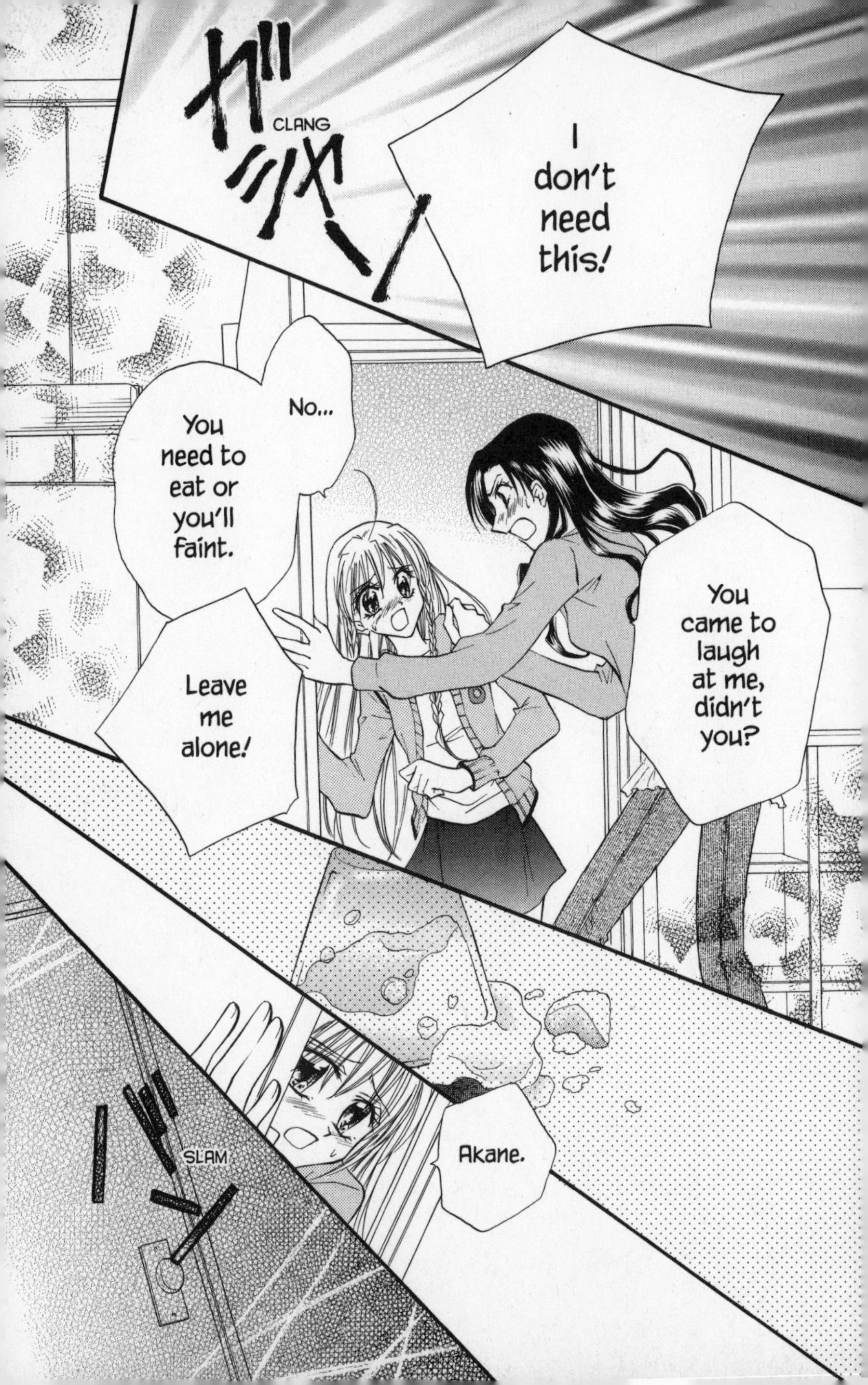
I don't need this!
ガシャン
CLANG
You came to laugh at me, didn't you?
No...
You need to eat or you'll faint.
Leave me alone!
Akane.
SLAM

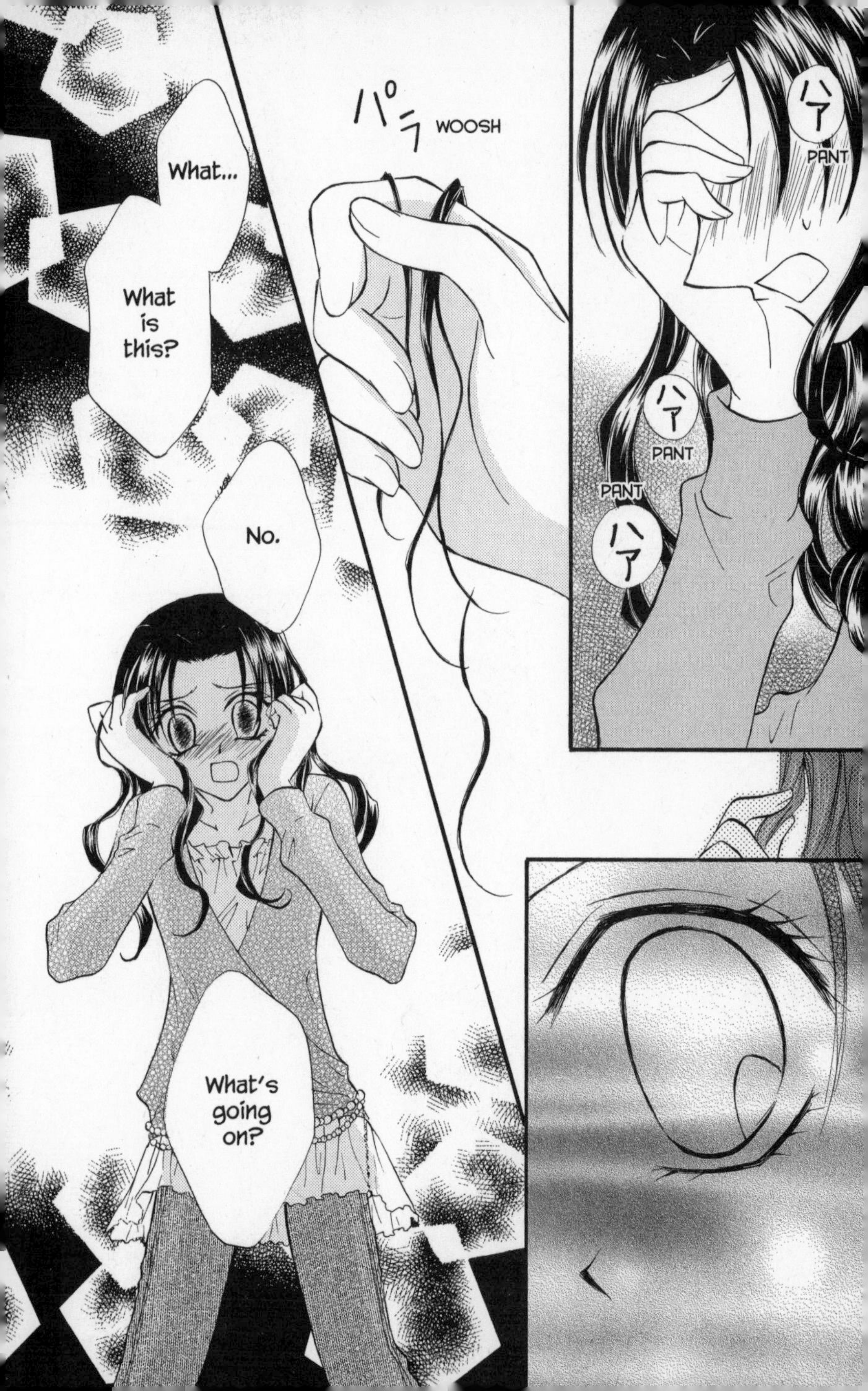
ハァ
PANT
ハァ
PANT
PANT
ハァ
パラ WOOSH
What...
What is this?
No.
What's going on?

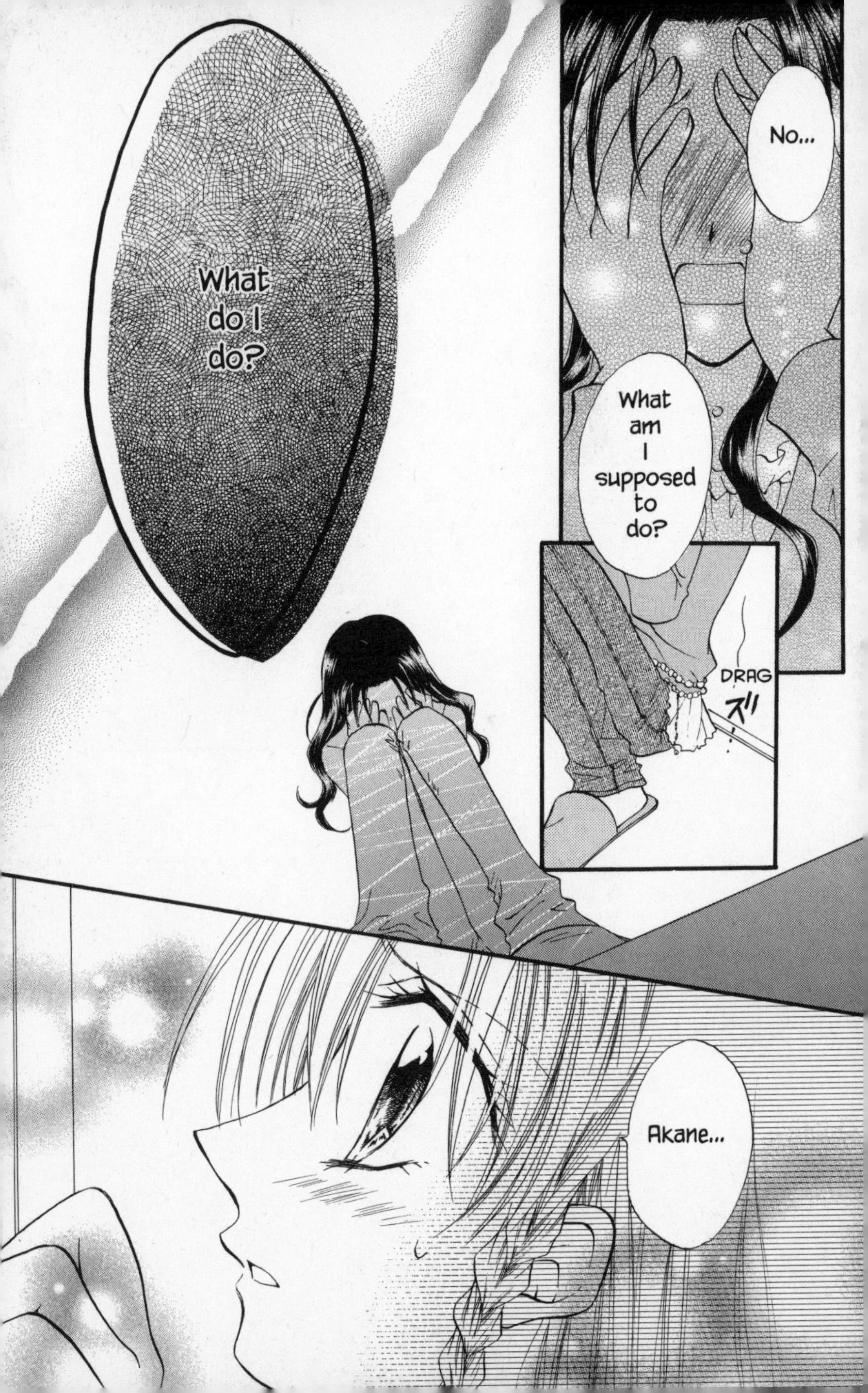
No...
What am I supposed to do?
DRAG
What do I do?
Akane...

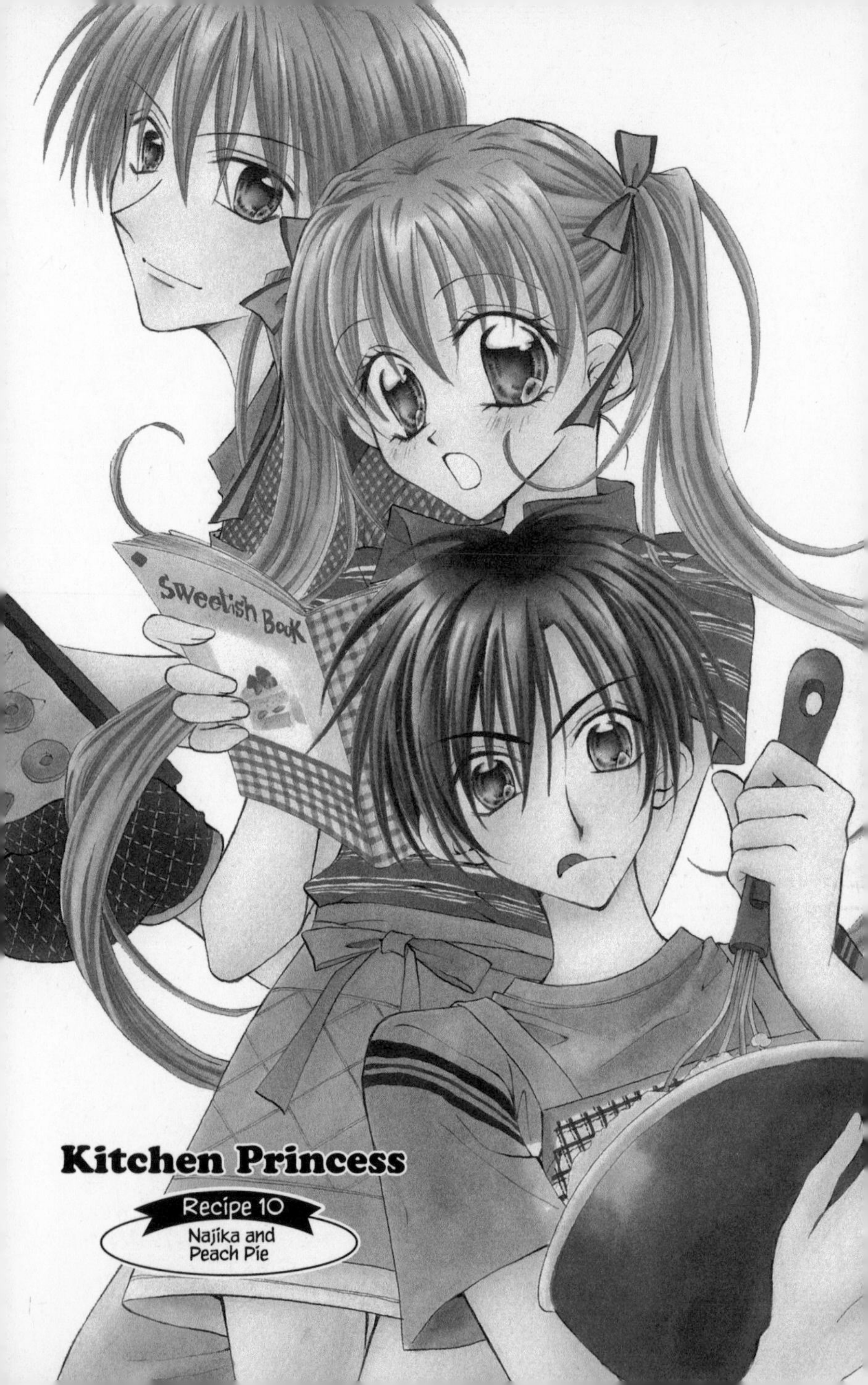
Sweetish Book
Kitchen Princess
Recipe 10
Najika and Peach Pie

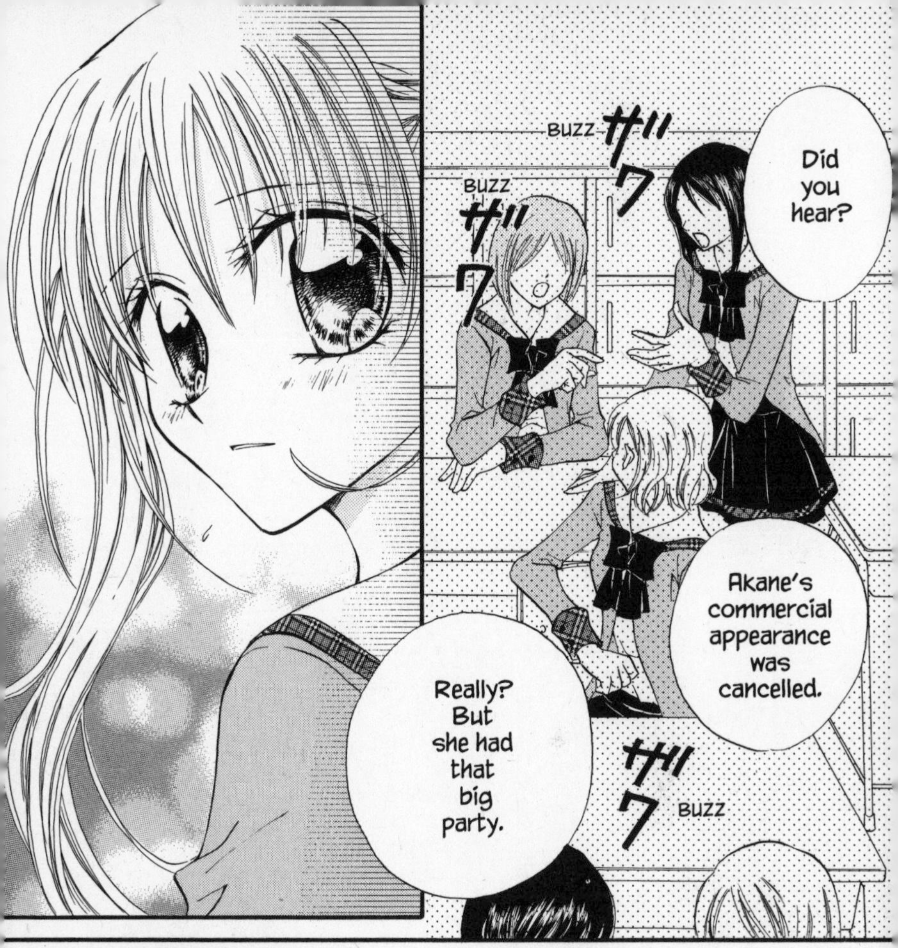
Did you hear?
BUZZ
BUZZ
Akane's commercial appearance was cancelled.
Really? But she had that big party.
BUZZ

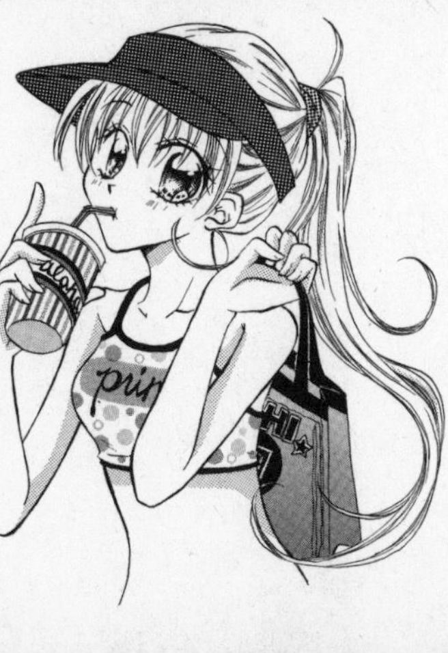

About Recipe 10's Splash Page

This is the first splash page that I let someone else do the background on! But I did give them a polka-dot pattern and a general idea of what I wanted. I was really looking forward to seeing what it would turn out like. It came out really good, better than I imagined, and I am very happy. ♥

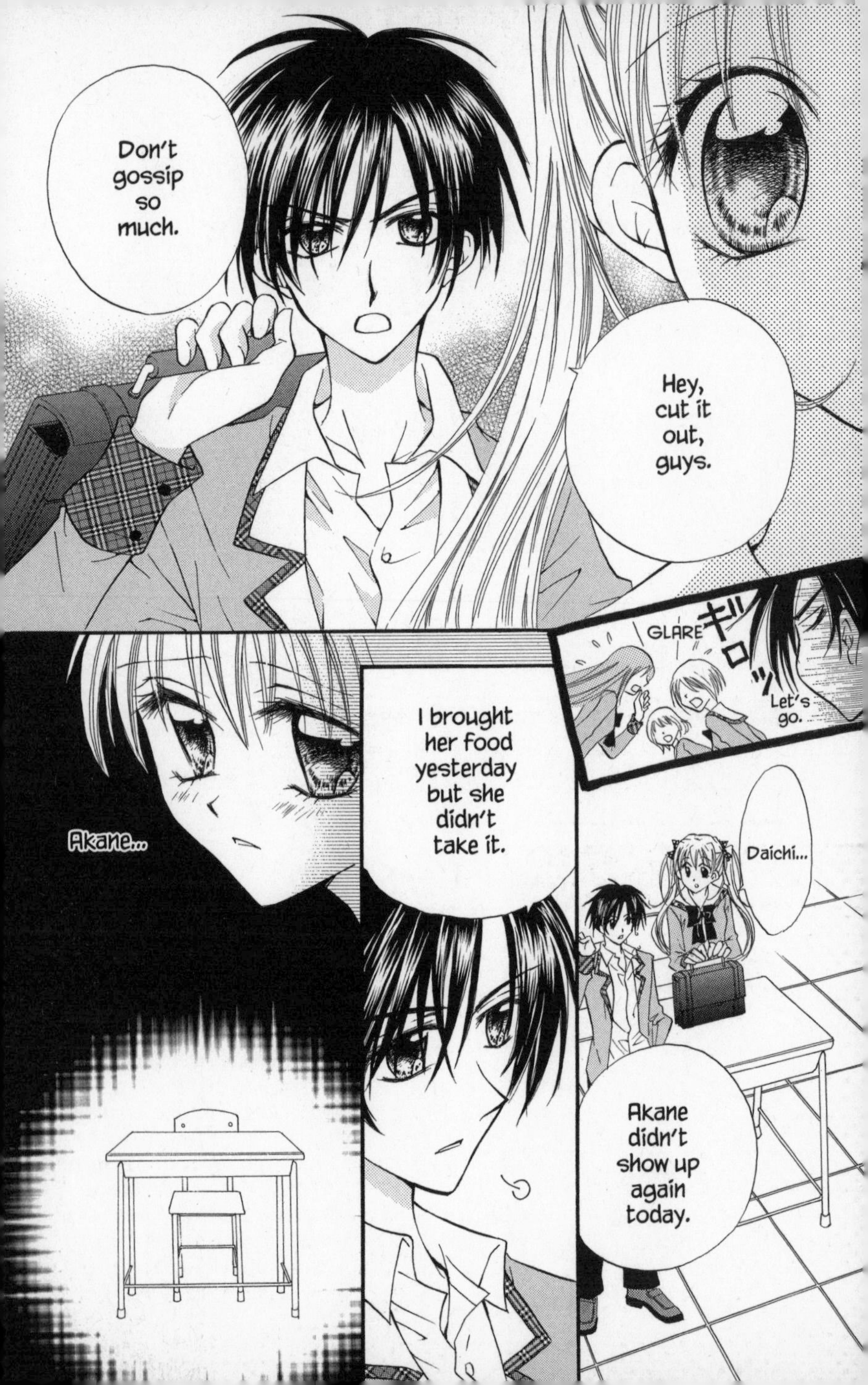
Hey, cut it out, guys.
Don't gossip so much.
GLARE
ギロッ
Let's go.
Daichi...
Akane didn't show up again today.
I brought her food yesterday but she didn't take it.
Akane...

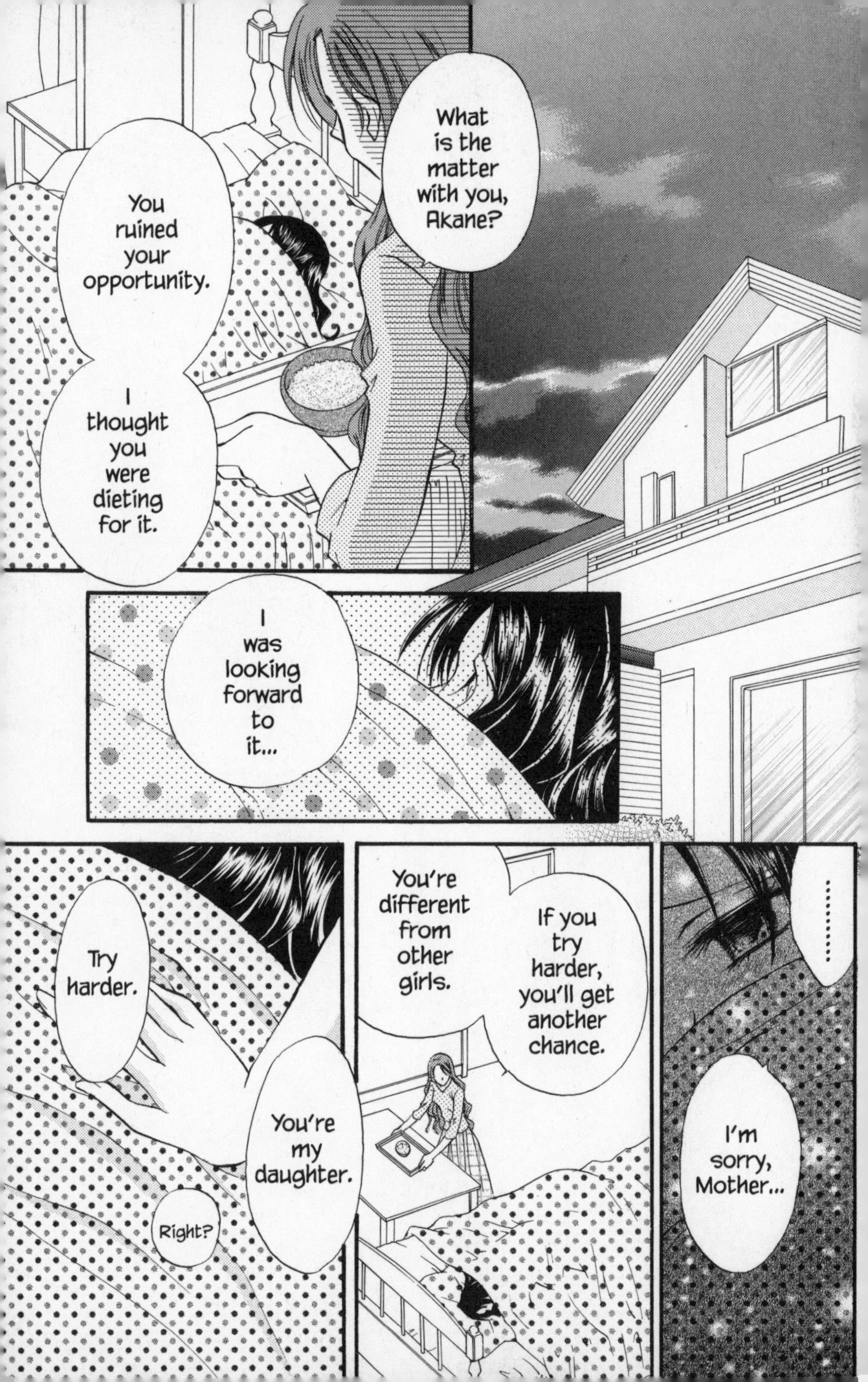
What is the matter with you, Akane?
You ruined your opportunity.
I thought you were dieting for it.
I was looking forward to it...
......
I'm sorry, Mother...
You're different from other girls.
If you try harder, you'll get another chance.
Try harder.
You're my daughter.
Right?

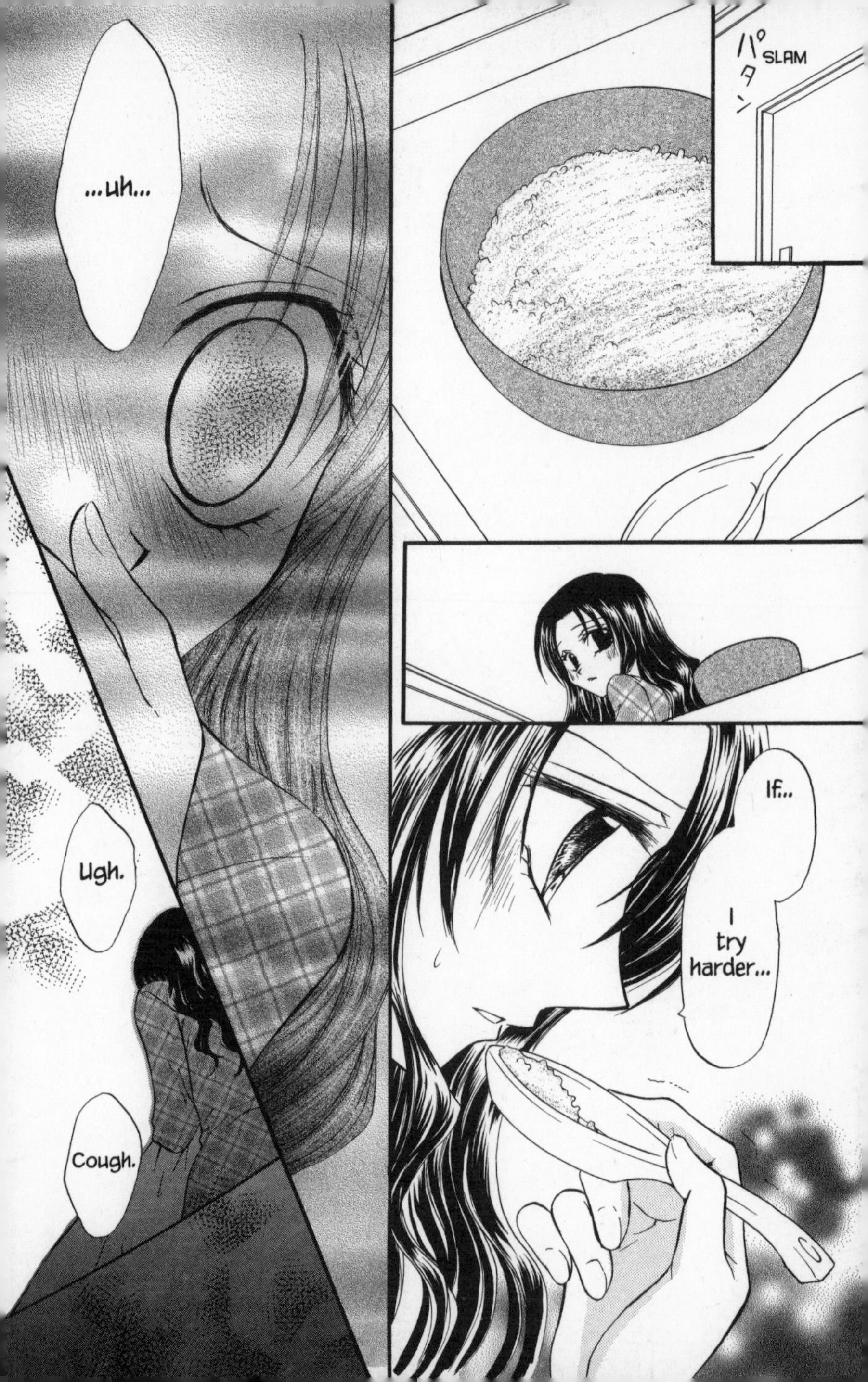
パタン
SLAM
If...
I try harder...
...uh...
Ugh.
Cough.

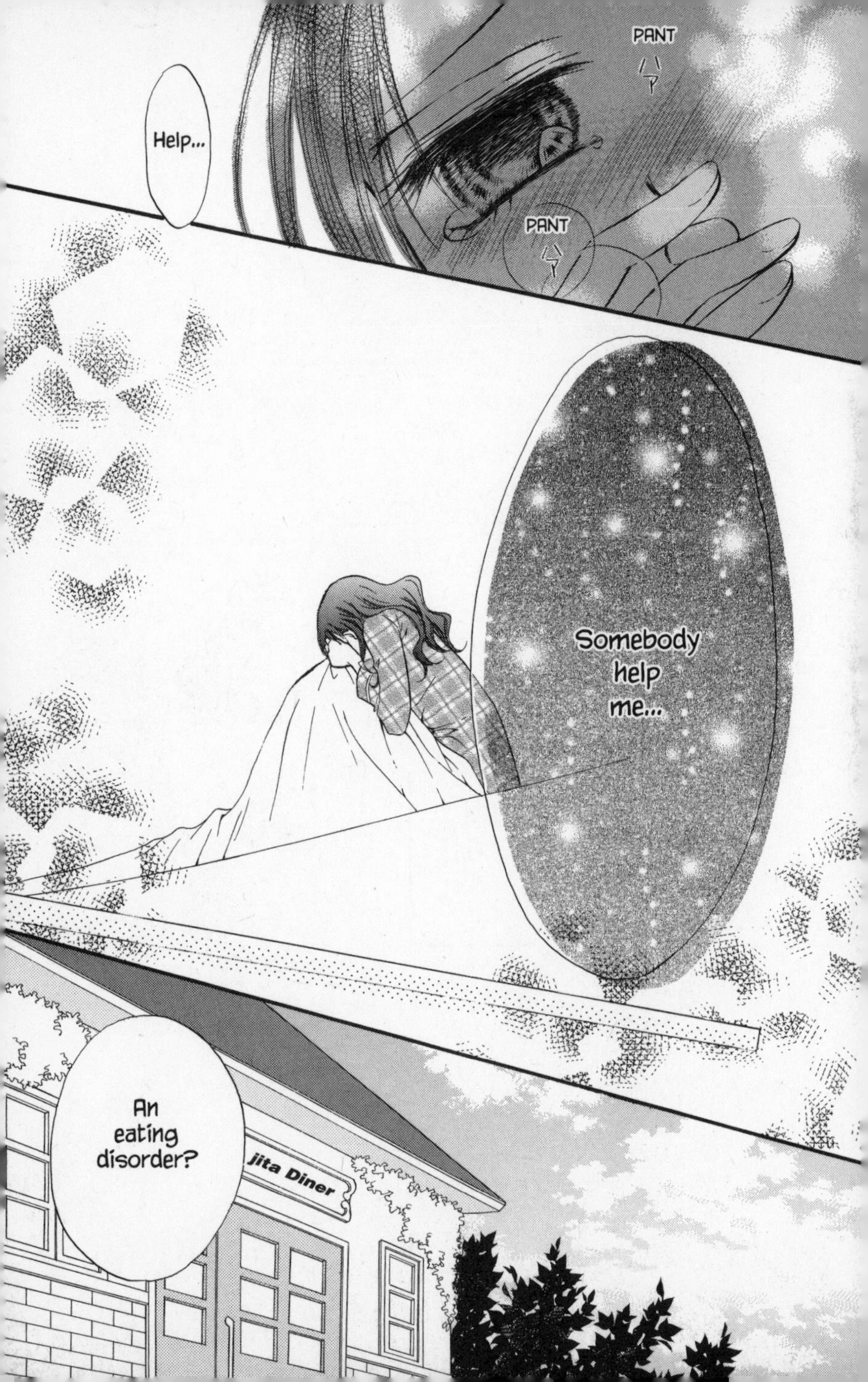
PANT
PANT
Help...
Somebody help me...
jita Diner
An eating disorder?

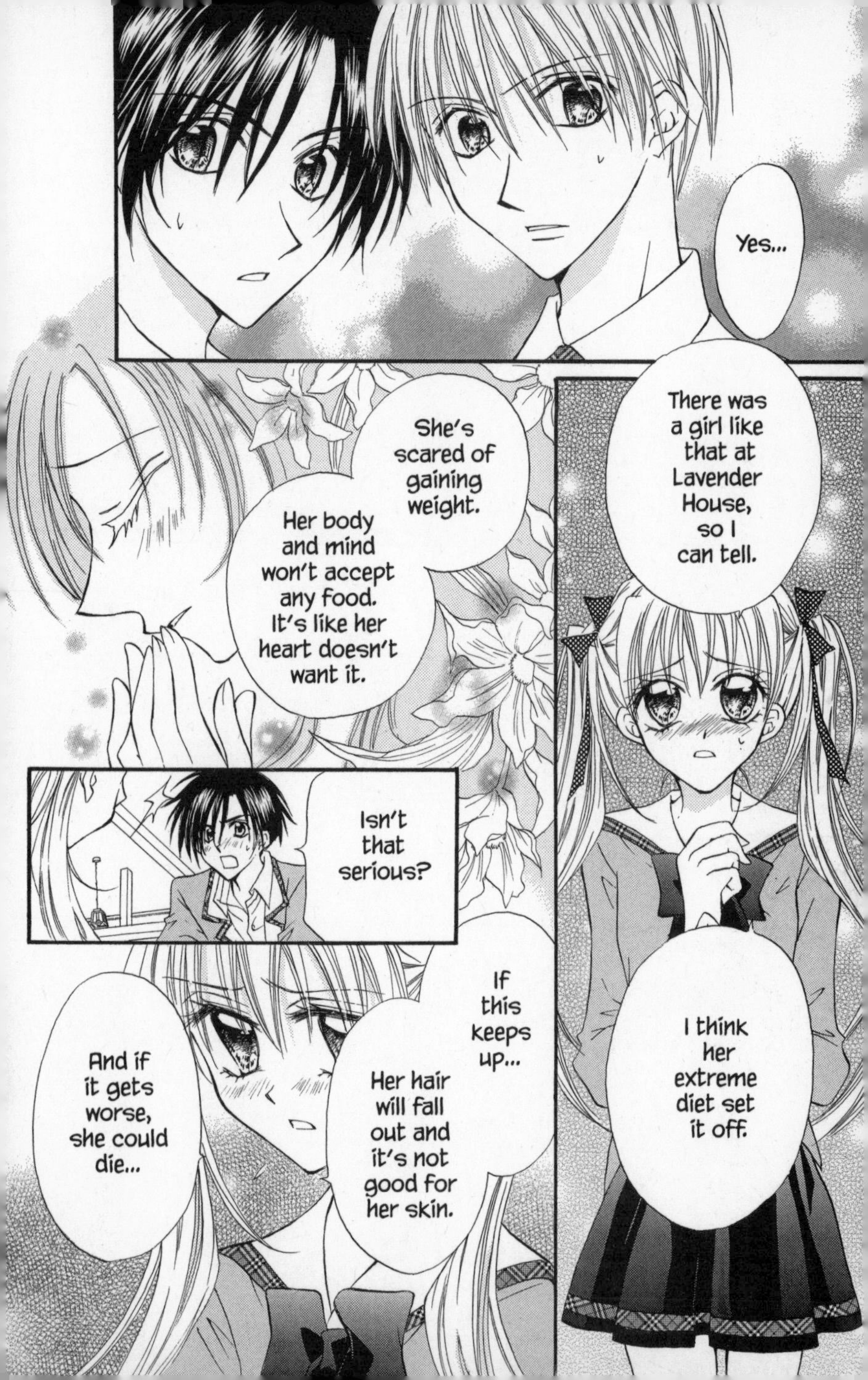
Yes...
There was a girl like that at Lavender House, so I can tell.
I think her extreme diet set it off.
She's scared of gaining weight.
Her body and mind won't accept any food. It's like her heart doesn't want it.
Isn't that serious?
If this keeps up...
Her hair will fall out and it's not good for her skin.
And if it gets worse, she could die...

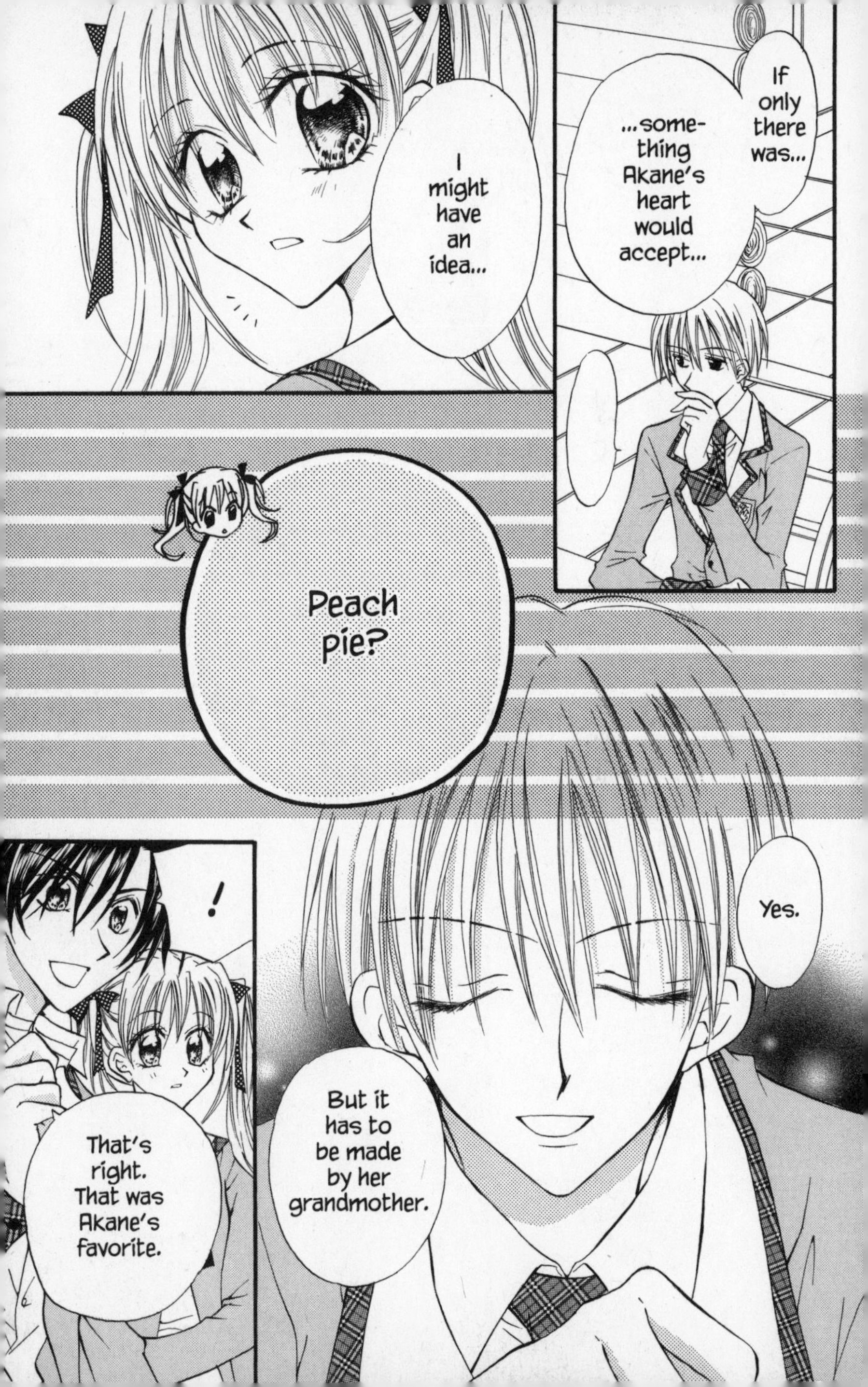
If only there was...
...some-thing Akane's heart would accept...
I might have an idea...
Peach pie?
Yes.
But it has to be made by her grandmother.
!
That's right. That was Akane's favorite.

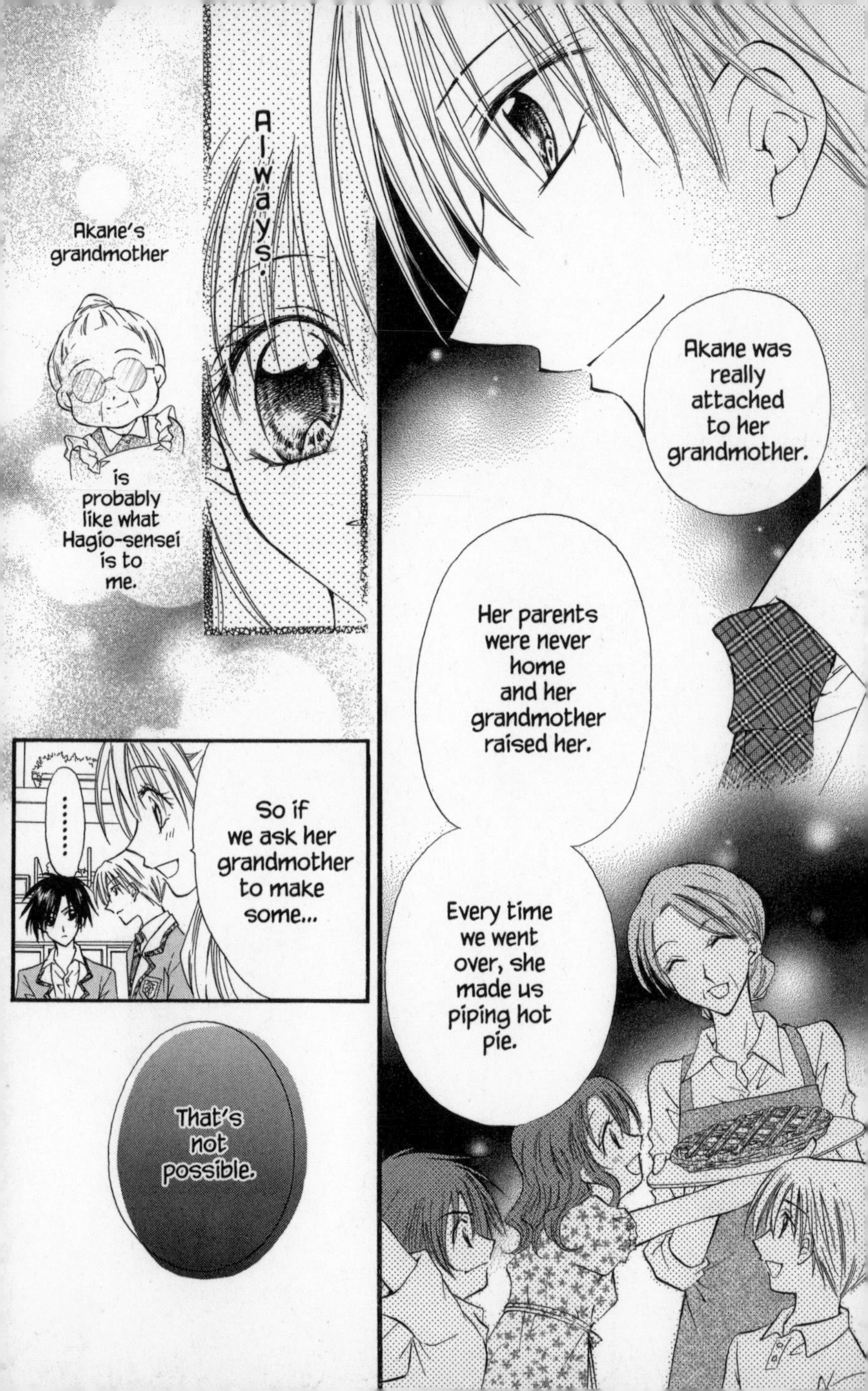
Akane was really attached to her grandmother.
Her parents were never home and her grandmother raised her.
Every time we went over, she made us piping hot pie.
Always.
Akane's grandmother is probably like what Hagio-sensei is to me.
......
So if we ask her grandmother to make some...
That's not possible.

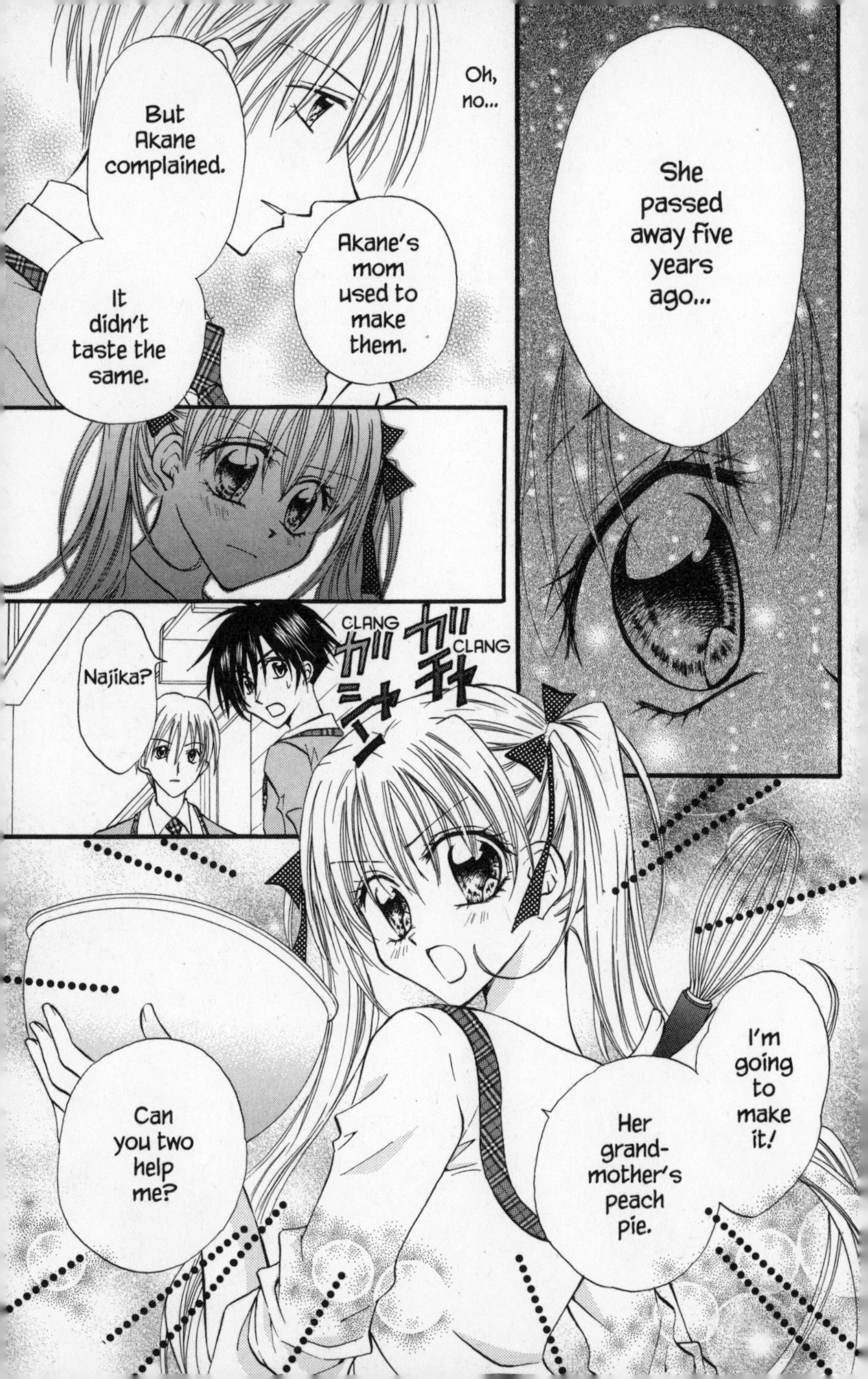
Oh, no...
Akane's mom used to make them.
But Akane complained.
It didn't taste the same.
She passed away five years ago...
CLANG
CLANG
Najika?
I'm going to make it!
Her grand-mother's peach pie.
Can you two help me?

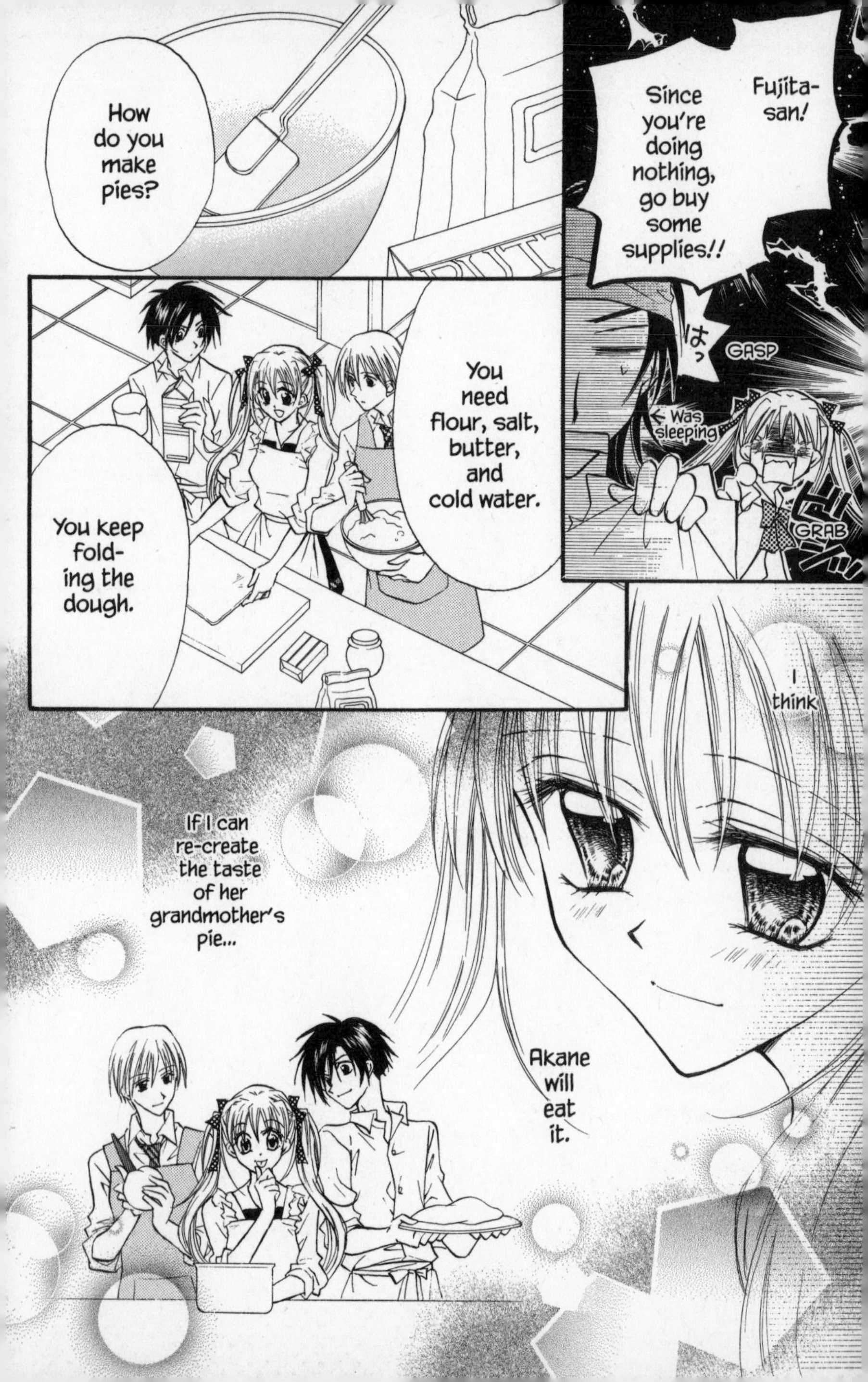

Fujita-san!
Since you're doing nothing, go buy some supplies!!
はっ
GASP
Was sleeping
GRAB
How do you make pies?
You need flour, salt, butter, and cold water.
You keep fold-ing the dough.
I think
If I can re-create the taste of her grandmother's pie...
Akane will eat it.

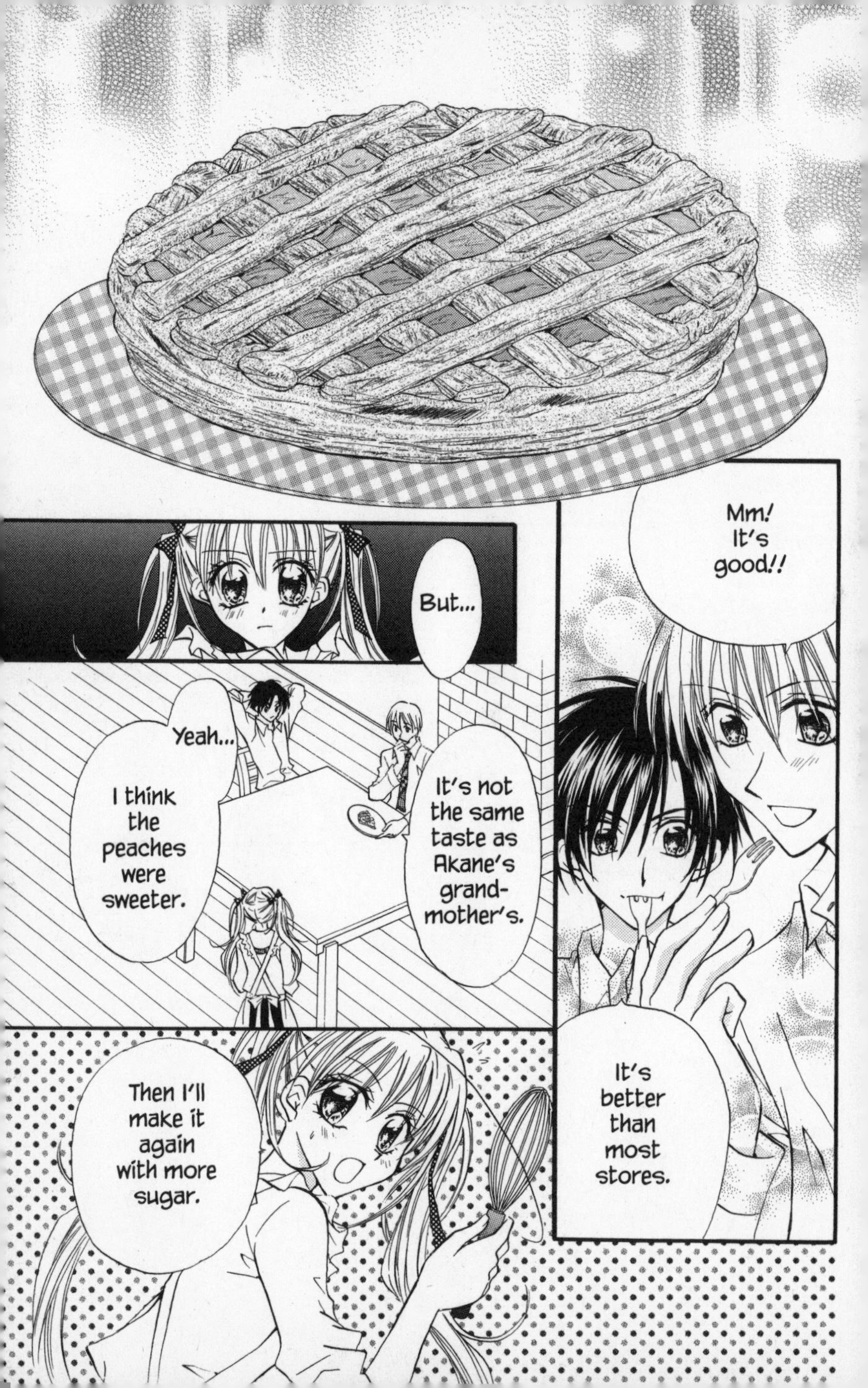
Mm! It's good!!
It's better than most stores.
But...
It's not the same taste as Akane's grand-mother's.
Yeah...
I think the peaches were sweeter.
Then I'll make it again with more sugar.

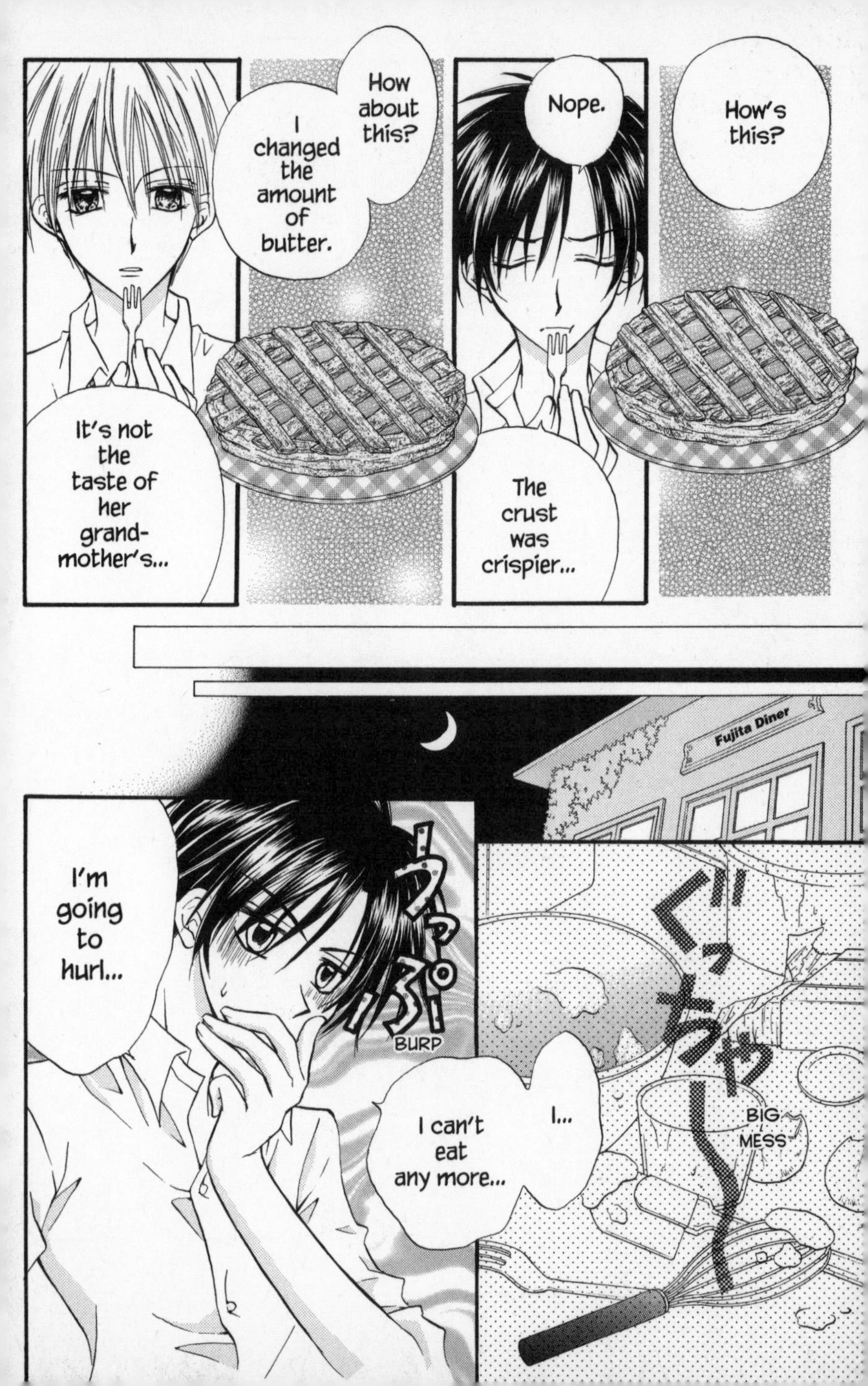
How's this?
Nope.
The crust was crispier...
How about this?
I changed the amount of butter.
It's not the taste of her grandmother's...
Fujita Diner
BIG MESS
I...
I can't eat any more...
BURP
I'm going to hurl...

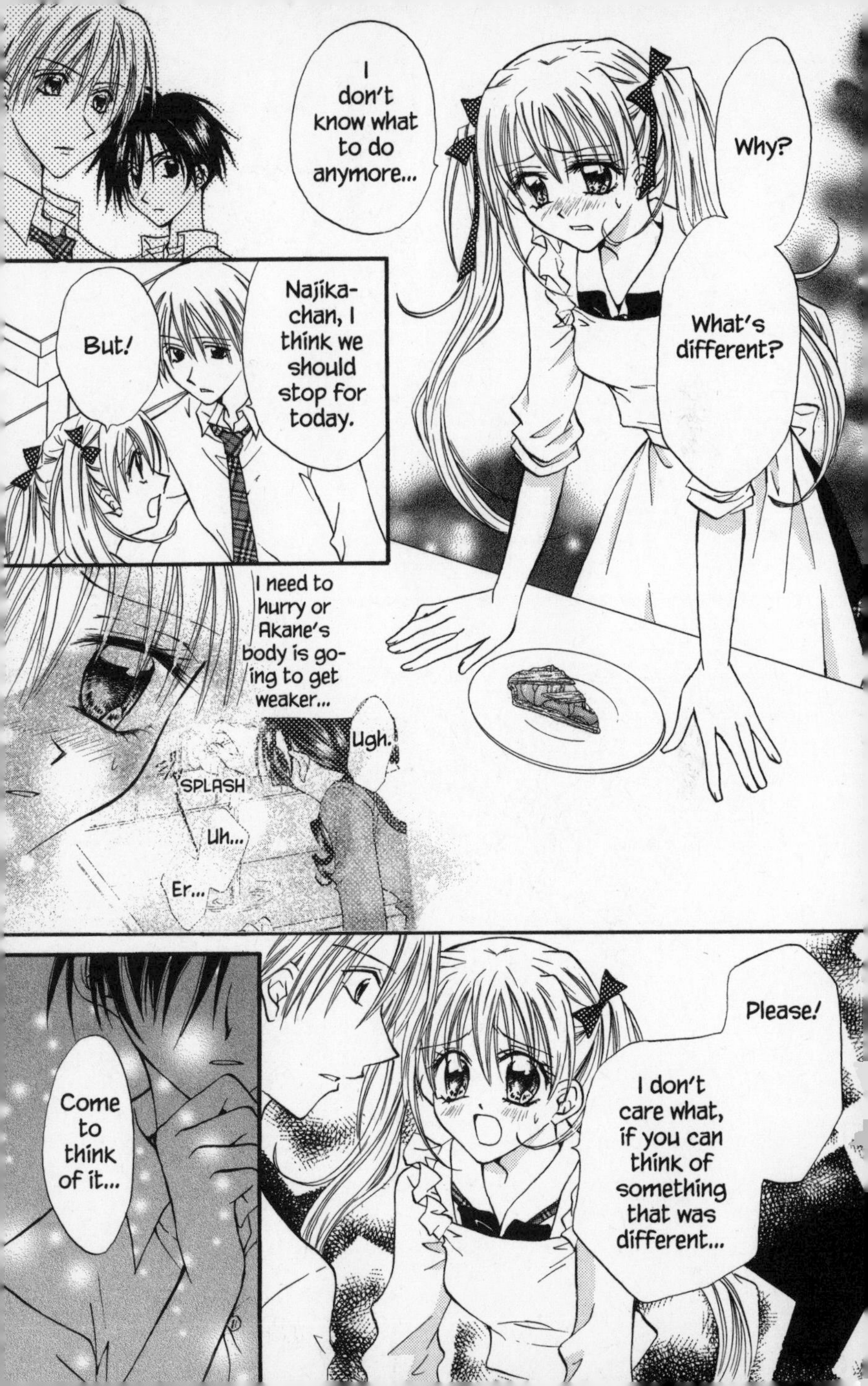
Why?
What's different?
I don't know what to do anymore...
Najika-chan, I think we should stop for today.
But!
I need to hurry or Akane's body is going to get weaker...
Ugh.
SPLASH
Uh...
Er...
Please!
I don't care what, if you can think of something that was different...
Come to think of it...

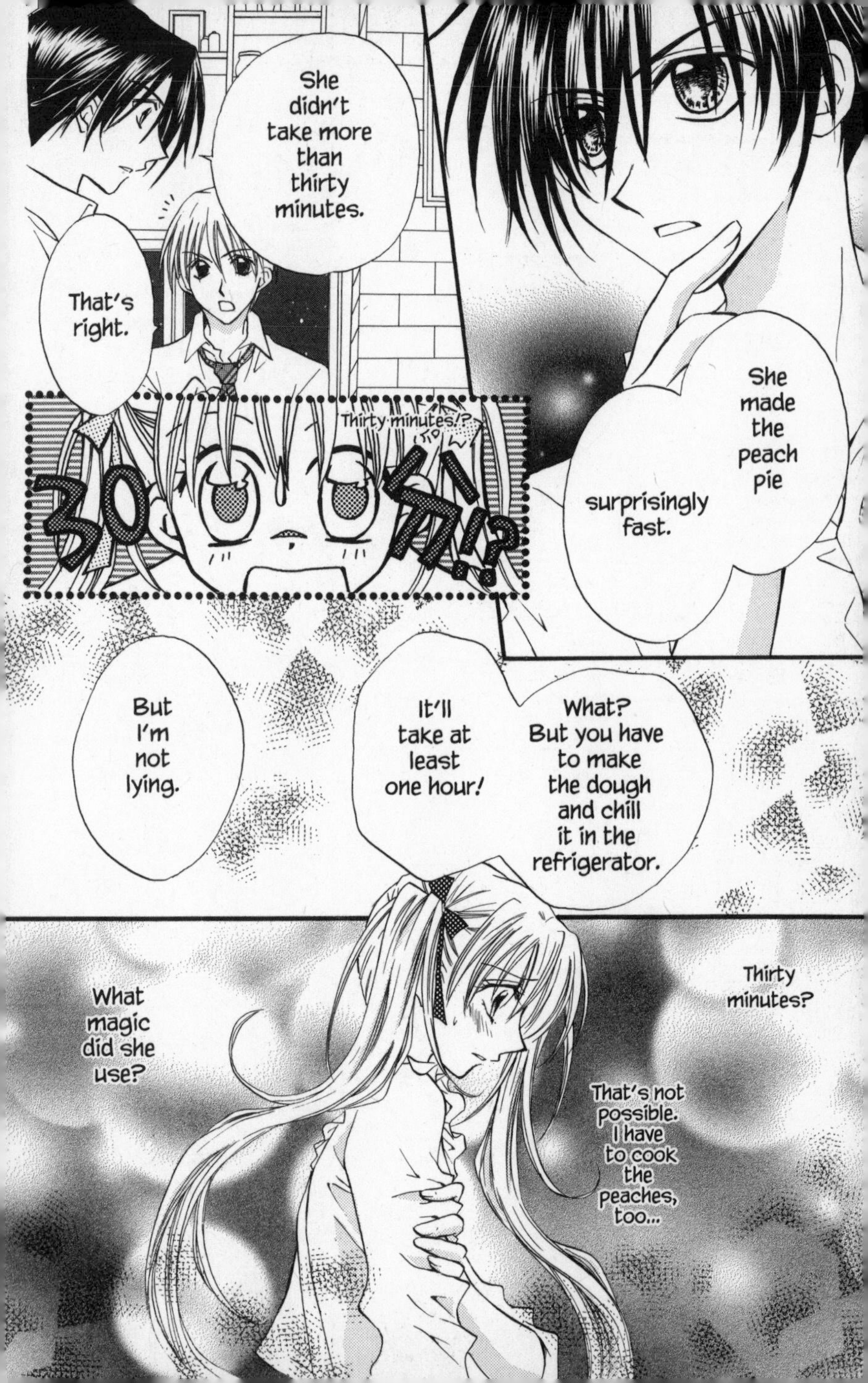
She made the peach pie
surprisingly fast.
She didn't take more than thirty minutes.
That's right.
30分!?
Thirty minutes!?
What? But you have to make the dough and chill it in the refrigerator.
It'll take at least one hour!
But I'm not lying.
Thirty minutes?
That's not possible. I have to cook the peaches, too...
What magic did she use?

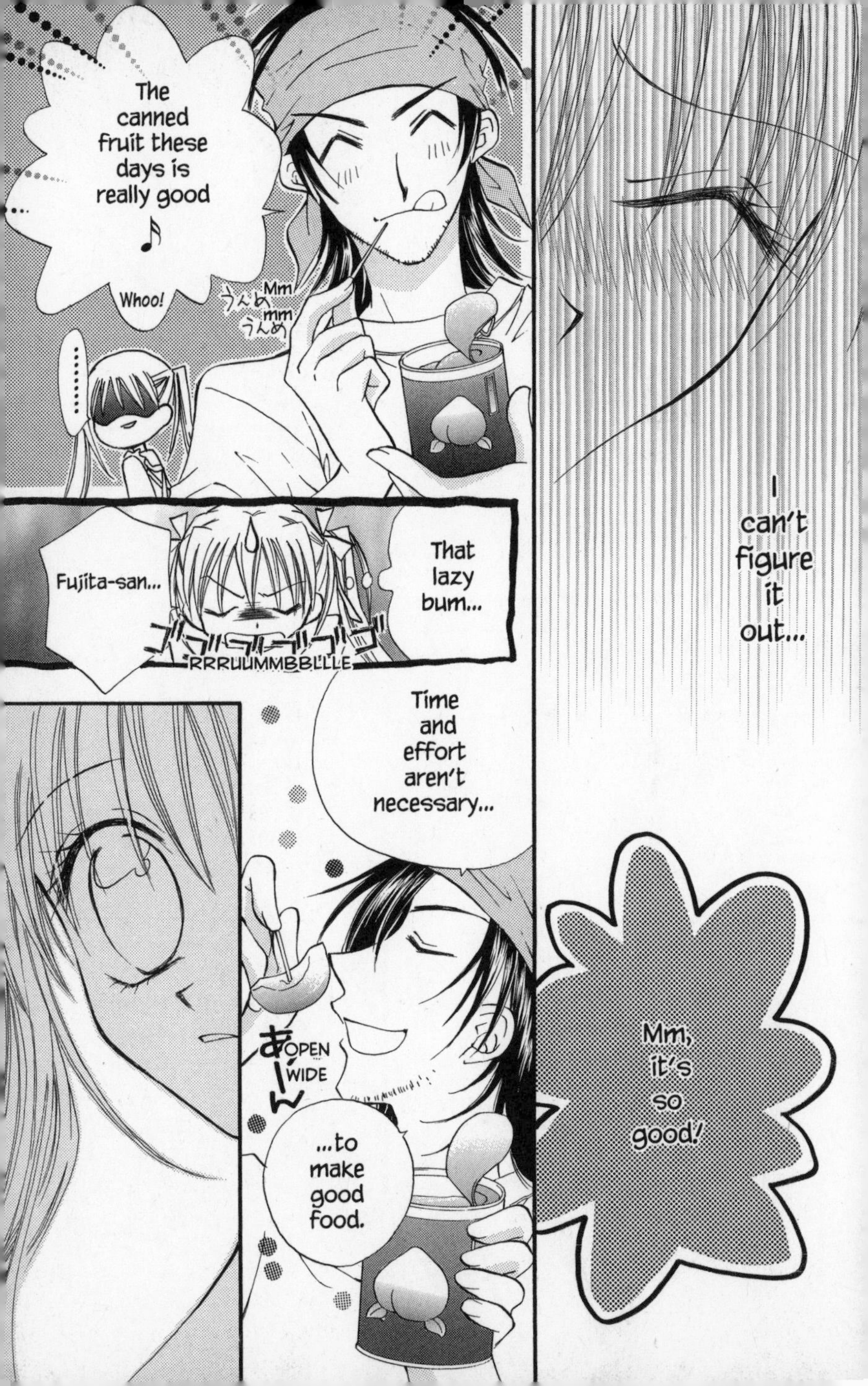

I can't figure it out...
The canned fruit these days is really good ♪
うんめ Mm
うんめ mm
Whoo!
......
That lazy bum...
Fujita-san...
ゴゴゴゴゴゴ RRRUUMMBBLLLE
Time and effort aren't necessary...
あーん OPEN WIDE
...to make good food.
Mm, it's so good!

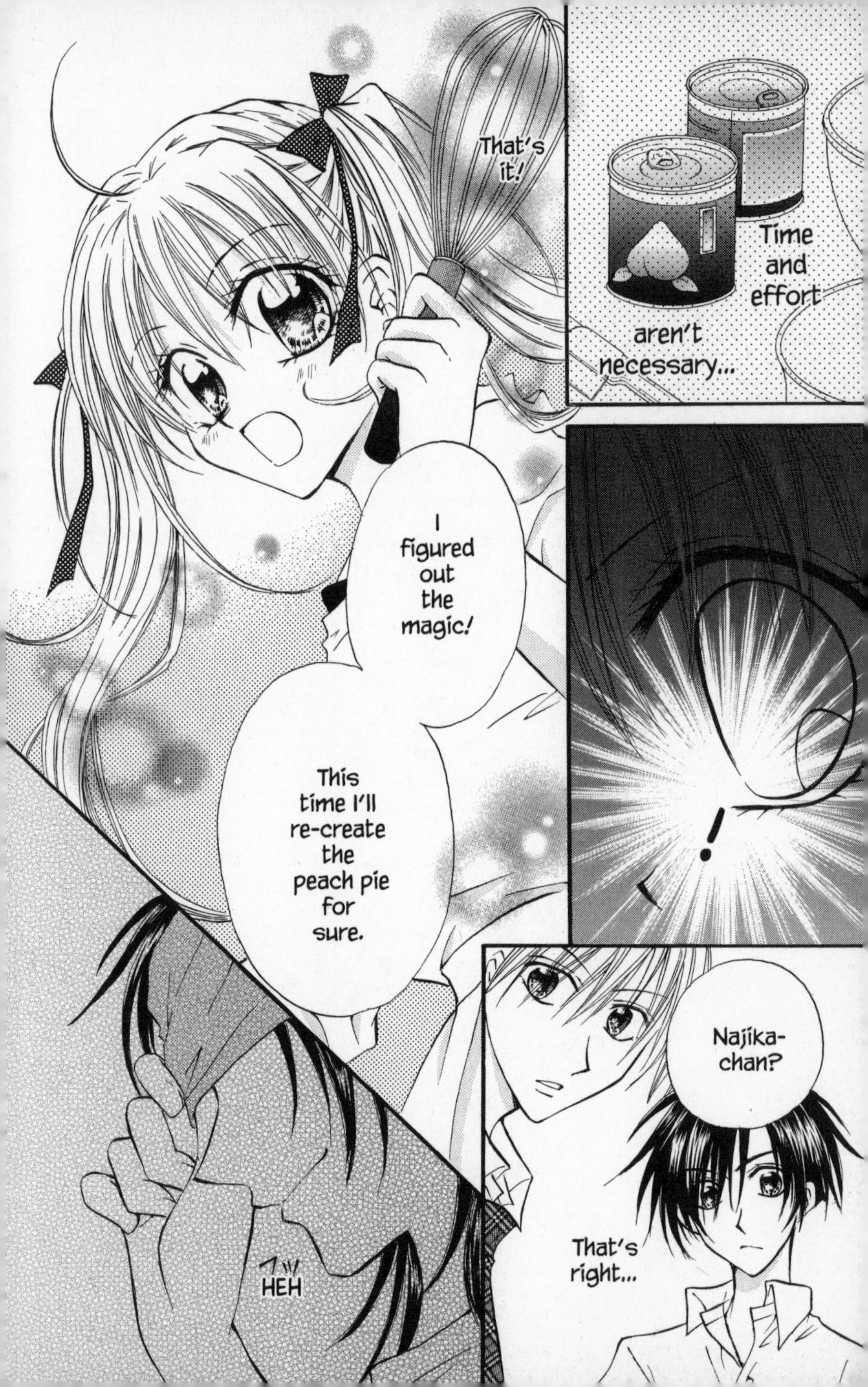
Time and effort aren't necessary...
!
Najika-chan?
That's right...
That's it!
I figured out the magic!
This time I'll re-create the peach pie for sure.
HEH

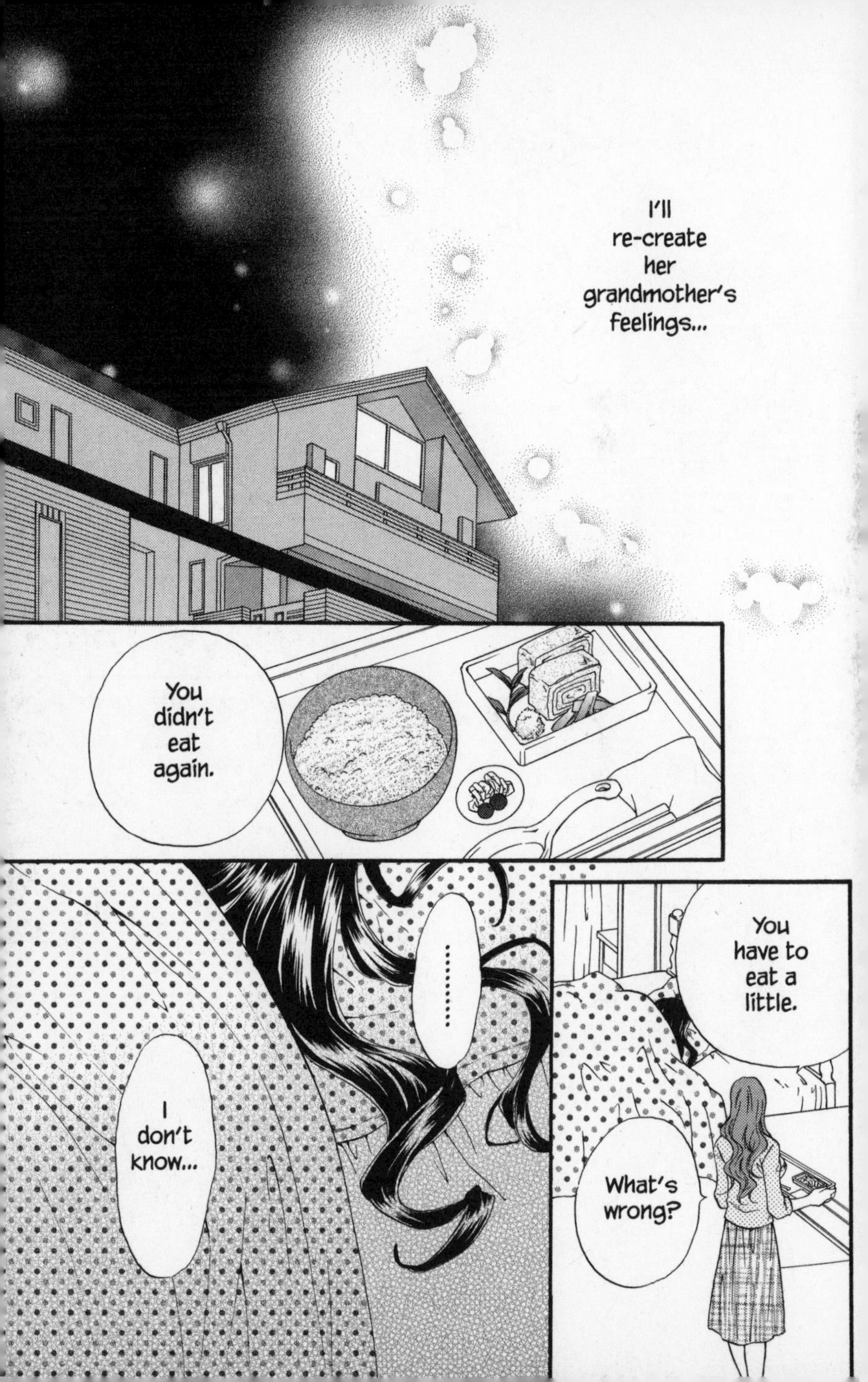
I'll re-create her grandmother's feelings...
You didn't eat again.
You have to eat a little.
What's wrong?
......
I don't know...

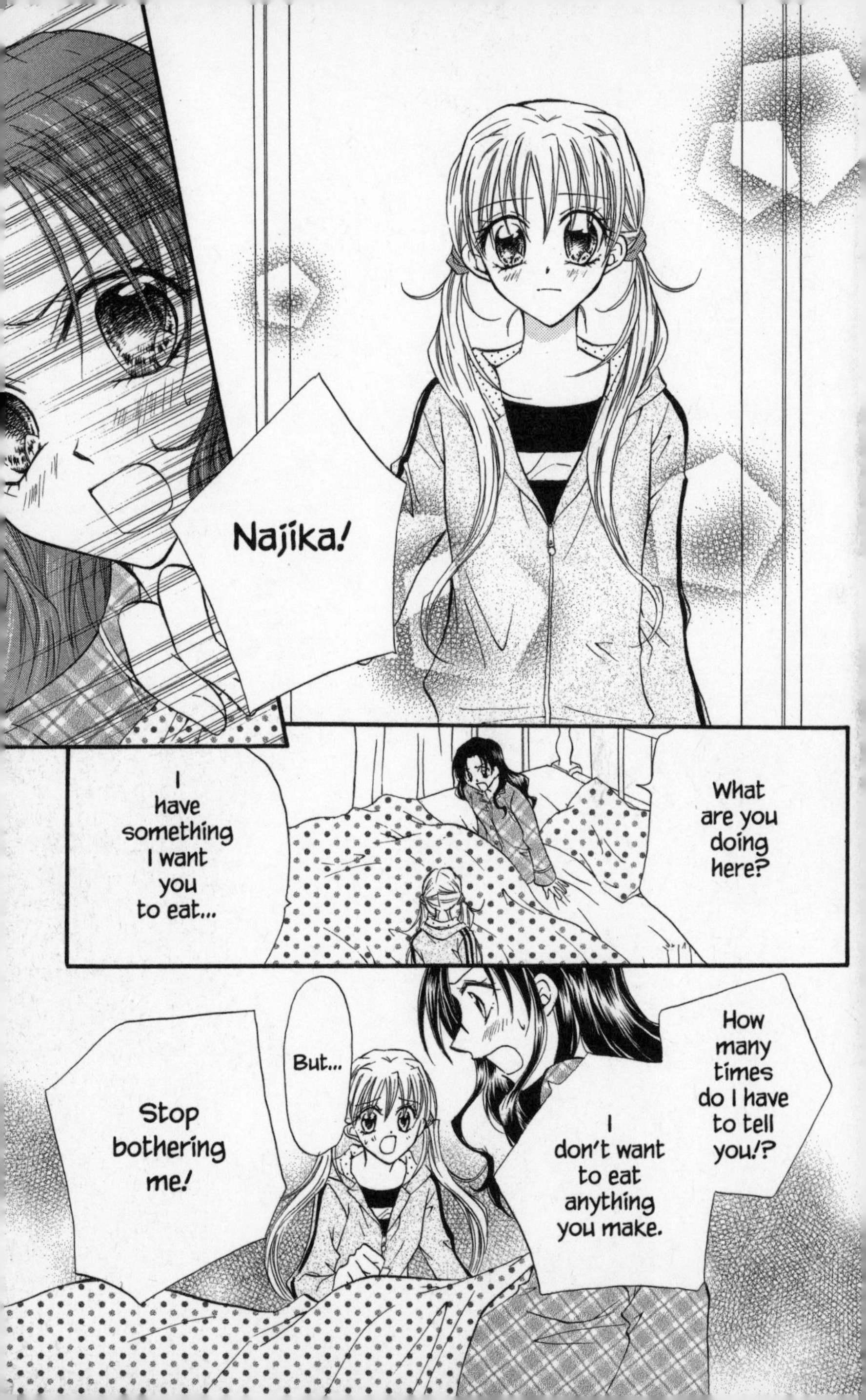
Najika!
What are you doing here?
I have something I want you to eat...
How many times do I have to tell you!?
I don't want to eat anything you make.
But...
Stop bothering me!

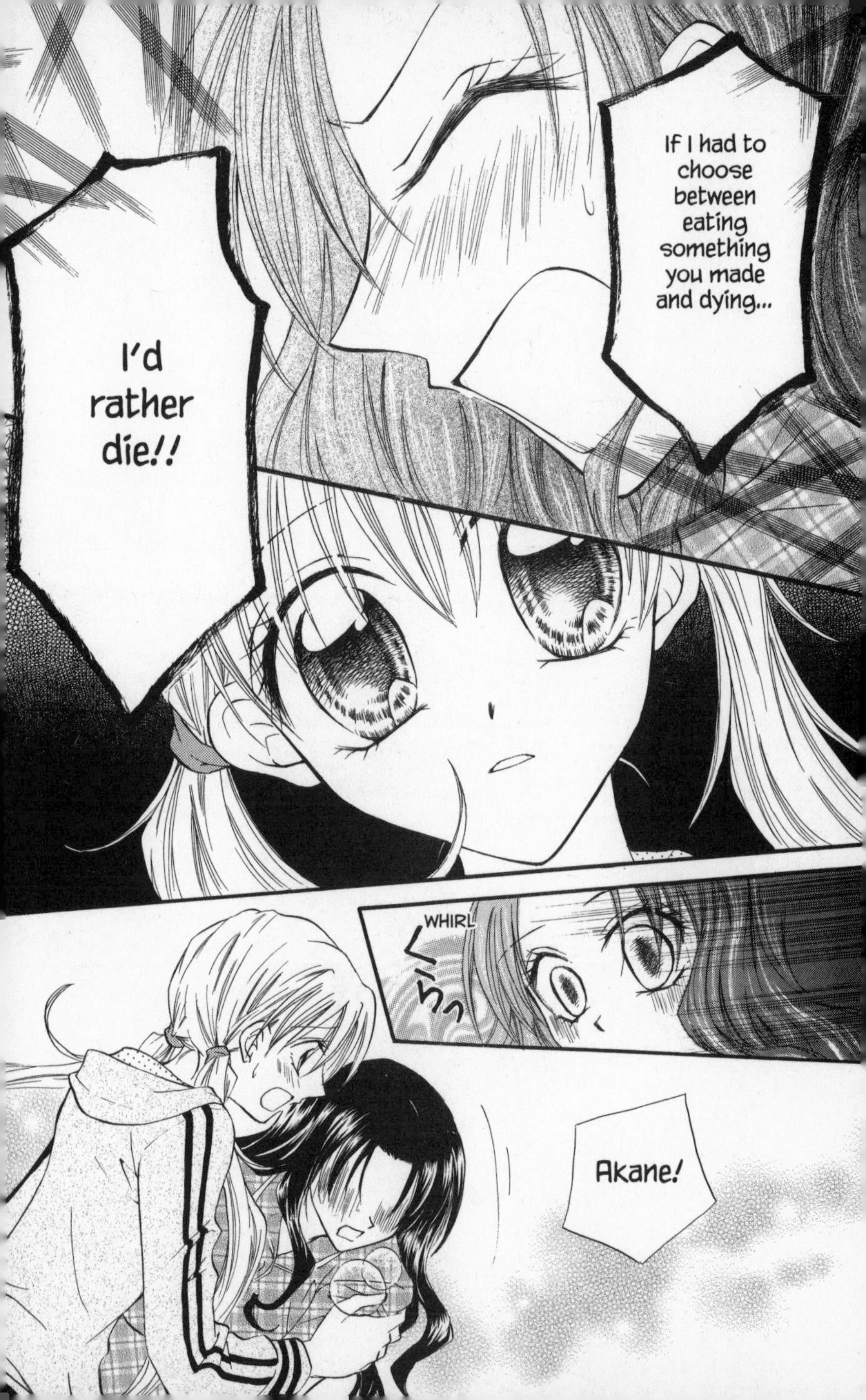
If I had to choose between eating something you made and dying...
I'd rather die!!
WHIRL
Akane!

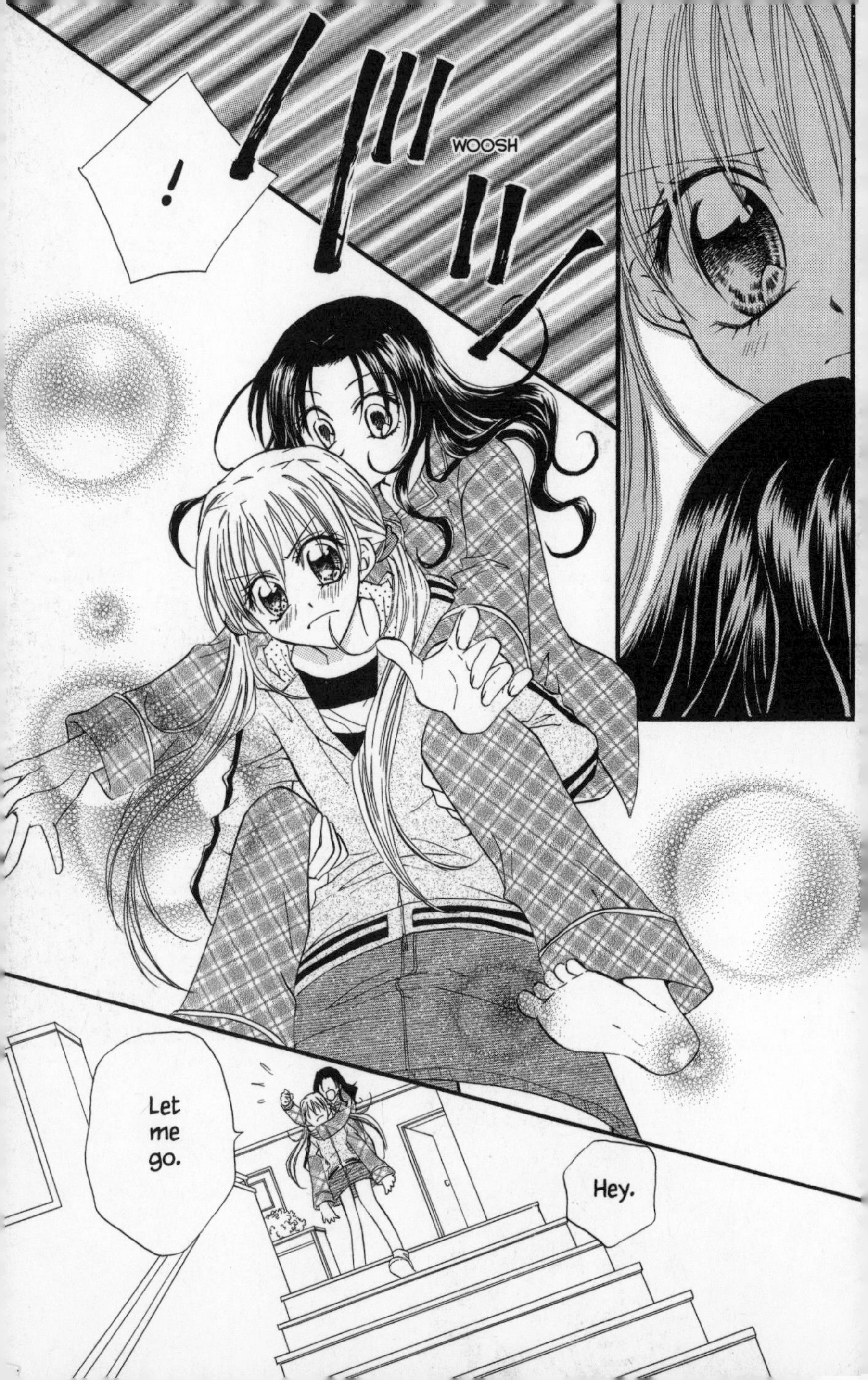
WOOSH
!
Hey.
Let me go.

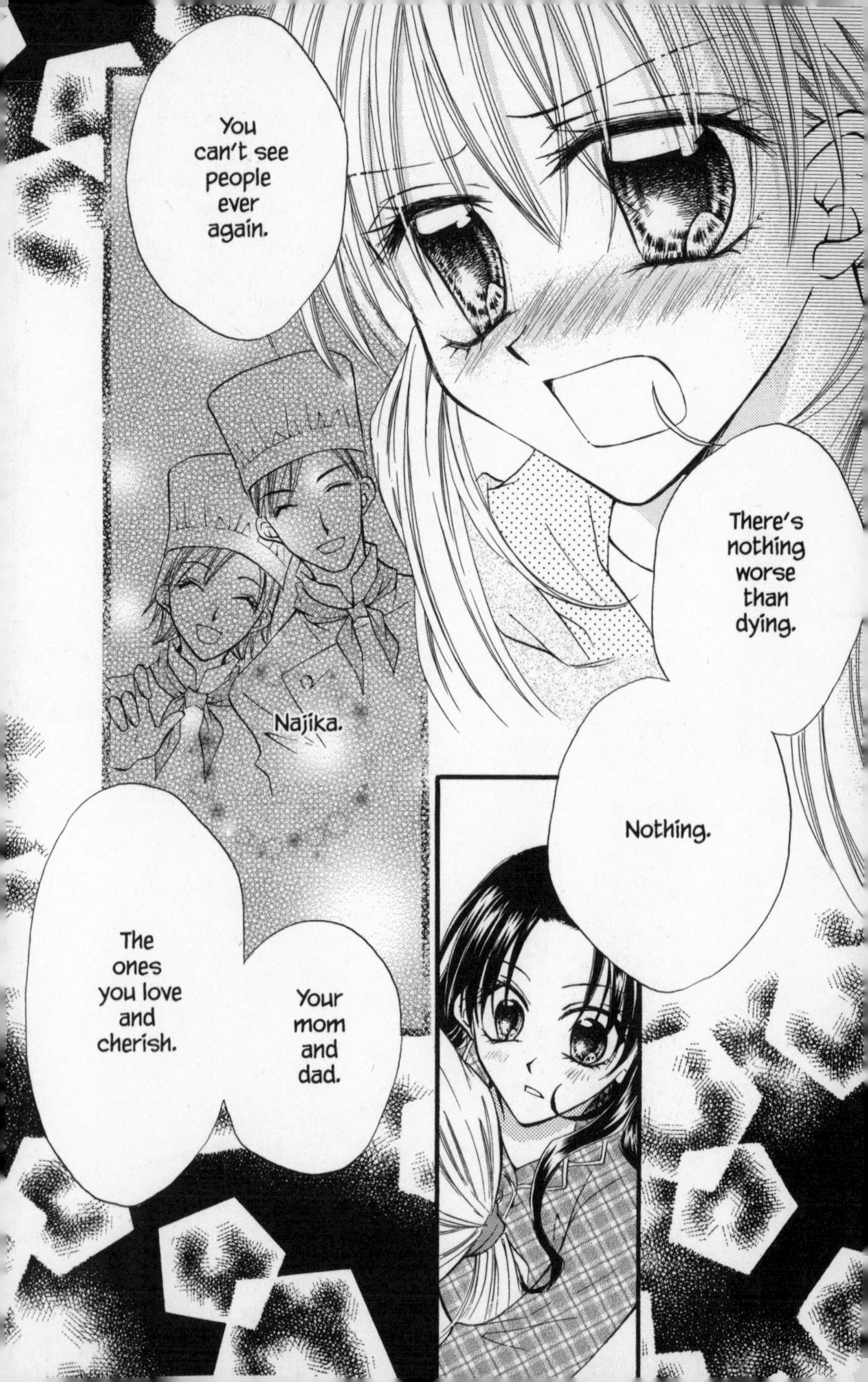
There's nothing worse than dying.
Nothing.
You can't see people ever again.
Najika.
Your mom and dad.
The ones you love and cherish.

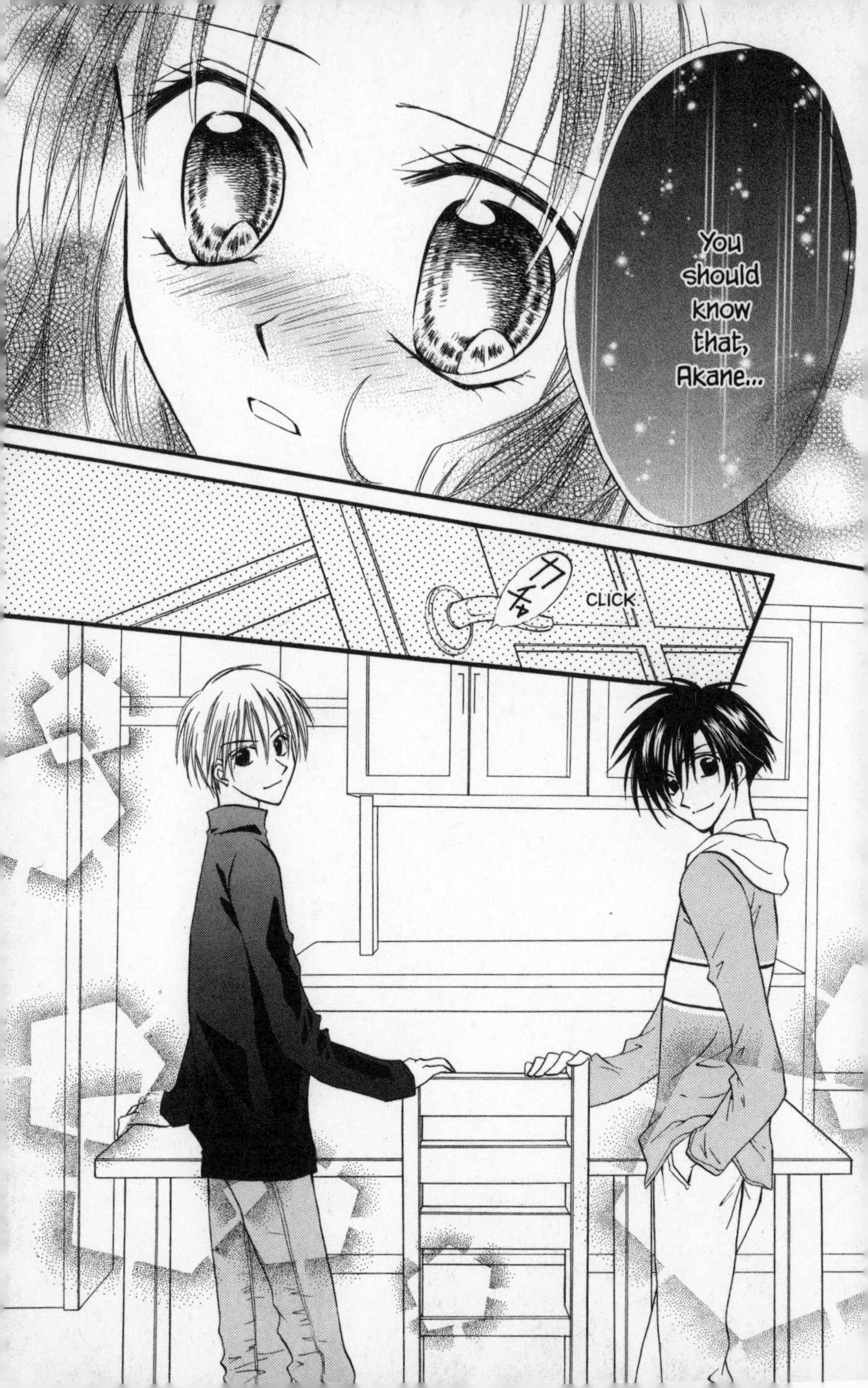
You should know that, Akane...
カチャ
CLICK

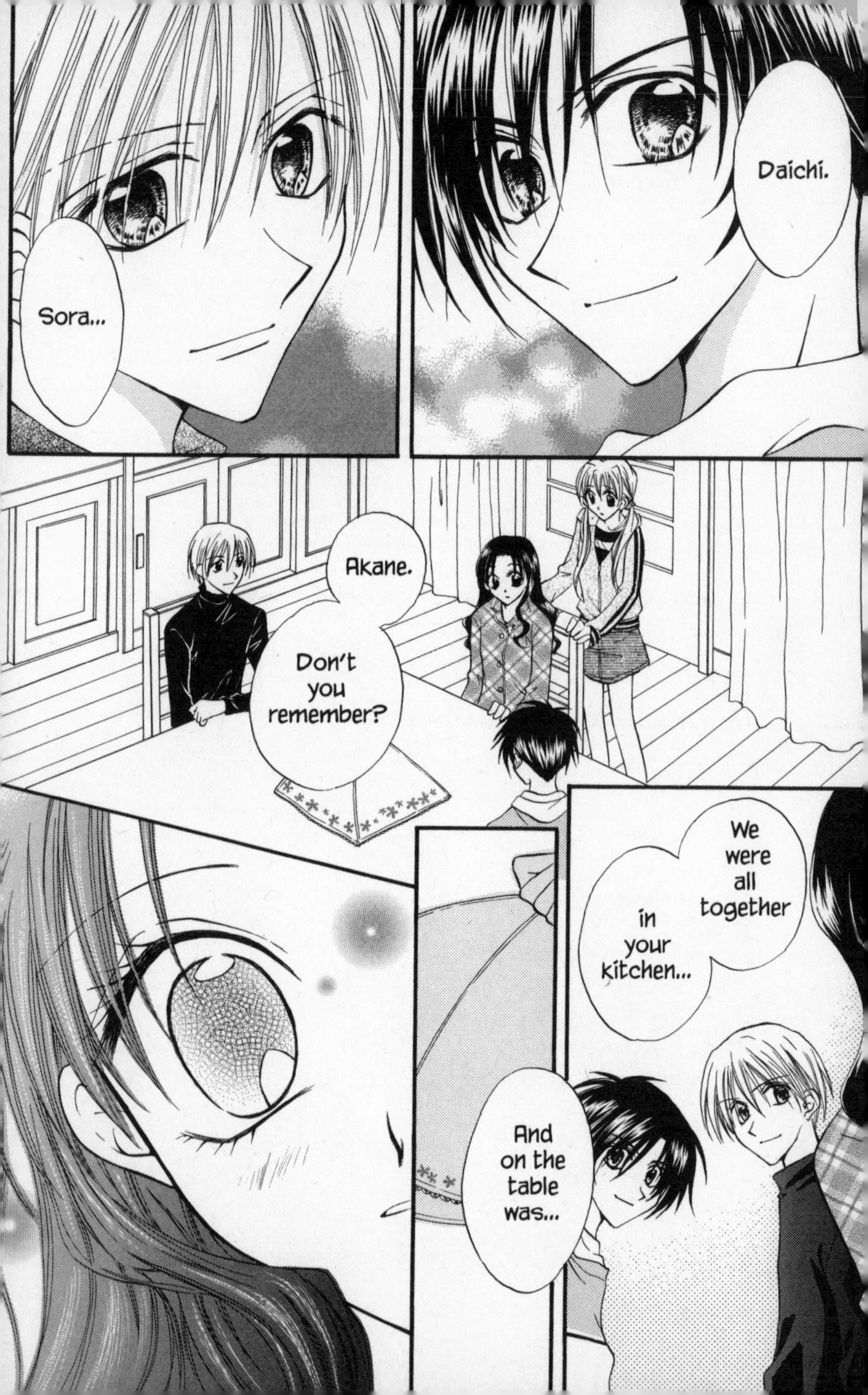
Daichi.
Sora...
Akane.
Don't you remember?
We were all together
in your kitchen...
And on the table was...

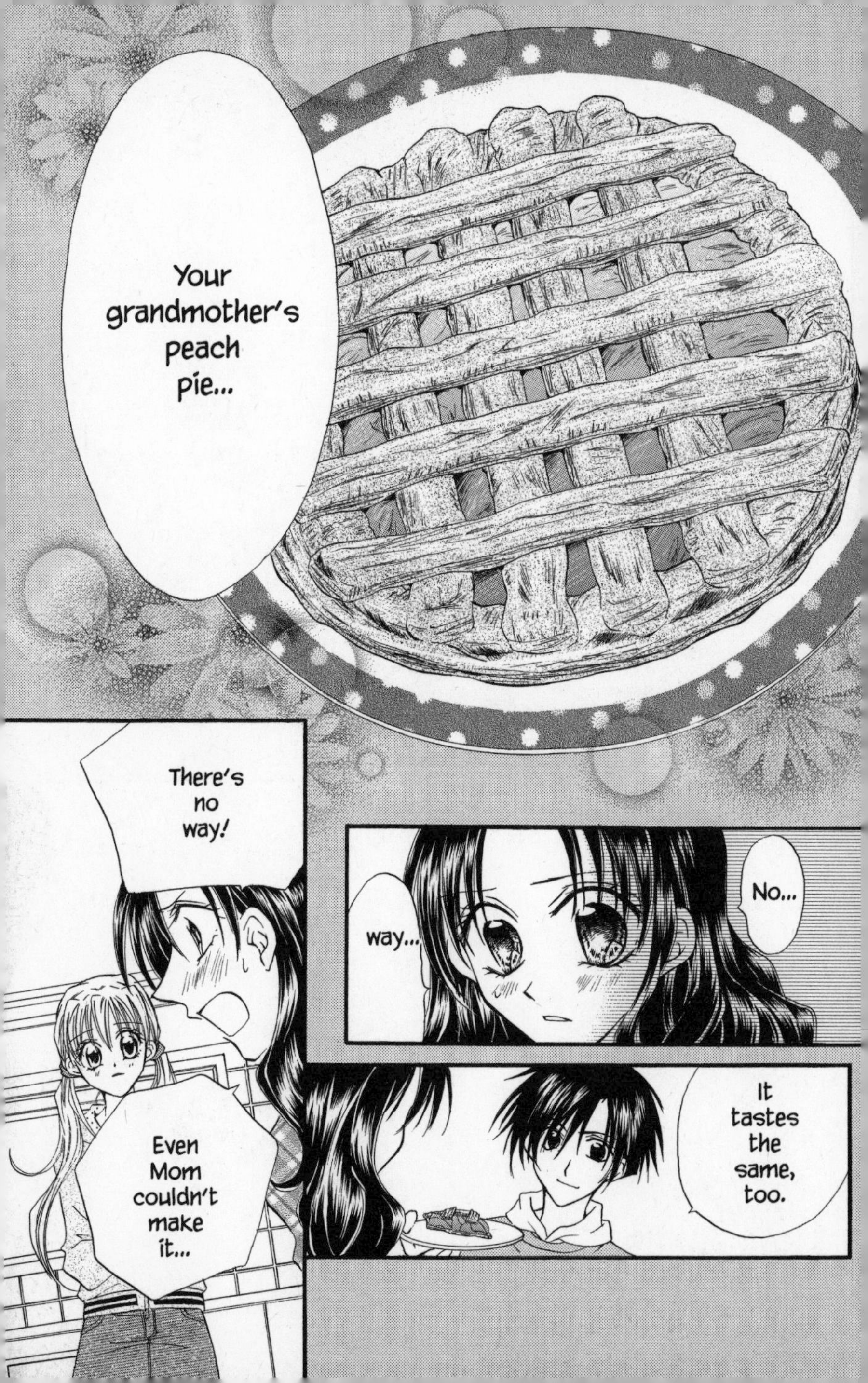
Your grandmother's peach pie...
No...
way...
It tastes the same, too.
There's no way!
Even Mom couldn't make it...

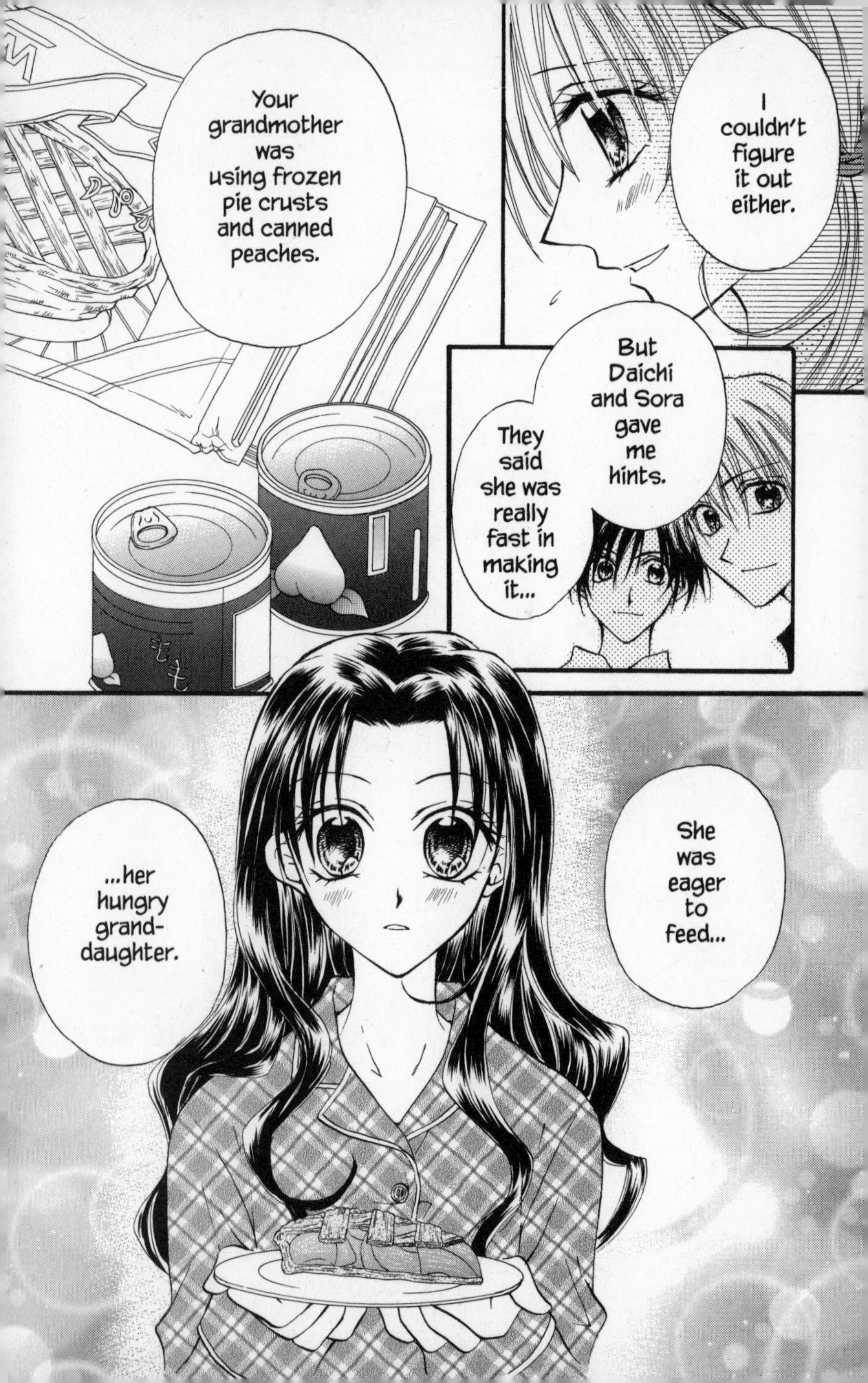
I couldn't figure it out either.
But Daichi and Sora gave me hints.
They said she was really fast in making it...
Your grandmother was using frozen pie crusts and canned peaches.
She was eager to feed...
...her hungry grand-daughter.

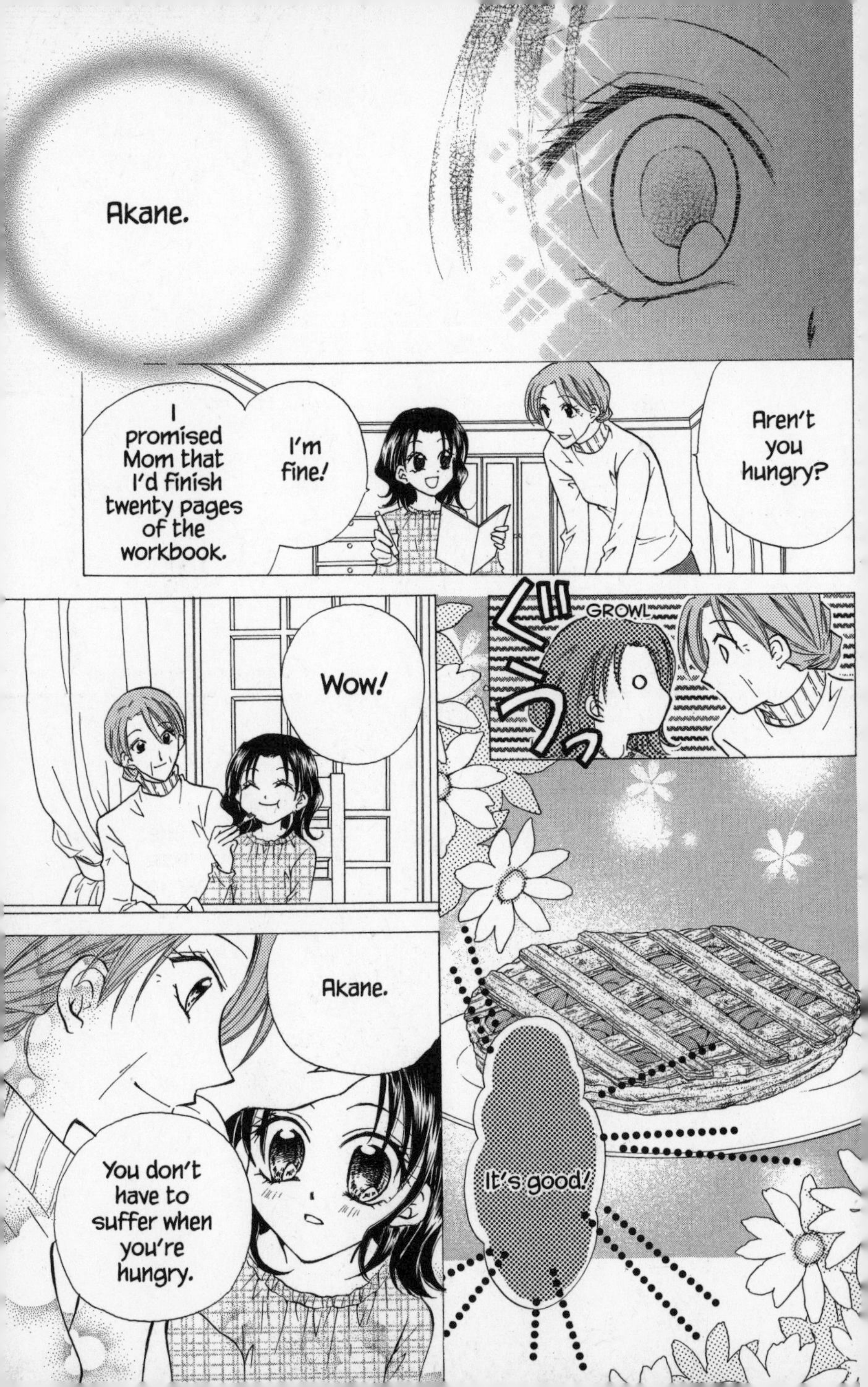
Akane.
Aren't you hungry?
I'm fine!
I promised Mom that I'd finish twenty pages of the workbook.
GROWL
Akane.
You don't have to suffer when you're hungry.
Wow!
It's good!

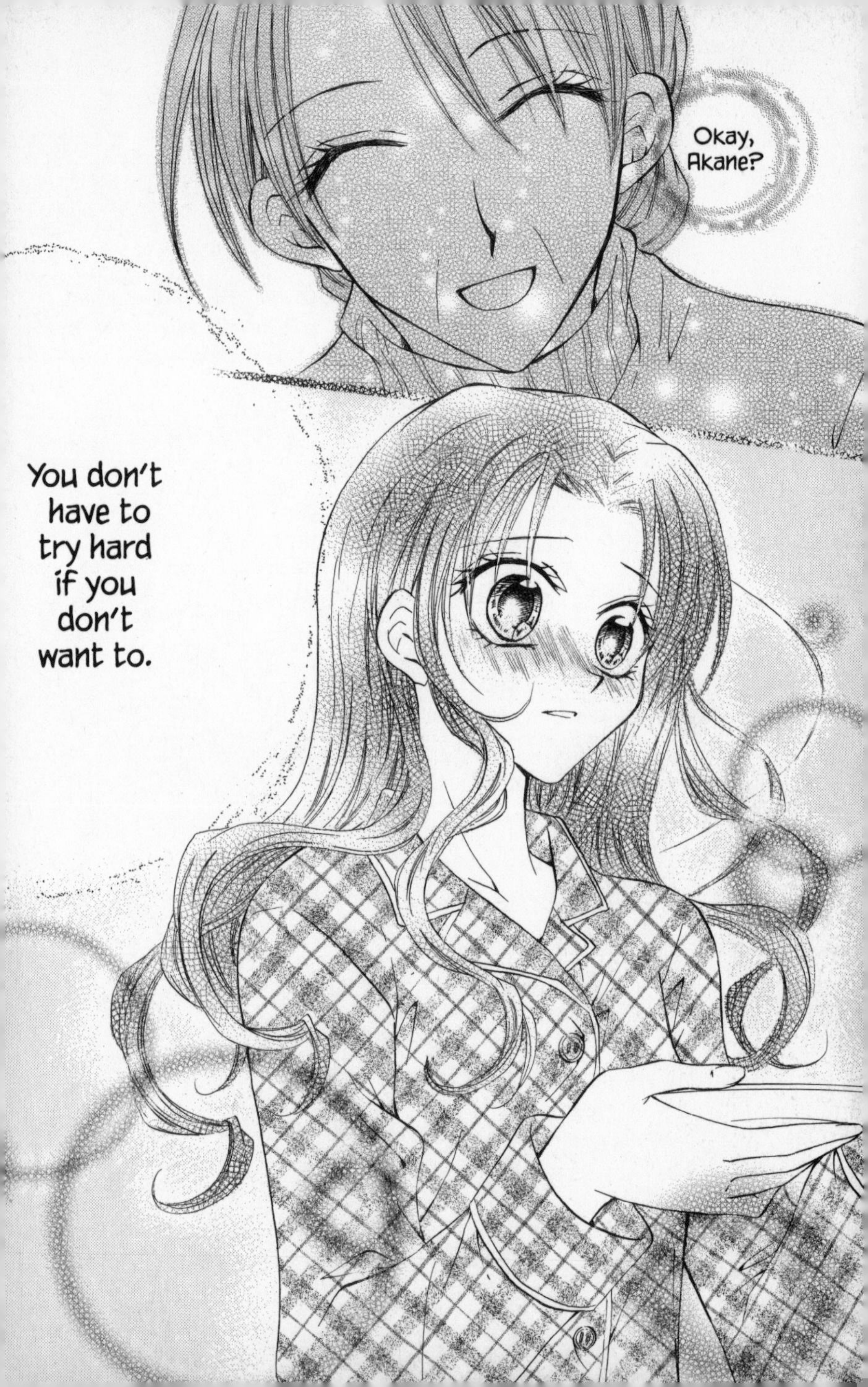
Okay, Akane?
You don't have to try hard if you don't want to.

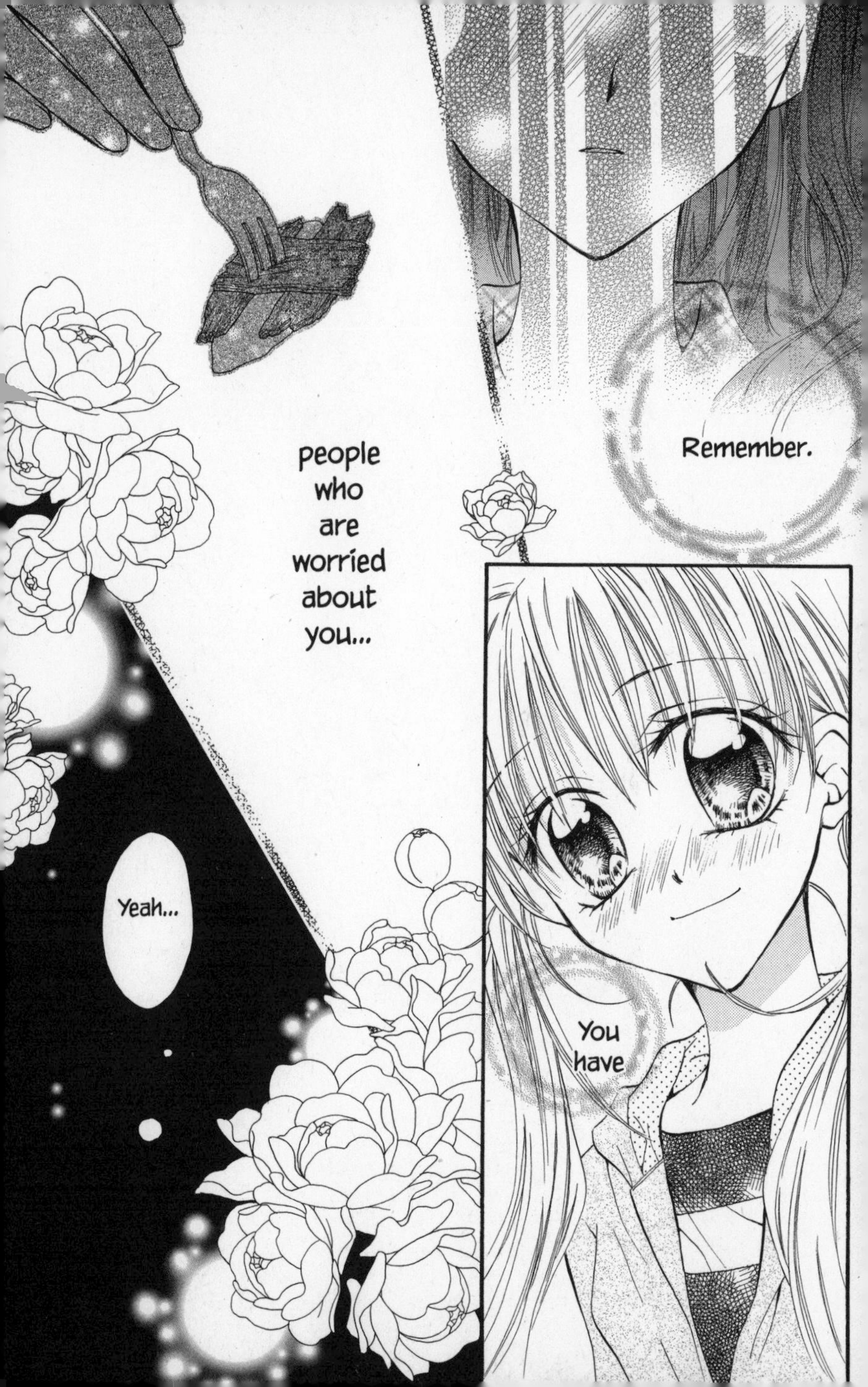
Remember.
You have
people who are worried about you...
Yeah...

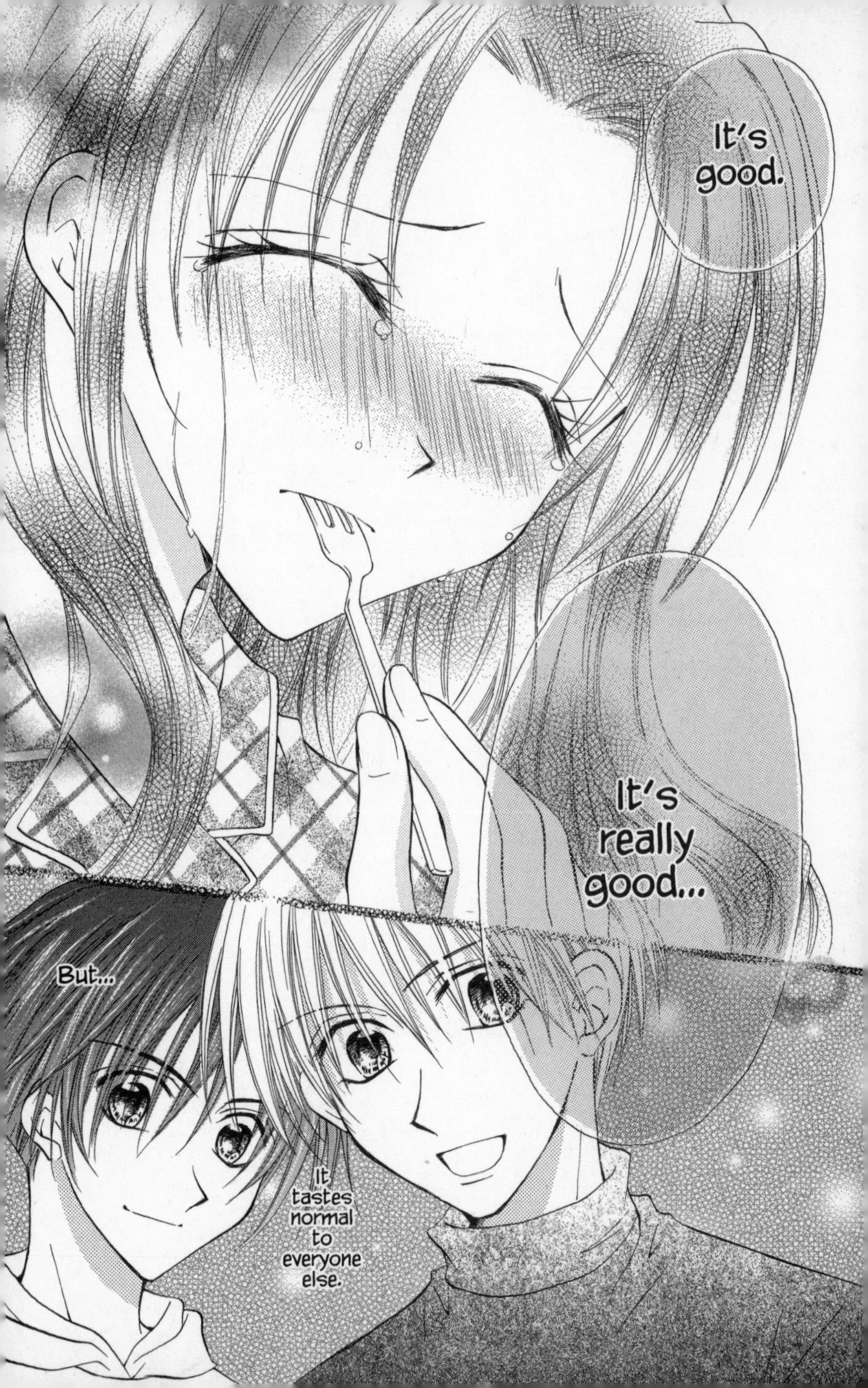
It's good.
It's really good...
But...
It tastes normal to everyone else.

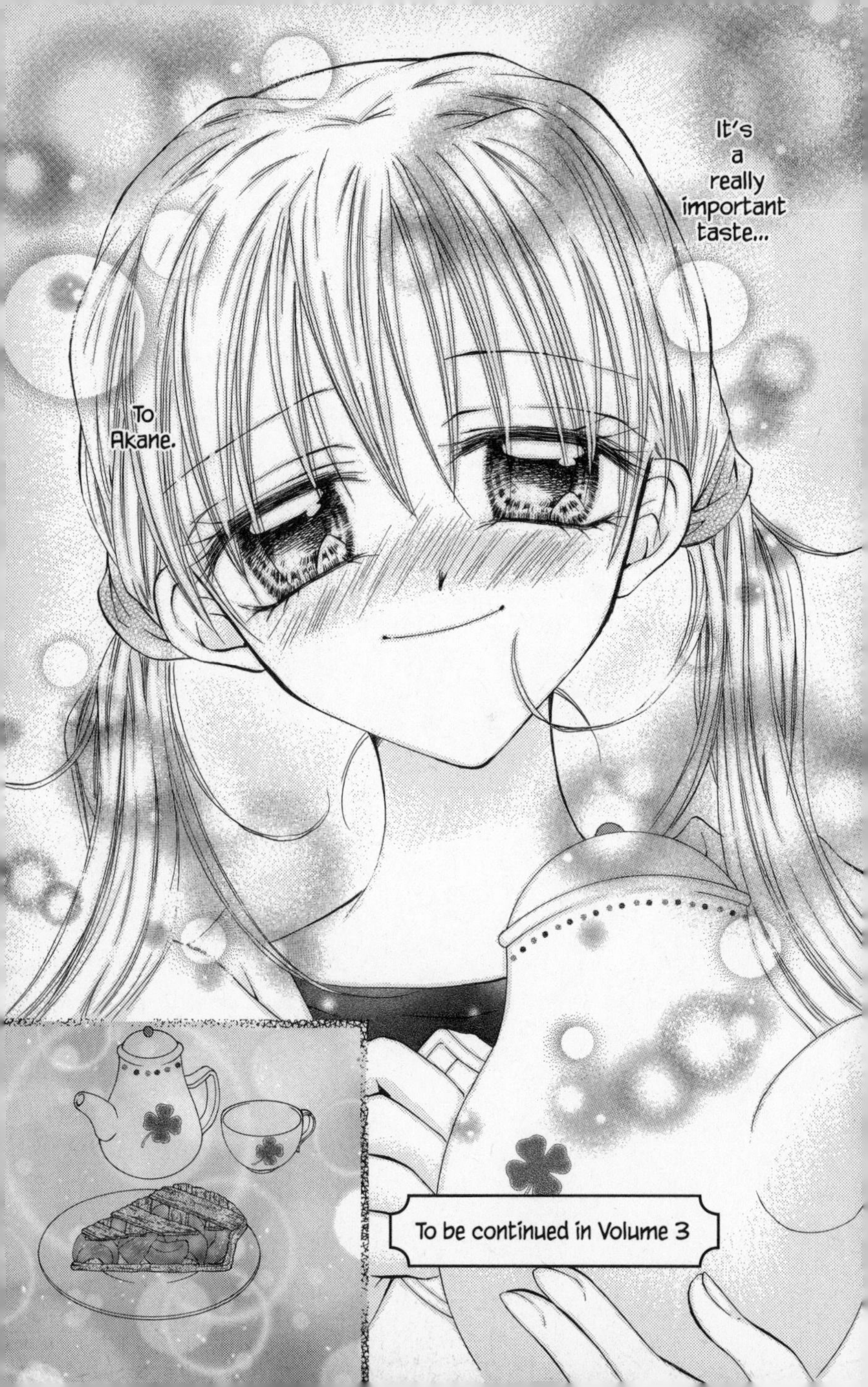
It's a really important taste...
To Akane.
To be continued in Volume 3

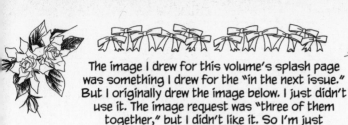

The image I drew for this volume's splash page was something I drew for the "in the next issue." But I originally drew the image below. I just didn't use it. The image request was "three of them together," but I didn't like it. So I'm just putting it here ♥

Please send letters to:
Nakayoshi Editorial Team
PO BOX 91
Akasaka, Tokyo 107-8652

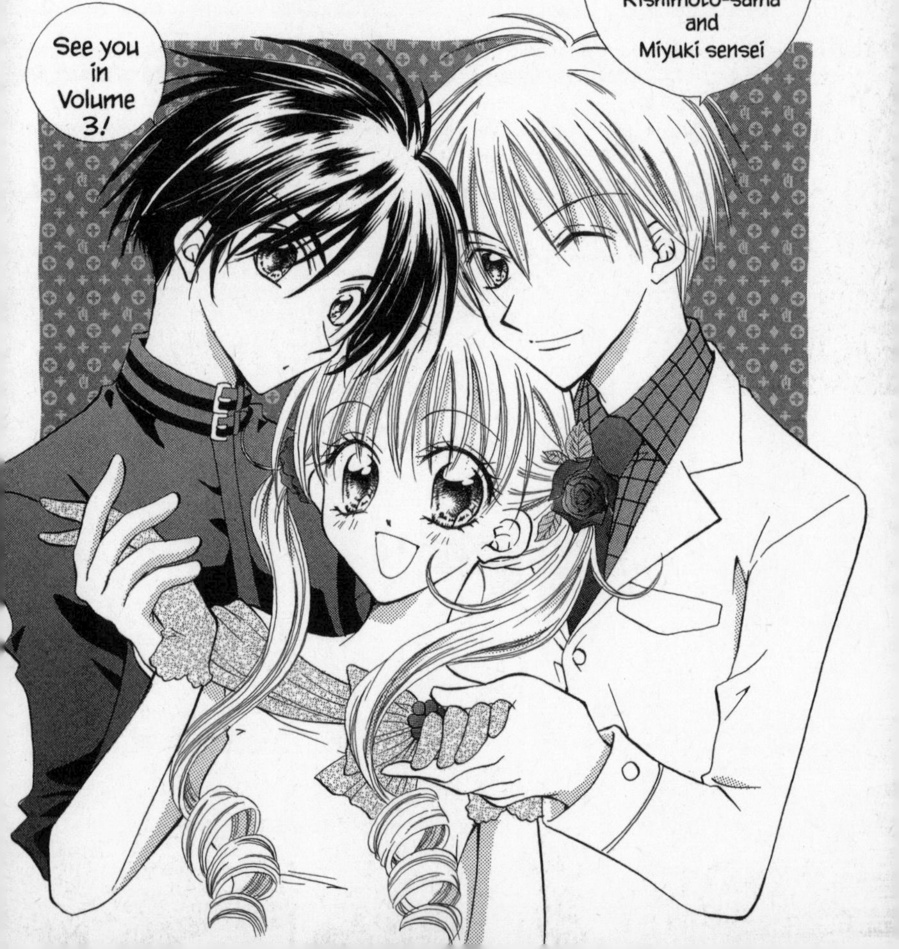
Thank you
Maruyama-sama
Shobayashi-sama
Marimo-sama
Kishimoto-sama
and
Miyuki sensei
See you in Volume 3!

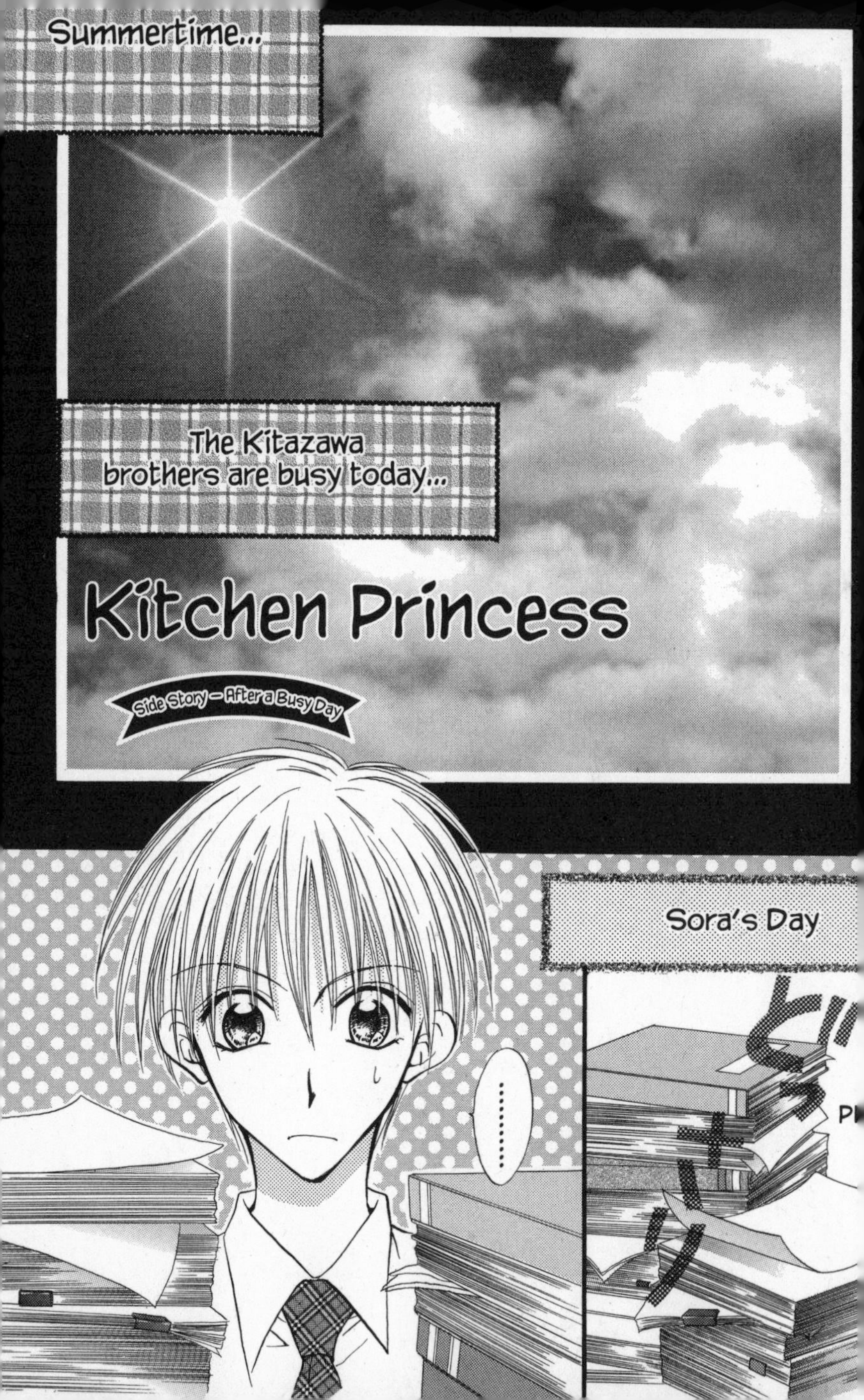

Summertime...
The Kitazawa brothers are busy today...
Kitchen Princess
Side Story – After a Busy Day
Sora's Day
......

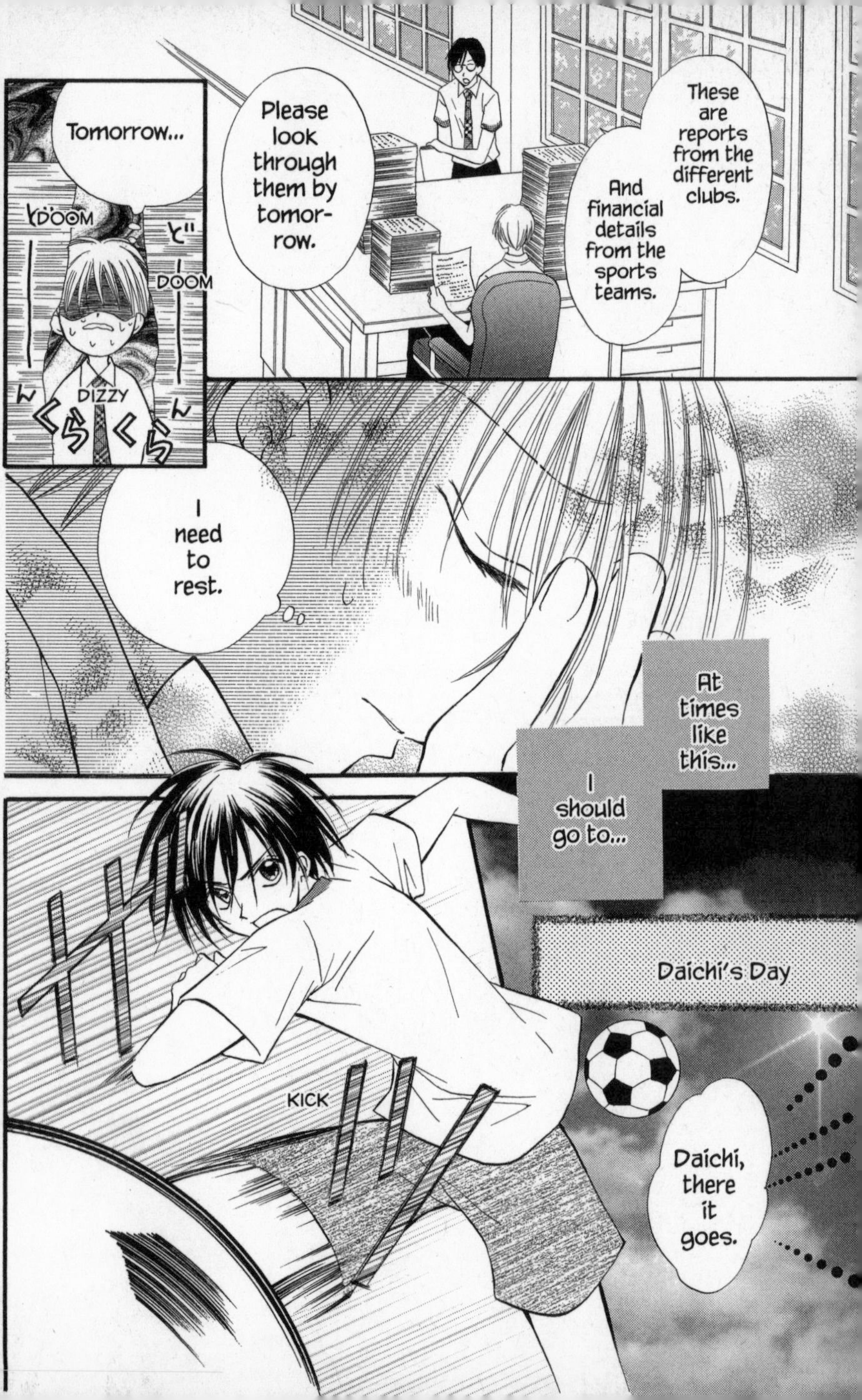

These are reports from the different clubs.
And financial details from the sports teams.
Please look through them by tomorrow.
Tomorrow...
DOOM
DOOM
DIZZY
くらくら
I need to rest.
At times like this...
I should go to...
Daichi's Day
Daichi, there it goes.
KICK

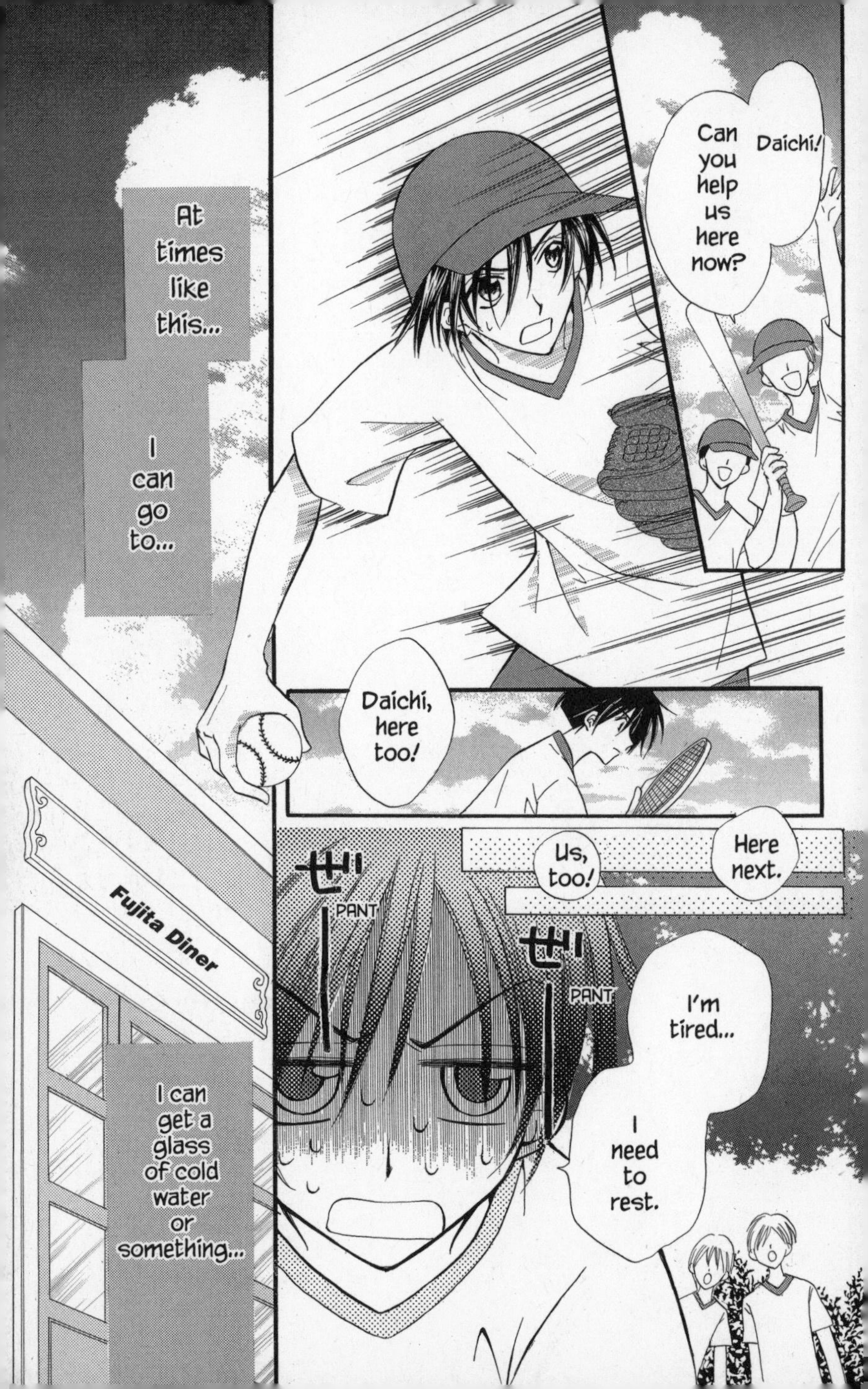

Daichi!
Can you help us here now?
Daichi, here too!
Here next.
Us, too!
ぜい PANT
ぜい PANT
I'm tired...
I need to rest.
At times like this...
I can go to...
Fujita Diner
I can get a glass of cold water or something...

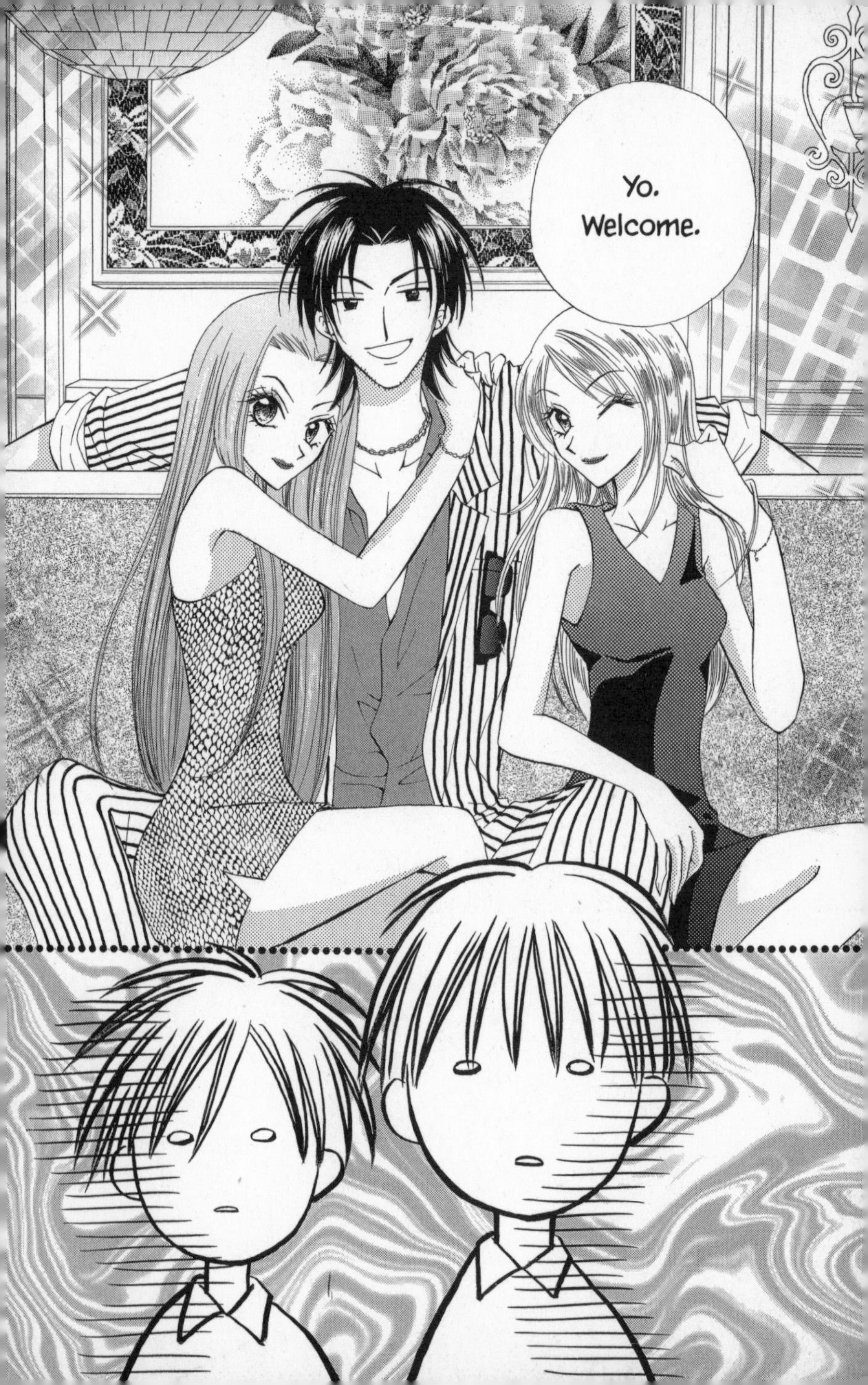
Yo. Welcome.

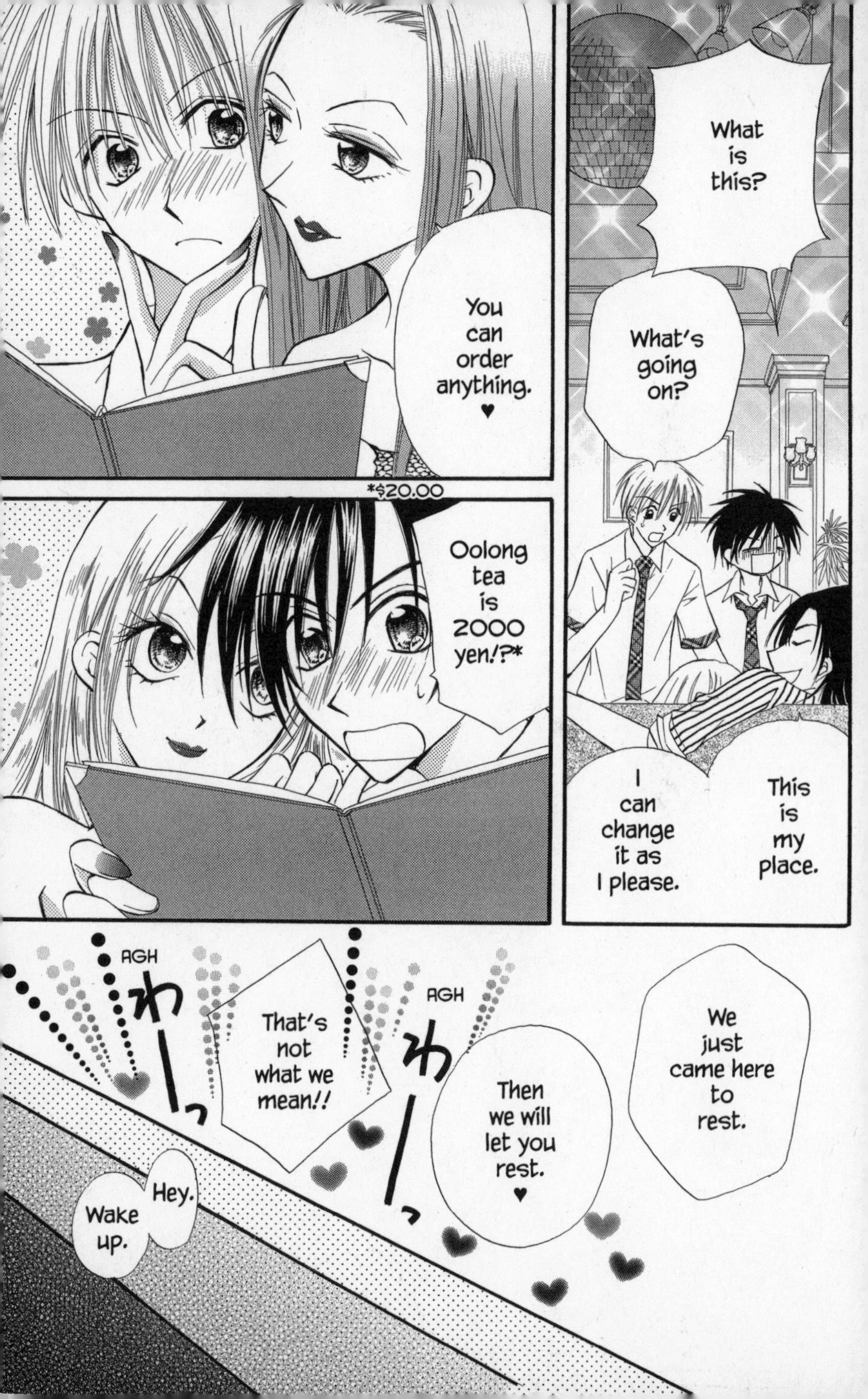
What is this?
What's going on?
This is my place.
I can change it as I please.
You can order anything. ♥
Oolong tea is 2000 yen!?*
*$20.00
We just came here to rest.
Then we will let you rest. ♥
AGH
わーっ
That's not what we mean!!
AGH
わーっ
Hey.
Wake up.

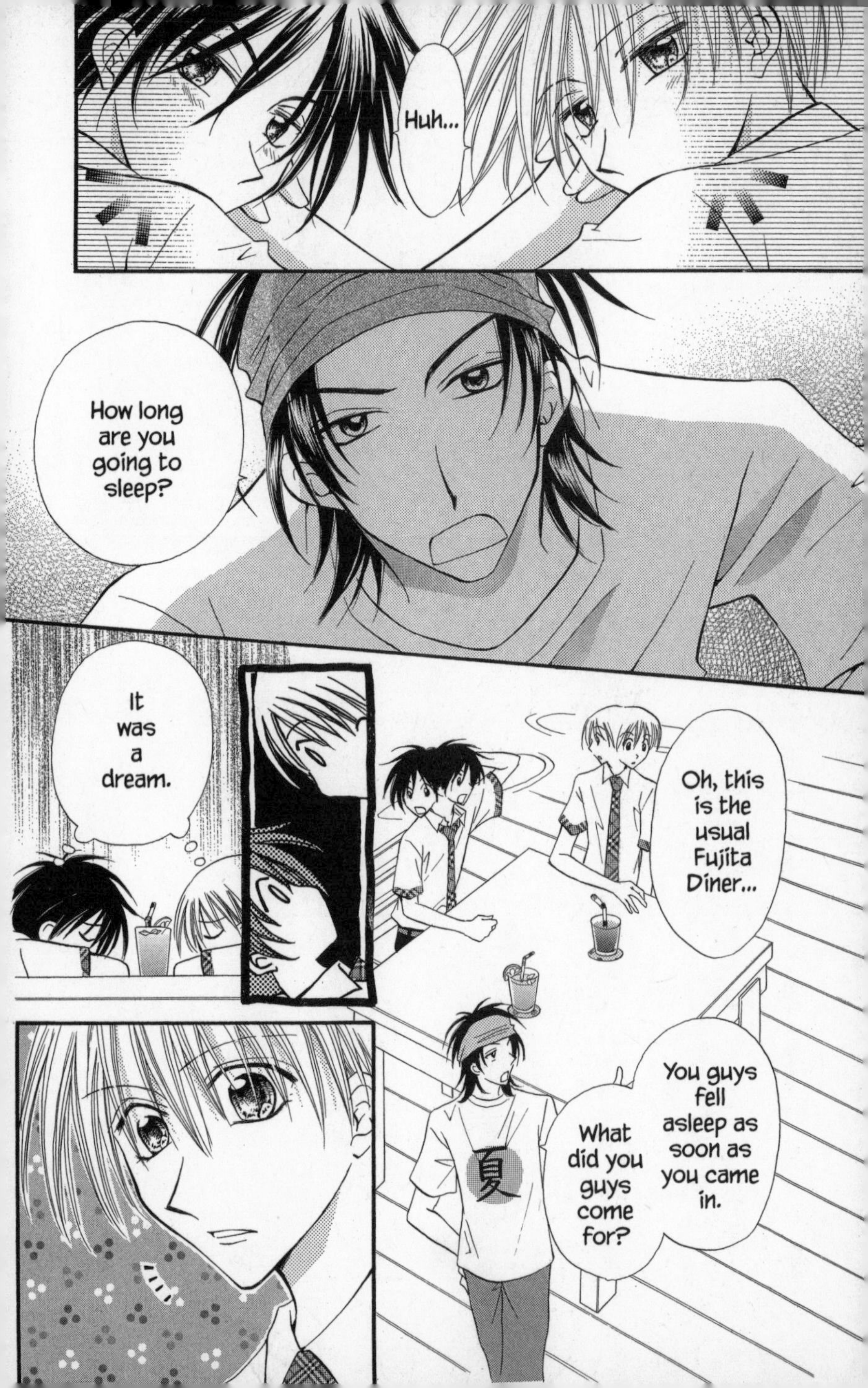
Huh...
How long are you going to sleep?
Oh, this is the usual Fujita Diner...
It was a dream.
You guys fell asleep as soon as you came in.
What did you guys come for?

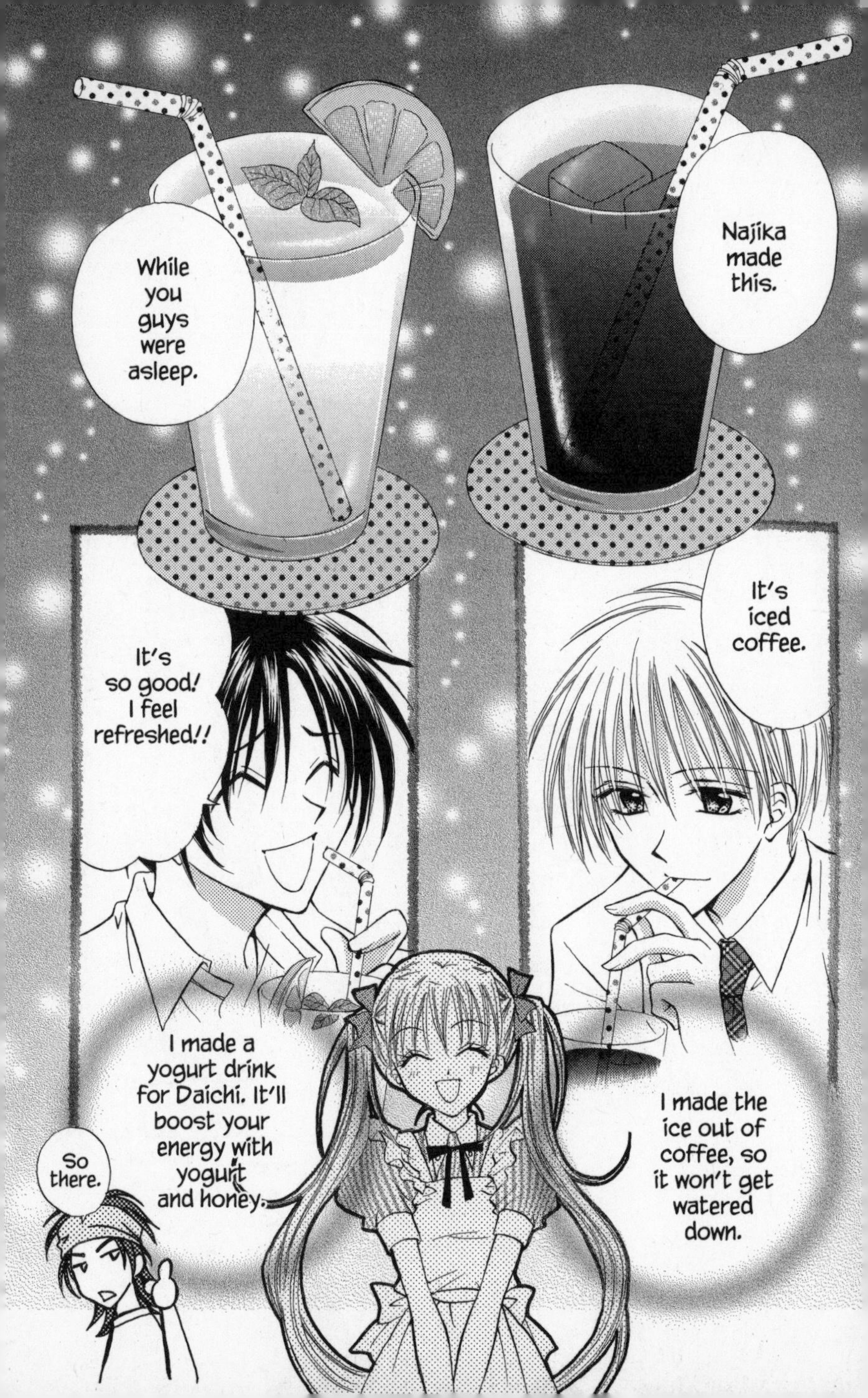
Najika made this.
While you guys were asleep.
It's iced coffee.
It's so good! I feel refreshed!!
I made the ice out of coffee, so it won't get watered down.
I made a yogurt drink for Daichi. It'll boost your energy with yogurt and honey.
So there.

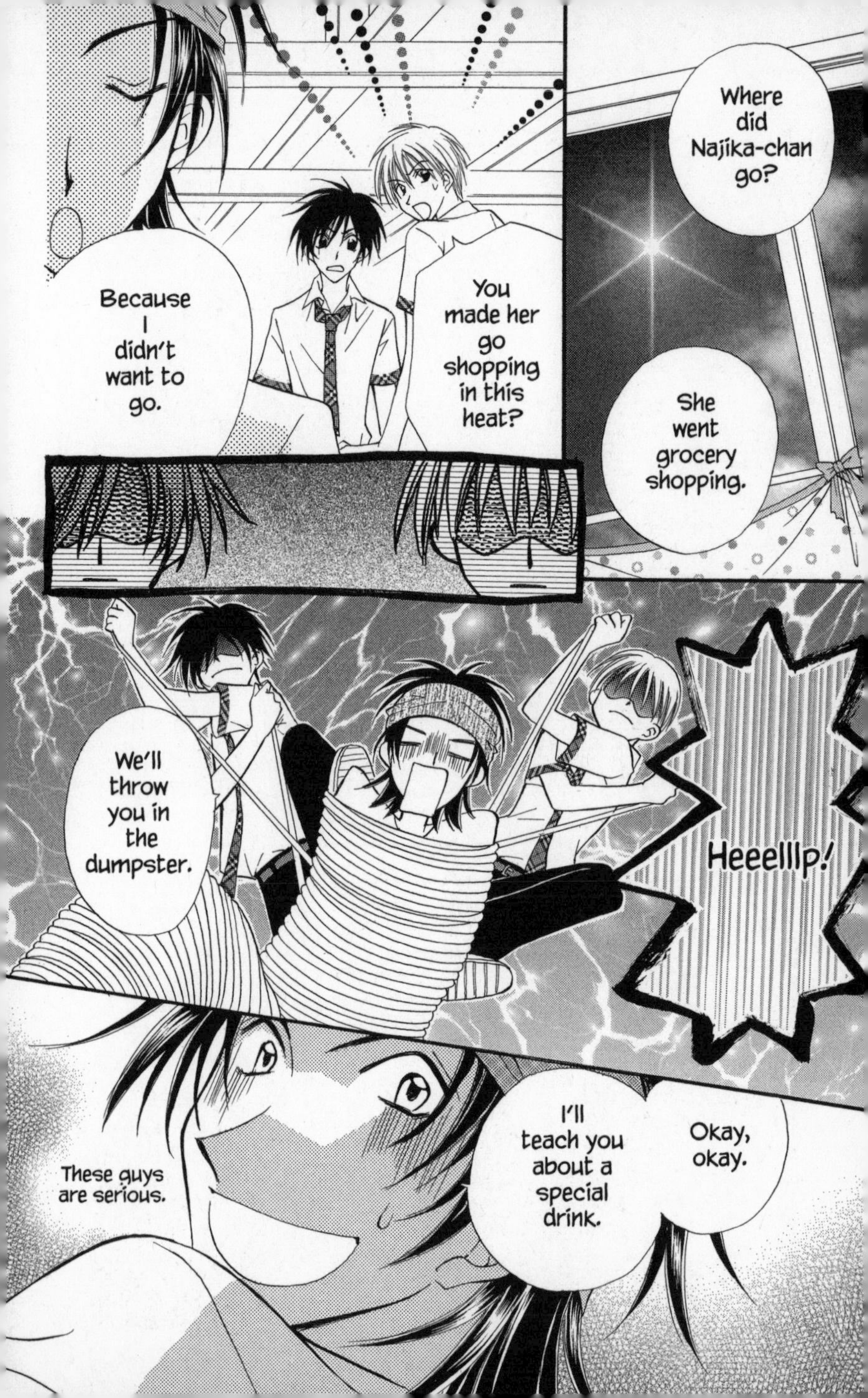
Where did Najika-chan go?
She went grocery shopping.
You made her go shopping in this heat?
Because I didn't want to go.
Heeellllp!
We'll throw you in the dumpster.
Okay, okay.
I'll teach you about a special drink.
These guys are serious.

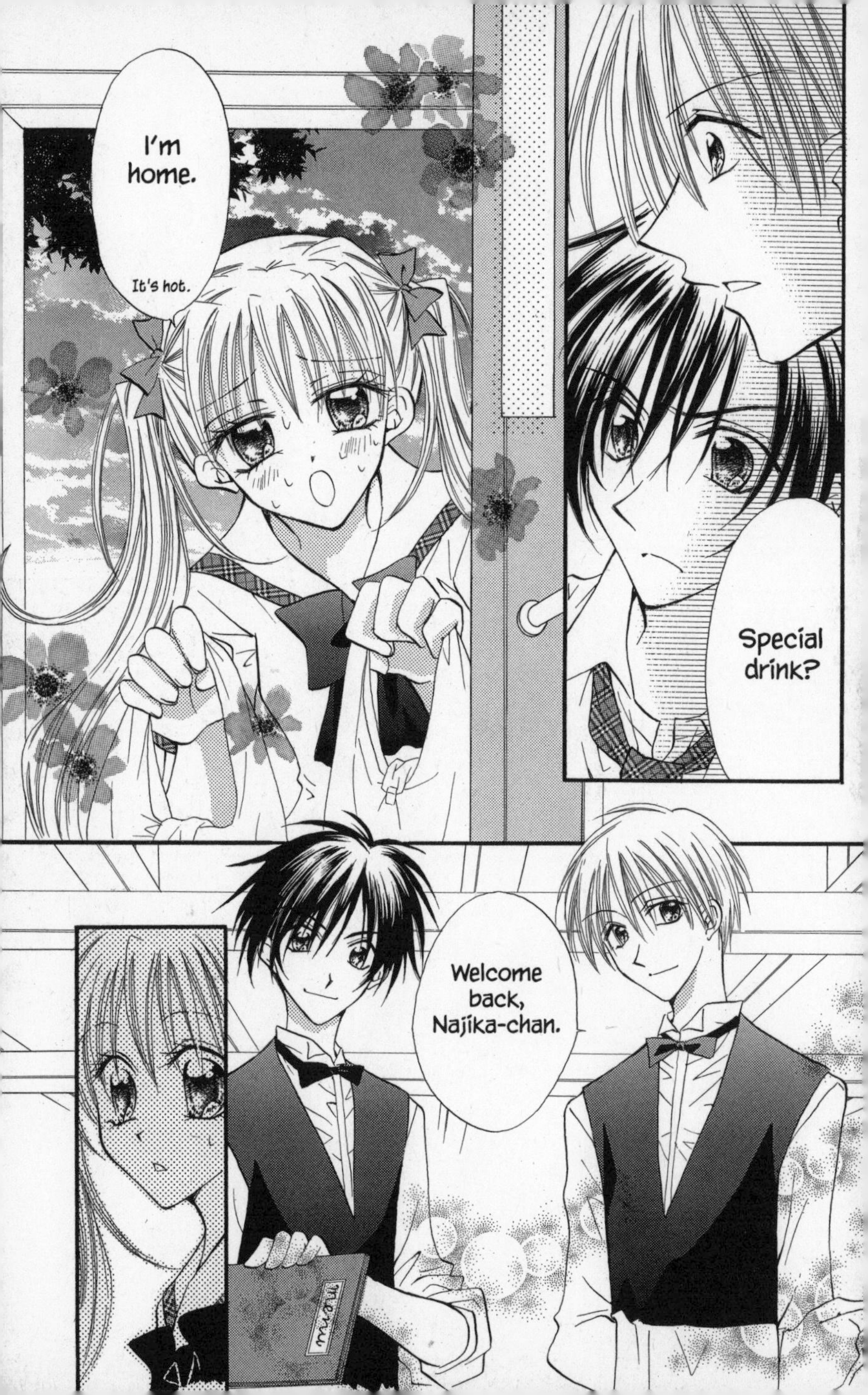
Special drink?
I'm home.
It's hot.
Welcome back, Najika-chan.
menu

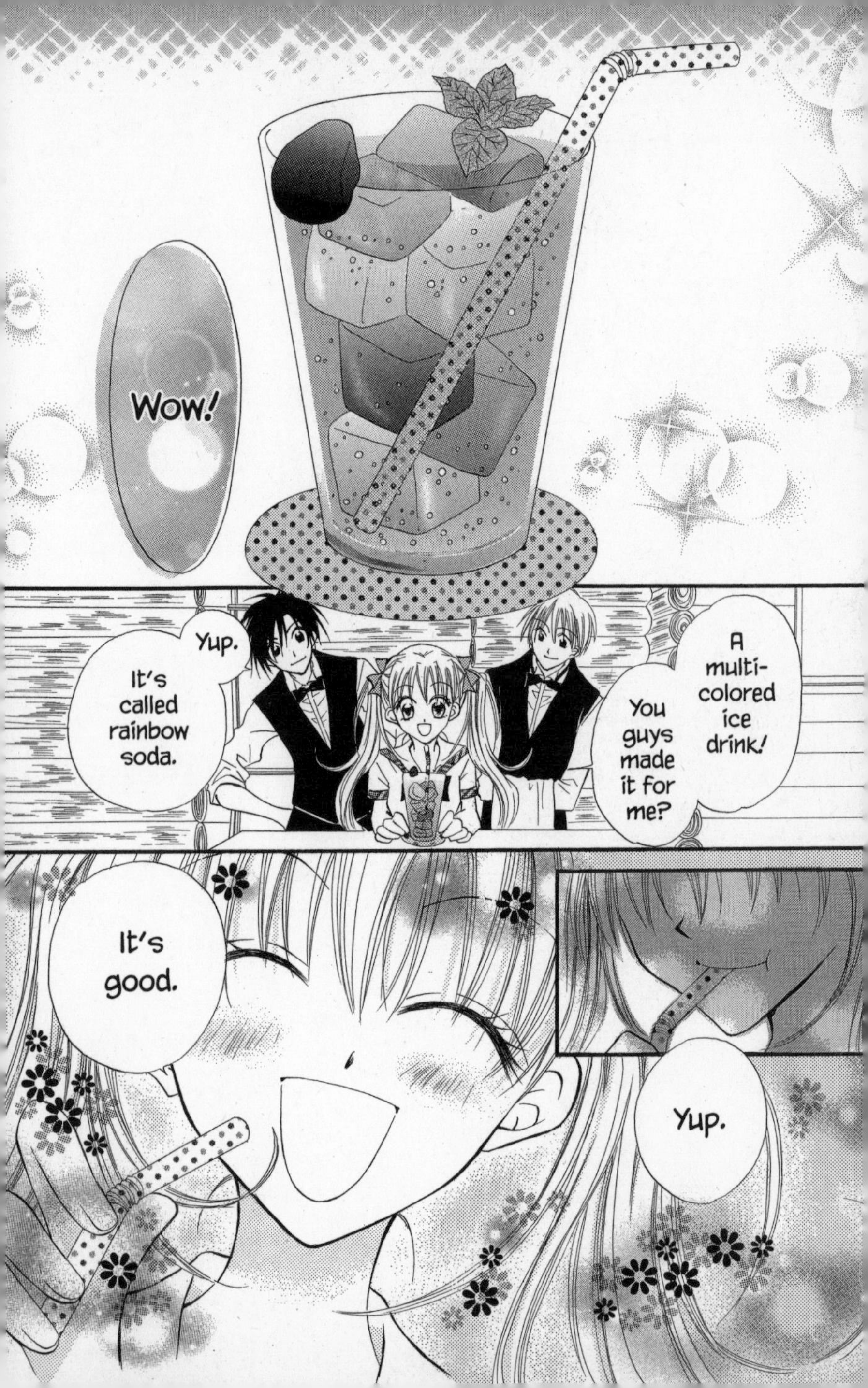
Wow!
A multi-colored ice drink!
You guys made it for me?
Yup.
It's called rainbow soda.
Yup.
It's good.

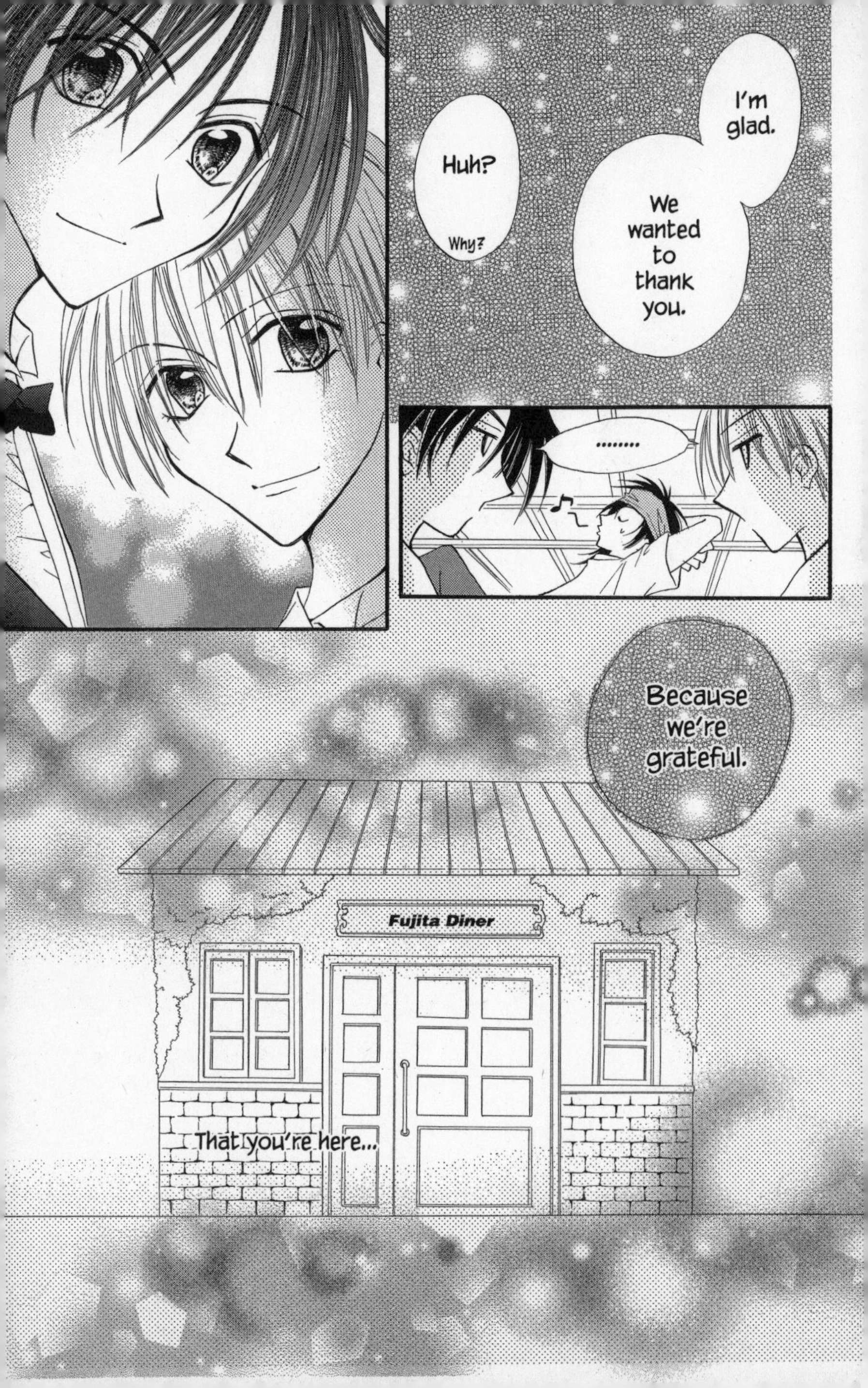
I'm glad.
We wanted to thank you.
Huh?
Why?
....
Because we're grateful.
Fujita Diner
That you're here...

Kitchen Palace

Did you enjoy *Kitchen Princess*?
In this section, we'll give you the recipes
for the food that Najika makes in the story.
Please try making them. ♥

Chocolate Macaroons

Tip from Najika.

It's also good if you substitute grated cheese for the cocoa!

Chocolate Macaroons

About 15 cookies. 70 g unsalted butter, 50 g soft flour, 50 g almond meal, 50 g corn starch, 4 tablespoons cocoa powder (no sugar), 3 tablespoons powdered sugar

How to make

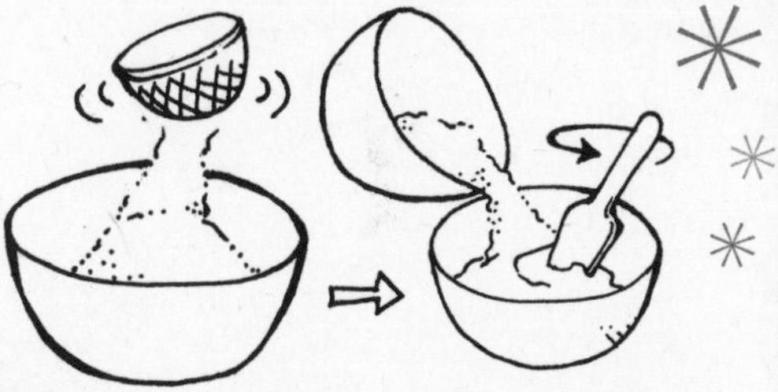

1 Leave the butter at room temperature to soften it. In a bowl, whisk butter with a wooden spoon.

2 Sift all of the other ingredients into a separate bowl, and add to the first bowl. Make sure it is a little moist.

3 Roll the dough into balls of about 3 cm in diameter. If you take some dough and squeeze it in your fist, and then roll it with both of your hands, it'll come out good.

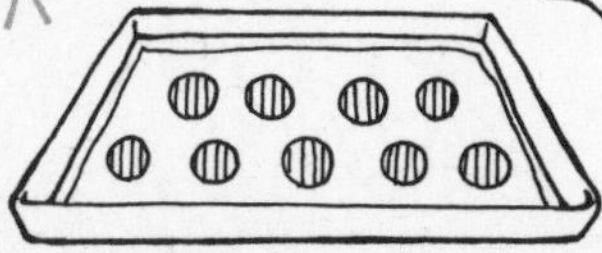

DONE ♥

4 Place the balls on a sheet of wax paper on a cookie sheet. Make sure to space them out 3-4 cm apart. Bake in oven for 15 minutes at 180 degrees Celsius (approx. 350 F).

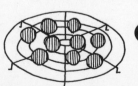

5 When done, take it out of the oven and cool.

This snack melts in your mouth and goes well with coffee or tea. You can wrap it nicely and give it away for Valentine's Day!

Tip from Najika.

The temperature of the oven depends on the make of the oven. So when you bake it, if the inside is still raw, try lowering the temperature and bake it longer.

Sponge Cake

One cake about 18 cm in diameter. 2 eggs, 1/3 cup sugar, 1/3 cup soft flour, 1 tablespoon unsalted butter. Frosting/Filling: strawberries, 3/4 cup whipped cream, 1 tablespoon sugar

How to make

1 Cut out a piece of wax paper to match the cake, and put it in the bottom of the cake pan. Make sure to have all the ingredients measured out and ready. Microwave the butter for about 1 or 2 minutes. Preheat the oven to 160 degrees Celsius (approx. 320 F).

2 Crack the eggs in a bowl and mix. Then add sugar until it all melts.

3 Put warm water (about 30 degrees C, 86 degrees F) in a big bowl. Place the bowl from step 2 inside and use a mixer to whip it up.

4 Sift soft flour into the bowl from step 3. After stirring, add the melted butter from step 1.

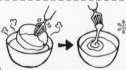

5 Pour the batter into the cake pan. Make sure to use both of your hands to tap the pan to take out any excess air. Then put the pan in the oven.

6 The sponge cake is ready when you stick a toothpick through it and it comes out clean! Once done, take it out of the pan and place it on a cake plate to cool.

7 Put sugar in whipped cream, and place the bowl in a bigger bowl with ice water and use a mixer to whip.

8 Wash the strawberries and cut off the stems. Cut them in slices and keep them aside. Cut the sponge cake in half and spread whipped cream on the bottom half. Place the strawberry slices on the whipped cream, and spread more whipped cream on top of that. Place the top half of the sponge cake on top of the bottom half.

9 Spread whipped cream along the sides and the top evenly. Decorate the cake using strawberries and whipped cream and you're done!

Everybody's favorite strawberry cake is so easy to make.

DONE ♥

Make the rice ingredients first! You can choose your favorite things to put with the rice. ♥ You can also change the rice to sushi rice!

Tip from Najika.

How to make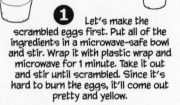

Cake of Rice

One cake about 15 cm in diameter. 4-5 bowls of rice, 3/4 cup salmon flakes, carrots 3 cm, a few daikon sprouts. Scrambled eggs: 2 eggs, 1 tablespoon milk, 1 tablespoon sugar, a little bit of salt. Flavored minced meat: 3 1/2 ounces minced meat, 3 tablespoons water, 2 teaspoons soy sauce, 2 teaspoons Japanese sake, 2 teaspoons sugar, a pinch of ginger

1 Let's make the scrambled eggs first. Put all of the ingredients in a microwave-safe bowl and stir. Wrap it with plastic wrap and microwave for 1 minute. Take it out and stir until scrambled. Since it's hard to burn the eggs, it'll come out pretty and yellow.

2 Wrap the carrot in plastic wrap and microwave it for 2 minutes. Once it cools down, peel it, wash it, and cut it into pieces.

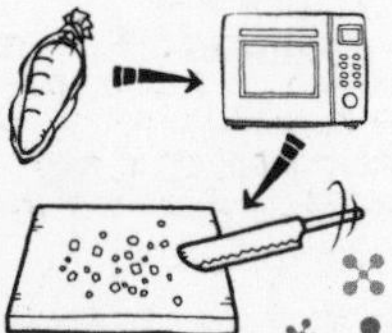

3 Next we'll make the flavored minced meat. First, grate the ginger. Put all the ingredients in a pan and stir well. Put it on medium heat and stir well until most of the juice evaporates. It is finished when the meat is a little moist.

4 For the daikon sprouts, cut off the stems and cut the sprouts into short pieces.

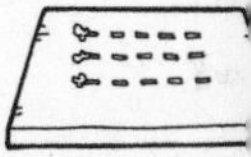

5 Take out the base of the cake pan and replace it with plastic wrap. Put the scrambled egg in and lay it out so it is evenly distributed. On top of the eggs, put in 1 cm of rice. Use the base of the cake pan to push the rice down so it will stay in cake shape.

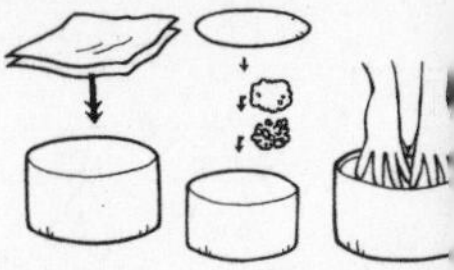

6 Remove the base and put in the following in order: salmon flakes, rice, minced meat, and rice. Make sure to push down each time you put in the rice! Leave in the cake pan for a few minutes, and when you think the shape is secure, remove the base.

Minced meat Salmon flakes

7 Place a plate facing down on top of the cake pan, and flip everything over. You should have the eggs on top. Remove the cake pan and the wrap on the sides.

8 Sprinkle the carrots and daikon sprouts on top of the egg and you're done. Cut and eat it like a cake!

It's easy and looks very attractive, so it's perfect for a party!

DONE

Yogurt Mousse

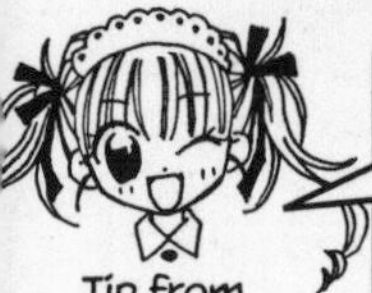

Tip from Najika.

Yogurt is made with fermented milk. Dairy bacteria is good for your stomach and intestines and works to regulate your system.

Yogurt Mousse

4 servings
1 cup plain yogurt, 3 tablespoons sugar, 1 cup whipped cream, 2 teaspoons gelatin, 3 tablespoons hot water

How to make

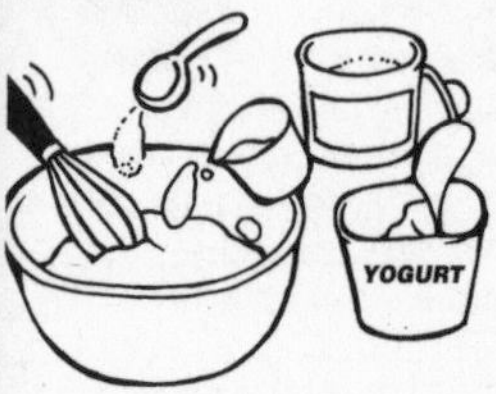

YOGURT

1 Mix the yogurt and sugar in a bowl.

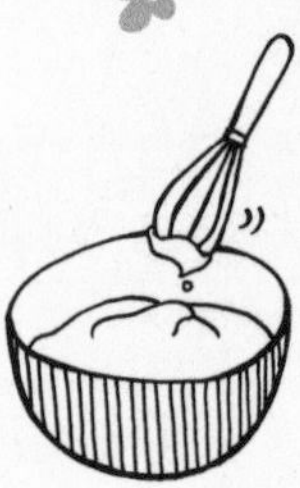

2 In a different bowl, pour whipping cream in and mix until it whips up. Make sure it has the same texture as the yogurt.

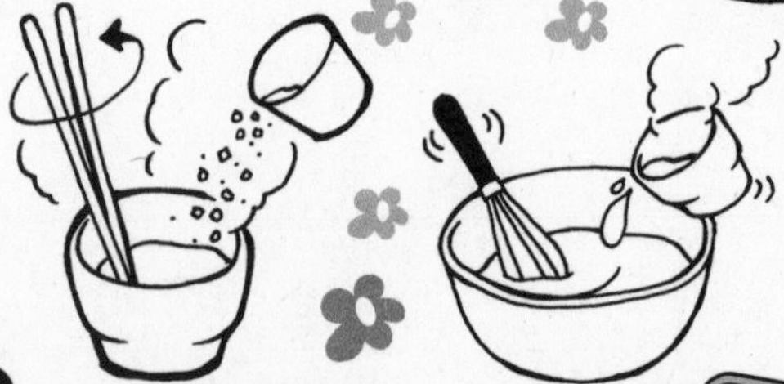

3 In a small bowl, put in hot water and pour the gelatin in. Stir as you are pouring the gelatin so it doesn't clump up. Stir until the gelatin is completely melted.

4 Put the hot water from step 3 in the yogurt and stir immediately. You have to be fast or the gelatin will clump up.

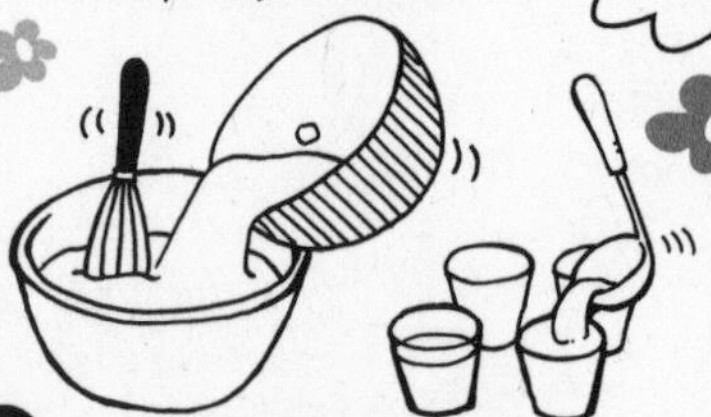

5 Add the whipped cream from step 2 into the bowl from step 4. After mixing them, pour the yogurt into glass cups and chill in the refrigerator for about an hour.

DONE ♥

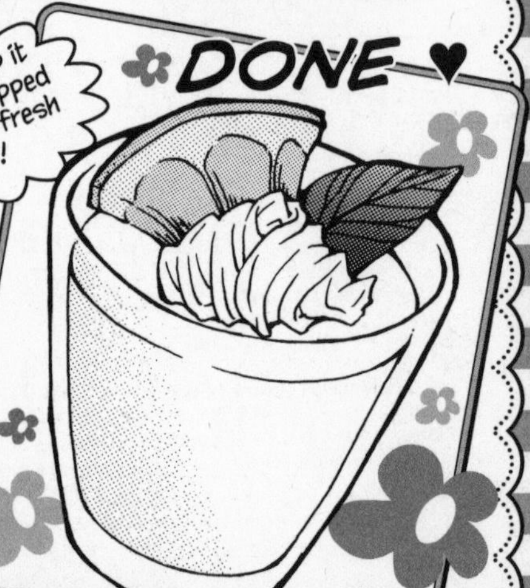

You can top it off with whipped cream and fresh fruit!

Peach Pie

Tip from Najika.

Anyone can make delicious pie if you use frozen pie crust. You can make other pies using apples or pears, too!!

Peach Pie

One pie about 18 cm in diameter. 2 to 4 sheets frozen pie crust dough, 1 can peaches, 2 tablespoons sugar, 1 tablespoon lemon juice, egg

How to make

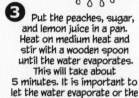

1 Take out the frozen pie crust dough from the freezer and thaw it at room temperature for about 10 minutes.
*Depending on the brand, the thawing time may vary. Check the instructions on the package.

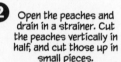

2 Open the peaches and drain in a strainer. Cut the peaches vertically in half, and cut those up in small pieces.

3 Put the peaches, sugar, and lemon juice in a pan. Heat on medium heat and stir with a wooden spoon until the water evaporates. This will take about 5 minutes. It is important to let the water evaporate or the pie will get soggy.

4 Lay the sheet of pie dough in a pie tin, and trim the excess dough. Poke holes in the base with a fork for air to go through.

5 Place the peaches from step 3 flatly in the pie tin, and surround the outside of the tin with a pie sheet strip of about 1 cm. Place more on top, crossing the strips.

6 Brush some egg onto the surface. This is important, since it helps the crust turn a nice color during baking. Bake the pie at 190 degrees Celsius (approx. 375 F) for 20 to 25 minutes.
*Depending on the oven, the amount of time may vary. Make sure to keep checking the pie so it doesn't burn.

You can make this in a short amount of time!

DONE

Side-Story Recipes

Fight the heat with a cool drink! If you keep the glasses in the refrigerator, they'll be even cooler!

Tip from Najika.

Cool Drinks

Yogurt Drink: 1/2 cup plain yogurt, 1 cup of milk, 1 tablespoon honey, 1 tablespoon lemon juice. Magic Iced Coffee: as much iced coffee as you like. Rainbow Soda: three or more types of juice (grapefruit, blueberry, cranberry, or anything you like), some cider

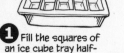

How to make

Rainbow Soda

1. Fill the squares of an ice cube tray halfway up with water.

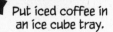

2. Add juice to each cube. As long as you are careful that they don't overflow into the next cube, you can make as many types as you want. It is important to mix it with water because if there is too much juice, it becomes sherbert-like and melts easily.

3. Once the ice cubes are ready, put them in a glass of cider.

Magic Iced Coffee

WATER

1. Put iced coffee in an ice cube tray.

ICED COFFEE

2. Once the coffee ice cubes are frozen, put them in a glass. Pour iced coffee in the glass and you're done. This way, even if the ice melts, the taste won't change. You can do the same thing with iced tea.

Yogurt Drink

MILK
HONEY

1. Put all the ingredients in a blender and blend. If you don't have a blender, you can put them in a bowl and use an eggbeater.

2. Put ice cubes in a glass and pour the mix from step 1.

You can top it off with a cherry or a lemon wedge to make it look cute! ♥

DONE ♥

Kitchen Princess

From the Writer

Thank you for reading Volume 2 of *Kitchen Princess*.
I am the writer, Miyuki Kobayashi.
In Volume 1, I explained Najika's, Sora's, and Daichi's names, but then I got questions asking about Akane's name. Everyone has a name referring to nature, so why is Akane's name a color? Why do you think it is?
Najika's name makes me think of a bright cloudless sky after the rain. Shiny and colorful like a rainbow—that's the image I have. On the other hand, Akane's name makes me think of the setting sun. The sky is deep red, and that is where I got her name. Also, I am getting letters about who's more popular—Sora or Daichi. For now, Daichi is a little bit more popular. I sometimes get letters saying, "I like Fujita-san more than the boys!" Very funny (laugh). I would like to finish by saying thanks to Natsumi Ando-sensei, our editor Kishimoto-san, and editor-in-chief Nouchi-san. I will see you in the exciting Volume 3!

About the Creator

Natsumi Ando

She was born January 27th in Aichi prefecture. She won the 19th Nakayoshi Rookie Award in 1994 and debuted as a manga artist. The title she drew was *Headstrong Cinderella*. Her other known works are *Zodiac P.I.* and *Wild Heart*. Her hobbies include reading, watching movies, and eating delicious food.

Translation Notes

Japanese is a tricky language for most Westerners, and translation is often more art than science. For your edification and reading pleasure, here are notes on some of the places where we could have gone in a different direction in our translation of the work, or where a Japanese cultural reference is used.

Hokkaido, page 11

Hokkaido is located in the northern part of Japan. It is the second largest island and the biggest prefecture.

Aniki, page 26

Aniki is the honorific term for "older brother," usually used by boys (or girls who are tomboys) starting in their younger teens. It is less honorific than *onii-chan* and *onii-san*.

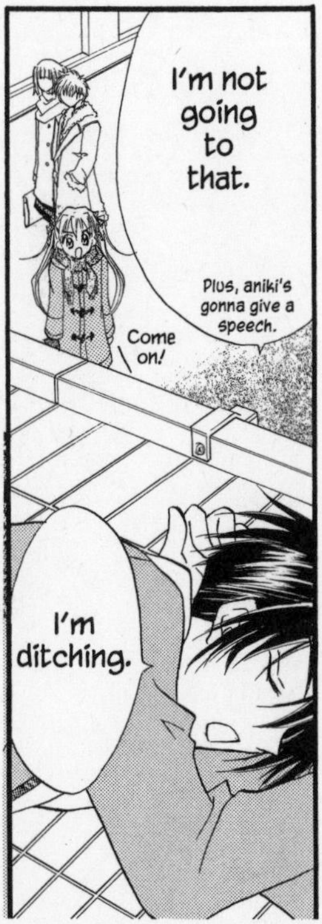
I'm not going to that.
Plus, aniki's gonna give a speech.
Come on!
I'm ditching.

Milkies, page 31

Milkies are a Japanese candy, similar to taffy. They are milky cream–flavored, hence the name. It is one of the signature candies of Fujiya, a major candymaker in Japan.

Akane, page 191

The character for Akane means "deep red" in Japanese.

Preview of Volume 3

We are pleased to present to you a preview from the next volume of *Kitchen Princess*. This volume is available in English now and will be part of the forthcoming *Kitchen Princess Omnibus* 2.

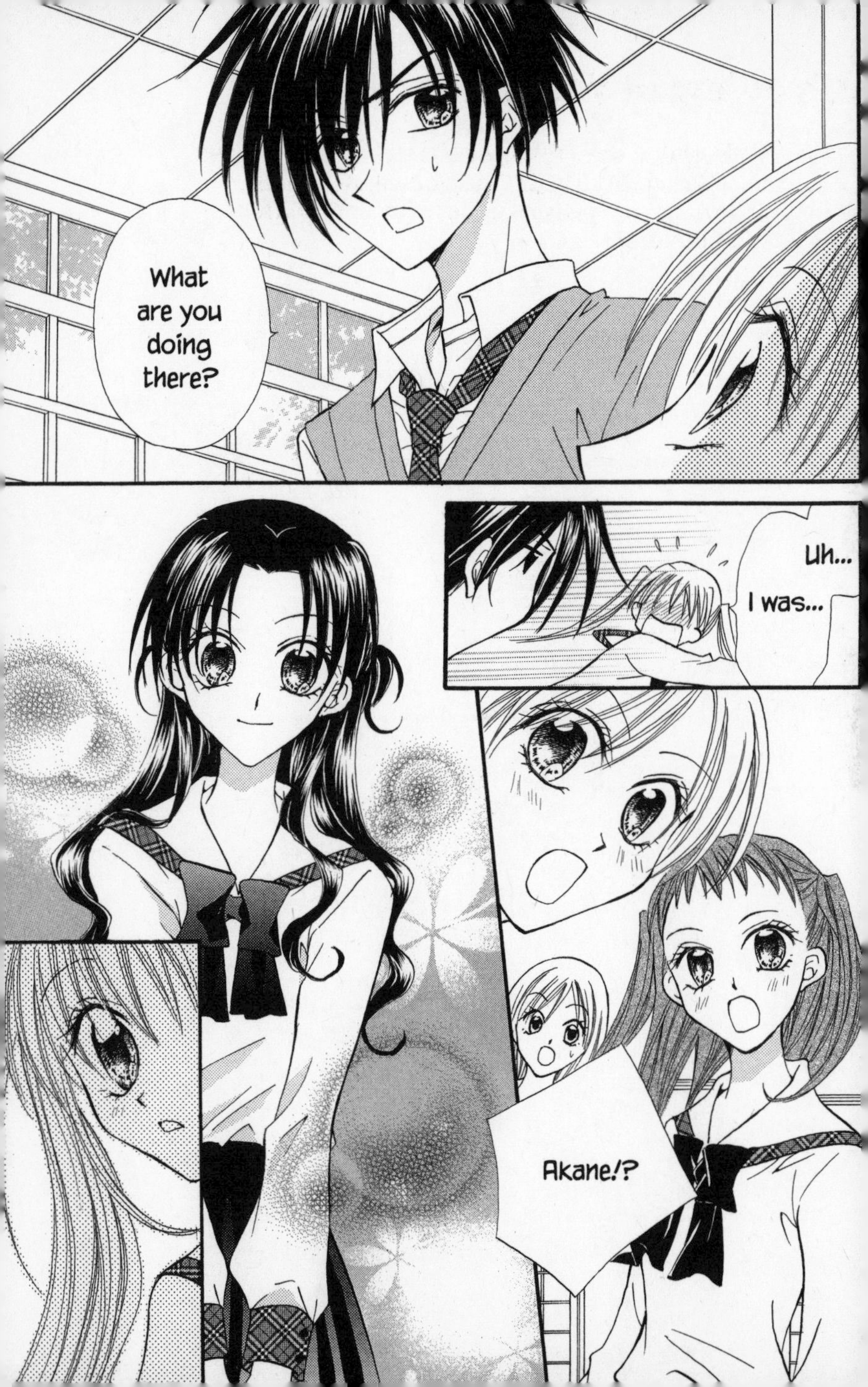
What are you doing there?
Uh...
I was...
Akane!?

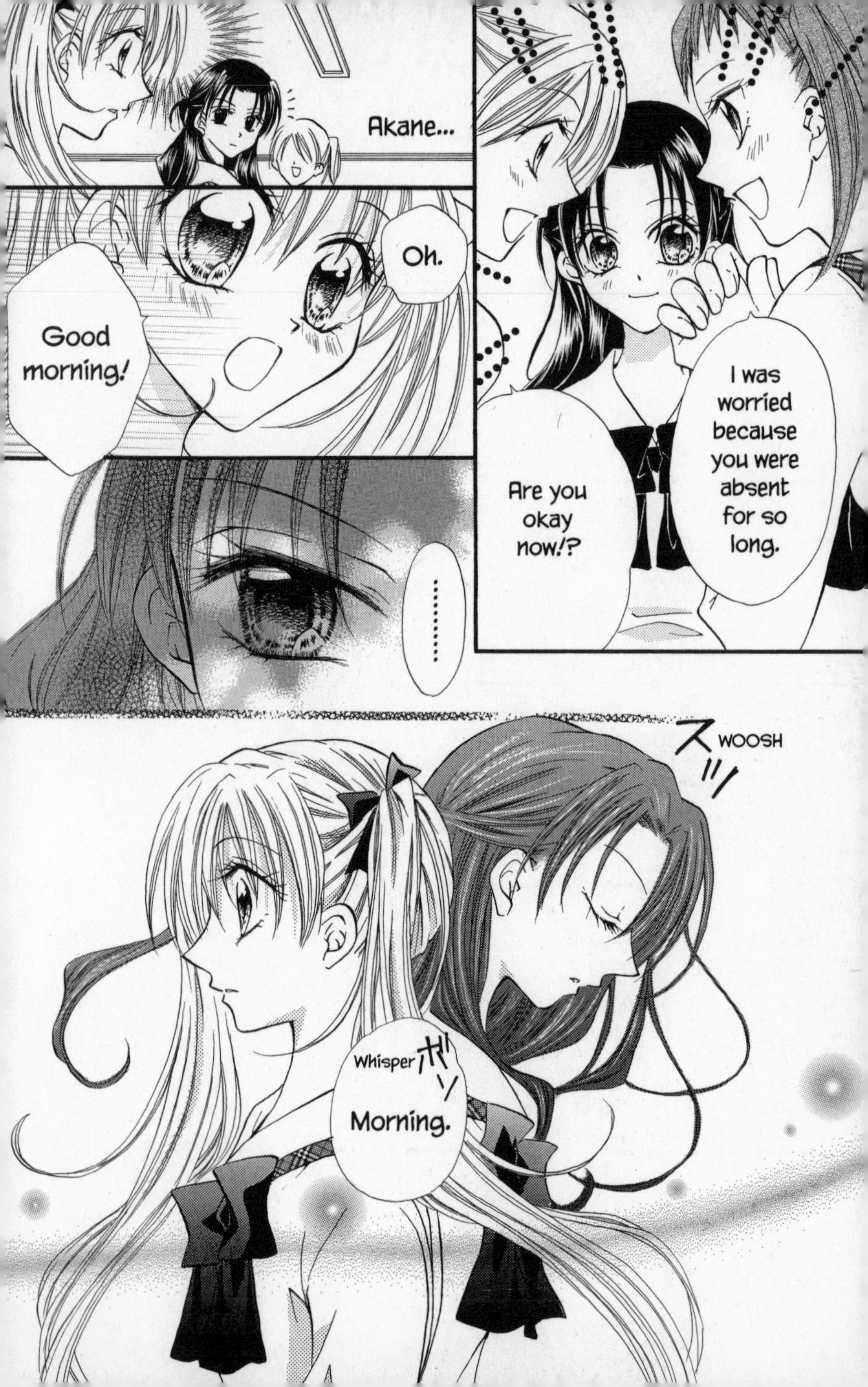
I was worried because you were absent for so long.
Are you okay now!?
Akane...
Oh.
Good morning!
......
WOOSH
Whisper
Morning.

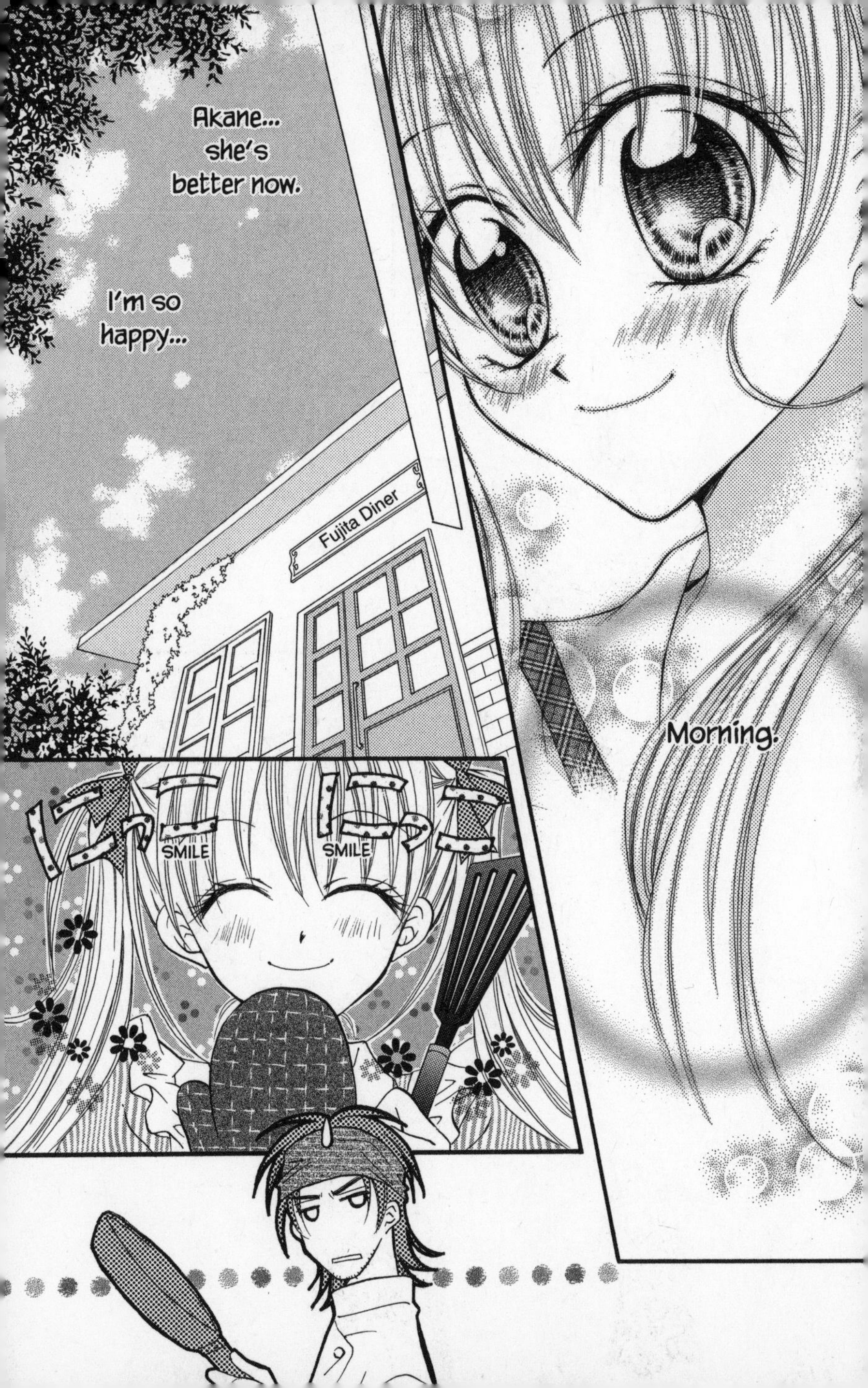
Morning.
Akane... she's better now.
I'm so happy...
Fujita Diner
SMILE
SMILE

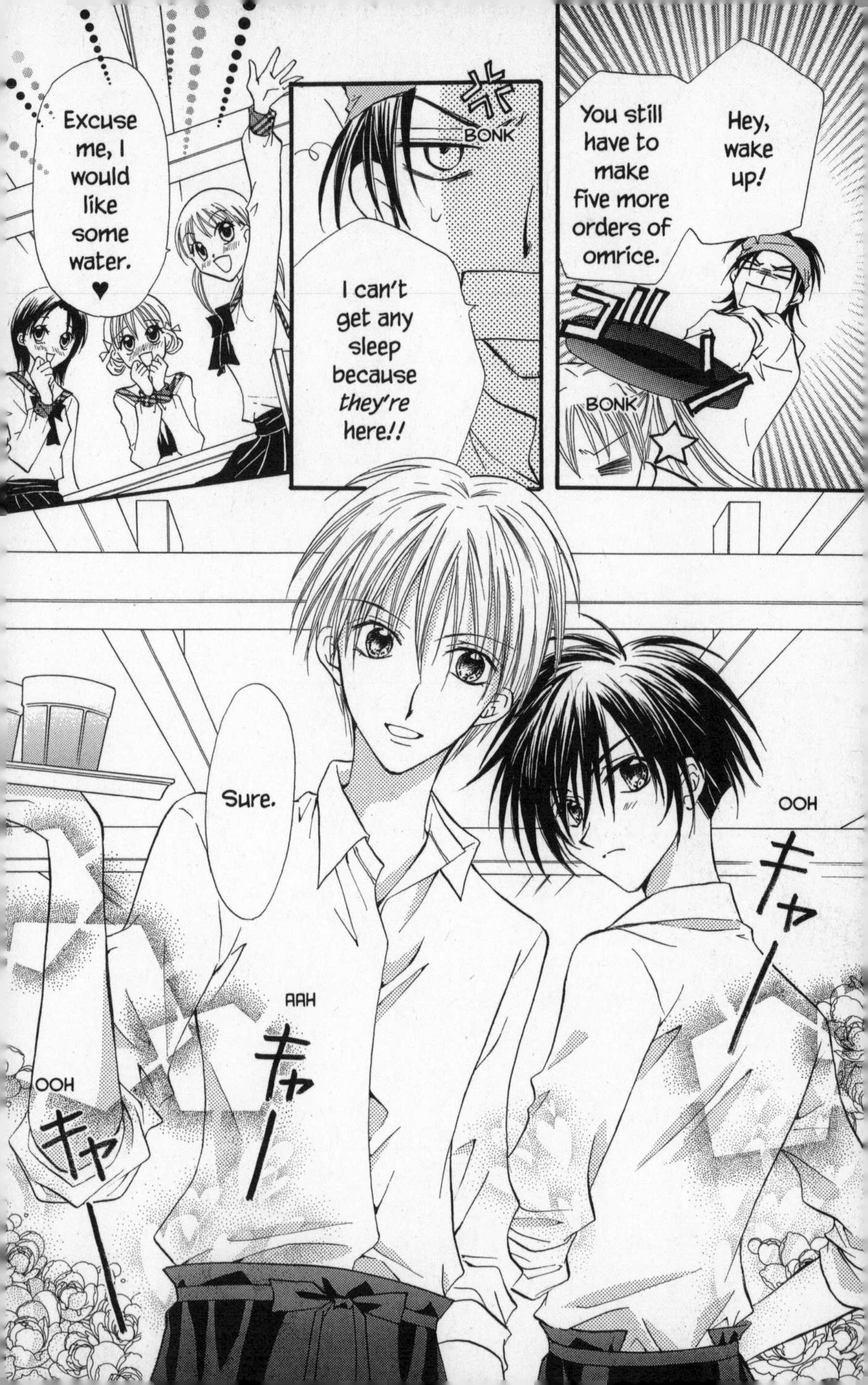

Hey, wake up!
You still have to make five more orders of omrice.
BONK
BONK
I can't get any sleep because *they're* here!!
Excuse me, I would like some water. ♥
OOH
キャー
Sure.
AAH
キャー
OOH
キャー

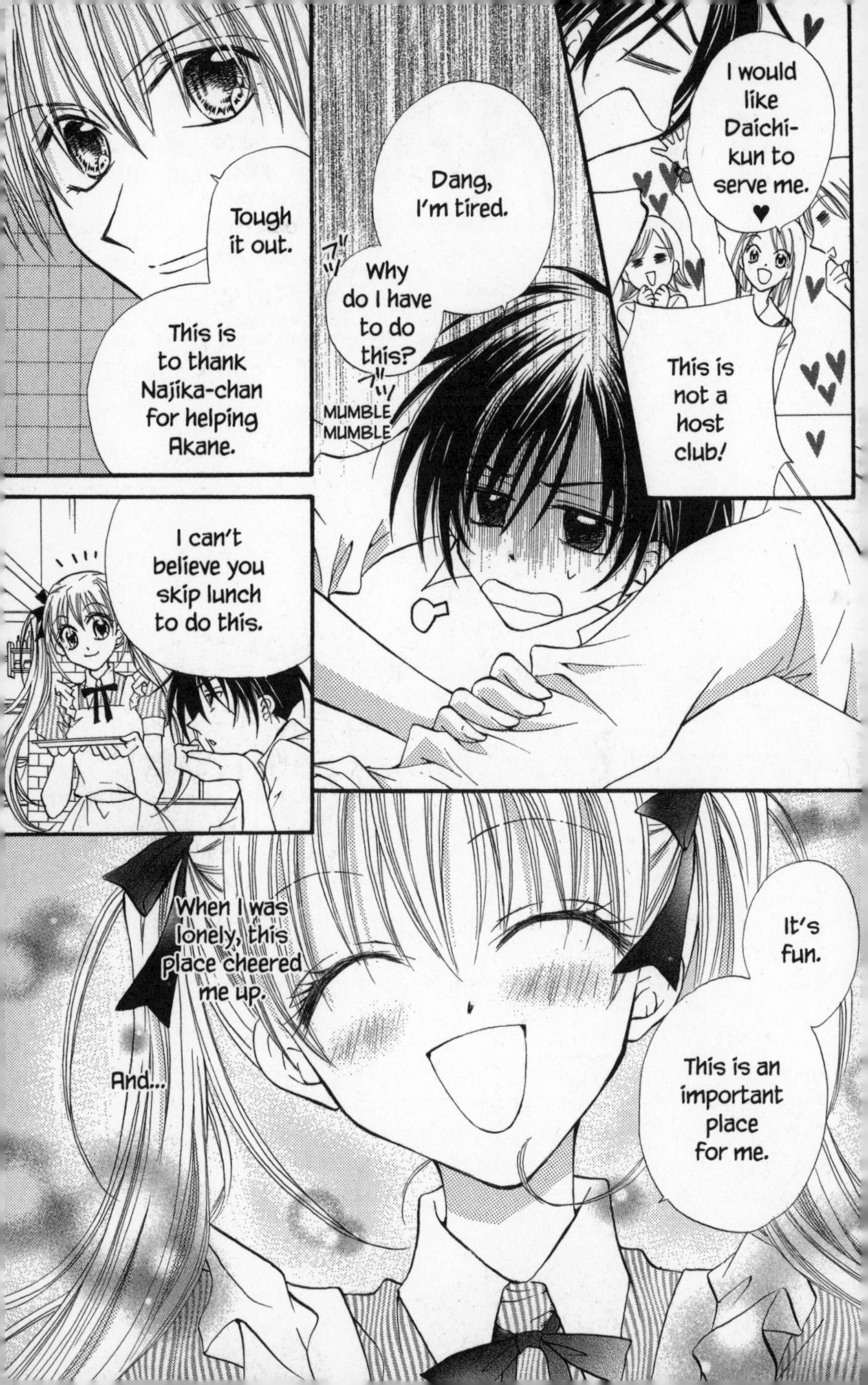
I would like Daichi-kun to serve me. ♥
This is not a host club!
Dang, I'm tired.
Why do I have to do this?
MUMBLE MUMBLE
Tough it out.
This is to thank Najika-chan for helping Akane.
I can't believe you skip lunch to do this.
It's fun.
This is an important place for me.
When I was lonely, this place cheered me up.
And...

TOMARE!

止まれ

[STOP!]

You're going the wrong way!

Manga is a completely different type of reading experience.

To start at the *beginning,* go to the *end!*

That's right! Authentic manga is read the traditional Japanese way—from right to left. Exactly the *opposite* of how American books are read. It's easy to follow: Just go to the other end of the book, and read each page—and each panel—from right side to left side, starting at the top right. Now you're experiencing manga as it was meant to be!